SCRIPTURE UNION

DAILY
BIBLE
COMMENTARY

Title entry

Genesis—Job

subi

SCRIPTURE UNION
47 MARYLEBONE LANE
LONDON, W1M 6AX

Holman

© 1973 Scripture Union
First published 1974
Reprinted 1977

ISBN 0 85421 387 2

Printed and bound in Malta by
Interprint (Malta) Ltd

Contents

Co-ordinating Editor—Rev. Arthur E. Cundall, B.A., B.D.

Maps and Illustrations—Jenny Grayston

Maps, Illustrations and Articles

List of Standard Abbreviations

AV (KJV)	Authorised Version (King James), 1611.
c. (circa)	about
cf., cp.	compare
e.g.	for example
f.	verse following
ff.	verses following
Gk.	Greek
Heb.	Hebrew
i.e.	that is
J.B.	Jerusalem Bible, 1966.
LXX	Septuagint (Greek Version of the O.T.)
NEB	New English Bible, 1961 and 1970.
NT	New Testament
OT	Old Testament
p.	page
pp.	pages
RSV	Revised Standard Version 1946 and 1952.
RV	Revised Version (American Standard Version) 1885.
s.v.	(*sub voce*) 'under that word'
v.	verse
vs.	verses
viz.	namely

General Introduction

The overwhelming response to the Scripture Union Bible Study Books, when originally issued during the period 1967–71, has led to the demand for their preservation in a more compact and durable form.

It will be recalled that the original intention of this series was to encourage the daily study of the Bible at greater depth than was possible with the Bible Study Notes. This allowed fuller discussion of introductory, textual and background material, whilst still aiming at devotional warmth, sound exegesis and relevance to daily life. It is heartening to know that this aim has, in considerable measure, been achieved. Moreover, the Bible Study Books have been widely used as the basis for group discussion in homes, colleges and churches, and some volumes have even been used as prescribed texts in Bible colleges! It is hoped that the new format will find an equally encouraging reception.

It remains true, however, that the principal aim of this series is to stimulate personal daily Bible study. Each main section contains material for a three-month period. The one exception to this is the section Ezra-Job which contains readings for a two-month period. Where it is suggested that two sections should be read together in order to fit a two or three-month period, they are marked with an asterisk. There is, of course, no obligation to adopt this suggestion. This particular volume, therefore, provides material for a period of approximately fourteen months. The complete series of four volumes will provide for daily readings over a five-year cycle, and will form a complete Bible Commentary. It is appreciated that few students will have the time available for a full consideration of all the questions set for further study. But since these are placed at approximately weekly intervals it would be stimulating and refreshing if time could be set aside once a week for the study of one or more questions.

The authors of the individual sections have been allowed the necessary liberty of approach within the general scope of the series. This provides for a certain variation which we trust will prove stimulating rather than disconcerting. All authors are united within the circle of evangelical, conservative scholarship and are widely respected within this field.

Opportunity has been taken to correct errors which escaped attention in the earlier edition and also to make limited revisions where necessary. The inclusion of further introductory articles, maps, diagrams and charts will, we trust, add to the value of this volume as an aid to the study of God's Word.

It is assumed that the reader will be using one of the standard editions of the R.S.V. (or one of the 'Study Bibles' based on it), and will therefore have the marginal references and footnotes of that Bible available; many of these references will not be repeated in these books, and users are therefore recommended to look up the R.S.V. references as a regular part of their daily study. If the R.S.V. is not available, then other modern versions such as the Jerusalem Bible, the New English Bible and The Living Bible, or the well-proven R.V. are recommended.

Introduction to the Pentateuch

The Hebrew Bible was divided into three main sections:

1. First in importance, and fundamental to the whole, was the Law, or Torah, which is synonymous with our word Pentateuch which was first used by the Alexandrian scholar, Origen, about A.D. 200. Pentateuch derives from two Greek words, and signifies a 'five volumed book'. This title witnesses to the distinct nature of each of the 'five components and also to their unity, cf. the Jewish reference to it as 'the five-fifths of the Law'.

2. The Prophets, the second section, was divided into two. In the Former Prophets were included what we would regard as the historical books, Joshua, Judges, Samuel and Kings (see article, Introduction to the Historical Books, p. 196). There were four books also in the Latter Prophets, viz. Isaiah, Jeremiah, Ezekiel and the Book of the Twelve Minor Prophets.

3. All other Old Testament books were included in the Writings, or Hagiographa ('Holy Books'), regarded as the least important section.

The New Testament gives clear witness to this threefold division, e.g. Luke **24.**27, 'Moses (a common synonym for the Pentateuch) and all the prophets'; Luke **24.**44, 'the law of Moses and the prophets and the psalms' (regarded widely as the most important book in the Writings and as a synonym for the whole).

The title 'Law' for the Pentateuch could be misleading, for although there is a great deal of legal material, both civic and religious, the basic framework is one of historical narrative. In fact, Law (Torah) derives from a Hebrew verb meaning to throw or shoot; as a noun it signifies law, instruction or direction, and possibly the second of these, i.e. instruction, is the most helpful description of the contents of the Pentateuch. It is primarily a book of instruction, covering, by direct precept, illustration or warning, most aspects of life.

We have already observed the importance of the Pentateuch for the whole Bible. Here the foundation of the great biblical themes is laid, including; the nature of God and His requirements; the effect of sin on the individual, the family and the community; the place of sacrifice; the concept of covenant—itself linked closely with the view of God's redemptive, saving activity—and many others. When we come to the historical books and the prophetic writings we see immediately the standpoint of the writers, based firmly on the revelation contained in the Pentateuch. Similarly, such expressions as, 'Oh, how I love thy law!' (Psa. **119.**97) show the derivation of the piety of the psalmists. Christians are apt to forget that the 'Bible' of the early Church *was* the

Old Testament. Christ saw His work as the *fulfilment* of the Law, an attitude followed by His disciples. The New Testament writers *assumed* the great truths of the Old Testament, making no attempt to re-lay this foundational revelation. Clearly then, the careful, reverent study of the Old Testament is a 'must' for the Christian.

A basic Mosaic origin for the Pentateuch is assumed in this series, although a full discussion of this question is evidently impossible. Suffice it to say that, now that the absurd extremes of documentary analysis have been widely rejected, there is a growing recognition on the part of scholars that Moses occupied a vital place in an important, transitional phase in Israel's history. Mosaic authorship of certain sections is specifically stated in Exod. **17**.14; **24**.4,7; Num. **33**.2; Deut. **29**.1; **31**.9, 24, and there is a consistent witness to this fact throughout the Bible (e.g. Josh. **8**.31; 2 Kings **14**.6; Neh. **13**.1; Dan. **9**.11; Mark **12**.26; Luke **2**.22; John **5**.46). It is likely that Moses used existent documents, particularly in Genesis. It is virtually certain that he drew upon a wide range of laws and customs current in the ancient Near-East, reshaping them where necessary. Possibly he utilized the talents of other prominent leaders such as Aaron, Joshua and Phinehas. Other sections, specifically noted, were given by direct revelation from God. Thus Moses was at times a compiler, an editor, a mediator and a sifter of religious traditions, giving, under the guidance of the Holy Spirit, a distinctive impress upon the whole. This does not rule out the probability of later additions designed to make certain references up to date or comprehensive enough to cover all contingencies, but the basic contribution was surely Mosaic. For further consideration of this reference may profitably be made to R. K. Harrison: 'Introduction to the Old Testament'.

Genesis

INTRODUCTION

Genesis gets its name from the ancient Greek translation of the book; the word means 'origin' or 'beginning', and the title is appropriate enough, for the book traces history back to the very beginning of time. Many of the great Biblical themes have their point of origin in *Genesis*—notably sin, judgement, salvation and promise. The pivotal character of *Genesis* is Abraham; the early chapters [1–11] gradually restrict the field of vision from the whole universe to the one individual, Abraham, while the rest of the book shows how God's promise to him of a great nation descended from him began to come true. How did the nation of Israel come into being? Why did it have a special relationship with God? How did it come to find itself in Egypt so early in its national history? These are the major questions *Genesis* answers for us; but it also affords us a matchless insight into human nature and God's character, and leaves us with a clear (though undetailed) impression of God's ultimate purposes for Israel and mankind. *Genesis* is thus the essential prologue not only to Exodus but to the whole Bible, not excluding the New Testament.

On questions of date, authorship and chronology, the Bible student should consult standard commentaries (those by D. Kidner and E. A. Speiser are outstanding in different ways), Old Testament introductions or Bible dictionaries. See also the chronological table on page 37.

Genesis 1.1—25   Man's Environment

If man is to make any sense at all out of life, and find any goal or purpose in it, he must come to some sort of terms with his environment and with his own nature; and before he can do that he must arrive at some sort of understanding of both. The Bible offers information and guidance on both topics; and its opening chapter begins with a consideration of man's environment—the material universe in which he finds himself. The universe is not described in coldly scientific terms, for that would be irrelevant to man's needs, but is presented from the human point of view (hence, for instance, the central position given to our planet). The narrative is not unhistorical, since the present situation can only be accounted for by some description of what brought it about, but the main emphasis is on the present, not the past. Gen.1 is above all theology. It was written in the first place, of course, for Israelite readers long ago, in a world very different in some respects from ours. Their

9

contemporaries believed in many gods, whereas ours are more likely to be atheists. For both the lesson is that in fact every facet of the universe was created, majestically and purposefully, by 'the only wise God' (Rom. **16**.27). Some have always been tempted to believe in fate in the stars (and the sun and moon, too); but man ought to view them as simply functional, providing light and giving rhythm to the universe (14–18). There is only one Source of power in the whole universe.

And what is it all for? Far from being overawed by our environment, we are to realize that it was planned and created for man's benefit. What might have remained formless and desolate (2) was systematically ordered by God in preparation for man's advent (cf. Isa. **45**.18). But for God's continuing activity, however, chaos would come again tomorrow. Gen. **1** is a call to faith and understanding.

Notes: V. 2: 'moving'—the verb seems to denote almost maternal care; hence the margin reading is improbable. V. 6: 'firmament' properly denotes something solid; its use here warns us against interpreting every element in early *Genesis* too literally. V. 24: 'cattle'—animals (not just cows), which man would domesticate.

What can be learned from this passage about the nature and character of God?

Genesis 1.26—2.3   Man's Place in the World

The ancient Mesopotamian 'Creation Epic', written in praise of the god of Babylon, depicts man in the lowest of categories, as a sort of afterthought, created as a lowly menial whose function was to carry out all the unpleasant and laborious tasks, thus allowing the gods to take their ease. Ancient Israel was undoubtedly acquainted with myths of this type, to which *Genesis* provided a startling contrast and corrective. In Gen. **1** man is no afterthought, but the crown and climax of creation; woman—so often despised and deprived in the history of mankind—holds the same high position in the divine order of things. Both sexes alike are presented not as abject slaves but as rulers, having world-wide dominion. Indeed, the human status is here more than royal; it is in some sense divine. What precisely is intended by the 'image' and 'likeness' of God has been much debated; on the one hand we ought not to restrict it too severely (e.g. to man's rationality), while on the other we must read it in context, noting that it is God's attributes as ruler and controller which are specifically linked with human functions. The passage, in other words, is primarily reminding us of our potential and our

10

responsibilities, rather than describing our natures; the Fall (Gen. 3) has somewhat modified the picture, but man still has the same high privileges and calling (cf. Psa. 8).

The implication of 2.1 ff. is that mankind *shares* God's 'rest', symbolized in the institution of the sabbath (the word 'rested', 2.3, is in Hebrew *shabath*). Even in the pattern of creation God was setting man an example to follow, and considering his physical needs; cf. Exod. 20.9 ff. This in effect presented the Israelite reader with another responsibility, his duty to keep the sabbath; nor is it without its lesson for us (cf. Heb. 4.1–11).

Notes: V. 26: 'image' and 'likeness' are virtually synonymous. Vs. 29 f.: it is disputed whether or not a vegetarian diet is intended; if so, the divine command meant 'a significant limitation in the human right of dominion' (G. von Rad). 2.1: 'host' (literally 'army') underlines again the orderliness of God's creation.

This volume cannot deal adequately with various problems arising in Gen. 1. The commentaries should be consulted, especially that of D. Kidner in the Tyndale O.T. Commentaries series. The following books provide a variety of viewpoints regarding the scientific and philosophical questions which are raised in connection with the creation narrative:

Christian View of Science and Scripture by B. Ramm, *Creation and Evolution* by D. C. Spanner, *The Scientific Enterprise and Christian Faith* by M. A. Jeeves, *Faith and the Physical World* by D. I. Dye, *Man's Origin, Man's Destiny* by A. E. Wilder Smith, and *Creation, Evolution and the Christian Faith* by R. Acworth.

How far does this passage give us guidance regarding our Christian duties towards our twentieth-century world and its inhabitants?

Genesis 2.4—25   Human Nature and Needs

The universals of ch. 1 now give place to the particular; man is now looked at in a different way, in the setting of the cradle of civilization, Mesopotamia. Human nature is here the primary consideration, and it is shown how God intentionally created man as a being with basic needs, and has always provided for those needs. Man is dependent, first, on the ground (7 ff.)—it remains 'home' even to today's astronauts! His cultural needs are hinted at in vs. 10–14; nor would he be happy in idleness (15). But above all his social needs are discussed (18–25); God's provision was the marriage bond, the family unit—on which man is as dependent today for his well-being as ever he was. The story of woman's creation (21 f.) emphasizes how intimate is the relationship between man and wife, and

11

distinguishes it from mere animal contacts. The divine intention was for a fully harmonious relationship, free from any hint of shame (25).

Our first forefathers found themselves, moreover, in a wonderfully well-stocked part of this earth; there was little they lacked, except for the knowledge of the whole gamut of human experience, with all its content of both good and evil, symbolized for them in one of Eden's trees. To hanker after this was the first prohibition uttered by God, and with it came His first warning to man (17). 'You shall die' is a threat of punishment, of life cut short, and does not imply that man was by nature immortal (3.22 makes it clear he was not); nevertheless, till now death was something outside their experience.

It is a difficult (and controversial) matter separating literal, historical event from symbol in early *Genesis*. Paul vouches (e.g. Rom. 5) for the factual truth of much of it, but some have felt at liberty to view certain elements as pictorial (perhaps the trees and the rib); Eden, for instance, is never said in Scripture to have changed or disappeared, but vs. 10–14 are clearly not a literal geographical description of some part of today's Middle East. The first readers will have found the imagery fully meaningful; the important thing for us is to discover what meaning lies behind the symbols—that is where divine truth lies.

Notes: V. 7: 'man'—Hebrew *adam;* 'ground'—*adamah*; cf. v. 23 (RSV margin). V. 8: 'Eden' meant 'a plain' in Assyrian, but the Hebrew sense 'delight' is probably also intended. V. 14: 'Hiddekel'— the Tigris. Vs. 19 f.: naming was an important function of ordering and ruling (cf. 1.28).

Examine the N.T. treatment of vs. 23 ff., and consider what other practical lessons the verses may hold for us.

Genesis 3 The Fall

Gen. 1 depicted an orderly universe, without an inharmonious feature; Gen. 2 portrayed man in an ideal setting, without a cloud on his horizon. But we know only too well that life is not like that; human tragedies abound, and it is difficult for many people to see any order or purpose in their environment. The fault is not that of the Creator, however; Gen. 3 proceeds to lay the blame squarely on human shoulders. The impulse to doubt God's word and to disobey was indeed devilish, symbolized in a serpent's form (cf. Rev. 20.2), but the decision was entirely that of human-kind—both sexes equally guilty, though both tried to shift the blame. The reality of temptation never exempts man from personal responsibility.

Thus man disobeyed his Creator at the dawn of time; but 'Adam', whose very name signifies 'mankind', is not only the first man (cf. Rom. 5.12) but also everyman (cf. 1 Cor. 15.22). None of Adam's sons ever escapes from Adam's sinful nature. Equally, we all suffer from the consequences of 'one man's trespass'. Gen. 3 should not be viewed as teaching that there were no thorns, thistles, etc., before the Fall, but rather that an evil conscience and separation from God together transform life into a wretched existence. Honest toil becomes irksome labour; the wonder of marriage becomes a matter of shame, lust and domination; the joy of bearing children becomes a source of physical anguish. Even man's control over the animal kingdom becomes a matter of danger and brute force (15). The figure of the serpent—unpleasant creatures by any standards—is particularly evocative, since serpents were proverbial for shrewdness (cf. Matt. 10.16) and also symbolic of primeval chaos.

So was Paradise lost. The most significant reality of the new era was death; life now could only come through procreation (20). There was, on the other hand, more point in the reference to the woman's seed (15) than the sacred writer ever knew. The story of God's grace to man had only just begun.

Notes: V. 22: 'like one of us'—i.e. immortal beings, including the cherubim (24), well-known symbols to the Israelites as attendants and messengers of God; see notes on Exod. 37 f.

In what respects can Jesus be viewed as Adam's counterpart? How far is the Christian still 'in Adam'?

Genesis 4 Problems of Society

Against the background of the gradual development of early civilization, this chapter impresses upon the reader the consequences of the Fall. Patently, no connected history of civilization is given; the casual mention of Cain's wife and city (17) makes it clear that many historical details have been omitted. In microcosm, we are shown a world of growing skills and accomplishments, with people moving in various directions and pursuing different professions. Man's questing mind and inventive abilities (which distinguish him from the animal kingdom) have always been a source of pride to him. But Gen. 4 offers him no congratulations; instead, it illustrates how the baser emotions, such as jealousy and vindictiveness, are just as much part of man's fabric, and that indeed man's diverse skills themselves result in disharmony and disunity—and death. Diversity of religious belief is hinted at in v. 26.

An important aspect of civilization has always been religious belief and observance. This chapter notes this feature also (without giving any account of its origins and beginnings), and shows that in this area of life, too, human nature can be just as ugly. The point of the story of Cain and Abel is not the question of the correct mode of sacrifice (each man brought merely what he had to offer), but that jealousy and murder can arise even between brothers and worshippers of the same God, in the very practice of their faith. If so, what hope is there of just dealings between unrelated individuals or peoples, of differing religious traditions, when their secular interests once clash?

Human generation and kinship feature prominently in Gen. **4**. This factor heightens the human tragedy and underscores man's desperate need for 'the ministry of reconciliation'. It also, however, points the way ahead, since it introduces the principle of divine choice and appointment (25); God was in His good time to provide salvation through His chosen men and nation.

Notes: V. 7 personifies sin, as a wild animal to be mastered (cf. **1**.28). V. 15: the 'mark' of Cain's safe-conduct illustrates divine mercy. V. 24 shows how urgently civilization requires law; see note on Exod. **21**.23 ff. V. 26 may suggest that relatively few worshipped the true God; the full import of the name 'Yahweh' was not revealed till the time of Moses (cf. Exod. **6**.3).

What guidance does the Bible give on correct attitude of mind in religious observance?

Genesis 5 From Adam to Noah

Here we have the first lengthy genealogy of the Bible. Such passages tend to strike the modern reader as boring and valueless, but it is self-evident that they must have been of considerable interest to their authors and original readers. There was, to begin with, a much greater interest in one's heredity and forebears than is common today. The Biblical genealogies were not artificial (although they could be schematized, cf. Matt. **1** and its omitted names); they were intended to underline genuine relationships, or to support legitimacy. For the Israelites, Gen. **5** served to link them directly via Shem (32) with Adam. From the historical point of view, its function is to indicate the long passage of time between the creation of man and the Deluge. The great ages ascribed to individuals are a problem; to some the suggestion that clans are intended rather than individuals is attractive, but it is difficult to apply, especially in the case of Noah. In any event, there is theological point in the gradually diminishing life-spans of *Genesis*, which are suggestive of the steady increase of sin in the world; the reality of death, sin's penalty, is prominent in this chapter again.

But if sin and death constitute the overall impression, a happier note is struck with four names. Adam was made in God's likeness, and this was a hereditary blessing, through Seth (1 ff.)—despite the Fall. Enoch achieved a renewed mysterious communion with God (24; cf. 3.8); and death was signally defeated in his case. Finally, Noah's birth was an occasion of promise—a promise that the consequences of the Fall were not irredeemable (29).

Notes: V. 1: 'Man' is in Hebrew *Adam.* V. 22: the Greek Version (Septuagint) interpreted the phrase 'walked with' as 'pleased'; cf. Heb. **11.5.** V. 29: 'relief' (or 'comfort') is a pun on the name 'Noah'; frequently in *Genesis,* it is not the strict etymology and meaning of names that is treated as significant, but their similarity to other (quite unrelated) Hebrew words.

Could we draw any lessons from our own heredity or from our family (or national) relationship?

Questions for further study and discussion on Genesis chs. 1–5

1. Would it be true to say that Gen. 1 presents the doctrine of a Creator rather than a doctrine of creation?
2. In what contexts are other O.T. references to creation located? What lessons are associated with creation?
3. What does the N.T. suggest will be the future of the created universe?
4. Should man's rule be exercised individually or collectively? Ought we to speak of the 'kingship' as well as the priesthood of all believers, in view of Rev. **5.10**?
5. What sort of 'rest' does the Christian look for?
6. Trace and study the 'river' symbolism of *Ezekiel* and *Revelation*; note also Joel 3.18; Zech. **14.8.**
7. Does each man have his own Fall?
8. Does Gen. 4 help to explain the bitterness that often exists between individual Christians, or between different Christian fellowships and denominations?

Genesis 6   Evil Reaches its Climax

The story of Noah begins here; it is a story of God's judgment upon evil and of His salvation for those whom He selected, in this case, Noah and his family. The principles of God's actions are set out clearly here; His purpose to bring a terrible disaster upon the earth was directly due to the sins of man. At the same time, those who were faithful to God were to be spared. It is recognized that man's wickedness involves all created beings (7); yet God will have mercy on them too (19 f.): Rom. 8.18–23 is a comparable passage.

The chapter opens with a rather cryptic passage (1–4), which the original readers must have understood better than we can, for v. 4 makes a tacit appeal to traditions of the day. Its general import is to emphasize the progress that evil made in that pre-Deluge world, and the total lack of moral restraint. 'The sons of God' (2)—a much discussed phrase—appears to mean angelic beings (cf. 1 Pet. 3.19 f.), and thus some glimpse of cosmic evil is afforded the reader. Far from there being any sense of conscience or repentance, it was the wicked who were called 'heroes' and 'famous men' (4, JB). But Noah stood apart from his contemporaries, 'blameless in his generation' (9).

The most significant theological term in the chapter, occurring here for the first time in Scripture, is 'covenant' (18). It was a guarantee to Noah of God's promised deliverance, offered freely to him; it was God's covenant, not a contract between equals. The story of salvation is the story of God's fidelity to His word and to the men with whom He has voluntarily entered into a special relationship.

Notes: V. 3: 'abide'—the Hebrew verb is obscure; several meanings are possible. V. 4: the Nephilim seem to have been giants (cf. Num. 13.33). V. 6 is pictorial language, speaking of God in bold, human terms; human wickedness could change God's attitude towards man, but not His mind or His overall purposes. Vs. 14 ff.: several words here ('gopher wood', 'rooms', 'roof') are of uncertain meaning.

In what ways does evil tend to be presented as good or desirable in our modern world?

Genesis 7   The Flood

The careful chronological data of the chapter draw attention to the historical character of the Flood story. Indeed, it would have occurred to no ancient Near Easterner to doubt the story, for there was a widespread folk memory of such a large-scale calamity; a number of versions of a deluge story have survived, the Epic of Gilgamesh being the most famous of them. The disaster was probably limited to the Mesopotamian region; the word 'earth' (17–24) is reasonably vague, and can often be translated 'country', while the Hebrew word for 'every' (4), 'all' and 'whole' (19) is much less precise than its English equivalents. Admittedly the total picture is almost cosmic, but that is because the author wished to emphasize that the disaster was a result of cosmic evil, and also to depict the scene as a reversal, in effect, of Gen. 1—Creation un-created, so to speak. Hence the allusion to waters below and above the firmament (11). Serious flooding of the Mesopotamian valley has always been a recurrent phenomenon, but Noah's Flood was clearly far worse than any since; and the writer is concerned to show that 'natural' disasters are in fact wholly in God's control, and that He acts in history in both judgment and salvation.

Verses 1–5 in many ways reiterate the details of ch. 6 (while giving greater precision about the number of animals); many writers have deduced from the repetition that the Biblical author was using more than one source document. From other points of view, it may be said that the paragraph serves to heighten the tension between meticulous preparation and inexorably approaching disaster.

Notes: V. 2: it is not clear whether 'seven pairs' or merely 'seven' (cf. AV) is meant; recent commentaries support the RSV. 'Clean animals' would serve both for food and sacrifice, in due course; hence their greater numbers. V. 5 (cf. 6.22): Noah's obedience to God is stressed. V. 16: 'the LORD shut him in'—the God supreme over all nature is also the personal God with whom Noah had close contact (cf. 6.9).

How far is it possible to see God's hand in the major events of more recent times? Have His principles of action in human affairs changed in any way?

Genesis 8   A Fresh Start

The chapter depicts the gradual restoration of normality to the scene; the very length of the passage emphasizes the magnitude and extent of the Deluge. The gradual abatement of the waters was a natural enough phenomenon, once the rains had ceased, but again it is the theological side of things which is uppermost in *Genesis:* in these natural events 'God remembered Noah' (1). The word 'remember' in Scripture has a great deal of practical significance— it means not just to recall to mind but to act appropriately.

Ararat (4) is a very mountainous region to the north of Meso-potamia, roughly equivalent to what we know as Armenia; no specific peak is mentioned. The raven (7), it may well be implied, could live on the corpses it found, for it is a carrion bird; but Noah waited for a sign, provided by the dove (10 f.), that there was once again vegetation to sustain life. Then Noah and his company emerged (18 f.), to embark on a new life. God renewed His command to the animal kingdom to multiply (17; cf. **1**.22), and set in motion again the regular seasons (22; cf. **1**.14). But a new principle is also to be seen (20 ff.); the first reference in the Bible to an altar now occurs. The sacrificial death of animals is accepted by God in lieu of the just punishment of the whole of mankind. And so through the institution of a sacrificial system God could offer mercy and promise, without obliterating the principle of retribution and judgement. Divine punishment would still from time to time afflict individuals, groups, localities and even nations.

Notes: V.11: the 'olive leaf' here symbolizes life, not peace. V. 13: 'the six hundred and first year' refers to Noah's age (cf. 7.6); Noah was in the ark almost exactly a year (cf. 7.7,10 f.).

The sacrificial system of the Tabernacle and Temple was done away with through the work of Christ; but had it any lessons to teach which are in danger of being forgotten nowadays?

Genesis 9   Universal Blessings and Universal Ills

The central theme of the chapter is the 'Noahic covenant' (8–17), now applicable not just to Noah's immediate family (cf. **6**.18) but also to his whole progeny—mankind from the time of the Flood onwards. This Biblical covenant was permanent and universal in its scope (10,16), and was unconditional in the sense that God promised never again, under any circumstances, to wipe out a whole generation in such a way (15). Nevertheless, God made certain demands upon man (4 f.).

This paragraph about God's unmerited favour and unchanging goodness is sandwiched between two passages indicative of man's unchanging weakness and sinfulness. Verse 1–7 are reminiscent of Gen. **1**, and yet present a darker picture, in which death plays a significant part; the animal kingdom is now man's prey, for food, while Cain's precedent in committing murder will be so frequently followed in the future that it necessitates legislation (6). Noah's own godly behaviour could do nothing to alter man's basically sinful character. The final verses (20–27) show that even in Noah's family circle there were moral flaws which would have their effects and results many years afterwards. Noah's drunkenness is not openly reproved, and it may have been due to ignorance of the potency of wine; he was the first to attempt viticulture (20), not agriculture (as RSV incorrectly states).

In vs. 4 f. we find certain pre-Mosaic rituals and legislation having

18

divine sanction, the one for its symbolic, the other for its practical, value; the law of blood revenge has always done much to preserve law and order in primitive societies, but it would clearly not be at all suitable for modern society. Hence neither regulation as it stands should be transferred to our statute books. Other means may well be necessary today to safeguard the sanctity of life. Similarly, vs. 25 ff. should not be used to justify any contemporary political viewpoint; the curse on Canaan was fulfilled in its subjugation by Israel 3,000 years ago (just as the immorality of Canaan's action here foreshadowed the later immorality of Canaanite religion). The fulfilment of v. 27 is more difficult to pin down; possibly the primary allusion is to the Philistines, who came from the Aegean area in the thirteenth century, overrunning the Canaanites in south-west Palestine and encroaching on Israelite territory there.

Notes: V. 13: 'I set'; the Hebrew verb seems to signify a past tense, and we need not assume that the rainbow itself was a new phenomenon. V. 25: 'a slave of slaves'—a Hebrew idiom for the lowest of slaves. V. 27: 'enlarge' is a word-play on the name Japheth.

Note the second part of v. 6; to what areas of modern legislation other than homicide could one apply the principle here enshrined?

Genesis 10   The World Repopulated

In Gen. 10 f. we have the second major genealogy of the book; the name lists bring us from Noah to Abraham, passing over in almost total silence the events of centuries. In the history of salvation, there was no significant figure between the two; but whereas Noah stood alone (with his family) in a desolate world, Abraham lived in a well-populated world, and he himself came into contact with a considerable variety of cultures. Gen. 10 f. introduce the reader to the changed circumstances. Chapter 10 mentions seventy nations in all, who occupied the eastern Mediterranean world—from Elam to Ethiopia, from Arabia to Greece (and Tarshish, v. 4, perhaps brings Spain into the picture). The list is not complete, but may be viewed as representative of all the nations contained within that general area; nothing is said of nations lying outside it, unless v. 32 includes *all* of them by implication.

The descent of Shem is listed in final position (21–31); the most important line is very often reserved till the end in the Bible's name lists. The general picture shows the Japhetic nations to the north, the Hamitic peoples to the south, of the Semites, but the lists indicate how involved the exact relationships were. Names occurring twice (e.g. Lud, vs. 13,22) show not only the mixed ancestry of the

19

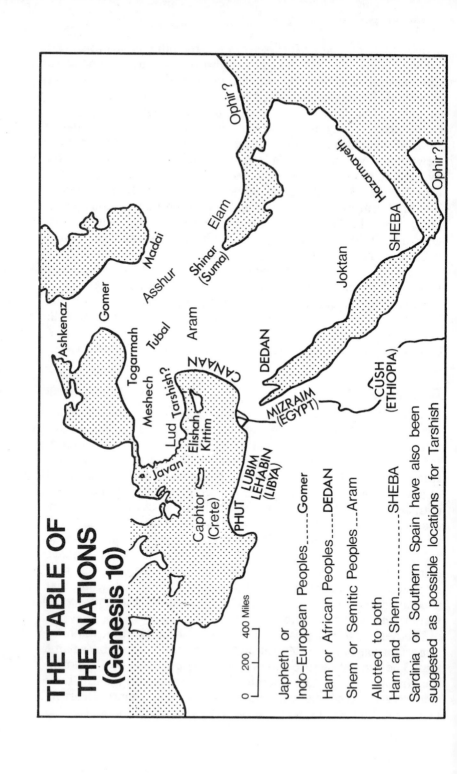

THE TABLE OF
THE NATIONS (Genesis 10)

Japheth or
Indo-European Peoples......Gomer

Ham or African Peoples......DEDAN

Shem or Semitic Peoples....Aram

Allotted to both
Ham and Shem.................SHEBA

Sardinia or Southern Spain have also been
suggested as possible locations for Tarshish

0   200   400 Miles

Ophir?

Hazarmaveth

Elam

SHEBA

Shinar
(Sumq)

Ophir?

Madai

Asshur

Joktan

Gomer

Ashkenaz

Aram

DEDAN

Togarmah

Tubal

Meshech

Lud   Tarshish?

CANAAN

Javan

Elishah
Kittim

Caphtor
(Crete)

PHUT

LUBIM
LEHABIN
(LIBYA)

MIZRAIM
(EGYPT)

CUSH
(ETHIOPIA)

peoples concerned, but also the fact that the father-son relationship throughout the chapter is used to embrace other relationships too, e.g. linguistic and political. (In the O.T. world son-ship seems to have been a status, and not necessarily or always a blood relationship.)

A particularly important name here is Eber (21)—i.e. the Hebrews, of whom Abraham was one (cf. **14**.13). For information on the various names, an up-to-date commentary or Bible dictionary should be consulted.

Notes: Vs. 4 f.: 'Javan' refers to the Greeks (Ionians), and 'the coastland peoples' are those of western areas, from a Palestinian viewpoint. V. 8: Nimrod is an early 'potentate' (JB) for whom a variety of proposed identifications have been made. Hunting was a very popular activity among later Assyrian kings, true to the proverb of v. 9. V. 14: the parenthesis should probably be placed after 'Caphtorim' (cf. Amos **9**.7).

What weight should be given to the phrase 'before the LORD' *(9)? How far does human greatness or achievement merit Christian support and approval?*

Genesis 11 Men and Movements

The genealogy of Shem, resumed at v. 10, is interrupted by the story of the tower of Babel. The ambiguity of the Hebrew word translated 'earth' (1,8 f.) results in the impression that the Babel episode caused the diversity of languages in the world as we know it. But different languages have already been mentioned (**10**.5,20,31); and the writer's attention is here centred on Babel itself rather than the whole earth as we know it. Probably no more than Mesopotamia is intended, and we may view vs. 8 f. as a theological description of some unrecorded political upheaval which resulted in local ethnic and linguistic confusion. Nevertheless there is true insight into the disharmony and discord which linguistic diversities still bring about.

Babylon (= Babel) became a byword for political arrogance: cf. Isa. **47**; Rev. **18**. Its proud, godless outlook is here taken back to its very earliest days. The proud city liked to think of itself as 'Bab-ili', 'the gate of God', but God Himself saw it as the home of confusion (9; Hebrew *balal*). There may be veiled taunts at Babylon in the description of makeshift building materials (3) and the minute stature, from God's standpoint, of the tower (5). Remains of similar temple towers are today still visible in parts of Mesopotamia.

Babel represents the teeming, restless world, intent on its own ends, a world made foolish by God's frustration of its purposes. But vs.

10–32, in introducing us to Abraham (called Abram till **17.5**), present a marked contrast; here man's acts and God's plans go hand in hand, quietly and in unobtrusive fashion, unseen by the Babels of this world. Verse 31 marks the first stage towards the land of Canaan; Haran lay over half way from Ur to Palestine. The two cities were similar, sharing the same religious culture, which may explain why Terah went no further; but Abraham had not yet reached his goal (see Acts **7.2** ff.).

Notes: V. 1: 'few words': a single language, not a small vocabulary, is meant (AV is better). Vs. 26,31: the personal name Haran is not in Hebrew identical with the placename. The phrase 'of the Chaldeans' located Ur for Palestinian readers. V. 32: some texts make Terah's age at death 145; this would fit in better with other data.

How far do modern political attitudes re-echo Babel's? Would you interpret present-day political tensions as divine punishment?

Questions for further study and discussion on Genesis chs. 6–11

1. Has Gen. **6.**1–4 any bearing on our situation today? How far do both good and evil permeate our society? Does Matt. **13** offer any guidance about our responsibilities in such a world?
2. What lessons are drawn from the Flood story elsewhere in the Bible? See especially *1* and *2 Peter*.
3. Examine the Biblical references to intoxicants. What precisely does the Bible have to say about them?
4. Is Col. **3.11** the reversal of Gen. **9.25** ff.? In what senses is any one nation 'superior' to another? Why, in God's purposes, do 'kingdoms rise and fall'?
5. From a Christian standpoint, should the United Nations be supported on the basis of Gen. **10,** or attacked because of Gen. **11.**1–9? Or is neither passage relevant?
6. How far is Acts **2** the N.T. counterpart of Gen. **11.**1–9?
7. Does the multiplicity of languages matter?

Genesis 12　　　　　　　　　　　　　　Abraham's Call

The rest of *Genesis* centres around four men—Abraham, Isaac, Jacob and Joseph. In the story of their lives and careers the Bible teaches the reality and the nature of God's choice of men to fulfil His purposes; these men were not simply the ancestors of the Israelite nation but men through whom God would provide salvation and blessing. The scene is set in this chapter. First, there was the divine call, command and promise (1 ff.); note how the promise goes beyond the individual and the nation-to-be. (The passive

sense of v. 3, cf. RSV margin, is implied in the reflexive sense.)
Vs. 4–9 tell in brief compass of the first visit of the chosen man to
the promised land; it was then inhabited by others (6), but already
was promised to Abraham's descendants (7). In this paragraph we
see Abraham obeying (4) and worshipping (7f.); places like Shechem
and Bethel were ancient sanctuaries, and in symbolic fashion Abraham
claimed them for the true God.

But v. 10 emphasizes the insecurity of Abraham's tenure; no
stigma appears to attach to him for his retreat to Egypt, but
Pharaoh's rebuke (18 f.) of his resort to half-truths was fully
deserved. His fear of Pharaoh was quite unnecessary, for the king
needed to fear Abraham's God; but Abraham's faith was not
flawless. However, even this episode so fell out—under divine providence—that
Abraham left Egypt a wealthy man (16,19). His
resort to Egypt during famine and his departure with Egyptian
goods foreshadowed the experiences of Jacob's family and the
exodus. The worldly success of God's people depended on Him,
not on their own efforts (v. 2 may be contrasted with 11.4).

Notes: V. 1: this call presumably came at Haran, not Ur, since
Abraham was to leave his 'father's house'. V. 6: 'the place': i.e.
a shrine. V. 11: Sarah's beauty at the age of 65 illustrates the problem
of the patriarchal life-spans. V. 13: the wife-sister relationship
(cf. 20.12) was common and prized among the ancient Hurrians,
whose culture was prevalent at Haran. V. 17: the 'plagues' were in
warning, not punishment.

What was the teaching of Christ regarding worldly possessions?

Genesis 13   Lot's Departure

Although it is not yet possible to establish the date of Abraham
with precision, the period 2000–1800 B.C. seems highly probable.
Historical documents of the period are lacking, but occasional
texts and archaeological excavations and study have provided a
fairly good idea of the background to Abraham's story. Palestine
was occupied by Canaanites and other pre-Israelite peoples (cf. v.
7); certain cities (like Shechem, Bethel, and Jerusalem) were already
in existence; but the hill-country was as yet sparsely inhabited,
and the semi-nomadic life pursued by Abraham was readily possible.
There was no bar to his looking north, south, east and west (14 f.),
no hint yet that military conquest would one day be necessary.

So there was peace and prosperity (2) for Abraham and his
nephew Lot, who till now had accompanied his uncle constantly;
but prosperity itself proved a hindrance to peace (5 ff.), and the

two men parted company. Lot found company of a very different sort (12 f.), and while he retained his own high standards of conduct (this is implied by **18**.22–32; cf. 2 Pet. **2**.7), his choice led him to a dead end (10), and to personal tragedy. His movements prefigured the territorial location of the Moabites and Ammonites (his descendants), and their loss of the Abrahamic blessing, close kin to Israel though they were. By contrast, Israel's glorious future and extensive territory was explicitly promised to Abraham (14–17). He continued to roam with his flocks, but Mamre, near Hebron in southern Palestine, seems to have served him as his home territory from now on (18).

Notes: Vs. 3,10: there is a vantage point near Bethel which gives a wide view over the Jordan plain. V. 7: the names Canaanites and Perizzites are used for all the pre-Israelite Palestinians; a fuller list occurs in **15**.19 ff. V. 12: the site of Sodom is thought to lie under the southern end of the Dead Sea.

To what extent can one legitimately moralize over Lot's actions? Can he be blamed for leaving Abraham, for instance?

Genesis 14 Melchizedek's Blessing

Here again Abraham appears in a clearly historical setting. It is to be hoped that an ancient record will soon be found which will identify some of the kings of v. 1 for us—the only certainty is that Amraphel is *not* the famous Hammurabi of Babylon, as used to be thought! Nevertheless the names all ring true both to the period and to the localities named. (The names 'Bera' and 'Birsha' [2], however, are probably deliberate distortions of the original names, since as they stand they appear to mean 'in evil' and 'in wickedness' respectively—a symbolic reference to the character of Sodom and Gomorrah.) The period was one of coalitions and confederacies; in this respect, too, the chapter is historically accurate. The confederate forces will not have been enormous, and Abraham's 'house' was by no means small (14); even so, his military action was probably in the nature of harassing the rear of the armies as they withdrew northwards.

The primary purpose of the chapter is to show how insecure Sodom was, for all its attractiveness, and how dependent Lot was upon Abraham; Abraham, on the other hand, would owe no debt to Sodom (21–24). But the best-known feature of Gen. **14** is the meeting of Abraham with the king of Jerusalem, Melchizedek (18 ff.), whose significance was greater than appears on the surface (cf. Psa. **110**.4; Heb. **5** ff.). This priest–king entertained Abraham

24

to a royal feast (18), and blessed him in the name of his God (El Elyon, in Hebrew), whom Abraham knew to be the one true God, the LORD (22). To him, therefore, Abraham could respond warmly and generously (20; cf. Heb. 7.4-7), thereby prefiguring Israel's debt of allegiance to the high priest and king in Jerusalem; but with Sodom's king Abraham had nothing in common.

Notes: V. 1: 'Goiim' usually means 'nations' in Hebrew; possibly 'barbarians' is roughly the sense here. Vs. 5-8 describe a clockwise, circular route to the south-east of Palestine. V. 14: 'trained men'; 'retainers' is more probably correct. 'Dan'—in fact called 'Laish' at the time, cf. Judg. **18**.27 ff.—was on the northern boundary of later Israel. V. 18: 'Salem' = Jerusalem, cf. Psa. **76**.2.

Does this chapter offer guidance regarding Christian duties where political debts, alliances or loyalties are concerned?

Genesis 15 Covenant Promises

Abraham had already been promised that he would father a mighty nation, which would have Palestine as its homeland (**12**.2,7); but as yet he had no child (2; cf. **11**.30). In conformity with customs that then prevailed (in the Hurrian civilization, for instance at Haran), he had evidently already nominated or adopted an heir, his slave Eliezer (2 f.); Eliezer could of course have become father to a nation on Abraham's behalf, but that was neither Abraham's wish nor God's intention. God gave Abraham a more specific promise now (4). In his quiet response of faith (6), Abraham demonstrated qualities very different from the arrogance of Babel, or the worldly wisdom of Lot. He was helplessly dependent on God, and humbly accepted that position; this attitude was the first since the Flood to merit the description 'righteous'. The fuller implications are brought out in the N.T., especially Rom. **4**; Gal. **3** and Jas. **2**.

Abraham's was a questing faith, however, and he now sought confirmation of the promise regarding the land of Canaan (8). The divine response was to enter into a covenant with him; the various details given emphasize both God's mysterious majesty (the fire pot and the torch of v. 17 symbolized His presence) and also His gracious condescension, submitting Himself to human covenant rituals of the day. It was, like Noah's, a unilateral covenant; but where the Noahic covenant promised God's goodness to all men, the Abrahamic covenant related only to Abraham's descendants, and constituted a promise of territory. On the face of it, the promise was unconditional, but it should be observed that the pre-Israelite Palestinian peoples were to lose the land because of their own misdeeds (16), while the fact that only in David's reign did Israel master the whole of the territory specified (18) suggests that that part of the promise, too, would be modified in accordance with Israel's response to God. In other words, this covenant made implicit moral and religious demands. At the same time, it revealed that the Egyptian sojourn and the exodus were no accident but part of God's overall design.

Notes: V. 16: 'generation' here means a full life-span, cf. v. 13. V. 18: 'the river of Egypt'—the Wadi el-Arish on the north-eastern border of Egypt, not the Nile. Vs. 19 ff.: i.e. not one of all these peoples would be able to stand in Israel's way, when the time came.

What promises made to Abraham are still offered to Abraham's children? On what basis may they be claimed?

Genesis 16   Ishmael's Birth

In begetting a son by his wife's slave girl, Abraham was following a well-established custom of the day, practised among the Hurrians of northern Mesopotamia. Such a child would be the heir unless the true wife afterwards gave birth to a son. Some Hurrian marriage contracts specified that a wife, if barren, must take steps to furnish a son by these means (note that Sarah took the initiative, v. 2); but no such stipulation had appeared in God's contract with Abraham! Abraham and Sarah can scarcely be blamed for impetuosity (note v. 3); but to the God who reckoned 400 years as but an interval of time (15.13), ten years were little enough. But if Abraham and Sarah were misguided, the fault was not Hagar's and certainly not Ishmael's, and God's care for and interest in them both is shown here. Ishmael, indeed, would in a sense reap the fruit of God's promises to Abraham, for he was to be granted an equally prodigious progeny (10)—numerous peoples who roamed in the desert areas south and east of Palestine (cf. 25.12–16).

The chapter is also an indictment of polygamy. Nothing is said in direct denial of the social conventions of the period, but the story well illustrates the tensions and passions engendered by polygamous unions. One can understand or sympathize with the feelings of both women, and also with the invidious position in which Abraham found himself; but most to be pitied is without question Ishmael, who would grow up to be at odds with all men, even his own kin (12). The 'wild ass' typified a free, independent and fierce spirit.

Notes: V. 7: Shur lay well south of Palestine, *en route* for Hagar's native Egypt. Vs. 13 f.: the Hebrew of Hagar's statement and of the well's name is difficult to interpret; the latter is taken by most

26

scholars to mean 'the well of the Living One who sees me'; Hagar expresses her astonishment at being permitted such close contact with God.

What legally sanctioned social conventions of our own day might be considered ill-advised, in God's assessment of them?

Genesis 17   The Sign of the Covenant

The repeated references to Abraham's age draw attention to the steady passage of time, and to the increasing improbability, by human standards, of his ever having a son by Sarah (1,17); his faith in God's promises was severely tested—but though he laughed, he obeyed. Thirteen years had elapsed since Ishmael's birth, and the lad was now on the verge of puberty, the age at which boys were circumcised in many parts of the ancient world. Whatever its origins (they are lost in antiquity), the rite seems to have served as a mark of tribal kinship, and was practised among most of the Semitic peoples and also the Egyptians. Ishmael was accordingly circumcised at the age of thirteen, although evidently it had not been customary in Abraham's family hitherto. It may be that Ishmael and his descendants were thereby permitted full kinship with other peoples of the Palestinian region, and that this was part of God's plan for blessing him (20).

Circumcision was adopted now by Abraham too, and all male members of the household (26 f.), but the divine instructions to him included two significant differences: first, the rite was hereafter to be carried out in infancy, not puberty (12); second, it was to be a sign, not of tribal kinship, but of a covenant relationship with God (10). For Israel, therefore, it was from the outset a religious, not social, rite. It could embrace those who were not born of Abraham's line (12), while its absence would exclude even those who were Abraham's own descendants from covenant blessings (14). It was not, therefore, a mechanical and meaningless custom, but a symbol of obedience to God. Thus the implicit demands of the covenant (see notes on ch. **15**) are now made more explicit, though v. 1 issues a call for a completely devoted life of obedience.

It now became clear to Abraham that Ishmael, blessed though he was, stood outside the special covenant relationship, and it was in this context that the specific promise of Isaac's birth was made to him.

Notes: Vs. 5,15: the new names signify a new beginning, although both 'Abraham' and 'Sarah' seem to be merely variants of their

27

earlier names. V. 20 contains a Hebrew play on words (cf. v. 17 f.), since 'Ishmael' means 'God hears'.

What are the values, and what the dangers, of religious ceremonials such as circumcision?

Questions for further study and discussion on Genesis chs. 12–17

1. How far is it possible to break away from one's environment? Would it be easier to obey God in a nomadic world than in our settled one?
2. Could the promises of Gen. **12.1** ff. be claimed by every missionary?
3. Was Gen. **12.1** ff. fulfilled in all respects in the N.T.?
4. Does Lot's choice of 'the cities of the valley' illustrate the futility, imperfection or godlessness of human reasoning? What part should reason and intelligence play in a Christian's decisions?
5. Does Gen. **14** offer any justification for war, in certain circumstances? Or should a Christian be a pacifist in all circumstances?
6. In the light of Gen. **15**.13–16, have we a duty to pronounce judgement on immoral acts on the part of nations today? If so, what should our principles of judgement be?
7. Study the N.T. references to circumcision. Ought Christians to bear some distinguishing mark?

Genesis 18 Impending Events

Some three months have passed, and the scene is high summer—a peaceful scene at the tent door, typical of Bedouin hospitality to this day. The visitors, however, were more than men (cf. **19**.1), and in speaking with them Abraham was conversing with God Himself (first indicated in v. 10). Their messages, moreover, were not the normal conventional conversation between visitors and host concerning news of the recent past but a declaration of the imminent future: Sarah's conception and Sodom's destruction. It is interesting to contrast Sarah's reaction to the former declaration with Abraham's response to the second; since fairly specific notice of Isaac's birth had already been given (**17**.21), Sarah's laughter denoted continuing disbelief, not the startled surprise Abraham had exhibited (**17**.17). In the laughter, however, the appropriateness of Isaac's name is again demonstrated.

The very close relationship and understanding between Abraham and his God are vividly portrayed in vs. 16–32. They were such that God put Himself under compulsion to reveal to Abraham a measure of the future, while Abraham for his part felt free to discuss the revelation and even to seek modification of it. There is a strong emphasis on righteousness in the passage; it is lack of it which dooms Sodom and Gomorrah (20), it is righteousness which should theoretically save them (24 f., etc.). Nor is v. 19 to be overlooked, where the purpose of divine choice is set out. Here was a lesson for future generations of Israel, not only that their duty was to live by God's standards, but also that they could exercise a preservative function in an evil society, for that is the point of vs. 22–32. Abraham's minimum was ten (32); Isa. **53** might be viewed as the continuation and climax of this passage, for it tells of the One who interposed Himself on behalf of the Many, bearing their sins in His own person.

Notes: Vs. 17 ff. lay the foundation for Abraham's title 'God's friend' (Isa. **41**.8); John **15**.15 f. similarly links the themes of friendship with God and divine choice. V. 33: 'his place' was Mamre (cf. v. 1).

What guidance does this chapter afford on the nature, function and effectiveness of prayer?

Genesis 19   The End of Lot's Story

The idyllic scene of the previous chapter could scarcely have a stronger contrast than Gen. **19**, with its account of the perverted carnality of Sodom, the violent destruction of the city and its neighbours, and finally the dismal end of Lot's career (we hear nothing more of him). Lot was not without courage (6), and he resisted the wishes of his fellow citizens to subject his guests to the sexual perversion to which Sodom has given its name (7); the incestuous relationship with his daughters (32–36) was neither with his consent nor his knowledge. Nevertheless he had deliberately made a permanent home among the men of Sodom, and his offer to them of his daughters (8) does him little credit. It is small wonder that his daughters grew to be little concerned about sexual morality, and had no respect for their father's person.

The destruction of the cities was God's judgement upon them; in more prosaic terms, the disaster was the result of an earthquake, which in this Dead Sea area produced emissions of inflammable sulphurous gases. Possibly it was falling debris which encased Lot's wife (26) (cf. the volcanic disaster to Pompeii in the first century A.D.). Later, the Dead Sea seems to have inundated the sites of the cities. We may well believe that the whole region was abandoned (31); most of the Dead Sea region still remains desolate and uninviting. However, Lot's daughters could have rejoined Abraham easily enough had they wished; instead they remained where they were, and their descendants later occupied the territory immediately east of the Dead Sea. The Moabites and Ammonites were thus close kin of Israel, but their unhappy origins would always be a barrier between them and Israel.

Notes: V. 1: the third visitor to Abraham (identified with the Lord) had not accompanied the other two (**18.**22). V. 3: 'unleavened bread' is quickly made. V. 4: 'to the last man' emphasizes that there were not ten righteous men in Sodom. V. 11: the word translated 'blindness' is unusual; clearly a supernatural affliction is meant. V. 22: the name refers back to v. 20. Vs. 37 f. preserve another Hebrew word-play: 'Moab' resembles *me'ab*, 'from a father', while 'Ben-ammi' would mean 'son of my kinsman'.

What duties have we towards our families and friends, inside our modern permissive society?

Genesis 20 Abraham at Gerar

The book of *Genesis* can often surprise the attentive reader; at this point, for instance, one would surely have expected the narrative to revert to Abraham (as indeed it does), to depict the firm qualities of his faith, and to relate at last the story of Isaac's birth. Instead, we seem to be back at square one, for we find Abraham repeating the deceitful and faithless deed perpetrated in Egypt early in his career (cf. **12.**10–19), and apparently without even the excuse of famine now. It is evident that Abraham was no plaster saint. But as in ch. **12,** so again now, God Himself rescues Abraham from his predicament, and enriches him with material goods in the process (14 ff.). Had there been no divine intervention, moreover, Abraham would have lost Sarah and forfeited God's promise to him of a son by her. Later generations of Israelites might well have paid better heed than they did to this record of the dangers of moral laxity (and its correlative, religious apostasy). It has often been argued that this chapter is simply a variant tradition of the incident recorded in ch. **12** (to say nothing of **26.**1–16)—the sort of suggestion which is equally beyond proof and disproof—but such an approach totally ignores the distinctive theological emphasis of the two passages (the earlier passage is concerned with the helplessness of Abraham and the loving care and protection of God; but the emphasis in ch. **20** is upon matters of faith and morality). Moreover, some new features emerge now; note the designation of Abraham as prophet and intercessor (7), for instance. His actions are given some measure of justification, or at least apology (11 f.). In the general context of the promises of Abraham's descendants, it is significant that the barrenness of Abimelech's family, which would in time inevitably mean the decline of his people (cf. 4,7,18), is causally linked with the absence of reverence or obedience to Abraham's God (11).

Notes: V. 1: Gerar was in the later Philistia, south-west of Mamre, but well north of the Negeb. V. 6: note that sin is an objective fact, which can be committed in all innocence. V. 12: see note on **12.13**. V. 16: a comparison of RSV with other English Versions will show how uncertain is the sense of the final clause.

Are there any principles here which should apply to a Christian in a pagan society?

Genesis 21.1—14 The Chosen and the Rejected

With masterly brevity, the long-awaited story of Isaac's birth is now told: the promise is fulfilled. Here was the first step in the creation of God's chosen nation, Israel, and the forefather, like all his sons, underwent the rite of circumcision (cf. **17.12**) at the age of eight days. The name 'Isaac' is probably an abbreviation for 'Isaac-el', '*God* laughs'; Sarah joined in the divine pleasure at the birth, her incredulous laughter now yielding to unadulterated joy (6). It is almost as if Isaac's birth brings universal 'laughter', for through Abraham's seed were all nations to be blessed (**12.2** f.). However, there was one individual whose 'laughter' (another form of the same Hebrew verb gives the sense 'playing') was unwelcome (9). The adolescent Ishmael may have been teasing the child Isaac in some fashion (cf. Gal. **4.29**); but if the shorter Hebrew text (cf. RSV margin) is original, its probable sense is that Ishmael was, by his very presence and uninhibited behaviour at the feast in Isaac's honour, usurping the latter's position—'playing the Isaac', as it were. In any case, Sarah's rather arrogant words of v. 7 led naturally to her jealous outburst of v. 10.

Abraham's reluctance to eject Ishmael was due first to natural affection, and also, no doubt, to the fact that displaced heirs like Ishmael were legally protected in the Hurrian society whose customs Abraham generally followed. But God's decision supported Sarah, not in her jealousy and hatred, but in her intuition that the two heirs to divinely promised greatness were bound to come into conflict if they remained together. It is instructive that while God's chosen man was Isaac (cf. Rom. **9.6–9**), yet He did not destine Ishmael to loss and suffering; since through Isaac universal blessings would come about (indeed since Ishmael too was a son of Abraham), Ishmael could not go unblessed.

Notes: V. 8: weaning probably took place much later than in modern western society; Isaac may have been as much as four years old. V. 14: 'child': the implication of RSV that Ishmael was a babe in arms is unfortunate and unnecessary.

In the light of Rom. 9, do you consider that the non-Christian world is destined to receive any blessings? If so, what would those blessings consist of?

Genesis 21.15–34 Beer-sheba

Once Israel was settled as a nation, her traditional northern and southern boundary towns were Dan and Beer-sheba respectively (cf. Judg. 20.1). Dan has already figured briefly in Abraham's career (14.14) as a place of conflict, from which Abraham drove foreign intruders headlong out of his promised territory. Now Beer-sheba comes into the story. It too appears as a site of conflict (25), which was, however, quickly resolved, at least for the time being (Gen. 26 tells of fresh trouble breaking out after Abraham's death). It was the chief town of the Negeb, a region (mentioned in 20.1) whose name means 'dry'; hence the importance of the theme of water throughout this passage, in connection with both Ishmael and Abraham. Wells in this region not only preserved individual human lives, but were equally vital as the basis of prosperity in herds and flocks.

As Ishmael fades out of the *Genesis* story, the reader is reminded once again of God's care for him and purposes for him. Previously his mother had from very similar circumstances turned back to Palestine and to Abraham (16.7–15); but now Hagar and Ishmael move permanently out of Palestine. Ishmael later took an Egyptian wife (21), but the prediction of 16.12 soon began to come true, for he avoided the settled civilization of Egypt, preferring a wild, nomadic, wilderness existence.

The treaty between Abraham and the king of Gerar attempted to safeguard the water-rights of both parties in perpetuity; hence the solemn oaths, and the appropriateness of the name by which God was worshipped in Beer-sheba, 'the Everlasting God'. Trees (33) could also be symbolic of stability and longevity. Beer-sheba, like Dan, became an important but corrupt sanctuary city in the later history of the nation (cf. Amos 8.14).

Notes: V. 15: 'cast' is not an ideal rendering—babyhood is *not* implied; better, 'abandoned' (JB). V. 21: Egypt was Hagar's homeland (cf. v. 9); Paran lay to the south of Palestine, to the north-east of Egypt. V. 25: 'complained'—the tense of the Hebrew verb suggests a continuing state of affairs. V. 31: 'Beer' means 'well', and 'sheba' both 'seven' and 'oath'; the paragraph suggests that the number seven had significance in oath rituals.

Beer-sheba's later importance to Israel no doubt had its origin in the events here recounted; how far is it a dangerous thing spiritually to dwell on past religious history?

Genesis 22   The Supreme Test of Faith

Heb. 11.17 ff. sees this chapter as the climax of Abraham's faith. One should not overlook Isaac's feelings and his ready submissiveness, but the spotlight is on Abraham throughout. Any parent can imagine something of his emotions; but it was more than his obedience that was being tested, it was his faith. The faith which had won him commendation (15.6) had been in God's promise of a son through whom a great nation would presently emerge; since then he had been taught that Isaac was the only son (cf. v. 2) who counted as far as this promise was concerned. Now he is commanded not just to witness but to carry out the very act which will cut off that life of such enormous promise. How could he both obey and retain his faith in God's promises? This cruel dilemma could only be resolved by yet greater faith, in a God whose every promise is fulfilled. Abraham did not fail, and his reward was to learn a fresh aspect of God's character (14).

The first-born was specially consecrated to God (cf. Exod. 13.1). Israel's neighbours sometimes sacrificed children to their gods, and the God of Israel had no less a claim on His worshippers; but He provided the way of escape (cf. Exod. 13.15). The principle of substitution was an important one, and laid a basis for the sacrificial system inaugurated under Moses and brought to its climax in Christ.

The important name in vs. 20–24 is Rebekah (23), who was to marry Isaac and give birth to the next generation of Abraham's promised descendants; Abraham's kin remaining in the Haran region were not forgotten, even though he had settled (more or less) in the south of Palestine. The related peoples who remained in the territory north of Palestine came to be called 'Aramaeans', their language 'Aramaic' (note the name Aram in v. 21). A related group who migrated to southern Mesopotamia were the Chaldeans (Hebrew *Kasdim*), whose ancestor may appear in this list as 'Chesed' (22).

Notes: V. 2: Moriah: 2 Chron. 3.1 suggests a theological, and possibly a geographical, link with the site of Solomon's Temple. V. 8: 'Himself'—better, 'for Himself'. V. 16: see Heb. 6.13 f.

In the light of the story of Abraham, what are the visible characteristics of a life of faith?

Questions for further study and discussion on Genesis chs. 18–22

1. Are there any practical ways in which we could emulate Abraham?
2. Does Gen. **18.**22–32 suggest that our function in society is that of intercession for it? How far does this passage exemplify our Lord's teaching on prayer?
3. Does Gen. **19** suggest that urban life and society are always more sinful than that in the countryside? Or are rural sins merely different?
4. What view does Rom. **1** take of sexual immorality and perversion?
5. In what sense was Abraham a prophet (**20.7**)? Have we any prophetic responsibilities, in view of 1 Cor. **14.**1–5?
6. Have you ever offered your children or your home back to God? What sacrifices would you be willing to make for Him?

Genesis 23   A Property Transaction

Abraham's life, latterly, seems to have revolved round the two fixed points of Mamre and Beer-sheba, and it was in the former vicinity that Sarah died; Mamre was very near the city of Hebron, known through most of the second millennium B.C. as Kiriath-arba. Though he had a treaty with Abimelech guaranteeing him water-rights, Abraham had never purchased any part of the promised land (cf. Acts **7.5**); he was content with a semi-nomadic life and with the glorious future in which he firmly believed (cf. Heb. **11.8** ff., 13–16). But the grim fact of death necessitated a permanent resting place, and Mach-pelah was his first and only acquisition of real estate. Here Sarah was buried, and in due course Abraham himself, Isaac, Rebekah, Leah and Jacob, too. 'In death', Gerhard von Rad has written, 'they were heirs and no longer strangers'.

For the acquisition of the property, Abraham had to bargain with some Hittites; the facts are given us in authentic detail. The typical oriental exaggerated courtesy is to be seen in the words of Ephron (11)—when he intended to exact a full and probably exorbitant price (15 f.)! Two other authentic features are the determination of Ephron that Abraham should take not only the cave itself (9) but the whole property (11), and the specific mention of trees (17). The laws of the Hittites (whose homeland lay in what is now eastern Turkey), it is now known, attached feudal obligations to property owners; and in their property transactions trees were regularly

34

listed. These Hittites were far from their homeland; perhaps they were a settlement of traders. (Conceivably, however, the term 'Hittites' in the O.T. includes other ethnic groups as well; many laws and customs were shared by a number of peoples, in any case.)

Notes: V. 2: Num. 13.22 recounts the rebuilding of this city, and possibly its renaming as 'Hebron'. V. 10: the city gate was always the place where business was transacted—the reference is to the city council, in modern terms.

In a society where a measure of ownership is inevitable, how far is it possible to emulate Abraham's disregard for his geographical environment?

Genesis 24 A Bride for Isaac

This, the longest chapter in *Genesis*, is devoted to a single theme, the story of how Isaac came to marry Rebekah. It is a charming narrative, in which the characters really come to life, even though to us the whole way of life depicted may seem strange and remote. Wonderful literature, agreed; but why, it might be asked, should so much attention be paid to a single event of a rather romantic and distinctly non-theological nature? To the Israelite reader of the passage, however, the topic would have seemed less insignificant, for Isaac and Rebekah were the parents of his whole nation: he owed his very existence to the events here related. Moreover, there is emphasis here on the purity of the stock; Ishmael had married an Egyptian (21.21), and Esau was to marry two Hittite women (26.34 f.), but for Isaac, the Israelite nation's sole forefather, as for Abraham before him, no such dilution of the chosen stock could be tolerated. Such were Abraham's wishes, expressed in the most solemn oath (3 f.), and the chapter confirms the rightness of his decisions by showing how God overruled in every detail of the story. It is interesting to note Abraham's insistence that Isaac must not leave the promised land (6), in view of the fact that Jacob and all his sons were to do so; the Israelite reader may have drawn the lesson that departure from the promised land was not God's intention for him, although it might at times prove to be God's punishment for folly and disobedience.

Notes: V. 2: the gesture served to make the oath more solemn. V. 10: Nahor was Abraham's brother (cf. v. 15). V. 27: 'in the way'— i.e. 'directly'. V. 30: the avarice of Laban's character is immediately noted. V. 33: the servant exhibited a remarkable degree of urgency, by eastern standards. V. 50: Bethuel (Laban's father) must have been very old, since Laban elsewhere speaks for him; the two men here comment that events had put it beyond their power to venture an opinion.

Does this chapter constitute an object lesson in divine guidance, or only in divine overruling, or both?

Genesis 25 Family Affairs

One generation gives place to another, as Abraham's life closes (8), and Isaac's sons are born (24 ff.). The picture is not so much of the inexorable passage of time as of the goodness of God; it was He who gave Abraham a full and happy life, and it was He who gave sons to Isaac, after Rebekah had experienced fully twenty years of barrenness (20 f., 26). In this way it is once more underlined that each generation was God's gift to His people. The theological principle of God's choice is also emphasized; just as Ishmael had been set aside, so too Esau, even though his mother was no concubine: Rom. 9.10–13 provides the commentary. At the same time, it is made clear that Esau had only himself to blame for losing the divine blessing—his birthright was the major share of the promised land. Jacob is already depicted as imperfect in character, but at least he did not despise God's promised gifts. However, even before their birth it had been foretold that the natural order would be reversed; the oracle was fulfilled in the subjugation of Edom (which had kings before Israel, cf. 36.31–39) to the Israelites under David (2 Sam. 8.13 f.).

The many names listed in 1–4, 13–16 of tribal groups descended from Abraham and thus related to Israel are of little interest to the modern reader. They all occupied the fringes of the great Syro-Arabian desert which encircles Palestine on the south and east, and are long since extinct. The point is that numerically and geographically they could have eliminated Israel in its infancy but for God's promises and protection.

Notes: V. 1: no time note is given; probably this marriage had taken place long before Sarah's death, but is only now relevant to the narrative. V. 20: Paddan-aram is another term for Upper Mesopotamia. V. 18: the final clause probably· refers to forays against related tribes. Vs. 25 f.: there are three word-plays here, 'red' linking up with Edom (cf. v. 30), 'hairy' with Seir (cf. 33.16), and 'heel' with Jacob. The meaning of Esau is unknown, but 'Jacob' is probably derived from a word meaning 'may God protect'. V. 30 depicts Esau as 'an uncouth glutton' (Speiser). V. 31: the sale of birthrights was perfectly legal under contemporary laws.

In what do immorality and irreligion lie, in the light of Heb. 12.15 ff.?

World of the Patriarchs

c.1800 B.C.	Abraham enters Canaan
c.1720 B.C.	Hyksos Dynasty established in Egypt
c.1690 B.C.	Joseph sold into Egypt
c.1670 B.C.	Jacob enters Egypt
c.1570 B.C.	Hyksos Dynasty ends
c.1309–1290 B.C.	Sethos I—the first persecuting Pharaoh
c.1290–1224 B.C.	Ramesses II—the second persecuting Pharaoh
c.1270 B.C.	The Exodus
c.1230 B.C.	Entry into Canaan

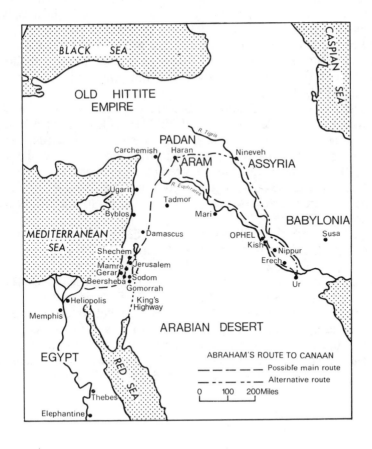

A constant theme of Abraham's life story had been the question of relationships with other people in and around Palestine; the promised land was no vacant one. The same problems confronted Isaac now, and it is at once impressed upon the reader that Isaac was little different from his father in the steps he took, and that God was just as faithful as He had ever been. The promises were renewed to Isaac, and he like Abraham before him was given prosperity in spite of a semi-hostile environment. Vs. 1–11 remind us of 12.10–19 and 20.1–18, but it is no 'duplicate narrative'; v. 2 explicitly recalls the former passage, while Abimelech's words in vs. 10 f. were based on ch. 20 and show that the lesson had already been learned that Abraham and his family must go unmolested. The rest of the chapter shows how Isaac's signal prosperity led to peace, and to the first fulfilment of the promise (4) that other peoples would seek to share in the blessing granted to Abraham's seed. The people in question were the forerunners of the Philistines, who arrived in force on the south Palestinian coast in *c.* 1200 B.C.; it is not certain whether Abimelech's people were actually related to the later Philistines or not, but it is clear that there could and should have been peace between Israel and Philistia, had both nations remained obedient to God.

The relationship of God's people to the land is one interesting aspect of the chapter. Isaac was forbidden to leave it as Abraham had done (2 f.); and he took the first steps towards settling in it, for agriculture demands a more sedentary life than sheep-herding (12). But intermarriage with its present occupants was an entirely different matter (34 f.); in that way lay bitter trouble for future generations of Israelites. Esau was thus the prototype of apostate Israelites.

Notes: V. 15: the Philistine action was designed to deplete Isaac's livestock and drive him from their territory. V. 26: the Abimelech and Phicol of 21.22 may have belonged to the previous generation; family names and titles often recurred in the ancient Near East. V. 33: 'Shibah' should perhaps read 'Sheba'; in context 'oath' (cf. vs. 28,31) is meant. Cf. 21.31; these parallel statements should not be taken as conflicting indications of how Beer-sheba got its name, but as comments on the appropriateness of the name.

Have we guidance here for settling disputes in a Christian manner?
How far is material prosperity still a sign of God's favour?

Paul's words in 1 Cor. **1.**26 f. could well serve as a judgement on Gen. **27.** Here are God's chosen family, deceiving and hurting one another, and endeavouring to assert their own will in the face of His plans for them. None of the four characters emerges blameless. Note the bitterness, hatred and separation which resulted, in punishment of their own follies; and yet the divine plans were never frustrated for a moment.

We know from ancient documents that in Hurrian circles (whose conventions the patriarchs seem to have followed) the words of a dying man were legally binding; and certainly Isaac thought he might be dying, though in fact he lived long afterwards. The situation thus gave his words to both sons a testamentary character. In general, the spoken word was more irrevocable in O.T. times than we would consider it today; all the more did this apply when the spoken word invoked the name of God. God purposed a special blessing for the younger son; and all unwittingly Isaac acted as God's agent and spokesman: the blessing could never be recalled.

The oracle to Jacob is plain enough, but—as RSV margin indicates —there is ambiguity in Isaac's wishes for Esau (39); we may even suspect that the ambiguity was deliberate. At any rate, there is no doubt that the promised land was more fertile than the terrain Esau's descendants came to inhabit. The 'one blessing' (38) for Esau was that one day he would assert his independence (40); this prediction was fulfilled when the Edomites broke away from Israel's control, as they were to do from time to time.

Rebekah's deceitfulness persisted to the end; she offered one (genuine) reason to Jacob for his departure, but quite a different one to Isaac.

Notes: V. 36 provides another Hebrew word-play, since 'birthright' and 'blessing' are very similar words. V. 44: 'a while' (literally 'a few days'): in fact, twenty years passed, and mother and son never met again. V. 45: 'bereft of you both'—since Jacob would be dead and Esau could well be indicted for his murder. V. 46: cf. **26.**34 f.

Was Esau's behaviour any more reprehensible than Jacob's? How wrong is deceit?

Jacob left southern Palestine on his self-imposed exile, and reached a point in central Palestine, Bethel, another famous sanctuary city in later Israel. It had been already claimed for Yahweh in token fashion by Abraham (12.8), and it was here that Jacob now had his personal encounter with Abraham's God. Each generation evidently needed a renewal of the promises of God, and they responded by renewing their covenant relationship with Him. The terms of Jacob's covenant are set out in vs. 20 ff.; and if there is a certain aura of bargaining in Jacob's words, that is fully in keeping with his character. Tithing (22) was to be compulsory under the law of Moses, but Jacob offered tithes voluntarily, in proportion to the prosperity that God might allow him; but all he requested from God was the bare minimum of food and clothing (20). The vital promise was still the land itself, and we can now see how that promise had been given and renewed at one locality after another within the Holy Land.

The unique dream at Bethel makes an interesting contrast with the story of the Tower of Babel (11.1-9). The staircase (more accurate than 'ladder', v. 12) is reminiscent of the temple-towers of ancient Mesopotamia; the phrases 'house of God' and 'gate of heaven' (17) stand in contrast to Babel's vaunted title, 'gate of the god'; and the lone individual going into exile may be compared with the scattering abroad of the men of Babel (11.9). But the initiative at Bethel was wholly God's, and His forgiving generosity stands over against the human arrogance displayed at Babel.

There is pathos in the brief note about Esau (6-9), as he endeavoured vainly to win back his parents' favour. The offending Hittite wives were not divorced, nor could Jacob's blessing be recalled. Esau's new wife was from within the family, but outside the chosen line.

Notes: Vs. 3 f.; cf. 17.1-8. V. 12: cf. John 1.51. V. 18: i.e. Jacob consecrated a memorial stone. V. 19: 'that place' (or 'shrine') was originally distinct from the city, though very near it (cf. 12.8). Vs. 20 f. (and the sequel) will have constituted a sermon to the sixth-century exiles.

To what extent are vs. 20 ff. an expression of faith? Is it ever proper to 'bargain' with God?

Questions for further study and discussion on Genesis chs. 23-28

1. If Abraham paid Ephron an exorbitant price for Mach-pelah, should we praise his generosity or rebuke his poor stewardship of money? How is a Christian to approach this sort of problem?
2. Isaac must not marry outside the family (Gen. 24); why do you

think some O.T. worthies (e.g. Joseph, Moses) were permitted to do so?
3. Should every Christian expect divine guidance as to his choice of husband or wife?
4. Are there any birthrights we are in danger of despising?
5. Should we conclude from Gen. 26.9 f. that deceit is only wrong when it has harmful results? How serious a sin is lying? What has the N.T. to say on the subject?
6. Why did not Jacob's deceit (Gen. 27) cause him to forfeit Isaac's blessing?

Genesis 29 Laban's Daughters

The locale of the narrative reverts to the Haran area, which Abraham had left long before (12.4), and it is not surprising to find numerous details in this chapter which can be paralleled in documents from the ancient city of Nuzi, another centre of Hurrian civilization; for instance, both the custom of vs. 24,29, and the brief and casual way in which it is referred to, can be paralleled. Jacob's servitude to Laban is another authenticated detail; we may surmise that Laban had no sons as yet, and was adopting Jacob as a slave-heir (see notes on ch. 15). The seven years to win a bride seems to have been a high price to pay, however, by contemporary standards.

Jacob's situation is strikingly different from that of his father. Isaac had won a bride in the minimum time without ever leaving the promised land, without relinquishing his heritage or becoming indebted to another man. But Jacob took nothing with him and was forced to become dependent for long years upon a man of formidable avarice and powers of deception. The fault, however, lay entirely on his own shoulders. There is irony not only in the deceiver being deceived, but also in the way that Leah displaced her younger sister with the man who had displaced his elder brother; moreover, her sons were the leading progenitors of the Israelite tribes, including Judah in particular. The chapter illustrates not only how human deeds bring their own punishment, but also how God uses such circumstances to further His own purposes.

All of Jacob's sons except Benjamin were to be born outside Palestine, interestingly enough; the very ancient credal statement of Deut. 26.5 testified accurately to Israelite origins. The significance given to the names of Leah's sons (31–35) relates to the rivalry between Jacob's wives—another argument against polygamy—and foreshadows the later inter-tribal frictions.

Notes: V. 10: Jacob's action was that of a very strong man (cf.

41

vs. 3 f.). V. 17: 'weak' may be correct, but AV 'tender' is still a possibility. V. 25: Leah would have been veiled at the previous day's ceremony. V. 31: 'hated' is too strong a word; 'unloved' or 'neglected' is the sense.

To what extent does the principle of retribution on this life still apply? What other principles govern prosperity and adversity?

Genesis 30 Problems and Prosperity

Jacob's large family began at last to foreshadow the promised great nation, which Abraham can have foreseen so dimly; nevertheless, there is untold pathos in the domestic intrigues depicted and hinted at in vs. 1–24. In a polygamous society, the status conferred by fertility is probably inevitable, and the resulting unmerited misery, here and there, undeniably tragic (cf. 1 Sam. 1). The most pitiful feature here is the sordid bargaining over the mandrakes (a narcotic plant fancied to hold sex-stimulant properties); God's grace in giving Rachel a son was at least attributed by her to the true Agency (22 ff.).

Bargaining and scheming were constant features of Jacob's life. His problem now was that he had no clear legal right to remove his wives and sons from Laban's household, and no title whatever to any of the property of Laban, who now had sons of his own (cf. 31.1). So the two men came to an agreement, and both indulged in underhand activities to defeat the other's schemes. Jacob's ploy (37–42), though apparently devoid of any scientific basis, was fully credited in the ancient world; here too the resulting prosperity of Jacob should be attributed to God and no other. God thus gave wealth to yet another generation of His chosen family, in spite of all the demerits of Jacob's character. The promise that blessing would overflow to other peoples too was also fulfilled for this generation in the wealth which Jacob brought Laban, and which Laban himself was obliged to acknowledge (27–30).

Notes: V. 3: 'upon my knees'—i.e. 'in my name and acknowledged by me'. V. 11: 'Gad' must in context mean 'fortune' (RSV margin), though the word also means 'troop' (cf. AV). V. 21: Dinah is mentioned, since her story follows in ch. 34. V. 32 is none too intelligible, and there is good reason to prefer the ancient Greek translation (the Septuagint), which speaks only of black sheep and variegated goats (see JB). Vs. 39 f. are also difficult; the suggestion that 'flocks' (39) refers only to goats, and so contrasts with the sheep (40), is attractive.

Temporary barrenness is a recurring theme of Genesis; what purposes may God have in denying children to some Christian homes?

Jacob's journey to the Haran region had permitted him to marry within the family, but it cost him dearly in terms of time and happiness. He now had to extricate himself from an unhappy and deteriorating situation, and from the clutches of a grasping and treacherous character; it is even possible that the 'sons' of v. 1 were adopted heirs and not Laban's own children. The end of the chapter sees Jacob safely back in the promised land (Gilead, v. 25, was a region of Transjordan), with an agreed frontier between him and Laban, but it took the personal intervention of God to bring this about; but for His overruling and help, Abraham and Isaac might earlier have become inextricably linked with Egypt or Philistia, and now Jacob with the Arameans. If the promise of Palestine awaited fulfilment centuries later, the freedom to live there was already granted by God, to each generation individually.

There are two recurring themes in the chapter, one legal, the other theological. The legal position of Jacob is discussed in several ways; his actions were justified by Laban's daughters, first (14 ff.), and finally ratified by Laban himself in the binding covenant at Mizpah (44–50). The strange incident of Rachel's theft of the household deities is connected with legal rather than theological issues, for such gods served then as title deeds to property in the Haran civilization; apparently Rachel hoped to win more than flocks and herds for her husband. The fate those deities suffered, however, is surely part of the theological fabric of the story. Those inanimate and passive objects stand in contrast to the God who revealed Himself to Jacob and Laban and brought their actions into His control. Note how both parties came to recognize Him as the God of previous family and personal experience. (The term 'Fear', v. 42, probably links up with 28.17.)

Notes: V. 19: sheep-shearing involved considerable festivities (cf. 1 Sam. 25). V. 21: 'the Euphrates' (literally 'the River'): perhaps the reference is rather to a river much nearer Gilead, in view of the mere seven-day journey mentioned (23 ff.). V. 24: Laban is warned to be careful what he says, not prohibited from all conversation with Jacob. V. 47: the names (in Hebrew and Aramaic respectively) show that this point, with its watchtower Mizpah, came to serve as a linguistic as well as political boundary.

In what terms could you describe God, in the light of your own or your family's experience?

Genesis 32 Meeting with God

From Mizpah Jacob continued to journey in a direction approximately due south, as the mention of Mahanaim (2) and Peniel (30) reveal. The river he crossed was the Jabbok (22), not the Jordan (though v. 10 suggests he looked wistfully at it). In other words, he made no attempt yet to enter Palestine proper, but headed straight for Esau's territory (later known as Edom), sending messengers ahead as he did so (3). His determination to put matters right with Esau was, however, matched by his fears—fears that Esau would exact a full revenge and that God might after all fail in His promises (11 f.). Hitherto he had attempted to achieve his ends by bargains and tricks; by now he seems to have learned to put himself in God's hands and to practise honesty in his dealings with other men.

The Jabbok, which flows through a deep east-west canyon into the Jordan, forms a natural frontier, and evidently Jacob viewed it as his Rubicon. It was entirely appropriate that at this stage in his career and his journey he should have a personal encounter with God, a mysterious and unique experience which left a permanent mark on him. Where Abraham had been content to listen or to discuss, Jacob must struggle, and oblige God to struggle with him. Similar defiance coupled with demands marked the career of his offspring after him, and they, like him, well deserved the name 'Israel' (28; see RSV margin), which occurs here for the first time in the Bible.

The various place-names of the chapter are all interpreted with reference to Jacob. The RSV footnotes explain most of them; 'Jabbok' (22) is a very similar word to 'wrestled' (*ye'abek*, v. 24). In later centuries, Israel's tenure of Transjordan was often insecure, and this record of such sites' connection with both Jacob and his God will have served as both reassurance and warning to Israelites who lived there.

Notes: Vs. 1 f.: Jacob took the vision both as a sign of protection and as guidance on how to act; 'messengers' (3) is the same word in Hebrew as 'angels', and 'companies' (7) is from the same word as 'armies', Mahanaim. V. 32: a detail nowhere else mentioned.

How far are we prepared to go to promote reconciliation between ourselves and others?

Genesis 33 Meeting with Esau

Whether or not Esau's intentions had been hostile—his large body of men may have been simply a precautionary measure—the

meeting of the two brothers proved amicable enough. Possibly Esau was disarmed by the way Jacob put himself in a defenceless position at the head of the caravan. The fact that Jacob did so can be attributed to the reassurance he had gained from his Peniel experience, for before that he had been careful to remain at the rear. The conversation that ensued between the brothers once again looks very like haggling (perhaps Jacob found it difficult to converse in other modes!), but on this occasion Jacob was not seeking to gain anything, and we may doubt if Esau was either. The conversation was really the reversal of their previous dealings with each other, Jacob now giving instead of stealing, Esau voicing affection instead of threats. The latter's disinterest in Jacob's wealth may well have been genuine, for it is evident that both men had prospered; Isaac's blessings and God's plans for both had already seen fulfilment.

However, Isaac's blessing for Esau had contained a less happy element (cf. 27.40), and no doubt this fact explains the way the two men now parted (12–18). Jacob had no wish to become Esau's close neighbour in Seir (many miles to the south), and he played for time, first residing in Succoth (a few miles west of Peniel) and then, when he could, returning to Palestine proper, travelling due west to Shechem. The narrative is extremely concise, and one could interpret it as implying that Jacob in the end cheated Esau once again; but this is scarcely credible, since it would make nonsense of the reconciliation just effected.

The past was thus forgiven, but not forgotten; it was his anxiety to put as many miles as possible between himself and Esau that led Jacob to settle, purchasing property outside Shechem. The city was in principle claimed for God and Israel (20); but trouble would not be long in coming.

Notes: V. 10: 'the face of God': cf. 32.30. V. 19: the family of Hamor was still prominent in Shechem in Gideon's time (cf. Judg. 9.28).

What do you consider the most important elements in effective reconciliations?

Genesis 34 {Conflict at Shechem}

Jacob's property purchase at Shechem led to a fresh problem of relationships, in its way comparable with Abraham and Isaac's experiences in Philistian territory (chs. 20,26). There were differences, however, firstly because the purchase itself made Jacob more attached to the Shechem area than Abraham or Isaac ever

45

needed to be where Gerar was concerned, and secondly in the fact that Jacob had a very much larger family, with their own individual viewpoints. His family were evidently adult by now; and in the light of 14.14 and 33.1 we may safely assume that Simeon and Levi were not alone when they attacked the city, even if the male citizens were largely incapacitated by the after effects of circumcision. The chapter makes it clear that Jacob's family were a formidable body of men (27 ff.) but were not yet powerful enough to withstand a concerted attack by the settled population (30).

It is small wonder, in these circumstances, that attempts were made to promote intermarriage and in every practical way to foster unity between the nascent 'Israel' and the men of Shechem. This city (destined to be of major importance in northern Israel) was inhabited by a pre-Canaanite people (uncircumcised Hivites, cf. vs. 2,14), who were willing to compromise (and so submitted to circumcision) but at the same time expected Jacob to do the same, in the first place submitting to their lower standards of sexual morality, in which they were true forerunners of the Canaanites. And Jacob himself was apparently ready to meet them half-way; to have done so would have meant the eventual absorption of Israel and the disappearance of God's chosen race. In this respect Gen. 34 offered a warning to later generations to beware of close ties with the Canaanites. At the same time, the actions of Simeon and Levi are certainly not commended; see the stern denunciation of them in 49.5 ff. The last two verses of the chapter leave us with the dilemma between meek acquiescence and treacherous violence.

Notes: V. 7: 'folly in Israel': i.e. a moral outrage by the standards Israel came to adopt. V. 12: the 'marriage present and gift' were for the bride's father and bride respectively. V. 24: 'all who went out of the gate': i.e. all able-bodied citizens.

What principles govern the rightness—or otherwise—of compromise?

Questions for further study and discussion on Genesis chs. 29–34

1. Why did God allow the patriarchs to practise polygamy? Is it invariably wrong, in every part of today's world?
2. Gen. 30 depicts both Rachel and Jacob as placing a credulous faith in the 'science' of their day; should we take a warning from this? Or should we simply note that God nevertheless rewarded their credulity?
3. How should a Christian set about coping with a treacherous and worldly schemer such as Laban was?
4. Make a study of the names and titles used of God in *Genesis*.

5. Do you approve of the methods used by Jacob to effect reconciliation with Esau? What would you have done differently?
6. 'Compromise' tends to be a good word in politics, a bad word in religion; should this be so? What room is there for compromise in matters of faith and practice?

Genesis 35 The End of an Era

Several threads of the story are here brought to their logical conclusion; Jacob's return to Bethel, the completion of his family, his reunion with his father at Mamre, the death of Isaac, and Jacob's last act in collaboration with Esau, are recounted. Two other deaths are recorded. On the other hand, the birth of Benjamin opened a new era, for now the story of the deeds and relationships of the twelve sons of Jacob can be fully told.

Geographically, a systematic journey southwards, from Shechem to Mamre, is depicted. Bethel holds the central position, in the journey and the story, for Jacob was under a vow to return to it (cf. **28.21** f.). He did so as if on a pilgrimage, taking every step to render his whole company holy, getting rid of household deities like Rachel's (cf. **31.19**), and magic charms ('the rings', 4), while God afforded immunity (from attack and also religious contamination) from local inhabitants. The clause 'when he came from Paddan-aram' (9) implies that all the intervening events, recounted in chs. **33** f., were unnecessary delays from a theological point of view; Jacob's blessing and future were both linked firmly with Bethel.

Benjamin was the only son of Jacob born in the promised land (the last sentence in v. 26 is clearly a generalization), and it is probable that he was born in the territory afterwards allotted to his tribe (cf. 1 Sam. **10.2**), rather than in the vicinity of Bethlehem, where the traditional site of Rachel's tomb is (v. 19 states merely that they were *en route* for Bethlehem).

Reuben's arrogant and immoral deed (22) constituted a claim to equality with his father (cf. 2 Sam. **16.21** f.); instead, it cost him his birthright (cf. 1 Chron. **5.1**). Already Jacob's three eldest sons had forfeited his blessing (cf. **49.3–7**).

Notes: V. 8: Deborah: cf. **24.59**. V. 18: 'her soul'—i.e. her life; in the O.T. the two terms are often synonymous. The point of the ehange of name from Ben-oni to Ben-jamin was that the former was ill-omened, while the latter carried overtones of good fortune.

How far is it a Christian obligation to make vows to God?

Verses 6 f. record the final parting of Jacob and Esau, which was due less to mutual incompatibility than to their God-given prosperity; so too had Abraham and Lot parted company (13.2–12). They separated, but their bond of kinship was never forgotten, and for many centuries the history of their two peoples was intertwined; the Herod family of N.T. times was Edomite (Idumaean). It was David who first made the Edomites subject to Israel (2 Sam. 8.14), and it seems very probable that the name-lists preserved in this chapter were brought into Israelite keeping during his reign (note the reference to kings of Israel in v. 31). Conceivably the names in vs. 40–43 refer to David's local administration in Edom. In other eras the Edomites proved something of a thorn in Israel's side; see Num. 20 and Psa. 137.7 ff., in particular, for situations both earlier and later than David. Gen. 36, by tracing their distinct history in outline fashion from Esau's time till David's, implies that God overruled in their affairs and preserved them as a people for His own purposes; they too were sons of Abraham. Not that they were of pure stock; this chapter does not gloss over their intermarriage with other groups, in particular the earlier inhabitants of the Edom area, known as Horites (20), who were perhaps related to the Hurrians of the Mesopotamian and Syrian regions. Another name which was destined to play some part in the O.T. story is Amalek (12).

Constitutionally, tribal chieftains (15–19) gave way to a non-hereditary monarchy (31–39). The kings were presumably elected, and kept court in their own home towns, just as Saul did at Gibeah.

The names Seir and Edom are generally synonymous in the O.T.; their strict application may have been to the eastern and western parts of the territory respectively.

Notes: See Kidner's commentary for discussion of the question of discrepancies in the name-lists. V. 37: 'the Euphrates' seems very unlikely in this context, and the literal rendering 'the river', referring to some local Edomite stream, is to be preferred.

In what ways should the Biblical doctrine of election affect our relationships with other individuals or communities? What responsibilities have Christians towards non-Christians?

Genesis 37 Joseph's Youth

With this chapter begins the final section of *Genesis*, and the story of Joseph. While Joseph was the elder son of Jacob's favourite wife Rachel, in the full list of Jacob's family he was last but one. Historically, however, the most powerful tribes were to be Judah and

Ephraim, which was one of the two Joseph tribes (cf. **41**.50 ff.), and for a long period Ephraim would be the stronger of the two. One of the unpredictable facets of history? No, says *Genesis*; the reason was that God's principle of choice was still at work—from Joseph's very boyhood. Hitherto, those not specially chosen by God, like Ishmael and Esau, found themselves outside the promised land; now it is revealed that even within the chosen race and the confines of Israel God exercised the same principle, selecting individuals and individual tribes, for leadership and other purposes. But while His choice was sovereign (cf. Rom. **9**.10–13), we are nevertheless shown that it was not arbitrary; Jacob's three eldest sons had already exhibited their unworthiness for prominence in Israel, and v. 2 now reveals how undeserving were his fifth, sixth, seventh and eighth. There remained three, including Judah, who still had priority over Joseph, but they too forfeited their place by their murderous hostility towards their young brother. There is irony in the fact that the man who saved the boy's life, and thus enabled him to climb eventually to power, was the eldest son, Reuben, who but for his own folly should have sired the leading tribe in Israel. Reuben's plan was to restore Joseph to his father (22), which could have been but a temporary rescue; but events overruled Reuben, and the narrator feels no need to identify the One who engineered them. God thus spared the life of another generation. Judah, of course, played his part, but in no very admirable fashion (26 f.).

Notes: V. 1: Jacob seems to have remained at Mamre near Hebron (cf. v. 14). V. 3: Joseph's 'robe' was in any case ostentatious; the traditional 'coat of many colours' remains a possible translation. V. 10: 'your mother' can only refer to Leah. V. 28 is rather confusing; if Midianites and Ishmaelites refer to the same people (which is quite possible, in view of Judg. **8**.24), then it was his brothers who 'drew Joseph up'.

To what extent were Jacob's and Joseph's actions ill-advised? What morals may be drawn from this chapter regarding human relationships in general?

Genesis 38 Judah's Maturity

Joseph is forgotten for the moment, apparently out of sight and out of mind, and the reader's attention is drawn to Judah, Joseph's rival for political power. The tribe of Judah indeed survived the northern kingdom, and went on to provide the chain of salvation down to N.T. times (cf. John **4**.22); moreover, Judah himself,

Tamar and Perez all figure in the genealogy of Christ Himself (Matt. **1**.3). For all that, Gen. **38** is no very edifying chapter as regards human behaviour —the significant characters are presented 'warts and all'—and again Scripture is emphatic that the chosen race did nothing to earn their election. For all their moral failures, God was good to them, permitting Judah to commence his occupation of southern Palestine, and granting him a family, thus honouring His pledges to Abraham, Isaac and Jacob. As before, He intervened and indicated a chosen line of descent, by denying children to Er and Onan, and giving Perez priority over his brother.

The story is true to the conventions of the day; indeed, the double standard of morality for male and female has been all too familiar throughout history. The custom of 'levirate marriage', i.e. marriage to one's elder brother's widow to provide an heir for him, was common in the ancient Near East, though it was an unpopular law (because of the financial and other obligations it entailed). All too common in Canaanite circles, too, was the custom of ritual prostitution, especially at festival times such as sheep-shearing (12 f.); its purpose was magical, to promote the fertility of the soil. Judah took some sort of warning (26), at least, and it was true that at a later date his tribe was less affected by Canaanite practices than was Ephraim (note Hos. **4**.14 f.).

Notes: V. 1: Adullam was in the centre of Judah's later tribal territory. V. 8: cf. Deut. **25**.5 f. V. 9 has no relevance to debates about birth control; Onan deliberately and consistently cheated Tamar of her social and legal right to an heir. V. 11: the parenthesis makes it clear that Judah had no real intention of letting Tamar marry Shelah. V. 30: 'Zerah' probably means 'bright', a reference to the scarlet thread.

In what respects was Tamar 'righteous' (26)? Is 'righteousness' a purely relative matter?

Genesis 39 Joseph's Morality

The locale of the narrative switches abruptly from southern Palestine to Egypt, where the fortunes of Joseph are now followed in considerable detail. Most of the stories in *Genesis* are told with reasonable brevity, but Joseph's adventures are recounted at some length, with no little dramatic effect. Thus the narrator brings home to the reader how long a process it was for Joseph to rise to power, how long it was before his brothers met retribution, and how long a time Jacob went uncomforted. In this first Egyptian episode, far from taking the first steps towards a position of authority, Joseph on the face of it descended even lower in the social scale, from slave to convict; yet in both situations, in fact, he showed himself worthy of the fullest responsibilities he could be offered. In many ways Joseph is presented to us as the prototype of the man of true wisdom; his actions are governed by careful reasoning rather than by social conventions, and by the fear of God (cf. Prov. **1.7**) rather than by natural human inclinations. We left Judah in ch. 38 in a position of full freedom of action but exercising very little self-discipline; Joseph stands in marked contrast, for he was another man's slave yet master of himself. In no sphere was the contrast more glaring than in sexual morality. Note how both men left behind a symbol of their moral standing, the one willingly, the other perforce (**38.18; 39.12**).

Joseph's wise and honourable behaviour merited him positions of trust; but note that the chapter ascribes his success not to himself but to God. His imprisonment was probably a mild enough punishment for the misdemeanour of which he was falsely accused, but if so it should be credited to a fresh act of salvation on God's part rather than to any suspicion on the part of Potiphar of his wife's veracity.

Notes: V. 6 contains an allusion to the rigid dietary taboos of ancient Egypt; cf. **43.32**. V. 14: the word 'Hebrew' is often in the O.T. used on the lips of non-Hebrews in a derogatory sense.

How far can one expect reward in this life for fidelity to a high moral code? Should one view Joseph's experiences as in any way a norm?

Questions for further study and discussion on Genesis chs. 35–39

1. Is there a Christian counterpart to 'putting away foreign gods' (Gen. **35.2**)? What does holiness mean in N.T. terms?
2. Could the ancient social conventions of Gen. **38** be translated into any modern equivalents? On what basis should local customs be evaluated?
3. How far was Jacob's skill in deception passed on to his sons? What characteristics are likely to be reproduced in our children?
4. How many of the precepts of *Proverbs* can you find exemplified in Joseph's early career?
5. Do you think Joseph is portrayed as an ideal character? Is it legitimate to view him as having foreshadowed Christ?

Dreams play a relatively small part in the Bible as a whole, but have an important role in the story of Joseph. God could (and can) make Himself known to man in a wide variety of ways, but dreams were evidently a rare medium of revelation. The dreamers here and in ch. 41 were Egyptians, and it is made clear that they expected their dreams to have significance; this outlook was typical of the Egyptians, who attributed predictive value to dreams, and wrote 'scientific' literature on their intepretation. God accordingly condescended now to make use of their dreams. We may view the dreams of Joseph (37.5–11) as having been a preparation for the role he now had to play. There is an interesting distinction, however, between his own dreams and those recorded here; the only question regarding the former pair was whether they had any significance or not; if they did, their meaning was only too clear—neither Joseph's brothers nor his parents needed any interpreter! But the Egyptian political prisoners' dreams were more opaque and an interpreter was essential. The grisly pun (19 f.)—'to lift the head' was normally an idiom signifying favourable reception—emphasized the confusing similarity of the dreams and yet their totally different connotations. Joseph, in filling the interpreter's role, was more than the wise and prudent youth of previous chapters; for the ability to interpret dreams could only be God-given. Thus, although his own conduct secured him promotion within the prison walls, it was God alone who provided the ultimate means of escape. Joseph, of course, saw the chance (14 f.), but the sequel (23) showed that human shrewdness was insufficient to secure his release.

The rank of the Egyptian prisoners was much higher than the English terms 'butler' and 'baker' suggest. Their offence may well have been of a political nature.

Notes: V. 3: Egyptian prisons were complex affairs, administratively, and it looks as if Potiphar was the superior of 'the keeper of the prison' (39.21 ff.). V. 8: in effect, Joseph discredited the Egyptian professional interpreters and wise men. V. 20: the rendering 'singled out' (Jewish Publication Society of America version) copes neatly with the ambiguous 'lifted up the head of'.

For what purposes does God sometimes unveil part of the future? Why, for that matter, does He normally hide it from us?

Genesis 41   From Prison to Palace

Now at last Joseph's dreams and godly behaviour were vindicated. All in a day, he went from a dungeon to a position of supreme power in Egypt; but thirteen long years had passed since his shepherd days in Canaan (46; cf. 37.2). The change in his fortunes was due to the Egyptian king's dreams—once again, the one reinforcing the other (32). These dreams were different again. Those of earlier chapters had been of no practical import, since there had been no suggestion that Joseph, the butler or the baker could do anything to avert the future their dreams portended; but to the interpretation of the king's dreams Joseph could add practical advice about the appropriate measures to meet the situation. Joseph again made it clear that dream interpretation was no mechanical thing (16); the result was that Pharaoh recognized Joseph to be not only 'discreet and wise' but also the vehicle of 'the Spirit of God' (38 f.). It is interesting that there is no hint of anyone's doubting the accuracy of Joseph's words; divine authority carries its own conviction.

Many details of the chapter are authentically Egyptian—for instance, Joseph conformed to Egyptian customs before confronting Pharaoh (14), for shaving was not customary among the Israelites and their forebears. The sun-god worshipped at On (the later 'Heliopolis') was called Ra, which appears as the last element in the name Potiphera (45). For other details, see the commentaries. However, the meaning of one or two words remains uncertain (especially Abrek [43], and Zaphenath-paneah [45]); above all, we have no way of identifying the Egyptian king, though he was probably one of the non-Egyptian 'Hyksos' kings and reigned about 1700 B.C.

Famine rarely afflicted Egypt and Palestine simultaneously, since their sources of fertility were different (Egypt depended on the Nile, not on local rainfall). Patently this was no ordinary famine.

Notes: V. 6: 'the east wind', coming from the desert, is always hot and unpleasant in Egypt. Vs. 51 f.: Manasseh and Ephraim are Hebrew, not Egyptian, names; this fact, like the meanings given them, harks back to Joseph's homeland, which he certainly did *not* forget!

Does this chapter warn the reader against viewing all human catastrophes as acts of divine judgement?

Genesis 42 Reunion

There was plenty of contact between Palestine and Egypt during the second millennium B.C., such as the slave trade which had brought Joseph to Egypt, and it is no surprise to find that word soon reached Jacob of the food supplies available in Egypt. The brothers' journey and meeting with Joseph followed inevitably;

their first act on meeting him immediately fulfilled his first dream (37.7). Their failure to recognize him was natural enough; he was twenty years older now, a mature man, he spoke in the Egyptian language (cf. v. 23), and in any case they were convinced he was dead (22). It now became apparent that their consciences were not totally dulled (21); and they were to show a concern for their father and their young brother (Benjamin) which had not characterized them in earlier days.

Joseph's actions were a strange mixture of love and resentment. He treated them like guests (25), and yet it could only add to their fears. His accusation of espionage would have rung true enough at the time, and then as now spying was an extremely serious charge; that too must have terrified them. The choice of Simeon, the second eldest, as hostage was inevitable once Joseph knew that Reuben had been his rescuer years before (22 f.). It is easy to condemn Joseph as vindictive and cruel, playing a cat-and-mouse game with his brothers; but they had after all been guilty of a particularly callous deed, tantamount to fratricide, and it is no wonder that Joseph wished to wring an apology from them before reconciliation could follow. In taking a hostage, moreover, he was primarily trying to ensure his brothers' return to Egypt. Their unbrotherly act would in fact leave a legacy of suspicion and jealousy among the tribes which reached a climax in the period of the Judges. It is noteworthy that the most jealous and aggressive tribe was to be Ephraim, Joseph's son's tribe (cf. Judg. **8.1** ff.; **12.1–6**).

Notes: V. 21: 'he besought us'—a detail not mentioned in ch.37. V. 22: it is not clear why the brothers assumed Joseph to be dead, unless they had convinced themselves of the truth of their own lies (37.31 ff.).

How far is forgiveness appropriate or desirable without prior apology or compensation? Are there any circumstances in which forgiveness ought to be withheld?

Genesis 43 The Second Encounter

Joseph's stratagem to ensure his brothers' return would have been of no avail, for Jacob was quite prepared to abandon Simeon rather than risk Benjamin; once again it was God, not Joseph's shrewdness, that produced the desired result. The increasing hardships created by the famine eventually forced Jacob's hand, though he still tried to ignore the plight of Simeon and the instructions to bring Benjamin. This time it was Judah who stood surety for Benjamin; twice over he and Reuben had shown that of the ten eldest sons of Jacob they possessed the greatest sense of fraternal care and responsibility. Hardship and frightening problems were not only affecting character but also bringing it to light for what it was.

The new encounter with Joseph produced nothing but exceptional generosity from him; Simeon was at once released, and all eleven were made Joseph's guests. For all his kind words, however, they could scarcely be expected to feel very relaxed; they were ready to fear the worst (18), and his accurate knowledge of their exact relationship (33) was calculated to disturb them afresh—or was it intended as some sort of clue to his identity? At any rate, despite their puzzlement, they had no intention of spurning their good fortune, and they made merry (34); besides, they dared not insult their host.

It is once again emphasized how Joseph's brothers fulfilled his youthful dreams (26,28). The depth of his emotions is again stressed, too (30); admittedly, he had no reason to feel vengeful towards Benjamin, who had been too young to join the conspiracy against him, and who was, moreover, his only full brother, the only other son of Rachel.

Gifts play a certain part in this narrative; the 'present' (11) was in the nature of tribute to an overlord, while Joseph's 'portions' (34) were the largesse of a man of high rank to his inferiors (cf. 2 Sam. **11**.8).

Notes: V. 32: it was evidently a cultic practice of the Egyptians to avoid ritual contamination caused by eating with foreigners. Strangely enough, the Jews came to adopt a similar practice centuries afterwards.

How far do we feel or exhibit a sense of fraternal responsibility within our local church context?

Genesis 44 The Climax

If the brothers were congratulating themselves on getting away on this second occasion without any mention of espionage and without leaving a hostage, their peace of mind was shortlived. Evidently they knew, this time, that their money had been returned to them (1), since they mentioned it to their pursuer (8); equally evidently, the discovery of the silver cup in Benjamin's sack took them utterly by surprise and dismay. One can imagine the temptation they must have felt to abandon Benjamin to his fate—the thought must surely have crossed their minds that he was perhaps guilty of the theft (Judah's words in v. 16 at least suggest this). It is now revealed what Joseph had planned; he was not simply tormenting them, but putting them to the test: would they put their own skins first by betraying Benjamin (as was explicitly suggested to them, 17)? To their lasting credit, they were now as unanimous in sacrificing themselves on Benjamin's account as they had been in their hatred and betrayal of the young Joseph. Judah was the spokesman, but the silence of the rest gave assent to his words. The narrator's literary skill is such that he has no need to write a word about Benjamin's feelings in all this, completely dependent as he was on the protective instincts of his brothers.

Judah emerges with more credit than anyone; it could be argued that he showed more consideration for Benjamin than did Joseph himself, though of course Joseph did not mean to deceive and frighten Benjamin a moment longer than was necessary. Historically, the events of Gen. **44** laid a basis for the later tribal relationships; Benjamin would be a small and relatively weak tribe, sandwiched between the powerful 'Joseph tribe' Ephraim to the north, and Judah to the south. Ultimately Benjamin would align herself with the latter, in spite of the closer relationship with Ephraim. Gen. **44** shows how Judah had lost his arrogance of ch.**38**, and now displayed a dignity deserving of future rule (cf. **49.**10).

Notes: Vs. 5,15: it is not clear whether Joseph really did practise divination, or merely wished the brothers to think so. V. 16: the 'guilt' Judah admitted to may have been intended in general terms, i.e. their present troubles could only have come from God as some sort of punishment.

How far are we prepared to profit by, or where possible make amends for, past mistakes?

Genesis 45 The Denouement

Judah's final words about his father, which showed his loving concern for Jacob, touched Joseph's heart, and he could keep up the pretence no longer; besides, his brothers had passed the test he had imposed upon them, and there was no further point in hiding his identity from them. So he let himself go, and allowed both tears and words to spill out freely. Very marked, however, is the contrast in his brothers' reactions, for they were quite literally speechless; throughout the chapter scarcely a word is attributed to them. It was not merely shock that had this effect, it was dismay (3), which Joseph rightly diagnosed as the result of a bad conscience (5). They could scarcely be expected to appreciate all at once the nature of the test he had set them, whereas they would immediately recall the accusations of espionage and the imprisonment of Simeon;

long afterwards they still feared Joseph's vengeance (**50**.15). (Indeed, it is interesting to note that although Joseph showed every sign of love and care for his family, he did not once speak explicitly of forgiveness. However, actions speak as eloquently as words.)

Possibly Joseph harboured mixed feelings towards his brothers; at any rate, he could certainly look back at their betrayal of him in a positive and intelligent way, seeing God's overruling in it all (5–8). It is clearly true that it was their jealousy and cruelty which had sent him to Egypt, thus enabling him to be in the right place at the right time; the sojourn in Egypt was no accident and was all part of the divine plan (cf. **15**.13). But at the same time one can be excused for wondering whether the desperate famine now and the years of oppression in Egypt which lay in the future were not in themselves a punishment for the brothers' treatment of Joseph.

Notes: V. 7: 'a remnant': the continuity of the people of God is a recurring Biblical theme. V. 8: 'a father to Pharaoh' was a frequent Egyptian title for outstanding administrators. V. 10: 'the land of Goshen': see notes on ch. **46**. V. 24: Joseph foresaw that there might well be recriminations among the brothers, as they faced the prospect of having to tell the truth to their father.

How is forgiveness best expressed? Should it always be explicitly stated?

Questions for further study and discussion on Genesis chs. 40–45
1. What different modes of divine revelation can you find in the Scriptures?
2. How should we view abnormal experiences in life? Would they usually serve some specific function in God's plans for us?
3. Should one expect a Christian statesman or politician to be more successful or far-sighted than a non-Christian?
4. How often does God make us wait for something? What effect ought such an experience to have upon our character?
5. How do we react when we undergo flagrant injustice?
6. Study the theme of forgiveness in the N.T.
7. What past untoward experiences can we now find purpose in?

Genesis 46   The Whole Family in Egypt

The single individual, Joseph, had gone from Canaan to Egypt in humiliating circumstances, lonely and destitute; that his way had been foreordained by God, he did not realize till years later. The picture here is very different. The effect of the genealogy is to emphasize that it was the whole family who went to Egypt; some of Jacob's grandchildren are here listed for the first time. Several modern scholars have argued that only a limited group of Israelites was ever in Egypt (and indeed a comparison of 14.14 with 46.27 may suggest that some of the Israelites' retainers and close associates were left in Palestine); but *Genesis* and *Exodus* are emphatic that the whole embryo nation underwent the Egyptian experience, and that every tribe without exception later enjoyèd the deliverance of God. They went unitedly; nor were they destitute, despite the famine (6); they travelled in state, with royal patronage, and with Judah perhaps going ahead as a sort of royal herald (the exact meaning and point of v. 28 are obscure). In these respects their eventual departure from Egypt offers instructive parallels and contrasts. Finally, they went at God's express instruction and with His blessing (2 ff.); Beersheba, the last place of worship on Palestinian soil on the route southwards, was the logical point for Jacob to seek divine guidance.

Egypt, however, was no paradise on earth; v. 34 is a reminder of the underlying hostility Egyptians felt towards foreigners. It was important, therefore, that the family should not be separated from each other nor integrated with the Egyptians. Joseph was determined that his kinsmen should reside in a region suited to their various needs—and one conveniently placed for eventual exodus! The land of Goshen, later known as the land of Rameses (47.11), was in the east Delta region, and is often identified with the Wadi Tumilat area; to date, the name 'Goshen' has not been found in Egyptian documents. This area was in antiquity not infrequently occupied by non-Egyptian semi-nomadic peoples.

Notes: V. 4: 'close your eyes'—i.e. at death. V. 12: for Er and Onan see ch. **38**. Vs. 26 f.: see the commentaries for a discussion of the numbers in this chapter.

To what extent do Christians today live in a hostile environment? How far should we seek to avoid 'integration'?

Genesis 47   Joseph's Arrangements

The central section (13–26) is concerned with the arrangements Joseph implemented to meet the desperate famine conditions. Egyptians and Canaanites alike were affected by his measures; Canaan was, either in fact or theory, under Egyptian control for most of the second millennium B.C. The severity of the famine is underlined by the fact of the enslavement of so many poverty-stricken people; it was only common practice then for a man to sell his own person when every other commodity had been sold, and Joseph cannot be blamed for the general economic systems that obtained. The 20% tax, too, was a familiar, and not immoderate, impost of the day.

By contrast, the Israelite community were better off than all their neighbours; while the latter were losing property and freedom, the family of Jacob were granted 'the best of the land' as a holding, plus all the food they needed (11 f.). Before long it became evident to all that they were enjoying an astonishing prosperity (27). The only Egyptian to profit was the king himself, thanks to Joseph (and note v. 10), while the Egyptian priesthood suffered less than most (22,26); it is worth observing that it was the crown and the religious powers who at the time of the exodus sought to obstruct God's purposes.

Jacob himself was more far-sighted than most, however; while others looked only at their present circumstances and made the best of them, he could see the past in perspective (9), and meant to plan for the future. His dispositions are set out for us in **47.29–49.**32; but his very first concern was for himself, that his own remains should return to the promised land (29 f.). He wanted no permanent association with Egypt. Joseph took the most solemn oath; for the 'thigh' symbolism see **24.**2. Jacob's final act (31) was no doubt equally symbolic, but its precise significance escapes us, and it is therefore not known whether 'bed' (Hebrew *mittah*) or 'staff' (Hebrew *matteh*), as the Greek O.T. and Heb. **11.**21 understood the word, is correct.

Notes: V. 2: 'five men'—presumably a representative number. V. 11: 'the land of Rameses' was the name used for Goshen in Moses' time (Rameses II reigned *c.* 1290–1224 B.C.).

Is it inevitable that we should accept and adjust to the prevailing social and economic systems of our own environment? Is it our business to investigate or challenge their morality?

Genesis 48 Jacob's Arrangements

History records that the twelve tribal territories of later Israel did not bear precisely the same names as the twelve sons of Jacob; the 'missing' names were Levi, whose descendants never occupied a tribal holding, and Joseph, from whom not one but two tribes claimed descent, namely Ephraim and Manasseh. It was therefore altogether fitting that Jacob, who as 'Israel' gave his name to the whole future nation, should himself constitute the two sons of Joseph as tribes-to-be, giving them the same status as Reuben and Simeon, his own eldest sons; vs. 12 f. describe an act of adoption. Indeed, they far outweighed Reuben and Simeon in tribal importance, for they came to occupy the whole central area of Palestine. Both were powerful tribes, but the more powerful was Ephraim, which in fact emerged as the strongest of all twelve; thus it happened that the youngest individual of all the tribal ancestors fathered the most powerful tribe. Our chapter shows that this turn of events was no accident, but was due to God's planning, revealed in advance to Jacob. The theme of God's sovereign choice thus runs right through *Genesis*, as time and time again the elder gives place to the younger. (Note, however, that the setting aside of the elder does not put him beyond the pale of God's love, goodness and mercy.)

Heb. 11.21 takes Jacob's blessing of Joseph's sons as the supreme act of faith in his life. His own father had given him the firstborn's blessing unintentionally and unwittingly, but Jacob put aside any wishes or preferences he may have felt, and gave directions for the future as God Himself meant it to be.

Notes: The relevance of v. 7 is none too clear; its implication may be that but for Rachel's premature death she might have borne more sons, who would have displaced Ephraim and Manasseh. Vs. 15 f.: 'Joseph' is here a collective term. The verbs 'led' and 'redeemed' are metaphors to denote loving care and help, drawn from the actions of a shepherd and a man's closest relative respectively. 'Evil'—i.e. 'harm' (JB). V. 22 seems obscure, but Gen. **34.** and Josh. 24.32 explain it; 'mountain slope' is the same word in Hebrew as 'Shechem'.

What past action in your life could be described as your supreme act of faith?

Genesis 49.1–12   Shadows of the Future

'Like father, like son' runs the tag; and by their characters and conduct Jacob's sons had long since presaged the characteristics the tribes descended from them would display. At the end of his life, accordingly, Jacob could give them some idea of what their future held. Each son was given an oracle, couched in poetic and. allusive language; the very antiquity of the poetry creates further problems of meaning. We need not doubt that Jacob was passing on divine revelations, but two points should be borne in mind: first, the predictions were not for the end of time (AV's 'the last days' in v. 1 is quite misleading), but for the period of the Israelite occupation of Canaan and of the judges; secondly, the revelation was of very limited scope, as is shown by the oracle to Levi, which conveys no hint of the important priestly offices that tribe would fulfil. Gen. **49** should be supplemented by and compared with Deut.

33, where the final words of Moses about the tribes are recorded.

Reuben and Simeon were the most southerly tribes, located on the east and west respectively of the Dead Sea, and both suffered from hostile pressures from the south; both had merited Jacob's anger (35.22; 34.30), and their tribal characteristics of pride and violence would earn the enmity of their non-Israelite neighbours. Simeon was no doubt largely 'scattered' in Judah's territory. Levi, too, suffered the loss of territory, but that tribe redeemed itself by later exhibiting its violent character in a good cause (Exod. 32.25–29), after which they put up their swords. They were granted cities throughout Israel (Josh. 21), and 'scattered' in that fashion.

Judah had already redeemed himself in Jacob's eyes, and nothing but good is offered him; victory, leadership and prosperity are all predicted for his tribe, which did indeed become the most powerful southerly tribe, and in the person of David provided the king for the whole nation. The general sense of v. 10 is that the tribe's independence and leading position would continue and culminate in the wide rule of one man; the reference is to David, who in turn foreshadowed his greater Son (cf. Rev. 5.5).

Notes: V. 4: 'unstable'—better, 'unbridled'. V. 7: God now speaks through Jacob. V. 8: 'shall praise' (*yodu*) is a word-play on the name Judah. V. 10: the RSV rendering has the support of Ezek. 21.27; both the marginal alternatives are improbable, since a place-name would be out of keeping with the general context.

How far could others predict our future, on the basis of our character and past conduct? What sort of future do we deserve?

Genesis 49.13–33   Jacob's Last Words

The minor tribes are briefly described in vs. 13–21; they were descended from Leah's youngest two sons and from the sons of the slave girls Bilhah and Zilpah (cf. 30.3–20), though they are not listed in the same order. There is no obvious reason for the change of order. We know very little of the characters of the individuals or of the later history of these tribes; hence these oracles are in part obscure to us, though the metaphors are informative and striking. As with Judah (8) there are some word-plays on the names, notably on Dan (= 'judge') and Gad (see RSV footnote). The wording of v. 16 suggests that the reference is to the northern area to which Danites migrated and where they founded the city of Dan (cf. Judg. 18), and v. 17 may well be an allusion to their capture of this city; if so, this whole section relates to the more northerly territories of Israelite Palestine. Zebulun is characterized by its maritime ·

61

trading interests, Issachar by its subservience under pressure, both Dan and Gad by their determination under pressure, and Asher and Naphtali by the fertility of their lands.

In central Palestine, Joseph's descendants would be signally blessed (22–26) above all their fellow tribes. Joseph's personal unhappy separation from his brothers (and at their hands) would be compensated for by his descendants' outstanding fertility and success. As for the tribe of Benjamin (27), its small numbers would prove no brake upon its vigour and courage.

Jacob's last thoughts were for himself, as he gave commandment regarding his burial. The only purchased possession in Canaan was Mach-pelah (cf. Gen. 23), and there lay his grandparents, parents and wife Leah (whose death is now mentioned for the first time); he had no intention of being separated from them, or from the promised land, in death. During his lifetime he had known far too much separation from home and family.

Notes: V. 14: 'sheepfolds' is uncertain; AV's 'burdens' may not be far wrong, heightening the picture of Issachar's servitude. Problems about the meaning of Hebrew words also render vs. 21 f. obscure; the sense of v. 18 is clear, but its relevance to its context is not. V. 26: 'separate' is really a cultic term (cf. JB, 'dedicated'), and there may be reference to the sanctuaries in Ephraim and Manasseh.

How is faith best expressed in conditions of sickness or old age? Can we take Jacob as an example to follow?

Genesis 50   Death —and its Sequel

We are apt to speak today of the finality of death, but this chapter raises doubts about the appropriateness of the expression. In the first place, one man's death can make considerable changes in the situation of those who survive him (Exod. **1**.8 illustrates this point afresh), as Joseph's brothers fully appreciated—and feared (15). At all costs, however, the unity of the family must be maintained in an alien world; Joseph showed wisdom as well as an exceptionally affectionate and forgiving spirit. Secondly, death was anything but final in ancient Egypt, whose religion has been described as a cult of the dead; every possible provision was made for the afterlife. The bodies of Jacob and Joseph were embalmed in true Egyptian style, but with a different destination in view—the promised land. Jacob's body was taken to Mach-pelah immediately, as a token occupation of Palestine by 'Israel'; but Joseph's coffin remained in Egypt, an ever-present reminder to the Israelites in Egypt that their destiny lay elsewhere, that they had a filial duty towards Joseph's remains, and that God had made promises to them through him. In his last words Joseph not only demonstrated his own faith (cf. Heb. 11.22) but in effect demanded faith from succeeding generations; this chapter will have been an effective sermon to the Jewish exiles in Babylonia many centuries later, with its themes of faith and hope and unity. The exiles in Egypt undoubtedly remembered his words: cf. Exod. 13.19; Josh. 24.32. In these various ways, therefore, Gen. 50 is far more than just the end of the story of the patriarchs.

Perhaps in part because of the Egyptian morbid concern with death and the afterlife, the O.T. says remarkably little about what lies beyond death—it is chiefly concerned to teach the living how to behave towards the living. Nevertheless the patriarchs' determination to be buried in Palestine is surely one evidence that they looked beyond the tomb; see also Matt. 22.31 f.; Heb. 11.9 f., 13–16. The final clause of 49.33 is another evidence. Death was *not* the end.

Notes: V. 3: the period of mourning was little less than for an Egyptian king! (The 'seven days' (10) was the customary Israelite period of mourning.) V. 22: God granted Joseph a lifespan considered by Egyptians to be the ideal one. V. 23: cf. 30.3 for the idiom.

Which is the less desirable attitude—to be too concerned with this life, or too concerned with the afterlife?

Questions for further study and discussion on Genesis chs. 46–50

1. Trace the stages of Jacob's spiritual journey to serenity and faith.
2. In the light of Gen. 49, have we a duty to offer our family, or other people, word-portraits of themselves? What similes might they find appropriate for us?
3. Study Gen. 50.15–21, and consider what part is played in present-day Christian divisions by (*a*) past history, (*b*) a guilty conscience, (*c*) lack of forgiveness.
4. What O.T. passages do offer a firm hope in resurrection and life after death? How has the N.T. reinforced that hope?
5. What preparations have you made for death? Do those arrangements (such as they are) display fear or faith?
6. What do you consider are the most important recurring themes in *Genesis*?

ROUTE OF THE EXODUS

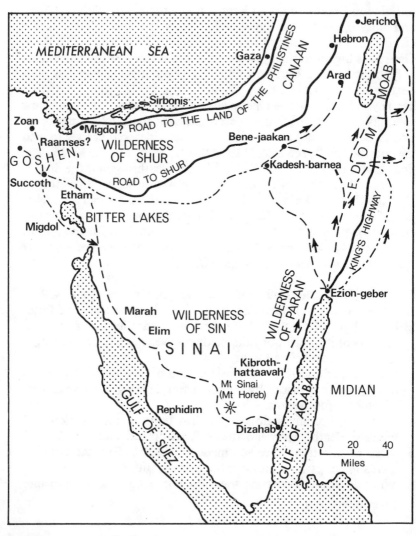

Probable route of Exodus — — — — —
Alternative routes — — · — — · —
Red(Reed) Sea, a northward or southward
extension of the Bitter Lakes

Exodus

Exodus ('Departure') like *Genesis* receives its English name from the Greek Bible. The sequel to *Genesis*, it is another book of beginnings, for it relates the story of Israel's birth as a separate nation, a birth surrounded by never-to-be-forgotten events—the Passover, the law-giving at Sinai, and above all the miraculous rescue of the Israelite people from a hostile environment. The book is very appropriately linked with the name of Moses, who was both the central figure of the narrative section of the book (ch. **1-19**), the mediator of the divine laws (**20-31**), and mentor and guide to Israel as they turned from apostasy to obedience (**32-40**). *Exodus* thus presents us with the constitution of the new nation, and introduces us to the man who was responsible for it; the events of *Exodus* and the work of Moses were fundamental to Israel's faith and history. Indeed, the rest of the O.T. would make little sense without the *Book of Exodus*.

As in *Genesis*, so in *Exodus*, the Prime Mover in all interplay of persons and events was God Himself, revealing Himself in both word and deed.

For additional information, *The New Bible Commentary* and the Torch Bible Commentary on *Exodus* (G. Henton Davies) can be consulted with profit.

Exodus 1   The Beginning of Oppression

If Jacob's descendants had remained happy and prosperous in Egypt, or had never multiplied greatly, then conceivably the exodus and the conquest of Canaan might never have happened. So the beginning of the exodus narrative is the story of the circumstances which made the exodus both possible and necessary. Factors in the situation were historical developments and personages, coupled with the overruling hand of God; observe the changes which took place between the eras of Joseph and Moses (1-10). One important development (7) was in direct fulfilment of God's promises to Abraham (cf. Gen. **12.2**; **17.6**). A change of dynasty may well be implied in v. 8; the first Pharaoh to oppress the Israelites was probably Sethos I (*c.* 1302-1290 B.C.), an early ruler of the 19th dynasty. His building programme in the north-east Delta region was completed in the reign of his son Rameses II, who gave his name to one of the store cities (11): Pi-Ramesse in Egyptian. No doubt the persecution had the effect of strengthening the bonds of the Israelite community, which might otherwise have lost its cohesion through growth and intermarriage with Egyptians and others. In fact, 'Israel' now became a nation for the first time, and the phrase 'the people of Israel' will now occur frequently. As regards their numbers, we should observe that 'the land' (7) is that of Goshen (cf. Gen. 47.27), not the whole of Egypt; on the other hand, probably there were more than two Hebrew midwives (15), but perhaps the names of only two were known to the writer.

Few redeeming features of the Egyptian rulers are portrayed in *Exodus*; but the people of God are not depicted as morally perfect. The midwives were plainly guilty of deceit, if only by telling half-truths (19); their reward was for obedience to God, not truthfulness (21).

Notes: V. 5: the Greek O.T. Version (Septuagint) has the figure 'seventy-five'; cf. Acts 7.14. V. 15: the term 'Hebrew' was used depreciatively in Egypt, to indicate a slave-caste. V. 22: i.e. the king now by-passed the midwives.

Note the different types of fear, and their consequences (9,12,21). How far are my outlook and conduct governed by fears of any sort? Whom or what do I fear?

Exodus 2 — The Training of a Deliverer

The story of Moses' infancy is well known—a tribute to the narrative skill of the writer. Not until v. 10 do we meet the name Moses, and to keep the secret, the names of his parents (Amram and Jochebed) and of his elder brother and sister (Aaron and Miriam) are not divulged. Thus dramatically Moses takes the stage: here is the man who will transform Israel's situation. He was not to act alone, however; this chapter shows how God directed the whole pattern of his life, from his earliest infancy. If vs. 1–10 emphasize his helplessness, vs. 11–14 acknowledge something of his impetuousness; yet even his folly had beneficial results for him. He came to owe a debt in three human directions: to Egyptian court education (10; cf. Acts 7.21 f.); to Midianite desert crafts (including tribal administration); but above all, of course, to his own people. He did not allow his relationship to Pharaoh's daughter to affect his feeling of kinship with the oppressed Hebrews (10 f.; 'his people' is literally 'his brothers'); Heb. 11.24 ff. explains why. A lesser man would have written them off after the experience of vs. 13 f.

The Midianites were related to the Israelites (cf. Gen. 25.2), and were well disposed to them until a later date (see Num. **22.**1–4; Judg. **6** ff.). They roamed widely in the wilderness area east of Egypt and south and south-east of Palestine, though their 'land' is usually located to the east of the Gulf of Aqaba. They may have worshipped the true God, but if so they later lapsed into idolatry (Judg. **8.**26). Moses' first contact with them was reminiscent of Jacob's experience in the Haran area (Gen. **29**); but there is this difference, that Moses already appears (for the second time) as a born deliverer.

Moses' training for leadership was not a short one, and meanwhile Israel suffered a great deal (11,23). Nevertheless, they were not forgotten; note the significant verbs in vs. 24 f.

Notes: V. 1: 'daughter' here means 'descendant'. V. 22: the second part of the name 'Gershom' seems to be linked with the Hebrew word *sham*, 'there'. V. 23 implies that there were two oppressing kings; the second was probably Rameses II (*c.* 1290–1224 B.C.). V. 25: the words 'their condition' are not in the Hebrew, and perhaps spoil the effect of the original.

Heb. 11.23–27 interprets this chapter as faith in action. How does our faith express itself in situations of prosperity or adversity, or during long periods when God does not seem to answer our prayers?

Exodus 3   The Call of Moses

The death of the Pharaoh and the undiminished persecution of Israel (**2.**23) made it both possible and imperative that Moses should return to Egypt, but we find him peacefully minding sheep, far away. Till now he had had no personal encounter with the God who had planned his life and career, but now this was signally remedied; the chief Actor in the exodus events now made His appearance, bringing to Moses' conscious attention His person, His character and His purposes. God revealed Himself first as the God of previous promise and fulfilment (6), who could therefore be trusted implicitly, and then as Yahweh, amplified as meaning 'I AM WHO I AM' (14 f.). Many interpretations have been read into and out of this phrase, but two seem particularly appropriate: here come together 'the revealed truth and infinite mystery of the nature of the true God' (J. C. Connell); and there is secondly the practical lesson for the future, ' "I am what you will discover me to be" ' (G. Henton Davies). It is possible that the name Yahweh had been neglected by Israel while in Egypt.

Moses was equally interested in his own character and abilities (11), but they were irrelevant. It is remarkable that 'the sign' offered to him would not be apparent until after he had accomplished his mission (12). Once the Israelites were rescued from Egypt, and had worshipped God at the holy mountain, their future possession of the promised land would be certain. The initial steps of faith would serve to increase and strengthen faith.

Moses' message was to be one of full deliverance, but in the first place the Israelites were to make reasonably innocuous requests from the Egyptians. The sacrifice in the wilderness (18) may have been arranged thus to avoid giving offence to Egyptian neighbours, to whom such sacrifices could have been abhorrent. But whether this is so or not, we may fairly interpret both the three days' journey (18) and the despoiling of the Egyptians (22) as symbolic of departure and of victory.

Notes: V. 1: 'Jethro' is the better known name of Reuel (2.18); several Biblical characters bore two names. V. 8: cf. Gen. **15.**18–21. The human analogy ('I have come down') emphasizes God's personal and close interest in His people. V. 22: they must claim their unpaid wages.

What aspects of God's character have most impressed themselves on you personally?

Exodus 4 The Road Back to Egypt

Moses was by no means the last O.T. character to feel unworthy of God's calling, and incompetent, too (cf. Judg. **6**; Isa. **6**; Jer. **1**; Ezek. **2**). He felt that there were two good reasons why no Israelite should listen to him, and despite God's unanswerable reassurances, he burst out rudely, 'Send anyone You will!' (13, JB). Verse 19 may well conceal a very real additional reason for Moses' hesitation and unwillingness; it is easy to find plausible, even theological, excuses for cowardice, but God is not deceived. Moses is depicted in Exod. 3 f. as a typical prophet, and in a sense vs. 14 ff., 27 ff. show prophet and priest ('Levite', 14) in an ideal teamwork; so it should always have been throughout Israel's history!

The 'magic' of vs. 1–9 may seem odd and puzzling to us today; but in a polytheistic world, the true God must show Himself no *less* powerful than His false rivals. Note the divine purpose of miracles (5).

En route for Egypt (v. 20 anticipates the end of the journey) Moses nearly met his death, probably through illness, at God's hands (24). Verse 24 f. are extremely concisely written, but the best explanation of them seems to be that Moses could scarcely instruct God's 'first-born son' Israel to 'serve' Him, and threaten the death of Pharaoh's first-born son if the king proved disobedient

(22 f.), while he was himself neglecting obedience to the divine ordinance of circumcision (cf. Gen. **17**.9–14) where his own first-born was concerned. Outside Israel, many ancient peoples practised circumcision at puberty or in manhood, not infancy, and it looks as if Moses had hitherto conformed to Midianite customs in this respect; but now Midian lay behind him.

This chapter exhibits in a variety of ways how God acts, not only in the supernatural (2–9), but also in revelation (19,27), natural (?) illness (24), and even the characteristic reactions of human beings (21). Pharaoh himself hardened his heart (cf. **8**.15), but this very fact contributed to, rather than thwarted, God's plans. It is also psychologically true that divine commands produce human rebelliousness (cf. Rom. **7**.7–10). See, too, Rom. **9**.14–24.

Notes: V. 20: 'his sons' were Gershom (**2**.22) and Eliezer (**18**.2 ff.). Note that Moses' shepherd's staff is now a symbol of God's power. Vs. 22 f. anticipate, and justify in theological terms, the tenth plague.

Is 1 Cor. **11** *(especially vs. 27–32) a fair N.T. parallel to vs. 24 ff.? Are there any practical lessons we could learn from such a study?*

Questions for further study and discussion on Exodus chs. 1–4

1. In the light of Exod. **1**.20 f., could it be said that happiness and prosperity are normally signs of God's approval of human conduct?
2. Should every Christian's early life be viewed as divine training for some future service?
3. To what extent are we indebted to non-Christians? To what extent should we be?
4. Do miracles occur today? If not, why not?
5. Noting Exod. **4**.10–17, and the subsequent career of Moses, consider whether natural gifts and talents are of much importance in Christian service.
6. What are the essential characteristics of a great religious leader?
7. Does our personal relationship with God compare more closely with Exod. **4**.10–17 or Gen. **18**.22–33?

Exodus 5.1—6.1   A Desperate Situation

Every effort was made to induce the Egyptian king to be reasonable. In a world of many gods and forms of worship, the Israelite request (1–3) cannot have seemed an extraordinary demand, and a king like Cyrus of Persia would have acceded to it (cf. Ezra **1**). But no few ancient kings took the view that their political supremacy meant the superior worth and power of their particular deities and therefore despised the worship of subject peoples. Hence Pharaoh's disparagement of Moses' God. He was in any case more interested in what he viewed as practicalities (4 f.)—a true materialist! Nevertheless, he had issued a religious challenge, in effect (2), and it was to be taken up.

The king's treatment of his Israelite slaves was, if anything, calculated to get less work out of them; but his primary intention was to 'divide and rule', by setting the Israelites against Moses and Aaron. Nor was he unsuccessful (20 f.). Moses once again had every excuse for abandoning his people, but by now he knew where to turn in times of perplexity (22 f.).'The reassuring word came that before long Pharaoh would be only too glad to get rid of the Israelites (6.1). The word 'now' is emphatic.

Notes: V. 6: 'the taskmasters' were Egyptian, 'the foremen' Israelite. V. 7: the function of the 'straw' was either to reinforce the bricks or to separate them from the moulds. V. 16: the last clause is of uncertain meaning; it could be rendered, 'You do wrong to your people'—describing the Israelites as Pharaoh's subjects (cf. v. 15, 'your servants').

What dangers do you see in your society of secular influences causing disharmony between Christians? Are such influences likely to be less dangerous, or more insidious, in a 'free' society?

Exodus 6.2–27   Moses' Call Confirmed

This chapter provides a breathing space in the rapid narration of events, and enables us to take stock of the situation—a broken, humiliated people (9), and a discouraged and despondent Moses (12,30). Neither was very heroic at this point in time. Much of vs. 1–13 repeats the content of chs. 3 f.; in a worsening situation, Israel is as apathetic as before, Moses equally unsure of himself. Indeed, whereas previously he called himself 'slow of speech' (4.10), he now claimed to have a positive impediment (12). But God's revelation of Himself was little different either; human failure and obstinacy made no alteration in His character, power or intentions.

However, there are a few significant differences from the earlier chapters. Here for the first time in the Bible (except Gen. **48.**16) we find the verb 'redeem' (6), a theological term of the first importance; it links the ideas of deliverance and of the resumption of a claim. Secondly, Pharaoh was now to be told in plain language that Israel would be leaving Egypt permanently (13), not merely to observe a wilderness festival. Thus the message of hope became clearer and stronger, despite the cruel circumstances.

The other new emphasis of the chapter is the interest in the person of Aaron, who was to be Moses' spokesman to Pharaoh (7.1) as well as to the Israelites (4.16). The genealogy (14–25) is more concerned with him than with Moses. Israel, both people and leader, needed a capable mediator, closely related to them, and they would need continuity in this priestly office, too; on this Heb. 7 provides a N.T. commentary.

Notes: V. 3 has been much debated, since if taken at face value it would contradict many passages in *Genesis* (from Gen. 4.26 onwards). The answer may be that it is the *content* of the Name that was a new revelation; Israel had not yet known Yahweh as Saviour and Redeemer. But see 'God, Names of' in *The New Bible Dictionary* for further discussion. Vs. 14 f.: Reuben and Simeon were the only sons of Jacob older than Levi, and so they serve here to introduce Levi's genealogy. V. 26: 'by their hosts'—orderly array, not panic-stricken flight.

What provision is made to meet the needs of 'the body of Christ'? See 1 Cor. 12.27 f., and consider how much you need, or help to supply, these provisions.

Exodus 6.28—7.24　　　　　　　　　The First Plague

The Egyptian ruler was given a final opportunity (7.1–13) to release Israel and save his own people from terror and disaster. God had His purposes even in the king's stubbornness (5), as Paul was later to emphasize (Rom. 9.17); but we are not led to picture Pharaoh as an unthinking automaton, unable to make his own decisions. Fully conscious of what he was doing, he firmly opposed Moses and Aaron (13). The result was a trial of strength and endurance. The ordinary Egyptian populace were to suffer, their fate bound up with their ruler's decision; in this world the innocent frequently suffer for their leaders' sins, but it must be remembered, too, that the Egyptians were worshippers of Egyptian deities, who are portrayed in these chapters as the real enemy of Israel's God (cf. 12.12). The Egyptians had to be taught a theological lesson (5).

The word translated 'serpent' in vs. 9–12 is not the customary one (used in v. 15, which probably refers back to 4.3), and it may mean 'crocodile', a creature typical of the Nile. If so, it would symbolize even more clearly God's victory over all Egyptian forces. The first plague (20–24) again afflicted the Nile, on which Egypt's whole life depended, and to which the king was paying a routine, almost certainly religious, visit (15). The plague closely resembled a regular natural phenomenon, but was evidently much more serious, and may have been caused by an abnormally high inundation.

The Egyptian magicians followed suit in a mere token fashion, but they were easily able to convince Pharaoh (22). Pure water was still obtainable (24), but they could scarcely make the Nile more red than it already was! The widespread nature of the plague (19) again shows that it was far from natural. We may guess that the land of Goshen was spared.

Notes: V. 7: multiples of forty may often be of imprecise reference in the Bible, meaning simply so many 'generations'; but it is less easy to reduce Aaron's age on this basis. On the plague sequence, see 'Plagues of Egypt' in *The New Bible Dictionary*.

With v. 23 compare Acts **18.***17. What should be our general attitude to the events that go on around us?*

Exodus 7.25—8.32　　Increasing Pressure on Pharaoh

The severe inconvenience of shortage of water was followed by three invasions by swarming creatures. There may well be a natural sequence here; the frogs are specifically linked with the Nile (3), which had figured in the first plague, and the gnats and flies could well have been associated with the stinking heaps of dead frogs (13 f.). There is certainly a theological point once again; frogs were regarded in Egypt as having divine powers and conveying fertility. But on this occasion their own fertility was Yahweh's doing (10), and it proved no blessing to the Egyptians, whose magicians could in some way add to the affliction but were evidently helpless to diminish it (7). Verse 18 possibly means that they tried to 'bring forth' the gnats out of the houses, rather than that they endeavoured to produce yet more insects. At any rate, the magicians gave up the unequal struggle at this point, and appear again merely as helpless victims (9.11).

The chief human interest centres on Moses and the king; their contacts were reasonably courteous thus far. Note that Pharaoh was (temporarily) prepared to go some way towards meeting Israelite requests (25,28), and Moses offered to meet him halfway, no doubt well aware that Pharaoh would change his mind, and that Israel's release would in the end be permanent. It is clear that the king was always ready to indulge in wishful thinking (note v. 10).

Israel's escape from the fourth plague (22 f.) suggests that they had been consistently spared; at any rate, no plague from now on afflicted them.

Notes: The RSV footnotes indicate that the meaning of vs. 12,23 is not absolutely certain; Moses' first words to Pharaoh (9) are also problematic (cf. AV). Nor is the precise identity of the two types of insect very certain. V. 27: see note on 3.18.

Can we profitably study Moses' use of tact and of straight talking (25–29)? Was he in any way compromising his position? Do you see here a precedent for religious tolerance?

Exodus 9 Increasing Stubbornness of Pharaoh

Now for the first time the plagues began to affect the persons and the pockets of the Egyptians; but the earlier disasters, predicted as they had been, could serve as a warning to any who cared to take heed (20). While Israel was God's special people, and Egypt the object of His anger, yet this chapter reveals His mercy and also His universal interests (15 f.). God was concerned that Egypt, as well as Israel, would come to know His character (14).

Pharaoh's reactions are again of interest. His stubbornness evidently did not mean total disinterest, but the very fact of discovering the truth and power of God's predictions led him to resist the more (7). Verse 12 is the first time that we read of God's action in hardening the king's heart, although it had been predicted (cf. 4.21; 7.3); as J. C. Connell comments, 'Wilful hardness begins now to be punished with judicial hardness.' There is no fatalism here; in his wiser moments, Pharaoh knew better than to blame God for his own actions (27). Rom. 1.18–32 provides a similar picture of human sins as a punishment for earlier hardness of heart. Pharaoh's arrogance is also mentioned (17).

The word 'all' in v. 6 is not to be over-pressed, in view of v. 20; the statement may be telescoped, i.e. 'all the cattle of the Egyptians were affected, many of them dying'. There were still animals left to be afflicted in later plagues, just as the timing of the hail-storm (v. 31 suggests early February) left crops to be damaged by the plague of locusts of ch. 10.

Notes: V. 5: 'Tomorrow . . .'—Pharaoh was given time to change his mind, just as he had hoped for a change of mind on God's part (8.10). V. 14: the Hebrew word for 'heart' nearly always relates to intelligence, not the emotions. V. 23: 'fire' presumably means lightning.

In view of vs. 15 f., consider how far you are fulfilling God's purposes for your life. What information does the N.T. provide regarding His purposes?

Exodus 10 Pharaoh's Last Chance

As the plague sequence moves towards its inexorable climax, the cumulative effects of the disasters can be clearly seen. Verse 15 indicates the damage to the crops, and v. 24 hints at the shortage of remaining livestock in Egyptian possession. By now Pharaoh's advisers at court are having second thoughts (7), and the king himself is beginning to waver, even though in the end all courtesy is set aside and Moses is summarily dismissed (28). It is striking that the benefits Joseph, with royal co-operation, had brought upon Egypt, were now dissipated by a stubborn king, through the instrumentality of another great Israelite. The king, quite apart from the rapidity with which he revoked his offers, was never prepared to make adequate concessions. Twice in this chapter he demanded hostages (10 f.,24); the word rendered 'little ones' (10) or 'children' (24) is a term which probably includes womenfolk.

The damage locusts can do is proverbial, and eloquent testimony to it may be found in Joel 1 f. But the ninth plague, thick darkness, may seem almost an anticlimax to the modern reader. It must have been caused by the *khamsin* wind, bearing westwards stinging sand and dust particles; 'darkness to be felt' is no metaphor. This plague again can be viewed as a natural phenomenon severely intensified. More significant, however, is the fact that it symbolized the utter defeat of the most venerated Egyptian deity, the sun-god Ra (whose very name the king, *Ra*meses, bore). It was no anticlimax that Egypt's chief god was the last to be signally defeated. It is noteworthy that the term 'plague' is not often used in *Exodus*; the disasters are significantly called 'signs' (2). It is in this light that the statement about God's making sport of the Egyptians is to be read; this is not gloating over human suffering, but a stern warning against the folly of idolatry and false worship. Cf. Isa. 44.24 ff.

Notes: V. 15: 'darkened'—more graphically, 'the ground was black with them' (JB). V. 19: 'the Red Sea' (literally, 'reed sea' or 'lake'): see notes on 15.4. V. 28: Pharaoh's threat, like his promises, was in fact quickly revoked.

To what extent do we utilize recent personal experiences as 'sermon material', in our own family circle or outside? When were we last conscious of God acting in 'history'?

Questions for further study and discussion on Exodus chs. 5–10

1. How many other O.T. leaders found themselves rejected by Israel?
2. The plagues form a significant part of the story of Israel's 'redemption' from Egypt; have they any N. T. counterpart?
3. What are today's false gods? Are they human beings or something else?
4. Are today's 'false prophets' capable of any signs and wonders?

74

What sort of thing do our contemporaries find particularly impressive?

5. How genuine were the confession and prayer of Exod. **10.16 f.**? How important is it to utter the 'right' words in our prayers?

6. If the Israelites had been a heretical sect and Pharaoh a Christian ruler, should we have described him as wise, firm and high-principled? What exactly do you understand by 'a hardened heart'?

How does hardness of heart show itself in Christian people?

Exodus 11   Prelude to the Final Plague

From a literary point of view, this chapter provides the reader with a breathing space, prior to the story of the whole complex of events surrounding Israel's departure from Egypt. The narrative here continues to describe the interview between Pharaoh and Moses, a sequence interrupted by vs. 1–3. One may view this paragraph either as God's silent message to Moses as he stood in the king's presence, or else as a previous revelation not passed on to the reader till this point in the narrative. One or two previous plagues had been unheralded, but full warning was given of the last one, which was to bring such tragedy on every Egyptian family. During the earlier disasters, the Egyptian populace had gradually taken an attitude different from the king's but they failed to dissociate themselves from him till too late; only after the tenth plague would they by-pass Pharaoh entirely (8).

Moses' 'hot anger' (8) is intelligible as the natural emotion engendered by such an interview. G. H. Davies has made the interesting suggestion that Pharaoh's delaying tactics had succeeded in preventing the feast in the wilderness at its proper time; there is no further mention of this feast, and it may be that the Passover replaced it—at the right time but in the wrong place, as it were. This speculation, if correct, would give additional reason for Moses' anger.

The Hebrew word for 'plague' (1) is here used, appropriately, for the first and only time in *Exodus*; it is a term which often describes serious infections and epidemics; a different Hebrew word is used in 9.3. A more frequent description of these ten disasters is 'wonder' (9 f.); i.e. they were 'portents' of God's power and of His judgement and salvation. The disasters are thus treated as of theological import from start to finish.

Notes: V. 4: 'midnight' refers forward a few days (cf. **12.3,6**). V. 5: grinding corn was viewed as the most menial of all tasks (cf. Isa. **47**.1 f.). The threat to the cattle may be due to the veneration paid to certain animals in ancient Egypt.

In the light of v. 2, consider how far political and national loyalties should be carried. What N.T. guidance have we?

Exodus 12.1–28 The Passover Feast

The stern warning to Pharaoh is followed by strict instructions to the Israelites. Till now, they had been spared by direct action of God from the effects of the plagues, but now their safety and· well-being, though still deriving from Him, were to be dependent on their obedience to His instructions. There would be special point in this fact if indeed the ritual now prescribed embodied the ritual of a known but presumably neglected feast, first mentioned in **3**.18. In other.words, Israel was being recalled to the worship of Yahweh, in cultic deed as well as on the spiritual plane. However, we know nothing of the rites of the older feast, save that it incorporated sacrifice. We may also see in the instructions here a test of Israel's faith and loyalty, since to sacrifice animals in Egypt could have led to even worse persecution (cf. **8**.26).

The ritual was also designed to be directly relevant to the situation, and in another respect, too, would constitute an act of faith; they must be in readiness to depart (11). The roasting of the lamb (8) may have been the quickest mode of preparation; later it might be boiled (Deut. **16**.7). Leaven (8) symbolized delay, in the first place, though it soon came to symbolize decay! Similarly, hyssop (22), an aromatic plant convenient for use in sprinkling, came naturally to serve as an emblem of purification (cf. Psa. **51**.7).

Notes: V. 2: the month was Abib, later called Nisan (cf. **13**.4; Esth. **3**.7). V. 3: note how Israel is already viewed as a 'congregation', with the possibility of excommunication (15). Vs. 11 ff.: the original meaning of the word 'passover' is obscure; it signified judgement for Egypt, protection for Israel, and the latter may be the meaning, in view of v. 27. Note the specific mention of Egyptian deities.

To this day, the Passover is a family festival for Jewish people, cf. vs. 3 f. Can Christians make any comparable 'sacramental' use of the home? Note another function of the home in vs. 25 ff.

Exodus 12.29–51 Exodus at Last!

The long period of waiting and preparation ended, almost in explosive fashion, with the demoralizing last plague, as the final judgement upon Egypt, and the immediate release of the Israelites.

Pharaoh was forced to change his mind, in more respects than one (31), by an event which brought the reality of divine judgement into his own palace (29). Although we might describe this final plague as an epidemic, it is quite impossible to account for its selectivity by any naturalistic explanation. Unanimously, the Egyptian king and populace sped the Israelites on their way. No longer could Pharaoh claim that he did not know Yahweh (5.2); he was now impelled instead to ask His blessing (32). As for the Israelites, they wasted no time in starting their journey; the first stage (37) has been estimated as about 30 miles. Verse 39 is more than an historical note; it explains why in later years unleavened bread continued to be eaten during the days following the passover meal. Similarly, vs. 43–49 (like 14–20) show a concern for ritual, and remind us that the 'historical' books of the Bible had always more to teach than history. The paragraph, relevant though it was to later celebration of the passover in Canaan ('the land', 48), arises directly from the historical situation, since 'a mixed multitude' (38) escorted Israel out of Egypt, and decisions had to be made about their place in or with the Israelite community.

Notes: V. 37: The figures (a round number, cf. Num. 1.46) undoubtedly seem too great; the Israel of David's day probably numbered no more. The Hebrew word meaning 'thousand' seems to have been ambiguous (e. g. sometimes it means literally 1,000, sometimes a 'clan-unit' [Judg. 6.15], sometimes 'a large number' as probably in Judg. 15.15), and this fact may account for some of the surprisingly high numbers of the O.T. For a detailed discussion of the problem, see J. W. Wenham in *Tyndale Bulletin* 18 (1967) pp. 19–53; Wenham himself computes *c.* 72,000 for the whole migration. V. 40: In the Greek Version the figure includes the period from Abraham to Joseph as well, i.e. the time spent in both Canaan and Egypt; this is followed by Paul in Gal. 3.17. Stephen, however, in Acts 7.6, follows the Hebrew text. V. 42: 'a night of watching': cf. Psa. 121.3 f. Vs. 46,49 emphasize the importance of unity in celebrating the passover, cf. 1 Cor. 11. With v. 46, cf. John 19.36.

With v. 42, cf. 20.8–11; what aspects of God's activity might Christians do well to emulate? What relevance has passover or sabbath for us today?

Exodus 13 Instruction and Guidance

The greater part of this chapter (1–16) is again concerned with ceremonial instructions; this time their import is specifically linked with the situation which will face Israel after the conquest of

Canaan (5,11). The passover feast is to be followed by a seven-day period during which no leaven must be eaten, with a final day of special festal celebration (6 f.). Thus Israel emerged from her exodus with two consecutive festivals, Passover and Unleavened Bread; either name could be used loosely for the whole festal complex, but the distinction between the two feasts was remembered into N.T. times (cf. Mark **14.**1) and beyond. It may be that both festivals had a prehistory (cf. **5.**1), possibly Passover having had a pastoral character, Unleavened Bread an agricultural one, but the events surrounding the exodus were to be the real and abiding basis for future celebration. Future generations need be told nothing of anything prior to the exodus (8,14 f.).

The twin festival was linked with a third ritual, the consecration of the first-born (1 f.,11–16). The 'first-born' theme has occurred several times in *Exodus* (**4.**22 f. and its fulfilment in ch. **12**). When the Egyptian first-born had perished, God had spared, not just the Israelites in general, but their first-born in particular. This historical event, too, was to be permanently enshrined in cultic observance. Where clean animals were concerned, sacrifice was laid down; the donkey—the only unclean domesticated animal—necessitated a different ruling (13); human first-born were different again (15; for fuller details cf. Num. **18.**15 f.).

Verses 17–22 provide a general picture of the Israelites in their new environment; the only specific detail of the journey is the mention of Etham (20), of uncertain location. The keynote of this paragraph is the theme of divine guidance. Israel had on the face of it exchanged cruel servitude for a life of deprivation and aimless wandering; from God she had needed deliverance, but now sought guidance and provision.

Notes: V. 3: 'this day'—the 15th Abib. V. 9: the observance of the feast, with its confessional statements like that in v. 8, demonstrates Israel's adherence to God's law; other peoples bore distinguishing marks or dress to indicate their obedience to their gods. V. 16 is of similar import; Jewish phylacteries are worn in fulfilment of it. V. 17 refers to the shortest route to Palestine; but it was guarded by a series of strong Egyptian fortresses. V. 19: cf. Gen. **50.**25.

Note how the confessional statement of vs. 14 f. links 'history and duty'. Find examples of this sort of 'creed' in the N.T.

Exodus 14   The Final Hurdle

The Sinai Peninsula (and indeed at this period Palestine itself) was under Egyptian control, so if the Egyptian king maintained his previous hostility, Israel's position would be precarious until at least she passed the various frontier fortresses and got out of range of the major part of his armies. Her own battle array (13.18) cannot have been very impressive as yet, nor had she any experience of warfare. Verse 2 could suggest some manoeuvring to elude Pharaoh, though vs. 3 f. scarcely support such an interpretation. At any rate the Egyptian king changed his mind once more and gave pursuit, and the Israelites were terror-stricken; they had escaped bondage, but were now threatened with a worse fate. But to assess the situation simply in these terms was to ignore the chief Actor in the whole series of events; Moses made no such mistake (13), and the miracle which followed resulted in his people's better understanding (30 f.).

How is this miracle to be understood? The Bible consistently sees God's hand at work as much in the 'natural' as the 'supernatural', a fact which can make it difficult for us to unravel the one from the other. Here both elements are present. Note the various factors instrumental in providing Israel's rescue (vs. 16,21,24,25,27), to which torrential rain might be added (see Psa. 77. 16–20), but v. 30 sums them all up under one Name. Verse 14 does not necessarily mean that no Israelite had to wield a sword; it means primarily that in the end-result God, not Israelite swords, would win the day (perhaps cf. 2 Sam. 18.8). Verse 25 shows the Egyptians retreating 'from before Israel'. Again, the 'wall' of waters (22,29) may mean no more than that the waters to the right and left provided a defence; the term may derive from the poetic imagery of 15.8. But whatever the mechanics involved, a miracle it plainly was, that an ill-equipped, frightened, infant community should make their escape, while their powerful and confident enemy should meet utter disaster.

Notes: V. 2: the location of the places named suggests that 'the sea' here was the Mediterranean; but 'the sea' of the miracle was not the Mediterranean (cf. 15.4, and see note). V. 3: evidently Pharaoh did not expect the Israelites to attempt a desert journey. V. 15 implies that Moses had prayed. V. 31: 'believed in': i.e. they committed themselves to the leadership of God, through Moses.

Does v. 15 suggest that prayer may sometimes be a substitute for faith and action? In what ways can prayer be wrongly used?

Exodus 15 Praise and Blame

The experiences of Passover and the Red Sea were permanently enshrined not only in the hearts of the Israelite community but also in their institutions and observances; not only in creed and ritual but also in joyful hymn—for we may well believe that vs. 1–18 were sung annually at Passover-time. In view of v. 17, the Jerusalem Temple will have been the most appropriate setting for the triumphant song. That is not to say that the hymn was composed in later Jerusalem, and is anachronistic here; on the contrary, it shows all the marks of being very ancient poetry, and nothing in it is incompatible with a thirteenth-century date. Due to its very antiquity, some of the words and expressions cannot now be translated with any certainty.

The hymn did more than exult over fallen enemies; it expressed the Israelite discoveries about their God—His power, His uniqueness, His love, His kingship. Above all, they had learned that their fathers' God could be claimed as their own (2). It also expressed their faith (14–17); if mighty Egypt could be so defeated, no minor power in Palestine posed any threat.

But the ransomed people's faith lasted a mere three days (22)! The harsh realities of desert life soon dispelled their joy and courage; human enemies can be destroyed, but who could tame the wilderness? Their anxieties were natural enough, and no word of rebuke was directed at them; but they should have taken note for the future, for by His gracious provision God 'proved them' (25). There is a forward allusion here, for the Hebrew word 'proved' is related to the place-name Massah (17.7), where the Israelites were to revert to their complaints.

Notes: V. 4 'the Red Sea' is literally 'the reed sea/lake', and nearly all scholars today place the miracle at one of the lakes which lay between the Gulf of Suez and the Mediterranean. (See 'Red Sea' in *The New Bible Dictionary*.) V. 12: 'the earth swallowed them': a collapse of the sea-bed has been suggested, but poetic imagery should rarely be taken so literally. Vs. 13,17: 'abode' and its parallels are difficult to pin down precisely; conceivably Sinai is meant in v. 13, Jerusalem in v. 17. V. 20: the description of Miriam could imply that she was Moses' *half*-sister; but cf. Num. 26.59. Vs. 25 f. anticipate the law-giving at Sinai. V. 27: Elim cannot be identified with certainty.

'There is more to a hymn than a good tune.' How do your favourite hymns compare with the one in this chapter for content, theology, or personal experience?

Questions for further study and discussion on Exodus chs. 11–15

1. Ought one to seek theological explanations for all 'natural' disasters (whether on a national or a personal level)? Or has such an approach its dangers?
2. Why did leaven come to symbolize evil? Study the use of this symbol in the N.T.

3. What comparisons can be made between the Passover and the Lord's Supper?
4. What did Paul mean by the phrase 'Christ, our paschal lamb' (1 Cor. 5.7)?
5. What sort of guidance and provision can a Christian expect? In what sense is this life a desert journey?
6. Note Exod. 14.31: ought we to repose a practical faith in anyone besides God?
7. Note Exod. 15.18: what evidences can you find of God's reigning in today's world?

Exodus 16   Divine Sustenance

In the desert, water tends to be a more precious commodity than food, and it is not surprising that the unpalatable waters of Marah had occasioned the first Israelite complaints; however, the luxuriant oasis of Elim had temporarily satisfied them on this score. But all too soon they became conscious of hunger. It is remarkable how swiftly Egypt had come to seem a desirable place; the cruel servitude was quietly overlooked, while the slaves' diet was now labelled 'fleshpots', i.e. 'pans of meat' (3, JB), a startling exaggeration. Once again Israel's complaints met with little rebuke, however; instead, their wants were supplied once more, in a timely and miraculous fashion. The quails (13) were a special delicacy to meet their immediate cravings; these birds migrate northwards in large numbers each spring across this region, flying very low. A later supply of quails is mentioned in Num. 11.31 ff., but this will have been a rare occurrence. The regular and constant provision in the desert (it lasted consistently till the Israelite armies reached Jericho, cf. Josh. 5.10 ff.) was manna. Verses 32–36 clearly relate to a time after the ark of the covenant had been made.

The quantity of the manna, the peculiarities of its appearance each weekend, and other features, show how miraculous its supply was; Psa. 78.24 appropriately calls it 'the grain of heaven'.

A particularly interesting feature of the story is the emphasis on the Sabbath. Clearly a form of Sabbath observance antedated the Sinai legislation (when it received a particular significance, cf. Ezek. 20.12,20; Neh. 9.14); 20.11, indeed, linking the seventh day with the Creation, hints at the great antiquity of its observance.

Notes: V. 15: see RSV margin. The word *man* may derive from an Egyptian word, or else represent a dialect (Arabic?) form of the word 'what?' (in classical Hebrew *mah*). For a fuller discussion of manna, see the commentary by G. H. Davies, and also 'Manna' in the *New Bible Dictionary*. Vs. 19 ff.: cf. Matt. 6.11. V. 32: On this occasion, God's goodness is to have a tangible memorial. V. 36: 'omer' occurs only in this chapter, but an 'ephah' is well known (probably *c*. 22 litres).

Note the two senses of God's 'glory' (7,10). What part may the glory of God play in a Christian's life and experience?

Exodus 17 Two Further Hazards

As the Israelites progressed stage by stage towards Mount Sinai, they faced one serious problem after another; these were dangers typical of the desert, but new to Israel, long used to the high civilization and culture of Egypt. The reality of God's unmistakable presence among them (cf. v. 7) did not in any way detach them from the normal facts and problems of daily life; but it did give them every reason for faith and hope. At Marah God had tested their faith (15.25); at Rephidim now they showed an increasing lack of it. Note how the roles were reversed (2). The verbs of Moses' statement in v. 2 were embodied in the place-names (7), as a long-standing testimony to the Israelites' behaviour; the Sinai experience did little to change their character, for in Num. 20.2–13 we find a virtual repetition of the whole incident.

But if Israel's faithlessness was recorded in the place-names, God's provision and promise at Rephidim were also recorded (14). From time immemorial the nomadic peoples of the Arabian deserts have lived partly by raids on others, in which life is held cheap. The Amalekites, however, had more serious intentions than mere plunder; they were seeking to prevent the Israelites from entering 'their' domain (the wilderness area south of Palestine), and hence from reaching Palestine itself. Moreover, they represented an inplacable hostility to the Israelites until the end of the eighth century (cf. 1 Chron. 4.41 ff.). Hence the divine anger and pronouncement of doom. See, too, Deut. 25.17 f.

This first victory over Amalek was achieved not so much by Israelite valour as by divine help and the leadership of Moses. Whatever the symbolism of his actions (11 f.)—perhaps prayer—the need for his constant supervision is stressed. The passage also underlines his need for active and able lieutenants; here we have the first mention of Joshua. Hur appears again only in 24.14 (apart from genealogical lists).

Notes: V. 6: 'at Horeb' seems strange (Rephidim was some distance from Mount Sinai, cf. 19.2), and some scholars think that the phrase has accidentally and erroneously crept into the text here. It is certainly a strange coincidence that the similar incident at the other Meribah took place not far from a Mount 'Hor' (Num. 20.22).

However, 'Horeb' may be the name for a range of mountains, of which 'Sinai' was one single eminence; since Rephidim cannot be located with certainty, it may have been near the Horeb range. V. 7: RSV margin 'Proof' may be misleading; 'Testing' or 'Trial' is preferable. V. 16: the meaning of the saying is obscure.

With v. 7 compare Psa. 22.1. Can one define when it might be 'wrong' and when 'right' to ask this sort of question? Does it depend on the answer expected?

Exodus 18   Jethro's Contribution

The Israelites were now getting near Mount Sinai; v. 5 may mean that the incident actually occurred at its foot, but 19.1 f. relates back to Rephidim. The Bible is often more interested in theological than in chronological sequence, so we are free to place this chapter chronologically after 19.1 f.; alternatively we may interpret the phrase 'the mountain of God' as the whole Horeb range (see note on 17.6), for the Hebrew word *har* can mean 'hill' or 'range'. In any case, the chapter belongs logically to its present context. The hazards of the preceding three chapters have highlighted the position of Moses; Israel's debt to him was incalculable, and he was still to serve his nation in many ways, but the struggle with Amalek had shown a hint of his human frailty. Moreover, 17.15 with 18.12 suggests a rather casual approach to sacrificial worship. The time had come when a more thorough organization was necessary, at all levels; and it is interesting that the very man who acted as priest on this occasion, Jethro, was the man who saw the need for it. Once again, it is not very clear whether he was previously a worshipper of Yahweh or not; possibly he worshipped Him and some other deities, too (cf. v. 11). At any rate, Midianite that he was, he readily acknowledged the supremacy of Israel's God in word (10), ritual act (12) and humble submission (23).

The immediate result was a judiciary organization, quite possibly on a Midianite pattern. All that was now required was the law for them to administer, and that could not be mediated through a Midianite; direct revelation from God must supply that. Verse 27 depicts Jethro as going his way; Moses was now making a break with the past.

Notes: Vs. 2 ff.: this is the first we hear of Moses' second son by name, and of Moses' sending his family away. They had all set out for Egypt (cf. 4.20); but probably Moses had at some stage anticipated that Pharaoh would injure them or use them as hostages. V. 14: 'sit' has here a judicial sense. V. 25: Num. 11.16 speaks of seventy elders who aided Moses; cf. Exod. 24.1.

How open should we be to the advice of non-Christians? Why do you think the arrangements suggested by Jethro were not given to Moses by direct divine revelation?

Exodus 19   The Holy Mountain

In midsummer the Israelite community reached its first goal, Mount Sinai, otherwise known as Horeb (see note on **17.6**). Here Moses had had his first encounter with the God who had guided and guarded him from his infancy; here the infant nation, which had likewise experienced divine deliverance and provision, was to have its first encounter with God, and in that encounter find maturity and purpose. At the outset the nation is reminded of its recent experiences and their inner meaning (4); the phrase 'on eagles' wings' expresses both 'tender care' (J. C. Connell) and 'safe transport' (M. Noth). Israel's privileged position and her proper function in the world is next set before the people (5 f.). The term 'kingdom' recalls **15**.18; their king is Yahweh, and He is about to provide their national constitution and laws. The people's response (8) is expressive, as G. H. Davies has pointed out, of optimism, enthusiasm and innocence; the contrast and disillusionment can be seen in Paul's words in Rom. **7.7** ff.

But before the covenant and the law came the encounter; in some sense God came within 'the sight of all the people' (11); yet note v. 21. Theirs was a terrifying experience, and they were right to be in fear (16,21). The various instructions given them emphasize the distance between God and sinful men, the holiness of God, and above all the need for mediation. An interesting feature of the chapter is its threefold prescription for priesthood; note vs. 6,22,24. The detailed prescriptions were yet to be given, but already the divine pattern was being set. Verse 24 makes Mount Sinai the prototype of 'the holy of holies' (cf. Heb. **9**.6 f.). It is particularly instructive that at this experience of such intimate contact between Israel and God, the election of Israel is put in its proper perspective, and the divine purpose for the whole world declared in germ (5 f.; cf. Isa. **49**.6).

The data of v. 18 have sometimes been interpreted of volcanic activity, but unnecessarily. While the precise location of Mount Sinai is still uncertain, the traditional general area (in the south of the Sinai Peninsula) has much to commend it; but there were no volcanoes there in historical times.

Notes: V. 13: 'the trumpet' may be figurative here, describing the howling of the wind through the mountains during a storm. Throughout the Bible, the trumpet symbolizes the presence of God, and special days of (or in commemoration of) His activity.

With v. 6 compare 1 Pet. 2.9. How far has the Christian Church fallen short in carrying out its intended functions?

Exodus 20.1–7   Three Principles of Worship

Here begins a long section (chs. 20–31) consisting almost entirely of instructions to Moses, and to Israel, through his mediation. It falls into three distinct parts, chs. 20; 21–23; and 25–31. Chapter 24 (which reverts to narrative) shows that one or both of the preceding sections was issued in documentary form, as part of the covenant made between God and Israel at Sinai. God had already commanded obedience to the covenant stipulations (19.5), and these are now outlined. First are given the ten commandments (literally 'words', 1); 34.28 calls them '*the* words of the covenant', i.e. they are the general principles in which all the specific 'ordinances' (21.1) are embodied. They are unsuitable for use as law, since they are not detailed enough, nor do they specify penalties.

The initial statement (2) is not a command but provides the basis of the covenant, drawing attention to the special relationship between Yahweh and Israel, and to the historical background to it. It is important to recognize that it is the nation as a whole which is addressed in the ten commandments; hence the reference to successive generations in v. 5. It is a political truism that the follies of one generation often create for a nation adverse effects of long duration; for Israel, the outstanding political folly would be idolatry and the worship of false deities. (*Judges* provides numerous examples of Israelite idolatry and its political consequences.) Verse 7 goes further and points out that a pretence of serving Yahweh exclusively will not suffice; the prophets were often to rebuke the nation for hypocrisy (cf. for example, Amos 4.4 f. or Isa. 48.1 f.).

The words 'jealous' (5) and 'showing steadfast love' (6) are two sides of the same coin. Both terms are difficult to translate adequately in English. The former does not have the unpleasant overtones of the English word; it relates to the covenant and signifies Yahweh's right to the undivided loyalty of His people; the marriage-bond metaphor, frequent in the O.T., adequately interprets the sense. 'Steadfast love' is expressly a covenantal term, 'covenant loyalty' being its basic meaning. Yahweh both gives and expects full covenant loyalty.

Notes: V. 3 is not concerned to deny the existence of other deities; they were, in a sense, very real, as objects of worship, in the

85

ancient world. V. 5: 'you' is the nation; see Deut. 24.16 for the warning to the individual. V. 7: the use of Yahweh's 'name' in magical practices is probably implied; perhaps cf. Acts 8.9 ff.

What forms might hypocritical worship take today?

Exodus 20.8–26 Precept and Warning

In the remaining seven commandments the attention is turned from the Creator to the creature; the sabbath day precept (8–11) looks in both directions, for the purpose was both humanitarian (implied here, and emphasized in Deut. 5.12–15) and ritual. The theme of man's following the divine pattern is drawn from Gen. 1.1–2.4. The differences between this paragraph and its parallel in Deut. 5 suggest that the stone tablets (cf. 24.12) contained the ten commandments in very brief form (note the brevity of vs. 13 ff.), and that the Biblical text offers precept and commentary together; the commentary, too, has divine authority (1; cf. Deut. 5.5).

It is interesting to compare v. 12 with v. 5; the previous generation needs as much forethought and consideration as the next one. And if religious error could bring about political disaster (5), social evils might culminate in exile (12). (Again, note that the address is to the nation, rather than the individual, although it must be carried out at the individual level. Thus the promise can legitimately be extended to the individual, cf. Eph. 6.1 ff.) Verse 12 reminds us that the aged and bereaved tended to fare badly in the ancient world.

The social demands of the law were just as much covenant stipulations as were the religious precepts; the covenant served to bind Israel together, as well as to unite the nation with her God. Hence the prophets, recalling Israel to the covenant, inveighed against social injustices as well as idolatry.

Verses 22–26 go into more detail about religious observance, but note that they are more negative than positive, and may well be read as a warning (in view of the events recorded in ch. 32). The patriarchs had left many shrines in Palestine; the danger was that the worship of Yahweh might be corrupted into idolatry or its equivalent. Note the stress on simplicity, modesty and unpretentiousness.

Notes: V. 17: 'covet' indicates more than a mere emotion; 'to scheme to acquire' gives something of the sense. The word 'house' is a comprehensive term, and includes all that follows. Vs. 24 f. presuppose nomadic conditions. 'Peace offerings': see 'Sacrifice and Offering' in *The New Bible Dictionary.*

How did Jesus interpret and extend some of the commandments? How would you apply them to present-day Christian living?

Questions for further study and discussion on Exodus chs. 16–20

1. Trace the manna theme in the N.T.
2. What is the N.T.'s teaching about testing and temptation?
3. How many O.T. instances can you find of non-Israelites who were used by God to teach or aid His people?
4. Are the ten commandments dated in any respects? How permanent is their relevance?
5. Attempt to frame ten 'commandments' (or whatever number seems appropriate) which might serve as principles embodying all the N.T. precepts.
6. What 'sacrifices' does the N.T. demand from Christians? What might be considered the Christian counterpart to the altar of Exod. 20.24 ff.?

Exodus 21.1–17   Slavery and Capital Offences

The next three chapters (often referred to as the Book of the Covenant, cf. 24.7) contain Israel's earliest lawcode. The laws are called 'ordinances' (1), a noun which in Hebrew derives from the verb 'to judge'; these were the articles of law by which Israelite lawsuits were to be governed. The imperatives ('You shall [not] . . .') of ch. 20 give place to 'when' and 'if'; i.e. this is case-law. It is all nevertheless closely linked with the overriding principles set out in the ten commandments (note how vs. 15,17 elaborate 20.12, for instance).

While Israel's origins and rescue from Egypt were unique to her, she was nevertheless very much part of the ancient Near East, and owed debts in many directions. It is not surprising, therefore, that her laws have much in common with the various lawcodes which have come down to us from this general area of the ancient world. In particular, comparisons between the Book of the Covenant and the lawcode of Hammurabi, the great Babylonian king of some centuries earlier than Moses, have often been made. Sometimes it is helpful to draw such parallels; for instance, parallel material in documents from the ancient Mesopotamian city of Nuzu has recently suggested to some scholars that 'marital rights' (10) might be a mistranslation, and that 'oil' or 'ointments' would be preferable. But it is equally important to recognize the distinct cultural and religious context of each code. The Sinai covenant constituted all Israel a brotherhood, and there is little here of the considerable class distinctions of Hammurabi's Babylon. However, the Israelite code set out to maintain law, not to overthrow the existing social order, and v. 2 immediately recognizes the fact that ancient society could not manage without the institution of slavery. But observe the humaneness of the slavery laws; in Israel the slave had personal rights, notably the right of eventual freedom. (The term 'Hebrew' [2] may be significant; it is a wider term than 'Israelite', and indeed Israelite slaves may not be envisaged here at all.)

Notes: V. 7 has a humane point; 'freedom' is not always beneficial. V. 13: see Num. **35.** Accidental or unpremeditated manslaughter is here provided for.

What N.T. guidance can you find on the question of Christian duties where civil laws are concerned? Can you suggest any present-day laws which might well be described as decreed for human 'hardness of heart' (Mark **10.5**)*?*

Exodus 21.18—22.17   Principles of Compensation

This whole section consists of case-laws governing forfeiture and restitution. Various principles had to be taken into consideration. In some cases punishment was appropriate and necessary (e.g. 20); in others, no fault attached to either party, but compensation for unintended injury had to be enjoined (e.g. 18 f.); both principles apply in the case of theft (e.g. **22.**1). There appears to be some tension in the laws relating to injuries done to slaves (**21.**20 f., 26 f.); the law had to recognize two factors, first that slaves had human rights and ought to be properly treated, the second that they constituted property. In our natural repugnance against slavery, we are inclined nowadays to forget that the humane treatment of slaves was not only a moral obligation but also common sense, if a master wanted good value from them.

The sanctity of human life is underscored in various ways; **21.**28 must be read in this light: the owner of an ox, if faced with the possibility of personal loss, would take every precaution against accident. Similarly, the *lex talionis* (23 ff.) must be read in its context; its very severity should have promoted the greatest care and respect for the persons of others. It must also be remembered that its function was in part to *restrict* vengeance (and take it out of the hands of the wronged individual or his family); contrast Gen. **4.**23 f. But if absolute justice demands full compensation, the law can always be tempered with mercy; in course of time money compensation was brought in to modify this law (as Num. 35.31 seems to imply).

As in lawcodes generally, there is some scope given for the discretionary decisions of judges and arbitrators; **21.**22 expressly names them, and at some other points the lack of detail and precision implies that the final decision was theirs. **22.**9 in particular implies, without specifying, some means of deciding whom God might 'condemn'.

Notes: **21.**32: 'thirty shekels' was no doubt the current slave value.
22.1-4: the RSV rearrangement of these verses clarifies the sense.
V. 9: ' "This is it" ' constitutes a claim to property. V. 13: the
'evidence' would prove the 'neighbour' had not been negligent.
V. 15: i.e. the price of hire covers risk of loss.

*Have the humane qualities of present-day lawcodes in any way
undermined the sense of the sanctity of life and the importance of the
individual? How compatible are justice and mercy?*

Exodus 22.18—23.19
Social Morality and Religious Observance

This final section of the covenant laws consists of forthright, unconditional directives, and so differs from the case-laws of **21.**2—
22.17. The first three verses bring some religious matters into the
judicial sphere, but most of the section is concerned to inculcate
proper attitudes (both in society generally and in the law courts)
and to govern basic ceremonial practice—the sabbath, the sabbatical
year and the three major annual festivals.

The concern for the poor and defenceless in society (**22.**21-27) is
a distinctive feature of the Israelite code, and arises directly from
the covenantal nature of Israel's constitution. Rich and poor alike
were bound together by the bonds of the same historical experience
(21) and of the same covenant with God. Verse 25, it should be
noted, is not prohibiting normal commercial practices, but defending the underprivileged from exploitation. Such fine moral attitudes
cannot be sufficiently safeguarded by law; hence the note of warning
of divine retribution.

Chapter **22.**18 ff. must also be read in the light of the covenant,
in which the Israelites voluntarily bound themselves to the exclusive
worship of Yahweh. The pagan customs so stringently prohibited
here constituted as serious a covenant breach as the breaking of any
of the moral and social laws. Indeed, the view is taken that if the
covenant were set aside in the religious sphere, general moral and
legal corruption would inevitably follow. It is therefore quite
improper to make this passage a pretext for religious intolerance.

Of the three festivals (**23.**14 ff.), it is the first, Passover–Unleavened
Bread, which holds pride of place in the section. It was far more
than an agricultural feast, in view of recent events. Note how
22.29 f.; **23.**18 also relate back to the Passover record (chs. **12** f.).
The other two festivals (**23.**16) were explicitly linked with the agricultural year. It is evident from the agricultural aspect of the Book
of the Covenant, as also from the recognition of class distinctions
in **22.**25 ff., that the passage of time is envisaged, and that many of

the prescriptions relate to the life of a settled community in Palestine. (Many scholars accordingly conclude that the Book of the Covenant reached its final form after the Israelite conquest of Canaan.)

Notes: **23.17:** 'males'—women were not excluded, cf. 1 Sam. **1.3** ff. V. 19 prohibits a Canaanite magical (fertility) practice.

How far is morality dependent upon religion? Is the 'true' faith in practice productive of the loftiest morality?

Exodus 23.20–33 Promise and Fulfilment

The academic world is today in possession of the text and details of a good many covenant documents from the ancient Near East, and comparative studies have illuminated our understanding of Biblical covenants in various ways. It is particularly interesting to find that the concept of a covenant relationship between a people and a deity is distinctive to Israel; the nearest parallel outside Israel was the Hittite type of covenant which linked king and people in a rather similar fashion. Both were 'suzerainty' covenants, i.e. agreements between unequal partners; the king (human, or in Israel's case, divine) could set out what stipulations he deemed necessary and command his subjects' obedience. But at the same time he bound *himself,* in some sense or other limiting his own freedom of action. So the Book of the Covenant ends with God making a number of promises to Israel—promises which, however, would in their fulfilment involve further demands upon the Israelites. The promises were thus conditional upon their obedience. Verses 29 ff. provide one such promise; it was not completely fulfilled until David's reign, and then only for a generation or two, because of the persistent disobedience of the Israelites to the stipulations here set out. Not only did they frequently indulge in pagan worship, in defiance of v. 24, but they were also ready enough to enter into covenants with Canaanite peoples (cf. vs. 32 f.). By its very nature the Sinai covenant was exclusive: 'no man can serve two masters'.

Notes: V. 23 lists the various contemporary occupants of Canaan; the list is abbreviated in v. 28. The verb 'blot . . . out' is a strong word, but probably has reference to national entity rather than to total extermination (cf. Psa. 83.4, where the same Hebrew verb is used). V. 24: 'pillars': upright stones sacred in Canaanite worship. V. 28: 'hornets': probably another plague is intended, although some scholars take the word as metaphorical. V. 31: cf. Gen. 15.18; 1 Kings 4.21. Here 'the Red Sea' is probably the Gulf of Aqaba.

To what extent are God's promises to us conditional? Are we in danger of forfeiting any of them?

In this chapter, too, interesting parallels with other covenants of the ancient world appear. They were regularly solemnized by the taking of oaths, by putting the stipulations in writing (and periodically reading them publicly), and by an appropriate ceremony of ratification. All of these elements appear in Exod. 24. There were no possible loopholes for Israelites to declare that they did not know or had forgotten the statutes and ordinances. Thrice now (3,7; **19.8**) they had made public declaration of their willing obedience.

A significant feature of the covenant ceremony is the role of sacrificial blood (5–8). This is typical of the Biblical covenants; see especially Mark **14.24**. We may view its function as atoning for the sins of the past—the Israelites were to start observing the covenant with a clean sheet, so to speak. But it also serves to draw attention to the fact that even in this solemn moment, willing to serve God as they were, their very first need was atonement.

But atonement (by means of burnt offerings, 5) is only half the story. The term 'peace offerings' may be better rendered 'fellowship (or "communion") offerings'; the chief point about the covenant was that it bound God and Israel into a close relationship (as the frequent O.T. marriage metaphor emphasizes). The Sinai covenant was no modern contract where neither party has the slightest personal interest in the other, and where they often never even meet face to face. On the contrary, the representatives of Israel had the closest possible contact with their God, in a unique experience (which must however be qualified by reference to 33.20; note that only the 'feet' of God are here mentioned specifically). The final words of v. 11 may well imply a fellowship meal.

Notes: Vs. 1,9: Nadab and Abihu were Aaron's sons (cf. **28.1**). V. 13: Joshua apparently went so far up the mountain, cf. **32.17**. V. 14: Aaron and Hur were to administer the law in Moses' absence. V. 16: the 'settling' of God's 'glory' has its N.T. counterpart in John **1.14**.

How far may the Christian today experience the 'glory' of God? See 2 Cor. 3.18. What do you understand by the word 'glory'?

Questions for further study and discussion on Exodus chs. 21–24

1. To what extent is it a Christian duty to have a revolutionary effect on society? See Matt. 5.13–16.
2. Is a 'Christian country' in any way comparable with the ancient Israelite community? How much consideration ought a Christian administrator or legislator to pay to non-Christians under his authority?

3. How would you attempt to apply Exod. **22**.25 in modern conditions?
4. Note Exod. **23**.19: are there any contemporary 'pagan' practices which as Christians we should carefully avoid?
5. Has the fact of the conditional nature of God's promises to Israel any bearing on today's political problems in the Near East? What moral criteria should a Christian apply to such political issues?
6. How many covenants can you discover in the Bible? Which were of most importance?
7. Trace the theme of God's glory through the Bible.

*Exodus 25   Furniture for the Shrine

Not the least important aspect of the Sinai covenant was its priestly content. Right at the start of the Sinai ceremony the divine word to Israel had constituted her 'a kingdom of priests and a holy nation' (**19.6**), but the covenant document itself contains very little of ceremonial instruction. A passage like **23**.14–17, however, undoubtedly implies some established ritual, either already known or else to follow immediately; we now find the latter to be the case. The ceremonial description begins with the furniture necessary for the shrine, and the first object discussed is the ark (10–22), usually referred to elsewhere as 'the ark of the covenant', by far the most sacred object to the Israelites. It was functional in several ways; as a box, it contained the twin tables of the law ('the testimony', 16); v. 22 sets out two other functions; and important aspects not mentioned here were its use in ceremonial and military processions (cf. 2 Sam. **6**.12–19; 1 Sam. **4**.3–11); admittedly these functions lent themselves to some misuse. Its lid was both a cover and a place of atonement (the Hebrew word translated 'mercy seat' embraces both these senses). The ark thus symbolized the presence of God, whether in the midst of His people or at their head when on the march.

The table (23–30) served to hold all the non-animal offerings made to Yahweh, while the lampstand (31–39), of course, supplied light within the shrine. The detail in the construction of all three items of furniture is represented as important and God-given (9,40), but its significance is not elaborated here (nor in Heb. **9**.1–5). See further discussion on ch. **37**.

Notes: Vs. 3–7: it has been suggested that these treasures had been taken from the Egyptians and Amalekites. Vs. 8 f.: 'sanctuary' is more literally a holy place, and 'tabernacle' a dwelling place. V. 18: 'cherubim': archaeology has revealed that these were like winged sphinxes; see article and illustration in *The New Bible Dictionary*. Vs. 31–39 are no longer completely intelligible, due to technical vocabulary and textual problems.

Consider the various functions of the ark of the covenant; how far can they be translated into N.T. terms?

*Exodus 26   The Tabernacle

The shrine itself is next considered; detailed instructions are given regarding its materials, its plan and construction, and the positioning of its furniture. Verse 30, like 25.40, emphasizes the divine authority behind the whole plan; it also reminds us that the detail of these chapters was not precisely the blueprint for the architects. One is often apt to forget that the content of such Biblical passages was intended to teach, explain and inspire, and not simply to record 'what happened'. The primary relevance of these chapters was for the ordinary Israelite worshipper of later generations; the tabernacle served as the basic model for Solomon's Temple, so the practical import of this part of *Exodus* remained instructive until as late as A.D. 70, when the Jerusalem Temple was finally destroyed.

It was the fashion in Biblical scholarship at one time to view these chapters as totally fictitious—the tabernacle was just a projection backwards of Solomon's Temple. But this view can certainly not be maintained today, especially since the ancient Near East has provided parallels of various sorts to the data here set out. The present trend is to view the data as having taken gradual shape, between the time of Moses and that of David. However, *Exodus* states categorically that the whole was completed in Moses' lifetime (cf. 40.16–33), and there is no concrete evidence which contradicts the Biblical statements. On the contrary, portable shrines exhibiting similar modes of construction were known in Egypt before Moses' time.

The shrine was divided into two compartments, separated by a veil (33), and the outer entrance was again screened (36). It is a mistake to look for symbolism in every detail of the tabernacle's construction—the 'frames', for instance, were of very practical purpose, to ensure that the whole edifice stood up! But there is undoubtedly genuine symbolism to be found; the elaborate fivefold curtaining not only served to protect the shrine in all weathers, it also hid the sacred contents from profane eyes, and must have provided extreme darkness inside. God's real presence was shrined in scarcely approachable mystery. The rich beauty and symmetry are also symbolic.

Notes: Certain of the data are difficult to understand now. See commentaries for details, and especially the article 'Tabernacle' in *The New Bible Dictionary.*

Study Heb. 9, and the differences between Israelite and Christian worship. What caused the differences? Do we profit by them as we should?

Exodus 27 The Tabernacle Court

The description of the tabernacle given in 25.10—27.19 moves progressively from the detail of the inner shrine (where the ark of the covenant was to be housed) outward to the sanctuary courts; the very length of the section underlines the distance that existed between man and God under the O.T. scheme of worship. Inside the court (9–19) would stand the altar (1–8), usually described as the altar of burnt offering (cf. 30.28) to distinguish it from the incense altar, which stood inside the shrine, and which is described in 30.1–10. Nothing is said yet about the sacrificial ceremonial; for the moment the attention is concentrated on the material content of the shrine. Hence we are not told how precisely the altar functioned; it is generally supposed that, being a hollow box in shape, it was filled with earth (cf. 20.24) which would absorb the blood from the victims on the altar. But if nothing is said about burnt offerings as yet, the altar nevertheless serves as a reminder that 'under the law almost everything is purified with blood, and without the shedding of blood there is no forgiveness of sins' (Heb. 9.22). To approach God, one had first to pass the altar of burnt offering; it was both the barrier to the shrine and the route to it. In turn, the altar's presence rendered the court holy, and so it, too, needed to be screened from prying eyes.

A further material requirement was the oil for the lamp (20) which leads naturally on to the mention of Aaron and the priests (21), out of strict chronological order, but providing the link with the next chapter. The chapter closes with another reminder that the prescriptions contained in it remained relevant for many generations of readers.

Notes: V. 2: the 'horns' were a very important, symbolic feature of the altar; note 1 Kings 1.50. V. 20: 'continually' refers only to night-time, as v. 21 and 1 Sam. 3.3 make clear.

Meditation: *Eternal Light! Eternal Light!*
How pure the soul must be,
When, placed within Thy searching sight,
It shrinks not, but, with calm delight
Can live, and look on Thee!

There is a way for man to rise
To that sublime abode:
An offering and a sacrifice,
A Holy Spirit's energies,
An Advocate with God.

(Thomas Binney)

*Exodus 28   The Priestly Garments

The description now turns from the shrine and its contents to the personnel who would supervise its services: the Aaronic priesthood. It is noteworthy that not a word is said about their moral or intellectual capacities. In N.T. times, the high priesthood was scarcely renowned for simple godliness; but then, neither was Aaron's own family—Nadab and Abihu were to perish miserably (cf. Lev. **10**.1–3), and their mention here (1) serves to underline the fact that the qualities of a priest were beside the point. Ultimately, no man is qualified: see Heb. **5**.1–4. The suitability of the Aaronic priesthood lay elsewhere: firstly, they were chosen by God Himself (cf. Heb. **5**.4); secondly, they could fully represent Israel since drawn from it (1); thirdly, their fitness depended entirely on their total obedience to the ritual laid down for them—indeed, their very lives depended on it (cf. v. 43).

There is an implied contrast with earlier practices; in *Genesis* we find the father of the family repeatedly acting as its priest, in a fairly simple and unelaborate ritual. With the giving of the Law at Sinai, a new era came into being, when great stress was laid on the holiness of God. To please Him, Israel must keep *all* His laws, ceremonial, moral, social, etc. The priesthood must themselves be holy, i.e. dedicated full time to His service, and keeping aloof from profane occupations. Their dress was evocative of 'glory and beauty' (40), little of themselves being visible. This was true even of the ordinary priests, while the high priest's rich vestments were symbolic of royal position. (There is an interesting parallel with the regalia of Phoenician kings, cf. Ezek. **28**.13.) Such royal robes were not always appropriate, however; note Lev. **16**.4,23 f.

Several functions of the priest are briefly noted here; see especially vs. 29 f. 'The Urim and the Thummim' constituted the sacred oracle, by which the people could ascertain God's will (its nature is not entirely clear, nor is the meaning of the two Hebrew words). The priest entered God's presence representing his people, then emerged from the shrine to give them God's directives.

95

Notes: Vs. 42 f.: the stress on decency is reminiscent of **20.26.** Breeches were very rare items of apparel in the ancient world.

What does holiness mean in N.T. terms?

*Exodus 29   Priestly Ordination

Till now all the instructions given relating to the tabernacle concerned material objects—if it is permissible to include the persons of Aaron and his sons under this heading. God had laid it down what the shrine should consist of, what its contents should be, and who should serve in it. Chapter 29 for the first time deals with ritual. In Lev. 1–7 full instructions regarding the sacrificial rites for all Israel are given, but the first necessity was that the priests themselves should take office in accordance with the ceremonies appropriate. Lev. 8 records the implementation of the instructions.

Chapter 28 outlined the proper apparel for the priests, but appropriate dress alone did not fit them for service. A number of symbolic acts were prescribed as rites of consecration; note the use of water (4), oil (7), sacrifices and blood (10–21), and other offerings to God (22–25). Water betokened purification, while the first sacrifice was explicitly a sin offering (14). Anointing was a well-known ceremonial act of the day; oil symbolized the bestowal of office, kingly or priestly. The offering of a whole ram (18) meant the total consecration of the priesthood to God (18,25). Finally, it is noted that the priests have some share in certain of the offerings (27 f., 31–34), but this is prohibited to the laity (33).

The elaborateness of the whole ceremony was multiplied sevenfold (35 ff.), emphasizing the meticulous care with which a holy God was to be approached. Yet His presence was real (45 f.). Despite all the laborious preparations which man had to make, it was in the end God who took the initiative in meeting His people (42 f.).

Verses 38–42 relate to the unvarying daily routine of sacrifice, not specifically to the rites of ordination. Cf. Num. 28.3–8.

Notes: V. 6: 'the holy crown'—the 'plate' of **28.36.** V. 26: 'your portion'—i.e. for Moses, who (uniquely) stood above the priesthood. V. 36: even the altar, constructed by sinful hands, would require atonement.

Note the parts of the body specifically consecrated in v. 20. What aspects of life today most require to be brought into submission to God, in your view?

Plan of the Tabernacle

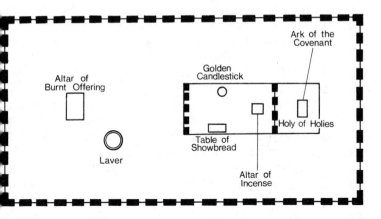

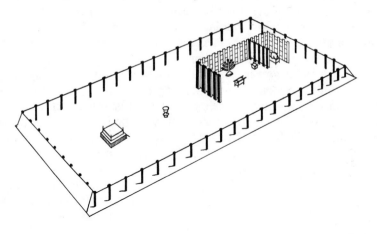

Outer courtyard: 146' x 73'.
Width of entrance at eastern end: 29'.
Overall dimensions of the sanctuary: 44' x 15'.
Dimensions of the Holy of Holies: 15' x 15'.
Approximate height of the Sanctuary: 15'.
(All figures are approximate to the nearest foot, allowing for a cubit of 17.49 inches.)

Exodus 30 Final Tabernacle Instructions

This chapter completes the detailed prescriptions for the sanctuary and its fittings. Two further pieces of tabernacle furniture are described (1–10,17–21), and instructions are then given regarding the making of anointing oil (22–33) and incense (34–38). These items might be styled as relatively less important contents of the sanctuary; otherwise the incense altar and the laver would have been listed with the other sacred furniture, in the context of ch. **25**. In a sense, the incense altar was an adjunct to the ark of the covenant: it was placed opposite the ark (6), and though outside the inner shrine, it was viewed as belonging to it (cf. Heb. **9.**3 f.). Similarly the laver served as an adjunct to the altar of burnt offering (20). But the very least important sanctuary contents had to be carefully specified; nothing must be left to chance, and nothing profane must penetrate the tabernacle courts. The corollary of this was that nothing sacred must be utilized outside the sanctuary, for secular purposes (32 f., 37 f.). The prohibitions of v. 9 clearly must have had relevance to contemporary cultic practices of some sort; 'unholy incense' was incense made otherwise than vs. 34 ff. specify. The adjective 'unholy' (more literally 'strange', 'foreign') came in course of time to mean 'pagan', 'idolatrous'. Its opposite, 'holy', frequent in this chapter, is a term emphasizing the distinction and separation between the sacred and the secular.

But all the elaborate service of the sanctuary would be costly, and vs. 11–16 indicate how financial needs were to be met. The census (12) is reported in Num. **1**. The equality of all Israelites before God and their universal need for atonement, was the basis laid down for their giving (14 f.). Verse 12 refers to an additional reason for paying a sum of money; 2 Sam. **24** tells of an occasion when a wrongful census was punished by plague.

Notes: V. 13: 'shekel of the sanctuary' may mean that this shekel weighed differently from the secular one. V. 18: the laver had a much more elaborate counterpart in Solomon's Temple; cf. 1 Kings 7.23–39.

What are the N.T. principles regarding giving?

Exodus 31 Holy Work—and Holy Rest

The instructions for the tabernacle were now complete—except for the architect's name! One would expect that such a sanctuary would require an appropriate priesthood, to use and care for all the sacred objects, and the data about Aaron in ch. **28** are natural enough; but even in the stage of its construction, the sanctuary, with its contents, must never be in careless or profane hands. As Aaron had been divinely selected for his tasks, so now were Bezalel and his associates. Again, Aaron and his sons required divinely ordained vestments in the fulfilment of their duties; Bezalel and his subordinates were similarly equipped by God Himself. Some Christians are inclined to divorce the guidance of the Holy Spirit from human abilities and intelligence; v. 3 supplies a corrective to such a misconception. Bezalel was given authority to use his own initiative (4 f.), provided he never departed from the basic plans (11).

The climax and seal of the divine instructions to Moses on Sinai was a restatement, in fuller and more urgent terms, of the fourth commandment (20.8–11). This again may surprise us, in view of the fact that Jesus more than once countenanced the breach of the sabbath, and that the Christian church celebrates the first day of the week instead. Its importance was twofold: firstly, its observance had humane points, as Deut. 5.12–15 makes clear; secondly, careful keeping of the sabbath was a sort of priestly function, the only one which could be practised in the workaday, secular world, far from the sanctuary. Naturally, it is the latter element which receives stress in this general context, although the final statement, 'was refreshed' (17), hints at the sabbath's practical value and benefit. Sabbath observance was in fact the acid test of the reality of an Israelite's religion, for it revealed his inward attitude to both God and man, and the true extent of his 'holiness', ceremonial and ethical; hence the stress laid upon it by some of the prophets (see especially Isa. 58.13 f.; Jer. 17.20–27; Ezek. 20.12–24).

Notes: V. 13: 'that you may know'—better, 'that it may be known' (i.e. the sabbath was a sign to the world). V. 18: 'written with the finger of God' is a metaphor, to draw attention to the authority of the law Moses carried.

Is the observance of the Christian Sunday the real equivalent of Jewish sabbath-keeping? Are we in any danger of retaining one aspect of the sabbath's significance while overlooking the other?

Questions for further study and discussion on Exodus chs. 25–31

1. Why do you think that a detailed blueprint for Christian worship, comparable with these chapters, is not given us in the Bible?
2. Compare and contrast Aaron's priesthood with those of Melchizedek and of Christ.
3. Make a list of the contrasts which should obtain between an Israelite priest and a Christian minister.
4. What role does anointing play in the N.T.?
5. What part should beauty play in Christian worship?

6. How far should Christ's words about the sabbath (Mark **2.27**) be applied to all Christian ceremonial and ritual?

Exodus 32 Apostasy and Punishment

Events now proved conclusively that God's choice of Israel as His special people was due to no virtues on their part. Their previous fears and complaints (chs. **16** f.) now turned to active rebellion against both God and Moses; Stephen's castigation of his fore-fathers was fully justified (Acts **7**.38–41). The very first thing they did for the covenant was to break it, there at the foot of Sinai; and it was the very first covenant stipulation (**20**.3) which they breached. The part played by Aaron is astonishing; it looks as if he endea-voured to transform their idolatry into a form of the worship of Yahweh (5). If so, it was an aberrant form, in direct contravention of the second commandment (**20**.4), and Aaron was blameworthy (cf. Deut. **9**.20). Chapter **32** contained a sermon for later generations, for the day came when the whole northern kingdom, priests and all, adopted a similarly corrupted form of Yahweh-worship: see 1 Kings **12**.25–33. Modern scholarship has established that the young bull image at Dan and Bethel was not really intended as a god, but as a pedestal or throne for Yahweh; but such a form of worship was scarcely distinguishable from the Baal cult, and led inevitably to syncretism, especially as the bull was a common fertility symbol in the Baal religion. In this chapter, the Israelites 'rose up to play' (6)—a verb with a frequent sexual motif—indicating how immorality immediately followed apostasy.

Punishment rapidly ensued; Israel deserved to be totally rejected by God, who could as easily have made a new Abraham out of Moses (10). But Moses again showed himself an outstanding medi-ator and intercessor; vs. 9–15 are to be read as a test of his character, not of God's real intentions (see 2 Tim. **2**.13). Even so, death struck down not a few; the plague (35) was perhaps consequent upon the noxious draught of v. 20. As for the unpleasant duty laid upon the Levites (25–29), it taught the lesson for future generations that it was for the religious leaders to take the strongest action necessary to secure the faith in all its purity.

Notes: V. 4: 'fashioned it with a graving tool': 'cast it in a mould' seems a preferable translation, in view of Aaron's absurd excuse in v. 24. V. 25: the precise sense of 'broken loose' is not clear. V. 33: 'My book': cf. Psa. **69**.28.

*How costly to us has our service of God proved? See v. 29, and Luke **14**.26 f.*

100

The thread which runs through this chapter is the theme of God's presence. The complex tabernacle instructions had not yet been implemented, so there was as yet no way to approach God's presence by means of careful ritual. Moreover, the whole community had been rendered unholy by the events of the previous chapter, even though the guilty had perished. God would not go back on His word and His promises, but Israel was unfit for any close communion with Him (1–3). They could only express their regrets in terms of mourning (4 ff.) and worship from afar (10). Meanwhile a temporary substitute for the tabernacle was established, in the care of the only two individuals who had been uninvolved in the apostasy, Moses and Joshua. But note its position (7); the symbol of God's presence could not be in the centre of His people till the covenant had been renewed.

Moses again adopted the role of mediator and intercessor. As Israel prepared to leave the holy mountain, with the threat of God's disfavour hanging over them, Moses felt that he needed a clear sign that God would be with them none the less. God promised the sign of victory in Canaan ('rest', 14), but Moses required a more tangible symbol; his request (15) was to be answered by a fresh law-giving and by the permission of God to build the tabernacle after all. It was at this point that Moses made bold to ask for something more; aware, as all saints have been, that his knowledge of God was imperfect, he asked for a full vision of Yahweh. He was asking the impossible; but he received the promise of a close acquaintance with the works and attributes of God, through an awe-inspiring mystic experience.

Notes: V. 6: the ornaments seem to have been used for the purposes of the tabernacle, cf. **38.8.** V. 9: 'the pillar of cloud': cf. **13.21** f. V. 11: 'face to face' is a metaphor denoting very close contact and communion. V. 15: the same Hebrew word serves for both 'presence' and 'face'; this fact may have prompted Moses' bolder request.

Israel was conscious of its distinctness (v. 16); in what respects can we Christians claim to be distinctive today?

Exodus 34   Covenant Renewal

Moses' intercession, and indeed, God's unchangeable plans, resulted in a renewal of the Sinai covenant, in circumstances and terms naturally very like those of chs. **19–24.** It was unnecessary, therefore, to list all the stipulations afresh; the ten commandments, for instance, are mentioned by name but not set out in detail (28). The promise of victory in Canaan was explicitly renewed (11), but the promise itself necessitated a stern warning; if at the very foot of Sinai, with nobody to blame but themselves, the Israelites had lapsed into idolatry, the dangers of apostasy would be very much greater in Palestine, where false religion was to be seen on every hand. It was appropriate, accordingly, that Israel should be reminded of the exclusive nature of her covenant with Yahweh (12–17) and that the specifically religious observances demanded of her should be rehearsed (18–23), to prevent any careless lapse into Canaanite ways. Specific pagan practices were again forbidden (25–28). In addition, the Israelites were commanded to get rid of all pagan symbols (13) and advised against social intercourse and intermarriage with idolaters (15 f.). In the event, their failure to observe their side of the bargain meant that their victories in Canaan were slow and partial and incomplete (cf. Heb. 4.6–11).

The renewal of the law and the covenant enabled Moses to have a fresh experience and revelation of God (5–8), as he had been promised (33.18–23). His previous encounter with God on Sinai had left no mark upon him that frightened his people, but things were different since their apostasy (29–35); they were now at one further remove from the glory of God. Paul, in 2 Cor. 3.7–18, reminds us that the reflection of the divine glory faded from Moses' face, and that the veil he wore served to hide that fact as well as the glory itself.

Notes: V. 11: 'drive out' means little more than 'conquer', for v. 12 indicates that many non-Israelites would remain. V. 13: 'pillars', 'Asherim' were sacred objects in Canaanite worship; the latter were wooden poles devoted to the goddess Asherah. V. 24: i.e. God would preserve the land from hostile attacks at festival seasons.

Note the privileged position and the responsibilities of the Christian, as set out in 2 Cor. 3.12–18.

Exodus 35.1—36.38   The Work Begins

The remaining chapters of *Exodus* are very largely repetitive of earlier chapters, especially 25–31; the RSV footnotes give detailed references to parallel sections. The order is not identical, but the chief difference is that where 25–31 gave instructions regarding the tabernacle, in the future tense, 35–40 tell of the execution of the instructions, and the past tense is employed. Such lengthy repetition was not unusual in ancient documents, strange though it may appear to us. If the point of the earlier chapters was that every detail of the shrine was designed by God Himself, the point of chs. **35–40** is that the shrine was constructed and erected in precise accordance with those details.

The work began with Moses calling a full assembly (35.1–19), where he gave warning that not even such sacred labours must breach sabbath observance, and then appealed to the willing generosity of the people, as he set the material requirements of the tabernacle before them. They responded warmly and unstintingly; in fact, they provided more than enough (36.2–7). Their response now was in marked contrast to their earlier rebelliousness. It is interesting to observe the history of their jewellery and ornaments; see 32.2 ff.; 33.4. ff.; 35.21 f.

Not only did they give, they laboured, men and women too, under the direction of Bezalel and Oholiab; 35.34 notes, as 31.1–6 did not, that these two men were capable teachers as well as craftsmen. Thus under their direction the hangings and outer frames were completed; the order was from the inner shrine outwards.

Notes: **35.3**: only here in the O.T. is fire specifically prohibited on the sabbath; in the context, fires required for metal casting are probably in view. **36.2**: 'come' is a word with priestly overtones; G. H. Davies comments, 'work was also worship'. **36.10–38**: 'he' is probably impersonal throughout (like English 'they').

Study Rom. **12,** *for a N.T. call to worship, with similar emphasis on effort and generosity.*

Exodus 37.1—38.31   The Sacred Furniture Completed

These two chapters record the construction of the tabernacle furniture (37.1—38.8), and the fittings for the sanctuary court (38.9–20). The order again begins with the inner shrine, and proceeds outwards; pride of place is once again given to the ark of the covenant (37.1–9), the central item of furniture in the tabernacle. It had, in fact, been made prior to the assembly spoken of in 35.1; cf. Deut. 10.1 ff. (Bezalel evidently acted as Moses' special representative in constructing it.) As for the bronze overlay for the altar (38.2), it was added at a later date (cf. Num. 16.39). Then again, the data of 38.21,25 f. relate to a time after the appointment of the Levites and of Ithamar (Num. 3 f.) and after the census (Num. 1). In other words, the description here is systematic rather than strictly chronological.

For brief discussion of the function of the ark of the covenant, see notes on ch. **25**. Its design was partly functional (i.e. a box) but partly symbolical; it was viewed as the throne of God, and thus betokened His presence in a special way. 1 Sam. 4.4 (cf. 2 Sam.

6.2) shows that it was the figures of the cherubim in particular which constituted the ark a throne. They were well-known accompaniments of royalty and deity in the ancient Near East (or they would have had no significance for the Israelites); similar figures adorned the thrones of Phoenician kings, for instance. (There can have been no danger of their drawing veneration to themselves, or they would have been prohibited under the second commandment.) In appearance they were winged sphinxes; see Bible dictionaries for illustrations. It is to be observed that the provisions of the Israelite cult in general were (a) similar enough to contemporary religious practices to be meaningful to the ordinary Israelite worshipper, (b) different enough to draw attention to the distinctive features of the Israelite faith and to the uniqueness of Yahweh.

Notes: **38.8**: the ministering women's functions are not known; the only other mention of them is in 1 Sam. **2.22**. Their mirrors were of bronze, not glass. V. **26**: see notes on **12.37**.

How far do we find or make our Christian practices meaningful, to ourselves and to our contemporaries?

Exodus 39.1—40.38   The Complete House of God

The making of the priestly vestments (no doubt including the Urim and Thummim, cf. **28.30**, although there is no specific mention of them) brought to an end the preparatory work for the tabernacle (**39.1–31**); the complete articles were brought to Moses, for his approval (**32–43**). It is explicitly noted, indeed stressed, that nothing was contrary to the divine design; it has been pointed out that the statement that everything was in accordance with God's commands occurs seven times in ch. **39**, seven times in ch. **40**! Moses was then able to consecrate the priesthood and the sacred objects in an anointing ceremony; this, too, according to the explicit instructions of God (**40.1–33**). Nothing was left to chance or to mere human initiative.

A new era now opened in the history of God's people—on a very appropriate date (**40.1**), two years after the exodus from Egypt. Moses, great leader as he continued to be, must now step back (**40.35**); the priesthood belonged to Aaron and his descendants after him (**40.15**). 'Perpetual' in this context means 'hereditary', and can be contrasted with the eternal priesthood of Christ (cf. Heb. **7**); in other words, Aaron, too, must one day step aside. Both Aaron and Moses were His forerunners, like John the Baptist (cf. John **3.28** ff.). And even at Sinai, in the days of their greatness, the emphasis is wholly on the One who designed, owned, and deigned to dwell in, the shrine just erected: see **40.34–38**. The tabernacle was the sign of His presence, in the midst of His people, while the cloud and fire were the signs of His guidance to the promised land. Whatever Israel's faults and problems might be in the future, these three signs offered the basic source of a joyful confidence in her God.

Notes: 39.43 is reminiscent of Gen. **1.**31; here was a new creation! 40.31: Moses' name is included, since he had priestly functions during the installation ceremonies.

Study Heb. **10.**19–25 *and its implications for us.*

Questions for further study and discussion on Exodus chs. 32–40

1. What are the chief reasons for apostasy in general? What are its chief symptoms today?
2. In the case of yourself or your local church, is there any danger of your aids to worship becoming 'idols'?
3. Do Aaron's actions (ch. **32**) illustrate the danger of trying to make Christianity conform to the convictions and thought patterns of our contemporaries?
4. Why do you think the Scriptures contain so much repetition? Would you consider that passages which are repeated are more important than others?
5. Study the theme of the presence of God in the Book of Exodus.
6. What is God's dwelling place, according to the N.T.? What has the N.T. to say about the Jewish Temple?
7. In what respects does *Exodus* tell an unfinished story? In particular, what was missing in the Sinaitic laws and cultic prescriptions?

Leviticus, Numbers and Deuteronomy

INTRODUCTION

The scene of Leviticus and of Numbers **1—10** is Mount Sinai, and the content of these opening chapters is as daunting as their setting. Yet their unremitting thoroughness gives its own witness to the complete seriousness with which God takes His covenant with His people: it is no casual or arm's-length relationship, but one which must shape and colour every inch and minute of life, to train up a people whose forms of worship, structures of society and minutest details of behaviour will reflect the holiness of God. Without these chapters we should have had little if any idea of the many facets of sacrifice to which the N.T. makes reference; the high and fearful demands of priesthood; the meaning of the rent veil of the Temple and the bearing away of sin which the great Day of Atonement expounded in advance; nor should we have heard the second of the great commandments, '. . . love your neighbour as yourself', nor understood the meaning of Jubilee and of Nazirites, nor pictured the array of Israel's camp and the order of their march.

By way of contrast, the remainder of Numbers (**11—36**) tells the absorbing story of reluctant, mutinous pilgrims and the eventual arrival of their children at the threshold of the Promised Land after a series of stresses, altercations and seductions which the N.T. treats as standing examples and warnings to the Church (1 Cor. **10.**1–13; Heb. **3**; Jude 5,11; Rev. **2.**14). Interspersed with these events are various laws, ecclesiastical (e.g. tithes, ritual cleansing, festal sacrifices) and civil (e.g. vows, inheritance, homicide), and the log of Israel's travels (**33**).

Deuteronomy tells of Moses' last, solemn charge to Israel. It has a warmth and eloquence all its own, and (as various recent scholars have pointed out) its pattern strikingly reflects the structure of a treaty covenant, with its preamble, historical survey, basic principles, detailed stipulations, confirmatory blessings and cursings, witnesses, and the injunction that copies of the covenant must be preserved and periodically read in public. For details, see the commentary. To make this preaching of the Law indelible, its challenge is summed up in the Song of Moses (**32**), and then the Pentateuch is brought to a fitting end by the oracle giving the destinies of the twelve tribes, and by the restrained but moving account of Moses' death.

Leviticus

1. THE FIVE STANDARD SACRIFICES: Leviticus 1—7
A. BASIC REGULATIONS: 1.1—6.7

Leviticus 1   The Burnt Offering

The broad regulations of this chapter are supplemented by further details in 6.8–13. But first note the setting, a characteristic O.T. blend of grace and judgement. Israel, liberated and brought into covenant, is encamped at Sinai, and the glory of the Lord has sealed the great enterprise of erecting the 'tent of meeting' (1; cf. Exod. **40.34**) where God will have fellowship with man. Yet this very glory has kept Moses at a distance (Exod. **40.35**), and Leviticus will constantly bear witness to God's overwhelming holiness.

By its name (lit., 'that which ascends') and by its ritual the burnt offering showed its Godward emphasis. It was the only sacrifice, among the five types in chs. **1—5**, which provided no food for either priest or worshipper. So the crown rights of God and the joy of giving *away* were established at the outset, while the gradation of values, from a bull down to a pair of pigeons, allowed everyone the opportunity to bring some gift. Each was of equal fragrance (9,13,17), when offered from the heart (Psa. **51.17, 19**); each on any other terms was an affront (Psa. **51.16**; **50.9 ff.**).

Yet sacrifice was harsh and violent, and the offerer was to know it, his own hand pressed on the creature's head (4; see comment on 3.2), his own act doing it to death. And his part in the proceedings, while it emphasized his personal responsibility, could not be construed as achieving his acceptance. True, the victim was his gift, but its atoning value (4) was *God's* gift (see **17.11**), while his own role was mere butchery (5,6: to kill, flay and cut up). It was the priest's part to give it the form of a sacrifice, bringing it to God. The bulk of the chapter is about this.

The O.T. knew the inadequacy of such victims (e.g. Psa. **40.6–8**) and of such priests (e.g. Lev. **4.3**). The N.T. finds in Christ the one real priest and sacrifice (e.g. Heb. **9.6 f., 11 f.**), who 'gave Himself up for us, a fragrant offering' (Eph. **5,2**; cf. Lev. **1.9,13,17**). Sanctified by Him (Heb. **10.14**), the Christian can become a living sacrifice himself (Rom. **12.1**), called to offer the worship and praise (1 Pet. **2.5**; Heb. **13.15 f.**) which are not drama but reality.

108

Concerning this offering see also 6.14–23; Num. 15.1–10. The word 'cereal' is a translator's convenience; the Hebrew simply calls it an 'offering', using a word which implies a token of homage. In these laws it is a technical term for offerings that involved no shedding of blood, so the translation is a fair one; but in Gen. 4.3–5 it is used equally of Cain's gift and Abel's, and there are other such passages. In civil life it stood for tribute or a formal gift: cf. Gen. 33.10; 2 Kings 17.3 f.; Psa. 45.12.

Offered to God, it was not only homage but the acknowledgement and dedication of His staple gifts. It made no atonement since it cost no life (cf. Heb. 9.22); but it was to accompany the blood-shedding sacrifices, as Num. 15.1–10 indicates. God was presented again with His own gifts, yet not in their natural state (there was a place for this: cf. v. 12; 23.10, etc.) but in the forms given them in human use: fine flour, not grain; oil, not olives; and so on. The domesticity of vs. 4–7, with their recipes and utensils (a griddle [5] was a metal baking-plate), reinforces the point, setting aside ordinary things, at their best, for God in token (the 'memorial portion') and for His ministers in actuality; using the unspoken language of hospitality, of the kind that Abraham and Sarah gave in Gen. 18.6 ff. when they entertained angels unawares. So Acts 10.4 describes the practical piety of Cornelius in terms of this offering (cf. vs. 2,9,16).

But there are no concessions to familiarity. Every feature of the memorial portion emphasized its holiness: its consecration by anointing (1; see on 8.10 ff.); its frankincense used up for God (2; cf. Psa. 141.2); its ascent in fire (2). The ban on honey and leaven (11) strikes the same note, for it only applied to fire-offerings, as v. 12 makes clear. These substances were among the minor luxuries of life, matters for gratitude (12; cf. 7.13), but more eloquent of God's bounty than of His demands (cf. Exod. 12.39; 13.7–9; Prov. 25.16).

Note, finally, 'the salt of the covenant' (13), a reminder of the table fellowship that had confirmed the bond between God and His people (Exod. 24.8–11). In this way every sacrifice was to contain an allusion to this host-and-guest relationship (see Ezra 4.14; cf. 'a covenant of salt', Num. 18.19; 2 Chron. 13.5). Such is God's fidelity; such, too, He expects from us (13) and, it would seem from Mark 9.50b, between us.

Nothing in this chapter gives any hint of what would have loomed largest in a human account: that this offering was festive, a meal as well as a sacrifice. This aspect will emerge in 7.11–36 (cf. **17.**1–7, and the further law of Deut. **12.**20–28), but the present concern is with more primary matters: the fitness of the victim (1,6), its slaughter by and for the worshipper (2a,8a,13a; see further, next paragraph), its blood hurled against the altar (2b,8b,13b), and the burning of what belonged exclusively to God (3–5,9–11,14–16). Without these the meal would have been mere camaraderie or a pleasant fellowship meal; with them its fellowship could be fundamentally 'with the Father', as the N.T. would put it, and thereby genuinely 'with one another' (see 1 John **1.**3,7).

The symbolism of laying one's hand on the victim's head (2, etc.) was that of substitution. The action largely spoke for itself, but any ambiguity is removed in Num. 8.10–19, where see comment.

The law against eating fat (16b,17) is elaborated a little in **7.**22–25. There is, incidentally, no conflict with this rule in Neh. 8.10, where a different word is used. Whether the fat was devoted to God as being the richest part (as Gen. 4.4 seems to imply) or, like the blood, as symbolizing life, we are not told; the food laws seldom offer their reasons. But by marking out (for a while—cf. Col. 2.16 f.) certain areas of life as God's preserves and not man's, the levitical laws gave a continual reminder of both sovereignty and grace. Sovereignty, in that it is for God to choose what He will give or withhold; grace, in that what He withholds He turns to our benefit. The blood (17) was 'given' back for better use than nourishment (**17.**11). The fat, 'as food offered by fire to the Lord' (11), was made the symbol of the fact that we do not feast alone, but play host to God Himself, by His gracious command. He dines with us, as well as we with Him.

With regard to the sin offering, see also 6.24–30. The scope of this sacrifice is defined by the word 'unwittingly', repeated in each paragraph (2,13,22,27). I.e. it was not the offering *par excellence* for a man convicted of his general sinfulness, for the Law could provide no single 'full, perfect and sufficient sacrifice'; rather, it met the kind of need indicated by Psa. **19.**12 as distinct from 13. Cf. Num. **15.**22–31. It could almost be called the Lapse Offering; for 'unwittingly' translates a word which implies not so much ignorance as stumbling or straying.

The degree to which different classes of offender affected others by their sin seems to be reflected in the descending scale of victims. The 'anointed priest' (3), whose sin involved the whole people, was probably the high priest, anointed more liberally than his fellows (cf. **8.**12 with v. 30; Psa. **133.**2). Verse 3 reveals the impossible burden of priesthood; Heb. **7.**27 f. names the only bearer of it equal to the task. But some such responsibility is inseparable from all leadership (cf. Jas. **3.**1; Heb. **13.**17).

Notice the strong emphasis on the blood, recovering the sinner's lost access to God. For his own offence (3–12) or the congregation's (13–21), the high priest could no longer minister in the sanctuary until blood had made atonement at the places where he would stand before God: the veil, the incense altar and, in the courtyard, the altar of burnt offering. The sevenfold sprinkling (6,17), the daubing of the incense altar's horns, and the pouring of the remaining blood round the main altar (7,18), formed a more elaborate sequence than the single rapid movement of throwing the blood against the altar, prescribed for the offerings of chs. **1** and **3**. The modified ritual for the individual, whether ruler (22–26) or private citizen (27–35), made the same point by being enacted at *his* customary meeting place with God, the main altar (25,30,34). See further, on **10.**12–20.

Amid these complexities, note the implied seriousness of the sins we might think excusable; but also the simple assurance of the refrain, 'the priest shall make atonement for him . . ., and he shall be forgiven' (20 [plural], 26,31,35). Study, finally, the challenging parable that Heb. **13.**11–14 finds in the instructions of vs. 12 and 21. 'Let us go forth to Him . . .'.

Leviticus 5.1—6.7   Sin Offering and Guilt Offering

The Sin Offering (continued, **5.**1–13). There is little doubt that these verses round off the regulations of ch. **4**, still speaking of the sin offering rather than the guilt offering (see **5.**14—**6.**7). Although **5.**6a,7a suggest the latter, they are subject to vs. 6b,7b, which are supported by vs. 8,9,11,12 in speaking of the sin offering. (Note that in **4.**13,22,27 the actions that demand a sin offering make the offender 'guilty', as do those of **5.**2–5; it is a somewhat similar linking of terms in vs. 6a,7a here.)

The pattern of **5.**1–13 is simple: first, some examples of offences that called for this sacrifice (1–4)—minor liberties taken with God's majesty and holiness; and secondly, the sacrifice itself (5–13), with the concessions to various degrees of poverty. It is probably vs.

111

11–13 that account for the word 'almost' in Heb. **9**.22; an exception that proves the absence of magical views of the inherent power of blood.

The Guilt Offering (**5**.14—**6**.7). For this, the distinctive notes are the costing of the sacrifice ('valued by you . . .', **5**.15,18; **6**.6; cf. 1 Pet. **1**.18 f.) and the more-than-full repayment of the damage (**5**.16, etc.). It portrays the element of 'satisfaction' in atonement, and of restitution in repentance; it is this term that describes the sacrifice of the Servant in Isa. **53**.10.

The first case here (**5**.14–16) refers to what Mal. **3**.6 ff. calls 'robbing' God: i.e. using for oneself the tithes, firstfruits, etc., which are God's due and therefore 'holy'; hence the monetary repayment in v. 16. The second case (**5**.17–19) seems to correspond to Psa. **19**.12, Jer. **17**.9, etc., in that some guilt is known only to God, and there can be atonement but not restitution. The third group of cases (**6**.1–7), which incidentally draws out some of the implications of 'Thou shalt not steal', makes classically clear the Biblical principle that no sin is purely a man-to-man affair. This emerges not only from the fact that manward restitution is not enough (the transaction of vs. 4,5 must be followed by the atoning sacrifice of vs. 6,7), but from the significant phrasing of v. 2a. The whole paragraph is an anticipation of our Lord's dictum, 'first be reconciled to your brother' (Matt. **5**.23 f.).

B. PRIESTLY REGULATIONS: 6.8—7.38

Leviticus 6.8—7.10 — Procedures for Four Offerings

Specialized though these directives are, they supply further insights into the rituals already prescribed in chs. **1**—**5**.

The Burnt Offering (**6**.8–13). Thoroughness and preparedness are demanded by the law of the altar fire: the sacrifice wholly consumed (9) and the fire always burning (12 f.). The vigilance that this required of the priests was matched by that of the singers (1 Chron. **9**.33; Psa. **134**.1 f.), and the beautiful figure of Psa. **5**.3 is clearly derived from v. 12. It is no far cry to the call of Luke **12**.35–40 or of Rom. **12**.11. Regarding the quarantine-like precautions of **6**.10 f., they will only seem excessive if one takes a popular estimate of holiness and sin, which they are designed to correct. The lesson was as unwelcome to ancient Israel as to modern man: see Ezek. **44**.6–8,15–19.

The Cereal Offering (**6**.14–23). Note the phrase, 'their portion of My offerings' (17). Part of the concern of vs. 14–18 is to teach a true attitude to 'giving and receiving' (Phil. **4**.15). The giver is shown that he makes an offering to God, not a dole to a dependant; and the receiver, that his share is by rights a gift from heaven, not simply the 'perks' of the job. Paul may have had this passage in mind when he developed the theme in sacrificial terms in Phil. 4.18.

The Sin Offering and Guilt Offering (6.24—7.7). The rituals for these were very similar, as 7.7 points out. The reason for the rule against eating the sin offering in the circumstances of 6.30 was doubtless that the priest was personally implicated in both cases where this ritual was prescribed: on his own account (4.3,6) or as a member of 'the whole congregation' (4.13,17). The distinction between his capacity as mediator and as worshipper is seen too in the different rules for the cereal offering (vs. 18,23).

The portion for the priest (7.8-10). After v. 7 it is convenient to list the portions allotted to the sacrificing priest on other occasions. The fact that these are God's bounty from offerings due to Him (see on 6.17) is not mentioned here: the recipients are given the security of a fixed share, as of right. The N.T. uses the matter-of-fact term 'wages' (Luke 10.7; 1 Tim. 5.18) in this kind of context. God may test His servants by shortage, but He does not show a preference for pauperizing them.

Leviticus 7.11–38   Procedure for the Peace Offering

The instructions in ch. 3 made no mention of the meal that followed the sacrifice, nor of the priest's allotted share; the whole concern was with making an acceptable offering to God. Now the secondary matters can follow.

Thanks, vows and freewill gifts (11–18). Notice the inclusion of leavened bread alongside unleavened (12 f.); see the comment on 2.11 ff. As for the requirement that the meat must be eaten the same day (15) or, in the case of vows and freewill gifts, within two days (16–18), its main purpose may have been to ensure that the feast was shared, and shared widely. The large company glimpsed in e.g. Deut. 12.18 f. would be almost a necessity for this, especially in the thanksgiving feast, whereas the celebration of a vow that had been heard, or of a gift that one was moved to offer, could be kept within a smaller circle if one desired it. While the risk to health could well account for the rule against keeping the meat for a third day (17 f.), the variation between one and two days points to another kind of concern, such as the one we have suggested.

How and what one might eat (19–27). The lesson conveyed by the distinction between clean and unclean (19–21) is touched on in the comment on 6.10 f., and the significance of the ban on fat and blood is discussed at 3.16b f. The phrase 'cut off from his people' (20, etc.)

first occurs in Gen. **17**.14, where the uncircumcised suffers this penalty because he has 'broken My covenant'. I.e., it is excommunication, not for inadvertence (which was quickly remedied: cf., e.g. **11**.24-28), but for arrogance. It is not said to be irreversible.

Wave offering and heave offering (28-36). The second of these terms should possibly be translated simply 'offering' (RSV) or 'contribution', i.e. something 'removed' from the main mass rather than 'lifted up' before God. But the latter gesture would have effectively conveyed the fact that the priest's share was first of all the Lord's, and 'heave offering' may well be the right translation. The 'wave offering' (30,34) was probably waved not from side to side but towards the altar and back (the verb is used of the movement of a saw in Isa. **10**.15), perhaps to indicate offering it and receiving it back from the Lord, in a gesture as simple in its symbolism as that of the 'heave offering'.

Questions for further study and discussion on Leviticus chs. 1—7

1. Leviticus (like Exodus and Numbers) literally begins with the word 'And'. Follow up this clue to its place in the total pattern of the Pentateuch.
2. How are we to regard these sacrifices? As the outsider's way back to God, or as the insider's pattern of worship?
3. Do you find any significance in the order in which the sacrifices are dealt with in these chapters?
4. Choose a N.T. reading to go with each of the five sacrifices.

2. THE PRIESTHOOD INAUGURATED: Leviticus 8—10

Leviticus 8   The First Stage of Priesting

At long last the instructions recorded in Exod. **29**; **30**.22-30; **40**.9-1. are due to be completed. The ceremony links together the high priest, his fellow priests and the place where they minister, in ritual differing with their various functions but united by the common feature of anointing or sprinkling with oil (vs. 10-12,30), which signified God's ownership (10c,11c,12c; cf. Gen. **28**.17 f.) or, in the case of men, His commission (e.g. 1 Kings **19**.16) and the endowment of the Spirit for particular tasks (e.g. Isa. **61**.1; 1 John **2**.27). The richness of oil also gave it the pleasant connotation of festivity (cf. Isa. **61**.3; Psa. **45**.7; **104**.15), and its pervasiveness made it an apt symbol of unity, as it spread its fragrance over the diversity of the high-priestly robes (cf. v. 12 with Psa. **133**). This diversity included the names of the twelve tribes of Israel, engraved on the stones set in ephod and breastpiece (cf. vs. 7 f. with Exod

114

28.9–12,17–21,29). Against such a background of anointed priests, prophets and kings must be seen the title of the Lord's anointed, the Messiah or Christ.

The Urim and Thummim (8) were apparently used for ascertaining God's Yes or No by drawing lots. Possibly these lots were matching stones, showing the answer according to whichever surface was uniformly uppermost when they were withdrawn from the breast-piece (cf. 1 Sam. 14.37,41 f., RSV)—while a lack of uniformity indicated no answer. But this is conjecture; what is clear is that God's answer was given or withheld at His own will. The contrast between this form of enquiry and those of divination and necromancy (where man attempts to pierce God's secrets) is firmly drawn: cf. Num. 23.23; 1 Sam. 28.6,7 ff.; Isa. 44.24–26.

The word 'ordination' ('consecration', AV [KJV], RV) in vs. 22, 28, etc., is from a Hebrew root connected with fullness. It is used of the 'setting' which a jewel fills (Exod. 28.17), and could possibly emphasize the 'installing' of the priests in office. But it is coupled with the term (lit.) 'fill your hand' (RSV 'ordain you') in v. 33c, which evidently refers to the symbolism of v. 27 whereby the priest was entrusted for the first time with the offerings which would be his lifelong concern.

The applying of blood to the right ear, etc., in vs. 23 f. signified its application to the whole body, since these were the extremities and the right side was valued above the left (cf., e.g. Gen. 48.13 ff.). Probably we should not read into it the further O.T. associations of, e.g. the ear with obedience (Isa. 50.5), etc., which obscure the real point here, the claiming of the man in his entirety, a living sacrifice for God.

Leviticus 9   The Priesting Completed

'The eighth day' (1) recalls the words 'It will take seven days to ordain you' (8.33), days of waiting at the threshold (8.35) as neither priests nor laymen (Moses was their priest throughout ch. 8). But by itself the vigil, though it emphasized the thorough preparation, still brought them no admission: only the blood of atonement could do this.

Following almost the whole gamut of offerings in vs. 2–4, there is the promise of glory (6), true to the sequence regularly found in the N.T. (e.g. Luke 24.26; Rom. 8.18 ff.; Heb. 2.9 f.); but here the mediator was the first to need atonement, and the suffering was not his own. RSV's 'Then' in v. 15 is useful in highlighting the preliminaries that had to take place before an imperfect high priest could save his people. Heb. 7.26 ff. makes the point and draws a contrast.

The blessing of the people (22) was no empty gesture but an effective transmission of God's power; an example of its meaning is shown in Deut. **28**.1-14. It was the special calling of the priests 'to bless in the name of the Lord' (Deut. **21**.5), and the priestly gesture of v. 22 was to be our Lord's parting one (Luke **24**.50 f.) after His fulfilment of 'the sin offering and the burnt offering and the peace offerings' (22).

Notice, finally, the tokens of God's presence (23 f.), majestic even in grace. The people's exultant and awestruck response shows two ingredients of worship, in primitive vigour—not softened by familiarity. To record a more modern reaction to God's presence, v. 24 might have had to read, 'they dragged themselves to their feet, and mumbled'.

Leviticus 10   The Priesthood Marred

Significantly, the priests are no sooner ordained than in trouble. Their special temptation is to presume on their position, and improve on their instructions. Cf. the pressure on our Lord to force the pace (Matt. **4**.6 f.); cf. the carnal deviations which Paul had to rebuke in the young churches (e.g. Gal. **1**.6; Col. **2**.8 ff.). The Church does not always take kindly to being under the word of God.

The fire and glory of vs. 2 f. throw back a fierce light on the episode of **9**.23 f., where it was the sacrifice that was consumed, not the offerer. They are also visible reminders of the judgement which even God's saving presence precipitates: cf. John **3**.17 ff.; Heb. **10**.26-31; **12**.25-28. Such is holiness, and the truth about it was the answer Aaron needed and accepted (3). David was to learn a similar lesson through Uzzah's fate (2 Sam. **6**.8-15), and Isaiah through Uzziah's (2 Chron. **26**.16,21; Isa. **6**.1 ff.).

The remainder of the chapter draws out some detailed implications of v. 3. (Further issues, which are quite crucial, emerge in ch. **16**.)

No respite from responsibility (4-7). To be unkempt (6a), in surrender to private grief, would be to become ritually unclean. Continuing to stand between God and man, as they must (7), they would then transmit wrath instead of blessing (6b). Cf. Samuel's sense of inescapable responsibility, in a different context: 1 Sam. **12**.23.

No strong drink on duty (8-11). How directly this injunction bore on Nadab and Abihu's offence, we simply are not told. But their fate underlined the danger of careless handling of what was holy. Verse 11, however, goes beyond physical to mental fitness for the priest's hardest and most neglected task: cf. Deut. **33**.10a; Hos. **4**.6-11; Mal. **2**.7 f.

The priest completes the sacrifice (12–15; 16–20). Once more the priest as mediator is distinguished from the priest as individual. As the latter, he was entitled to the parts of certain offerings as his emoluments (14 f.); but as the former, he played a vital part in the ritual of an offering's acceptance (12 f., 17,19b). The climax of some sacrifices was their ascent in smoke; of others it was the bringing of their blood inside the holy place (4.6 f., 17 f.) or the holy of holies (16.14 f.); while of others it was their consumption by the priest in the sanctuary (v. 18 agrees with ch. 4 that the last of these applied when the second did not). In this last case, priest and victim together were to 'take away' iniquity (17b, RV marg.) and make atonement (17b)—not by the priest's eating a sin-laden carcase, for it was 'most holy' (6.25), but by his completion of the bringing of the slain victim before God. This identification of priest and sacrifice made all too little sense when Aaron (19b) or any son of his was the mediator. The discord would only resolve itself in Christ (Heb. 9.23–28).

3. THE CLEAN AND THE UNCLEAN: Leviticus 11—15

Leviticus 11   'Taste not, Touch not'

Food laws (11.1–23,41–47). Several of the names, especially of the birds, are of uncertain meaning to us; and the generalizations about certain classes (e.g. vs. 3,9 f., 20) offer no reason for the rules that apply to them, only a simple guide to their use (e.g. 'chews the cud', in vs. 5,6, is a convenient, not a technical, description). Different principles may have governed different examples, cultic in some cases, hygienic or aesthetic in others; what mattered for the Israelite was that God had drawn these distinctions and made them an object-lesson in practical holiness.

The old view that the pig (7) was banned chiefly as a danger to health, rather than as an animal prominent in heathen rites, is vigorously defended by W. F. Albright (*Yahweh and the Gods of Canaan*, 1968), who points out that the creatures of vs. 5 and 6 are also disease-carriers, not cultic animals. (Possibly the camel [4] was prohibited in order to keep the classification of v. 3 uncomplicated by exceptions). Albright also notes the distinction between free-swimming and mud-burrowing aquatic creatures (9–12), which broadly corresponds to their possession or lack of fins and scales, and has special relevance to the transmission of disease in places where water is slow moving.

The disqualifying element in vs. 13–19 appears to be that these are birds of prey, ritually unacceptable because of the blood they consume. In vs. 20–23, 29 f., 41 f., an aesthetic principle may enter in, to exclude creatures that are repulsive-looking as being demeaning to the eater; but the main consideration seems to be their close contact with the earth (contrast v. 21 with 41–43), which calls to mind the curse on the serpent in Gen. 3.14.

With regard to these regulations in general, notice the opportunity they were to provide in Isa. **66.17** of offering studied insults to God. This is one extreme; the other is Pharisaism; the gospel delivers us from both (cf. Rom. **7.4–11**; **8.2–4**; Col. **2.16–23**).

Defilement by contact (**11.24–40**). The reference of v. 26 is evidently to carcasses, as in the rest of the passage. The rules for decontamination, strict as they are, take account of practical necessities. The 'quarantine' is short (24b, etc.) and the cleansing straightforward (e.g. 28,32). This moderation, together with the distinctions made in vs. 32–38 between relatively washable and unwashable, absorbent and non-absorbent materials, and between different quantities and states of water in vs. 34,36, implies a commonsense approach which discourages Pharisaic extremes at the same time that it reiterates the central lesson, 'Be holy, for I am holy' (44 f.; cf. 1 Pet. **1.16**).

Leviticus 12   Defilement by Childbirth

This unpromising chapter was to give rise to the first two events recorded of our Lord after His birth, and set the scene for the prophecies of Simeon and Anna: Luke **2.21–39**. It not only prepared the conditions in which His birth 'under the law' (Gal. **4.4**) would be made plain from the start (cf. Luke **2.22,27,39**), but provided our only secure clue to His initial poverty (8, cf. Luke **2.24**).

The terms 'unclean' and 'clean' which dominate this group of chapters are ceremonial, not moral; cf. the expression 'their purification' in Luke **2.22** (RV, RSV), which refers to the infant Christ's involvement in His mother's uncleanness by the law of v. 2b (its provisions are set out in Lev. **15.19** ff.). A child's sinfulness from its conception onwards (Psa. **51.5**) is not in view here; see further on vs. 6–8. But while Scripture regards marriage and procreation as God's good gifts (e.g. Psa. **127.3**; Heb. **13.4**), it also makes this area the first to come under judgement at the Fall. There may be an intended reminder of Gen. **3.16** in this law; possibly, too, of the promise of Gen. **3.15** in the shortened period of uncleanness for the birth of a boy (2–4,5). The boy's circumcision, however (3), may have counted towards the cleansing, as some have suggested.

The two stages of ritual uncleanness (the week or fortnight and the additional 33 or 66 days) were at two levels of stringency: in the first period the mother's uncleanness was, so to speak, contagious

118

(2b,5a, cf. **15.**19 ff.), while in the second it only debarred her from holy things and places (4).

In the purifying rite (6–8), the burnt offering, with its emphasis on dedication, preceded the sin offering. This unusual order (in contrast to, e.g. **8.**14,18; **9.**7; **14.**19) tends to confirm that the thought of personal sin was not prominent here; the cleansing was 'from the flow of her blood' (7), not from any guilt attached to marital intercourse or childbirth. Notice, finally, that the element of dedication, implicit in the burnt offering, was uppermost in Luke **2.**22, where the occasion was used as the opportunity to give back Mary's firstborn to the Lord.

Leviticus 13   Defilement by 'Leprosy'

According to a leading authority on leprosy, Dr. R. G. Cochrane, 'the modern disease of leprosy bears no resemblance to that described in the Bible' (*Biblical Leprosy*, Tyndale Press, 1961), and this view is endorsed by various O.T. scholars. The same Hebrew term applies to certain mildews and fungi in materials (**13.**47–59; **14.**33–53) as to the several kinds of sores and infections described here, whose symptoms (and, above all, curability) distinguish them from the leprosy we know. For suggested identifications, see the commentaries.

The priest's careful procedure, with its provision for a three-stage examination where necessary (e.g. vs. 4–6), is an impressive diagnostic exercise. But ritual defilement rather than physical contagion was the point at issue, though the two would coincide in many cases. The chief signs of a defiling malady were, variously: depth, local bleaching of the hair (3,20, etc.), active spread (7,22, etc.) and rawness (10,14, etc.). In connection with the last of these, note vs. 9–17 which show why such lepers as Gehazi, 'as white as snow', were not automatically isolated (2 Kings **5.**1,27; **8.**4 f., cf. perhaps Num. **12.**10–15). This condition, perhaps leukoderma, was repulsive, as Aaron's appalling description of Miriam makes all too plain (Num. **12.**12), but only called for isolation if open sores broke out (Lev. **13.**14–17). The whiteness, incidentally, confirms that what we call leprosy is a different disease, since 'the lesions of leprosy are never white' (R. G. Cochrane, ibid.).

The torn clothes, etc., of v. 45 were signs of mourning (cf. **10.**6; Ezek. **24.**17), as though the banished man were mourning his own death; yet the words 'as long as he has the disease' (46) hold out some hope, which the next chapter will reinforce. The intense signs of grief and shame put this ceremonial defilement in a class by itself, and support the view that it was intended to illustrate the havoc of sin. This impression is strengthened by the fact that leprosy was inflicted as a judgement on at least three people in the O.T. (Miriam, Gehazi and Uzziah) and by the allusion to the leper's cleansing which is made in the penitential Psa. **51**.7 (cf. Lev. **14**.6 f.). If the passage on mildew in a garment (47–59) is in mind in Jude 23, it provides another indication of the moral symbolism of this chapter.

Leviticus 14 The Cleansing of 'Leprosy'

(*i*) *In a human sufferer* (1–32). The procedure, summarized, was first the patient's examination and clearance (the ritual must be based on truth), then the first purification rites and partial restoration (4–9), finally, on the eighth day, the sacrifices for atonement (10–20, 21–32).

The hyssop (4), a bushy plant, was evidently to be bound to the cedar stick with the scarlet material, to make a mop for the sprinkling mentioned in v. 7. Its somewhat similar use at the first Passover (Exod. **12**.22) gave it an obvious appropriateness, as did the cedar's resistance to decay and the scarlet stuff's blood-red appearance. All three were also used in preparing the cleansing water described in Num. **19**.6.

The 'running water' (5) was understood in later Judaism to mean water taken from a spring (implying its purity) but held in the bowl which received the blood. It would be hard to imagine a more vivid symbolism of death, cleansing and liberation (on the last of these see below, on v. 53) in all of which the healed man was made a participant by the sevenfold sprinkling (7; cf. 1 Pet. **1**.2). Note the purifying by water and blood, and the explicit pronouncement (7b) which resolved any ambiguity which the actions might have had concerning the crucial question—for sacraments without words establish nothing.

The subsequent atoning rites (10–20 or 21–32) are remarkable for prescribing the whole range of sacrifices except the peace offering (which no doubt was often voluntarily added for a thanksgiving celebration), and for treating the reclaimed man almost as if he were a priest, earmarked for God with blood and oil (14,17, cf. **8**.23,30). [*Note:* The 'log' of oil (10) was about ⅓ litre.] It was a characteristic divine gesture of grace superabounding where, in picture, sin had abounded.

(*ii*) *In a house* (33–53). With this, compare the 'leprosy' in a garment, **13**.47–59. As with the food laws, these regulations make good sense physically, but were primarily a means of sharpening the Israelite's sense of what is clean or unclean before God. This is clear from the ritual regulations of vs. 46 f. (inadequate as health rules) and especially those of vs. 48 ff., closely akin to the means of purifying the human leper. Incidentally the release of the living bird (53) in connection with cleansing a house suggests that it symbolizes a removal of uncleanness (cf. the scapegoat, **16.22**) rather than a resurrection, both here and in v. 7. In all these areas it is made very clear that the bold symbolism of the ritual was to be the counterpart of practical action that was equally bold, realistic and ruthless in excluding every sign of corruption.

Leviticus 15   Defilement by a Discharge

The subject is of discharges from the genital organs, and the pattern of the chapter is symmetrical, dealing first with pathological (1–15) and normal (16–18) cases in males, and then with normal (19–24) and pathological (25–30) cases in females, before leading on to a statement of the law's purpose (31) and the summary (32 f.).

The isolating effect of an abnormal discharge was second only to that of leprosy, cutting off the person concerned not only from the sanctuary (31) but from almost any share in social life. The restrictions of, e.g. vs. 4–12 amounted to a perpetual quarantine, whereas those of vs. 16–18 involved no one else and were quickly over. In the case of women, the regulations for normal and abnormal states differed only in duration and in requiring sacrifices for the latter group (29 f., cf. 14 f. for males). On v. 24 see comment on ch. **18.19**.

So the chapter illuminates the plight of the woman afflicted for twelve years with an issue of blood, and her 'fear and trembling' (Mark **5.33**) at the discovery of her contact with the crowd and with Jesus. Her case shows up the limitations of the Law, which could isolate uncleanness (31) but could not cure it (cf. Gal. **3.21** f.).

What is left unsaid here is that the commonest cause of persistent discharges is gonorrhoea, a disease of promiscuity. While some who suffered under this law would be innocent (and were not accused by it), others would know that they had themselves to blame, and would find the analogy between ceremonial and moral defilement uncomfortably close.

Verse 31 is an important statement of the principle involved in this group of laws, soon to be rigorously enforced in Num. **5.1–4**. In the Exodus period the searching implications of God's presence were shown by immediate interventions (cf. **9.24**; **10.2**). At other times the warning, 'lest they die', was implemented by more gradual or inward processes (e.g. Ezek. **18.31**; **24.21–23**; John **8.24**; **15.22**), but never withdrawn. Access to this perfect holiness is for 'hearts sprinkled clean' and 'bodies washed with pure water' (Heb. **10.22**). The positive side of this is indicated by the unusual verb for 'keep . . .

separate', which is the root of the word Nazirite—a reminder of Israel's high calling, a people consecrated to special service.

Questions for further study and discussion on Leviticus chs. 8—15

1. What aspects of the priesthood of Christ are illustrated by the garments, the ordination rites and the duties of Aaron and his sons?
2. In what sense does the N.T. show that earthly priests are obsolete (see Heb. **5—10**), and in what sense is the Church 'a holy priesthood' (see 1 Pet. **2.5**; Heb. **13.10–16**)?
3. Study the relation of Col. **2.16** f. and Mark **7.18** f. to the laws on the clean and the unclean in, e.g. Lev. **11**. What did Christ abolish in Mark **7.1–23**, and what did He retain?
4. In the light of Question 3, do you think it a fair summary to say that the Christian is bound by the moral laws of the O.T., but not by its ceremonial and civil regulations? If so, what is the present value of the latter two? What other N.T. passages throw light on this?

4. THE DAY OF ATONEMENT

Leviticus 16   The Way into the Holiest

This chapter is one of the most important in the Law, and looms large in the Epistle to the Hebrews. It was given urgency by its tragic context (1).

The fact that the high priest's own access to the Holy of Holies had to be won by sacrifice (11–14) before he could re-enter on his people's behalf (15 ff.), was proof enough of the priesthood's inadequacy (cf. Heb. **5.3**; **7.27**; **9.7**). The cloud of incense, to hide God's throne from Aaron 'lest he die' (13), re-emphasized the lesson; in fact the whole chapter calls attention to man's distance from God by the very thoroughness of its procedure, from the opening warning, 'not to come at all times' (2), to the closing emphasis on the ubiquitous defilement of sin (33).

Verses 6–10 use the common O.T. technique of presenting an outline account before coming to the fuller details, which follow in vs. 11–22. The word Azazel (8,10,26) need not be a name; it should be understood in the light of vs. 20–22, which would support the meaning 'dismissal' (RV marg.) or 'entire removal' (BDB Lexicon, p. 736). In later Judaism, Azazel is the name of a demon, but this could have originated from a misunderstanding of this very passage. The Septuagint, the earliest Jewish translation, has simply 'dismissal'. Just as the first ceremony (11–14,15–19) is the classic llustration of atonement as opening the way *in* ('within', vs. 2,12,15; cf. Heb. **9.12**; **10.19–22**), so the scapegoat ritual exemplifies supremely the concept of having sin laid 'upon' the victim (22; cf. Isa. **53.4–6**; I Pet. **2.24**) and taken 'away' (21; cf. Psa. **103.12**; John **1.29**; see also comment on Lev. **14.53**).

The high priest, divested of his customary robes for the plainness of white linen, emphasized, by his appearance and by his ritual washings (4,24), the sole preoccupation at this stage with purification from sin (cf. Rev. **19.8**). After this, the 'glory and beauty' of his full attire (Exod. **28.2**) marked his return to his people to mediate in their sacrificial worship, even though the emphasis remained on its value for atonement (24).

The fulfilment far outstripped the foreshadowing, not only in the more radical divesting of the true High Priest and in His subsequent enthronement, 'crowned with glory and honour' (Heb. **2.9**; **10.12**), but in the value and efficacy of the sacrifice, made not 'once in the year '(34) but 'once for all' (Heb. **9.12**), and opening 'heaven itself' (Heb. **9.24**) to all the redeemed. And while the Aaronic high priest returned to his waiting people only to 'make atonement' immediately again with fresh sacrifices (24), the glory of the fulfilment is that Christ 'will appear a second time, sin done away, to bring salvation to those who are watching for Him' (Heb. **9.28**, NEB).

. A HOLY NATION: Leviticus 17—27

Leviticus 17   Precious Blood

That God is a jealous God—i.e. that there is no trifling with His Covenant nor with His prerogative as Creator—is made clear in two ways: by His concern for Israel's loyalty, and by His forbidding all invasion of His rights over life (exemplified here by blood). It is also clear that this attitude is love, both by the 'harlot' metaphor of v. 7 (cf. Paul's expansion of it in 2 Cor. **11.2**) and by the redemptive use which God assigns to the blood which He claims (11). These two concerns colour the two parts of the chapter.

No neglect of God's altar (1–9). To secularize a potential sacrifice, killing for private use an animal fit for a peace offering (1–4), is denounced as not only butchery but a step to treachery, since dues withheld from God are soon used against Him (7), and secularism is a vacuum waiting to be filled. The satyrs (7) were probably visualized as goat-like demons. Their cult reappears in 2 Chron. **11.15** and perhaps 2 Kings **23.8**. If it resembled that of early Greece it was orgiastic.

The rule summed up in vs. 3 f. would no longer be practicable when Israel spread out over the promised land (see Deut. 12.20 ff.), but that of vs. 8 f. continued in force (Deut. 12.13 f.). Its neglect led to religious anarchy, as Hos. 8.11 and the books of Kings reveal.

The sacredness of blood (10–16). The background to this legislation is as old as Noah (Gen. 9.3–6); a standing reminder of man's limited rights over his fellow creatures. In the New Covenant the principle of both halves of this chapter are expected to be responsibly worked out in freedom (cf. 1 Cor. 10.14–33).

Verse 11 is important for its clear statement of God's initiative in atonement. His 'I have given it for you' reverses the direction of flow that prevails in man-made religions, where the worshipper gives in order to receive. The background in Gen. 9.3–6 and Exod. 21.23 ('life for life') confirms that the shed blood is regarded here in its normal sense, as evidence of violent death, not (as some have tried to argue) as a store of quasi-magical vitality. This is expressed even more plainly if the last phrase is translated (as J. A. Motyer has suggested) 'at the cost of the life', as the Hebrew certainly allows; but it does not depend on any one translation. What this verse faintly foreshadows, the N.T. brings into full view, tirelessly proclaiming God's 'unspeakable gift' in 'the precious blood of Christ'.

Leviticus 18 Sexual Sanity

The first and last paragraphs (1–5; 24–30), insisting that Israel must rise above heathen ways, enclose two blocks of sexual laws on incest (6–18) and on other kinds of unchastity (19–23).

Verses 1–5. The refrain, 'I am the Lord your God', already found at 11.45 and at the head of the Ten Commandments (Exod. 20.2) opens and closes the chapter, and motivates the rest of the book (see especially ch. 19). What *He is* must govern what we do. Its negative corollary, 'You shall not do as they do' (3), has its Christian equivalent everywhere in the epistles: e.g. Rom. 12.2; 1 Cor. 6.9–11, etc. In such a context the law of God is seen as the boon it ought to be it is our inveterate sinfulness that has turned v. 5b into an accusation, as in Gal. 3.12 (cf. Gal. 3.21; Rom. 7.10).

Verses 6–18. The ruling concern of these laws is not with genetics (although they are genetically beneficial), but with social decency. E.g., there is no blood tie between the would-be partners in vs. 14–18, but a family bond whose relationships must be kept distinct from those of sexual union. It develops the principle of Gen. 2.24, where the same distinction is made for the protection of both marriage and the family. The prohibition in v. 16 is not in conflict with the law of levirate marriage (Deut. **25**.5 ff.), but refers to the (presumably divorced) wife of a living brother. Notice the improvement made in v. 18 over the customs that prevailed in Laban's circle (Gen. **29**.27), although the law still allowed polygamy, whose threats to family stability are reflected in several of these regulations and in the revealing word 'rival' (18).

Verses 19–23. The heinousness of these offences mounts with each example. That of v. 19 is treated as a minor offence in **15**.24, but as a major one in **20**.18, the difference evidently being between inadvertent and deliberate violations of the command. All the remainder, i.e. the sins of vs. 21–23, were capital offences; see ch. **20**. The children handed over to Molech (21) were possibly in some cases given to be temple prostitutes (the context of sexual sins and the absence of the words 'by fire' from the Hebrew here give some support to this), but there are other passages where it is clear that Molech received children as burnt offerings (e.g. 2 Kings **16**.3 with 2 Chron. **28**.3; Jer. **32**.35). The sharpest denunciations here ('abomination', 'perversion') are reserved for the deliberate depravities of vs. 22 f., a climax comparable to Rom. **1**.26 f.

Verses 24–30. The closing paragraph has the same basis as the opening one (see on vs. 1–5), but stiffens the commands with warnings. It is instructive to see various faces of judgement: as a divine act ('I am casting out . . .; I punished', 24 f.), as self-inflicted decline (they 'defiled themselves', 24, cf. v. 30), and as nature's retribution on the unnatural ('lest the land vomit you out', 28). To these, vs. 28 f. add an impressive note of impartiality, and Gen. **15**.13–16 one of unhurried progress to a just conclusion.

Leviticus 19   Unclassified Ordinances

The unifying thread of the chapter is personal, namely the holy Lord Himself (2,3,4,10,12 . . .). That He had said a thing, was enough; one obeyed for His sake, not for one's own moral satisfaction. Jesus was to show that some aspects of the law, while all were binding, were 'weightier' than others—and yet were the very ones which tended to be neglected (Matt. **23**.23), since the legalist loves what he can measure.

All the major types of legislation meet in this miniature Pentateuch. The substance of six of the Ten Commandments is found in vs. 3,4,11,12; a sample of sacrificial law in vs. 5–8; Deuteronomy's concern for the poor and weak in vs. 9,10, 13,14, and its emphasis on the inward disposition in vs. 17,18; while an extreme example of technical purism in v. 19 rubs shoulders with the great commandment of v. 18 on the love of one's neighbour, which is given a searching interpretation, almost anticipating the Gospels, in v. 34. Other characteristic themes of the Law are equally prominent; it is instructive to make a list of them and of related passages in Exodus to Deuteronomy.

On matters of detail: v. 16 probably means giving false witness in a capital trial. In v. 17 note the same openness in dealing with a grievance as our Lord prescribed in Matt. 18.15. In v. 20, Jewish tradition influenced the AV[KJV]'s unwarranted translation, 'she shall be scourged'. The RV's 'they shall be punished' also outruns the plain Hebrew, which is (cf. RSV) 'an inquiry shall be held'. In many civilizations inquiry has included torture (cf. Acts 22.24), but the O.T. stands out in contrast, nowhere countenancing it.

In v. 23, 'forbidden' is literally 'uncircumcised'. Like the heathen, this was out of bounds; and even when this ban was lifted, the fruit must be for God before it could be for man. Sound farming, like sound hygiene in ch. 11, was made a parable, and a vehicle of obedience and devotion. This is the method of the Law; its Christian equivalent, which should be no less thoroughgoing, is the maxim of 1 Cor. 10.31. This motive prompts the obscurer as well as the plainer regulations of the remaining verses: e.g. vs. 27 f. refer to superstitious practices (possibly originating in attempts at self-disguise, for fear of spirits) unworthy of servants of the one Lord. His service may be exacting; it is also liberating: cf. Psa. 119.45.

Leviticus 20   Unclassified Ordinances (continued)

The brief law against the worship of Molech in 18.21 is now expanded (1–5). God's name was 'profaned' (3; cf. 18.21) not only by being linked, through His people, with such atrocities, but by the very notion that He should share His bride with others (cf. 'playing the harlot', 5c).

The name Molech almost certainly denotes a deity worshipped as king. It may be significant that other 'kingly' deities had to be similarly placated (2 Kings 17.31b). It was part of God's justice that those who rebelled against His constructive kingship and laws should find themselves saddled with a tyrant and with 'statutes that were not good', fastened on them, as we should say, by the very logic of their choice (Ezek. 20.23–26).

Stoning (2) appears to have been the standard form of execution (cf. John 8.5 with Deut. 22.22). It emphasized the people's corporate responsibility to administer God's sentence; it also brought home to the prosecution witnesses the gravity of their action, since they had to cast the first stones (Deut. 17.7; cf. also Lev. 24.14).

An apt comment on the prohibition of spiritualism (6) is the story of Saul, whose attempt to stamp out the practice confirms the antiquity of this law (1 Sam. **28**.3), and whose recourse to it in the end, when God was silent, brings out its character as an attempt to go behind God's back. The practice is consistently and vehemently condemned in the Law (Lev. **19**.31; Deut. **18**.11), and was punishable by death (v. 27; cf. Exod. **22**.18). Neither the cruelty perpetrated against innocent suspects in our own history, nor the existence of charlatans, alters the reality or the gravity of this offence against God.

Verses 10–27 continue to deal with matters already raised in earlier chapters. It is difficult to be certain of the distinctions between the terms 'cut off', 'bear his iniquity', and 'die childless' (see vs. 17–21 especially). The first of them may be a term for execution (cf. vs. 3–5), but its use elsewhere in purely ritual contexts points in those cases to banishment or excommunication (e.g. Lev. **7**.21,25,27). Perhaps the context determined the nature and duration of the sentence; in v. 17, etc. the similarity of the offences to those of vs. 10 ff. suggests the death penalty. 'Bear . . . iniquity' (17,19) might be paraphrased 'take the consequences'. 'Childless' (20 f.) is too precise a word to translate the Hebrew, since the latter (lit. 'stripped') has the meaning 'childless' in Gen. **15**.2 but not in Jer. **22**.30, where it indicates disgrace or destitution.

Notice again the guiding light of all these laws, in vs. 7,8,24,26. The heart of the covenant is expressed in v. 26c: 'that you should be Mine'. It is the sufficient reason for the high demands of the rest of the chapter and of the whole Law.

Questions for further study and discussion on Leviticus chs. 16—20

1. The notes on ch. **16** point out three aspects of atonement illustrated there: viz., access to God ('within'), the bearing of sin ('upon'), and its removal ('away'). Where in the Bible are these various aspects expounded more fully?
2. Blood, as life laid down, is said in **17**.11 to have special atoning value (cf. Heb. **9**.22). Collect and study the sayings of our Lord and of Heb. **9** and **10** on this.
3. The comment on **18**.24–30 speaks of the 'various faces of judgement'. Study these in conjunction with Gen. **3** and **4**, and with Rom. **1**.24–32.
4. Follow up the lines of study suggested in the second paragraph of the comments on ch. **19**.

Leviticus 21 Priestly Purity

The three paragraphs of this chapter point to an ideal of priesthood in which the private concerns of the priest are swallowed up in those of his ministry (1–15), and in which the sacrificer is as un-blemished as the sacrifice (16–24, cf. 22.19–25). The ideal is expressed in the clear-cut terms of outward practice and physique, which made the regulations workable while making at the same time the spiritual and moral implications very plain.

What was alien to God's holiness, whether technically (e.g. a corpse, 1 ff., 11) or morally (7,9), must be alien to those who would handle holy things, who could be defiled not only by contact (11) but by surrender—for that appears to underlie the mourning rites of vs. 5,10: by one's disfigured and dishevelled state one immersed oneself in the calamity. A priest, by contrast, especially the high priest (10), was reserved for God, and must be intact for Him. See also on 10.4–7. Note that while the regulations of vs. 1–15 were without concessions, those of vs. 16–23, which were beyond a man's control, distinguished between the right to offer sacrifices and the right to partake of them (22). Fitness to mediate must be, by token, absolute; fitness to benefit was not by merit but by inheritance and grace.

The continuing relevance of the chapter derives from the twofold nature of the priesthood. (i) It was mediatorial, and pointed towards 'a high priest, holy, blameless, unstained' (Heb. 7.26). This aspect of priesthood is fulfilled, without remainder, in Christ (Heb. 10.11–14). (ii) It was a company of men called to a holiness whose constant demands overrode the 'changes and chances' of life, for the sake of others. This aspect is, or should be, fulfilled in the Church (cf. 1 Cor. 7.29–31; Heb. 13.15 f.; 1 Pet. 2.9).

Notes: V. 4: 'as a husband' ('being a chief man', AV[KJV], RV): the abrupt Hebrew suggests a damaged text; there is no agreed solution. Ezek. 24.16 f. tells against the RSV's translation here, since Ezekiel's behaviour was expected to appear startling, priest though he was. V. 10: 'hang loose': this is also the verb used of the people's disarray in Exod. 32.25 and Prov. 29.18. 'Nor rend his clothes': cf. Mark 14.63.

Leviticus 22 More about Priests and Offerings

Various defilements (1–9). In contrast to the long-term disqualifica-tions of ch. 21, these are mostly brief and superficial. But they become serious (9) if they are taken lightly (note this principle: cf. Matt.

.19), since the distinction between holy and profane is the great heme of these laws.

The priestly household (10–16). The principle here, as in, e.g. Exod. 2.43–49, is that the privileges of the house are only for the committed, not for those who have a foot in another establishment (as in vs. 10,12). So the slave has the advantage in this respect over the free man. The inclusion of the priest's household at his table is no relaxing of the law, as vs. 14–16 re-emphasize; notice the responsibility of the priests to see that holy things are not cheapened and thereby made a source of guilt (14–16).

Unblemished victims (17–25). Priest and sacrifice alike were to be perfect specimens: see **21.**16–23; cf. Heb. **9.**14, where 'Christ . . . offered Himself without blemish to God'. The obvious importance that a sacrifice 'be accepted . . .' (19) is not forgotten by Paul in Rom. **12.**1 f., speaking of the Christian's acceptable self-offering; contrast the grudging sacrifices of Mal. **1.**8 ff. As regards the degree of imperfection tolerable in a freewill offering (23), A. Bonar points out that such a gift reflects the offerer's sense of gratitude, inadequate as it is, rather than God's atoning provision, and he contrasts the narrowness of the former with the breadth of the latter (*A Commentary on Leviticus*, p. 390). In v. 24, translate the last clause 'You are not to do that in your country' (Jerusalem Bible; cf. RV)—i.e. not use these methods, nor (25) offer such animals bought from foreigners. Holiness, with its rejection of a 'maimed or worthless sacrifice', went hand in hand here with mercy (cf. the law against human castration, Deut. **23.**1).

Calves and lambs (26–30). Here again, ritual and humane considerations seem to unite in motivating these regulations. With the provision of v. 28, cf. Exod. **23.**19b, which may be a counterblast to fertility magic; but cf., too, such simple restraints on human callousness as those of Deut. **22.**1–4, 6–8, etc.

The unifying theme: holiness (31–33). The petition 'hallowed be Thy name' would express the aim of each part of this law. For the Christian this prayer has implications that are no less multiform, and no less searching.

Leviticus 23   The Sacred Calendar

This chapter has its complement in Num. **28,29,** which prescribes the sacrifices for these (and other) occasions. To the Christian it is remarkable for God's seal on its main outline, in the Gospel events. 'Christ our Passover' (1 Cor. **5.**7) was sacrificed during the feast of that name, against all human attempts to avoid that period (Matt. **26.**5). 'Christ the first fruits' (1 Cor. **15**:20,23) was raised

129

'on the morrow after the sabbath', the day of presenting the firs
fruits (Lev. 23.10)—for the sabbath in question was that of th
passover, from which the feast of Pentecost, meaning the fiftietl
day, was reckoned (15 f. cf. Acts 2.1). Pentecost itself (15–21), a
which the first harvest of the gospel age (John 12.24; Acts 2.41
coincided with the O.T. wheat festival, was again a time of God';
choosing, not man's. Finally, the N.T. uses the symbol of th
vintage, the final ingathering (39–43, cf. Exod. 34.22), for the comin
judgement of the world (Rev. 14.18, cf. Rev. 19.15). But in both
Testaments this event is dominated by the theme of liberation (40,43
Rev. 15.3 f.).

Significantly, the Day of Atonement (26–32, cf. ch. 16) has lef
no comparable mark on the N.T. except in the comparisons drawr
between its limitations and the perfection of the work of Christ
See the points of contrast in Heb. 9,10.

Notes: V. 3: 'a holy convocation': this is one of the few, bu
sufficient, specific indications in the O.T. that the sabbath was
prescribed for public worship as well as rest. V. 5 (margin): 'between
the two evenings': i.e. probably, between sunset and nightfall.
V. 22: neighbourly love breaks in, amongst the technicalities, cf.
19.9 f. V. 32: 'from evening to evening': this reckoning probably
does not spring from Gen. 1.5 (which states that evening drew on,
not that it began the day) but from the concern to prepare for the
morrow.

Leviticus 24   Unbroken Homage

The sanctuary light (1–4). The force of the word 'continually' is
limited by the phrase 'from evening to morning' (3). I.e., the lamp
was to burn by night without fail, but apparently not through the
day. Cf. Exod. 30.7 f.; 1 Sam. 3.3.

The imagery of the lampstand reappears in Zech. 4.2 ff. and in
Rev. 1.12,20; 2.5; in both of which places it portrays the Church,
though there is little hint of this here. Situated outside the veil but
within the tent, accessible to the priests alone, it served the ends of
worship (cf. Psa. 134.1) rather than witness, along with the altar
of incense (cf. Psa. 141.2; Rev. 5.8) and the table of showbread
which stood with it. The N.T. balances this by calling the Church
to bring its light out of seclusion (Matt. 5.14–16; Phil. 2.15).

The showbread (5–9). This 'bread of (God's) presence' was placed
on a table that was plated with gold and laid with golden dishes,
spoons, flagons and bowls (Exod. 25.23–30), a display fit to suggest
a banquet in His honour. But the plain food prescribed as the offering
spoke of His concern not for the exotic and elaborate, but simply

r a complete Israel (cf. the twelve loaves) presented to Him in
rder (6), purity and perpetuity.

A blasphemer and the law of retribution (10–23). The ugly incident
f vs. 10 ff. jarring against the theme of 'holy' and 'most holy' (9)
akes a pointed comment on the human material available. Moses'
fusal, however, to be hurried into a decision (12) is instructive in
self; it also emphasizes the divine authority of the ensuing death
ntence. The law of retribution (17–22), reaffirmed from Exod.
.23 ff., upheld the principle of an equivalent as against an arbitrary
nalty. It is important to realize, first, that the law itself used the
rinciple flexibly (see Exod. **21.26** f.), and secondly that the N.T.
ndemns its use, not in the context of public law (cf. Rom. **13.3** f.),
ut in that of personal relations (Rom. **12.19**; Matt. **5.38** ff.).

As a postscript, the deaths of Jesus and Stephen for blasphemy
ow what happens when a just law falls into the hands of the
ejudiced—those whose religion finds expression in the words
hey stopped their ears and rushed together . . .' (Acts **7.57**).

eviticus 25 Sabbatical Year and Jubilee

he Jerusalem Bible divides the chapter (preferably to RSV) after
22, analysing the second portion as 'Consequences of the holiness
f land and people', with the subtitles 'a. The land: redemption of
nded property' (23–34), and 'b. The people: loans and enfranchise-
ent' (35–55).

Verses 1–22. However sound the principle of a fallow year, it
ould invite disaster to observe it everywhere simultaneously (as
e chapter seems to require), but for the divine promise of vs. 20–22
f. **26.10**). The jubilee, with two fallow years in succession (11),
tensified the test of faith to an extreme; for the whole ordinance
eant taking one's hands off the most basic things of life, to concede
at they were primarily God's. This was too much for pre-exilic
rael, whose land had to wait for the captivity to enjoy its sabbaths
6.34 f.; 2 Chron. **36.21**).

Verses 23–55. The basis of the law that made property inalienable
as not the rights of man but the crown rights of God ('the land is
line', 23), which were incidentally a man's best protection. It was
o accident that Naboth lost his vineyard to a king who had lost
is faith (1 Kings **21**; cf. Isa. **5.8,12**). As well as limiting what money
ould buy, the emphasis on God's primacy raised the question of
ow money should be made and spent (35–38), and whose servants,
timately, were the men you seemed to own ('For they are My
rvants' 42,55). (On the economics of v. 37, see on Deut. **23.19** f.).
here the law discriminates between Israelite and foreign slaves

131

(45 f.), it does so by stressing the special generosity due to a 'brother (35,36,39, etc.), not by disparaging the stranger or refusing him leg; status (see Lev. **24.22**). If the N.T. goes far beyond this (Gal. **3.28** the O.T. has already made a notable beginning.

On the relation of this law of slavery to that of Exod. **21.2 f** and Deut. **15.12 ff.**, evidently there was a distinction between thos whose slavery was enforced for theft or debt and those who too refuge in it for security (39; cf. A. H. Finn, *The Unity of the Pente teuch*, pp. 169 f.), contracting for a potentially longer term of service but a better status (39 f.) and an option of redemption at any tim (48 f.).

Leviticus 26   A Concluding Charge to Israe

This appeal was to be echoed, forty years later, in the parting word of Moses, where its substance is re-shaped into the blessings an cursings that clinch a covenant.

The basic loyalty (1,2). The decalogue opens with the same emphasi as this, in its four Godward commandments, which Israel's subse quent history shows to have been the crucial issue for her (see e.g. Hos. **4** for the social effects of her wavering allegiance).

The blessings of obedience (3–13). The good things of this para graph are only marginally the ordinary fruits of sound living. Goin far beyond natural achievement, it is God's ordering, protecting conquering, fertilizing, and liberating presence that is the specia promise of these verses. Note the assurance that is the essence o salvation, in vs. 12 f. (cf. Rev. **21.3**); note, too, the striking close '. . . and made you walk erect'; cf. Psa. **40.2**.

The pains of disobedience (14–46). There is a controlled crescend of divine wrath revealed here. The repeated 'sevenfold' (18,21,24,28 the lengthening paragraphs, the deepening disasters (whose clima lies beyond even the cannibalism of v. 29, in the utter demoralizatio of vs. 36–39) are held nevertheless within the strong framework o God's forbearance, seen in the search for signs of repentance (14a 21a,23,27), in the limited duration, implied in the phrase 'as long as (34 f.), and in the assurance that the ancient covenant will surviv (44 f.). The humbling contrast between man and God shows clearl in the parallel phrases: 'they spurned My ordinances . . . Yet . . . will not spurn them' (43 f.).

Note: The expression 'enjoy its sabbaths' (34,43) should perhap be rendered 'fulfil . . .' etc., since the verb is that of v. 43b, 'mak amends', where it expresses the idea of satisfying a creditor. A similar vocabulary is used in Isa. **40.2**. On these 'sabbaths', see o **25.1** ff.

The assessment of vows (1–25). The money values in this chapter were laid down to enable a gift in kind to be replaced by one in cash with some degree of realism.

(i) *People* (1–8). An example of such a vow is Hannah's offering of Samuel, although hers was irrevocable (1 Sam. 1.11). The sliding scale was concerned with approximate economic, not spiritual, values; it reflected something of the actualities as one presented to God possibly the 'fag-end' or possibly the full strength of a life; so guarded against hypocrisy, while leaving room for hard cases (8). The truth that all are fundamentally equal before God is expressed elsewhere, in the law that assessed each person's 'ransom' at a mere half-shekel, regardless of wealth (Exod. 30.11–16).

(ii) *Animals* (9–13), (iii) *Houses* (14 f.), (iv) *Land* (16–25). Here again the concern is partly to combat hypocrisy (10a), vacillation (10b) and wrangling (12), but partly, too, to clarify the relation of vows to the laws on landholding and the jubilee (16–25).

Special cases (26–33). With the notion that one can put God in one's debt with what is already His (26,30), compare Luke 17.10; 1 Cor. 4.7. The meaning of 'devoted' (28 f.) is quite distinct from 'dedicated' or 'vowed', being a special word for the things and people due for extermination (cf. Jericho) by a divine decree. It was this command that Achan and King Saul tried to circumvent.

The tithe (30–33) was no innovation: Jacob had vowed it to God at Bethel (Gen. 28.22), and Abram had tithed his battle spoils to Melchizedek as priest (Gen. 14.19 f.). The N.T., finally, adds its own reminders (to those that are implicit in this chapter) that a legalistic spirit can misuse the best of laws. See our Lord's comments on cash assessments in Matt. 23.16–22, on tithing in Matt. 23.23, and on twisted vows in Matt. 15.4–9.

Questions for further study and discussion on Leviticus chs. 21—27

1. From the contexts in which 'holy' is used in these chapters (and in chs. 17 ff.) what are the chief implications of this word?
2. God's acts of creation and redemption underlie the round of festivals in ch. 23. Has this anything to teach the Christian about patterns of worship, or has the N.T. left such a scheme entirely behind?
3. What lessons about material wealth can we learn from ch. 25?
4. What insight does ch. 26 give us into the ways of God and man?

Numbers

Numbers 1 The Census

The events of the opening chapters are dated a month after the erection of the tabernacle (Exod. 40.17), and a fortnight after the first wilderness passover, recorded in Num. 9. The census is a military one (3,20,22, etc.), setting the tone of this book, in which Israel, seen in the Book of Exodus mainly as a liberated people, and in Leviticus as a consecrated people, is faced now with fighting its way into its inheritance—a task it will initially refuse.

The military emphasis may have left its mark on the method of numbering the tribes, where it has been variously conjectured that the word for thousands may have originally meant in this context 'clans' (as in Judg. 6.15), 'officers' (cf. Zech. 9.7, AV[KJV], RV), 'trained men' (from a verb to learn), or 'military units' (cf. Num. 31.14, where 'hundreds' might stand for similar but smaller units). Possibly such military companies were numbered by their nominal value rather than their current strength. The subject is discussed by J. W. Wenham, 'Large Numbers in the Old Testament', *Tyndale Bulletin* 18 (1967), pp. 19–53.

Verses 47–54. The Levites, exempt from soldiering, had an indispensable role as mediators (53). Negatively, compare vs. 51,53 with the sharp lessons of 1 Sam. 6.19 f.; 1 Chron. 13.9 f.; 15.2 ff.; positively, compare this living wall between tent and people (53) with the shield of intercession when Moses 'stood in the breach . . . to turn away (God's) wrath' (Psa. 106.23), or when he was stationed to intercede above the battle in Exod. 17.8–13. On such apparent inessentials 'hung the issue of the day', then as now.

Numbers 2 Israel in Array

Two things plainly emerge from this chapter: the value set on good order, and the centrality given to God. As to the first, clearly there was, and is, much to be gained in efficiency by eliminating uncertainty and the friction of jockeying for position; yet the smooth running could still conceal deep jealousies (cf., e.g. Judg. 12.1–6; 2 Sam. 19.43). Note that our Lord refrained from fixing a similar 'seating order' among His twelve, preferring to educate them by exposing their rivalries and expounding the ultimate realities of rank (e.g. Mark 9.33 ff.; 10.35 ff.).

God's centrality was symbolized not only in camp, where the tent of meeting, surrounded by the tribe of Levi, was the focus of the inward-facing square formed by the twelve other tribes (2), but als‹ on the march, where the holy things and their bearers were assigne‹ to the mid-point of the line (17). An incidental effect of such ‹ pattern of march was to distribute responsibility, since the honour o forming the vanguard or rearguard was matched by that of constitut ing the central bodyguard to the tabernacle and its treasures.

God 'in the midst' (cf. v. 17) is a recurrent topic in Scripture seen from afar in the ideal pattern of Israel in Ezekiel's visio‹ (Ezek. **43.7**; **48.35**); encamped among us, unrecognized, in th Incarnation (John **1.**14); present in the assembled church (Matt **18.**20); and visible in full glory in the new creation (Rev. **21.**3 **22.**3), where the pattern of the desert camp of Israel reappears transfigured, in that of the twelve-gated city of God (Rev. **21.**12–14) See also on **5.**1–4.

* Numbers 3   The Tribe of Lev

(i) *The priests* (1–4). The death of Nadab and Abihu for sacrileg‹ is recounted in Lev. **10,** where Eleazar and Ithamar are shown takin; over their duties at once (Lev. **10.**12 ff., 16 ff.), so vital was the rol‹ of mediator. Of the two families, Ithamar's had gained the primac‹ by Eli's day, but abused its trust and was subordinated again to th elder branch (cf. 1 Sam. **2.**30 ff.; 1 Kings **2.**26 f.).

(ii) *The Levites, in relation to the priests* (5–10) *and to Israe‹* (11–13). The two words, 'given' (9) and 'Mine' (12), express th‹ exacting vocation of the Levites, at once lowly and lofty—a fai‹ sample of all divine service. Chapter **8** will describe their initiatior into their new office

(iii) *The numbering and division of the Levites* (14–39). In the nex chapter fuller details are given of the duties of the three branches o the tribe. Here we may note that children, from a month upwar‹ (15, etc.), were numbered among the consecrated (cf. vs. 40 ff.) although they would not do actual service before thirty (**4.**3,23, etc. or, for some duties, twenty-five (**8.**24).

[N.B. (*i*) The fact that the Amramites were already a clan (27 suggests that Amram was a distant rather than an immediate pro‹ genitor of Moses (Exod. **6.**18,20). This agrees with other chrono logical data and with genealogical conventions.

(*ii*) In v. 28 the Septuagint's 8,300 corrects a scribal slip whereb‹ a 3 had evidently become a 6 by the omission of one letter (cf. th‹ total, v. 39)].

Note the precision of the camping stations, with the four sides o the tabernacle each flanked by its particular group (23,29,35,38), s‹

that priests and Levites made a camp within a camp, interposed between their brethren and divine judgement (cf. **1.53**).

(iv) *The Levites as substitutes for the firstborn* (40–51). The emphasis throughout this passage, on God's unconditional claim on the lives concerned, should counteract the notion that man gratuitously confers upon God his vote or his service. With the claiming of the firstborn, compare that of the Christian's whole family: 'Otherwise, your children would be unclean, but as it is they are holy' (1 Cor. 7.14).

On the assessment of the firstborn's redemption, i.e. the price of release from service, cf. the note on Lev. **27.1–8**. Here, their involuntary obligation is assessed at a 'flat rate' corresponding to the lowest of the charges in the former passage, where a contract had been freely entered into.

* Numbers 4 — The Tribe of Levi (continued)

(v) *The duties of the clans* (1–33). These tasks have already been broadly indicated in **3.25,29–31,36** f. The details that are now filled in help to emphasize the unapproachable holiness of the sanctuary. If the tribe of Levi had to insulate Israel from exposure to the tabernacle (**1.53**), the priests must shield the Levites themselves against contact with what it contained. After the instructions for covering the holy vessels (5–15), v. 20 clinches the object-lesson with perhaps the strongest warning in the whole law on the lethal impact of holiness on the intruder. This (with v. 15b) is the context of the judgement on the men of Bethshemesh and on Uzzah (1 Sam. **6.19**; 1 Chron. **13.10**), when these warnings were found to be more than words. David's reaction to the second incident, passing from anger and fear to obedience and joy (1 Chron. **13.11** f.; **15.2–15, 25–29**), shows how unpalatable but how potentially fruitful is God's rebuke to man's casualness.

(vi) *The census of serving Levites* (34–49). The qualifying age of thirty refers to the duty of carrying the tabernacle and its vessels. Liturgical duties began at twenty-five (**8.24**). At a later stage, when there was no longer a portable tabernacle, David redesigned and enlarged the pattern of Levitical service, and brought forward the starting age to twenty (1 Chron. **23.24–27**).

2. MISCELLANEOUS DIRECTIVES: Numbers 5,6

Numbers 5 — 'None of us lives to himself'

Expulsion of the unclean (1–4). Fuller instructions on uncleanness are given elsewhere (Lev. **13.45** f.; **15.2** ff.; Num. **19.11** ff.): here they are put into effect, and their basis explained in v. 3b (which is the basis of all holy living).

Restitution, and priestly dues (5–10). The expression 'breaking faith' (6) is the same as that used of marital infidelity in vs. 12,27 since our Godward relationship has much in common with marriage. It is striking that a wrong done to a fellow man is viewed first and foremost as done against God (see on Lev. **6.**1–7).

The accused wife (11–31). This is the nearest approach in Scripture to a trial by ordeal, a favourite procedure in ancient times. But it differs crucially from most of these trials, first, by looking not to the potion itself but primarily to the Lord (21) for the verdict, and secondly, by requiring a demonstration of guilt rather than of innocence. (Generally in such trials the accused was tested with something deadly, but here with nothing physically potent enough to cause the drastic damage of v. 22.)

The test was by exposure to holiness: holy water, holy ground (17) and, placed in the woman's own hands, an 'offering of remembrance' (15b), i.e. an offering that lodged an appeal to God for action against sin.

The ritual, like all Biblical rites, would take effect not automatically as if by magic, but as the instrument of God's will in accordance with truth. The curse would not operate unjustly (Prov. **26.**2), but it could not be side-stepped, with its writing made an ingredient of the potion (note incidentally this early use, apparently, of parchment and ink, 23) and its terms accepted with the double Amen (22).

But vindicated or not, the accused wife could only be deeply humiliated (see, e.g. v. 18) and the marital relationship violently strained by such a procedure (to which, characteristically, tradition was to add further degradations). Whether a husband resorted to it or not depended on the man he was (cf. Matt. **1.**19). But the existence of such a law could leave no doubt of the extreme gravity of adultery in the eyes of God. As a postscript, in case the male should suppose himself entitled to more lenient divine judgement, see Hos. **4.**14 (RSV).

Numbers 6 The Nazirite Vow

The ruling idea of the term 'Nazirite' comes out in the kindred words translated 'separate', 'separation', 'consecrated' (18) and 'consecration' (19) in this chapter, all from the root *n-z-r*. The Nazirite was set apart from some aspects of normal life, to be more conspicuously available for God. The negative and positive sides are shown in the three abstentions and in the clinching verse, v. 8.

The vine (3 f.) was one of the minor luxuries of settled life, in contrast to the simple fare of the nomad (cf. Jer. **35**.6 f,). The unshorn hair (5) may have had the symbolism found in Exod. **20**.25; Deut. **15**.19, where things set apart for God must be given Him intact. Ceremonial cleanness (6 f.) was the precondition for worship, and the Nazirite must be as constantly ready as the high priest himself (cf. v. 7 with Lev. **21**.1–3,11). The vow could be lifelong (cf. Samson, Samuel, John the Baptist) or temporary (cf. Paul in Acts **18**.18, and the four men of Acts **21**.23–28; the latter seem to have been carrying out the conditions of vs. 9 ff.).

All of this bore special witness to the pilgrim spirit and the self-dedication and purity of life which were fundamentally the calling of every Israelite. It is worth noting that while this vow was to be treated most seriously (cf. Samson's tragedy; see also Amos **2**.11 ff.), it was a particular expression of holiness that was not required of everyone, nor a matter of extra merit, as Matt. **11**.18 f. proves.

The priestly blessing (22–27). The explanatory v. 27 is important, and is further illuminated by, e.g. Exod. **20**.24b, where God promises to meet His people with blessing wherever He records His name. The inclusive term, 'bless' (23), is expounded by its companion words, ranging from protection (24) to the concord which is the positive content of 'peace' (26). But the dominant note is personal, with the varied expressions in vs. 25,26a for enjoying not only God's benefits but His smile.

Questions for further study and discussion on Numbers chs. 1—6

1. Look up the references to God 'in the midst', in the final comment on ch. **2**, and find further examples and developments of this theme.
2. 'They shall not . . . look upon the holy things even for a moment, lest they die' (**4**.20). If this was the fate of an intruder (see notes), study the similarities and differences in the reception given to a genuine seeker (e.g. Gen. **32**.24 ff.; Exod. **33**.18 ff.; Isa. **6**; 2 Cor. **3**.18; etc.).
3. 'The spirit of jealousy' (**5**.14). This is the same word as 'zeal', and can be used in a good or a bad sense. Study this word in Scripture, and pinpoint the good qualities of which the bad ones are a corruption.
4. Discuss the bearing, if any, of the Nazirite's special vocation (see second paragraph of Notes on ch **6**) on the varied patterns of Christian living. How relevant is 1 Cor. **7** (e.g. vs. 7 ff., 17 ff.) to this?

3. THE TABERNACLE SERVICE INAUGURATED: Numbers 7.1—10.10

Numbers 7 The Best for God

The gift of wagons (1–9). This presentation, to greet the erection of the tabernacle, was clearly a voluntary gesture, taking Moses by surprise (4 f.). It is worth observing both the passive and the active role of Moses in receiving divine guidance about it, in that he waited for God's will to be made plain (4–6)—since not every human offer is serviceable for His work; and that he took care to think out the apportionment of the gifts so as to comply with his existing instructions (7,8, especially 9; cf. ch.4)—thereby avoiding the well-meaning blunders of David and others as in 2 Sam. **6**.3 ff.

The offerings for the altar (10–88). The twelve identical offerings, furnishing the altar with the main requirements for worship, gave every tribe an equal share in what would be done and offered there; and the twelve days (11) led up towards the climax on the fourteenth: the first Passover since Egypt (cf. Exod. **40**.17; Num. **7**.10; **9**.1–3).

The voice from the Mercy Seat (89). While God had many ways of speaking (e.g. **12**.6 ff.), certainly plain, audible utterance was one of them (cf. the boy Samuel's experience: 1 Sam. **3**.4 ff.). As to the place from which the voice was heard, the description makes it clear that God was not contained or embodied in the ark or cherubim, but enthroned on and attended by them (cf. Pss. **80**.1; **99**.1, etc.); and the terms of the verse are reminders of the conditions of a divine-human meeting: namely, atonement (the basic meaning of 'mercy seat') and covenant (the significance of the 'testimony' in this phrase; cf. **10**.33, etc.), whereby the militant holiness signified by the cherubim (cf. Gen. **3**.24; Ezek. **10**.2) is turned to man's salvation instead of his destruction (Psa. **18**.6–19).

Numbers 8 The Living Flame

The seven lamps lit (1–4). On the symbolism of the lampstand in Scripture, see on Lev. **24**.1–4. Some idea of 'the pattern' of it (4) can be gathered from the bas-relief on the Arch of Titus in Rome, where the Temple's lampstand is shown among the spoils captured from Jerusalem in A.D. 70. By then, as Heb. **8**.5; **9**.2,23 f. explain, the earthly sanctuary and its furniture had been superseded by the realities they portrayed.

The living sacrifice (5–26). This occasion may have been in Paul's mind in the writing of Rom. **12**.1, where, as here, the prelude to the living sacrifice is seen to be atonement and the discarding of the old life (cf. v. 7 with e.g. Rom. **6**.3 f.). On the expression 'wave offering' (11), see on Lev. 7.28–36; the Levites may have been led to the altar and back to their place. The act of laying hands on them (10) has an important bearing on the theology of sacrifice, since v. 16 (with its phrase, 'instead of') makes it clear that the Levites were offered as substitutes for their fellows. The gesture that signified this was repeated immediately afterwards, when the Levites, for their part, laid their hands on the animals that were to be their sin offering and burnt offering (12).

Another matter clarified here is the term 'consecrated' (17), and its companion words 'sanctified', 'holy', etc., which represent the same Hebrew root. It is used here to sum up a group of non-technical terms which display its different facets: e.g. 'separate(d)', 'Mine' (14), 'wholly given' (16; lit., 'given, given'), 'taken' (18). It emerges from the same context that God is generous with what He takes. 'I have taken' (18) is closely followed by 'I have given' (19). The Levites were withdrawn from one sphere to serve in another (where a greater variety of work awaited them than appears from this passage by itself: cf. 1 Chron. **23—26**; 2 Chron. **17.8** f.; **19.**8). Even after retirement they were to reckon that they could still be of use (25 f.). And the Church continues to profit from the many psalms which are the legacy of Asaphites and Korahites (e.g. Pss. **73–85**), sons of Levi.

Numbers 9.1—10.10   Worshippers, Pilgrims, Warriors

The second Passover (9.1–14). The difference in kind between the first and all subsequent Passovers would be especially vivid on this occasion, when memories of the night of judgement and liberation were fresh. *Then*, salvation had been in the making, now it was a fact to build on, and the feast was kept not to ensure it but to celebrate it: cf. Exod. **13.**8.

The supplementary law recorded in vs. 6–14 was invoked in Hezekiah's day, and was stretched still further at the king's intercession (2 Chron. **30.**2 ff., 18–20)—an incident which confirms the impression given here of a régime that was merciful and adaptable, for all its intolerance of the arrogant and the careless. The incident is one of several that show the development of the law, as new matters came up for decision; but Moses' humility (8; cf. note on 7.1–9) ensured that this case-law was as divinely authorized as the basic statutes.

The cloud and fire (9.15–23). This token of God's presence came to be known as the Shekinah, from a verb 'to dwell'. It had been visible at the first stage of the Exodus (Exod. **13.**21; **14.**19), and its presence now above the tabernacle showed that God accepted this as

'My house' rather than 'your house' (cf. Matt. **21**.13; **23**.38). In the cloud's removing or resting (17 ff.), Christians may still see an expressive metaphor for the guidance they can expect, in the quiet indications of God's will for their movements.

The silver trumpets (**10**.1–10). These, or their successors, are portrayed on the Arch of Titus, with the table of showbread and the lampstand (see on **8**.1–4), and were distinct from the rams' horn (*shophar* or *yobel*) sounded at, e.g. the battle of Jericho or the year of jubilee. Their military function (like that of bugles), to call the camp to specific action, seems to have determined their symbolic use as a call to God to rally to His people (9b). The same thought, but without the overtones of danger, is implied in the trumpet call at sacrifices and festivals, as if to say 'Lord, come to us!' (10). The 'trumpets and . . . horn' of Psa. **98**.6 are of more than musical significance: they voice the nations' jubilant prayer.

So this paragraph appropriately rounds off the inauguration of the tabernacle, and looks ahead to action, as Israel prepares to march, to fight and to feast.

4. THE MARCH RESUMED AND HALTED; Numbers 10.11—14.45

Numbers 10.11–36   As an Army with Banners

The order of march (11–28). Israel had been encamped at Sinai for nearly a year (11; cf. Exod. **19**.1), attending to the priorities: law, covenant, worship, community. Without these, Canaan would be a second Egypt. But the march, too, was a preparation, a training in orderly co-operation, as here, in readiness for the campaign, and an exercise in walking by faith. It was a demanding mixture of routine and unpredictability, such as God may still prescribe for the pilgrim.

The means of guidance (29–36). The general guiding of Israel by the cloud was no substitute for local knowledge. Moses, for all his years in Midian, was not desert-bred, and, to his credit, knew his limitations and the value of an expert's eye for detail (31). In time to come, his welcome for a genuine ally would not go unrewarded: cf. Judg. **5**.24 ff.

The stirring invocation at the beginning and end of journeys (35 f.) pictures the Lord as ranging ahead of His people, clearing a path for them. Note that the second prayer does not visualize Him as confined to the vicinity of the ark, for this merely halts and the people gather round it; whereas the Lord returns from the fray, to station Himself again in the midst. Psa. **68**, which opens with the prayer of our v. 35, magnificently develops the theme of the march of God, not only through the deserts but through the skies (Psa. 68.4,33), and of His enthronement at the sanctuary, which becomes the centre of not only Israel but the world.

Numbers 11   Discontent, and Coals of Fire

To take part in the greatest expedition in history and to be obsessed with the diet, was to be ludicrously small-minded. Apart from Moses and a few others, these men revealed themselves to be no pilgrims, but only refugees like their camp followers (4; cf. Exod. **12.**38). Even the least visionary of them might have foreseen a certain scarcity of fish (5)! But the N.T. advises us to view these chapters less as a casebook than as, potentially, a mirror (1 Cor. **10.**6), and it has its own tale of similar incongruities to add (e.g. Mark **9.**31–34; 1 Cor. **11.**20 f.), which present-day Christians, if they searched their hearts, could supplement. As to the manna (7–9; cf. Exod. **16.**14 ff.), human perversity disdained a food which was nevertheless pleasant, versatile (8) and a gift from God (Exod. **16.**15)—just as it would disdain, eventually, the Bread of Life (John **6.**35 ff.).

Verses 10 ff. reveal something of the strain of Moses' isolation, which had brought him to the verge of breakdown. To the over-wrought, God is understanding and constructive: there is no rebuke for Moses' tirade, or even for the scepticism of vs. 21 f.; only the practical answer of the double intervention (16 f., 18–20). The sending of the quails is a classic example of judgement by a surfeit of the thing one has craved. The enduing of the seventy elders with the Spirit raises the interesting question of their relation to the leaders chosen in Exod. **18.**24 ff. and to the seventy elders of Exod. **24.**9–11. If the three groups are identical (cf. the wording of v.16) it may imply that the attempt to share responsibility had broken down through spiritual disunity, of which Eldad and Medad's absenting themselves was a sample. The true remedy was to partake of the same Spirit (the Lord's, 29b), whose bestowal on this special occasion was marked by a temporary sign (25c,d) possibly like that of Pentecost. Moses' reply to the zealous Joshua (28 f.) is a model for every leader, and has good reason to be called Christlike: cf. Luke **9.**49 f.

Numbers 12   Disunity at the Top

With the deviousness of malice, Miriam and Aaron dressed up their rancour as religious principle. To have objected openly to the newcomer would have been an admission of simple jealousy, so the single point of contact between the actual (1) and the pretended issue (2), namely the person of Moses, was made their target. The fact that Miriam is named before Aaron and was the only one to be punished, suggests that it was she who resented the new 'first lady' (1) and was the instigator of the attack, manipulating the pliant Aaron, who had once before shown himself susceptible to the suggestion that his talents were wasted (Exod. 32.1).

The 'meekness' of Moses (3) was not a matter of temperament (cf. Exod. 2.11 f.) but of subordinating his personal interests to those of God and His cause, leaving his vindication in God's hands, like the true Servant in Isa. 50.5–7. A less misleading adjective would be 'humble'. In passing, the bearing of this verse (3) on the authorship of the book is no different from that of the 'he' which is used everywhere of Moses in these narratives except where he is spoken to or speaking (e.g. 11.11 ff. and most of Deut.). I.e., the books of Moses were compiled from his own written records (cf. Deut. 31.24), but in the form of biography, not autobiography.

In vindicating Moses, God dealt first with the slander, which had been that convenient alloy, a half-truth (Moses was unique in responsibility and intimacy [7 f.], not in prophetic function), and after that, with the slanderers (9 ff.). It is instructive that the high praise of v. 7 is used in Heb. 3.2–6 to show how far he himself is surpassed by Christ. It is the difference between steward and son: cf. Gen. 15.2–5.

On Miriam's 'leprosy', and the phrase 'white as snow', see on Lev. 13. Moses' intercession for her (13) was wholly in character: cf. 11.2; 14.13 ff.; etc. In this respect, too, he showed the mark of the great Servant (Isa. 53.12c), which is also the badge of His household (Matt. 5.44; 1 Pet. 3.9).

Numbers 13   The Reconnaissance

The fact that God was the commander of the enterprise might have seemed to make this survey superfluous. But the searching questions of vs. 17–20 make it clear that He does not excuse His servants the normal burdens of fact-finding, value-judgement and responsible decision. His army must not be one of conscripts or passengers, but of volunteers who have espoused His cause and counted the cost; it is the only way for omnipotence to work alongside finite men without swamping them. (Those who 'play at God' sometimes forget how He does it Himself.)

Accordingly we find every tribe represented (1–16), the whole length of the land inspected, and the rough taken faithfully with the smooth: the gigantic grape-cluster (23) matched the news of less inviting giants. There can be no subsequent complaint of a blind choice.

The sequel illustrates the diametrically opposite assessments ('well able', 'not able', vs. 30 f.) which can be made of exactly the same data; for the visible facts were not yet in dispute, only the invisible— and these not explicitly, at this stage. Caleb (soon to be joined openly by Joshua: **14.**6 ff.) exemplifies the realism of the spiritually minded, in viewing the picture in its frame, the will of God; the rest show the limited realism of the carnally minded by forgetting to give this so much as a thought. These two approaches not only divide the converted from the unconverted: they are present as alternatives with every situation that meets the Christian.

Notes: V. 22: the wording of the references to Hebron in Genesis suggests that in Abraham's day it had not yet received its present name. V. 32: 'So they brought ... ', rather, 'And they brought ...'. I.e., they are now changing their tune from v. 27, regardless of inconsistency. To say that the land devoured (i.e. could not support) its inhabitants was incompatible with both the welcome evidence of the fruit and the unwelcome evidence of the giants. V. 33: the Nephilim occur only here and in Gen. **6.**4 (AV, 'giants').

Numbers 14 The Great Refusal

The force of the time-note 'that night' (1)—since the spies had returned in daytime (cf. **13.**26c)—is that the night was deliberately given up to lamentation, with the inevitable result seen in the morbid fantasies of vs 2 f. (Paul and Silas knew better than to court this danger, Acts **16.**25.) Moses now had to listen to hysterical death-talk (2) such as he himself had indulged in (**11.**15); but theirs, unlike his, was defiant: note the ugly mood of v. 10.

The stability of the true servant, proof against fear or favour, is finely displayed here. In face of fear, all four who are named in vs. 5 f. (including Aaron, loyal again after his repentance in **12.**11) lean hard into the will of God. The prostration in v. 5 is to the Lord, in full view of ('before') the crowd, and the speech of Joshua and Caleb pivots on His purpose and calling (8). Tested next by the favour held out in v. 12b, Moses can rise above it through his overriding concern for his Master's good name (13 ff.), not his own. Here it is interesting to see the lasting impression evidently made on him, months before, at the 'cleft of the rock' (Exod. **33.**22), when he had learnt that God's glory resides in His goodness (Exod. **33.**18 f.; **34.**6 f.), for his prayer now regards the 'power' of the Lord as made 'great' (17) supremely in the exercise of His longsuffering (18 f.).

With God's startling proposition (12; see on Deut. **9**.14) compare John **6**.6: 'This He said to test him.' The test crystallized, and thereby strengthened, Moses' sturdy devotion; indeed the insight he displayed was itself God-given, as shown above.

Since God's mercy, however, is not laxity, as Moses had acknowledged (18b), the forgiveness of Israel (20) excluded the persistently impenitent (22; note 'ten times'). On this, we may observe that (*i*) their judgement granted them the fate they asked for; (*ii*) their children suffered, for a while, on their account (33, but 31); (*iii*) God's vision, unlike theirs, ranged far outside the immediate time and place: see the great prospect of v. 21.

The final episode, vs. 39 ff., strikes a note which is heard in many sayings in the Gospels: that second thoughts can come too late, and the opportunity be over. For the name Hormah (45) see on **21**.1–3.

Questions for further study and discussion on Numbers chs. 7—14

1. In the note on **11**.28 f. a comparison is drawn between Moses' reply to Joshua and Christ's reply to John. Besides the points noted in the N.T. specifically (e.g. 1 Cor. **10**.2; Heb. **3**.2), are there any illuminating comparisons and contrasts to be drawn between Moses and Christ? (E.g. Num. **11**.10–15 with Luke **9**.41 ?)
2. Note all that Moses said in reply to the criticism of him in ch. **12**. In 2 Cor. **12** and **13**, compare Paul under attack. Is there a common motive behind their divergent methods?
3. What lessons does the N.T. draw from Israel's great refusal in the wilderness? See especially Acts **7**; 1 Cor. **10**; Heb. **3** f.

5. FURTHER LAWS AND LAWLESSNESS: Numbers 15—19

Numbers 15   Ritual Additions and Clarifications

Accompaniments to a sacrifice (1–12). It is here that we learn that the animal sacrifices of Lev. **1** and **3** must be accompanied by cereal food and wine, perhaps to make use of the conventions of hospitality to encourage and express a festive, ungrudging approach. In this spirit, Paul regarded his possible martyrdom as the libation that would crown the sacrifice (Phil. **2**.17; 2 Tim. **4**.6).

A foreigner's sacrifice (13–16). The rule that homeborn and alien stood, so to speak, on level ground before the altar, paved the way towards the total equality preached in the gospel (Gal. **3**.28). Note that this stranger is a sojourner, no casual visitor, and must be committed to God's covenant by circumcision (Exod. **12**.48 f., cf. Gal. **3**.27). It is an equal sharing in the grace of God. For other aspects of a foreigner's equality before the law, see, e.g. Lev. **18**.26; **19**.34; Deut. **24**.14,17,20 ff.

The first for God (17–21). This offering was a yearly thanksgiving for a land and crops of one's own (19) after the necessary spoon feeding in the wilderness, cf. Josh. **5**.12. It celebrated a proper coming-of-age, not with arrogance but with thankfulness for the means of self-support, and recognition of their Giver.

Lapses and defiant sins (22–36). The requirement of sacrifice for even unwitting sins (22–29) is a powerful lesson in holiness—as long as it does not reduce sacrifice to the status of a fine or a licence (cf. Amos **4**.4 f.). The severity of vs. 30 f. is the O.T.'s answer to this, and Psa. **51**.16 f. shows how it should be taken: to induce repentance, not despair. The right attitude to the two extremes of sin envisaged in this law is seen in Psa. **19**.12–14.

Verses 32–36, taken alone, might seem an example of an unwitting sin savagely punished, but vs. 30 f. supply the context and the offender's motive. It is this that can turn the most trivial gesture into a fundamental challenge. Note that the matter was not dealt with in hot blood (34).

Tassels (37–41). It was this part of Christ's garment that the woman of Matt. **9**.20 touched, and this that the Pharisees liked to enlarge (Matt. **23**.5). Some writers have held that in view of v. 32, with v. 39b, the blue cord was to bring heaven to mind even as one looked earthward. A Jewish calculation finds in the numerical value of 'tassel' in Hebrew, plus the customary number of knots and threads, a reminder of the 613 precepts of the Law. Dare one suggest, however, that this fashion of the time was adapted to serve a memory-helping purpose no more mysterious than that of a knot in a handkerchief? (cf. v. 39).

Numbers 16   The Rebellion of Korah

This classic revolt (Jude 11) was the most determined challenge of all, with its coalition of sacred and secular leaders (1), its canvassing of prominent names (2b), and its broad front of attack (3, 13 f.). This breadth was in fact a weakness, since the credibility of the claim to universal holiness ('every one of them', 3) was hardly enhanced by the frankly material values of vs. 13 f. Probably there was a genuine difference between the two groups, the one actuated by envy (cf. vs. 9 f.), the other by greed (13 f.); the former group too small-minded to realize that their quarrel was with God (11, for they agreed to the test, 16–19), and the latter group too shortsighted to distinguish their gaol from their goal. It was now Egypt, not Canaan, that flowed for them with milk and honey (13).

With a lesser man than Moses, v. 4 would have read, '. . . h¢
drew himself up'. It is the man of small moral stature (it has beer
said) who must stand on his dignity. Moses, here and elsewhere, i:
sufficiently the servant of God (see on **12.3** and **14.5**) to be maste:
of himself and to submit the whole question to heaven (5). Eve¡
his angry rebuttal in v. 15 is a plea to his judge, not a counterblas
of abuse.

The genuineness of this stance was proved by the intercession o
both Moses and Aaron for their enemies, twice over (22,44–48)
The second of these is a striking action-picture of the strict meanin;
of intercession, i.e. interposing on another's behalf. Cf. especiall
v. 48 and Isa. **53.12**; **59.16**.

Note: Korah's picked men, the 250 who tested their claims witl
incense, were destroyed by fire (35 ff., cf. vs. 6 f.), whereas evidentl
Korah himself (see ch. **26.10**), his accomplices, and all who stoo¢
with them (27), were engulfed (31–33). But the fact that Korah'
sons escaped (cf. **26.11**), to the lasting benefit of Israel (cf. 1 Chron
6.22 ff., esp. v. 28; see also the headings of Pss. **42,84**, etc.), show
that the warning of v. 26 gave an equal opportunity to all.

* Numbers 17 The Sign of Aaron's Ro¢

The demonstration with the rods, which were the leaders' tokens o
office (for this reason the Hebrew for 'tribe' is 'rod'), supplied ;
sign that was not only visible but lasting. A comparison of v. 1⁰
with Heb. **9.4** suggests that initially Aaron's rod (with the jar o
manna mentioned in Exod. **16.32–34**) was placed in front of the ar:
(perhaps outside the veil, where it could be seen), but later deposite:
inside it. By the time of Solomon, however, the only remainin
contents of the ark were the stone tablets of the Decalogue (
Kings **8.9**).

The antecedents and the sequel of this incident are both instructiv¢
Aaron's rod had already authenticated its owner's call, to any u¡
prejudiced enquirer, by its part in the deliverance from Egyp'
see, e.g. Exod. **7.9** ff., 15 ff. This was conveniently forgotten. An
the present sign, for all its kindly implications of supernatur:
promise and fulfilment (8, cf. Jer. **1.11** f.), was the excuse to dive¡
popular resentment from Aaron to the God who had confirme
His choice of him (12 f.). The clearer the sign, and the surer th
appointed mediation, the deeper was the wound to pride. There i
hardly a plainer justification than this for the N.T.'s distrust ¢
signs as solvents of scepticism: cf. Luke **11.29** ff.; **16.30** f.; 1 Co¡
1.22 ff.

148

Numbers 18

Priests' and Levites' Responsibilities and Rewards

Access to holy things (1–7). The meaning of 'bear iniquity' in v. 1 is virtually 'be held responsible'; its implications vary with its contexts (cf., e.g. Exod. **28**.38; Lev. **5**.17; **10**.17; **16**.22). Here the setting emphasizes the perils that surround the realm of holiness: see chs. **16,17**; especially **17**.12 f. The gulf between laymen and Levites, which the rebels denied in **16**.3, and between Levites and priests (**16**.5–11), is now precisely defined, and the divine initiative in this arrangement is reiterated in the words 'gift', 'given', etc. (6 f., cf. **8**.14–19).

Priestly perquisites (8–20). The emoluments were ample, and their quality first-class (12); at the same time there were reminders that God's service has its high demands. Some of the meals were sacramental, eaten ceremonially as though on God's behalf, in token of His acceptance of the sacrifice (9 f.; see on Lev. **10**.12–20); others, while more domestic (11,19), were still hedged about with certain formalities (11c,18). Above all, the ban on landed property (20) was a test of where one's treasure was (see comment on **35**.1–8). The behaviour of the sons of Eli was to show, one day, how contemptuously a covetous priest could regard his dues (1 Sam. **2**.12–17). On the phrase 'a covenant of salt' (19), see on Lev. **2**.13.

The tithe for the Levites (21–24). On the antiquity of the tithe see on Lev. **27**.30–33. But like all matters of obedience, its observance fluctuated with the nation's piety. Both Malachi (**3**.8–10) and Nehemiah (**13**.10–12) had to rouse their contemporaries to take it seriously enough to support the Levites.

The Levites' tithe for the priests (25–32). This 'tithe of the tithe' (26) has an interesting bearing on the antiquity of the Law (cf. Y. Kaufmann, *The Religion of Israel*, pp. 191 ff.), in that a tithe from the numerous Levites of Moses' day would easily support the priests; whereas the proportions were reversed after the Exile, when few Levites returned to Jerusalem. The fact that this law, an embarrassment after the Exile, remained intact, to the detriment of the priests, is good evidence that the books of Moses were already regarded as unalterable at that date.

Numbers 19   The Ashes of a Heifer

This provision for ritual cleansing is the subject of a 'how-much-more' comparison in Heb. **9**.13 f., showing that the old institutions were 'a copy and shadow' (Heb. **8**.5) of the realities of the N.T., which surpass them at two points in particular: the intrinsic value

of the sacrifice and the inwardness of the cleansing. At both these
points this chapter cries out for fulfilment, by its tantalizing
inadequacy as much as by its clarity of symbolism. The inadequacy
is not only that of the victim (almost the proverbial sacred cow!)
but of the tediously slow cleansing (12,19) and the wholly external
realm in which it operated. The conscience, as Heb. 9.9,13 f
points out, was untouched. At the same time the symbolism is
all too plain in its emphasis on man's predicament, barred from
God by the presence of death (11 ff., 14 ff.) which is part of his
world, and isolated from his fellows by the contagion of his defilement (22). (The prophet Haggai was to use this regulation as a
parable of the spreading taint of a single matter of persistent
disobedience [Hag. 2.10–14].)

This negative aspect is balanced, to be sure, by the varied symbols
of atonement, in which nothing is spared to make the sacrifice as
complete as it can be (see on Lev. 14.4 for the cedarwood, etc.).
The pains that were taken over this were a pledge of God's concern,
but a pledge is no permanent resting place. Taught by such a chapter
as this we can share the relief with which the gospel was intended to
be greeted, as it swept away the need to pick a cautious path through
largely unavoidable hazards, and enabled sinners to 'draw near . . .
in full assurance of faith, with . . . hearts sprinkled clean from an
evil conscience' (Heb. 10.22), set free to attend to matters of substance, unmixed with those of shadow.

6. FINAL JOURNEYS AND ENCOUNTERS: Numbers 20—33.49

Numbers 20   The End of an Era

The smiting of the rock (1–13). Moses, recalling this fatal episode
in Deut. 3.26, put the blame of his sin on Israel, and this aspect
of the matter is endorsed in Psa. 106.32 f. Yet it remained his sin
and Aaron's; and its seriousness lay not in any technicality (such as
the spoiling of the type of the once-smitten Christ) but in the fact
and effects of unbelief (12). It is a surprising diagnosis, since Moses
and Aaron seemed to show more anger than doubt—though there
is a hint of the latter in the emphasis laid (in the Hebrew) on the
phrase 'out of this rock?'. But their unbelief went deeper than
any doubt of God's power; fundamentally it was a distrust of His
attitude. Like Jonah, they were in no mood for mercy, whatever
God might say. So they misrepresented Him, and His name was
not 'sanctified' (12). An ambassador can hardly do worse by his
sovereign. (*Note:* Meribah ['strife', 13] was also the secondary

name of the scene of an earlier conflict [Exod. **17**.7]. Both are recalled in Psa. **95**.8.)

Edom's intransigence (14–21). The generosity of Esau (Gen. **33**.4) was not copied by his descendants, whose hatred of Israel, not without provocation (1 Kings **11**.15), grew more and more implacable: cf., e.g. Obad. 10–14. On the 'King's Highway' (17) see *New Bible Dictionary*, p. 700, where it is pointed out that 'datable ruins' bear witness that the road passed through occupied territory at this time. Israel's avoidance of a clash (21) is worth noting; their battles were fought, in the ensuing campaigns, only by divine permission or command.

The death of Aaron (22–29). This was not only death but disappointment (24); it made clear at the outset the imperfection of human priesthood, which would never rise much higher than Aaron, and would sink at times disastrously lower. The priesthood's double weakness, of mortality and sin, is pointed out in Heb. 7.23–28, in utter contrast to the priesthood of the 'Son who has been made perfect for ever', and who 'always lives to make intercession'.

Numbers 21 Harsh Realities

A war of annihilation (1–3). In view of the distinction in Deut. **20**.10–18 between inhabitants of Canaan and enemies elsewhere, it is significant that it was a Canaanite community against which God accepted this vow. The name Hormah (3) is related to the verb 'utterly destroy' (2 f.), a term used by Israelites and non-Israelites to imply a war that is also a kind of crusade.

The brazen serpent (4–9). The epithet 'fiery' (6) is enigmatic; it may have arisen from the painfulness of the wounds. The people's rapid change from abuse to entreaty (7) is reminiscent of Pharaoh himself; expediency was all. In such a context the patience of Moses (7c) and the mercy of God stand out in their true colours as 'love to the loveless shown'. At the same time, the remedy, free as it was, was for the individual to accept, by an act of trust as feasible as it was decisive. Our Lord used this incident, with its presentation of God's judgement (8a) as the instrument of His salvation (8b), to picture Himself as crucified, and to expound the offer of life—but now eternal life—to the individual who trusts in Him (John **3**.14 f.).

By a familiar process, the brazen serpent later became venerated as holy in its own right (2 Kings **18**.4), whereas its only significance had been functional.

The journey towards Pisgah (10–20). After the discouraging detour to avoid Edom (see on Deut. 2) the route was now northward again, up the east side of the Dead Sea. The 'Book of the Wars of the Lord'

(14) is evidence of Israel's concern to preserve in writing even the well-remembered songs of its great occasions (cf. Josh. **10.13**; 2 Sam. **1.18**). The snatches of song in vs. 14 f., 27 ff. may have served the same kind of purpose (but in terms of boundaries) as our 'thirty days hath September . . .'. Perhaps the verse in vs. 17 f. was a working song like a sea shanty; but its theme of water in the desert is evocative of more than physical resources (cf. John **4.13** f.).

Victories over Sihon and Og (21–35). The kingdom of Sihon (21–32), destined for Reuben and Gad, was a stretch of Transjordan from the gorge of the Arnon (half-way up the Dead Sea's eastern shore) to that of the Jabbok, about 30 miles to the north. Bashan (33–35) was a rich pasture land still further north, in the region of the Sea of Galilee; half of Manasseh would settle there. So the eastern part of the inheritance was already won, and the first giant slain (Deut. **3.11**; Psa. **136.17–22**); no small token of victories to come.

Numbers 22 The Hiring of Balaam

Israel's thrust to the north, described in ch. **21**, had now been followed by a return southward, still east of the Jordan, to the plain near the end of that river's course towards the Dead Sea. It was the final halting place before the invasion of Canaan. Here Moses would give his parting discourse (Deut. **1.5**) before ascending mount Nebo to die (Deut. **34.1,5**).

Midian (4,7), in temporary alliance with Moab, was a far-ranging desert people, whose hordes would be a scourge in Gideon's day (Judg. **6.5**), although one branch of them, the Kenites, had thrown in their lot with Israel (**10.29** ff.; Judg. **1.16**).

For all his vacillation between good and evil—more accurately, because he rated money above either of them—Balaam is unequivocally condemned in Scripture (2 Pet. **2.15**; Jude 11; Rev. **2.14**, cf. Num. **31.16**). We may be surprised that God tossed him up and down as He did, forbidding the enterprise (12), allowing it (20), opposing it (22); mystifying him (23–30), chiding him for not seeing the invisible (32 f.); extracting his withdrawal yet refusing to accept it (34 f.). But He knew the man He was dealing with. Note the implications of the pious words of v. 19, in conjunction with v. 12: that to line Balaam's pocket God might be induced to reverse the destiny of a nation. It was clear enough in what sense he reckoned the Lord to be 'my God' (18). To such a man, the only thing stronger than the love of money was the fear of death, and these experiences were well calculated to produce it. Nothing that Balak could say would now move Balaam from the position of v. 38, try as he still would to serve both masters.

On the speaking ass, there seems as little need to fret about the mechanics of this as of any other miracle. It was as timely and purposeful as all Biblical signs: in this case a deflating reminder to the expert in visions and utterances that under God the very beast he rode could see what he himself was blind to (vs. 23,31), and prove a better prophet than he. Note that Balaam got the worst of the exchange not only with the angel (34) but—reduced as he was to a monosyllable (30c)!—with the ass. Cf. 2 Pet. 2.16.

Numbers 23 Balaam's First Two Oracles

The seven pairs of offerings (1,14,29), impressive as they might seem, were a caricature of true worship: a gesture to Yahweh at the shrine of a rival (Baal, 22.41) or, later, at artfully selected places (13,27), using a sub-personal technique ('to look for omens', 24.1) designed to circumvent or change His mind, not to advance His interests. All these devices were totally ineffective, as Balaam soon discovered (24.1). So far from manipulating God, he found himself speaking the potent words which gave effect to God's will.

(i) *A people apart* (7-10). Through Balaam's eyes, as he surveyed the myriads in this no-man's-land, came the impact of the truth (cf. 'What do you see?', Jer. 1.11,13; Amos 8.2), but the words were from God (5). Israel's special calling, and her recognition of it (cf., rightly, RSV's 'reckoning itself', v. 9), form a major theme of the Pentateuch, to persist throughout history. In alluding to 'the dust of Jacob' (10) God confirmed the ancient promise to Abraham (Gen. 13.16; cf. 17.5) in which the N.T. would discern the whole Church, Jew and Gentile alike (Rom. 4.16 f.). On v. 10b, Matthew Henry made the famous comment that 'there are many who desire to die the death of the righteous, but do not endeavour to live the life of the righteous'.

(ii) *An invincible people* (18-24). Balak's attempt to change the oracle by controlling what the prophet could see of Israel (13) only provoked the classic statement of God's unchangeability (19) and an account of how *He*, not merely the prophet, saw His people (21). The translation of v. 21a is complicated by the fact that Hebrew often uses the same word for an act and its consequences; hence the RV has 'iniquity' and 'perverseness', where the RSV has 'misfortune' and 'trouble'. But the usage of the two Hebrew words rather supports the RSV's other translation of them in Hab. 1.3 (an interesting echo of this verse) by 'wrongs' and 'trouble'. I.e., God saw Israel not as the wanton troublemakers that they were

153

in Balak's eyes, but (21b) as His own army, triumphant agents of His own work (23b).

If the first vision, then, confirmed the promise to the patriarchs, the second emphasized the redemption from Egypt and the shattering conquests that lay just ahead for Israel. It was encouragement from a most unexpected quarter.

Numbers 24   Balaam's Closing Oracles

Perhaps his own words, God-given, against the diviner's art (23.23) helped to wean Balaam from his omens (1), i.e. the superstitious study of random movements and patterns (cf. Ezek. 21.21). He was beginning to glimpse the personal, purposeful rule of God.

(iii) *Israel in peace and war* (3-9). As the margin shows, the last word of v. 3 is obscure; and there are still more suggestions. But 'opened' is perhaps supported by later Hebrew and Aramaic. 'Closed' makes sense if it is part of a progress traced by the other verbs; but this is not very apparent, and it involves a slight change in the Hebrew pointing (as does the meaning 'perfect' or 'sound').

Israel's orderly array (2) conjures up to Balaam a peaceful landscape, very different from the waste land where they are now encamped. It is a watery picture, one of those scenes where the spaciousness (6a, 'that stretch afar') and the informality (6b) of God's design blend happily with man's tidy cultivation ('gardens beside a river', 6) and busy contrivances (the 'buckets' for irrigation, 7). For any community, particularly the Church, this could be a parable of its best pattern, and a reminder that but for God's gifts, (cf. 'water' and 'seed', 7), all would be desert.

The warlike conclusion repeats much of 23.22,24 to confront Balak again with the folly of resisting what God has miraculously begun. Once more this process is traced back beyond the Exodus (8) to the patriarchal call (9b; Gen. 12.3). With the mention of Agag (7), so impressive then, so unimpressive now, the antiquity of the oracles suddenly obtrudes itself, to make Israel's continuity all the more striking. Agag was evidently a hereditary name or title for the Amalekite king (cf. Amalek's prestige in v. 20): the name reappears in 1 Sam. 15.8 f., 32 f.

(iv) *Star and sceptre* (15-19). Balaam used no preliminary rituals now. He even showed some personal involvement and emotion (17a,23); yet the sequel proves that there was no repentance (25.2; 31.16). The immediate horizon of vs. 17-19 seems to be the reign of David, as the list of conquests indicates. But in Jewish thought the 'star' was also messianic. Our Lord takes up this title, as 'the root and the offspring of David, the bright morning star' (Rev.

154

22.16). With the 'sceptre', compare Gen. **49.**10, a still earlier prophecy of David and, it would seem, of his greater Son.

(v) *Supplementary prophecies* (20–24). Balaam's vision travels beyond Saul and Amalek (1 Sam. **15**) to Assyria (Asshur) and its deportations (22), and on again to Assyria's own fall (24). Ships from Kittim (Cyprus) refer to Roman sea power in Dan. **11.**30, but hardly here, since Assyria had fallen long before Roman times. Even so, the range of Balaam's vision was immense.

Questions for further study and discussion on Numbers chs. 15—24

1. Starting with the references in the note on Num. **15.**13–16, supplemented if possible by others from a concordance, study the place given to the stranger and sojourner in Israel. Is there anything here to guide modern societies in their relations with alien minorities?
2. Some aspects of intercession are suggested in the comment on **16.**22,44–48. What further insight into its meaning and function can we gain from other parts of Scripture?
3. What can the Christian learn from the tithe laws, as given in Num. **18.**21 ff. and in Deut. **26.**12 ff.? Does the N.T. offer any guidance on the subject?
4. What warnings should we take from Balaam's acts and attitudes, and what lessons from God's handling of him?

Numbers 25   Disaster at Peor

The Moabite's seduction of Israel was a deliberate stratagem after the failure of their original plan. It was Balaam himself (**31.**16) who conceived the idea—one that was sufficiently diabolical to be recognizable again in the tactics employed against the church in Rev. **2.**14, and indeed wherever a frontal assault is replaced by a policy of enticement. The N.T. dwells on both aspects of this affair: the spiritual disloyalty (Rev. **2.**14) and the physical lust (1 Cor. **10.**8)—or, in modern euphemisms, a new theology and a new morality. Note, too, the expression 'yoked' (3,5), which may have influenced the language of 2 Cor. **6.**14 (lit.).

By the conspicuous fate of the ringleaders, retribution had to be displayed before God as sufficiently meted- out (4c). Such a background emphasizes the curse that rested on a hanged man (Deut. **21.**22 f.—but the word is different) as the visible object of God's judgement. Such was Christ for us (Gal. **3.**13).

Verses 6–15. Retribution continues to be the theme, and atonement (13) is effected by an act of stark justice. It is the complement of **16.**46 ff., where the atoning act took the form of interposing

155

the person and work of the priest between the wrongdoers and their due—an act which owed its efficacy to the real interposition to be made one day by Christ, vicariously judged.

On the detail of the number of victims given in v. 9 and the 23,000 mentioned in 1 Cor. **10.**8, L. Morris points out (Tyndale Commentary, *1 Corinthians*) that 'obviously both are round numbers, and in addition Paul may be making some allowance for those slain by the judges' (Num. **25.**5). On the divine 'jealousy' which dominates vs. 10–13, see on Lev. **17.** Note, too, that Zimri was no mere youth caught in an unguarded moment, but a man of standing (14) who flaunted his trophy before the whole penitent congregation (6). It was a cool and undisguised challenge, which Phinehas was wholly right (cf. Psa. **106.**30 f.) to accept.

Verses 16–18. Retribution remains the theme of the chapter to the end. This time it is corporate, but not merely nationalistic: Midian is treated as a source of apostasy, and the reprisal was to be Moses' last campaign (**31.**2). Note, too, that the Kenites, converts to Israel from Midian (**10.**29 ff.; Judg. **1.**16), were not penalized.

Numbers 26   The Second Census

This is again a military census (2), like that of ch. **1,** expanded by the names of clans within the tribes (substantially those of Gen. **46** and Exod. **6**) and by a few comments. It is here that we learn of the escape of Korah's sons (11; see note at the end of ch. **16**).

The tribal figures vary unpredictably from those of the earlier census; e.g. Simeon (14) has dropped catastrophically, Manasseh and Ephraim have virtually exchanged totals (but perhaps their names should have come in their usual order) and other tribes have shown rapid growth or loss, leaving the grand total, however, very little altered. On conjectured interpretations of these figures, see on ch. **1.**

If this is unexciting reading, the occasion itself was notable. It was a prelude to action and a fulfilment of prophecy. The former of these is implied in vs. 52–56, where the tribal totals are related to the coming inheritance; and the latter is explicit in vs. 63–65, which make as good a summary of the book of Numbers as one could wish to find. The N.T. finds this a very live object-lesson for Christians: see 1 Cor. **10.**11; Heb. **3.**12—**4.**2.

Numbers 27   Two Problems of Continuity

A test case of inheritance (1–11). Some other examples of the law's growth or clarification through new cases can be found in Lev.

24.10; Num. **9.**6–14; **15.**32 ff. On this occasion, as before, Moses showed a remarkable openmindedness—open, that is, to God (5), whose will he did not automatically equate with ancient custom. The five daughters, for their part, were admirable for their courage and spirit; and thanks to this constructive reaction on both sides to a problem which might have been nursed as a grievance, the whole incident publicly demonstrated God's approachability and care for individuals, far more vividly than an existing statute in the law book would have done. For us, too, it may have light to throw on God's purpose in subjecting us to situations in which we find ourselves deeply disturbed and temporarily baffled.

Joshua to succeed Moses (12–23). The long shadow of Moses' approaching death, an event which will not occur until he has given the discourse which occupies Deuteronomy, already points to the approaching era of conquest and settlement. Moses himself, to his credit, thinks of his people's need rather than his own disappointment, and so Joshua is commissioned, not in spite of him, but at his fervent request. It is the way God prefers to work: cf. Matt. **9.**38, in a passage which suggests that our Lord may have had the present incident in mind (cf. Matt. **9.**36 with our v. 17; but cf. primarily 1 Kings **22.**17).

By placing his hands on Joshua, Moses was openly commissioning him (18 f.) and sharing with him his authority (20). Deut. **34.**9 adds that through this act Joshua was 'full of the spirit of wisdom', although our v. 18 shows that already in some degree he possessed the Spirit (as his previous military and moral leadership bore witness). Together, the two passages indicate that he was freshly empowered for his new tasks in the act of being set apart for them (cf. 2 Tim. **1.**6 f.).

He must receive God's instructions, however, through the high priest (21), unlike Moses, to whom God spoke face to face (**12.**8). Henceforth the functions of leader and mediator of revelation would remain distinct until they were united again in Christ, God's Prophet, Priest and King.

Numbers 28 and 29 The Calendar of Offerings

The companion to these chapters is Lev. 23, which covers much the same ground but is not confined, as this passage is, to the sacrificial materials. The scheme here is to cover first, the daily, weekly and monthly statutory offerings (**28.**1–15), and then, to work through the calendar of feasts, etc., from Passover to Tabernacles (**28.**16—**29.**38), concluding with a note that the catalogue took no account

157

of the more spontaneous occasions, and that it was faithfully communicated to the people by Moses (29.39 f.).

Two things emerge clearly from this formidable list. The first is the great importance attached to the regular continuity of worship, morning by morning, evening by evening, sabbath by sabbath, and month by month. Each of these must persist regardless of the extra demands of the others and of the festivals: see the recurrent phrase beginning with 'besides . . .', in 28.10b,15b,24b, etc.; see also 29.6a.

The second feature is the progress to a climax in the seventh month, whose events occupy the whole of ch. 29. The festive beginning, with trumpets and a holiday (29.1); the solemnities of the Day of Atonement (29.7–11; cf. Lev. 16); and the elaborate eight-day feast of Tabernacles (29.12–38), made it the crown of the year. But the sequence within those eight days is surprising, with the number of sacrificial bulls diminishing daily from thirteen to seven, and then abruptly down to one on 'the last day of the feast, the great day' (as John 7.37 puts it). This decrease is so opposed to human ideas of climax that it is hard to resist the conclusion that the Author of these regulations shaped them to the pattern of the true consummation, in which sacrifice would cease.

Note, finally, that the liturgical year was linked to two symbols of onward movement, one recurrent and the other non-recurrent. The first was the march of the seasons from spring (Passover time) to autumn (cf. Exod. 23.16). The second was the march of Israel from Egypt, through the wilderness (which the Booths or Tabernacles commemorated, Lev. 23.43) towards the promised land. Both the O.T. and the N.T. see this as a miniature of God's scheme of human history (see opening comment on Lev. 23) from the redemption of His people to the time when the world will know Him as King (Zech. 14.16) and the harvest of the earth be reaped (Rev. 14.15 f.).

Numbers 30   Responsibility for Vows

The aim of this chapter was simply to state a person's obligation concerning the vows he undertook (2), and to clarify the position of those who were not wholly free agents: a daughter at home (3–5), a wife (6–8), and a widow or a divorced woman (9–15). The principle binding the father or husband was that he must own or disown such a vow once it came to his notice, without delay or vacillation. Silence gave consent.

To turn from this straightforward rule to the legislation in the Mishnah, and to the glimpses of contemporary attitudes which appear in the Gospels, is to be reminded of the uncertainties and quibbles which beset any law code (obliged to decide, e.g. what phrases just escape classification as vows) and of the cynical manipulations (Matt. 15.5) and absurd values (Matt. 23.16–22) which man's perversity imposed on such material.

Our Lord did more than indict the conscious hypocrite. His outright 'Do not swear at all' (Matt. 5.33–37, cf. Jas. 5.12), however, is evidently addressed to us as individuals in our personal dealings (along with the rest of the maxims of Matt. 5), since the N.T. allows both angels (Rev. 10.5) and men (2 Cor. 1.23) to make affirmations by God when they are acting as His spokesmen. Indeed, God Himself, as Heb. 6.13 ff. points out, used this means of confirming His promise. As to vows, Paul could use them with a clear conscience (Acts 18.18; 21.23–26), and while Scripture records some disastrous examples (e.g. Jephthah's and Herod's) it tells of others (e.g. Jacob's and Hannah's) that were highly fruitful.

What is always wrong, the 'evil' (Matt. 5.37) that our Lord was concerned to stamp out, is the arrogance of arming our assertions or our prayers with a trump card of appeal or promise. A true character does not need the former, or a true faith the latter. Jesus and His brother James both point us to the sterling simplicity of a genuine Yes or No, which is worth exactly what the speaker is worth.

Numbers 31   Vengeance against Midian

Abhorrent as this story must be, it is important to see it in its own terms. I.e., this avenging of Israel (2) was no private vendetta but 'the Lord's vengeance' (3) executed at His insistence, in face of at least a partial reluctance on Israel's part (14 f.) and as punishment for a specified outrage (16; see ch. 25). The equivalent term to 'vengeance' in N.T. quotations is *ekdikēsis*, retribution, in which the idea of judicially giving a person his deserts is prominent. Note that Balaam now received the penultimate wages of sin (8, cf. v. 16, and comment on ch. 22).

The character of the massacre as a cleansing operation was borne out by the quarantine requirements (19 f.) and the ritual use of fire and water (23; this verse incidentally throws light on the meaning of Luke 3.16). The mention of 'atonement' through handing over the portable spoil (50) shows that this act was a restitution of forbidden treasure (53), which had put the camp in jeopardy as Achan was to put it at Jericho (Josh. 7.1). The roles of executioner and beneficiary, which go ill together, were to overlap only within the strictest limits.

The whole grim episode, with its imperfect agents, its dividends and its inclusion of the innocent with the guilty, is a microcosm of a creation that groans and travails, even though it is under providential rule (Rom. **8.**20,22). At the same time, its pattern of retribution foreshadows, however distortedly, the ultimate retribution of the Last Judgement, committed (John **5.**22; 2 Thess. **1.**7 f.) to hands which are wholly to be trusted and were first dedicated to salvation.

Numbers 32   'Do Not Take Us Across the Jordan'

It was common sense for Reuben and Gad to match together needs and resources: 'cattle' and 'a place for cattle' (1,4); but it was shallow to decide so much by reference to so little. They were fortunate in having to submit their case to the authorities (2) and be faced with other aspects of the matter. As always, a godly and frank observer could weigh up, better than they, their existing obligations (6), the effect of their example (7), the context of past events (8), and above all, the relation of their choice to their vocation (15). Since their impulsiveness and self-interest were all-too-human traits, the incident has a timeless relevance to decision-making of all kinds.

The revised proposal of vs. 16 ff. was a fine example of constructive response to criticism: neither tamely withdrawing nor obstinately persisting, but looking for a synthesis on the basis of what is right. The new plan required faith as well as courage, since the undefended cities, however well fortified, would invite immediate attack. The faith was well founded, and the happy outcome is recorded in Josh. **22.**

As for the later history of these tribes (who were joined by half Manasseh, headed by the clan of Machir: 33,39 ff.), their relative isolation became sometimes a temptation to aloofness (Judg. **5.**15b–17a, but 14b), and always a lure to their enemies (e.g. 1 Sam. **11**; Amos **1.**13; and cf. the place-names in Num. **32.**3 with those of Isa. **15**, an oracle against Moab). For all this, the eastern side of Jordan was an enrichment to Israel, for its beauty (Song of Sol. **4.**1), its balm (Jer. **8.**22), its fertility (Mic. **7.**14), and, not least, for the most famous of its sons, Elijah the Tishbite (1 Kings **17.**1; 2 Kings **1.**8), whose rural simplicity was to challenge the sophistication of the throne at a turning point in Israel's history.

Numbers 33.1–49   The Log of the Journey

Concealed in this forbidding chapter, v. 2 is seldom encountered, but its importance is far-reaching, as evidence of not merely a natural concern to remember the Exodus events in substance, but a divine command to record them with precision. Other allusions to records written by Moses occur in Exod. **17.**14 (after the first attle); **24.4–8**; **34.27** (covenant documents); Deut. **31.**9,24 (the law as expounded in Deuteronomy).

Forty stopping-places are named here (this excludes Rameses, the starting point), eleven of them belonging to the first three months' journey to Sinai (5–15). Two of the places in this section, Dophkah and Alush (13), are mentioned only here, and there are many more such in the rest of the chapter. It emerges, too, that the list is not exhaustive (unless it tacitly distinguishes between a bivouac for the night and a formal camp), since it names no stage-points for the three-day journey in v. 8, or for the 70 miles that separate Ezion-geber from Kadesh (36). It seems likely that the number of places transferred from Moses' log to this chapter was consciously limited to forty, a very appropriate total. Apart from the first and last years' movements (for the latter, see vs. 37–49 and the notes on **1.**10 ff.) scarcely any pattern can be reconstructed—which is again appropriate enough to the restless monotony of the years of wandering, though it is partly due to our inability to identify more than a few of the sites. With vs. 31 f. cf. Deut. **10.**6 f. and comment.

. THE PROSPECT OF CANAAN: Numbers 33.50—36.13

Numbers 33.50—34.29 Realistic Planning

Policy towards the Canaanites (33.50–56). It is again made clear that Canaan is to be not merely a national home for a refugee people, but a holy land. No fraternization, no mingling of religions (52), no scramble for the best places (54) must jeopardize this conception, which God takes with frightening seriousness (56). Notice, in passing, the combination of human planning and divine arbitration envisaged in v. 54, in that there was evidently to be a preliminary survey and division of the land into viable holdings of different sizes, and a classification of tribal strengths, before the specific apportionments were made by lot within this framework. The double-harness of hard thinking and prayerful submission is a permanently valid principle of decision-making.

The bounds of the land, and the territorial commissioners (ch. **34**). There is a similar list in Ezek. **47.**13–21. Israel came nearest to possessing the full extent of its inheritance in the reigns of David and Solomon, though the coastal strip remained in the hands of the Philistines and of Tyre and Sidon even then. Not all the places are known, but enough are identified to give a fairly clear outline, for which a Bible atlas can be consulted. As regards certain names: 'the Brook of Egypt' (5) is the Wady el Arish, about 100 miles east of the Egyptian border-fortresses. 'Mount Hor' (7) is obviously not

161

the southern mountain of that name where Aaron was burie (20.22 ff.), but another in the north, so far unidentified. 'The entranc of Hamath' (8) should probably be rendered 'Lebo-Hamath', abou 50 miles north of Damascus, near the source of the Orontes. 'Th sea of Chinnereth' (11) is known in the Gospels as 'the lake c Gennesaret' (or of Galilee or Tiberias).

On vs. 13–15 see ch. 32. Of the leaders in vs. 16–29. Caleb was th only survivor of the first generation, as was pointed out in 26.6! His fellow survivor, Joshua, was already marked out for more tha tribal leadership (27.18 ff.). Caleb, by his spiritual singlemindednes: was to prove as unflagging as men half his age: see especiall Josh. 14.10–14.

Numbers 35

Cities for Levites (1–8). Although the Levites were not altogethe landless (2 ff.), they had no continuous stretch of territory to ca their own, and were probably never given their full rights in th 48 cities allotted them. They had to remind the authorities to mak the allocation (Josh. 21.1 ff.), and if Hebron and Shechem are an criterion (Josh. 21.13,21) Levites were not noticeably dominant i the places they were supposed to own (cf. 2 Sam. 2—4; Judg. 9 Moses foresaw that having 'no portion or inheritance', they woul share the insecurity of 'the sojourner, the fatherless and the widow (Deut. 14.29). The intention of the law, however, was that the should be posted throughout Israel as disseminators of God's trut (Deut. 33.10), enjoying a modest security through their allotmen of tithes, cities and glebe land (Num. 35.3), yet dependent on Go as their true inheritance (18.20). See further on chs. 8 and 18.

Cities of refuge (9–34). These six cities, three on each side of th Jordan, are named in Josh. 20.7 f. There is the true flavour of anti quity in 'the avenger (*gō'ēl*) of blood' and in the role of the congrega tion (12) and the elders of the offender's city (Deut. 19.12). A Sinai God had promised to provide a refuge (Exod. 21.13 f.), whic would replace or supplement the altar which sufficed in the wilder ness. Only in a city could the law for manslaughter be applie (25 ff.), or a refugee await trial (12) without the risk of starvation Adonijah and Joab, who resorted to the altar (1 Kings 1.50; 2.28) were guilty of a different crime, that of treason, on which the kin could make an immediate decision.

This law supplied a workable means of replacing blood-feuds b public justice, with proper rules of evidence (30) and tests to dis tinguish murder from manslaughter (16–24), changing the kinsma status from private avenger to agent of the court (Deut. 19.12) ho must settle an account for which otherwise God would hold he nation liable (Num. 35.33 f.). This penalty of death was laid own for mankind in general, not Israel alone, in Gen. 9.6. Cf. Rom. 13.4.

It is tempting to see typical significance in 'the death of the high priest' (25,28) releasing the manslayer. Perhaps Heb. 9.16 f., with ts use of a non-sacrificial aspect of Christ's death, gives some ncouragement to the idea. But what is taught unequivocally here s the sanctity of human life (cf. Gen. 9.6b), which made even ccidental killing a serious enough matter to restrict the offender's iberty until the end of an era.

Numbers 36   A Problem of Inheritance

t is instructive to see this fresh development in a matter that was aised and seemingly settled in 27.1–11. The new clause in the law vas God-given like the rest ('according to the word of the Lord', 5), ut each stage had first presented itself as a problem which gave ause for concern, and the present one arose out of an apparent clash of divine commands (2a,b,4). In such a case there must be a ynthesis, because God's word is self-consistent. Here, the answer demanded faith and obedience, by limiting an heiress to marry only vithin her father's tribe (8). This was perhaps no great sacrifice, n an age less dominated by individualism than our own. But we an be grateful to this procession of sisters not only for enlivening hese pages with their engaging names, but for providing one of he few contemporary examples of doing 'as the Lord commanded' 10), to end this book of selfwill and wasted years on a note of ncomplaining co-operation.

Questions for futher study and discussion on Numbers chs. 25—36

1. 'When a man vows . . ., he shall not break his word' (30.2). We know our Lord's teaching on this in Matt. 5.33 ff.; but what about simple promises? What guidance can we get, from Biblical events and pronouncements, as to when, if ever, a promise should be broken?
2. What view does the O.T. take of exterminations (by human agency, as in ch. 31, and by non-human as in ch. 16)? What exterminations (of these two kinds) does the N.T. mention, and how does its view of them compare with that of the O.T.?
3. 'Be sure your sin will find you out' (32.23). Find other sayings which present the sinner as a threatened or hunted man (e.g. Gen. 4.7; Psa. 140.11; . . .), and his punishment as something he has set in motion himself.

Deuteronomy

OUTLINE

THE PARTING CHARGE OF MOSES

1. THE PRELIMINARY RETROSPECT: chs. 1—4

2. THE COVENANT EXPOUNDED: chs. 5—26

A. THE BASIC PRINCIPLES: 5—11

5 'Face to face at the mountain'
6—11 'Him only shall you serve'

B. THE DETAILED REQUIREMENTS: 12—26

12 A Single Sanctuary
13 Penalties for Subversion
14 Laws on Mourning, Eating and Tithing
15 The Year of Release
16.1–17 The Three Great Feasts
16.18—17.20 Justice and True Worship
18 Priests, Levites, Charlatans, Prophets
19 Safeguards of Justice
20 The Wars of the Lord
21 The Restraint of Lawlessness
22—25 Miscellaneous Laws: Social, Sexual and Symbolic
26 'Flowing with milk and honey'

3. THE LAW PRESSED HOME TO ISRAEL: chs. 27, 28
27, 28 Blessing and Cursing, Inscription and Declamation

4. THE COVENANT'S CONTINUING CHALLENGE: chs. 29–31
29 'You stand this day before the Lord'
30 'Therefore choose life'
31 Changing Leadership, Unchanging Law

5. OUR HOPE FOR YEARS TO COME: chs. 32—34
32 The Song of Moses
33 The Blessing of the Tribes
34 The Death of Moses

164

THE PARTING CHARGE OF MOSES
I. THE PRELIMINARY RETROSPECT: Deuteronomy 1—4

Deuteronomy 1   Recalling the Great Refusal

The geographical details of v. 1 cover a wide area, and are probably a digression arising out of the term 'the wilderness', to remind the reader of the journeyings which that word should bring to mind. The expression 'beyond the Jordan' (1,5) is more accurately rendered in the region of Jordan', since it can be used of either the near or the far side in relation to a speaker: cf. 1 Kings 4.24 (=5.4, Heb.), Isa. 9.1 (=8.23 Heb.).

There is a skilful selection of details throughout the chapter. The time note in v. 2 adds irony to that of v. 3a, an eloquent contrast between the achievable and the achieved! The allusion to the officers and judges (9–18) was equally to the point, being both heartening and challenging: it was proof of God's promise-keeping, by the reminder of what had wonderfully developed since Abraham (10; cf. Gen. 15.5), and it faced the leaders again with the high responsibility they already shared with Moses. They would have no excuse for collapsing when he was taken from them (and the hard cases of v. 17b would still be catered for, as 17.8 ff. was to point out). There was force, again, in characterizing the wilderness as 'great and terrible' (19 cf. 8.15; 32.10), since it highlighted the wonder of their safe conduct (cf. the vivid metaphors of vs. 31 ff.), the perversity of their fathers' refusal of the 'good land', and the disaster which a second rejection would invite.

Making itself heard through all the warnings and reproaches is the call to go forward in faith. As an object-lesson, Caleb and Joshua, at the forefront of the inheritors of the land, are contrasted with Moses, the last survivor of the disinherited (34–40). Moses, though he had also earned his own punishment (Num. 20.12), stands here as head of his disobedient people, suffering on their account (37) though not in their stead (Exod. 32.32 f.). This had been the price of their drawing back; but the price of pressing on unbidden had been just as high (41–46). Both warnings were relevant to the approaching campaign, in which, as always, courageous and obedient faith would be the condition of victory.

Deuteronomy 2   The Wanderings and First Conquest

'The Red Sea' (1) here means its eastern horn, the Gulf of Aqabah, with the port of Elath or Ezion-geber (8) at its northern tip. For

165

Israel it had meant turning south, away from Canaan (cf. **1**.40), t
pace out the course they had cravenly chosen for themselves, littl
as they liked it in the event (Num. **21**.4). In its truth to the logic c
the situation it was a penalty typical of God's judgements.

Now, after 38 years of nomadism (3,14), the meandering ha
turned to a march; yet the theme of this chapter is the tight contro
of this movement by God's decrees. The theme is given extr
depth by the 'asides' which show how others entered *their* inher
tances by divine allotment (note especially 12b, cf. 5,9,19,21b–22
Any idea that to be the chosen people was to be a master race wa
ruled out as early as this. They had their allotted place in it
appointed time (Gen. **15**.13–16), with no more absolute freeho
than had their heathen predecessors (Lev. **18**.28; **25**.23). Amc
would have to remind them of this forgotten lesson (Amos **3**.1 f
9.7 ff.).

In contrast to the peoples of vs. 1–19, the Amorites (26–37) wer
ripe for judgement (Gen. **15**.16; see also comment on Deut. **3**.6
and God now enhanced their king's aggressiveness (30; cf. Nun
21.26–30) to bring about his ruin (cf. Rom. **9**.17 f.). It was anothe
aspect of divine judgement; cf. the first paragraph, above.

Notes: Some of the names of the early inhabitants in vs. 10–1
20–23, occur also in Gen. **14**.5 f. Some are alternative names fo
the same people (11,20). For details, see the *New Bible Dictionary*
On v. 29, with its apparent disagreement with Num. **20**.21; Deu
23.3 f., a possible explanation is that not all the outlying settlement
followed the hostile policy of their leaders, and Israel was glad t
do business with such groups. (So G. T. Manley, *New Bible Com
mentary.*)

Deuteronomy 3 The Retrospect Conclude

The policy of extermination (6), already used against Sihon (2.34 f.)
was to be standard procedure against the peoples that Israel wa
to dispossess, but was not to be employed against any and ever
enemy. See **20**.10–15,16–18, where the reason for this discriminatio
is explained. God alone has the right to pronounce such a sentenc
(which is a special case of His universal sentence of mortality
Psa. **90**.5 ff.); and it is worth noting (*a*) that the first two extermina
tions in Scripture were independent of human agents and fallib
motives (Gen. **6**.7; **19**.24 f.); (*b*) that the Canaanite massacres le
room for a Rahab and her family, as the Genesis ones left room fo
Noah and Lot, with theirs; (*c*) that our Lord's advice is to trea
reports of violence and tragedy chiefly as signs of a world unde
judgement, rather than as material for moralizing (Luke **13**.1–5

17.26–37); (d) that final judgement will correct the approximations that are inevitable in temporal judgements (Luke 10.12 ff.). See also on Num. 31, throughout.

King Og (11), as the last of the giants (AV[KJV]), with his 13′ 6″×6′ 0″ iron bedstead, has had some translation queries raised about him. Was his iron bed perhaps a basalt sarcophagus, and can Rephaim mean 'giants'? But the familiar interpretation is probably right. A huge sarcophagus is an unlikely trophy to transport to another kingdom, and both 'iron' and 'bed' are common words. And Rephaim, though it is an elusive term, has associations with hugeness in 2.10 f., 20 f., and was translated 'giant' in the Greek of Josh. 12.4 and elsewhere.

On vs. 12–22, see on Num. 32. Verses 23–29 faithfully reflect the tantalizing situation of Moses, which has already made itself felt in 1.37 f. The former reference (where see comment) seems to belong to the beginning of the wanderings, where Moses himself was guiltless. The present one certainly belongs to the end (23), but even so, Moses' guilt was incurred under Israel's provocation (cf. v. 26 with Psa. 106. 32 f.), and God's refusal was couched in terms that may well have comforted Moses by their striking resemblance to the great promise to Abram: cf. v. 27 with Gen. 13.14.

Deuteronomy 4   'Therefore . . .'

The retrospect has covered grace and judgement: no promise, no warning, has failed. And all has been verifiable: 'Your eyes have seen . . .' (3). Yet its meaning can be missed or forgotten (9), so this chapter sees to it that history does not degenerate into reminiscence but makes its mark on belief and action.

'The word' (2) is the first emphasis: vs. 1–14. Its character as unalterable truth (2,9,13) and as a challenge to the will ('statutes . . . ordinances . . . commandments') made this a humbling revelation, but a steadying one to live by, independent as it was of fashions of thought, and manifestly superior to any existing system (6 f.).

The second emphasis is on *the invisible God*. The theme has arisen in connection with His self-disclosure through words: 'no form . . . only a voice' (12). It dominates vs. 15–31 with the reiterated warnings against idolatry and (19) against astral worship; warnings whose relevance subsequent history was to confirm. (The force of v. 19b is that the stars, etc., are objects created for the benefit of all, not powers controlling national destinies.) The implied seriousness of idolatry, which at first sight may seem as exaggerated to us as it did to them, was not primarily through its denial of truth (though this is exposed in v. 28) but through its breach of the covenant

167

(23 f.). Because this was a personal bond between the Lord and Israel, any flirtation with other gods or substitute-figures would be as radical a betrayal as adultery would be in a marriage. So idolatry, a marginal sin to human eyes, could only lead to national disaster (26).

The third emphasis is on God as *the only God* (32–40). From a simple comparison of Sinai and the Exodus with any events attributed to other gods, the passage builds up to the twin statements of absolute monotheism in vs. 35, 39,which are as emphatic as anything in Isa. **40** ff., where the doctrine is often said to be first encountered. Intertwined with such a theme, note the pattern of grace, e.g. in the sequence 'He loved . . . and chose . . . and brought you out . . . to bring you in, to give you . . .' (37 f.).

Verses 41–49 mark the transition from the preliminary discourse to the main speech of the book (chs. **5—26**). Verses 41–43(cf. Num. **35.9** ff., esp. v. 14) round off the former, and vs. 44–49 look forward to the latter (note the terms of v. 45a ,which suit the material of chs. **5—26** better than that of chs. **1—4**). Verse 46a sets the scene; vs. 46b–49 digress to recall the initial conquests that were the pledge of the full inheritance.

2. THE COVENANT EXPOUNDED: Deuteronomy 5—26
A. THE BASIC PRINCIPLES: 5—11.

Deuteronomy 5   'Face to Face at the Mountain'

It is important to relate the 'statutes and . . . ordinances' (1) to the bigger reality, the 'covenant' (2) whose ends they served—somewhat as the rules of a household serve but do not constitute the family or the marriage. Chapters **5—11** dwell on the covenant partnership itself, of God and Israel, partly by recollection, partly by instruction and appeal. It is settled at the outset that there are no merely derivative members, who must share in the covenant at second hand (2 f.). To the second generation as much as the first, the Sinai confrontation was to be reckoned their own, 'face to face' (4). It is an O.T. counterpart, in its sphere, of the 'once for all' and the 'today' of the gospel.

The ten commandments (5.6–22). On these ten 'words' (22, cf. **4.13**, lit.), see further on Exod. **20**. In 4.13 they are equated with the covenant, since they were its title-deed or 'marriage-lines', for which the 'ark of the covenant' might be called the deed-box. The opening phrase (6a) expresses God's side of the mutual self-giving which is the essence of a covenant, and vs. 7–15 spell out man's side of it— somewhat as a marriage vow specifies the love, honour and obedience implied in the bride's response. The 'manward' commandments

16–21) continue the same theme, for they are the acid test of our Godward profession (cf., e.g. Jer. **7**.9 f.). The slight variations from the Exod. **20** version (chiefly v. **15**'s mention of Egyptian bondage, instead of the Creator's rest, to encourage sabbath keeping; also a smaller change in v. **21**) suggest a preacher's greater degree of freedom than a reader's; perhaps, too, they point to a structure consisting of a brief command (e.g. 'You shall not covet') followed by a more flexible expansion.

The overwhelming presence (**5**.23–33). This vivid memory of Sinai is a significant prelude to the law, especially the ritual law, revealing as it does the unbearable impact of holiness on the sinner. It was a standing reminder that the law's elaborate screen between God and the worshipper was no show of aloofness but a necessity, begged for by man himself. Ponder the contrast, by grace, between Rev. **5**.16 and Rev. **22.4**.

Deuteronomy 6   The Heart of the Matter

Verses 4 f., known as the *Shema* ('Hear . . .'), were picked out as the primary commandment, not only by our Lord, but by others of His day (Luke **10**.25 ff.) and by traditional Judaism. It is part creed, part command; and the warmth of the latter flows rightly from the personal emphasis of the former, with its reiterated name Yahweh . . . one Yahweh' and its echo of the covenant in speaking of '*our* God'. This is a monotheism that is reached, not by elimination of other hypotheses, but by revelation, explicit and by name, with grace at its heart in the self-giving implied in His commitment to His people.

'You shall love . . .' (5) is the only motivation that makes Law fruitful, for God's commands are given to define how love must show itself in different contexts, not how little one can get away with, or how much merit one can acquire. 'Heart and soul' denote the whole range of one's being, and 'might' denotes the intensity (cf. Eccl. **9**.10—but a different word) of one's loving. The addition of 'mind' in the N.T. quotations only makes explicit what is implied in 'heart' in the O.T., which includes both mind and will. 'Soul' is almost synonymous with 'self'. For the three words together, see 2 Kings **23**.25.

The people of a book (6–9). As against most religions, which inculcate routines, God looks for knowledge and understanding (cf. also v. 20), and sees the home and the common round as its school. As against the modern fear of overdoing matters, He requires His teachings to be the very stuff and pattern of a family's life (7); as gladly worn as a ring or an ornament; as obvious as their front door (8 f., cf. **11**.18–20). (It was a mistaken literalism that invented phylacteries [text-cases worn on the arm and forehead], as a comparison with Exod. **13**.9,16; Prov. **3**.3, indicates.)

'*That it may go well with you*' (3,18, cf. 24). This is a constant theme of Deuteronomy, which marries the idea of absolute obligation (e.g. vs. 1,13,25) with that of finding fulfilment in life. In human systems of ethics these tend to be alternative rather than complementary criteria; it is God's total authority and perfect love which bring them together. Cf. the two halves of v. 24, where this harmony is perfectly expressed.

Deuteronomy 7 Israel and the Gentiles

(i) '*No covenant . . ., no mercy*' (1–5). For the identities of the 'seven nations' (1), as far as they are known at present, see a reference book, e.g. the *New Bible Dictionary*. On the word for 'utterly destroy' (2), see on Num. **21**.1–3. Cf. vs. 25 f. here, where 'accursed thing' (*ḥērem*) is the corresponding noun. The 'pillars' and 'Asherim' (not 'groves', AV [KJV]) of v. 5 appear to have been stone and wooden representations of, respectively, a god (El or Baal?) and the principal Canaanite goddess Asherah.

(ii) '*Chosen*' (6–11). This key paragraph on the choice, or 'election', of Israel gives no encouragement to the complacency, pride or speculation it might be expected to provoke. Complacency is forestalled by the emphasis on the end in view (to be 'holy' and to be 'His', 6, cf. the similar stress in Eph. **1**.4–6) and by the warning that they are to take no liberties (10 f.). Pride is punctured by the 'not because . . .' in v. 7 (cf. **9**.5 and the gospel's 'not because . . .' in, e.g. Tit. **3**.5). And there is no room for speculation in face of the clause 'because the Lord loves you' (8), which puts the matter beyond argument—unless we think to judge divine love by human. The paragraph as a whole encourages humble confidence in the One who has begun and continued (8 f.) so surprising a thing.

(iii) '*Blessed above all peoples*' (12–16). Deuteronomy visualizes a people and country that will be the envy of the world. This eager anticipation, which keeps breaking through, is strong evidence of the genuineness of its professed setting, looking in from the outside to a land of plenty, and ahead to great possibilities. The blessings of these verses will be elaborated in **28**.1–14.

(iv) '*You shall not be afraid of them*' (17–26). Whether the 'hornets' (20) were meant literally or symbolically (cf. Isa. **7**.18), this was a reminder that fresh 'signs' and 'wonders' (19) would meet the new situation. But note the deliberate limitation decreed in v. 22, an important verse for interpreting the conquest summaries in Joshua which are themselves balanced by, e.g. Josh. **13.1** ff.), and for understanding God's frequent choice of gradual or modest conquests in the spiritual war. He knows how much His people are ready to handle and consolidate.

Deuteronomy 8 'Facing either Poverty or Plenty'

The temptation of Christ has illuminated this passage for us through His complete acceptance of v. 3b, not as an irksome demand, but as the secret of life. His later saying, 'My food is to do the will of Him who sent Me . . .', bears out the abiding reality this had for Him. For Israel it was a lesson learnt grudgingly, if at all. In fact the two attitudes to miracles implied in vs. 3 f. reveal the extraordinary insensitivity of sinful man to God, even when His power is on display. The manna was as unwelcome as a new coinage or a new hymn tune ('which you did not know, nor did your fathers know'!), and the sustained miracle of v. 4 seems to have aroused no particular gratitude. It was not proof that was lacking, but willingness to be convinced.

With relative affluence ahead (7 ff.) God's praise could be sung in a new key (10), but temptation would also take a new form (11 ff.). Yet it was still, at bottom, pride that was the snare: not the pride that objects to being 'pushed around', as in vs. 2 ff., but the unconscious complacency of the prosperous.

With regard to the 'iron' and 'copper' of v. 9, it was a happy irony that the chief source of these would be found in the Arabah, the tract of country between the Dead Sea and the eastern tip of the Red Sea (see on ch. 2), which was part of the 'great and terrible wilderness' (15). The most bitterly resented phase of the wanderings (Num. **21.4** ff.) had in fact traversed a region which would help to make Solomon's fortune. Some of God's best gifts to Israel (as to us) were those that were least inviting and least immediate.

Questions for further study and discussion on Deuteronomy chs. 1—8

1. 'No form; . . . only a voice' (4.12). What were the main reasons for the O.T.'s emphasis on this point, and for Israel's reluctance to accept it? In what ways is it still a live issue?
2. The N.T. quotes the last six commandments several times, but not the first four (5.6–15). Is this because it covers their subject-matter more searchingly? Study the N.T. teaching on these four areas.
3. 'What is the meaning . . .?' (6.20). Has the answer to this question anything to teach us about explaining our faith to an enquirer? Examine what it says, and how it puts it.

4. Show how Gen. 3, by its account of man's negative choice and its cost, helps to illuminate Deut. **8.3b** .What example would you choose to illustrate it positively?

Deuteronomy 9   'You are a Stubborn People'

This chapter is an important companion to the statement in 7.6 ff. on God's choice of Israel. There, they were reminded of their political insignificance; here, of their moral unworthiness (4 f.), which the rest of the chapter expounds as essentially that of their mutinous spirit. Not the sins of weakness but those of defiance are picked out here, with the Golden Calf as the most revealing example—man's outrageous footnote to the deed of union with his Maker. The breaking of the tablets by Moses (17) incidentally makes their character fully clear as the certificate and summary of this covenant (cf. 11b), not as a detached statement of the moral law. His action dramatized the threat of annulment which God had pronounced in v. 14, a sober threat which would not have broken the promise to Abraham but would have channelled it now through this one descendant of his.

Since this part of Deuteronomy was specially in our Lord's mind in His forty days of fasting, it may be that the two fasts of Moses, as covenant mediator (8) and as intercessor for a rebellious people (18,25 ff.), formed the background of His own thinking at this time. Certainly, Israel was in no less perilous a state then than in Moses' day.

As a matter of narrative technique, note the tendency to stress a subject more than a time-sequence. E.g., v. 11 adds the note of time after v. 10 has dwelt on the detail of what was given and received. Similarly, vs. 18–20 hasten to tell of the intercession, before v. 21 fills in an earlier detail (The RSV's 'Then', in v. 21, is unjustifiable; it is a circumstantial clause, i.e. 'As for the sinful thing . . .'), and vs. 22–24 pile up further sins of Israel before v. 25 picks up the threads of v. 18 again with greater fullness. This freedom to follow up a theme while the narrative pauses, or to jump ahead and return later for the missing pieces, allows the story to make its own emphases. (A classic example of the technique is in Ezra 4, where the modern reader must enclose vs. 6–23 in brackets, or lose his way entirely.) It is not hard to see where Moses wished his emphasis to fall.

Deuteronomy 10   Divine Patience

Concluding retrospects (1–11). We can be grateful for Moses' first-person account of the new covenant-tablets, since v. 4 clears up the ambiguity of Exod. **34**.28, to show that the Lord Himself inscribed them. In v. 3 the meaning may be that Moses made a chest which served until Bezalel's permanent ark was ready (Exod. **37**.1–9; cf. **40**.20), but it is more probably another example of an anticipatory detail and a delegated task (see the final comment on ch. **9** above).

The parenthesis of vs. 6 f. seems to be editorial, being in the third person—perhaps an extract from the same 'log' that Num. 33 drew upon (see comments there), v. 6 telling of a return over the same ground as Num. **33**.31. The death of Aaron is brought to mind, no doubt, through the recollection of Sinai (cf. **9**.20). In vs. 8 f. Moses is again the speaker (notice the personal touch, '*your* God'), and Sinai/Horeb is the scene, the time-note in v. 8a referring to Exod. **32**.26–29 completed by Num. **3**.14 ff. So the bracket in the RV/RSV should be closed after v. 7, not after v. 9. Moses' thought has again reverted to the crisis at the foot of Sinai and to the great intercession, which he recounts for the third time: vs. 10 f., cf. **9**.18,25.

The only right response (12–22). With the purposeful 'And now—' (a common expression in letters of O.T. times, to introduce the main topic), Moses sums up the issue before Israel, in an appeal which will reach its climax in the last paragraph of ch. **11**. In terms of treaty-making, the customary preamble and historical survey, already heard, are now followed by the 'declaration of basic principle' (von Rad), before the detailed stipulations of chs. **12—26**, and the clinching blessings and curses of chs. **27—28**.

Notice how many of the themes of the foregoing chapters are rapidly reviewed in vs. 12–22: the great commandment (12), the beneficent laws ('for your good', 13), the monotheistic faith (14), the election of Israel (15), etc., etc. It is a good exercise to search out the passages which speak again here.

Deuteronomy 11   The Only Right Response (concluded)

A loving obedience, which nevertheless takes no liberties with God, is the substance of this appeal. It is put quite directly in the exhortations of, e.g. vs. 1,13, 22,and in the frank reminders of the first and last paragraphs, but it also comes through, indirectly, in the tone and spirit of the central sections. The speaker's delight at Israel's prospect of living in direct dependence on heaven (11), after the tame predictability of Egypt, that man-made kitchen-garden (10), is not the usual human attitude, which prefers a more controllable situation. To the self-willed, the promise of v. 12 is an intrusion, and the warning of vs. 16 f. an example of unfair pressure; but

Moses speaks as a lover of God, and calls his hearers to the same commitment.

So there is no middle way contemplated. For each household the goal is total exposure to the word of God (vs. 18–20 repeat the striking demand of 6.6–9 in very similar terms), and for the nation the choice between blessing and cursing must be dramatized as a deep divide (the two mountains, Gerizim and Ebal [29] rise about 3,000 feet on either side of Shechem). But if these demands are extreme, they are realistic. They are not only true to the sovereign rights of deity, and to the best interests of His people (cf., e.g. v. 9), but they are reinforced by the fact that Israel owes her past salvation (4 ff.) and future victory (23–25) entirely to God.

Note: The parenthesis in v. 2 leaves very little room for argument over the historical setting of Deuteronomy. To see the book (as some do) as the work of later preachers, speaking to their own age in the Mosaic tradition, is to make this negative either meaningless or insincere, for its plain words would convey the exact opposite of the truth.

B. THE DETAILED REQUIREMENTS: 12—26

Deuteronomy 12
A Single Sanctuary

The multitudinous laws of the next fifteen chapters are unified by the central theme of right relationship with God. The point of the present chapter, reinforced in its opening and closing paragraphs against paganism (1–4,29–31), is that Yahweh is *One*, and His single place of worship is to proclaim the fact and keep it steadily before His people.

Notice the emphasis on His own choice of this place, a point made six times in the chapter, since human religion loves to multiply superstitions at hallowed spots, while God on the contrary elects to 'put His name and make His habitation' (5, cf. v. 11) at a focal point. 'Name' implies a well-defined self-disclosure, and 'habitation' a settled place among His people. Gilgal, Bethel and Shiloh were temporary centres, but the chosen place would not be named until Jerusalem became the site of the Temple (1 Kings 8.16,29; 9.3). This in turn was superseded when 'the Word became flesh and dwelt among us', and worship was freed from physical sanctuaries (John 1.14; 4.21,23).

The other emphasis is on joy (7,12,18), a characteristic note in Deuteronomy. Here it arises out of the twin facts of material blessings (peace, e.g. v. 10, and plenty) and the warmth of fellowship, divine and human. Note the recurrent phrase, 'before the

174

Lord' (7,12,18), and the inclusiveness of the hospitality in the same verses.

Critical study of the chapter has chiefly fastened on its practical changes of sacrificial law. Lev. 17.3 f. laid down that no animal suitable for sacrifice might be killed 'secularly', but Deut. 12.20 ff. looks forward to relaxing this. Ingenious minds have speculated that this new procedure was tailor-made for Josiah's reformation (cf. 2 Kings 23.8, etc.); but it makes perfect sense in its own terms. It took little foresight to realize that what was suited to the encampment in the wilderness would no longer serve in the enlarged territory (20) that awaited Israel. The same concern for purity of worship motivates both chapters: see Lev. 17.7; Deut. 12.13 f.

As for the need of such purity, v. 31 reminds us that this was—and remains—no doctrinaire concern. There is no limit to the deliberate cultivation of evil, once the light of God has been quenched. Man then grows to love, and even revere, 'everything which the Lord hates'.

Deuteronomy 13   Enticement to Apostasy

Unlike many penal codes, which prescribed death for comparative trivialities, God's law kept it for major outrages against the human person and, as here, against the theocracy. Note in v. 5c one of the Biblical principles of punishment: a concern for the purity of society. This does not figure much in modern theories, which give most prominence to society's physical protection, to the criminals' reform and to deterring potential offenders. The last of these is the motive in v. 11; but underlying all three paragraphs is the implied concept of retribution. The penalty is exacted 'because' (5,10) the offender has done a specific thing which deserves it, and which is satisfactorily proved against him (14). Cf. Rom. 13.3 f. On execution by stoning, see on Lev. 20.2.

The test of a prophet by his attitude to the Lord, regardless of his signs and wonders, was a live issue in the days of Jeremiah (Jer. 23.16–22) and Ezekiel (Ezek. 13), and will remain so to the end (Matt. 24.24), for even Christians can be dazzled by the miraculous. Verses 1–5 take precedence over the further test of 18.22, which applied to cases where the prophet's loyalty was harder to assess.

Note, finally, the witness of vs. 12–18 to the disinterested motive for the ritual destruction of heathen cities. Here, with the same sentence passed on an Israelite community, its character stands out as a duty that overrode all self-interest and natural compunction.

The value that God attaches to undivided, but not untested,

loyalty (3b,4) could hardly be more emphatically proclaimed—nor the difference between His valuation and, for the most part, ours. Cf., in the N.T., the unfashionable plea of 2 Cor. 6.14—7.1.

* Deuteronomy 14 Laws on Mourning, Eating and Tithing

For the forbidden mourning customs (1 f.) see on Lev. 19.28, and for the food laws (3–21) see on Lev. 11, where the list is virtually identical, and on Exod. 34.26 for v. 21c. But the opening words of our chapter (1a) give a new tone to these injunctions, making the kind of appeal which our Lord used in Matt. 5.45 for His much higher demands. They are a landmark, too, in God's revelation, as S. R. Driver points out, in assuring the individual Israelite of the sonship which had hitherto been ascribed only to the people as a whole (cf. Exod. 4.22).

In the tithe law (22–29) there are some differences from that of Num. 18, for which more than one explanation has been suggested. One is that in Jewish tradition a second tithe was given, over and above that of Num. 18, and that every third year this (or even a third tithe) provided a charitable local feast as in vs. 28 f. (see on Deut. 26.12 [Septuagint]; cf. Tobit 1.7 f.; Josephus, *Antiquities* IV. viii. 22). Alternatively, this law may have been given to supersede that of the wilderness period, adjusting the Levite's share to the more abundant produce of Canaan.

The principle of v. 29b is one of the constants of Scripture, expressed in some memorable sayings, e.g. Prov. 11.24 f.; Isa. 58.10 f.; Luke 6.38; 2 Cor. 9.6 ff. It is true often enough in the material realm; always in that of the spirit. It will be the theme of the next chapter.

* Deuteronomy 15 The Year of Release

The opening of the chapter is similar to 14.28 f. in style and spirit, and the last words of 14.29 become its refrain (15.10,18). It is an exercise in faith and charity, not in hard-headed economics, as vs. 7–11 make clear—although v. 18 precludes any pose of moral heroism. Nowhere is it clearer than here that law without love is self-defeating, for its best intentions can always provoke the worst of responses (cf. especially v. 9).

In the realm of debts and slavery an Israelite's preferential treatment (3,12) should be seen for what it claims to be, the kind of help one expects within the family ('his brother', 2,3,12). It is no unfairness to one's business acquaintances that one's dealings with them should be financially sound rather than emotionally motivated; cf. 23.19 f.

The clash between v. 4a and v. 11a is more apparent than real; the former speaks of what will happen 'if only you will obey . . .' (5), and the latter of what is in fact foreseen. Cf. John **12**.8.

The law on slavery is either more explicit at one point than that of Exod. **21**.2 ff., in mentioning the release of a woman slave as well as of a man (12), or else it has been modified in the forty years' interval. The former is more probable, as the Exodus law was chiefly concerned with a slave's marriage before or after entering the household (Exod. **21**.3 f.), a point which plays no part here. But what is vital to the whole enterprise is generosity (cf. the first paragraph, above). For lack of substantial help (as in v. 13 f.), of fellow-feeling (15) or of goodwill (18), emancipation has sometimes turned out to be more devastating than slavery itself; it is characteristic of Deuteronomy to urge that this should not happen.

The firstlings for God (**15**.19–23). This reaffirms the law of Exod. **13**.2,11–16, given in the context of the deliverance of the firstborn. The point of v. 19b is that man must not take a first cut of what is God's. Is there an implied allusion to this in our Lord's use of an unused colt for His triumphal entry?

Deuteronomy 16.1–17 The Three Great Feasts

(i) *Passover* (1–8). Certain changes have been introduced to bring out the distinction between the once-for-all deliverance from Egypt and the annual remembrance of it. Enough is retained to bring it vividly to mind (note the references to Egypt in vs. 1,3,6), but the daubing of the doorposts with blood, which was the high point of the first Passover, has been abolished: the threat to the firstborn is a thing of the past. Further, there is emphasis on 'the place which the Lord will choose' (2,6,7)—for Israel will have *arrived*. Their fathers had eaten the Passover scattered and enslaved: their sons would be free and united. (Our Lord endorsed a Jewish continuation of this line of development by eating the meal reclining; contrast John **13**.23 with Exod. **12**.11).

(ii) *Pentecost* (9–12); (iii) *Booths* (13–15). On the meaning of these feasts see on Lev. **23**.15 ff., and the last two paragraphs of the comment on Num. **28,29**. Here the characteristic concern of Moses' preaching is not so much with the externals of these occasions as with the spirit of them, warm with devotion to God and friendly care for people of all sorts (note the breadth of vs. 11,14). The 'booths' (13) are explained in Lev. **23**.42 f., and are seen in use in the lively description of Neh. **8**.14–18.

In the summary of the three feasts (16 f.) notice the emphasis on giving, as an essential part of worship (16b) and as a testimony to God's prior gifts (17). The principle of v. 17 is taken up by Paul in 1 Cor. **16.**2 as a guide to weekly offerings, not only thrice-yearly ones.

Deuteronomy 16.18—17.20 Justice and True Worship

The theme of 'Justice and only justice' (**16.**20) is interrupted in **16.**21—**17.**7 by an even greater concern of this book, namely 'Yahweh and only Yahweh'. This still speaks to us, particularly when the 'contributions' of other faiths are urged on us. God leaves no room 'beside' His altar: see **16.**21. And on the relevance of this to justice itself, see **12.**31 and comment.

The highest court (**17.**8–13). Hitherto, Moses himself had been the arbiter of hard cases (**1.**17); now his work was to pass to a judicial panel, whose composition seems intended to be both lay and priestly (9). This was how Jehoshaphat interpreted it, giving special jurisdiction to the chief priest in religious cases and to the lay governor in political ones (2 Chron. **19.**11). The high authority of their office (10–13) is upheld by Christ in Matt. **23.**2 f., and its equivalent in a non-Israelite context is expounded in Rom. **13.**1-7 and 1 Pet. **2.**13–17.

The office of a king (**17.**14–20). How prophetic a charge this was, subsequent events would show. So apt were the warnings of v. 17 to Solomon that some writers have been tempted to re-date them in a later age—forgetting that for any king, David included, wives and money meant status and power; also that the danger of choosing a foreign king (15) was an issue hardly worth raising once the monarchy was established, but an open possibility before that. As for the king's duty to copy the law (18*), there was a modified acknowledgement of it at the first king-making (1 Sam. **10.**25) and perhaps a formalized trace of this at subsequent accessions (cf. 2 Kings **11.**12), but there is no record of any king making his own copy and studying it daily. The whittling away of an absorbing activity for the whole person into a formal gesture on a public occasion is rather characteristic in human affairs.

Questions for further study and discussion on Deuteronomy chs. 9—17

1. Study Deut. **10.**12–22 along the lines suggested in the concluding comment on that section.
2. 'You shall rejoice' (**12.**7,12,18). How do the circumstances that

---

* The Septuagint, mistranslating 'copy' as 'second law' (*deuteronomion*), gave us here the word that has become the title of the book.

are shown here help to produce true joy? What other sources of it are mentioned in Scripture?

3. In **14.**1, the motive for a high standard of behaviour is that 'you are sons of the Lord . . .'. Search out other motivations in Deuteronomy which argue from the past, present or future. Is there a place for each of these in Christian preaching?

4. Deuteronomy emphasizes 'Justice . . . justice' (**16.**20) as fervently as it emphasizes love. Is it true to say that justice is the primary form that love must take in public administration?

Deuteronomy 18   Priests, Levites, Charlatans, Prophets

The support of priests and Levites (1–8). As this short passage has been something of a critical battlefield it calls for a few technical comments. (*i*) In v. 1a, the RSV adds the words 'that is', thereby creating the impression that all members of the tribe of Levi were priests. This is grammatically unnecessary (Deut. **17.**1 has the same Heb. construction to express first a small group and then a larger one). If an explanatory insertion is needed, 'and' (AV [KJV]) is fully justified and manufactures no discrepancies. (*ii*) The additional priestly right to the animal's cheeks and stomach may have been an innovation at this moment, or a confirmation of an unwritten practice. (*iii*) A *Levite's option* (6–8) to minister at the holy city (instead of, e.g. teaching in the country districts: cf. 2 Chron. **17.**9) is equated by some writers with the country priests' deportation to Jerusalem in Josiah's reformation (2 Kings **23.**8 f.)—which creates a gratuitous contradiction between Deut. **18.**7 and 2 Kings **23.**9. But it would be surprising if such a perverse equation produced no problems for those who make it!

Ritual murder and the occult (9–14). Child-sacrifice and spiritualism are placed side by side, not only here, but in Lev. **20.**1–9, where see comments. Those who would defend the one may need to ask themselves why God associated it with the other, and why He considered all magic black, from ritual murder down to fortune-telling, in the long list of 'abominable practices' here.

The coming prophet (15–22). Here is the positive gift for which the foregoing prohibition is meant to clear the way (like all God's prohibitions). Instead of dark hints from mediums and omens, Israel will have the explicit words (note the plural, vs. 18 f.) of God, open to verification (21 f.). The criterion given here, that of prediction fulfilled, needs however to be partnered by that of **13.**1–5 (see second paragraph of comment on ch. **13**). Peter and Stephen were to quote this prophecy in their proclamation of Christ (Acts **3.**22; **7.**37). For us, this passage also brings the reminder that Jesus not

179

only lived out but spoke out God's truth. We are to take His every
word as authoritative, as He Himself demanded (John 14.10).

Deuteronomy 19   Protection for the Vulnerable

Cities of refuge (1–13). Little needs to be added to the comments
already made on this subject at Num. 35. Moses adds here the
practical provision of roads (3), and an illustration of the law of
manslaughter (5). The 'three cities' of v. 2 were to be in Palestine
proper, since three had already been appointed in Transjordan
(4.41–43). The 'three other cities' (9) beyond these six were never
appointed, as far as we know, because the ideal territory promised
to Abraham 'from the river of Egypt to . . . the river Euphrates'
(Gen. 15.18) was never occupied. David subdued and took tribute
from such an area, which Solomon inherited (1 Kings 4.21), but it
remained foreign and was soon lost. Verse 9 therefore expresses a
proviso which is implied even in the most forthright of God's
promises, for these are never made to relieve us of our obligations;
only of our anxieties.

The landmark (14). This was basic enough to find mention in the
ceremony of cursing in 27.17 (15–26), and to be proverbial, not
only in Israel, but beyond (Prov. 22.28; Job 24.2, cf. the Egyptian
Amenemope, ch. vi). Land was one's livelihood, and that of one's
posterity as well.

Laws of evidence (15–21). Not only capital charges, as 17.6 might
have suggested, but all (note threefold 'any', 15) must be properly
attested. This left its mark even on the dubious trial of Jesus, where
the lack of convergent evidence exposed the inadequacy of the case
against Him. The two further clauses here, the provision for divine
arbitration (17, cf. 17.8 f.; see on Lev. 8.8) and the merciless penalties
for false witness (19,21; see also on Lev. 24.17–22) were excellent
safeguards against every contingency but one: a régime of corrupt
priests or judges. So the law gave Jezebel no difficulty (1 Kings
21.8–14), and Caiaphas little enough. This would have been no surprise
to Moses, who had no illusions about officials (16.19), or about the
coercive power of law (see on 15.1 ff.). For his definition of the spirit
in which alone the law can be truly kept, see again v. 9.

Deuteronomy 20   The Wars of the Lord

Procedure before a battle (1–9). This is the exact opposite of a
'commonsense' approach, (*a*) in its appraisal of resources, rating the
invisible above the visible (1,4); (*b*) in its concessions to the preoccupied and afraid (5–8); (*c*) in its sequence of events, whereby the

commanders are picked last (9). Yet it is not irrational: the priorities are realistic, as history showed repeatedly from Joshua to 2 Chronicles.

The 'officers' of v. 5 were assistant administrators rather than military leaders (cf. v. 9). In Exod. 5.14 the name is used for foremen, and in Deut. 1.15 for local officials. The concessions which they proclaimed in vs. 5–8 were probably designed not only to relieve personal hardship but to ensure that those who fought were the totally committed. This was certainly the motive in v. 8; and if fear is infectious, so is frustration (5–7; cf. 28.30). There is surely concern, too, for the wellbeing of society, for military values are not treated as paramount: there are others implied here to take priority over them.

Rules of war (10–20). As regards the distant cities, v. 11 is illustrated by the story of Gibeon in Josh. 9. Evidently the harsh terms of v. 13 applied only to those who chose to fight on, as Elisha's indignant question in 2 Kings 6.22 makes plain.

The distinction between cities far off and near (10–15,16–18) was not military but judicial: the nations of v. 17 were ripe for judgement, and a threat to morality (18). On the policy of extermination, see notes on ch. 3, first paragraph.

Verses 19 f. give their witness, with vs. 5–7 above, against 'total war'. Though exceptions could be decreed by God (2 Kings 3.19), this general rule for Israel introduced a restraint which, in von Rad's words, 'is probably unique in the history of the growth of a humane outlook in ancient times'.

Deuteronomy 21   The Restraint of Lawlessness

The unknown murderer (1–9). Num. 35.33 had already established that to leave a murderer alive was to make the nation a party to his crime. The present passage allows no shelter behind the fact of ignorance—nor does it provide a formal substitute for the murderer if he is known: hence the animal sacrifice must be accompanied by the vivid disclaimer of vs. 6–9. (Had Pilate heard of this ritual? More probably its own eloquence accounts for its use in both contexts.)

The woman captive (10–14). Given the fact of war, enforced marriages could be as constructive a sequel as any, if the vanquished were treated with love. The law was sensitive to the woman's plight, giving her time (13) to adjust to her situation unmolested, and protecting her afterwards from exploitation (14). The shaven head and pared nails (12) would seem to represent her farewell to her former existence (cf. Lev. 14.8 ?), as she discarded, too, the humiliation of captivity (13a), to have them replaced by the new growth and garb of her life as an Israelite. All of this acted out the Biblical marital principles of mutual respect and commitment, encouraging the attitudes that would make for a true marriage, even though (cf. v. 14a) it could not compel them.

The unloved wife (15–17). The unhappy families of Genesis (see especially Gen. **37.3** f.) are a living comment on this law, which cuts back the evils of polygamy but has no illusions about the quality of its fruits. The strong Hebrew expression, 'loved and . . . disliked' (lit. 'hated'), is the equivalent of 'loved and unloved' or of 'one loved more than the other': cf., e.g. Luke **14.26** with Matt. **10.37**.

The rebellious son (18–21). Cf. **13.**6–9, and comments on that chapter. Filial obedience (cf., e.g. Rom. **1.**30; 2 Tim. **3.**2), is the first test of a man's acceptance of higher grades of authority, on which all order and stability depend. But see Eph. **6.**4.

God's curse on the hanged (22 f.). As S. R. Driver points out, hanging in the O.T. seems to have been the sequel, more often than the method, of execution (note the sequence in vs. 22 f., as in Josh. **10.**26 f.; 1 Sam. **31.**8,10; but 2 Sam. **21.**9)—which emphasizes its purpose as an exposure to contempt and execration. This is the passage which Paul quotes to show that Christ hanging on the cross became 'for our sake an accursed thing' (Gal. **3.**13, NEB). See also on Num. **25.**4.

Deuteronomy 22

Miscellaneous Laws, Social, Sexual, and Symbolic

Chapters **22**—**25** contain a profusion of brief laws, some grouped round a common subject (as in vs. 13–30 here), but most of them unarranged. The kindliest and the most unsparing, the lightest and weightiest, are heaped together without apology, since all are from God, although the reader is not excused the task of judging their relative importance and their place in the scheme (cf. Matt. **23.**23). See the opening comments on Lev. **19.**

Verses 1–4,6–8 are good examples of the partnership of love and law. Love is the motive in each case, but law directs it into wise and practical forms—e.g. summoning us to active help instead of neutrality or passive sympathy (2–4), teaching us self-restraint and respect for life (6 f.), and laying upon us the duty of taking precautions for other people's safety (8).

Verse 5 arises out of the scriptural concern to guard the built-in distinctions of God's creation. It does not specify particular forms of dress for the two sexes; these will legitimately vary with time and place. What is condemned is the perverted misuse of current custom; and since this is 'an abomination to the Lord' we are to regard this law as permanent, and respect its wisdom. The N.T. is no less emphatic against all tampering with sexual distinctions (cf., e.g. Rom. 1.26 f.; 1 Cor. 6.9, AV[KJV], RV).

Verses 9–12, however, are laws whose symbolism served a temporary purpose, like that of the food laws, to educate Israel in the pursuit of purity. Cf. the comments on Lev. 19.23 and (for v. 12) Num. 15.37–41.

Laws on chastity (13–30). Although the sentence of death could be commuted or waived (cf. Matt. 1.19; John 8.7), the fact that most of these laws carried it shows the intensity of God's concern over pre-marital loss of virginity (13–21), adultery (22–24), rape (25–27), fornication (28 f.) and incest (30). Note that although marriage largely made amends for the fornication of vs. 28 f., it did not make full amends (29a), and the couple were required to stand by the lifelong obligations that were implied in the sexual act (29b). With this serious estimate of this kind of offence, cf. 1 Cor. 6.13b–20.

Deuteronomy 23   'Closed are its Gates to Sin'

Membership of the assembly (1–8). These provisions should be read, not as rebuffs for the handicapped, but as stipulations designed to guard the Church of the O.T., and to express in vivid physical (1), social (2) and historical terms (3–8) its calling as a company of the redeemed, without blemish or reproach, a people apart and yet not a wholly closed community (cf. 'the tenth generation', 3; 'the third generation', 8). Verse 1 incidentally offered Israel protection against the influence of cruel contemporary practices (see also on 25.11 f.), and the rare word for 'bastard' in v. 2 may mean the child of an incestuous marriage: a further discouragement, if so, of deliberate social decadence. Other passages show that the genuine seeker, whatever his condition or origin, was always admitted: cf. v. 1 with Isa. 56.3–5 (see also on Lev. 21), and cf. v. 3 with the unreserved welcome to Ruth the Moabitess. Such a welcome was by grace; such a law made grace visible.

Seemliness in the camp (9–14). Although hygiene was well served through the rule of vs. 12 f., holiness, not health, was the main concern. It is the same theme as in ch. 20, where victory depends on 'the Lord . . . that goes with you' (20.4). The words of v. 14 are as pointedly relevant to the Church as to the armies of Israel.

The runaway slave (15 f.). This humane law is in striking contrast

183

to other ancient codes, which fixed rewards for returning a slave, and penalties (even death: Hammurabi 16) for harbouring one.

Cultic immorality (17 f.). Business, religion and lust pulled together in the Canaanite cults, which hallowed cultic fornication as a fertility spell for the crops and cattle. 'Cult prostitute' is lit. 'holy woman' (17a) and 'holy man' (17b)—a pungent commentary on pagan thought. 'Dog' (18) is a contemptuous term for the male prostitute.

Usury (19 f.). Verse 20 shows that lending at interest is not intrinsically wrong, only inappropriate within the 'family'. Lev. 25.35 f. indicates the context that is in mind: not a business venture seeking capital but a poor man seeking help, whose plight must not be your profit.

Vows (21–23). The note of caution found here reappears with a characteristic addition of verbal pepper in Eccles. 5.4–6. Peter seems to echo the principle of v. 22 in his rebuke to Ananias in Acts 5.4.

Hospitality and its abuse (24 f.). Another reminder of the relevance of love (here in the form of elementary courtesy) to every level of human relations.

Deuteronomy 24 — Firmness and Kindness

Divorce (1–4). The RSV corrects the translations of the AV(KJV), RV here, bringing to light the fact that the first 'if' launches a series of hypothetical events leading straight to the 'then' of v. 4. I.e., the concern of the passage is not to recommend divorce in certain situations (as in AV[KJV], RV) but to decree that if such a step is taken it must be irrevocable. It thereby protected a wife against being virtually lent to another man, and it discouraged hasty action. So, while permitting but not commanding an existing practice (as our Lord pointed out: Matt. 19.7 f.) it brought that practice under better control and upheld the dignity of marriage. Jeremiah incidentally used this law in a heart-searching analogy throughout Jer. 3.

'*A kindness in His justice . . .*' (5–22). There is perhaps no better demonstration than this chapter of the guiding concerns of God's law. Where it is precise and hard (concerning the divorcee, 4; or the kidnapper, 7; or quarantine, 8 f.; or non-transferable guilt, 16), it is no less beneficent than where it is strikingly generous. All the rulings are examples of true justice, in that they are matched to the actualities of the case, although some of these are matters that count for little in official human reckoning, e.g. the founding of a happy marriage (5), the self-respect of the man who begs a loan from you (10 f.), or the fact that a poor man 'sets his heart upon' getting his wages punctually (15). It is specially worth noting that by making these benefits a matter of law, not merely of exhortation, God secured them to their recipients as of right. He has always liked to turn His beggars into princes (1 Sam. **2**.8).

Note: Vs. 8 f.: The leprosy rules are found in Lev. **13** f. The allusion to Miriam (9) was presumably to emphasize that no exceptions could be made: not even for an exalted victim or intercessor, or to avert great inconvenience (Num. **12**.14 f.).

Deuteronomy 25   Miscellaneous Laws

Forty stripes (1–3). Paul's five beatings with 'the forty lashes less one' (2 Cor. **11**.24) were controlled by this law; the custom of omitting one stroke had come in to protect the court—not the prisoner!—from the risk of miscounting. In this passage, however, the penalty must be regulated 'in proportion to his offence' (2, cf. Luke **12**.47 f.), and the offender's human dignity must be respected: note the wording of the important caveat of v. 3b, and cf. the similar concern in **24**.10 f.

The unmuzzled ox (4). Paul's use of this verse to prove the duty of the Church to pay its workers (1 Cor. **9**.8 ff.) is an important witness to the relevance of the Mosaic law above and beyond its immediate context. Enough is commanded elsewhere to uphold the literal meaning of such a rule as this (e.g. Exod. **23**.12; Deut. **22**.6 f., cf. Prov. **12**.10), but God's self-consistency forbids us to stop there: we must go on in our giving to accept His valuation of human beings as worth 'much more' to Him than His other creatures.

Levirate marriage (5–10). This institution, which owes its name to the Latin word *levir*, brother-in-law, demonstrates the primacy of the family in Israelite law, overriding personal inclination and convenience. It incidentally shows that physical descent was not everything; a family was not merely a genetic but a legal or spiritual entity, and its continuance did not depend on the single thread of heredity. Twice in our Lord's ancestry this provision came into effect: Gen. **38**; Ruth **4**.

Indecency (11 f.). A somewhat similar item is found in the Middle Assyrian Laws (A. 8). The Biblical law seems deliberately framed to ignore extenuating circumstances, and so to fix absolute limits to what is permissible in an emergency. A general implication is that *not* all is 'fair in love and war'; a particular one is that God insists on the privacy of the sexual organs, and (as **23**.1 confirms) abhors interference with them.

Commercial honesty (13–16). The law is realistic in banning, not

185

merely the actual use of false weights and measures, but the possession of them (the reader can reflect on this principle and possible applications of it: cf. Rom. 13.14b).

Amalek (17–19). As in 23.3–6, the events of the wilderness are treated with special seriousness, as being a time of decision and destiny—a miniature of His whole drama of judgement and salvation, with life or death confronting each participant. Cf. the treatment of the Exodus theme in Isa. 40 ff. and in 1 Cor. 10 and Heb. 3 f.

Deuteronomy 26   'Flowing with Milk and Honey'

Firstfruits, and the story behind them (1–11). This is evidently the other half, the worshipper's part, of the 'Easter Day' ritual commanded in Lev. 23.9–14 (where see comment). The prescribed 'response' (5) enlarged the worshipper's horizon far beyond the bounds of simple gratitude for the promise of another annual crop. The wonder of seedtime and harvest is overshadowed by the greater miracle, the rise of a populous nation from the most meagre beginnings (5), and the story of its peril, rescue and triumphant arrival in the promised land. This is the Biblical perspective, rejoicing in 'all the good which the Lord . . . has given' (11), but still more in the facts of vocation and redemption. In the phrase 'a wandering Aramaean' the reference is to Jacob, most of whose family ties were with Paddan-aram. 'Wandering' is not the equivalent of 'nomad', a man whose roaming is purposeful, but of a creature in jeopardy like the 'lost' sheep of Psa. 119.176.

A declaration after the three-year tithe (12–15). (The Septuagint of v. 12 reads '. . . the second tithe you shall give to the Levites . . .', supporting, if it is reliable, a point discussed at 14.22–29, above.) On the forbidden activities of v. 14, see on Lev. 21, especially the second paragraph of comment. As for the prayer of v. 15, its position is significant, following the account of shared wealth and loyal obedience (12–14), since this is the scriptural sequence: e.g. 'Give, and it will be given to you' (Luke 6.38); 'Honour the Lord with . . . the firstfruits . . .; then your barns will be filled with plenty' (Prov. 3.9 f.). Examples of this principle, in matters spiritual as well as material, are found in every section of the Bible.

The peroration (16–19). The whole chapter has played its part in concluding the great exposition of the covenant, begun in ch. 5, by turning its attention towards the crowning blessing, the promised land. Now comes the challenge to work out in detail (16) the implications of the mutual commitment which is the core of the covenant ('You have declared . . . and the Lord has declared . . .', 17 f.).

186

Note the stress on 'this day' (16,17,18), for the original covenant was not part of a dead past (5.3)—there is no such thing with God's deeds: Eccles. 3.14, cf. Luke 20.38—and therefore the new generation must be confronted with it afresh. See 27.9 f.; 29.1; and for the Christian, Heb. 3.13-15.

Questions for further study and discussion on Deuteronomy chs. 18—26

1. 'That same prophet shall die' (**18.20**). What kinds of offences attracted this penalty in Deuteronomy, and what purposes was it meant to serve (e.g. **19.13,20** . . .)?
2. 'You may not withhold your help' (**22.3**). Follow up this line of thought, to see how far it is taken in the O.T. (e.g. Exod. **23.4 f.**; Prov. **24.11,12,17**; **25.21**; . . .) and in the N.T.
3. In the comment on **24.5-22** it is claimed that the 'precise and hard' enactments in that chapter are as beneficent as the obviously generous ones. Do the examples given there bear this out? If they do, can the same be said of the laws outside this chapter?
4. The scriptural sequence, 'Give and it will be given to you', is mentioned in the comment on **26.12-15** as one that can be illustrated from every section of the Bible, in matters spiritual as well as material. Is this so?

3. THE LAW PRESSED HOME TO ISRAEL: Deuteronomy 27,28

Deuteronomy 27

'. . . The Words of this Law very plainly'

Word and sacrament: monument and feast (1–8). In Moses' day it was common for an emperor to insist that his vassals should exhibit copies of his treaties with them, and have them regularly read in public. God decreed both these forms of reminder: the first, as here, being the display of the written law, clinched by a sacred meal, and the second being its public reading, as laid down in **31.10** ff. If this is one 'fingerprint' of the antiquity of the chapter, the command to build an altar on Mount Ebal (4), near Shechem, is another; for this strategic spot was well suited to celebrate an invasion, but was not destined to be the national sanctuary.

Back to the present (9 f.). Note the return to 'this day (9) . . . this day' (10), to counterbalance the emphasis of this chapter on the future, 'over the Jordan' (2,4,12). The covenant must not be a dream projected towards Canaan, any more than it must be a bare

187

memory of Sinai (see on **26.16**–19), for salvation may be rooted in the past and crowned in the future, but its effective moment is 'now': cf. 2 Cor. **6.2**.

The ceremonial blessing and cursing (11–26). On the dramatic setting for this, see on **11.29**. The imperial treaties of this time were reinforced with curses for disobedience and blessings for obedience, as here. It is another feature that fits the period. Here, to be sure, only the curses are actually enumerated, but the disposing of the tribes on opposite hills, with their two roles broadly corresponding to their ancestors' high or low ranking (the disgraced Reuben, the handmaids' sons and the youngest son of Leah being assigned to the mount of cursing), confirms that the ceremony presented both alternatives. And this is true of the next chapter, where Moses returns to 'this day' (**28.1**) and his present audience. The twelve curses here give special emphasis to offences which tend to escape human justice (either through secrecy [15,17,18,24] or through judicial corruption [19,25]), and to those that strike at the roots of society by flouting authority human and divine (16,26), or sexual decency (20–23). These are still the points where national decadence tends to begin and grow.

Deuteronomy 28

'All These Blessings . . . All These Curses'

Important as were the procedures planned in ch. **27** for a future occasion, it was the present that was paramount and that kept breaking into Moses' discourse (**27.1,9,10**: 'this day'). Chapter **28.1** can be read straight on from those interjections, and treats the hearers of Moses as bound up with the Israel of every generation ('you . . . you . . . your . . . your').

It is perhaps the most eloquent and moving chapter in an unusually eloquent book. Its structure is simple, consisting basically of two matching paragraphs of blessing and cursing in almost identical terms (1–6,15–19), suited to the kind of antiphonal ceremony that was described in **27.12** ff., each of which is then expanded in a longer prophetic discourse (7–14,20–68).

The leading themes of Deuteronomy are prominent in the passages of blessing (prosperity, victory and [9 f.] vocation), and are used to add to the poignancy of the negative passages (e.g. vs. 47,48,63). The latter are built up with extraordinary skill, not only in surpassing one climax with another, but in varying the large-scale descriptions with intimate touches of terror and pathos—e.g. vs. 32,34,37, and notably vs. 65 ff.

Still more impressive, however, is the fact that some of the worst of these calamities are encountered again, not as prophecy, but as history: cf. especially vs. 37,53–57,65, with the harrowing testimony of Lam. 4. On the relapse into savagery under siege, H. Butterfield's chapter on 'Human Nature in History' (*Christianity and History*, ch. 2) is illuminating, especially in pointing out the part played by 'the orderings and arrangements of a healthy society' in concealing from us 'the volcano that lies in human nature', which can burst into activity all too easily when there is a serious enough shift in our circumstances.

4. THE COVENANT'S PERENNIAL CHALLENGE: Deuteronomy 29—31

Deuteronomy 29   Covenant Renewal

This rededication of Israel to its bond of union with the Lord is the immediate purpose of Moses' farewell address, and the whole book therefore displays the pattern of a contemporary covenant ceremony, with its preamble and historical review (chs. 1—4), its general and particular requirements (chs. 5—11, 12—26), its preservation in writing (10.1–5; 27.1–8; 31.24 f.), its periodic proclamation (31.10–13) and its reinforcement by curses and blessings (27.11—28.68). For God's covenant refuses to be relegated to the past (cf. 5.2 f. and note); it binds the new generation, summoned to take the oath of allegiance ('the sworn covenant', 12), and it reaches forward and outward to 'him who is not here with us this day' (15). The last phrase may have been in mind when our Lord prayed 'not . . . for these only, but also for those who are to believe in Me through their word' (John 17.20)—embracing the whole circle of the covenanted throughout time and space (John 17.23), as present together to His view.

But there is no glossing over the immediate situation, in which Israel is as dense and disobedient as, one day, Isaiah would find her, and as she would still be in the gospel age (cf. v. 4 with Isa. 6.9 f. and its quotation by Jesus and Paul in Matt. 13.14 f. and Acts 28.26 f.). The reason for this is stated both in terms of the sinner's *incapacity* to see what stares him in the face (cf. what is said of the natural eyes in vs. 2 f., and of the eyes of the understanding in v. 4, which only God can open), and of his *defiance* of God's will (18 f.), for which he is wholly accountable.

The N.T. takes up the warning of v. 18 in Heb. 12.15, where the familiar phrase a 'root of bitterness' needs the present context to clarify its meaning. What sounds there like a mere provocation to

189

dissension or lowered standards is shown here to mean a prolific and stubborn source of apostasy. The phrase 'moist and dry alike' (19) is a characteristic mention of opposite extremes to denote a complete range of things, implying here that the judgement on such an apostasy would sweep away the whole nation, the innocent with the guilty. The threat of 'an overthrow like that of Sodom' (23) was all too nearly realized even in Isaiah's day (Isa. **1.**7–9), a full century before the Exile.

Verse 29 is one of the key statements of the scope and purpose of revelation, to be pondered for the limits it lays down, the assurances it offers, and the end it has in view. It should be the remembered motto of every theologian, preacher and student of the Word.

Deuteronomy 30 'With All Your Heart'

The promise of restoration (1–10). If the curses outweighed the blessings in ch. **28,** this passage shows grace superabundant where sin abounded. Note the 'when', not 'if', in v. 1; God knew what they would choose.

He knew also the shallowness of a repentance only born of hardship (cf. Hos. **6.**4; **7.**14); hence the necessity of the proviso repeated in vs. 2b,6b,10b, and of an inward work of grace to make it possible. The promise of v. 6 (complementing the command of **10.**16) is essentially that of the New Covenant which Jeremiah would prophesy in Jer. **31.**33. Those who point out, rightly enough, how little the covenant of Josiah's day touched the heart of Israel, must not blame Deuteronomy which prompted it; for no book of the O.T. emphasizes heart religion more.

The accessible Word (11–14). This memorable passage takes us gently to task for making a mystery of what God has made plain, just as the great statement of **29.**29 rebukes our hankering after what He has kept secret. Here is the true function of the law, as God's wisdom broken up small for man, for repetition and reflection (as in **6.**6 f.) which will issue in action (14). But this bringing of the word within man's reach was only a foretaste, as the N.T. shows. The pre-existent Word Himself would become flesh (John **1.**14), and Paul would be able to re-expound our passage in explicit terms of Christ, brought down from heaven and up from the dead (a realm even more inaccessible than 'beyond the sea'), and in terms of the gospel confessed and believed, to issue in salvation (Rom. **10.**5–10).

'Therefore choose life' (15–20). Once more, law and love are named in partnership (16), as in the teaching of the N.T. (e.g. John **14.**15; Rom. **13.**10). It is only when law is treated as the means of

salvation that it is brought into conflict with the gospel (e.g Rom. 10.5–10, as above).

So 'life and good' (15) were man's to choose (19) but not to earn. The O.T. itself would bear witness to this and to salvation by grace through faith (e.g. Psa. 130; Psa. 143.2,7,8), just as the N.T. would call us to the good deeds that follow salvation (e.g. Rom. 8.4; Eph. 2.8–10). In our passage the unit is the nation, and the issues are stated in terms of its inheritance. But the equation in v. 20 is true for the one or the many: 'loving the Lord . . . means life'.

Deuteronomy 31   Changing Leadership, Unchanging Law

The transience of the most ageless of men is felt with some pathos in v. 2. So the paragraphs of this chapter alternate between the themes of proper change (1–8, 14 f., 23) and proper permanence. Moses' uplifting words to Israel and Joshua in vs. 3–8 were to remain in Joshua's memory and be divinely brought back to him on the eve of invasion (Josh. 1.6 ff.). How wholeheartedly Moses handed over to him can be judged from Num. 27.15 ff., where the appointment is shown as the answer to his own prayer (see comments there).

Verses 9–13,24–29. The periodic reading of the law, which used to be thought the fancy of a later age, accorded in fact with the conditions laid down in imperial treaties of the time of Moses, as did the depositing of this document in the sanctuary (cf. vs. 24–26). Note, too, the calling of 'heaven and earth to witness' (28), which corresponds, but in a very different form, to the clause which summoned various gods as witnesses to those agreements. (This feature persisted in the later treaties.)

So God turned familiar patterns to good account, bringing out the strongest features of the spoken and written word—the spoken having the direct appeal that a living voice can make to a great assembly, and the written having the accuracy that is needed for a binding agreement or constitution.

To all this, instructively enough, God added the special impact of song (19,21 f., 30), with its grip on the memory and its demand for expression ('it will live unforgotten in the mouths'—not at the back of the minds—'of their descendants' [21]). It is still one of the many good reasons for using song in worship and instruction, and for seeing that the song is striking and substantial.

191

Deuteronomy 32 — The Song of Moses

This poem should be read with its object in mind: to be a standing witness to Israel of the sin and folly of apostasy, which God could see 'already forming' in His people's mind (31.21). So the past tenses of vs. 15–18,19–21, are 'prophetic perfects', referring chiefly to coming events which were already present to Him, although indeed Israel had turned to demons and false gods even in the wilderness (Exod. 32.1; Lev. 17.7; Num. 25.2). Those who date the song later than Moses, to account for its allusions to an Israel corrupted by prosperity (15) and chastened by defeat (36), ignore this predictive, forewarning purpose (see especially 31.20 f. for these very points.)

The pattern is as follows:

(i) *Introduction* (1–3). On the appeal to heaven and earth (1), see on 31.28. Cf. 30.19; Isa. 1.2.

(ii) *Generous God, graceless people* (4–9). 'The Rock' (4) is a favourite term in this song (15,18,30 f., 37) and in many others, evocative of all that is enduring (Isa. 26.4), towering (Psa. 61.2) and protecting (Psa. 62.2); yet it carries no suggestion of the impersonal —see vs. 6,18. 'Sons of Israel' is in the standard text of v. 8, but the Septuagint seems to have read 'Sons of *El*' (God) in the text it translated, and it is followed by the RSV. If this is right (it may not be), it contrasts the heathen, under the tutelage of principalities and powers (cf. Dan. 10.13,20 f.), with Israel which enjoys the loving care of God Himself. In any case, the disputed meaning of v. 8 should not distract attention from its remarkable companion, v. 9 (strange treasure for God, then and now!).

(iii) *Loving nurture* (10–14) *and careless scorn* (15–18). In v. 10 'the apple of His eye' means 'the pupil . . .' In the beautiful picture of the eagle and its young (11), Moses employed one metaphor ('flutters . . .') which had portrayed God's Spirit creatively moving over the waters in Gen. 1.2, and another ('bearing them . . .') which God had used in Exod. 19.4 of transporting His people out of their enemies' reach to meet Him at His chosen place. 'Jeshurun' (15, cf. 33.5,26; Isa. 44.2) has the sound of an affectionate name based on the word 'right' (cf. 4b)—sadly ironical here. The demon-worship of v. 17 is seen in more terrible colours in Psa. 106.37, and an unwelcome sequel to the 'new gods' is recorded in Judg. 5.8.

(iv) *Provocation and counter-provocation* (19–27). How purposeful is God's harshness can be seen by comparing v. 21 with Rom.

10.19; **11.**11 ff.; and how restrained it is, from vs. 26 f.; cf. Ezek. **36.**23–28.

(v) *God and the no-gods* (28–42). The argument of the section is that although a final overthrow of Israel could only be the Lord's doing (30, cf. v. 26)—for the heathen gods are worse than useless (31–33)—the heathen themselves would misconstrue this (27–29). Therefore, the final reckoning will leave no room for doubt, and the reversal will be complete (34–42). Note the emphasis on divine retribution ('vengeance', 'recompense', 'requite'), which is taken up in Rom. **12.**19b. Note, too, in v. 39 the forerunner of the great monotheistic statements of Isa. **44.**8; **45.**5, etc. The song, as God intended (**31.**19), was the seed of some of the profoundest teachings of both Testaments.

(vi) *Doxology* (43). If this should be thought too fierce, see Luke **18.**7 f.; but it is judicial vengeance, not human spite (Luke **9.**54 f.; Rom. **12.**19).

The song delivered; the singer dismissed (44–52). Hard as this decree may seem, the fact remains that henceforth Moses' words were to be his greatest legacy, eclipsing even his deeds. It was the right moment to be called away.

Deuteronomy 33   The Blessing of the Tribes

The companion to this chapter is Jacob's blessing of his sons in Gen. **49.** By definition, it looks ahead to their settlement in Canaan, and is therefore not to be dated by the conditions it predicts. (On the name Jeshurun [5], see on **32.**15.)

The prayer for *Reuben* (6) foresaw the danger of the tribe's decline and fall, exposed as it was to Moab, east of Jordan. But Judg. **5.**15 f. shows Reuben refusing the costly involvement with his fellow Israelites through which this prayer might have been answered.

Judah's blessing (7) should read as in the RV: '. . . with his hands he contended for himself; And [or But] thou shalt be a help . . .'— i.e. his danger, as a great tribe settled in the south, would be isolation and self-sufficiency. Largely through David, Judah's leading role in Israel as foretold in Gen. **49.**10 was indeed fulfilled. Incidentally, an echo of the missing Simeon's name may be intended in the opening word 'Hear' (cf. Gen. **29.**33, margin), for Simeon was destined to be merged with Judah. See on Num. **26.**14.

Levi (8–11) was perhaps tested and striven with (8) in the persons of Moses and Aaron, for whom Meribah was a fateful spot (**32.**51). The renouncing of family claims in v. 9 probably refers to the incident of Exod. **32.**29. It may also be a reminder of the total dedication still required of them—anticipating that of the Christian disciple. Note also the teaching duties of this tribe (10a); see references in the comment on Lev. **10.11**. For 'Thummim', etc. (8) see on Exod. **28**.30; Lev. **8**.8.

Commenting more briefly on the rest: the Temple was to lie just within *Benjamin's* border (and its courts apparently in Judah); hence the allusions to his favoured lot (12). 'His dwelling' may therefore mean 'God's dwelling' on Benjamin's hills, and the Christian can see his own privilege foreshadowed here (John **14**.23). *Joseph* (13–17), represented by *Ephraim* and *Manasseh* (17), was to occupy the 'choicest' part of the land: extensive, central and very fertile. Yet Hosea would have to say, 'All his riches can never offset the guilt he has incurred' (Hos. **12**.8).

Zebulun and *Issachar* (18 f.) were to live in the north, as were the remaining tribes of this chapter, except *Gad* (20 f.), which settled east of Jordan. In v. 19 the RSV has gratuitously inserted 'their', whereas the reference *may* be to the temple mount (Exod. **15**.17; Isa. **2**.3). In any case 'Galilee of the Gentiles' is called to bless the nations that enrich it (19); and we may remember that Zebulun was to include Nazareth (cf. Isa. **9**.1–7).

On the aggressive *Dan* (22), see Judg. **18**. *Naphtali's* 'lake' (23) was the Sea of Galilee. *Asher* ('Happy') (24) seems not to have lived up to its great possibilities. Did the refused challenge of Judg. **5**.17 become a habit?

The doxology (26–29) owes its magnificence partly to its exuberant vitality (e.g. 26,29b), but even more to its great range of vision, taking in height and depth, the fierce and the tender, blessings of peace and of war, defence and attack. God, to Moses, was no nebulous or neutral dignitary.

Deuteronomy 34 The Death of Moses

The *narrative*, as elsewhere, speaks of Moses in the third person, and v. 10 implies that it was written a longish time after his death. But Moses' own words, the bulk of the book, were written by himself and carefully preserved (31.24–26). See also on Num. **12**.3.

Two traditional sites for v. 1, Jebel Neba and Jebel Osha, are discussed by G. T. Manley (*The Book of the Law*, pp. 63 f.), who writes of the second of these, 'The view from this peak corresponds so minutely with the description here given as to impress anyone who has been privileged to see it'. After an eyewitness account of the panorama, this author concludes, 'The description is as true as the view is marvellous'.

It is hard to resist a comparison between this mountain scene and that of the Temptation (Matt. **4.8**). Here, the One who 'showed him all the land' (1) is the patient, scrupulous Lord whose best gifts are responsibilities not lightly granted (4) or lightly taken up (for Canaan was still an enemy stronghold), but are part of a design that is bigger than personal hopes and disappointments, and than death itself (see Luke **9.30**). In the other scene the deceiver offers power and glory for a single gesture. But the glory is false, and the gesture would cost the One of whom it is asked all that He owes elsewhere, and all that He is. It was the same in Eden, and the pattern is still unaltered.

The book ends by looking forward as well as back, for the future was in good hands. 'The spirit of wisdom' which filled Joshua (9) is elsewhere indicated to be *the* Spirit (Num. **27.18**). Even the note in vs. 10 ff. on the uniqueness of Moses as a prophet has its own content of hope, in view of the reiterated promise of **18.15,18**, which was to live on in the expectation of Israel (John **1.21**: Acts **3.22**) until it was fulfilled beyond all imagining.

Questions for further study and discussion on Deuteronomy chs. 27—34

1. The curse of **27.26** must have seemed too sweeping to be seriously faced by most of its readers, for whom the curse of **21.23** was perhaps more of a talking-point after the crucifixion. Paul was enabled to wrestle with the truth of both curses. Follow his reasoning in Gal. **3** to its triumphant conclusion.
2. '. . . Till you are destroyed' (**28.45**). In view of v. 46, in what sense should we take this? Study the relation between God's covenant and His judgement in this chapter and in Hos. **1—3** and Rom **9—11**.
3. With a reference Bible (RV references are the fullest) find out how much the Song of Moses (ch. **32**) shaped the language and thought of later writers.
4. Compare the blessings of the tribes in ch. **33** with those of Gen. **49**. What can we learn from this of the 'open-endedness' of God's promises and warnings (cf. Jer. **18.1–10**)?

Introduction to the Historical Books

Four of the major historical books, namely Joshua, Judges, Samuel and Kings form the Former Prophets in the second main section of the Hebrew Bible. We would include Chronicles, Ezra and Nehemiah, and possibly Ruth and Esther amongst the historical books, although these are all placed in the third section of the Hebrew canon, the Writings.

But even this enlarged list does not include all the books which have a historical basis, for at least three of the books of the Pentateuch (Genesis, Exodus and Numbers) could come within this category. Indeed, it would be fair to say that the whole biblical revelation is a revelation in history, it is certainly not the creation of theologians. There is a revelation of God and His activity in the affairs of men and nations which can appropriately be called 'progressive revelation' (c.f. Heb. 1.1f.). However, the emphasis must be placed on the second word, the movement is from God to man, not vice versa. The implication of this is that there is a divine purpose in and behind the events of Israel's history—biblical history is teleological in character (i.e. motivated and directed towards a particular end).

Some explanation must be ventured as to why the Hebrews included apparently historical books amongst the Prophets. Possibly it was because these books were believed to have been written in prophetic circles, or because prophets such as Gad and Nathan, Elijah and Elisha, etc. figure prominently in them. But a deeper explanation lies in the conviction that in the historical books, the fundamental principles concerning God and His requirements are declared as clearly as in the prophetic oracles. The prophets could and did declare 'Thus says the Lord', but the mind of God was equally apparent in His judgements or blessings in the facts of history. For this reason E. J. Young has rightly spoken of 'interpretative history'. The writers were not concerned to document every fact of history, they were selective, and could pass over a king of undoubted secular importance, like Omri, in comparative silence (1 Kings 16.23–28), whilst giving attention to the humble women who ministered to Elijah and Elisha and to the testimony of a slave-girl (2 Kings 5.2f.). Modern historians might regard this as unbalanced, but the Hebrew historians were perfectly entitled to their point of view. Their purpose was primarily religious; to teach and to illustrate the lesson that the way of loyal obedience to God brings blessing, whilst the opposite pathway leads to disaster. G. W. Anderson aptly comments, 'the historian ... is three parts preacher'.

Possibly this helps to explain the anonymity of most of the writers. They were not in the least concerned to draw attention to themselves, their concern was for the honour of God. Modern authors could take this leaf out of their books! We know of Ezra and Nehemiah, and Samuel, Gad and Nathan are mentioned by name (1 Sam. **10.25**; 1 Chron. **29.29**; 2 Chron. **9.29**), but that is all. Their sources are more clearly defined, they include:

  i. The Book of Jashar (Josh. **10.**13; 2 Sam. **1.**18)
 ii. The 'Court History' of David (2 Sam. chs. **9–20**; 1 Kings chs. **1,2**).
iii. The Acts of Solomon (1 Kings **11.41**)
 iv. The Book of the Chronicles of the kings of Judah and the Book of the Chronicles of the Kings of Israel, mentioned respectively fifteen and seventeen times by the editor of the books of Kings.

To this list we must probably add references to the prophetic narratives and the Temple archives.

Further details may be found in the Introduction to the individual books. But as a general comment on the historicity of the whole, note the words of G. T. Manley: 'The treatment of the Old Testament history by Christ should be carefully studied. He never cast doubt upon its main outlines or its minutest details. He mentions the incident of David and the shewbread (Mark **2.**26), the glory of Solomon (Matt. **6.**29), the visit of the Queen of Sheba (Matt. **12.**42), Elijah's mission to the widow of Zarephath (Luke **4.**26) and the healing of Naaman (Luke **4.**27). He believed in its historical truthfulness, and we may unhesitatingly do the same.' Our ever-increasing knowledge, through archaeological research, of the contemporary world of the ancient Near-East, leads us to the same conclusion.

TRIBAL DIVISIONS IN ISRAEL

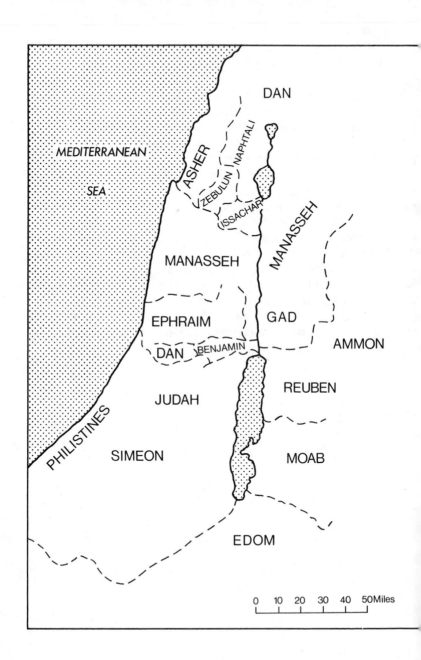

Joshua

INTRODUCTION

Joshua, like the other books treated in this volume, and numerous others in the O.T., is anonymous. It is wiser and more reverent to accept this fact than to try to find an author. It is also unnecessary to ask when it took its present form, for the matter in it is very old, often contemporary with the events described.

It is not a history of the Conquest, but falls into three clearly distinct sections:

(*i*) The mighty acts of God during the Conquest (chs. **1—12**);
(*ii*) The fulfilment of God's promise (chs. **13—22**);
(*iii*) A warning for the future (chs. **23, 24**).

Joshua 1

Joshua's appointment as Moses' successor is recorded in Num. **27**.18—23 (Deut. **34**.9); the reasons behind it will be found in Ex. **17**.8—13; **24**.13; **32**.17; **33**.11; Num. **14**.6—10.

Although Joshua knew that the conquest of Canaan could not begin until Moses was taken, his death was a heavy blow. There is a double call to courage: physical, as the military leader (6); and moral, in the keeping of the Law (7). God's giving waits on our readiness to accept (3); He never gives us blessings merely to be stored away in a spiritual bank waiting till we think we need them.

A careful study of the times involved in ch. **2** will show that the chapter must be fitted in after **1**.10—this is not unusual in Hebrew historical writing. The "three days" (11) are counted from the spies' return. Note the balance between God's guidance and human wisdom. Joshua was to enjoy special guidance (**5**.13—15, *etc.*), but he had also to acquaint himself with as much Scripture as then existed (7,8). The same principle holds good for us, except that as there is more Scripture for general guidance, we are likely to get less special guidance.

Palestine is not a country where military operations were possible the year round. We are not to think of the two-and-a-half tribes as separated completely from their families for six years or more; see

14.7,10 (just under 39 years elapsed between Kadesh Barnea and the crossing of the Jordan). There will have been "home leave" for some outside the campaigning season, while a flow of young men will have replaced the ageing, killed and wounded. The answer of the two-and-a-half tribes illustrates the principle that the true leader must always be out ahead of those he leads. From these tribes themselves we learn that God has no favourites. If we ask for special favours, we shall find that we are expected to pay a special price for them (*cf.* Num. **32**). They were also to learn too late that their unwise material asking brought spiritual loss.

"Moses the servant of the Lord" (1): "servant" means "slave". This is the same title of honour as borne by the prophets (Amos **3.**7), Paul (Rom. **1.**1, *etc.*), and our Lord (Isa. **52.**13, *etc.*).

Joshua 2

It was as right and proper for Joshua to send his spies as it had been for Moses earlier (Num. **13.**1,2, Deut. **1.**22,23). Normally God does not want us to be ignorant of what we have to face. The young men were betrayed, not by clothes or language, but by a certain freedom of bearing peculiar to the desert-dweller. Rahab was certainly a religious prostitute attached to the sanctuary, and as such a person of standing. The suggestion that she was an innkeeper comes from a deliberate false etymology given by the rabbis to the word translated "harlot" to save her honour. In going to her house the spies hoped to escape notice and to enjoy a measure of religious sanctuary. The king had to ask Rahab to hand them over (3).

Fear is a two-edged weapon, which we should use with care. It caused Rahab, who had obviously recognized who the men must be, to try and win the favour of their God by befriending them. It drove the others in Jericho to an even more stubborn resistance.

In vs. 15—21 we have a kind of story-telling common in the O.T. (The whole chapter is an example of it.) Clearly Rahab did not carry on a long conversation (16,21) in a loud whisper after the spies were already on the ground at the foot of the walls. We are first told of what she did (the important thing), and only then of the guarantee given her.

The "scarlet cord" (18) was not the rope used to let them down; that would have been far too conspicuous. It will have been only just visible to the keen-eyed Israelites below, while awakening no suspicion among the townsmen. The spies could give no unconditional guarantee to Rahab and her family. No sign attached to their clothes would have been sufficient to protect them in the excitement and hurly-burly of the capture of Jericho. They had to be protected by the easily identifiable house as Noah and his family were by the ark.

When Prof. Garstang excavated the ruins of an earlier Jericho, thinking they were Joshua's city, he found that part of the wall remained standing when most collapsed. The same probably happened to the section with Rahab's house (*cf.* **6.**20,22). Its high position prevented its roof from being overlooked (6).

How many people recognize us as Christians when they see us?

Joshua 3.1—4.18

The story carries straight on from **1.**10,11. Old Jerusalem is just about 2,500 feet above sea level; Jericho and Shittim about 850 feet below. From Jericho the floor of the Jordan valley slopes gradually downward for about six miles and then drops steeply about 150 feet to the trench (here 1,200 feet below sea level) about a mile wide through which the Jordan flows (the Dead Sea is 1,285 feet below). The trench is filled with jungle growth through which the river twists like an inebriated snake. It was not the river so much as the jungle that was difficult to cross, the fords of Jordan (**2.**7) being as much ways through the jungle as across the river. In spring the flooding of the Jordan (**3.**15) fills the trench, so they had a raging torrent, in places nearly a mile wide, between them and Jericho. Two agile young men might cross, but not the women, children, and cattle.

By the collapse of the banks the river was blocked at Adam (**3.**16), sixteen miles to the north. This happened to our knowledge in A.D. 1267, 1906, and 1927, with people crossing dryshod. The miraculous was not in the means but in God's complete control of Nature, so that it happened, not by chance but at the exact moment God willed it.

The gap between the ark and the people (**3.**4) was designed to impress on the people that this was entirely God's doing. It needs no explaining why the circle of stones was set up in Gilgal (**4.**20), but what of the circle in the river itself? If faith failed and scepticism laughed at the miracle, God could always dam the river again and let men see the hidden stones. There needs to be a sure memorial to God's salvation, hidden from men, in our hearts, to which we can look when men deny the reality of God's power.

The Levitical priests (**3.**3). The death of Nadab and Abihu (Lev. **10.**1,2) cut down the number of legitimate priests available. When local sanctuaries multiplied after the Conquest, there were not enough priests, and some accepted the task without God's call or sanction. The story is at pains to stress that only legitimate priests had the right to carry the ark.

What form does the danger of outrunning the ark of God take in Christian experience?

Joshua 4.19—5.15

Israel's last night in Egypt was the fifteenth of the first month. Now, forty years later, all but a couple of days, the purpose of the Exodus was accomplished (**4.**19). Canaan as a type is explained in Heb. **4.**9,10; it is not a picture of heaven, but of that stage in the Christian life where we have learnt that it is not our effort but Christ's power that matters.

The dismay of the kings of Canaan (**5.**1) must apply even more strongly to Jericho. As the people moved down from Shittim (**3.**1) they must have been seen from the walls of Jericho. Doubtless before the miracle happened the west bank was lined by soldiers from Jericho. They must have fled in terror as they saw the water disappearing. That would be why they made no attempt to molest Israel in the next few days.

The command to make flint knives (**5.**2) was probably intended to stress the entirely new beginning. Nothing they had brought across Jordan should be used for the purpose. The command for a second circumcision, which, taken literally, would be impossible, presumably means that the rite would now have a deeper meaning than when it had been commanded to Abraham (Gen. **17.**9—14). *Then* it was a pledge of a promise; *now* of a fulfilment. Life in the wilderness must have been very difficult and strenuous, so the neglect of circumcision can be understood. The "rolling away of the reproach of Egypt" lay in their new position as free men with a home. As long as they were in the wilderness they had not achieved the purpose of the Exodus.

Passover coincided with the barley harvest (11; *cf.* Lev. **23.**9—14 with v. 15, which shows that the sheaf was brought in Passover week). The "old corn" rightly disappears in R.S.V. (11). The manna ceased when it was no longer needed. Special provision by God can be a sign of immaturity rather than of special spirituality.

Joshua's vision (**5.**13—15) is to be compared to Moses' (Exod. **3.**2—5). It was his divine commissioning for his task. The purpose of the vision was not to give Joshua any special instructions—these he received, presumably through the high priest, whenever it was necessary—but to create a reverent attitude of heart and mind. We can easily become more interested in special guidance than in a right relationship with the Guide.

Thought: Obey Rom. **12.**1,2, *and you will have guidance when you need it.*

Joshua 6

We find one reason for God's long delay in giving Canaan to the Israelites in Gen. **15.**16. "The iniquity of the Amorites" was the misuse of sex in the name of religion, which acted as a moral poison inside and outside Palestine. Before He punished them, God gave them ample time for repentance. Now He was bringing in Israel as His executioner. That the behaviour of v. 21 was not normal for Israel is shown by Deut. **20.**10—18. In addition the case of Rahab (23) shows that any Canaanite could have saved his life by sincerely accepting God's will and repudiating his past.

The Conquest mostly followed normal methods, but it had to start with a ceremony that would reveal its true nature. The presence of the Ark, not normally taken into battle, the silent ranks of armed men, until the shout of victory was raised (16,20), and the solemn blowing of the rams' horns, all stressed that this was a solemn religious ceremony. Then the destroying of all that could be destroyed, and the handing over of the remainder to God (19,24) went beyond the normal to show that they were not common plunderers but emissaries of God's judgment.

The marching ceremony was not very long, once the few miles from Gilgal had been covered. They could easily march round Jericho, while keeping out of bowshot from the walls, in twenty minutes. How gruesome to the inhabitants of Jericho the final two hours and more of silent marching with the wailing of the rams' horns must have been! The fall of the walls, like the crossing of Jordan, was probably due to God's supernatural use of the natural. The Exodus had been marked by considerable earthquake activity (Exod. **19.**18, Judg. **5.**4, Hab. **3.**6, Psa. **114.**4), which may have so weakened the walls that they were more ready to collapse when the time came.

It was God's purpose that Jericho, probably the oldest continuously inhabited settlement in Palestine (as shown by Miss Kenyon's excavations) should remain a ruin for ever as a token of His judgment on the past; this did not include the neighbouring groves of palm trees (*cf.* Deut. **34.**3, Judg. **1.**16, **3.**13). For the fate of the man who defied the curse see 1 Kings **16.**34.

Joshua 7

If God's punishments are to be understood by those He punishes and their contemporaries, He must act according to standards they understand. For the man of Joshua's time, when a thing was devoted, or put in the ban (*cherem*; so **6.**18,19, **7.**1), it had a curse on it which demanded its destruction. Anyone taking devoted articles into his house or tent automatically brought the curse on it and all in it. Achan's family was not killed as an extra punishment on Achan but because they had come under the curse, as had the cattle and the tent (24). If we think such a punishment unfair, we must not forget that Achan knew the penalty of his action; if God had acted otherwise, he and others would have thought that God had condoned the act of rebellion.

Joshua's self-confidence (4) was not the cause of the defeat, but if he had asked God first, he would have discovered the sin without the defeat. The despair of Joshua and the people was due not to the size of the defeat but to its unexpectedness. The clearly implied rebuke in v. 10 is due to Joshua's assumption that God was at fault. He should have realized that the fault must be Israel's, even though he could not know the exact reason. Joshua's preoccupation with God's great name was, of course, mainly a preoccupation with his own safety.

Spare a thought for Achan's agony as he witnessed the choice of the lot drawing inexorably nearer to him (16—18). Joshua says, "Tell the truth" (19a); by acknowledging that the result of the lot was correct, Achan would give glory and praise to God.

The Valley of Achor is one of the deep, dark ravines that cut into the mountain backbone of Palestine from the Jordan Valley; it can be no longer identified, but it was still known in the days of Hosea (**2.**15). "Achor" means "trouble", and so 1 Chron. **2.**7 changes Achan's name to Achar, the Troubler. It is the troubling of Jesus Christ on the cross that really creates a door of hope for humanity. There are grounds for thinking that it was Achan's sin that started the cleavage between Judah and the other tribes. The desolate mound of Jericho was the abiding memorial of Canaanite sin; the cairn in the Valley of Achor that of Achan's.

Joshua 8

This portion gives the story of the fourth lasting memorial erected by the Israelites in Canaan. The stone circle at Gilgal testified to God's faithfulness, the mound of Jericho to Canaan's sin, the cairn in the

Valley of Achor to Judah's sin, and the ruins of Ai to the sin of the people's self-confidence.

Now, even though they had the right to expect God's blessing, they used a very simple stratagem to gain a complete victory. The knowledge that God is on your side is no reason why you should not use the sense God has given you. God does most of His wonders through His gifts to men, once they are surrendered to Him.

The chapter introduces us to problems we cannot answer. The ruins of Ai that have been dug up were destroyed before 2000 B.C.—*i.e.*, in or before the time of Abraham. It may be that tradition has attached the name Ai to the wrong site, or that it had been so recently re-occupied that what was left of Joshua's destruction was washed away by heavy rains.

More important is the problem of Shechem. Nothing is said of the capture of the area between Ai and Shechem, because the population was very thin, without walled cities. It was only shortly before the Conquest that the means had been discovered for making the cisterns hewn in the limestone rock watertight. Until these had become general, in parts where there were no perennial springs there could be no great density of population. In contrast Shechem was an ancient town and we are told nothing of its capture. Yet the complete people (33,35) held a service just outside its gates (*cf.* also 24.1). It is probable that when the city came into Jacob's hands (Gen. 34), he gave it to a related group of Habiru (Hebrews), who may already have had some faith in Jehovah. When Israel entered Canaan, they will have linked up with them. This would explain the language of Judg. 9, where the citizens of Shechem are Israelites, but feel themselves superior to Israel. The law written on the plaster of the altar (*cf.* Deut. 27.2) was probably the law of Deut. 12—26. It was certainly not the whole Law.

Questions for Further Study and Discussion on Joshua chapters 1—8.
1. How does the teaching of Joshua chapter 1 compare with the Christian ideal of leadership given in Mark 10.42—45?
2. What can we learn about the principles of guidance from the account of the crossing of Jordan?
3. What is the significance of the fact that God did not punish the inhabitants of Canaan in the way that He did those of Sodom and Gomorrah?
4. How far does ch. 7 throw light on the story of Ananias and Sapphira (Acts 5.1—11)?
5. How do we relate the story of the events at Ai to the general question of discipline in the Christian Church?

Rahab (ch. 2) both feared Jehovah and trusted Him, so she was able to save her life and that of her family as free persons. The leaders of Gibeon's four-city confederation feared Jehovah, but did not trust Him, so they saved their lives but became slaves (27).

Israel was on its guard. Its leaders were not going to come to terms with any local people (7), but they knew that they were allowed to with those at a distance, outside the promised land (Deut. 20.10—15). The deceit used was fairly transparent, but a judicious touch of flattery guaranteed that the obvious questions would not be put. There is always something heartwarming for most of us when we hear that God's dealings with us are being spoken of by people at a distance. If we remember how unimportant the most important of us are, we are likely to be suspicious of those who sing our praises without having known us.

The most important lesson of this chapter is its warning that there are actions we can commit as Christians which we cannot retract. The Gibeonite confederation lay strategically at a most important point, especially while Jerusalem lay in Jebusite hands. It is not surprising that Saul in his "zeal for Israel" tried to eliminate this foreign population (2 Sam. 21.2). He succeeded in forcing the population of Beeroth to emigrate (2 Sam. 4.2,3). The price he had to pay was first the assassination of his son Ishbosheth (2 Sam. 4.7), and then the judicial execution of seven sons and grandsons (2 Sam. 21.8,9). The severity of the punishment, quite apart from the seven years of drought on Israel, which he officially represented before God, indicates the enormity of his sin. The final picture we have of Gibeon is that it had become the great high place of Israel (1 Ki. 3.4, 2 Chron. 1.3,5).

The most obvious example of a responsibility we take on ourselves without having the right to terminate it is marriage. There are many aching and impoverished Christian hearts because natural desire was accepted as an indication of God's will. But we must look further. Our promises do not need the strengthening of an oath to be binding (Matt. 5.37). No Christian has the right to break a promise because it suits him (Psa. 15.4). If we feel that we have made a major mistake, we must pray for grace to glorify God in the mistake.

Joshua 10

Gibeon's action gave Israel a firm grip on the centre of the hills; this thoroughly alarmed the main towns in the area. Immediately Israel had to learn that a partner not chosen by God was an unreliable ally. But just because Israel remained true to his promise, where it seemed a gain not to, God gave him special help.

The "great stones from heaven" (11) are hailstones. We then have a quotation from a book of poetry—*The Book of Jashar* (*cf.* 2 Sam. 1.18) is one of Israel's lost books; it would seem to have been a collection of old national poems. Being poetry, it is hard to interpret, and various explanations are offered of the exact miracle described in vs. 12,13, but that a miracle happened is clear. A full discussion by E. W. Maunder, a former Astronomer Royal, may be found in *The Astronomy of the Bible* or *The International Standard Bible Encyclopedia*. He points out that from Gibeon *via* Beth-horon to Azekah and Makkedah (10) is twenty-seven miles, far more than could have been covered by fighting men in the time; in addition they had time to capture the city (28). The most reasonable explanation of v. 15 is that it ends the account of the victory with that of the victorious return, though the mopping-up operation must have happened before it (16—28).

These verses create difficulties just because of the completeness of the mopping-up. It is very hard to reconcile the account of complete annihilation with 14.6—15, 15.13—19, Judg. 1.8—15. The difficulty lies not in an apparent reconquest, but in the need of one after such a complete massacre of the population; even had some survived, they could not have increased enough in the interval. The most likely explanation is that we have here the account of a "combined operation". As Judah marched south (see notes on Judg. 1), Joshua swept round the coastal plain, and the country was caught in a pincers' operation. Because Joshua was the over-all general who had done the planning, the whole campaign is described as his work. The cave at Makkedah can be regarded as the fifth of Israel's monuments, this time of his greatest victory.

Joshua 11

When the occupying Israelites moved north of Shechem, they were faced by a line of fortresses cutting them off from the great plain of Esdraelon, Jezreel, or Megiddo (17.11—13; Judg. 1.27), but light-armed troops, like those of the Israelites, could slip between them very easily, especially at night. It was probably their infiltration into the plain that alarmed Jabin, king of Hazor (1). On older maps the name "Waters of Merom" (5) is generally put against the small lake north of the Sea of Galilee. Modern maps call this Lake Huleh and link the waters of Merom with Merom in the heart of Galilee. Israel's sudden attack was the more effective because the chariots could not be used in the hill country. They had been brought for a battle in the plain.

If we put vs. 12,13 together, we find that Israel destroyed the weaker towns that could be rushed, but left the stronger ones, except Hazor, uncaptured. This was particularly serious and inexcusable in the case of the cities mentioned in 12.21—23, whose kings had been killed. The probable reason is that the people were getting tired of fighting (cf. 18). Since only the highlights of the Conquest are given us, we are apt to think it was much shorter than it was in fact. Christians are always in most danger when they feel tired and think it does not matter whether or not they complete their task. It was just these cities that created one of the most serious dangers in the period of the Judges (Judg. 4,5).

"The Negeb" (16; 10.40—today, Negev) means all the land south of Hebron and Lachish down to the limits of cultivation. Owing to the uncertain rainfall agriculture is hazardous and much of the area is left to semi-nomads. The Anakim (21), or sons of Anak, were the remains of a particularly tall tribe among the earlier settlers in Canaan. They made the spies think of the pre-Flood giants (Num. 13.33; cf. Deut. 9.2). They were probably not very formidable, for they had already so dwindled as not to be mentioned among the peoples of Canaan (Gen. 15.19—21), unless, indeed, they are the same as the Rephaim. It is always the same; we tend to judge by looks.

Joshua 12

If at all possible, study this chapter with a good Bible map beside you. Better still, draw an outline map of Palestine, marking the places mentioned, making a difference between places captured and those where the town was left, even though the king was killed.

In vs. 1—6 we have a summary of Num. 21.21—35; 32.1—42. "The Arabah" (1,3,8) is here the Jordan Valley from the Sea of Galilee southwards; the term is sometimes confined to the more desert portions round the Dead Sea and south of it. "The Sea of Chinneroth" (3)—i.e., the Sea of Galilee; the name is probably derived from kinnor, a harp, there being a similarity in the shape.

"Mount Halak" (7), the Bald Mountain, site unknown; it is just possible that "Baal-gad" may be Baalbek. The lowland (8)—i.e., the Shephelah, or low hills between the central hills and the coastal plain. For the Israelite living in the hills they were low, the more so as he had given up hope of conquering the plains. The "slopes": a term is used which cannot be identified with certainty. It probably refers to the steep slope down to the Jordan Valley and the Dead Sea. "Goiim in Galilee" (23): R.S.V. is almost certainly correct in following the Greek with Galilee, rather than the Hebrew with Gilgal. "Goiim" means nations, but it is likely that Harosheth-ha-goiim (Judg. 4.2) is intended.

It would be unfair to suggest that the Church is unwilling to thank God for all His many mercies, but on the whole it is unwilling to indulge in detailed and specific thanks. If we were to train ourselves to recognize God's goodness act by act and detail by detail, many of us would come to think more highly both of God and of the Church. Much of our despondency comes from failing to see how much God has really achieved. On the other hand, such detailed thanksgiving would also make us more detailedly conscious of what had not been attained. Experience shows that the more we turn our attention to God's acts, the more we are aware of our falling short. This list is an excellent example, because it repeatedly reminds us of how much had been left undone, in spite of God's mighty acts.

Joshua 13.1—14.5

We may be surprised at the great detail in this section of *Joshua* (chs. 13—21), but these are the title-deeds of the children of Israel. Whatever the later fate of a tribe, its members could always say, "This is the land that God has given us." Where enemies had conquered it in whole or in part, the record stood as a reproach and a testimony to sin.

Read vs. 1—6 with Judg. 3.1—4. This is not a complete list of the unconquered, but of those God did not intend to be conquered by the first generation. It is always God's will that we should leave something for those that follow us to do. They lay not in the land but round it. Because the Israelites did not conquer what they should have, they never fully conquered these extra territories, but only made them tributary, and some (the Phoenician territory, 6) not at all.

We are told that half-Manasseh did not conquer Geshur and Maacath (13). The former is the region to the east of the Sea of Galilee, the latter the eastern slopes of the upper Jordan Valley leading up to Mt. Hermon. Absalom's mother was a daughter of the king of Geshur (2 Sam. 3.3; 13.37). Psalm 42 was written by one who lived near or in Maacath (6); it gives a picture of the rude and godless people that grew up in the mixed frontier area.

The treatment of the Levites (14) had a deeply practical motive.

Whenever the holding of a religious office is made to depend mainly on birth and not on special religious qualifications it will gradually accumulate power in the hands of the family concerned, so that it will gradually become a threat to the good of society. God made hereditary the position of the Aaronic priest and of the Levite, but put a limit on their ability to become rich.

The difference between the two-and-a-half tribes east of Jordan and those west of the river is that those east asked for what they wanted (Num. **32.**1—5)—this is not directly stated of half-Manasseh but we can assume they made their wishes clear enough. The rest accepted what God gave them. Already in ch. **22** we find the former beginning to wonder whether they had not made a mistake. Certainly their lands were always most open to attack.

Joshua 14.6—15.12

There are no grounds, once we realize that Hebrew historical writing is not tied by strict chronological order, for placing **14.**6 after **13.**1—**14.**5, or even after ch. **12.** It seems impossible not to link it with Judg. **1.**1b—20. This can be placed best, though without certainty, after the sin of Achan and the capture of Ai; this in turn would permit "the pincers' movement" suggested in the notes on ch. **10.** As is clear from **18.**1, Judah's lot was allocated before the general partition, as were also those of Ephraim and half-Manasseh (**16.**1). We no longer know why, but priority in God's giving does not imply favouritism. If Judah was to go up first against the Canaanites (Judg. **1.**1), it was only fair that he should have his portion first.

Caleb made a discovery that many others have made. The exercise of his faith acted as a kind of general tonic. It is not that faith always cures physical weaknesses, but it is a marvellous help towards making the maximum use of what God has given us. Many complain of weakness and lack of gifts because they have never learnt by faith to use what they have. Caleb is specially mentioned in connection with Judah, because he was not an Israelite but a Kenizzite (14), from one of the Midianite clans. It was fitting that the foreigner should have been received into Judah, for "to him shall be the obedience of the peoples" (Gen. **49.**10).

With what loving care the boundary of Judah is traced! Were it not that some of the place-names cannot be identified with absolute certainty, we could draw the frontier on the ground today. It is exact even in the most unlikely places. The South boundary runs through desert, where it might be claimed that frontier delimitation was of no

mportance, but it is accurately given for all that. Note that the Valley
of Achor is within Judah's bounds (7). Very many Christians have no
nterest in discovering what God has given them and therefore never
enjoy it. In addition they spend much of their time in coveting or
trying to cultivate the possessions of others. This is one of the most
potent sources of Christian dissatisfaction.
*Many a collision between Christians comes because they try to use the
same track.*

Joshua 15.13–63

The first part of our reading continues the story of Caleb (see also
Judg. 1.10—15). From the latter we see that this was no isolated
campaign by Caleb. He belonged now to Judah and together with
Judah he fought. Othniel was his nephew; such marriages were at the
time both common and favoured (*cf.* Gen. 20.12, 24.47, 29.15—19).
Those Greek MSS that read "he urged her" (18) are probably correct.
Field in the O.T. normally means open country, in many cases un-
tilled because it was unsuitable. Presumably the area round the
springs (19) is meant. For Negeb see note on 11.16.
   Most of the latter part (20—62) is an appendix put in by a later
editor giving the organization of Judah under the monarchy after the
time of Solomon. Solomon, for various practical reasons, was not
able to use the old tribal boundaries. He divided the land into twelve
portions, normally near the old divisions (1 Kings 4.7—19; vs. 13 and
19 refer to the same region, Geber having been replaced by his son).
When the kingdom was split under Rehoboam, Judah was divided
into twelve administrative districts to emphasize its claims to remain
the true Israel, even if the Northern Kingdom bore the name. The
paragraph division in R.S.V. is intended to bring this out, but it is in
one point misleading. A very little study should convince you that vs.
45—47 belong together. For all that, there are twelve sections, for
after v. 59 in Hebrew a group of towns has fallen out; it has been
preserved in the Greek—*viz.* "Tekoa, and Ephrath (the same is
Bethlehem), and Peor, and Etam, and Kolon, and Tatam, and Sores,
and Kerem, and Gallim, and Bether, and Manahath; eleven cities and
their villages." These eleven form the tenth section. Only in the fifth
section (45—47) is no number of places given, and that because the
section is mainly imaginary. It consists of the Philistine land which
Judah failed to hold at the first (*cf.* Judg. 1.18,19). David was able to
make it tributary, but already under Solomon the Philistines had freed
themselves, and so this section remained a dream and a grief.

211

V. 63 is a second appendix. Jerusalem was virtually reckoned to Judah (see note on ch. 18 at end). In Judg. 1 we are told how Judah did not deal adequately with Jerusalem, because it was not in its portion; now it was a thorn in its flesh. This was one of the causes helping towards the split under Rehoboam.

Questions for Further Study and Discussion on Joshua chapters 9—15

1. How does the story of Israel and the Gibeonites (ch. 9) apply to the people of God today?
2. "Israel's greatest victory (ch. 10) was won defending those who had put their trust in them." What does this imply for us?
3. In what sense may "giants" left over from the past (ch. 11) trouble us in the Christian life?
4. Trace the theme of the hardening of men's hearts, from chapter 11 v. 20, through Exod. 4.21, Isa. 6.10, Matt. 13.13—15, and Rom. 9.17*f.*
5. What is the tribute frequently paid to Caleb's character (ch. 14) How far is the refusal to rest on one's past achievements an ingredient of true faith?

Joshua 16,17

If we can see some reason why Judah received his portion in advance none is apparent for "the descendants of Joseph" (**16.1**). It is not unreasonable to suppose that the pride of Ephraim, which becomes so prominent in *Judges* and which finds an earlier expression in **17.14** lay behind it.

Reuben was Jacob's first-born, and therefore the birthright of a double portion in the inheritance was his. By his sin he forfeited his right (1 Chron. **5.**1,2), which automatically went to Joseph as first born of Jacob's other wife. This meant in turn that in the distribution of the land the descendants of Joseph were entitled to two portions This was not done by giving both Ephraim and Manasseh a portion for it is here clearly said that the allotment was to the descendants of Joseph, who divided it among them. The birthright was satisfied by giving Manasseh, the first-born of Joseph, an extra portion (**17.**1,5,6,17)—*viz.*, east of Jordan. For **17.3** see Num. **27.**1—7.

The arrogance of the Joseph tribes is seen in **17.16**. They were not prepared to bring the hill country under cultivation (see note on ch. **8** for the reason why it was thinly populated—without adequate water supply it had not been worth clearing the forest trees and scrub) and were equally unprepared to conquer the plain. In addition they had been given what was in many ways the best part of the country. 7.11—13 suggests a particular act of meanness. It seems that Issachar and Asher had voluntarily ceded part of their territory, because they felt they could not tackle the strong fortresses. Manasseh accepted the territory, but did little to dislodge the Canaanites. Note the subtle difference between 16.10 and 17.12; Manasseh *could* not, but Ephraim *would* not. In fact Gezer did not become Israelite until the time of Solomon, and then it was the dowry Pharaoh gave his daughter (1 Kings 9.16).

"The chariots of iron" (16,18) were wooden chariots strengthened with iron plates—they could be burnt (11.6,9). It was not the actual chariots that dismayed the Israelites but the differing concept of war that lay behind their use. They were based on stable lines of infantry, while the Israelites fought as irregulars, who could easily be cut to pieces by the quickly moving chariots.

Joshua 18

We are inevitably heirs of the past, and so was Israel. Some of their most important towns were already old when Abraham saw them. But their religion, in spite of resemblances in the sacrificial ritual, had nothing to do with Canaan's past. Archaeology has shown that Shiloh was first built by Israel. They wanted their chief sanctuary untainted by memories of Canaanite religion. At first, it seems clear, "the tent of meeting" was moved around a certain amount. Was it at Shechem at 24.1? It was at Bethel in Judg. 20.27,28. Finally in 1 Samuel 1 we find a temple at Shiloh. Excavations have shown it to have been the same size as the Tent. Probably this was still standing, but a building would have been erected around it to protect it from the elements.

The slackness blamed by Joshua (3) may well have been due to an unwillingness to settle down. It was fine to have a "promised land", but the reality showed the need for learning new skills and engaging in hard work. That is for many the disappointing side of God's gifts; they are always given that we may serve the better. Even His rest is linked with a yoke (Matt. 11.28—30).

Joshua, in his God-given wisdom, did not allow himself to be involved in the distribution of the land beyond presiding at the casting of the lots (10). The tribal portions were not arbitrary, but represented real natural divisions of the country, even though modern methods of transport have often hidden that fact.

Even though the division of the seven portions was by lot, God clearly overruled it, so that tribes which had reasons for feeling close to one another were normally together. Benjamin, the other Rachel tribe, accordingly found itself next to the Joseph portion. These boundaries are not to be regarded as unchangeable frontiers. We have in this list an apparent contradiction. "Kiriath-jearim", under the name of Kiriath-baal, is in v. 14 allocated to Judah (*cf.* **15.60**), but in v. 28 it is claimed as Benjaminite. The border may have fluctuated a mile or two. In this case, however, it may be linked with the fact that the other three towns of the Gibeonite four-city confederation were on Benjaminite territory (25,26). The memories of the original inhabitants may, for the time being, have been more potent than the official demarcation. Benjamin also owned an uncaptured Jerusalem.

Joshua 19

We gain the impression that here we have to do with one of the worst bits of sharp practice in the Bible. "The portion of the tribe of Judah was too large for them" (9): yet it had been allocated to them by God. In fact, though Judah had the largest area west of Jordan, so much of it was desert or poor pasture land that effectively it was probably no larger than any other. The Simeonite towns will be found in the first (**15.28,29,30,31,32**) and fourth (**15.42**) divisions of Judah; the position was reasonably fertile, but lay along Judah's weakest frontier. Judah had failed to hold the coastal plain; now he was willing that Simeon should be a shield against eventualities. In v. 2 read with Greek, Beer-sheba, Shema (*cf.* **15.26**) . . . ; there is a name too many. In v. 7 add Tochen (*cf.* 1 Chron. **4.**32). As a result Simeon found it very hard to keep a separate existence, and Judah found itself without its shield (*cf.* Judg. **15.**11, 1 Sam. **27.**6).

In the description of Zebulun's lot it is clear that the names of seven towns have dropped out at the beginning of v. 15; Jokneam, Kartah, and Dimnah can be supplied from **21.**34*f.* The Bethlehem mentioned is, of course, not the better-known one in Judah.

The reason why the boundaries of Issachar and Asher are only partially given is explained by **17.**11; the handing over of certain towns to Manasseh made the drawing of an exact boundary impossible. The extension of Asher's boundaries to Sidon (28) and Tyre (29) is again an ideal; it is doubtful whether they ever held the territory. At the time Sidon was more important than Tyre. It seems obvious that "Judah" (34) is a scribal error. This and others are due to the inherent difficulty in copying out little-known names.

Several of Dan's cities (41) will be found in the second division of Judah (15.33), while Ekron is claimed by them both. With the withdrawal of the Danites these cities, when conquered by Judah, are included in its territory. For v. 47, *cf.* Judg. 18. It is not clear whether all the tribe of Dan moved, but probably not. The failure of Dan to maintain its position was mainly due to Judah's failure to hold the coastal plain. Because Dan never really occupied its area, its boundary is not given.

Joshua 20

This chapter must be read in the light of Num. 35.9—28. In particular "until he has stood before the congregation for judgment" (6, also 9) is explained by Num. 35.24,25.

Man can never restore life, once he has taken it, and so the Bible regards even innocent manslaughter as a major fault, and so does not forbid the age-old custom of the avenger of blood. The Law protects the innocent man but inflicts a very heavy penalty. Not only had he to leave home, but he was confined to the bounds of the city of refuge (Num. 35.26,27), probably a distance of two thousand cubits—*i.e.*, a thousand yards—from the walls (Num. 35.4,5). For an agriculturist, with no skill as an artisan, this must have been most irksome. The making of the high priest's death the limit of time during which he was at the avenger's mercy, if he left the city, was partly due to the fact that the high priest was the only regular official personage at the time. At the same time there is a veiled type pointing to Jesus Christ, the great high priest. The lying-in-wait at the city boundaries was equally irksome for the avenger, so we may be sure that many cases were settled by a money payment.

Unfortunately this was one of the laws which were little observed in the wild period of the Judges. There is no suggestion in 2 Sam. 3.26—39 that Abner should have been safe in Hebron. Equally David did not suggest to the widow from Tekoa (2 Sam. 14.4—11) that a city of refuge was the solution of her problem. It was not until royal power and justice grew strong that true justice could be enforced.

All six cities, as commanded by Moses (Num. 35.6), were Levitical cities. This was doubtless to ensure a fairer first hearing, when the man reached the city (4). To increase the effectiveness of the cities, apparently such were chosen as already had a certain sanctity. The cities east of Jordan are too little known to us for an opinion to be given, but "Kedesh" (7) itself means "holy", Shechem was marked out by the great post-Conquest covenant renewal (ch. 24), and

Hebron was bound up with memories of Abraham and his walk with God.

God's very stress on the sanctity of human life should increase our sense of awe at the sacrifice of Jesus Christ.

Joshua 21

By the giving of cities to the Levites we must understand, not that they were inhabited exclusively by Levites—they quite obviously were not—but that they were afforded adequate room within the walls to build their houses (*cf.* Lev. 25.32—34). Then the land up to a thousand yards in every direction belonged to them (Num. 35.5,6), though apparently, they were to use it for grazing purposes only, not for agriculture. This was to remind them that their stake in the land was a different one (18.7).

God's overruling of the lot is seen particularly in the descendants of Aaron (13—18). Not only were they well placed for the temple that would be in Jerusalem, but with the division of the kingdom they found themselves automatically in Judah. For Anathoth (18) *cf.* 1 Kings 2.26, Jer. 1.1.

This dispersal of the Levites ensured that in every tribe there would be some who were specially acquainted with the Law and would be able to teach it. Even more important was that they were inextricably bound up with the fortunes of the people. In our highly organized modern society it is all too easy for the believer to live to himself washing his hands of his unbelieving neighbours. Not so in Israel. A number of the towns will be recognized as having remained unconquered, so some of the Levites remained homeless for a long time. In the case of Gezer (21) they had to wait until the time of Solomon and even then they found only smoking ruins (1 Kings 9.16). Gibeon with its Canaanite population, became a priestly town (*cf.* 1 Kings 3.4, 2 Chron. 1.3,5), so they were constantly reminded of the fault of their ancestors. When invaders, pestilence, drought came over part of the land because of the people's sin, there were always some Levites involved.

If you will mark the Levitical cities in the measure your map allows you will see that the tribal giving was generous. They allotted some of the choicest sites in the land to them—*e.g.*, Hebron, Libnah, Debir Gibeon, Shechem, Taanach, Kadesh, Jokneam, Ramoth-Gilead Mahanaim, Heshbon.

Joshua 22

At long last the time for return home had come, and the long labour of the two-and-a-half tribes had finished. They had paid a heavy price for their choice of territory, even if they went back rich (8). But it was not until they reached the Jordan that they fully realized what they had done. While, presumably, there were no particular difficulties in crossing, yet they saw what a barrier it really was, and how easily those on the other side could be thought of as living in another land. That they were not mistaken is shown by the language of the rest of the people, when they heard of the building of the altar (11*f.*); "on the side that belongs to the people of Israel" is a phrase that virtually disowned the people on the other side.

The making of the altar was not in itself forbidden at that time. But there had been no appearance of God, no theophany, to justify it Deut. 12.5,11,14,18—language which envisages the possibility of God's choosing more than one place, as in fact He did). Then it was an ostentatiously large altar (10) and a copy of the one in Shiloh (28). In the rash judgment of the other tribes it was the setting up of "nonconformist" worship. They did not stop to think that the altar was on the wrong side of the Jordan for that. If we would only stop to think at times, we would realize that actions we disapprove of may in fact have other explanations than the apparently obvious ones.

It is striking that it was an altar they erected as the symbol of their unity with their brothers. They knew that the only real link between them was spiritual. It has today come to be realized more fully than earlier that, until the rise of the monarchy, the tribes were in fact independent units. It was their loyalty to one God and to one central sanctuary that bound them together in a union, the efficiency of which depended on the reality of their faith at any given time. In fact the eastern tribes seem to have backslidden less than some in the west. No special acts of idolatry are recorded of them, and in the dark hours under Ahab it was from Gilead that Elijah came (1 Kings **17**.1).

Joshua 23

There are many who think that this chapter and the next describe the same event; this is quite likely, because the Bible is not averse to such descriptions from differing standpoints. Such an interpretation will not affect our understanding of the chapter.

"All Israel" (2) is, unless the opposite is clearly stated (*e.g.*, **8.35**),

217

always to be understood in such contexts of the whole people as represented by their leaders.

The first main point is a positive one (6,8), that they must remain true to God's revelation, as they had received it. It is not enough to keep from evil; one must positively do good in the way it has been revealed.

The second is the danger of compromise. The day was to come when Jesus Christ was to demonstrate by the power of the Holy Spirit that He could move among the worst of men and yet keep Himself "unstained from the world" (Jas. 1.27). Until then it was God's will for His people that they should be separate from the heathen—stories like those of Daniel show that God's power was sufficient to keep His loyal ones, when the lack of separation was not of their choosing. The history of Israel in the O.T. is less one of apostasy and more one of compromise with heathen neighbours; this led in turn to a worship which God refused to accept as being in any sense worship of Him at all.

The third is the need of loving God (11). As in the N.T. the love should be based on what God has done (9,10). No mere separation and mechanical keeping of God's will can ever be adequate. It is the attraction of God that drives out the attraction of the surroundings.

The fourth is a warning against intermarriage (12,13). The story of Ruth is evidence enough that there was no mere nationalistic or racial prejudice behind the warning. But Ruth had come to love God, thanks to the example Naomi had set her, before she ever met Boaz. In marriage man and wife become "one flesh" in a new union, and to this both contribute, probably fairly equally. It is useless one or the other thinking that love will lead the other to Christ. The believer can give all in the marriage, but the unbeliever will also contribute his or her all. The believer cannot lift the partner to salvation, but the unbeliever will go far in making unbelief the dominant factor.

Joshua 24

In this chapter the need of determined choice is stressed. Joshua knew that it was better to choose wrong than not to choose at all. The man who is never sure, who does not know his ideals, his loyalties, his beliefs, is like a half-dead fish floating all the time downstream. Joshua held out three choices to Israel.

First there were the gods their ancestors had worshipped before Abram ever heard and followed the voice of God (2,15). In v. 14 it is made clear, what in any case was obvious, that Joshua was not suggesting a revival of the past. Whatever may have been true of the eading Patriarchs, Gen. **35**.2—4 was for most participants a merely outward ceremony.

The next possibility was the adoption of the gods of the conquered people (15). It is true that they had shown themselves powerless in the presence of Jehovah, but at least they claimed to be thoroughly modern and "scientific". They promised a true control over agriculture, fertility, and sex generally. Even though they had been defeated and largely annihilated, the peoples of Canaan felt themselves intellectually and culturally miles ahead of the Israelites.

The third and real possibility was Jehovah. In vs. 3—13 Joshua stressed the goodness and power of God. His very greatness made single-minded loyalty essential (14). We may find it hard to believe that old loyalties could persist over such a momentous four centuries, but that is the way with men. It is remarkable how much of mediaeval Catholicism, and even old paganism, lies hidden in much modern Protestantism. The answer of the people was an obvious one. They protested that they had no intention of serving anyone but Jehovah (16—18). The evangelist can overlook that under certain circumstances and in certain surroundings his message can be accepted as obvious. So Joshua told them brutally that they could not serve Jehovah (19). Conversion is the work of the Holy Spirit. The type of life God demands (not merely expects) from the regenerate is a supernatural one, which only the Holy Spirit can create.

For vs. 29, 30 *cf.* **19**.49,50, Judg. **2**.8,9.

Questions for Further Study and Discussion on Joshua chapters 16—24.

1. What weaknesses in Israel are shown by **16**.10 and **17**.12,13?
2. What is the contemporary spiritual counterpart to Israel's failure (**15**.63, **16**.10, **17**.12*f.*)?
3. Study carefully Joshua's answer to the complaint of the Joseph-tribes (**17**.14—18) and analyse the qualities which it revealed.
4. We learn a great deal about the geography of Palestine from chs. **13**—**21**; we can admire the wisdom of God in the way He arranged matters. What lessons can we reasonably deduce—by analogy, not allegory—for the Church today?
5. Relate your reading in Joshua ch. **22** to the matter of Christian unity today.
6. What in ch. **24** is the sin above all others that Joshua warned against? Why does Scripture condemn it so severely?

Chronology of the Judges

c.1230 B.C.	Conquest of Canaan
c.1215 B.C.	Death of Joshua
c.1200 B.C.	Othniel—Mesopotamian oppression
	Philistines enter Palestine
c.1170 B.C.	Ehud—Moabite oppression
c.1150 B.C.	Shamgar—Philistine oppression
c.1125 B.C.	Deborah and Barak—Canaanite oppression
c.1110 B.C.	Gideon—Midianite oppression
c.1075 B.C.	Abimelech
c.1070 B.C.	Jephthah—Ammonite oppression
	Samson—Philistine oppression
c.1050 B.C.	The battles of 1 Sam. **4**
	Shiloh destroyed
c.1045 B.C.	Samuel
c.1020 B.C.	Saul's reign commences

Israel in the Judges Period

Judges

INTRODUCTION

Judges is anonymous, just as is *Joshua*. Very much of it is very old an
even contemporaneous with the events described, but the book a
such does not seem to have received its final form till the reign o
Ahaz or Hezekiah; *cf.* **18.**30 with 2 Kings **15.**29.

The book is not a history of the period, but **3.**7—**16.**31 give us ai
account of God's power in deliverance through the "Judges". I
should be remembered that there is no real claim made to chrono
logical order. Several of the Judges could have been contemporaries
This heart of the book is preceded by a section (**1.**1—**3.**6) explainin
how the troubles came to happen and is followed by two appendice
(chs. **17,18** and **19**—**21**) showing some of the disorders that coul
exist at the time.

Judges 1.1—2.5

This portion is largely Israel's roll of dishonour, a record of what i
left undone. For its understanding we must grasp that "After th
death of Joshua" (**1.**1) is the name of the book as a whole. The death
of Joshua is not given till **2.**8,9, and it is clear that the incidents in ch.
are all, or almost all, from his lifetime.

For vs. **8**—**20** see notes on Josh. **14.**6 and **15.**13, and for the cam
paign in general those on **10.**29—**38**. The easiest explanation of vs. 1,
is that the sin of Achan caused such bitter feelings against his tribe
that God saw fit to separate Judah for the time being from his
comrades. We know nothing of Bezek nor of Adoni-bezek, so we car
throw no extra light on vs. **4**—**7**. The fact that he was brought to
Jerusalem is no hint that he was its king (*cf.* Josh. **10.**1). "The city o
palms" (16): see note on Josh. **6**. There is no need to see any link
between v. 17 and Num. **21.**1—3. "Hormah" means "Put in the ban"
or "Given over to destruction". Actually there was a considerable distance between the two sites. For vs. 18,19 see note on Josh. **15.**45—47.

Judah and Simeon had burnt Jerusalem (8), but evidently because
it was not in their territory they could not be bothered to do the job

roperly. By the time Benjamin tried it was too late. Though not
trong enough to form a physical frontier, Jerusalem created a
sychological one which helped increasingly to separate Judah from
1e North.

Mark the uncaptured cities, so far as you are able, on a map. It may
urprise you to see what a strategic position they occupy. Just as
erusalem helped to isolate the South, so did the towns along Esdrae-
on isolate Galilee.

"The angel of the Lord" (2.1) should probably here be rendered
The messenger of the Lord"—*i.e.*, a prophet. Hebrew MSS indicate
1at there is a gap in v. 1 after "he said". Although we are so near the
Conquest, we have already reached one of the turning-points in
srael's history. The people might weep and sacrifice, but God never
ermitted them, from then on, even when they captured *some* of the
nconquered cities, to clear out their inhabitants. In other words,
srael never reached the limits of even a more restricted land, and
1ey never had it entirely to themselves.

Judges 2.6—3.6

Baal" means in itself "owner" and could be used for any god
vho was considered to be in some special way owner of a place
r district. By the Israelite period it had come to mean especially
he sky-god who was the bringer of the rains. Owing to the vital
mportance of rain for Palestine, he had become the most important
f the Canaanite gods. Ashtoreth (plural "*Ashtaroth*", 13) was the
reat goddess of the earth and fertility. The prophetic writers of the
3ible were not interested in introducing their readers to the rather
loody and distinctly pornographic details of Canaanite mythology.
hey simply lumped all the male gods together as Baals, the female
nes normally as Ashtaroth; but see 3.7.

That is not all. The gods of the Canaanites were all Nature gods—
.e., they were the spirits that made Nature work and were ultimately
ubject to the laws of Nature. Jehovah was the Creator of Nature,
utside it and its Controller. Every effort to regard Him as greater
han, but in some way like, the Canaanite gods so lowered Him that
he writers call that Baal-worship also. There is little evidence for a
omplete abandonment of Jehovah-worship or of the independent
vorship of the Canaanite gods. It was, however, obvious that such
god would use other gods to help him out, and that he would have a

wife. So other deities were honoured beside Jehovah. This is the back‑ground suggested in **2.**11—13; but *cf.* **10.**6.

A judge (*shophet*) is not one who enforces the law, but one who is deliverer. It is in this sense that Israel's deliverers are called judge: Since they were deliverers because the Spirit of God rested on them they will afterwards have been called in to act as judges in a mor literal sense. Since law cases at this time were all civil ones—*i.e.*, th person wronged brought an action against the one who had wronge him, and perjury was looked on with much more indulgence tha with us—it often needed spiritual wisdom to discover the truth 1 Kings **3.**16—28 gives us an example of Israelite judicial wisdor at its highest.

Question: How can the "down-grading" of God be practised b Christians today?

Judges 3.7–31

The first judge is Othniel; after his time Judah ceases to play an significant part in the book, except in the second appendix. "Mesopo tamia" (8): more likely northern Syria than the area east of th Euphrates. The oppressor's name means "Cushan Double-Wicked ness". This is obviously a playful pun on his real name. The firs judgment was a warning and came from one at a distance, whos existence was independent of the completeness or incompleteness o the Conquest.

"Asheroth" (7): plural of Asherah. Asherah was a Canaanit goddess, and so the plural can be used like Ashtaroth (**2.**13) for th female deities in general. It is occasionally used for an image of he (*e.g.*, 1 Kings **15.**13, 2 Kings **23.**7). Normally it means the sacre wooden pole erected in every Canaanite and Canaanite-typ sanctuary, representing the female element in deity, even as the stone or pillar (*mazzebah*), beside it represented the male element. A.V (K.J.V.) "grove" is most misleading.

The fact that the next oppressor did not penetrate further int Israel than Jericho—for "the city of palm trees" (13) see note on Josh **6**—suggests that his burden affected almost entirely the Benjaminites which is perhaps the reason why his tyranny was allowed to last for 1 years (14). Ehud's plan called for very careful timing. He had t obtain a private audience with Eglon on the pretext of a divin message. Gilgal (19) was not far from Jericho, and Eglon's guard:

may have seen him turn back there—at "the sculptured stones": perhaps an account of the crossing of the Jordan had been engraved on them (Josh. 4.20). Then he had to gain enough time not merely to save his own life, but also to seize the fords of Jordan before the Moabites could make up their mind what to do. The Moabites did not realize he was left-handed (*cf.* 20.16) and so did not suspect the sword at his right side. Note that the Ephraimites were ready to follow, but not to lead; we shall meet this trait again later.

There is no suggestion that Shamgar was an Israelite (*cf.* 5.6), nor is he introduced in the ordinary way. He was probably a Canaanite, for whom the Philistine penetration into the land was as unwelcome as for the Israelites. God is under no obligation to use one of His own people for the liberation of His people.

Judges 4

Now Israel's chickens have really come home to roost. The Canaanite cities of Galilee and the plain of Esdraelon had recovered from the mauling they had received in Joshua's day, and they threatened the whole of northern Israel. It looked as though the whole work of the Conquest might be nullified. The events are told us in two versions. The triumphal psalm (ch. 5), composed immediately after the victory, is put second, because the prose account (ch. 4), written a little later, gives us a more balanced, though also incomplete, picture of what happened. The two have to be put together.

In ch. 5 we see the campaign as a challenge to all Israel, to which some tribes respond. From ch. 4 it is clear that the real initiative lay with Zebulun and Naphtali (10, 5.18); Issachar, so far as his position in the plain allowed, probably also joined the main force (5.15). Barak, marching from Kedesh, led his forces almost past Jabin's capital (see map) and took up his position on Mt. Tabor (6), where Sisera could not ignore his presence. In fact Barak and his men were the bait in God's trap. Sisera hurriedly gathered his forces and marched to overwhelm him. Before he could attack, Barak's men rushed down on him (5.15) with the storm behind them. Half blinded by the rain the Canaanite ranks broke, and the chariots were bogged down in ground which was soft at the best of times (5.20,21). It will have been then that the other tribes attacked from the rear and the rout was complete.

While the broken army swept down the plain to Sisera's town at the gap where the Kishon flows towards the sea (16), Sisera turned desperately northwards (*cf.* 11), hoping probably that he could reach Hazor. Barak must soon have discovered that Sisera had escaped and turned north after him, only to find him dead (22).

It is often claimed that Jael was only protecting her honour. The men were away, doubtless hovering like vultures to strip the dead, and the only place where Sisera would be hidden was the women's portion of the tent (the men's lay open). Had he been found there by her husband on his return, it would have meant her death. This is true, but it is clear also that Jael did not share her husband's friendship for the Canaanites (17); it was her deliberate way of helping God's people, though it involved her in major risk.

Judges 5

The text of this ancient psalm has in places been poorly preserved. This helps to explain some of the striking differences between modern versions such as the R.S.V. and the N.E.B. on the one hand, and the A.V. (K.J.V.) on the other.

In vs. 4,5 we do not have a picture of God coming to Israel's aid from Sinai, but a contrast between God's power as shown at the time of the Exodus and the grim reality of the recent past (6—8).

Judah and Simeon are not mentioned, because for them to have come would have been to imperil the secrecy essential to the whole operation. They would have had to march past Jerusalem, which could have sent an urgent message to Sisera. Machir (14) stands for Manasseh (Josh. 17.1), rather peculiarly, for he had settled in Bashan and certainly the half-tribe west of Jordan is included. Gilead (17) stands for Gad. No tribe under the religious league then prevailing could be forced to come. But for a city within a tribe that had marched to withhold its help was another matter. That is why such a bitter curse is spoken against Meroz, a city of Manasseh (23). It implies that it had been put in the ban and would be destroyed. We can understand Asher and Dan; both were finding it hard to maintain their position at all. But Reuben and Gad illustrated the danger of being the other side of Jordan; they did not feel really involved.

The modern mind finds it hard to appreciate the barbaric satisfaction in Jael's act and the mockery of Sisera's mother. It was a hard and cruel time, and doubtless the hand of Sisera had been very heavy; v. 30 shows how they expected the Israelite villages to be looted after the victory. The real thing is that we are in the O.T. and in the period before the great prophets at that. God had still much to teach His people, and we need not be surprised that Deborah, though prophetess, should have felt such satisfaction. Do not forget, either, that these people would not have existed if God's commands had been properly carried out at the Conquest.

Judges 6.1–35

Periodically, for reasons that remain unclear, the nomad population of the desert increases until there is an explosion. So it was in the time of Gideon. The Midianites and their allies (3) were specially helped by the fact that, though the camel had been used earlier, its full domestication had just been carried through. With their camels they swept up the Valley of Jezreel and through the plain of Esdraelon and finally down the coastal plain, but they could not go far in the real hills. They should have been checked by the line of cities covering the great trade route, but though they had lost their power through Deborah, they had not been captured; they probably looked on grimly, rejoicing that their Israelite neighbours were suffering more than they. Though it is not recorded, it must have been a specially difficult time for the tribes east of Jordan.

In estimating Gideon, do not take v. 15 too seriously; it is typical Oriental self-depreciation. Remember also **8.18,19**. It seems fairly clear that in his dealings with the angel (11—22) Gideon sensed that he was in touch with the supernatural, but was not sure until the miracle took place. (Angels, who must not be mixed up with the cherubim, always appear in the normal form of men!) As the story develops, it becomes clear that his father is one of the leading personages in Ophrah. His is the altar (25), probably to Jehovah, worshipped as though He were a Canaanite god, because the care of the sanctuary, clearly a communal one, had been entrusted to him (28).

Gideon knew perfectly well that one or other of the servants would betray him quickly enough. We need not doubt that Joash had been very proud of the altar entrusted to him, but the prospect of losing a third, and possibly last, son made him quick-witted. We ought to apply his argument to our own circumstances. We are all too ready to defend God, where we think His honour is concerned. We should be far more ready to assume that God will look after His own honour, if our lives are such as to honour Him. The expression in v. 34 is particularly striking. Literally translated it is, "But the Spirit of the Lord clothed Himself in Gideon"; this did not mean the end of Gideon's personality.

We have already seen that Gideon was no reckless hero. He was willing to do God's will provided he was sure that it *was* God's will. The two signs asked for show how heavy the dew can be at certain times of year—the miraculous element does not lie in its quantity. The first sign was unnatural, but possible, because the fleece would be more likely to attract dew; the second surpasses man's understanding.

Gideon's camp was on the flanks of Mt. Gilboa (7.1). The first test put to his troops was in accordance with Scripture (Deut. 20.8), but in such a period of spiritual declension we may be sure that it had not been heard for a long time. "And Gideon tested them" (3): this translation is pure guess work; the Hebrew makes no sense at all. There seems to be no doubt that there has been a transposition in the Hebrew of v. 6. Those who lapped were those who went on all fours, those who put their hands to their mouth were those who knelt. There is no clear suggestion that there was any criterion of merit in the selection. Gideon was simply to choose whatever group was the smaller.

"He sent all the rest of Israel every man to his tent" (8) must be interpreted in the light of the sequel. Once the attack was launched there was no time for reinforcements; vs. 23,24 must have been prepared for before the battle, and similarly those sent off must have been told to hold themselves in readiness.

It would be interesting to know why Purah is specially mentioned (10,11). There must be some tale of great loyalty behind it. Gideon had done his part; now God showed him that He had been doing His. He had created among the Midianites this apparently irrational fear (14), which made them ready to panic at the slightest provocation. The braying of the rams' horns in the darkness, the war cries, and the lights would have tried better nerves than theirs. Once the camels panicked, all hope of a stand was gone. With every shadow an enemy the initial death roll must have been terrible (22). The Midianite army scattered widely north and south in the Jordan valley.

Judges 7.24—8.32

In this portion we have an excellent example of how much of Israel's early history was written. There is a conflict between 7.25 and 8.4. It seems that the writer had two contemporary accounts before him. That in 7.24—8.3 was taken from one told in Ephraim; while 7.19—23, 8.4 *seq.* were taken from the story told in Ophrah. The writer so joined them as to leave an obvious and indeed self-explanatory seam.

It is important to note how God used Gideon's natural impulses. Zebah and Zalmunna, the great tribal kings, slept with an elite camel corps around them. They were far too well-disciplined to panic, and they were able to extricate themselves from the rout without difficulty. Others would have thought the job well done with the death of Oreb and Zeeb (literally Raven and Wolf), but the duty of revenge drove Gideon on until the two kings were in his hands.

The reluctance of Succoth (5) and Penuel (8) to help Gideon was due to the measure in which Trans-Jordan had been exposed to the Midianite peril. These cities had probably been able to maintain themselves only by humiliating treaties with the Midianites. Gideon's cruel treatment of them was probably because their whole policy had made it easier for the Midianites to cross the Jordan and raid unchecked.

Gideon refused to become the first king of Israel (23), but he was it, all but the title. Abimelech could assume (9.2) that his sons would succeed him in his position. Gideon made an ephod (27—however we understand this unexplained term, it must have been pretty solid to judge by the amount of gold that went into its making), thereby showing that he was prepared to make religious innovations, a power contemporaries attributed to kings. Then he had many wives (30), which was one of the standard ways in which kings distinguished themselves; we seldom find a commoner with more than two wives. So here we see the religious organization of the people already beginning to break down because of a fundamental lack of loyalty to Jehovah. Once the position with the Philistines became acute, the cry for a king would become so strong that God would give way.

We see also the mounting pride of Ephraim, which would ride for a fall, when a rougher man than Gideon met it (see 12.1—6).

Judges 8.33—9.21

We are told this story, partly to give us a picture of society as it was breaking down when the check of true religion had virtually vanished, partly because of the lasting shock it gave to Israelite consciousness (cf. 2 Sam. 11.21). We are probably intended also to see in it God's judgment on Gideon's pride, even if he was not prepared to take the final plunge and *call himself* king.

"Baal-berith" (33) means "Baal of the Covenant" and is the same as the El-berith of 9.46. Clearly it is the God of Joshua's covenant (Josh. 24.25) Who is being so worshipped, but with all sorts of Canaanite

229

corruptions. For Shechem see note on Joshua **8**. The detail that all Abimelech's brothers were killed "upon one stone" (5) can only mean that this semi-pagan virtually offered them up as a human sacrifice to guarantee his kingdom. This will hardly have extended very far from Shechem itself. Most Israelites did not want to have anything to do with Abimelech, but equally they were not concerned with avenging the wrong done to Gideon's family (**8.35**).

Presumably Jotham's striking parable was given while they were still at the coronation ceremony. The point about it, which is often missed, is the complete uselessness of a king of the trees. All he can do is to "sway over" them (9,11,13), or act as "shade" for them (15), which, of course, the trees do not need. God is the king of the trees, and equally of Israel. So any king they can appoint can only be ornamental, an unneeded figure-head. To liken Abimelech to "the bramble" (14,15) was really an insult to the bramble, in spite of its weakness and treachery.

A careful reading of Israel's history will show that it was very rare for someone from a second-class marriage, like Abimelech (18), to rise to a position of leadership. A prophet might well do so, for in the sight of God all men stand equal. We can test it by finding whether the man's father is mentioned. Jotham knew that treachery begat treachery, and that there is very little honour among thieves, so he rightly foresaw that judgment would come from their own midst.

Judges 9.22–57

The two things by which men judged a king were whether he guaranteed justice and security on the roads. By acting as highwaymen the Shechemites gave Abimelech an extremely bad name. We are not told anything of Gaal's antecedents, but since birds of a feather flock together, he was probably leader of a bandit gang. We cannot fully understand his drunken boasts (28). Evidently the Shechemites chose to forget how they came to be in the city and claimed that they were descendants of Hamor (Gen. **34.2**). "Did not the son of Jerubbaal ... serve the men of Hamor?" may be a reference to the help Abimelech received from the Shechemites.

Obviously Gaal was drunk (28), but Zebul, who can have had only a handful of armed men, realized that if he was allowed to take root in Shechem, he would soon be its lord. The next day the hardly sober Gaal had to face Abimelech's army (34—40) and was so badly mauled that Zebul's few men were able to expel him and the remainder of his band. The Shechemites thought the matter was settled, but they little knew "the bramble". They were his relations, while he needed them (2), but now he wiped them out (42—45).

"The Tower of Shechem" (46) seems to have been the fortress guarding the sanctuary, which was outside the walls of the town. Probably the people who took refuge there thought that they were claiming some sort of sanctuary, but by this time Abimelech cared as little for God as he did for relationship (46—49). Shechem occupied too important a site to remain long in ruins (*cf.* 1 Kings **12**.1).

Thebez is some little distance north of Shechem. It may have accepted Abimelech as king and now decided it had had enough of him, or he may have started a mad career of conquest. At any rate his treatment of Shechem called out a desperate resistance in which the women joined. A millstone well thrown crushed his skull, but proud and self-centred to the last he thought only of how to save his reputation. As 2 Samuel **11**.21 shows us, his desperate gesture was in vain. There was no one to take over the reins of power he had dropped, and the thought of kingship slipped for the moment once more into the background.

What are the parallels between Abimelech and Absalom?

Questions for Further Study and Discussion on Judges chapters 1—9.
1. Analyze the reasons why Israel failed lamentably to drive out all the inhabitants of Palestine. See **1**.34*ff.*, **1**.19, **1**.25, **1**.28, **1**.33.
2. How can Jael's deception (**4**.18) be justified—if at all?
3. Consider ch. **5** and discuss in what ways we are involved in difficult situations because of the past failures of God's people. Also what difficulties may we be creating for our successors?
4. What can we learn from the dealings of the Spirit of God with Gideon to help us understand His work in the life of a believer?
5. What unchanging principles of victory in the warfare with God's enemies are emphasized by the experience of Gideon?
6. "The sins of the Church are seldom the active doing of evil, but normally the cowardly acquiescence in evil already done." Discuss this in the light of chs. **8, 9**.

Judges 10.1—11.28

It is today widely believed that those judges of whom next to nothing is told—*viz.*, **10**.1—5, **12**.8—15—were those whose duty it was to know and recite the law at the great political meetings of Israel, when the tribal alliance met at the central sanctuary to carry out its business, mainly judicial.

At this point Israel's religion had reached its lowest point until the reign of Manasseh (2 Kings **21**.1—9). The debasing of Jehovah, and the honouring of other gods beside Him, led to positive idolatry, which was not entirely cleared up until the reforms of Samuel (1 Sam. **7**.3,4). To the growing pressure of the Philistines, to which the story of Samson will introduce us, there was suddenly added the much heavier and doubtless cruder oppression of the Ammonites (**10**.7—9). Apparently it was only then that they realized what the eighteen years of Ammonite overlordship in Trans-Jordan had meant. Even then it was left to the latter to do the fighting, when the Ammonites heard that their serfs were stirring once more.

So far as we are able to reconstruct the old Israelite marriage laws and customs, Jephthah was a fully legitimate son of Gilead, because he had been legally accepted by his father (**11**.1). In the lawlessness of the time he was not able to establish his rights after his father's death, and so became a bandit chief in the wilder parts of Trans-Jordan. In their moment of despair the men who had been so unjust to him had to eat humble pie and beg the terrible bandit chief to come to their help. They had to drink the cup of humiliation to the dregs and accept Jephthah virtually as a local king. "Leader" (11) is the word used in 1 Sam. **9**.16, **10**.1, where it is translated misleadingly "prince". The agreement was solemnly ratified at Mizpah (11).

With all its barbarity the ancient world had more concept of international right than is often the case today; war needed justification (12). Ammon conveniently forgot the real history of the area. Whether it had ever belonged to them, we do not know. If so, it had been taken by the Moabites, from whom Sihon wrested it (Num. **21**.26—30). In any case, their having made no move for three hundred years made their claim invalid (26). Many have taken offence at Jephthah's speaking of *Chemosh* (24) as though he really existed. Why should a bandit chief have a better theology than his contemporaries?

Judges 11.29—12.15

Contrary to wide-spread opinion, human sacrifice was not common in the Near East at this time, nor probably at any time from 2500 B.C. on. Therefore, when it was offered, it was on occasions of outstanding importance. Jephthah knew that if Israel lost the battle, it would be the end of Israelite rule, in Trans-Jordan at any rate. So he was prepared to buy victory at the highest price he could pay. Secretly, in spite of v. 35, he must have realized the strong possibility that it would be his daughter. Every attempt to prove that Jephthah did not keep his vow is valueless (39). If you think that no priest would have carried out the sacrifice, re-read **10.6**. The corruption of idolatry cannot be eliminated overnight. In that barbarous and cruel time the mourning (38,40) was not for her premature death, but because she had been unable to fulfil her function as a mother.

There seems to have been something pathological about the pride of Ephraim. They did not rise against Moab until Ehud had borne the brunt of the day (**3.27**); they did not stir against the Midianites until Gideon had broken their power (**7.24**); they ignored the needs of Trans-Jordan for 18 years until Jephthah had won a decisive victory. Though they were the strongest tribe, only the minor judge Abdon (**12.15**) came from them. Now they turned on Jephthah, but received no smooth words from that grim and embittered man. There followed a decisive defeat, which along with those of 1 Samuel **4.2,10** changed the history of Israel. Without them Ephraim would never have agreed to a non-Ephraimite king, but none of the other tribes would have agreed to an Ephraimite one.

It is a very strange fact that even in our own days people living in what was then Mount Ephraim suffer from the same defect of speech. It suggests that probably many of the so-called Arabs of Palestine are in fact descendants of the old tribes, who have long ago forgotten their identity as they have changed their religion.

The Bible warns us against rash promises to God, or for that matter to man. Obviously Jephthah should not have made his promise, and yet he had a higher regard for God than many who think that their promises are just like pie-crusts. A true priest would have shown him the right way, which would not have been a simple cancelling of the promise.

Judges 13

The strangest figure among the Judges is Samson. His story simply cries out for an allegorization the text will not stand. We automatically protest that such a man could not have been chosen by God. Probably many an Israelite felt the same way; this is probably the reason why the angel appeared before his birth, and why he wore the long hair of a Nazirite (5), though we gain the impression that this may have been the only part of the Nazirite vow he kept (Num. **6.2—8**).

The Philistines moved south with the "sea peoples" to attack Egypt by land and sea (between 1200 and 1190 B.C.). They were completely defeated, and apparently placed by Rameses III in the area we associate with them, to guard the desert approach to Egypt. There they were a military elite in the midst of a predominantly Canaanite population, whose language they quickly adopted. They gradually extended their power, first for Egypt's benefit, and then, as Egypt grew weaker, for their own. They evidently acted with wisdom and moderation, for although by Samson's time they were in unquestioned control of Judah (15.11), there seems to have been no outcry. If God had not acted, Philistine influence would have spread to such a degree that it could hardly have been eliminated. Since Israel was not yet prepared to fight for his freedom, God raised up a man with a private grievance, whose killing of Philistines did not involve his people. Since they were a military elite, their death mattered more than that of the rank and file of their forces.

As with Gideon, Manoah and his wife did not know they had to do with an angel until they saw the miracle, though his wife had some suspicion (6). It is quite probable that Manoah suspected the genuineness of the message, but blessings on his wife for a breath of sound common sense (23).

There has almost certainly never been another Samson among the people of God, but there have been many other strange characters. We are very unwilling to learn that God wants to use all the gifts He has given, while we should like to confine Him to our respectabilities. We are accustomed to hear of the unusual on the mission field, but find it hard to make room for it at home.

Judges 14

"At Timnah he saw one of the daughters of the Philistines" (1). The story begins as naturally as all that. A young man goes through the spring landscape with his parents, in his eyes the light of love. His heart urges his feet faster than his parents can or wish to go, so he is here and there, seeing what there is to see. A lion in the first fullness of his strength is nothing to Samson in his present mood, but as he rejoins his parents, he remembers what an embarrassment his unwonted strength can be to them, so he is quiet about the encounter. Evidently Manoah is well-to-do. While the young couple talk, the parents haggle, until the clink of silver outweighs the voice of racial pride. A little later they come down for the wedding, dressed in their best, and Samson idly goes to have a look at his lion, and is met by bees. There is plenty of time before the wedding feast, so he shares out the honey. Life is very sweet.

At the wedding feast the guests begin to make fun of the country bumpkin from the hills, and their tongues are sharper than the bees stings, so he silences them with a riddle. Every spare moment in the feasting a solution is offered, each one wilder than the last, until, when the third evening of the wedding week is past, the screw is put on the bride, and she puts it on Samson. With a shock he realizes that you do marry your wife's relations. Hoping against hope he tells her the answer, but it is no shock as they gather for the last instalment of the feast to be told the answer.

In wild anger he left the house and ran at top speed the twenty-three miles to Ashkelon. The first thirty decently dressed men he could lay hold of he killed and early in the morning staggered in with his arms full of clothes. He flung them at the feet of the terrified guests and made off for home. "That's what comes of marrying your daughter to an Israelite" was the general verdict; to stop the bride's tears she was hurriedly married to the best man. Unfortunately they forgot that Samson was in love.

Judges 15.1—16.3

The fiercer the anger the sooner it cools. Love begins its work again, and Samson is going downhill happily with a kid to pacify his abandoned wife. He soon finds, however, that there is no wife and only the offer of a chit of a girl who leaves him cold. Revenge is sweet, however. With a Rabelaisian imagination he snares three hundred foxes. As the sun goes down, he ties them tail to tail with a lighted torch between. The maddened animals scatter far and wide, and all is tinder dry. Peace steals over the strong man as he sees the Philistine grain and olive trees go up in flames. He would have let the matter end there, but God had other purposes.

An inquest next morning on the damage soon established the cause, and summary injustice was done to the Philistine and his daughter. This was serious. After all, up till then it had been a family quarrel, but now his wife had been murdered, so Samson inflicted summary justice and retired to let things blow over (8). The Philistines would have done well to let sleeping dogs lie, but they decided that the master-race could not stomach an insult like that. The pique of the Judeans (11) showed that they regarded the whole matter as an inconvenient private quarrel. As Samson stood free before the Philistines, he looked round for a weapon and saw the jaw-bone of a donkey newly dead. With all its teeth in place it formed a terrible weapon. By the time the fight was over, the ground was littered with dead Philistines. A natural spring suddenly broke out, not one from

235

the jawbone. The misunderstanding came from the fact that the place was called after the famous jawbone (*lehi*).

There is no evidence that Samson went on killing Philistines. He was satisfied, and they probably decided to leave well alone. But it was insulting, when he apparently put his head into a noose by going to Gaza, and infuriating to find one's town gates ornamenting a hillside deep in Judean territory. That story must have been told and retold in every inn from Thebes to Babylon. Doubtless this was not the only trick he played. So injured honour demanded he must be eliminated.

Judges 16.4–31

The closing scenes in Samson's life could well have been greatly misunderstood. The valley of Sorek was in the debatable land between Israel and the Philistines. Delilah could have been entirely respectable, quite possibly a widow; she was almost certainly an Israelite, otherwise the five 'lords of the Philistines' would not have offered her the enormous bribe of 5,500 shekels (5)—thirty shekels was considered to be the value of a slave. There are no reasons for thinking that Samson did not marry Delilah. If we are in a hurry to condemn her, let us ask ourselves, whether there is not a price, which need not be in money, which might make *us* disloyal.

The cause of Samson's downfall was self-confidence. He cannot have been unaware that Delilah was plotting, though he was probably far from guessing the full truth. His attitude, when his head had been shaved, shows that his strength had never been merely a natural one, but was the special gift of the Spirit.

He had dishonoured the Philistines, now they would dishonour him. Grinding at the mill was the work of the women, above all the slave-women (*cf*. Exod. **11.5**, Isa. **47.2**). Now he must play blind man's buff in grim earnest to the honour of their god (25). That to the very last it was a personal quarrel between Samson and the Philistines is seen in his final prayer. He would die with his honour at least partially saved.

Palestine at the time did not know the arch, and only from Lebanon could timber long enough to span a large hall be brought. So shorter lengths were laid from wall to pillar, and pillar to pillar. On softer ground, as in the coastal plain, the pillars stood on large, flat stones to prevent their sinking in the soil. Samson's exploit lay in shifting the pillars off their supports, with the resultant collapse of the roof. It will have been at least a generation before the Philistines felt strong enough once more to attack Israel (1 Sam. **4.**1). The veteran warriors who perished in the ruins of the house of Dagon could not be so easily replaced. As we stand at the tombs of Jephthah and Samson, we may well think, "two extraordinary men!", but without them how different would the future history of Israel have been, if indeed there had been any!

Judges 17

Here we pass over to a picture of what life was really like. The story could be later than the time of Samson, but is probably earlier.

A woman, finding that someone has stolen 1,100 shekels from her, utters such blood-chilling curses on the thief that her son finds he cannot sleep at night and owns up. At the time a curse was looked on as a sort of wild animal to be let loose on the trail of the evil-doer. All she could do was to let loose an even stronger blessing that would overtake and destroy the curse (2), though we gain the impression that she was better at cursing than blessing. To reinforce the blessing the mother consecrated the silver to Jehovah, but then decided that He ought to be satisfied with two-elevenths of it (though perhaps another eleventh went on the rest of the shrine). We may judge that the graven and molten image both refer to the same thing, a bull image (Exod. 32.4, 1 Kings 12.28—in both cases a young bull rather than a calf is meant) to serve as throne for the invisible god. What use is a perfectly good shrine without a priest? A son had to serve for the time being, until a wandering Levite turned up. Levites were many, jobs few, and Micah, for the time, rich. So he was willing to become priest for the family for a good wage, board and lodging, and a new suit each year. As for Micah, he was in the seventh heaven with delight. "Now I know that the Lord will prosper me, because I have a Levite as priest" (13). The curse was dead and buried.

We may well wonder what such a family is looking for on the pages of Scripture, until we remember that this is merely a picture of what was. How much better, however, are our own times? It would be interesting to know how much church furniture, how many church buildings, have been an effort to bribe God with part, maybe a generous part, of ill-gotten gains. There is many a church and many a service where it would cause embarrassment if we asked, "Why is this here? Why do you do that?" Some might even suggest unkindly that "God's call" seems at times strangely linked with higher salaries.

237

Judges 18

The self-willed individual is often merely a representative of a self-willed society. Before we blame the tribe of Dan for seeking fresh fields, we should ask ourselves how much help they had received from the other tribes. Their fault lay in asking neither the other tribes nor God. The inquiry through the Levite (5) was made merely because the opportunity was handy. If it is objected that this (6) could not have been the voice of God, the answer is that if God had treated the Church as it deserved, there would be no Church.

It is not surprising that the five spies were enchanted with what they saw (9,10). Dan lies in what is perhaps the loveliest part of Palestine. Then, while the main roads passed through their portion in the coastal plain, there has never been more than a secondary road past Dan. They passed out of fighting and out of history. The five did not realize that the oracle of encouragement had been the voice of grace. They thought that the Levite's cultic collection was particularly potent, so they decided to take it along (14), as though God could be forced to go from place to place. Micah had forgotten, when he engaged the Levite, that a man who sells himself will always sell himself to a higher bidder, if the opportunity offers (20).

The Danites were a good-humoured lot. So long as they had their own way they had no grudge against the Ephraimites. No one was hurt, no house burnt down, the Levite came of his own free will, and Micah—? They needed the shrine more than he did, so what about it? No wonder Samuel had to begin by judging the people (1 Sam. 7.6) before God gave the victory. All concepts of inter-tribal responsibility had vanished. The possibility of justice at Shiloh was virtually forgotten.

At the end of the story the carefully preserved anonymity of the Levite is removed (30). He is seen as a descendant of Moses (probably not all links in the genealogy are given). The reading "Manasseh", which is found in the A.V. (K.J.V.), is due to a deliberate modification of the Hebrew text, by which the reader is invited to say Manasseh. The rabbis said, Even Moses had bad descendants; why should that be held against him? Under Jeroboam Dan graduated from a silver bull to a golden one (1 Kings 12.28f.).

Judges 19.1—20.11

That this story is almost certainly older than chs. 17,18 is shown by 20.28. There is also much more respect for inter-tribal justice.

Because we have become civilized, and most of us can forget what the natural man can do, at least if we stop reading the crime news, this chapter shocks us far more than does the previous story. For the Bible this is merely a story of natural man in his cruelty, self-preservation, and sensuality; the unfaithfulness to God and the ignoring of His revealed will shown in the former story were far more reprehensible.

Reading between the lines, it is fairly easy to reconstruct the background of chs. **19—21**. Benjamin, for reasons that are never hinted at, decided to leave Israel's religious alliance. That is why the Levite was treated as a foreigner to whom the men of Gibeah owed neither hospitality (**19.**15), nor security (**19.**22—25). The Levite summoned an emergency meeting of the alliance (**19.**29) to claim justice. By the refusal of the Benjaminites to carry out their alliance obligations (**20.**13), the other tribes found themselves in the same position as did the United States of America, when the slave states wished to secede. The constitution made no provision for this, so the only way out seemed to be war.

The Levite's wife is called a concubine (**19.**1), probably because she had no dowry. It was obviously a regular marriage. The urging of hospitality by his father-in-law is typically oriental. It shows why Rebekah was in such unmaidenly haste to go (Gen. **24.**54—58). The attitude of the servant towards Jebus (**19.**11) shows that Jerusalem was fairly careful to remain on good terms with those who passed by. There may have been an inn in Jerusalem, but Gibeah was too small for one. They were uncommon in small places, and the rendering "inn" in Luke **2.**7 must be regarded for this reason with suspicion (*cf.* N.E.B.). It is difficult to judge actions among people whose whole standard of values is different. For us the old man's suggestion was abominable (**19.**24), but for him his duties as host had to come first— he had to protect his guest. Equally the Levite had to see to it that his host came to no harm. The Levite's version puts him in a better light than he deserved (**20.**4,5).

Judges 20.12–48

The first mistake made by Israel was to accept the Levite's testimony without hearing the other side (4—7). No man can be relied on to give the whole truth in his own case. Then they passed sentence without hearing the defence (8—11). Then they bound themselves by a rash oath, even before Benjamin had a possibility of accepting their point of view. Next they expected Benjamin to accept the charge and verdict, though they had not been present when it was passed (12,13).

239

Finally they first made up their minds that it must be war, and only then did they ask God how it was to be waged (18). They gave God no chance to suggest another solution. Sorrow in the Christian life comes often from the prayer for God's guidance on the path of our own choosing.

Benjamin was obviously in the wrong and punishment had to come to them. But behind Benjamin's wrong lay also the sins of Israel, and so judgment had to begin there. Judah's selfishness over Jerusalem (see note on 1.8) led to their bearing the brunt of the first day's defeat (18). All the tribes were to blame that a considerable portion of Benjamin's territory was Canaanite (Josh. 9), and so their turn had to come the next day. Above all, however, they were to blame that they had put a portion of God's people in the ban. It is the end of this chapter that should sicken us far more than the story of Gibeah.

If God put the people of Canaan and later the Amalekites (1 Sam. 15.3) in the ban, He did so in His wisdom and patience—Canaan had waited since the time of Abraham (Gen. 15.13—16), the Amalekites from the time of the Exodus (Exod. 17.14). Even when God acted directly, He gave the contemporaries of Noah warning, all the time the ark was in building, and the cities of the plain the years of Lot's living among them. Here, however, Israel assumed that because Benjamin had separated itself from the people of God, therefore it had separated itself from God; because Israel had put Benjamin in the ban, God had too. We have here virtually a prophecy of the many bloody pages in Church history where "heretics" were annihilated to the glory of God. The one real difference is that Israel repented (21.2,3), but the persecuting Church did not.

Judges 21

Israel had sown the wind and was now reaping the whirlwind, but even so had not learnt. One may admire them for sticking to their word; one would admire them more, if they had laid their predicament before God. But even at this late stage, there seems to have been no realization of their folly. If things had gone wrong, God was to blame (15). Repeatedly we imagine that we know the will of God and set out to do it with boundless self-confidence. Then, when things go awry, we feel that God has let us down.

With typical human logic they try to cure the effects of blood-letting by further blood-letting (8—12). We need feel less sympathy with Jabesh Gilead, because, like Meroz (5.23), it knew the risks it was running, But even when we grant this, it is only a demonstration of the folly of human wisdom. The later links between Jabesh Gilead and Benjamin are surely a pure coincidence (1 Sam. **11**.1—11; **31**.11—13).

The book of Judges ends with a scene that would belong better to a pantomime or slapstick film than the real life of the Bible. The elders of Israel stage a glorious "let's pretend" to prevent their technically breaking their promise. Four times over the author assures us (**17.6**; **18.1**; **19.1**; **21.25**) that there was then no king in Israel. God had given them a political system, which in its three stages of local government, tribal unity, and inter-tribal justice and common action based on a loyalty to the one God, was almost ideal, especially under the conditions then existing. But the loyalty to God was short-lived, and even while it existed (chs. **19—21**), it was purely fleshly, a keeping of the letter of the law. Once that went, the whole system began to dissolve. No one reading *Judges* can doubt that the monarchy was preferable to the chaos which then was, and yet the monarchy represented spiritually a major fall. This is a point that we need to take seriously. Some are proud, it may be rightly, of the purity and Scripturalness of our church order. But when we compare the life of our community with that of one on whom we look down, we all too often find there is more Scriptural order among those we affect to despise than in our chaos.

Questions for Further Study and Discussion on Judges chapters 10—21.

1. "A true priest would have shown Jephthah the right way, which would not have been a simple cancelling of the promise." What might this "right way" have been? Has it anything to teach us?
2. Was Samson's silence (**14.9**) based on humility, or due to an awareness of having violated his Nazirite vow? Was this the "thin edge of the wedge" that was to lead in due course to a far more serious violation of his vow?
3. Summarize the lessons which Samson's experience teaches us in the matter of Christian living today.
4. Why was Israel twice defeated (ch. **20**)? Was the third campaign against Benjamin pressed home too ruthlessly?
5. How do the latter chapters of Judges illustrate the principle that "sorrow in the Christian life comes often from the prayer for God's guidance on the path that we have already chosen"?

Ruth 1

Ruth seems to throw a gleam of sunlight backwards over the dark pages of *Judges* and to show that the humble virtues could flourish even then. Such is not its real purpose, for in the Hebrew Bible it stands among the Writings, separated from *Judges*. It was doubtless written to show how a Moabitess figured in the genealogy of the great king David, and possibly to plead for a hand of welcome to those who came to Israel from outside.

Rainfall was very uneven in times of drought (Amos **4**.7,8), and so Moab might occasionally have more rain than Bethlehem, but the move and a ten years' sojourn (4) point to a desperately poor family for whom emigration could not worsen their lot. It follows that Orpah and Ruth must also have come from poor families, probably without dowries. By marriage they became members of the Elimelech family, and death did not release them from that fact. Naomi had, as head of the family, a legal claim over them, but she was equally under obligation to find them husbands, hence the, to us, strange language of vs. 11—13. Had she been able to offer a good dowry with the young widows, it would have been different; instead she gave them their freedom.

Ruth is not explained to us. It is easy to read more than we should into "and your God (shall be) my God" (16). By her marriage she was under obligation, outwardly at least, to serve Jehovah, and that obligation became stronger once she went to His land. Was she merely expressing this? In all probability through Mahlon and his family she had come to serve Jehovah because she wanted to. It is clear that both the widows had come to love Naomi, and there may have been a stirring of sacrificial love in Ruth's heart that made it impossible for her to leave the pitiful widow. We shall probably do best if we look on her as one of those little ones whom Jesus held up as an example to His followers.

At a time when one of the few excitements of life was a pilgrim feast or an enemy raid, and under circumstances where Elimelech's house and field must have been carefully looked after by near relatives, there is nothing surprising in Naomi's being quickly recognized (19). In fact Naomi was bringing back with her far greater riches than she realized.

Ruth 2

The fields of Bethlehem lie at various levels, and so the grain does no

242

ipen all at once, and the harvest period (23) could last some time. Ruth was exercising her right in going to glean (Lev. **19**.9,10; **23**.22), but especially in a time like hers much would depend on how it was interpreted. When she started, one large field, divided into strips among various owners, was being reaped. She was working in Boaz' section, when he came. It looks as though it was a case of "like master like man"; the friendly answer of the head servant had kept her in that section.

Ruth need not have been surprised that Boaz knew about her (10). The men of Elimelech's clan must have been very interested in Naomi's return, for there was property involved; but harvest and the slow pace of the east ensured that no immediate steps would be taken by anyone. "Keep close to my maidens" (8): first came the men with the sickles, then the "maidens" to make the sheaves, and finally the gleaners.

"An ephah of barley" (17)—*i.e.*, just under a bushel. This shows a side of Ruth's character we often overlook. To glean that amount in a day meant, even allowing for the extras (15,16), an extraordinarily hard day's work in great heat. She was not allowing her mother-in-law to starve, if she could prevent it. That she could bring home that amount and also have a bit of her lunch left over (18) immediately showed Naomi that her treatment had been exceptional. She suspected that unexpected developments might be round the corner, but for the time being she kept her thoughts to herself.

Ruth 3,4

In a land with strict segregation of the sexes a private conversation between a man and a woman, especially if she was young, like Ruth, was almost impossible without destroying her reputation, and his too (*cf*. John **4**.27). On this night, with the joy of a good harvest in his heart, Boaz was quite exceptionally sleeping out of doors; for all we know, it may have been to guard against thieves—in any case Naomi knew the local customs. Ruth bared his feet, for there was no more effective way of waking him quietly without a start than by letting his feet grow cold. When he did wake, in the moonlight he saw a woman lying there quietly. We must picture a conversation carried on in mere whispers, after which Ruth could slip away quietly, none knowing that she had been there. "Spread your skirt over your maid-servant" (**3**.9): to this day, in some Arab clans, a man will show that he claims a woman as wife as of right by passing the skirt of his robe round her.

In what follows we are not dealing with Levirate marriage (Deut 25.5—10, Matt. 22.23—28). There is no evidence that this was ever under any circumstances, extended from a brother to the next of kin Further, Boaz' words (3.10) show that, whatever her duty to Naomi Ruth was under no obligation to him. She could have tried to catch a young man by her beauty. The clue is given by the next of kin' objection (4.6); he was afraid of impairing his own inheritance. H really came into the picture because he had a pre-emptive right to buy the ground (Lev. 25.25), so there was no point in anyone else's doing it, until he knew whether the right would be exercised.

Clearly Naomi's bit of land can have had little cash value. In th understanding of an age more merciful in many things than ours it price was board and lodging so long as she lived. At her age it seemed a bargain until the next of kin realized that it also included the care o Ruth, who might easily outlive him. The question of marriage wa altogether another. At that time it was understood that a woman had a right to children; if a young woman came to live in a house in any capacity she would in due course become the wife of the head of the house or of one of his sons. Quite clearly the part about perpetuating the name of the dead (4.10) was more pious talk than reality, for the genealogy of David is always reckoned through Boaz and no through Elimelech and Mahlon.

"Boaz went up to the gate" (4.1): it was only the exceptionally large city like Jerusalem that had more than one gate. So the earl riser could be sure of catching anyone he wanted, as he went out to work in the fields.

Questions for Further Study and Discussion on the book of Ruth.
1. What evidence is there in this book that Boaz was a genuine man of humble faith in God?
2. In what sense does Boaz reflect and exemplify the Person and work of Jesus Christ?
3. Analyse the various forms which human love and mutual responsibility take in the book of Ruth.

and 2 Samuel

amuel, one book in Hebrew manuscripts, though divided in printed libles, may have received its name because Samuel is the first great haracter in it, or more likely because he first gave the impulse to this ype of prophetic historical writing. The author—we might better say ditor—has shown how the book is to be divided by his use of ummaries at the end of sections. Following these indications we lave:—

A.	The Book of Samuel	1 Sam. 1—7
B.	The Institution of the Monarchy	1 Sam. 8—12
C.	The Book of Saul	1 Sam. 13–15
D.	The Book of David the King	1 Sam. 16–2 Sam. 8
E.	The Book of David the Man	2 Sam. 9—20
F.	Appendix	2 Sam. 21—24

Section E, which was written by a contemporary, really ends with Kings 2. The striking differences between R.S.V. and A.V. (K.J.V.) are more often than not due to the very difficult text of the Hebrew. R.S.V. often follows the early Greek translation which, as the Dead Sea Scrolls show, often preserves a more accurate text.

I Samuel 1

Elkanah was a Levite (1 Chron. **6**.19—28, 33—38, *cf.* 1 Sam. **8**.2). He is called an Ephraimite because of his home—*cf.* Judg. **17**.7. V.3 does not mean he ignored two of the three pilgrim feasts, but that this was a special family sacrifice (*cf.* **20**.28,29). It is probable that the number of portions was a ritually fixed matter leaving Elkanah no choice. We have only gradually mastered the art of reading and praying without speaking aloud. Hannah's bitterness enabled her to pray within herself, but her lips still moved (12,13), something Eli had previously always linked with drunkenness.

Hannah's prayer must not be regarded merely as a natural desire for a child, but must be interpreted in the light of **2**.1—10. It is widely held that mothers in Israel wanted sons in the hope of being an ancestress of the Messiah. We gain the impression that it was rather their deep passion to fulfil the functions for which they were made and Hannah's thanksgiving supports this. If God has given us gifts, it is normal that they should be used. If they were not used, it was regarded as a reversal of the Divine order. This was, of course, before the N.T. revelation of the possible sacrifice of self to achieve the Divine purpose.

"When she had weaned him" (24): with us it is the exceptional baby that is not weaned by nine months. In the Near East a boy may not be fully weaned till three years old, and there are numerous special cases recorded where he was not weaned till five. So we may be certain that the pictures which show Hannah pushing a babe-in-arms into Eli's embarrassed arms are wrong. By the time he was taken to Shiloh he was a boy who could well fit into Eli's household.

We would think that Hannah had done more than enough to show her gratitude, but she brought a handsome thank offering with her as well. In her prayer she spoke of giving Samuel to God (11); now she is lending him (28). She was not holding back something she had promised, but she had come to know God better. She now knew that such giving could never break the link between parents and child. This she symbolized by her annual gift of a robe (2.19); he was still enfolded in his mother's love.

1 Samuel 2

Much in our modern educational systems has a sociological rather than educational motivation. It is felt that the best should come to the top irrespective of the parents' position and money. In an ideal society this would be so. Apart from v. 5, there is nothing in Hannah's song that has any obvious bearing on her case, but it is not Samuel she is thanking God for. She is overjoyed that in her God has demonstrated that principle of righteousness by which the injustices of life are checked and its wrongs reversed. Her own disability had created in her a passion for the vindication of God's purposes. This song served Mary as a pattern, when it was her turn to praise God (Luke 1.46—55).

The actions of Hophni and Phinehas are seen in all their darkness when we remember that in every ritualistic religion the details of the ritual are seen as at least as important as the personal sanctity of the priest. By their ignoring of ritual—even if it seemed unimportant—they showed their complete contempt for God. As might be expected there was soon contempt for the moral law as well (22).

Eli was of the family of Ithamar, not of Eleazar (*cf.* 1 Chron. **24**.3; **6**.4—10). Trustworthy Samaritan tradition claims that Eli had secured the high-priesthood because of the youth of the rightful heir in the family of Eleazar. If this is so, it aggravates the guilt of his weakness with his own sons and helps to explain the drastic punishment prophesied here (27—36) and in **3**.11—14. Note that in *Chronicles* the genealogy of Eli is passed over in silence; it can only be inferred. We can trace some of the steps by which the judgment of God was carried out: the death of Hophni and Phinehas (**4**.11), the murder of the priests at Nob (**22**.11—19) and finally the banishment of Abiathar (1 Kings **2**.26,27).

Ritual in itself is fundamentally unimportant. By the infringement in v. 13 there was no guarantee that they would get more than their share, and in v. 15 it was mainly a question of throwing their weight about. Such infringement is like rudeness. When this comes of ignorance, the wise man will overlook it. When it is deliberate, it springs from moral corruption. So it was with these young priests. Eli rebuked them for their immorality but overlooked that their disrespect to God was really something worse.

1 Samuel 3

If we think back to the days of Abimelech, Jephthah, and Samson, we need hardly be surprised that the prophetic voice was seldom heard. In such a period none would think much of it that a Levite was allowed to sleep in the temple (2). The going-out of the lamp need not point to carelessness. Exod. **27**.20,21 and Lev. **24**.2,3 imply that the lamp did not burn by day. So the mention of the lamp may mean simply that it was quite dark.

We are apt to think that the voice of God is so clear and distinct that it cannot be confounded with any other. This can be far from the truth, so the boy Samuel has to learn his first lesson as prophet. The message was not needed by Eli; he had been told more than that. But he was a great enough man, with all his weaknesses, to let Samuel know that he had heard aright. It was also God's way of letting Eli know that he must give Samuel his chance to act as a prophet, whenever God chose to speak. In addition, because Eli was a kindly old man, Samuel found it easier to take the first step in passing on a message that was very hard to deliver.

"The Lord . . . stood forth" (10): the picture seems to be of God's coming from His cherub throne behind the veil to Samuel in the holy place. "Samuel lay until morning" (15): in the light of vs. 5,6,9, it seems clear enough that it meant that he went to sleep again. That was as it should be. The voice of God should transform life and yet so mingle with it as to let it continue its normal tenor. "Let none of his words fall to the ground" (19)—i.e., God did not allow any of them to go unfulfilled. There is always a measure of contingency in prophecy, varying from case to case (cf. Jer. **18**.1—10). Samuel was to become virtually a second Moses, so God was careful to build up his reputation by not giving him messages the outcome of which might be changed by repentance.

Do we give God a chance of speaking to us, or would He have to wake us up to do it? Do we even want Him to speak to us?

1 Samuel 4

The Greek has an indubitably correct insertion in v. 1 showing that the campaign was started by the Philistines. They had recovered from their losses under Samson and were out to conquer the whole land. The first battle was perhaps the worst defeat suffered until then by Israel. They decided that God had left them in the lurch. It did not seem to occur to them that it might be due to their sin, nor are we told that any greeted Hophni and Phinehas as birds of ill omen when they came with their sins into the camp (4). Their idea was that God should be *forced* to fight for them. If He was not willing to do it for their sake, He would have to do it for His honour's sake. We do not do this quite so grossly, but the equivalent is not unknown among us. In the sequel God was to show that He was perfectly well able to look after the ark and His honour, but He was not going to be bullied by His people. Probably wrong confidence was linked with cowardice; possibly the unexplained reference in Psalm **78**.9 is to this battle (cf. 60,67).

The tragedy of Eli was that he was a man of greater spiritual perception than execution. He knew well enough that the fetching of the ark was a spiritual error, and he could expect no good from his sons' having to accompany it. Jeremiah **7**.12,14, **26**.6,9 tell us of the end of Shiloh. Excavations have shown, what in any case might have been assumed, that it was destroyed at this time. The Philistines will have marched straight there and burnt the temple, not out of wantonness, but because it was the outward symbol of Israel's unity. Apparently there was just time to rescue the most sacred objects—cf. 2 Chron. **1**.3,5. The remainder of the priests moved to Nob (1 Sam. **21**.1—6, **22**.9,10,18,19). So Israel was left without even the outward symbols of a unity that had almost completely disappeared.

The story of Phinehas' wife (19—22) is one of the most touching in

248

he Bible, but she was wrong. The glory of God had indeed departed, but not because the ark of God had been captured; the ark had been captured because the glory had already departed.

I Samuel 5.1—6.18

Once the ark had been taken to Philistia, God began to see to His honour. The adventures of Dagon (5.2—5) were secondary; they were merely a warning that the ark had better be kept from idol temples. Far more important was, as the Greek has at the end of 5.12, wherever the ark came "the land swarmed with mice" (*cf.* 6.5). Since O.T. Hebrew makes no distinction between the mouse and its bigger cousin the rat, we may well assume that the reference is to the latter, and that the tumours are plague boils. With one stroke God had undone the effects of the two Philistine victories. The terrible mortality made it impossible for them to follow them up. Otherwise there would have been nothing to prevent Israel's complete incorporation into Philistine territory.

The Philistine priests (6.2) were canny men; they knew that the woes of Philistia looked like cause and effect, but they knew also that there is such a thing as coincidence. So they advised the return of the ark to Jehovah with a guilt offering (6.3)—one of the indications of how close in outward form the Israelite sacrificial system was to the Canaanite. But Jehovah should be required to bring His ark home. Any self-respecting cows would at once have doubled back to their calves (6.7). In fact they protested vigorously against the constraint of God upon them (6.12).

For more than half a year the ark had been in Philistia (6.1), while Israel lay too stunned to know what would come next. Then the impossible, the incredible, happened. Impelled by an invisible power the ark came back. It is not surprising that the great stone in the field of Joshua of Beth-shemesh was shown for centuries after as the place where God began the transformation of His people's history. But something had happened. Until then the ark had been the mysterious guarantee of God's presence. The simpler and more superstitious may even have believed that God not only sat enthroned above it on the wings of the cherubs, but possibly even lived in it. But now they had seen it captured and the old respect had gone. Man would always rather have a magic instrument of some kind than the unchanging character of God.

In what ways do we today not trust God to look after His own honour?

249

1 Samuel 6.19—7.14

To many it seems impossible that God should kill seventy of the small town of Beth-shemesh, of hardly more than 3,000 inhabitants because they looked into the ark, while the Philistines had been allowed to take it with apparent impunity (but with what a sequel!) The difference was that the Israelite knew that he did wrong, the Philistine did not. As the margin shows, the Hebrew text presents a major problem with its addition of 50,000 men; they are clearly differentiated from the 70 of Beth-shemesh. Those who explain it of those drawn by the news from the neighbourhood may be right, but we are safer in regarding it as the remains of a text which cannot be restored with certainty. For the time being the ark had to wait in safe and respectful custody in Kiriath-jearim (2).

We are frequently plagued by those who believe that revival is just round the corner, if we have only faith enough. There are times when God has to inflict deadly drought in the Church before He can bless. Samuel waited twenty years before he made his call to repentance; anything earlier would have led to the merely superficial. Three steps may be noted: right relationship with God (4); right relationship with men (6, "Samuel judged the people"); victory over the enemy (11). The victory was on the same ground as the previous defeat (4.1,2; 7.12), the name in the earlier passage being given in anticipation.

Earlier liberal writers made a great deal of vs. 13,14, pointing out that chs. 13,14 show us the Philistines in the heart of Israel, and so the story here is dismissed as valueless. Common courtesy demands that the compiler of *Samuel* be granted as much insight as his critics. Except in chs. 13,14 the fighting from now on is always in the border districts, and we nowhere find that Israelite cities have to be re-captured. The plain meaning is that the victory of Eben-ezer ended Philistine occupation, though not Philistine power.

Samuel must be regarded as the real restorer of Israel's religion. In the period from Saul to Solomon we find very little trace of any deeply corrupted religion, and even the use of the name Baal gradually dies out.

Thought: God wants you to win your first victory on the field where you have been defeated.

1 Samuel 7.15—8.22

The one thing Samuel was not permitted to do was to set up more than an interim political settlement. The mention of the four places, not ery far apart, regularly visited by Samuel shows that he was not repared to choose a new centre to replace Shiloh until the people by alling for the ark showed that they wanted a renewal of the old eligious alliance. But they obviously blamed the shortcomings of the lliance and not their own, so the stop-gap system continued.

Samuel obviously hoped that his sons might follow him, but he did ot allow his father's love to blind him. They had first to be tested, nd they failed. The people had rejected the past; they could not trust 3od to raise up a successor to Samuel; anyway they wanted someone o lead their armies rather than praying down a miracle. All that emained was that they should lose their spiritual individuality and ecome "like all the nations" (5). This phrase forms the sting in their equest. While God had fixed the priesthood in a hereditary line, He vas free to choose the right man for civil leadership. This freedom hey wished to abolish by introducing a hereditary king.

In their spiritual obtuseness they did not even realize that it might e taken by Samuel as a personal rejection; after all, he was approach-ng "retiring age". It was God they were rejecting (7), for they were efusing all that Samuel stood for. He who represents God must xpect to be rejected, when God is rejected.

The Law contained no real place for a king; Deut. **17**.14—20 was nadequate to fix his constitutional place. So vs. 10—17 must be egarded, not as a prophecy of what the king would do, but as a tatement of what he was constitutionally entitled to. Though the eople were too anxious to have a king to realize it, these powers iltimately meant the destruction of the then existing economic attern. The social evils condemned by the prophets stemmed iltimately from these powers. It would be no use complaining then 18), for they had brought the situation on themselves. The story of he monarchy is of a continual, steady decline, which it had no power o arrest, because it was not essentially God-willed.

Questions for Further Study and Discussion on 1 Samuel chapters 1—8.
1. Consider the place and effect of prayer in family life, with special reference to 1 Samuel ch. **1.**
2. How far is Hannah's song a prophecy, and Samuel's birth a pledge, of the coming of Christ?
3. What does the story of the Ark and its structure have to teach us about the place of visible symbols of God's presence among His people today (Jer. **3.**16*f*)?
4. Study Samuel as a man of intercessory prayer (a priestly function) in **8.**6, **12.**19—25, Psalm **99.**6, Jer. **15.**1.

5. "He who represents God must expect to be rejected when God i[s] rejected."—How does this principle work out at the present time[?]

1 Samuel 9.1—10.8

The story of Saul contains certain difficulties we cannot now answe[r] with certainty. This comes partly from the compiler's havin[g] obviously used information from different sources. This sectio[n] comes, clearly enough, ultimately from Saul himself. He is calle[d] "a young man" (2); by the ordinary usage of *bachur* he would not ye[t] have been married, and this is borne out by his being fairly obviousl[y] under the guidance of the family slave. Yet apparently immediatel[y] after he becomes king he has a son who is a choice warrior (13.2[).] Either the earlier part of his reign has not been recorded, or the perio[d] between his first and second anointings was longer than the stor[y] suggests (*cf.* the language of 10.7).

To understand their arrival at Ramah remember that Saul and th[e] slave had lost their way. The slave had probably heard someon[e] speak of the seer without guessing his identity; hence the readiness t[o] pay him a fee for his guidance (8). It would be interesting to kno[w] when the truth dawned on Saul, and what his feelings were as he wa[s] treated as the honoured guest with an enormous portion of meat i[n] front of him (9.24).

He was anointed prince (*nagid*—9.16; 10.1). This was a purel[y] secular title, giving him no religious rights such as the pagan king[s] had. We shall see some of the implications later. The signs, apart fro[m] the third, had no intrinsic importance, but were merely confirmation[s] of Samuel's words. We should never despise God's ability to mak[e] Himself known in the everyday. For 10.2 see Jer. 31.15. It is clear tha[t] Rachel's tomb was shown at Zelzah, near Ramah, on the borde[r] between Benjamin and Ephraim. It is not important how this is to b[e] reconciled with Gen. 35.19. If the traditional understanding is correc[t] Rachel was only one of many to have more than one grave attached t[o] her in the popular mind. "A garrison of the Philistines" (10.5) is th[e] least likely rendering of a word that may mean also "a representativ[e] of . . ." or "a pillar of . . ."—*i.e.*, a military trophy. The same am[-] biguity is found in 13.3. There is probably no link between 10.8 an[d] 13.8—14, and the command is not explained.

The prophetic exercises of the group that met Saul (**10.**5,10) were apparently of the kind we sometimes meet today in Pentecostal circles. When they are the product of the Holy Spirit, they can have a tremendous influence on a person; and so it was with Saul (**10.**6). Then, as now, these phenomena could also be more an expression of a man's personality than of the Holy Spirit. Hence the surprise of many, who considered Saul was not of that type. A wiser man answered, "Who is their father?" (12)—*i.e.*, when the originator of the phenomena was the Holy Spirit, who could limit His choice of prophets? Clearly Saul's uncle, presumably Ner (**14.**51), had heard some rumours, perhaps that Saul had been guest of honour at Ramah, but wisely he kept silence (**10.**14—16).

There are some unexplained details in the drawing of the lots. Did Saul not have to draw himself (21)? Perhaps he bolted before they realized he had drawn it. It is one thing to know in private that God has chosen you; another to appear in public as the chosen. Presumably v. 25 refers back to **8.**11—17. The Greek may be right with, "about a month later . . ." for the last sentence of ch. **10.**

The way the story is told in **11.**4, it looks as though Jabesh-Gilead had from the first placed its trust in Saul. Their vagueness in v. 3 was simply not to alert Nahash. But had Nahash not heard? Probably he had, and the raid was intended to express his derision of the new-made king. In his pride he did not think of keeping watch for what he might do. With **11.**7 *cf.* Judg. **19.**29; Saul's method had evidently been traditional for the summoning of an emergency meeting of the tribal alliance, which had never been forgotten. God had given Saul the heavy task of building the bridge between the traditional and the unknown future. So He linked him with the Judges by marking out through his prophesying that he had the Spirit of God, and also by the style of his first victory. But he had to go on, so his remaining victories bore another pattern. If we criticize Saul, let us remember his greatness of spirit at the first.

Thought: In an ungrateful world Jabesh-Gilead remained grateful (**31.**11—13).

Samuel 12

The honeymoon was rudely ended by Samuel. Presumably his address was given at Gilgal, when he considered that they had had enough of rejoicing.

First there is the accusation of ingratitude (1—5). The very call for a king was an expression of ingratitude towards Samuel. In addition the whole proceedings had not shown much thought for the feelings of the old judge. The mention of his sons (2) was merely to show how long he had served them. It will be a great thing for us, when we reach retiring age, compulsory or voluntary, to be able to do so with a clean sheet. Samuel can add, "The Lord is witness" (6).

Then there is the accusation of ingratitude towards God (6—12). As God had told him (8.7), Samuel made it clear that the demand for a king was only one form, and that not the worst, of a continuous ingratitude. R.S.V. wisely replaces the meaningless "Bedan" (11) with "Barak"; the difference in Hebrew is small. There is no necessary contradiction between v. 12 and 11.1; Nahash may well have been increasing his power for some time.

Thirdly we have the conditions for God's blessing under the new terms (13—18). The bringing of a thunderstorm at a time when one may occur naturally about once a century may seem childish and unworthy of the old prophet. The Israelites found it very hard to believe at one and the same time that Jehovah was God of both Nature and history. At the time they had no difficulty with Him as God of history (*cf.* 8,9,11), but their honouring of the Baals (10) showed their difficulty in believing that He was God of Nature also. So God's control of Nature had to be demonstrated. It was not so much that their asking for a king was wicked (17), but their asking betrayed their essential wickedness.

It is most important that we learn the lesson of v. 20. As Israel with the Gibeonites (Josh. 9), our sin may cause something to happen that was not in God's will. Instead of trying to root out that which cannot be removed, we must learn to live with it, letting it remind us of our sin, so that we walk the more closely with God. We may even find at the end that God has used the fruit of our sin for His glory and our final good.

1 Samuel 13

For many, v. 1 in R.S.V. must come as a sort of brutal challenge. The damage to the text was at first doubtless accidental, but if scribes made no attempt to find the correct figures from other MSS, it was a Spirit-inspired judgment on the reign of Saul as a whole (*cf.* 1 Chron. **10,** where Saul's death only is recorded). Strangely enough, the other details that have come down to us are too fragmentary for us to make any valid guess at the length of Saul's reign.

Saul realized at once that the quality of a small standing army was worth more than the quantity of the militia, which was effective only for a short campaign. For Jonathan's action (3,4) see note on **10.5**. On the whole, "and the Philistines heard of it" would suit a trophy pillar best. We should follow the Greek at the end of v. 3 and render, "and the Philistines heard of it, and proclaimed, 'The Hebrews have revolted.'" "Hebrews" is the name used by foreigners (19, **14.**11); when it is the people speaking, it is "Israel" (4,20).

As remarked on **10.8**, we cannot easily link **13.8** with it. Saul had his "army chaplain" (**14.3**,18), and there was bound to be a priest at a sanctuary as great as Gilgal. Saul was merely looking for an excuse to act as priest himself—*i.e.*, he wanted to extend his power from the civil to the religious sphere, and it was this that caused his rejection (14).

In a hilly land like Palestine it would call for a much longer and more complete control than the Philistines ever exercised to eliminate all the smiths. The sea peoples (see note on Judges **13**), including the Philistines, owed their military power largely to their use of iron rather than bronze weapons. They had been willing to sell iron agricultural implements, but not weapons, nor the "know-how" of working iron. There will have been smiths in Israel able to work the despised bronze, but not iron. The Philistine blacksmiths' charges were exorbitant: a *pim*—*i.e.*, two-thirds of a shekel—for the larger, and one-third for the smaller, articles.

Thought: The last five minutes of waiting are often the most difficult!

1 Samuel 14.1–46

The Philistines had marched up by the passes of Aijalon and Beth-horon, had seized part of the central ridge and had gone further east to Michmash. Here they were separated from Saul's position in Geba (*cf.* 2 with **13.5**, **14.5**) by a deep ravine. They had virtually isolated Benjamin from the centre and north. The raiders went north, east and west, but not to the south, held by Saul. The general site of Jonathan's exploit is known, but not the exact place; in any case the crossing of the ravine, even today, is difficult.

The plan was that they should go down to the ravine bottom (8). If the Philistines said they would come down to fight them, they would await their coming (9); if they were challenged to climb up on the Philistine side, they would do so (10). Once they started climbing, they would probably have been invisible to those above, so it is not clear whether the Philistines dismissed them as mad, or whether they jocularly waited until they reached the top. No sooner had the panic started, than it was continued by the earthquake (15).

The ravine was narrow enough for those at Geba to see the panic but not to be sure of its reason. It could have been a trap, so Saul, to discover God's will, called for Ahijah and the ephod (so the Greek quite apart from 7.2, there is no evidence that the ark was used for discovering God's will), but before it was given, the reality of the panic seemed to make it unnecessary. Saul's oath (24) belongs to those superstitions which think that God is more likely to listen if men indulge in unnecessary self-denial. If God withheld His answer (37), it was because He often takes our stupidities as seriously as we mean them. R.S.V. is wrong in suggesting that the people ate the blood (32); they ate the animals *on* the blood—*i.e.*, they made no attempt to cook them away from the blood-stained earth. R.S.V. has rightly followed the Greek in v. 41. It is unlikely that we are meant to press "so the people ransomed Jonathan" (45); if there was any price paid it was that of an incomplete victory.

1 Samuel 14.47—15.35

These verses in ch. **14** are intended as a summary—*i.e.*, we are passing from the history of Saul to the coming of his successor. Everything told us from here on about Saul is in the light of David. Note that as a warrior Saul was very successful (see also note on 2 Sam. **1**.24). "Ishvi" (49) is indubitably Ish-bosheth (2 Sam. **2**.8). His name was really Esh-baal (1 Chron. **8**.33, **9**.39). Later scribes changed Baal to "Bosheth" (shame), but here to *yo* (from Yahweh), corrupted to *vi*. Abinadab (**31**.2) has accidentally dropped out. For this use of *bosheth*, *cf*. Mephibosheth with 1 Chron. **8**.34, **9**.40, and Jerub-besheth (2 Sam. **11**.21) with Judg. **6**.32.

As you will have seen from *Joshua*, the stringency with which the ban was operated varied from case to case. Here (**15**.3) it was as absolute as in the case of Jericho (Josh. **6**.17—19) and Ai (Josh. **8**.2). If this was not carried out (15,20,21), it must have been because Saul thought he understood God's will better than Samuel and informed his captains accordingly; note his genuine surprise in v. 20. Once again he was trying to assume religious rights, and so he was rejected once again. The fact that he had once "prophesied" (**10**.10) did not make him a greater prophet than Samuel.

Before you feel sorry for the Amalekites, remember that they had been given more than 200 years to repent. Their original sin (Exod. **17**.8) had been a breach of fundamental desert law, the attempt to monopolize the water supply, and doubtless they had not changed. Samuel's words to Agag (33) should be sufficient for anyone with an imagination.

Man's first sin was disobedience. It may very well be that Saul persuaded himself that Samuel had misunderstood God's will, just as the serpent persuaded Eve that God did not really mean what He had said. But whatever excuse we make for Saul, his action was as disastrous for him and his family as Eve's for mankind. Should you think that the people were carrying out God's command indirectly, for there is no reason to think that vs. 15,21 are in any way an attempted evasion by Saul, remember that most of the sacrifices would have been peace offerings, and these were for the most part eaten by the worshippers. You are not giving much to God if you will be the chief beneficiary of the gift.

Samuel 16

Samuel's sacrificing had been a regular part of his former activity; Saul's anointing had not changed his rights in this respect, and so he had probably continued his practice. But the breach betweeen him and the king was such public property, that the elders of Bethlehem were alarmed at his coming. They asked him, "Does your coming mean peace?" (4)—*i.e.*, "Is it for our good?"

There was no reason why David's anointing should have been understood as an anointing as king; prophets could be anointed (1 Kings 19.16). In view of Saul's growing uneasiness and suspicion it is probably better to render not "in the midst of his brethren" (13), but "from the midst"—*i.e.*, privately. David was not given the unnecessary outward gift of "prophecy" like Saul, but he received the inward reality of the Spirit.

For the Hebrew understanding, "an evil spirit from the Lord" (14) created a rather different impression than it does for us. With us it suggests a spirit that was morally evil, as is the case in the N.T.; here it merely conveys the thought that the outcome of his working was calamitous for Saul. It is worth noting that the accurate rendering is: "continuously tormented him". The fact that his courtiers suggested a purely natural remedy, which was successful for the time being, shows that Saul was not regarded as a case of demon possession in the N.T. sense.

The description of David as "a man of valour, a man of war" (18) virtually forces us to assume some lapse of time between his anointing and his taking up an official position at court, which we must not

257

exaggerate in its first stages. He was appointed as "one of his armour bearers" (21).

In the light of difficulties raised by the next chapter we must stress that v. 22 creates the impression of a full-time entry into the royal service. In addition, the very painful nature of Saul's illness makes it very improbable that Saul would have permitted David to go very far from the court. It seems that the story of Goliath (see notes on ch. 17) is earlier, but because it did not lead to an appointment at court, it is put later, as being of no special importance in the working out of the Divine purpose.

1 Samuel 17.1–54

We must look briefly at the main difficulties of this story, mainly because they are so often insisted on in schools and colleges. They are: (a) If David had been Saul's harper and armour-bearer, he would have had no difficulty in going direct to Saul (31); (b) vs. 33—36 are hardly compatible with 16.18; (c) ignorance of David's identity (55—58) is hardly explicable; (d) David's periodic return to the work of a shepherd (15) seems unnatural.

In the Greek (*Codex Vaticanus*) 17.12—31 and 17.55—18.5 are missing. If we could accept this as correct, the problem would largely vanish; but the translator probably omitted the verses just because he saw the difficulty. If on the other hand we assume that the story is earlier than that in 16.14—23, though probably after the anointing, then most (not all) of the difficulties vanish. We would have to see in v. 15 the effort of a late editor to explain an obvious problem. Another pointer to an earlier date for this story is the fact that no effort was made at the time to implement the promise that he should be Saul's son-in-law; if he was merely a lad, he was too young for marriage. The argument based on 2 Sam. 21.19 is dealt with there.

The reason why the two sides faced one another harmlessly for forty days (16) was because "the valley of Elah" (2) was little more than a ravine; anyone trying to cross it in the face of the enemy would be going to almost certain death. David could do it only because he was responding to Goliath's challenge; by the rules of the contest he had to let him cross.

David expected a victory, not because he was an Israelite and Goliath a Philistine, but because he interpreted Goliath's words as a challenge to God Himself (45—47). We must always be prepared to distinguish between our cause and God's. They are not necessarily the same. But behind the confidence lay an assurance based on doing

is duty. Whenever (better than "when" in v. 34) lion or bear inter-
fered with his sheep, he dealt with them as a matter of course. We shall
not do great things for God unless we learn to do the lesser as well. If
God had looked after him while he did his duty, how much more
when he was God's champion?

"His tent" (54)—probably God's tent, cf. 21.9. "To Jerusalem":
presumably David had the head pickled and hung it in his banqueting
hall after he had captured Jerusalem.

Samuel 17.55—18.30

From this point until David settled in the Philistine country (27.1) it
is impossible to fix the chronological connection between many of the
stories. We must not assume that because two stories stand side by side
the second must necessarily flow out of the first. Normally this
problem will not be discussed in these comments.

Saul had been privately anointed by Samuel, so he had every reason
for expecting that he would do the same to someone else, so we can
easily understand his eyeing anyone rising to prominence with
suspicion. So there is nothing unnatural in vs. 8,9. "He raved" (10):
literally "he prophesied"; R.S.V. is, of course, correct, but it throws
light on how some of the less reputable prophets behaved. "And Saul
cast the spear" (11): David would not have waited for the second
attempt; render "prepared to throw".

At this stage Saul still knew what he did in his fits of semi-madness,
so in his fear of consequences he detached David from the court. This
led only to increasing successes for David, and to his becoming
steadily better known and loved throughout the country. God's hand
was so obviously in it all, that "Saul stood in awe of him".

In his hope of driving David to suicidal rashness Saul remembered
the promise he had made when Goliath was challenging Israel
(17.25). Why he did not keep it, we do not know. He may have
married off Merab in one of his fits of gloom. Michal's love for David
rather changed the position (20), and Saul decided he had better press
ahead. David's diffidence (18,23) must not be interpreted too literally.
It did represent the poverty of David's family; David could not afford
to give the king a gift of the conventional size. Far more important,
however, was the compulsion David was under not to do anything that could be interpreted by Saul or his enemies as a sign of
plotting.

The Philistines were the only neighbours of Israel that did not
practise circumcision (cf. Jer. 9.25,26). Normally, when one wanted

to count the enemy dead, one cut off a hand. In this case the foreskin
were a guarantee that the dead were Philistines.

Saul was a tragic figure but quite typical. He knew he had been
rejected by God, but for all that he thought he could fight God's
rejection.

**Questions for Further Study and Discussion on 1 Samuel chapter
9—18.**
1. What reasons are there that made Benjamin a suitable tribe to
    provide the first king?
2. Consider ch. **13**: (*i*) does God specifically test an individual
    today? (*ii*) what is the relationship between usefulness to God
    and obedience to Him?
3. In what way do the excuses which Saul made (ch. **15**) find
    expression among Christians nowadays?
4. "David was not chosen king by God because of his musical skill,
    but without it he might never had become king." Work out the
    implications of this in terms of Christian vocation.
5. Contrast the way in which Saul and David met the challenges of
    life. What can we learn from these?

1 Samuel 19

We are now introduced to the gradual break-up of Saul. His awe and
fear first made him try to get someone else to bear the responsibility
of murder (1). This is one of the corruptions of power. Saul would
have claimed ignorance, while the murderer would have claimed
superior orders! Next day Saul swore solemnly that David would not
be put to death (6), yet a few weeks later he tried to pin him to the wall
(10). That this mood was not passing madness is seen in his attempt
to arrest him and his deliberate challenge to Samuel.

He was not then mad enough to flout a basic convention of Eastern
life: a man must not be disturbed at night in his own house. Saul's
men simply watched the door till dawn. How there came to be
teraphim in David's house we are not told. If we accept the translation
of vs. 13,16, we can hardly suggest that he was ignorant of its existence,
even if, as probable, it belonged to Michal. But both Genesis 31.19,34
("household gods"—*teraphim*), and the generally small size of
religious images at the time, are against the concept of a man-sized
image, which the traditional translation suggests. A more likely
rendering is, "Michal took the *teraphim* and put them by the bed"

3). In popular thought all serious illness was due to evil spirits, and he *teraphim* were placed beside the bed to guard it. The black goats-air rug and the crumpled clothes were enough to suggest someone in the bed. Saul's complete egomania is shown by his question to Michal (17).

God gave Saul one more warning. He deliberately challenged the spiritual authority of Samuel, with whom David had sought sanctuary. A mysterious power streamed out from Samuel's prophets and immobilized Saul's soldiers, presumably in the same way as it did Saul. When Saul himself intervened, madly thinking that his kingly power was greater than the power that had made him king, he found himself helplessly walking the last few miles and then caught up in the spiritual exercises, until he lay exhausted and half naked in a trance for a day and a night. What might have been a spiritual uplift became his shame. The question once asked in surprise now became a sneer (24). The sign of God's favour had become one of God's forsaking.

Samuel 20

At this point we must either see chronology dislocated or understand that Saul was by now suffering from schizophrenia, and was no longer conscious of what he had done during his mad fits. Only in one way or the other can we reconcile the murderous assaults of ch. **19** with the expectation that David would be at the royal table (6,18,19,26,27). Note that Jonathan seems to have no idea of how far things had gone (2). We can see something of the nature of the time in the struggle between Jonathan's trust in David and his fears (14—17).

Saul's general mental instability is seen in vs. 24—34. Jonathan evidently acted as Royal Chamberlain, and so Saul assumed that any courtier who was absent would have cleared himself with him (27). But when he found that Jonathan had acted within his powers, he flared up in fierce anger, and ordered David's immediate arrest and execution (31). When Jonathan asked for a motive for the verdict, he was himself threatened. "Saul cast his spear" (33): see note on **18.**11. "Because his father had disgraced him" (34): obviously it had been Jonathan who had been disgraced. The insult to his mother—Saul's wife!—conforms to quite a common Oriental type, and is not really meant to involve the mother as well.

The plan of vs. 18—22, 35—41 was based on the fact that the whole of David's future might depend on his avoiding the accusation of plotting against Saul, the Lord's anointed. Had the news got round that the warning to leave the court had come from Jonathan, he would have had to flee and join David, and no one would have believed that there was not an active plot against Saul. The limits of the plot were, of course, the saving of David's life—quite another matter.

Jonathan went out with one of his pages. He told the boy to fetch any arrows he might shoot. As the boy went, he shot over his head. The boy soon reached the arrow (37), but by then he had shot two even further, so the boy had to go further still (38). When he had brought back the three arrows (20), he was sent back to the city with the bow and arrows. This should have been all (40), but David, seeing that the coast was clear, came out of hiding. Evidently the friends had a premonition that they might not see one another again.

1 Samuel 21.1—22.5

Should David have fled from Saul's court? It is more than difficult to say, but he certainly should not have done it in the way he did. He was so broken by his emotional parting from Jonathan that he went unprepared and without a plan, so everywhere he came he brought danger to himself or others.

It is difficult to evaluate the story of Ahimelech. 22.15 shows us that we do not have the whole story in vs. 1—6. The Oriental's penchant for minding other persons' business means that the conversation may in part have been intended for Doeg and anyone else who might overhear. In any case, David's plight without food and weapons shows how unplanned his flight had been.

The next step confirms the impression. There were too many widows and orphans in Gath who hated his name. In addition some may have thought it a foolhardy act of spying, for news of his final break with Saul will not have preceded him. In the very jaws of death David suddenly came to himself and pulled himself together. He had been mad to go to Gath; good, he would play the madman properly. Since it was believed that the mad had been touched by the gods, he was under their protection and was allowed to go, if he wished.

On his return to Judah, David found that the news was abroad. Immediately he was joined by his relations. With Saul in the mood he was, they had no choice (*cf.* his treatment of the priests, 22.18,19). Even his old parents had to be brought to safety (22.3,4). David knew that they could not stand an outlaw's life, and he may have expected that the memory of Ruth, the Moabitess, in his ancestry would make the king more willing to receive them.

Unexpectedly David found other adherents as well (**22.2**). There are always some who are dissatisfied, but it takes much to make a man willing to be an outlaw. Justice is more than the enforcement of the letter of the law; it is seeing that right is done. Saul had become so concerned with his fears and suspicions, that he had lost the ability to put himself into another's shoes and discover what was really right.

"The stronghold" (**4,5**): in the first case it probably means "so long as he was an outlaw". The second is more difficult, but probably refers to an otherwise unnamed place in Moab. "The forest of Hereth" (**22.5**) was probably at Horesh (**23.15**), south of Hebron. A forest was wild, broken land covered with scrub.

1 Samuel 22.6—23.18

The immediate effect on Saul, when the mystery of David's disappearance was cleared up, was to feel sorry for himself. There is little spiritual hope for a man in this condition, when he persuades himself that everyone is wrong except himself. Saul may have discovered about Jonathan's farewell to David, but it is more likely that the accusation is the fruit of his own guilty conscience. That Doeg had kept silence until then shows how mad Saul was capable of being. Doeg was completely devoid of scruples, but he knew that Saul was capable of flying at him in a mad rage and killing him. "All his servants" (**22.6**)—*i.e.*, his courtiers.

Ahimelech knew he was treading on thin ice. He probably told Abiathar not to come with him to Saul, but to be ready to flee. That he came to David with an ephod (**23.6**) suggests that he had had his bag ready packed. We do not know whether it was Doeg that destroyed Nob (**22.19**), but if he did, he was acting on Saul's command. Treason to him was now treason to God, and those guilty had to be put in the ban.

Once again we meet David's essential planlessness. He had not asked himself how 600 men would occupy themselves doing nothing in the wilder parts of Judea. The grim realities of outlawry have little relationship to Robin Hood in the merry greenwood of Sherwood. The incursion of the Philistines (**23.1**) enabled David to go on building up his reputation as saviour of his people, while Keilah's position in the centre of Judah showed up Saul's decreasing ability to guard his kingdom.

We must not be too hard on Keilah for its willingness to hand over David, for it was too small to be able to resist Saul's army for long.

Unless he was prepared for full-scale civil war, to rely on Keilah was absurd. The apparent contradiction between 23.13 and 14 is probably explained by Saul's keeping a number of agents spying on David's whereabouts, but only taking action when he thought he had trapped him.

Jonathan, with a vivid sense of the strain on David, went "to strengthen his hand in God" (16). Small-minded men criticize him for not joining David. They forget that Saul was still the legal king. David neither killed him nor fought him, but only dodged him. No one had the right to leave Saul's service, till life in it was made impossible. Choice is not always as obvious as some would have us believe.

1 Samuel 23.19—24.22

We may easily excuse Keilah (23.12), but not Ziph. They had a right to demand that David move out of their territory, but not to betray him. The two geographical descriptions (19,24) place David down towards the Dead Sea ("in the Arabah", 24), southward of Ziph, on the other side of Jeshimon (*i.e.*, the Wilderness of Judea). Thanks to the treachery of the Ziphites Saul very nearly caught David (26), but God saw to it that the news of the Philistine raid came in the nick of time.

"Engedi" (23.29) is one of the very few spots in this wild area where there is constant fresh water. The description "Wildgoats' Rocks" (24.2) for the heights above Engedi is most expressive as any who have seen them will know. The very effort to move an army here was a sign of madness. For David's men the coincidence that Saul chose just their cave was sign positive that God had arranged it to give David his opportunity of revenge (4). David accepted the Divine overruling, but as an opportunity for showing his abiding loyalty. He was so great-hearted that he even regretted having put Saul to the shame of a damaged dress.

David had in these desperate days learnt the lesson that he must leave his wrongs and vindication in the hands of God. It is not easy to judge how far David was in fact telling the truth, when he put the cause of Saul's hatred on others (9; 26.19). It may have been simply politeness in seeking to minimize Saul's fault (*cf.* note on 26.19), or in fact there may have been jealous men who, seeing how the wind was blowing, kept stirring up Saul's infatuation.

As with David in Gath (21.10—15), the sudden realization of the presence of the angel of death sobered Saul for a moment. He realized that the moral greatness of David marked him out as the coming king (20). Unlike the occasion in **26**.21, when the shock and the impression were less, Saul did not suggest his return to court, for he knew he could not trust himself.

How petty is Saul; how great is David! Why should David kill Saul's family, if he does not kill Saul himself? Yet Saul demands an oath from him, but offers nothing himself. Saul was not going to swear to David, for secretly he was looking forward to the next access of madness, when he could forget and try once more to kill David. "Stronghold" (22) may refer back to **23**.29.

1 Samuel 25

At the time it seems to have been a special honour for a man to be buried in his house (1; *cf.* 1 Kings **2**.34). For someone who did not know the story, ch. **24** ended on a note that seemed to promise reconciliation; ch. **25** begins with the knell of coming doom—the one man who could have reconciled them was dead.

Let your imagination work on the story of Nabal and Abigail. How did outlaws in Jeshimon live? There were no king's deer to shoot, as in Sherwood. We see them acting as unofficial police, protecting the region against raiders (16). But then the "insurance premium" had to be paid (6—8). Nabal could have refused politely, but he had probably already drunk too much (36), so he insulted David as well as refusing (10,11,14). David might have accepted a refusal, but injured honour had to be cured by bloodletting (13).

That Abigail could lay hands at once on such an amount of food (18), even allowing for the smaller size of the "loaves", shows the scale of the feasting and the folly of Nabal. David's answer shows that he understood the real reason behind Abigail's concern (32,33). Once human standards are allowed to dominate our thinking, there is no limit to the complications that may ensue. Human standards demanded that David avenge his honour, but had he done so, he would have had a massive blood-feud with the influential Calebite clan on his hands, and Judah would never have been able to ask him to be king. He waited; Nabal had a stroke (37), which in the popular mind was clearly an act of God, and so a vindication of David's honour. He also gained an intelligent wife (42) who allied the Calebites to him.

It must be looked on as sheer coincidence that David's third wife (43) had the same name as Saul's (**14**.50). The Jezreel is that of Josh. **15**.56, not far from Maon and the Carmel of this story. By these two

265

marriages David had gone a long way towards securing himself in the far south of Judah.

The previous chapter ended on a note where reconciliation was still possible; this ends with every hope gone. 2 Samuel 3.13—16 can be explained only if Saul's action in re-marrying Michal was completely illegal and invalid.

1 Samuel 26

You will know a man by the company he keeps. At their former approach to Saul (23.19) the Ziphites were probably moved by the thought of gain. Now there is some of the malignity apparent which we have seen in Saul. They were probably made jealous by David's growing influence to the south of them. David's growing safety is seen in his not trying to avoid Saul. Now it is rather David who is the cat and Saul the mouse.

Saul had probably encamped on a flat hill-top. By climbing a higher hill David could see all the details in the moonlight. Saul slept at the heart of the camp—the rendering "the place of the wagons" (5, R.V.) is impossible, for they could never have been brought there—and his men were around him. Just as at Engedi God had led Saul to David's cave, so here He had poured "deep sleep" (12) on them.

It was probably a mere impulse that sent David climbing into the camp, but once again he faced the temptation of taking his future into his own hands and triumphed over it. If we compare the two incidents, we shall see that there is a sharper edge to David's words here. The losing of Michal had wounded him deeply, and he had realized more than ever before how utterly implacable Saul really was.

Did David himself believe the words, "Go, serve other gods" (19)? Probably not, but many at the time thought that once the frontiers of Israel were crossed, one was no longer under the direct control of Jehovah, unless one was fighting for Him. We must not forget, however, that when one had left Israel, there was no possibility of public worship. The very fact that David spoke like this shows that he was already toying with the fatal idea of going to the Philistines.

Note David's courtesy even under these circumstances. He attributed Saul's actions either to God—this would call for a sacrifice by David to appease Him—or to the advice of evil men (19). He never suggested that Saul himself was the person to blame. There is on David's part a respect for the powers that be as ordained by God which we seldom meet today.

Are we really convinced that God's power is the same and shows itself the same, wherever we may be?

1 Samuel 27

The Christian's fainting fits are an element we do not always sufficiently allow for, and which, but for the grace of God, may radically damage his spiritual life. What made David go to Philistia? First of all, I imagine, sheer tiredness. To have to go on living month after month in Jeshimon will sap the finest constitution and cause the most finely tempered mind to cry out for relaxation. Then, for some at any rate, it is almost impossible to grow accustomed to the abiding presence of the angel of death. Each new threat to his life came with renewed force, with the impact of all the previous efforts behind it. Then the mounting impression of Saul's malignancy will also have had its effects. There are many on whom contact with the diabolical has a laming power. His marriages will also have made him conscious of the life he was asking his wives to lead. Then, with David we repeatedly have the impression of a man of impulse, of one who acted first and thought afterwards.

David was in quite a different position from when he first went to Achish (21.11). Everyone knew now that he had broken irreparably with Saul, and so there was no question of his being a spy. Then his 600 hardened men made him a most valuable mercenary captain. The worst danger he exposed himself to was being regarded in Israel as a turncoat and traitor. Deep-rooted hatred against him and his men in Gath caused him to be moved to Ziklag, a former Simeonite town (6).

A mercenary captain had to justify his existence, and that in Achish's eyes was the raiding of Israel. Instead he raided the desert tribes, probably on friendly terms with the Philistines. For "the Geshurites" (8), *cf.* Josh. 13.2, not to be confused with the north-eastern Geshur (Josh. 13.11). The murder of women and children during raiding, unless the ban had been laid on a people, was considered despicable and reprehensible. David had to sink to the lowest depths conceivable to hide what he had been doing (11). To that he had to add hard lying. We should not forget this side of David, with its moral degradation.

Can you say, "I waited patiently for the Lord"?

1 Samuel 28

As things went from bad to worse Nemesis suddenly overtook David He was unexpectedly called to march with Achish against Israel. In his mental agony he used high-sounding but meaningless words (2) Achish understood them as a declaration of loyalty and made David the captain of his bodyguard. We leave David in his sore agony, for Saul who was in worse agony.

Saul, like not a few others, had to have guidance, not out of love for God but for fear of making mistakes. When they think they know the right course, they will ask no one, but it is almost impossible to stir them when they are in doubt. That was Saul's position, when he suddenly found himself cut off from every form of guidance (6). He collapsed, though there is no evidence that he was in special danger The change of direction of Philistine attack does not suggest an all out attempt to break Israel, but rather an attempt to strengthen their weakening grip on the great trade route.

Saul did not turn to other gods—let that be said on his side—but to the wise and kindly old man who had first turned his feet to the paths of greatness. He hoped to get into touch with him through "a medium" (7)—a far better translation than "witch". The outcome is not an affirmation but a rejection of the truth claimed for spiritism No one was more terrified than the medium herself (12). Whom, or what, she expected we are not told, but it was certainly not Samuel That God permitted Samuel to return is no evidence that mediums normally have such power. All that Saul gained by flouting God's commandment was a knowledge of the future that effectively and completely lamed him. God's withholding from us of an effective knowledge of the future is one of His most gracious acts. Most of us would either break under the knowledge, as did Saul, or abuse it.

A look at a map will show you that to reach Endor from Mt. Gilboa Saul had to skirt the Philistine army at Shunem. He could easily have been killed before the battle, and it would have been better for Israel if he had been.

Why should we expect God to guide us, if we ask Him only when it suits our convenience?

1 Samuel 29

When men are at their wits' end, then God displays that the impossible to them is child's play to Him. The story goes back to before **28.4** to Aphek in the coastal plain (4.1), where the Philistine units joined and were reviewed. One more drop in the cup of David's degradation awaited him; the Philistine commanders proclaimed that he was not to be trusted. In spite of his desperate plight we may well judge that they were wrong, but David deserved it. He was in a plight like that of Sir Launcelot, of whom Tennyson wrote:

> *His honour rooted in dishonour stood,*
> *And faith unfaithful kept him falsely true.*

With grim irony the writer depicts Achish apologizing profusely to David for sending him home. He had no idea that this was David's happiest hour. David, when he realized that this was final and irrevocable, played for safety. He put on a scene and protested vigorously against the indignity done to him. Fortunately he did not overdo it, so that Achish remained without suspicion. Try to picture the scene next morning as the Philistines marched north and David and his men south. Doubtless they had to accept many a jeer and gibe they did not venture to answer. The psalm itself may have been written later in David's life, but the striking picture of Psalm **124**.7 must surely have come to David that morning: "We have escaped as a bird from the snare of the fowlers; the snare is broken and we have escaped."

God gave David encouragement on his way as well. He received unexpected reinforcements, which were very soon to prove most acceptable (1 Chron. **12**.19–22).

In ch. **30** we shall find how David's fortunes reached their lowest point only to mend and rise rapidly. So here is the point where you would do well to revise the story of David up to date. Try to judge what were the factors which were to make of him a king according to God's own heart. Do some of the weaknesses we meet in these years of suffering reappear later? In the account of him as king do you find earlier traits appearing? Can you think of passages in the Psalter which seem to link with his experiences in these years?

1 Samuel 30

David and his men had no premonition of evil; they could have covered the sixty miles from Aphek quicker. There is no contradiction between the mention of the Amalekites (and 27.8) and ch. **15**. A numerous nomadic tribe will never be sufficiently concentrated to be wiped out in one operation. There is no suggestion that the raid was intended as revenge. The Amalekites knew that the Philistines, including David, had marched against Israel; from vs. 14,16 we see it was a general raid. The "Cherethites" were Philistines. Ziklag was

269

less able to resist, because it did not include veteran soldiers too old to march on active service.

The extent to which David's disgraceful conduct had marred his image in the eyes of his followers is seen in their willingness to stone him (6). "David strengthened himself in the Lord his God . . ." "Bring me the ephod" (6,7): this is the first time since Judah was left that we hear such language. David had finally been brought to an end of himself, and from now on his fortunes changed.

The exhaustion (10) was due as much to the inordinate weeping (4) as to the march to and from Aphek. The lack of watch by the Amalekites was because they knew the Philistines to be far away (16). It would have been impossible to mount an effective attack in the dark. David attacked at first light and continued until dark (17). Since no other camels are mentioned, these are all that will have been available. The rehabilitation of David by his victory is shown by the spontaneous acknowledgement of the booty as his (20)—*i.e.*, everything that had not been taken from Ziklag itself. We must not be too hard on "the wicked and base fellows . . . with David" (22); they had not been set much of an example ever since David chose the downward path.

In the list of Judean cities a couple of alterations should be made. "Bethel" (27) is Bethul (Josh. **19**.4); "Aroer" (28) was east of Jordan, so read either Adadah (Josh. **15**.22), or possibly Ararah.

Those who, like David, have turned to God in their deepest distress have been repeatedly amazed at the speed with which He has been able to change their fortunes.

Thought: "My strength is made perfect in weakness."

1 Samuel 31

The choice of Mt. Gilboa for Israel's position revealed the eye of a good general. It was a position of great defensive strength, and whatever the Philistine plans, they could not ignore a force stationed there. Yet, if we are to believe the Amalekite's story, and there is no valid reason for not doing so, the Philistines used their chariots in the battle (2 Sam. **1**.6), which would have been impossible on the mountain slopes. Clearly, instead of staying in his defensive position, Saul, in his despair, marched down the slopes to ground where all the advantages were with the Philistines.

Then, as earlier, the Israelites were not able to face the chariot charge, and fled. We do not know whether Saul could not flee, or did not deign to. Probably he tried, with his crack troops around him, to slow up the flight, retreating foot by foot. He saw his three sons fall near him. To break the stubborn resistance the Philistines brought up their archers and severely wounded Saul. He did not want to share the fate of Samson, and so took his life. "All his men" (6): in the setting, clearly Saul's body-guard is meant. They remained true to him to the last.

"The other side of the valley" (7)—*i.e.*, the north side. This verse confirms the opinion expressed on **28.4** that the Philistines' purpose was to strengthen their hold on the trade route. They conquered only the southern strip of Galilee and that part of Gilead opposite Beth-shan (not even as far south as Jabesh-gilead). The view so often found in modern books that Israel lay helpless at the feet of the Philistines lacks Scriptural foundation.

Saul's body deserved better treatment, for he and his sons had fought gallantly. We should be glad that the men of Jabesh-gilead at least guaranteed him decent burial (*cf.* also 2 Sam. 21.12—14). The modern tendency is to translate v. 12 "and they anointed them there" instead of "and burnt them there". Though quite possible, the mention of "their bones" (13) makes it improbable. Putrefaction had almost certainly set in. In addition, if the Philistines traced the bodies to Jabesh-gilead, it would be almost impossible to identify bones.

Saul took his life rather than be dishonoured, and yet his corpse was dishonoured. This points to the central weakness in his life. He was a man who had been touched by God and so could not do without God. Yet he was never willing to give unconditional trust and surrender.

Questions for Further Study and Discussion on 1 Samuel chapters 19—31.

1. What does ch. **19** teach about sacrificing love? Relate this to the cost of our love for Christ (*cf.* 1 Cor. **13**).
2. How does David's "exile" relate to Christian experience today? What special temptations beset us in times of spiritual "exile"?
3. Consider the teaching that we may draw from ch. **22** on the subject of jealousy (see also Prov. **6.34, 27.4**, Rom. **13.13,14**).
4. What example does David give us in his behaviour in ch. **24,** and how should this be expressed in our relationships with other people?
5. What warnings and examples can we draw from the behaviour of Nabal and Abigail (ch. **25**)?
6. Is the gain from temporary expediency ever worth the price paid (ch. **27**—see 2 Chron. **19.2**, James **4.4.**)?

271

7.   How far was David's success as a king the outcome of his experiences of suffering in earlier years?
8.   How does 1 Samuel illustrate the truth that "God is not mocked; for whatsoever a man soweth, that shall he also reap"?

2 Samuel 1

Long before the Philistines could find Saul's corpse, a keen-eyed human vulture had seen where he had fallen. As soon as the fighting had moved on, he had stripped him of the royal insignia and had headed south. Had he simply contented himself with bringing the news and the insignia to David, he might have been well rewarded, but he made the fatal mistake of thinking that David was a man with a deep dislike for doing his own dirty work.

Many scholars have built card-houses on the difference between the Amalekite's story and that in the previous chapter. They forget that with nineteen men out of twenty his perversion of facts would have reaped a rich dividend. David's question, "Where do you come from?" (13) finds its explanation in the thought of the time. David knew already that he was a foreigner. If he had been simply in transit, his action might have been condoned as committed in ignorance. When he said, "I am the son of a sojourner," he proclaimed himself one who was allowed to stay in the country on condition that he was subject to its laws. If Saul's armour-bearer did not feel justified in killing Saul, how much less an Amalekite! True he did not actually deserve the death penalty, but, if for the sake of gain we say we have broken the law, should we complain if the law has its way with us?

There are too many textual difficulties in David's lament for them to be mentioned, beyond the fact that the conjectural emendation in v. 21 (R.S.V.) is very doubtful. In v. 24 we have an incidental tribute to the qualities of Saul as king. It does not mean that Saul had a roving eye and a lively sense of feminine beauty. Since women were not touched in normal theft and raiding, a family's surplus assets would be turned into gold and silver ornaments worn by them. David means that by his wise rule Saul had created a prosperity which was reflected in the dress and ornaments of the women; the interpretation that booty taken in war is meant is much less likely.

Though Jonathan took first place in David's lament, there are no grounds for thinking that his mention of Saul was not entirely sincere. Saul, the God-chosen king, had virtually every quality that might be desired except submission to God's will. It may well be that in many ways he was a more outstanding man than David, but the atter possessed the virtue the former lacked, and that made all the difference.

2 Samuel 2

Though David asked God whether he should return to Judah and where, we are not told that he asked whether he should accept the throne of Judah. We cannot know what God's answer would have been, but David's action (see comment on **5.5**) was fraught with fateful consequences.

The message to Jabesh-gilead (5—7) was more than well-earned praise. Official messengers normally knew the message they carried. On their way they will repeatedly have been asked about their mission and message and have repeated it. This both made the fact of David's kingship quickly known and carried the hint that he would not turn down a request to be king of Israel as well.

Ish-bosheth raises many problems—for his name see note on 1 Sam. **14.49**. Apparently he was not at the battle of Mt. Gilboa; neither wife nor child of his is mentioned, and he was quite unable to maintain his dignity against Abner, even when he spoke treason (**3.6**—11). There are only two possibilities which might meet these facts. He could have been a mere lad, but this is contradicted by v. 10 and his place among Saul's sons in 1 Sam. **14.49**. Or he could have been mentally retarded, or a cripple, or in some other way unsuited for kingship. This would explain the discrepancy between his two years' reign (10) and David's seven-and-a-half (11). It will have taken Abner five years to force him gradually on a reluctant Israel, the names in v. 9 showing the stages: "Ashurites" were almost certainly Asherites—*i.e.*, Galilee.

The two kingdoms were at peace until, with Benjamin accepting Ish-bosheth, they had a common frontier. A chance meeting of contingents at the frontier town of Gibeon (12,13) led to the proposal for a little "sport" from Abner (14). Twelve young men—*i.e.*, without wives and children—were chosen on each side. Had one side or the other won, had there been even one to outlive the others for a few minutes and so claim victory, honour would have been satisfied. But faced by a complete draw (16) a general fight was unavoidable. Joab's veterans won a complete victory, but his brother Asahel was killed by Abner, and he was not the man to forget.

273

2 Samuel 3

It is unlikely that either kingdom wanted to break or win territory from the other, but bloodshed created blood feuds, and so more bloodshed, with the North regularly getting the worst of it. Gradually Abner began to show the cloven hoof (6). Clearly he had put in Ish-bosheth so that later he might quietly slip into his place. The harem of the dead king became the property of his successor. By taking Rizpah (7) Abner was making his first step towards claiming the throne. When Ish-bosheth did not take it lying down, Abner saw that his plans would not go through smoothly; he decided that he had more to gain from being second to David than to Ish-bosheth. One can hardly call it treachery; it was too open for that (9).

For "Michal" (13) see comment on 1 Sam. 25.44. By her return David became, after Mephibosheth, who was virtually debarred by his lameness, the leading claimant to the throne of Israel once it was vacated by Ish-bosheth, who might have been glad to abdicate. It is strange that the oracle of v. 18 was not mentioned earlier; it could hardly have been invented by Abner.

There is no reason for suspecting Abner of treachery against David, and it is unlikely that Joab really suspected him (25); he was preparing for his own treachery. "I am this day weak" (39): in the Semitic world the custom of the blood feud was of such antiquity that even the law of Moses did not try to abolish it; it only alleviated it; *cf.* notes on Josh. 20. Here it is not even suggested that Joab did anything wrong in avenging himself in Hebron. Plainly in the period of the Judges the very existence of cities of refuge had been virtually forgotten. David knew that the blood feud ate at the roots of true justice and government. He was also aware that the death of Asahel was more an excuse than a reason for the murder of Abner. Joab knew that if David made an agreement with Abner, he would take second place after David. But if he was called to account for murder, he could appeal to the "divine right" of the blood feud. It is not until 14.11 that we find David willing to grasp the nettle.

2 Samuel 4.1—5.5

The vultures of the past began to gather round Ish-bosheth. Saul in his efforts to eliminate the descendants of the old Gibeonite league (Josh. 9) tried plain murder (21.1,2). In the case of Beeroth the inhabitants thought it best to move (2,3). The most likely interpretation of this story is that Rimmon was able to hide his identity and continue in Beeroth. His sons had been waiting for their chance for vengeance. This, by all the standards of the time, they would have been entitled to, provided they had not entered Ish-bosheth's service. The freely taken oath of loyalty bound them to him.

Poor Ish-bosheth! He could not even afford a man as porter, and the woman had to combine the post of doorkeeper with kitchen chores. The very different readings in A.V. (K.J.V.) and R.S.V. of v. 6 have essentially the same consonantal text in Hebrew. It is charitable to suppose that in bringing Ish-bosheth's head to David the brothers were not looking for any reward, except, probably, of having a place among his retainers. Their conception of the nature of revenge made them think that David would share it.

If David had been asked on what authority he had had the brothers, or for that matter the Amalekite, killed, he would doubtless have answered that there were some offences so heinous that every man of good will, who had the ability, should deal with them. The modern paraphernalia of law and order has been so developed that it is rare for the private individual to play much part in ensuring justice. This has led to a wide diminution of a sense of moral reprobation towards the more reprehensible law-breaker. It is considered narrow-mindedness if one does not want socially to welcome the drunken driver who has killed, or the adulterer. There is something genuinely refreshing in David's spontaneous outburst of righteous anger.

Mephibosheth (in 1 Chron. 8.34, 9.40, "Meribbaal"—note the long genealogy of his descendants; Jonathan's loyalty was rewarded in this way) was, next to Ish-bosheth, the one real descendant of Saul left. So the writer interrupted the story in 4.4 to tell us of him, and so mitigate in measure the grim story of Ish-bosheth's end.

"He reigned over all Israel and Judah" (5.5): the policy of being made king of Judah first (2.4) was beginning to bear fruit, for it was no longer a single kingdom. Judah and Israel were now separate kingdoms sharing one king.

2 Samuel 5.6–25

The Philistines, having apparently given up hope of a complete conquest of the hill-land of Israel, were not concerned about the existence of two weak and warring kingdoms, the more so as David was presumed friendly in spite of the slur on his honour (1 Sam. 29.4). The union of the kingdoms, however, spelt danger for them, and they attacked at once. That both attacks were directed towards the valley of Rephaim (18,22) suggests that their policy was to split the two

kingdoms before David could effectually amalgamate them. A com
parison of v. 17 with **23**.13—17 suggests that the latter incident is from
this period, and that the struggle was longer and fiercer than the bare
account of victory suggests. Notice, especially, that under apparently
identical circumstances God's guidance varied (19,23). 1 Chron
14.12 explains the ambiguous v. 21.

The above assumed that vs. 17—25 preceded vs. 6—10 in time (that
they do so is obvious, from vs. 11–16). This is a *priori* probable and is
confirmed by "went down to the stronghold" (17). One never "goes
down" to Jerusalem in the Bible; David would not have abandoned
the strongest point in Central Palestine if he had just captured it. The
inversion of order is intended to stress the position of Jerusalem in
David's plans. He had intended its capture as his first act of statesman
ship.

Benjamin, by failing to capture Jerusalem, had lost all claims to it
Because David captured it, not with the help of the national militia
but by his own personal retainers ("his men", 6), the city became his
property. This made it the more suitable as a capital, for it was no
attached to any tribe. The translation of v. 8 is sheer guesswork, the
Hebrew text being clearly corrupt. The usual explanation, that the
city was captured by Joab's climbing up the shaft connecting the city
with its water supply (1 Chron. **11**.6), is probable, though not certain

The mention of a palace and an increasing family is an oriental way
of stressing David's security. Saul, as archaeology has shown, never
found time for building himself a proper palace; he was too involved
in constant fighting for such a peace-time occupation.

In v. 20 "Baal" in *Baal-perazim* obviously means "Jehovah"; also
"Eliada" (16) is "Beeliada" in 1 Chron. **14**.7. It was not until the end
of David's reign that this use of Baal as a title for Jehovah officially
vanished.

2 Samuel 6

The moving of the ark to Jerusalem was not merely an act of piety, or
even a step towards making Jerusalem the religious as well as the civil
centre of the people. It was even more David's affirmation of a return
to the ideals of the pre-monarchic tribal union, which had centred
above all about the ark.

When the Philistines returned the ark on a new, cow-drawn car
(1 Sam. **6**.7), they were doing the best they could, short of sending for
some Israelite priests to carry it back, so God had accepted their
action. Failure to realize His condescension made some think that H

had accepted this as a superior method, and so, although it was well known that the ark should be carried by the priests (13), it was assumed that the Philistine method should be followed. Whenever we think that we know better than God's revelation, we are apt to run into serious trouble.

"Baale-judah" (2) is "Baalah" (1 Chron. 13.6)—i.e., Kiriath-jearim. David, ignoring the real reason for Uzzah's death, assumed that Jehovah objected to the ark's being moved and so left it in the house of Obed-edom to see what would happen. When he heard that the ark had brought blessing with it (12), he decided that the removal was not the cause of Uzzah's death and decided to try again. When the first six paces were safely past, David in his intense relief brought a sacrifice (13).

In the Near East until recently it was normal for someone wishing to show special honour to one going in procession to dance before him scantily dressed. His own self-humiliation by scanty dress and wild dancing exalted the one being honoured—so it was with David. His wearing of "a linen ephod" (14) was hardly a claim to priestly or Levitical status, but rather an indication that he was engaged in a sacred ritual.

What are we to say of Michal (16—23)? She had been sorely tried, and we are given no indication of her feelings towards Palti, or Palti-el (1 Sam. 25.44, 2 Sam. 3.15). But the very harshness of David's answer leads us deeper. Michal had been brought up as a king's daughter, and David as a poor farmer's son. Michal had come to respect appearances, and David knew that before God they were meaningless (1 Sam. 16.7). In despising David she was rejecting God's standards.

Is this something we do, without realizing it?

2 Samuel 7

For the writer, David's wars (8) were incidental, and so he handled the other great policy decision of the reign first; v. 1 clearly refers to a fairly late date in his life. Even a prophet can be carried away by what he considers obviously right. If we immediately warm to a new proposal for our church or for some other Christian interest, it is the more reason for examining it most carefully in prayer.

By Divine law the Israelite altar had to be of earth or unhewn stones (Ex. 20.24)—the bronze altar of the Tabernacle was a frame to be filled with earth—and the sanctuary was a tent. In other words, when Tabernacle and altar moved on, there was nothing to indicate that God had been worshipped there, and so no one spot would permanently be regarded as more holy than another. A temple especially a magnificent one, would be regarded *literally* as God's house, and its site as peculiarly holy. God permitted the building of a temple for the same reason that He permitted a monarchy. The people had fallen so far spiritually, that they could no longer do without it.

The promise to David, "the Lord will make you a house" (11) could, of course, have been made at any other period in his reign, for it is in no sense a reward for his offer to build a temple. But given just here it is for the hearing ear the reminder that it is men and no buildings that God wants. By his prayer (29) David showed that he realized that any such promise contained a conditional element "Your throne shall be established for ever" (16): this is a promise with a double fulfilment. Taken as conditional, and using the normal secular understanding of the Hebrew translated "for ever", the nineteen generations of the Davidic monarchy were an ample fulfilment (*cf.* 19). Taken in the light of later promises the passage become Messianic, and looks forward to One Who should be the perfect dwellingplace of God on earth.

David knew that the promise was not enough in itself; it had to awaken a certain attitude of mind, and so he prayed for a blessing (29). The lesser knelt (in Hebrew "to bless" is linked with the word for "knees") before the greater, and with empty hands held out, awaited their filling in the giving of the blessing.

2 Samuel 8

David's wars, here recorded in summary fashion, give us the impression of wanton aggression, but where we have additional information the picture changes, and we see that David was no fighter for the love of it.

"After this" (1): the information is extracted from the royal chronicles, and refers to the sequel to 5.17—25. "Methegh-ammah" the older interpretation is "the bridle of the mother city"—*i.e.*, a strong point which was essential to the safety of Gath (*cf.* 1 Chron. 18.1). As the most inland of the Philistine cities Gath had always been the spearhead of their attacks on Israel, so its loss meant that from then on Philistia ceased to be much of a threat. The more usual modern explanation is "David took the leading reins out of the hands of the Philistines"—*i.e.*, Israel, not the Philistines, was now dominant in Palestine.

While the defeat and capture of Moab need not surprise us, the barbarous treatment of its warriors should. Nearly two-thirds of the prisoners were massacred (2), though "one full line" shows that a certain minimum of mercy was shown. Jewish tradition is that the king of Moab had David's parents killed (*cf.* 1 Sam. **22.**3,4), but this may have been invented to explain the cruelty. An attack in the back, like Edom's, during the Syrian campaign is more likely.

For more detail of the war with Syria see **10.**6—19, from which we see it was forced on David. David made himself king of the nearer Syrian territory of Damascus, but was only overlord of the more distant areas. With v. 13, *cf.* title of Psa. **60** and 1 Kings **11.**15,16. Obviously at the height of the struggle with the Syrians Edom attacked him in the rear; the terrible vengeance exacted suggests there was treachery as well. The result of all this fighting was that David became king of Judah and Israel, Edom, Moab, Ammon and Damascus, as well as overlord of the other areas mentioned.

With vs. 15—18 *cf.* the somewhat later list, **20.**23—26. David was in charge of justice (15). Read "Abiathar, the son of Ahimelech" and probably "the son of Ahitub" (17; *cf.* 1 Sam. **22.**11,20, 2 Sam. **20.**25). "Recorder" (16): better "remembrancer"; he had to keep David up to date with business and make his decisions known. "David's sons were priests" (18): "priest" is probably used in its secular sense— *i.e.*, as having immediate access to the royal presence.

Questions for Further Study and Discussion on 2 Samuel chapters 1—8.

1. What does David's lament reveal about his qualities of character (ch. **1**)?
2. In the light of ch. **2** consider the way in which human codes of honour can be taken too far.
3. What does ch. **3** have to teach us about the dangers of compromise, in the light of God's Law? Compare Deut. **17.**17.
4. What is the New Testament answer to the claim that the story of Uzzah (ch. **6**) illustrates a primitive view of a God of wrath of most uncertain temper? (See Heb. **10.**28,29).
5. What are the great themes and the searching questions revealed in David's prayer (ch. **7**)?

2 Samuel 9.1—11.1

From here to **20.**22, and then 1 Kings **1,2**, we have a history written by someone at the court of David, who was in touch with all that was going on—Abiathar and Ahimaaz, the son of Zadok, are popular guesses. Obviously **9.**1 must have happened soon after **5.**3. "Servant" (**9.**2,9)—*i.e.*, slave; there is nothing incongruous in his having slaves also (**9.**10). David recognized Mephibosheth as Saul's legal heir, and gave him honourable status at court, but in such a way as to keep him under supervision if there was any talk of revolt by supporters of Saul's dynasty.

Evidently Nahash, the old adversary of Saul (1 Sam. **11**), had helped David during his flight from Saul (**10.**2). We cannot explain the wanton light-heartedness of Hanun and his ministers. **10.**6 suggests that they had expected David to swallow the insult; a greater could hardly have been devised. Perhaps they thought him preoccupied with the Philistines. That some preoccupation existed is shown in David's sending only part of his forces—"the host of the mighty men" (**10.**7)—and that only when the Ammonites had hired a large mercenary army. It was so well known that Ammon had only one city of any size—*viz.* Rabbah (**11.**1)—that the identity of the city in **10.**8,1 is not indicated. The threat of the mercenaries removed, Joab returned; David's vengeance could wait.

Hadadezer evidently had his ambitions and recognized in David a dangerous rival. David's immediate reaction (**10.**17) probably took the Syrians by surprise. The site of "Helam" is uncertain, but it was probably in the Damascus area. "Forty thousand horsemen" (**10.**18): 1 Chron. **19.**18, correctly "forty thousand footmen", *cf* **8.**4,5. That number of "horsemen" would imply well over 10,000 chariots, hardly a possible number. The same verse gives 1,700 chariots; the 1,000 has dropped in *Samuel*, cf. **8.**4. **8.**4,5 shows that the campaign was in two stages and the total footmen were 42,000.

With the return of the proper campaigning season the turn of Ammon had come. David has repeatedly been blamed for staying in Jerusalem. We must first remember **21.**15—17, which almost certainly took place earlier; this was the recognition that a king meant more than merely a war leader. Further, the feeling throughout the story and the only explanation of the Ammonite folly, is that David was preoccupied with some other unspecified difficulty, internal or external. Let us leave judgment to the only One entitled to judge.

David had a summer-room on the palace roof (*cf*. Judg. **3**.23), which was the highest point in Jerusalem. Bath-sheba belonged to court circles and she must have known that David might see her. "The daughter of Eliam" (3): if this is the Eliam of **23**.34, Bath-sheba was Ahithophel's granddaughter, but the link is never made (see comment on **15**.31).

Both David and Bath-sheba seem to have assumed that Uriah would regard the royal attentions to his wife as an honour. So long as the child could theoretically be his, the proprieties had been observed. There seems to have been nothing particularly secret about the affair; Uriah probably had his suspicions and just "would not play ball". The force of v. 11 is probably: "The ark is housed in a tent; the bulk of the people sleep in the fields, because it is harvest time; the army sleeps as best it may." It seems impossible not to see an implied rebuke of David. There is no suggestion that the ark was with the army.

If Joab knew the motive behind David's letter, he was not the man to make any bones about it. He was probably none too sorry to get David down to his own level. David envisaged a clumsy plan for getting Uriah killed (15). Joab improved on it: he was not concerned if others lost their lives, too (16,17). "Jerubbesheth" (21)—*i.e.*, Jerubbaal, or Gideon; Baal has been replaced by *bosheth* (shame), with a change of vowels for euphony (see comment on 1 Sam. **14**.49). In the whole foul story David's answer is perhaps the most degrading part (25).

Uriah was one of David's special group of thirty, his mighty men (**23**.8—39). No disloyalty is recorded of them, but David was disloyal to them. We cannot help asking ourselves how genuine Bath-sheba's lamentations were.

If we read the histories of kings and great men of other nations, we shall find many another such story, though the husband generally saw in time on which side his bread was buttered. Until recently kings were often regarded as above the law, and men applauded their vices so long as they did not hurt the taxpayers' pockets. But God makes no exceptions to the demands of His moral law.

2 Samuel 12

Doubtless Nathan's duties included watching out for cases of injustice which had failed to reach the king's ears. So there will have been nothing in his story to awaken David's suspicions. For us it would, at the worst, have been a case of robbery with violence. David, with a far truer understanding of justice, took the revelation of the rich man's character into consideration. Our sentimentalists would object to death penalty (5) *and* fourfold restitution (6). But what good did the death penalty do to the poor man? It is easy so to be occupied with law as to forget that it should be a servant for the achieving of justice.

"You are the man" (7): David had passed sentence of death on himself. Before giving the two main charges, Nathan stressed the enormity of David's action (7,8): God had saved David, made him king, and though he had been one of Saul's retainers, had given him legally all that had been Saul's (there is no suggestion that he had actually married any members of Saul's harem). Surely God would have given him anything else reasonable. The first charge is murder to gain another's wife (9,10); the penalty, the continuance of "the sword" in his house. The second charge is adultery (11,12); the penalty, the open degrading of his wives.

David confessed his sin frankly, and Nathan pronounced the remission of the death penalty, but brought forward a new charge (14). The R.S.V. text is based on the probably correct supposition that "enemies of" was introduced by the scribes for reverential reasons. God exacts a penalty for the way He has been despised—*i.e.*, the death of his son. The first penalty, that for murder, can be seen not merely in the death of Amnon, Absalom, and Adonijah, but also in the bloodshed under Athaliah (2 Kings 11.1) and various later assassinations. The second penalty, that for adultery, was mitigated but not abolished (16.21,22).

David's reaction when his son sickened and died (15—23) was a public acknowledgement of God's justice; mourning for him could have been interpreted as dissatisfaction with God's action. God's love to Solomon was shown above all in his living, which in turn was a sign of grace to the forgiven father. The name Jedidiah is not found elsewhere.

Rabbah lies on a hill above the Jabbok. "The royal city" or "the city of waters" controlled the access to the water supply. Its capture meant that Rabbah could not long resist. David put the Ammonites to forced labour.

Amnon's passion for Tamar can on the one hand be understood. Many wives, many children, the boys separated from the girls after five or six; there would not be the sense of belonging together that exists in a normal family. On the other hand, as his sudden revulsion showed (15), there was something pathological in it. Like the evil spirit that had come on Saul, God's hand was behind it, as is further shown by David's nephew's part in precipitating the tragedy (3—5). It is usually maintained that v. 13 shows that marriage between half-brother and sister, though forbidden by the law, was still practised. More likely Tamar was desperately clutching at straws to save herself.

"David was very angry" (21): David is attacked on all sides for his softness to his sons—it is hardly fair to apply 1 Kings 1.6 to them all— but such charges show lack of psychological understanding. At the time crimes committed within the family, like Amnon's, were the sole concern of the family and above all of its head. So David was free to punish as he wished. But how was he, who saw the punishment for his own sin being worked out before his eyes, to punish the guilty?

How did Jonadab know (32) that Amnon only had been killed? For that matter, how did Absalom guess at once (20) that Amnon was the cause of Tamar's grief? Was it a mere coincidence that in removing the man who had wronged his sister, Absalom also made himself heir-presumptive to the throne? Perhaps Absalom had planted Jonadab in Amnon's household to ruin him. If Tamar was involved in his ruin, what of it if Absalom became king? Otherwise it is hard to account for his self-control, which gave Amnon no positive reason for suspecting his hostility (22); no one seems to have suspected his motive even when he specially stressed his invitation to Amnon. The drunkenness of the feast gave Absalom more time to get away.

In 1 Kings 1.17 there is a reference to David's oath to Bath-sheba that Solomon should succeed him. It will have been a private one, but suspicion as to its existence must have been rife. There was not yet an established custom that the eldest son should succeed, but it will have been regarded by most as natural. Ambitious Absalom will have felt compelled to establish his position while Solomon was still young.

2 Samuel 13.37—14.27

Geshur was independent, but its king probably paid tribute. Had David insisted, Talmai would probably have had to hand over

Absalom, his daughter's son. David had probably no wish to insist and was secretly pleased that he was spared dealing with Absalom.

Joab seems to have been a single-minded patriot, whose loyalty to David was bound up with his conviction that the greatness of Israel depended on him. If he obviously thought that the greatness of Israel meant also the greatness of Joab, that was a blind spot that many such men have shared. At this point (1) he was moved with affection neither for David nor Absalom, but by the wish to settle the question of the succession. After some hints to David (cf. 19), he decided to appeal to David's sense of justice.

The widow's story was not uncommon (4—11). One son of a widow accidentally killed the other and was evidently hidden by her. The heads of the family, with whom authority lay, insisted on justice and blood for blood. The widow's plea was that this involved greater injustice for her. She was in fact asking the king to declare that royal justice stood higher than family justice and the bloodfeud. Having extracted an oath from David (11), she charged him with wrong in overruling the law for her but not in the far more important case of Absalom, where the welfare of the land as a whole was at stake (12—14). She ended (15—17) by suggesting that it was her own trouble that had brought her to the king, and that the other matter had just slipped out.

David saw through this at once, and gave Joab permission to have Absalom back, but would not let him come to court. This was not imperfect forgiveness but the clear statement that he would not recognize him as successor. David did not allow affection to blind him to the realities of Absalom's character.

The Semites suffered from the same delusion as the Greeks, and others since. Beauty of heart and body, or ugliness of heart and body, do not necessarily go together. Absalom's perfect physical beauty prevented men's seeing his selfishness and worthlessness. His hair was probably worn in many plaits as is the custom with many Bedouin men today. There is no contradiction between v. 27 and **18.**18. His sons probably died young.

2 Samuel 14.28—15.29

With one like Absalom compromises are useless. He found that as long as he was debarred from court he was no nearer his ambition (**14.**32). Joab soon realized that he had judged wrongly, but he had a tiger by the tail (29,30). David had to recognize that the compromise would not work (33).

David is blamed for not acting, when Absalom adopted royal pomp, but at the time it was not royal pomp in Israel, it was only showing off. Behind the story as it develops there is a cool master mind. It can hardly have been Absalom's; he does not create that impression. It could have been Jonadab's, but he is not mentioned again; the traditional identification with Ahithophel is probably correct. Note that in the rest of this story the northern and southern kingdoms are carefully identified as Israel and Judah.

Absalom tried to win the North, Israel (2,6). Why the average person believed him is a mystery. Obviously there were delays, and the disappointed litigant will always believe that the judge has been less than fair. But if the woman from Tekoa could reach the royal presence and have a full hearing it suggests that Absalom was doing some hard lying.

He had his eyes on the North, so he went south to Hebron to be crowned! The two hundred Jerusalem guests (11) were intended to confuse David, who could not know who was loyal to him. That is why he abandoned Jerusalem (14). When treachery is abroad, the open country among those one can trust is better than the doubtful security of walls. He was accompanied by his retainers, mighty men and mercenaries. "And Ittai the Gittite" has dropped out in v. 18 before "and all the six hundred Gittites". David made a distinction between Ittai and the other mercenaries. The latter had been long enough in his service to owe him loyalty, the former had not had time really to owe him anything.

David was not unwilling to fight; Absalom was too bad a man to let him tamely become king. But he was not willing to let the superstitious say that he had triumphed by forcing God to take his side, so he sent the priests back, but enrolled them in his schemes.

If it is asked why Israel so easily rejected David, and Judah remained passive, the answer is that, once danger is past, it comes naturally to very many to resent true greatness. We prefer to celebrate it in retrospect.

2 Samuel 15.30—16.19

"Ahithophel is among the conspirators" (31): the opinion is often met that Ahithophel was acting in revenge for the dishonour done him through his granddaughter (see note on 11.3). Such a theory gives him a great-grandson of twelve, if not more. Would he at that age have offered to lead a risky and strenuous night attack (17.1)? Normally for an oriental to see a daughter or granddaughter in the royal harem was welcomed, for it meant a sure road to advancement. The theory also assumes that he wanted to destroy his granddaughter, for that would have been the sure result of Absalom's victory.

Hushai (for "Archite", see Josh. 16.2) was "David's friend" (37); this was an appointment of extreme confidence at court. "You will be a burden to me" (33) shows that he was elderly.

It is difficult to know what to think of Ziba. He must have had a genuine loyalty to David, for Mephibosheth would lose his favoured position once Absalom triumphed, and Ziba might have to pay heavily, if it was known that he had helped David. That he was exaggerating is certain (3), but it is possible that it was not all lies. We need not doubt the truth of Mephibosheth's words in 19.26,27, and yet the cripple may have had harmless daydreams of what he might have been, which in the moment of crisis may have made him dither long enough for Ziba to go off without him. His presence with David might have kept men like Shimei quiet. The gift to Ziba (4) was of very considerable value and presumably made him a free man.

Shimei was a distant relation of Saul's. He probably believed the worst rumours about the deaths of Abner and Ish-bosheth, and placed the worst construction on 21.1—9. David's restraint came from his recognizing that though Shimei's curses were groundless, he could have cursed him for the sins he had committed. In picturing David's withdrawal, we should not forget that apart from the soldiers there were many women and children. David was not the only one to bring his family with him.

Even Absalom was somewhat shocked by the fulsomeness of Hushai's greeting. The complete cynicism of his answer (18) won Absalom's confidence, for he thought he had found a man of his own character.

2 Samuel 16.20—17.29

"Go in to your father's concubines" (16.21): though the king's son took over his father's harem as part of his property, there is no evidence that, in Israel, he had any sexual relations with them. That would have been incest. Ahithophel's advice showed not merely fiendish hatred of David, but virtually caused Absalom to disown David and all he stood for. Absalom was a simple character, driven by ambition, but behind him were some who wanted to change the whole basis of the Israelite state.

Hushai triumphed over Ahithophel because he understood Absalom better. If we compare Ahithophel's "Let me choose ... and I will" (1) with Hushai's "You go to battle in person" (11), the difference is obvious. At the same time there was more in Hushai's advice than is often recognized. To control an army of twelve thousand in a night attack over the very difficult and broken ground between Jerusalem and the Jordan was a major task. If it succeeded, it would be fatal to David, but the wiser of Absalom's counsellors could see the possibility and result of failure. Ahithophel, in his bitter disloyalty, discounted the loyalty of those with David.

"Ahithophel ... hanged himself" (17.23) : if we could know with certainty the cause of his suicide, we should understand the hidden forces behind the rebellion much better. Here are two considerations: (a) Ahithophel had been the real power behind Absalom's plotting, and he could have expected to be the power behind the scenes after his triumph. But now he had taken the bit between his teeth and had been carried away by crude flattery (17.11—13). There was no certain future for Ahithophel. (b) He had a premonition of coming defeat. He had been carried on unerringly by a daemonic force. It had been checked, and he knew the end had come.

David's reception at Mahanaim, Ish-bosheth's former capital, was warmer than he could have dared to expect. "Shobi" (27) was Hanun's brother (10.1). David had evidently appointed him regent in Ammon, and he reaped the gratitude of loyalty. "Machir" had looked after Mephibosheth (9.4), and now he repaid David's kindness. "Barzillai" will have been the leading personality of Gilead.

2 Samuel 18.1—19.8

The frequent suggestion that David was showing distrust or resentment by putting Joab over only a third of the army (18.2) is baseless. In fact the ground between Mahanaim and the Jordan is so broken that no fully co-ordinated battle front was to be expected. For "the forest of Ephraim" cf. Judg. 12.4. The battle can never have been started on such broken ground. Though Absalom had nominated Amasa as general (17.25), it is doubtful if he was even on the battlefield, where Absalom was in personal command. David's experienced generals manœuvred him in his inexperience into drawing up his army with the broken ground behind him. The moment he began to retreat his lines were irreparably broken, and no further organized resistance was possible.

Whether Absalom could have been caught by his hair in the traditional way is doubtful. The Bible says it was his head, not his hair, that was caught. The runaway mule will have driven his head with such force into a fork of the branches as to stun him and leave him hanging. Joab's complete ruthlessness was common property (13), but here he judged rightly that Absalom had to die.

Joab's messenger was not "Cushi" but a "Cushite" (21)—*i.e.*, a Negro slave. Joab could not anticipate how David might receive the news; he might in his anguish even kill its bringer. Ahimaaz, on the other hand, foresaw the brutality with which the slave would announce Absalom's death, and he wished to spare David a little. Joab probably misjudged his speed and better knowledge of the ground (23) when he allowed him to run also. By his strong hint (29) Ahimaaz must have prepared David for the Negro's brutally triumphant proclamation.

Let us judge Absalom as we will and David's treatment of him as we may, we have no right to condemn David in the hour of his overwhelming grief. "Would I had died instead of you" (33) is the broken-hearted confession of a man who knew that he had killed his son by his sin. However much Absalom contributed to it; however much evil men stood behind him and pushed him on; quite literally he had died because David had murdered Uriah. Joab clearly had no understanding for the deeper causes of his grief (**19**.5,6).

2 Samuel 19.9–43

David behaved about Absalom much as he had about his baby boy (**12**.20). He could not call the dead back, but he could start mending the broken pieces. He had to walk warily and not rush things. Israel had deposed him (note how their language in v. 9 bore out the premonitions of Josh. **22**.24) and Judah was sulking, not very sure what to do.

With a little judicious prompting the latter responded enthusiastically (11—15), perhaps even too much so. Interestingly, Benjamin, at least in part, foreshadowed what would happen under Rehoboam, when they took the side of Judah. Their brief experience under Absalom had convinced all but the fanatics among them that the old days of Benjaminite grandeur under Saul had gone for ever. We cannot tell whether Shimei had had a change of heart, or whether he acted in sheer policy (16,17). David would have been glad to punish him, but had he done so, there were thousands of others who would have feared his wrath, and in fear resisted. Ziba remains an enigma (17); we still do not know whether it is love for David that is driving him, or the fear that certain lies might be coming home to roost.

There is a harshness about David's reply to Mephibosheth (29) that repels us. Yet the fact remained that Ziba had helped David when it mattered most, while Mephibosheth sat helplessly and uselessly in Jerusalem. David had bigger tasks facing him than getting to the bottom of the story. History tells us no more of Chimham (37), but Jeremiah **41.**17 suggests that David gave him a property near Bethlehem out of his private estate.

Judah's action had a tragi-comic result. The news of Judah's action spread quickly, and by the time David was ready to cross the Jordan representatives of half Israel were waiting for him (40). On the way up to Jerusalem a fully representative delegation had come to meet him. They were annoyed, for they seemed to think that their talk had created a sort of option on David, until they made up their mind. To make matters worse, Judah had virtually kidnapped David—*i.e.*, the fords of Jordan at Gilgal were on Israelite territory, but Judah had ignored this. We are not told what was said in the slanging match that followed, but tempers ran high. David had been a little too clever.

2 Samuel 20

Where tempers run high, people act without thinking. Sheba, a Benjaminite, evidently nursed the tribal grudge against David. His call to the delegation to abandon David had startling results (2). David had to leave the matter until he could establish himself in Jerusalem (2,3). Those who had come to meet him at the Jordan were only representative delegations, so he sent Amasa, the new commander-in-chief (**19.**13), to raise the Judean militia at top speed. Though Amasa was used to depose Joab, the choice was wise, because Amasa had been Absalom's commander-in-chief (**17.**25). Amasa had not the organizational skill to accomplish the task in the time set, so David had to send off his regulars under Abishai (6,7); Joab went as one of the mighty men.

Amasa, hearing what was afoot, rushed north with all the men he had gathered and reached Gibeon first (8). In killing Absalom Joab had killed for the state and the dynasty; now he murdered for the good of Joab himself. He had so arranged his sword, that as he started to embrace Amasa for the kiss of peace, it dropped into his free hand. As soon as they did not have Amasa's corpse to trouble them, the militia, accustomed to Joab's leadership, followed him. So Joab calmly slipped back into the position of general.

It was soon obvious that Sheba's revolt was an anti-climax. As

soon as his companions recovered from the angry words, they slippe
away, and the only ones to join him were his own clansmen (14). As h
marched north the cities shut their gates to him until he found refug
with his small band of men in the far north at Abel-beth-maachah.

Why its citizens received him, we do not know, but as soon as the
saw that Joab was in earnest, they called for a parley (16). That it wa
conducted by a woman suggests that the contingent Abel had sent t
Absalom's army had not yet returned. As soon as the townsme
realized what was really involved, that was the end of Sheba (22) an
of the fighting.

For vs. 23—26 cf. **8**.16—18. This is slightly later, for now we mee
"Adoram in charge of the forced labour" (cf. 1 Kings **4**.6; **12**.18)
though this was a widely used form of labour in lieu of taxes, it wa
deeply resented. Sheva is a variant spelling of Seraiah (**8**.17; cf.
Kings **4**.3); he was a foreigner, whose name did not lend itself t
Hebrew spelling. "Ira the Jairite" will probably have been a privat
secretary (cf. **8**.17,18).

2 Samuel 21

We now begin the appendix and read of various important matter
which had no obvious place in the earlier chapters.

Vs. 1—14 deal with a legacy of sacrilegious murder David inherite
from Saul. Continual famine caused by inadequate rain convince
David that there must be unexpiated sin over the land; a divine orac
declared that it was the result of Saul's breaking the oath sworn in th
days of Joshua (Josh. **9**.15) to the members of the Gibeonite league (se
comment on **4**.2,3). The Gibeonites, when summoned to David'
presence, indicated that they wanted an expiation that they as non
citizens were not entitled to ask (4). When assured they could as
freely, they demanded the death of seven of Saul's sons, indicatin
that a money ransom would not be accepted. It is often suggested b
liberal scholars that the whole matter was too opportune for Davi
not to have been rigged, but it is doubtful whether any of those hange
could ever have made a serious bid for the throne. The materna
devotion of Rizpah (10) could have lasted from April to October, bu
there may have been a few late showers about the end of April. Th
Gibeonites probably had primitive ideas about God, so the leavin
of the bodies on the gallows was to let God see that punishment ha
been inflicted. We shrink from a story like this, but no one can break
solemn oath with impunity. God's punishments come in the way tha
those that suffer them understand best.

The stories of David's battles began with his killing of Goliath; they end with his nearly being killed by another giant (15—17). The incident must have been near the end of the struggle with the Philistines, when David had consolidated his position as king of the two countries. This leads to the mention of the death of some other giants. There can be little doubt that 1 Chron. **20.5** contains the correct version of v. 19. "Jaareoregim" must be read as Jair. With this change the differences are small in Hebrew. There are those that would read "and Elhanan the son of Jesse . . ." claiming that Elhanan was the personal, David the throne-name of the killer of Goliath. This is possible, but highly improbable.

2 Samuel 22.1—23.7

In this section David's work as a psalmist is summed up and typified by two psalms. The former (**22.2**—51) is the same as Psalm **18**. A comparison between the two versions would be profitable, for it would show that both have been copied with care, but for all that minor changes have slipped in. This psalm was chosen by the editor of *Samuel* because it is a commemoration of God's care and protection generally and not in one particular incident in his life. The latter is "the last words of David" (**23.1**—7). It was not included in the Psalter, for it is not suited to public worship in spite of its great beauty. "Last words" need not be understood as meaning that he spoke them on his death bed. In the evening of his life, as death drew near, he summed up his experiences of God and of life.

David's experience of God was primarily as "Saviour"—*i.e.*, Giver of victory (**22.2**—4). He had repeatedly found himself on the verge of death, but God had always heard him (5—7). It is only the general context that shows that the dangers of war are intended here; it would have been equally true of other dangers. In the elaborate language in which he describes God coming to his aid (8—16) David implies that He used all the resources of Nature in helping him. He then describes his deliverance (17—20). This was due not merely to grace, but because he sought to walk according to His will (21—25), and above all because he was humble (26—31). He sings of the grace and help of God (32—43) by which he had become potentially the ruler of the world (44—51). Had God willed that he should extend his campaigns, he would have been equally successful.

Because his Last Words might be heard beyond Israel, David introduces himself (**23.1**) and claims inspiration (2,3a). He then uses two pictures of the righteous ruler (3b—5). The righteous king dispensing justice is like the sun rising on a clear morning before things are hidden by haze and dust. Things are seen as they really are with all the sophistries and lies of men defeated. Then he is the refresher of men as he has been refreshed by God. The righteousness continues with his descendants (5). Finally, from bitter experience, he gives a picture of the character, danger, and worthlessness of evil men (6,7).

2 Samuel 23.8—24.25

David instituted an order of thirty mighty men, perhaps in Ziklag to act as his bodyguard. If there are thirty-seven here (39), and another sixteen in 1 Chron. **11,** it is because some members were promoted to higher office and some died, and the vacancies were filled. *Samuel* stops at Uriah as a reminder of David's unfaithfulness to the faithful. The three (8—12) are included in the thirty, as are Abishai (18,19) and Benaiah (20—23). To obtain the thirty-seven names we must add Joab. He is implied but omitted because his crimes made him unworthy of his place.

Ch. **24** stands in its present position not for chronological reasons but because it looks forward to *Kings* and the building of the Temple, for which it is a direct preparation. "Again" (1) may refer back to **21.**1—14. The reason for God's anger is not even hinted at. At the time the wrongness of the census, felt even by a man like Joab (3), was so obvious that the writer has not explained why. It is sometimes suggested that it was because the half-shekel tax was not paid (Exod. **30.**11—16). For all we know, it may have been, but Joab's language implies an objection to the census as such, not to the neglect of an important ritual detail. The same applies to David's confession of guilt (10). It is likely that David was contemplating a change in the military organization, which would need a knowledge of the man-power at his disposal (*cf.* 9).

The punishment, by which David lost seventy thousand men (15), would be an appropriate one, if such was his fault. If it is objected that it is unfair on those who died, the answer may lie in the un-explained anger of v. 1. David showed his wisdom in letting the punishment be inflicted entirely by God (14).

The variety in the spelling of Araunah's name (*cf.* 1 Chron. **21.**15) is probably because it was a Hittite name (*cf.* Ezek. **16.**3), hard to fit into Hebrew. It may be that, in contrast with Gen. **23.**11, Araunah was genuinely giving the site to David (22,23) as his contribution to the stopping of the plague. But this was David's offering for David's sin, and so it had to cost David.

Thought: What you have gained from these three months' studies depends on how much time and effort you gave.

Questions for Further Study and Discussion on 2 Samuel chapters 9—24.

1. In ch. **11** trace the links in the chain of temptation and sin (vs. 2—4,8,13,15).
2. Can you find material in verses like **13.26,36,** and **39** for drawing a comparison and a contrast between David's love for his sinful sons and God's love for His sinful family? Can you trace New Testament parallels to David's thought in **16.**10 that God can bring good out of evil? How effective is this in countering the desire for revenge?
3. What philosophy of history can we see in **17.**14?
4. How may we fall into the trap of giving the impression that we have greater "shares" in Jesus Christ than anyone else (**19.**43)?
5. Study **22.**2,3 in the light of Luther's words, "The whole of religion lies in the personal pronouns."
6. How many attributes of God can you find in **22.**8—20?

THE BOOKS OF KINGS

In human terms the book which we know as 1 and 2 Kings tells the story of a couple of petty neighbouring states, originally united under one ruler, in the ancient Near East over a period of some four centuries until they were successively swallowed up by their larger neighbours who were bent on the ancient equivalents of "colonial expansion", or (to be more up-to-date) "liberation". (It is a pity that the ancients did not know these fascinating euphemisms for territorial aggrandisement, but used such *outré* terms as "conquest" and "subjugation".) As such, the story is one of absorbing interest, and it comes to life all the more readily in these days when we see young nations asserting themselves and larger nations busily extending their spheres of influence. The book of Kings truly proves that there is nothing new under the sun.

But there is much more to the story than this, however true and vivid this book is as a piece of secular historical writing. The two nations of Israel and Judah were the split components of a people whom God had chosen to be His own possession, and their history was written by men who saw in the various events the outworking of the hand of God. They believed that the history made sense if interpreted according to the basic philosophy that a nation which truly worships God and keeps His covenant with all its moral obligations will live in security and prosperity, but a nation which turns to idolatry and immorality will suffer from want and oppression, and only a tiny handful of pious people will escape its inglorious fate. The presentation of history in this form is clearly of the greatest significance, for, if the interpretation is truly in accord with the facts and is not an alien pattern imposed upon them, it shows that the God Whom Israel worshipped is the Lord of history and is deeply concerned about both the worship and the morality of His people. He is actively involved in their history both as Judge and Redeemer. The implications of this for the modern world are very considerable. If this interpretation is indeed true, does God still act in the same way in the history of the nations—and in individual lives?

The story recounted here was probably completed in essentials by about 600 B.C., but did not reach its final form until some time during the Jewish captivity in Babylon. Its authors are unknown. They had a variety of documents to help them, court and other official records, and cycles of stories about the great prophets. What we now know as two separate books was written as one volume, to be read through continuously from beginning to end.

THE KINGS OF JUDAH AND ISRAEL

(Simplified from the table in *The New Bible Dictionary* (*I.V.F.*), pp. 219-221. Names in brackets indicate alternative forms, and names in italics represent periods of co-regency. Nearly all dates are approximate only.)

1010	David	
970	Solomon	
JUDAH	ISRAEL	
930 Rehoboam	Jeroboam I	
913 Abijam (Abijah)		
910 Asa		
909	Nadab	
908	Baasha	
885	Elah	
884	Zimri	
	Omri	Tibni (rival king till 880)
873	Ahab	ELIJAH
872 *Jehoshaphat*		
869 Jehoshaphat		
853 *Jehoram*	Ahaziah	Battle of Qarqar (853)
852	Jehoram (Joram)	ELISHA
848 Jehoram (Joram)		
841 Ahaziah		
Athaliah (*Jehoash—minor*)	Jehu	
835 Jehoash (Joash)		
813	Jehoahaz	
798	Jehoash (Joash)	
796 Amaziah		
792	*Jeroboam II*	
790 *Azariah*		
781	Jeroboam II	AMOS
767 Azariah (Uzziah)		HOSEA

753	Zechariah	
752	Shallum	
	Menahem (Pekah—dated his reign	
750 *Jotham*	from this year)	
743 *Ahaz*		
741	Pekahiah	
739 Jotham	Pekah	
731 Ahaz	Hoshea	MICAH
729 *Hezekiah*		ISAIAH
722	FALL OF SAMARIA	
715 Hezekiah	Invasion of Sennacherib (701)	
696 *Manasseh*		
686 Manasseh		
641 Amon		
639 Josiah		ZEPHANIAH
609 Jehoahaz (Shallum)		JEREMIAH
Jehoiakim (Eliakim)		
597 Jehoiachin (Coniah, Jeconiah)		EZEKIEL
Zedekiah (Mattaniah)		
587 FALL OF JERUSALEM		

Israel during the United Monarchy

CYPRUS

● Hamath

Arvad

Kadesh

Riblah

Zedad

Byblos

PHOENICIA

ZOBAH

Berothai

MEDITERRANEAN SEA

Helbon ●

Lebanon

Hermon

● Damascus

Sidon

Tyre ●

Abel ●● Dan

Hazor

Accho ● Cabul

Carmel

Sea of Chinnereth

Ashtaroth

Nobah ●

Dor

Megiddo

Ramoth-gilead

● Edrei

ARABIAN DESERT

Jezreel

Dothan Gilboa

Mahanaim?

Shechem

R. Jordan

Joppa ●

Shiloh Adamah

AMMON

Bethel

Gibeah AI Jericho ● Rabbath-ammon

Jerusalem Gilgal

Heshbon

Ashdod

Bethlehem

Ashkelon Gath Hebron

Medeba

Gaza ● Lachish

Dibon

SALT SEA

Gerar

Beersheba

MOAB

● Kir-hareseth

Bozrah

Kadesh-barnea?

EDOM

Sela ●

Teman?

O   20   40 Miles

Boundary of the Empire ⋯⋯⋯

Territory conquered by David ▨▨▨

Administrative Districts of Solomon − − −

Ezion-geber

1 Kings 1. 1-31

THE REIGN OF DAVID (1010-970): (1) *Adonijah's Attempt on the Throne.* The opening two chapters of 1 Kings present us with the somewhat pitiful spectacle of the last days of King David, now very old and no longer in full control of his kingdom or even of his court and family.

Adonijah was probably the eldest surviving son of David (2 Sam 3. 3-5), and as such could command for himself a fair degree of support among the older and more conservative counsellors of the king. There was as yet no fixed rule of succession to the throne, and Adonijah may have hoped to over-rule the king's earlier promise of the succession to Solomon, David's son, by Bathsheba (1. 13). It has indeed sometimes been suggested that no such promise had been made, and that Nathan and Bathsheba played a trick on the king's failing memory, but this view scarcely accords with what we know of Nathan's upright character and with the fact that Adonijah did not invite Solomon to his "accession feast" and its accompanying sacrifices at *En Rogel* just outside Jerusalem.

Nathan acted swiftly to warn Bathsheba of the danger in which both Solomon and they themselves stood if Adonijah's bid for the kingdom gained support and succeeded: by all the precedents of ancient *coups d'état* their lives would be forfeit. They therefore arranged to secure an audience of the king in which they would successively appear and acquaint him with what was going on behind his back: how could Adonijah's elevation of himself and a regal celebration, held without the presence of such stalwart supporters of the king as Zadok and Benaiah, to say nothing of Solomon, be in accord with any command of the king?

Although David had displayed weakness, both in his lax upbringing of his sons (1. 6) and in clinging to the semblance of power, he could act decisively enough when necessary, and when he learnt of the plot he was not slow to confirm his promise to Bathsheba and take steps to put down the trouble.

How far were David's difficulties in his later years due to his own weakness of character?

1 Kings 1. 32—2. 12

(2) *David's Last Days.* David acted swiftly enough to nip Adonijah's conspiracy in the bud. He instructed those of his courtiers whom he knew to be loyal and trustworthy to take Solomon immediately on his own royal mule down to the Spring of Gihon (the Virgin's Spring

in the Kedron valley and anoint him as king and then to seat him on the throne. Taking a body of troops (**1**. 38; foreign mercenaries are meant, *cf.* 2 Sam. **15**. 18), the men carried out David's instructions to the accompaniment of lively popular support. Solomon was anointed with oil from a horn kept in the tent of God, and the trumpet proclaimed his accession as co-regent with his father.

The noise of the trumpet broke in upon Adonijah's premature celebrations, and he sought the sanctuary of the altar; by claiming this refuge he assured himself of protection from being the victim of summary vengeance without the opportunity of a trial, and Solomon for his part was content to bide his time.

After an unspecified lapse of time (*cf.* 1 Chron. **22**. 6—**29**. 25) David died, but before his departure he gave some instruction to his heir. The first part of it was lofty and pious in tone. Solomon was to play the man and follow the law of God given by Moses; this would ensure his own prosperity and the secure maintenance of the dynasty (**2**. 2-4). But how is this advice to be squared with the worldly wisdom which follows it (**2**. 5-9)? While Solomon was to show loyalty to the family of Barzillai and give them a royal pension (*cf.* 2 Sam. **17**. 27-29; **19**. 31-40), he was to take vengeance on Joab, the commander of the army (and a supporter of Adonijah!), and upon Shimei who had once cursed David (2 Sam. **16**. 5-14; **19**. 16-23). In the case of the former it could be argued that David, as his superior, shared in the blame for his murder of Abner and Amasa (2 Sam. **3**. 26-30; **20**. 8-10) and wished to clear himself of blood guilt, but the command to dispose of Shimei was a plain evasion of his own promise to him of immunity.

Such acts of treachery were typical of the measures needed to ensure the safe establishment of an ancient king, but remain inexcusable. The line between legitimate political action to secure a desirable end and what is illegitimate is easily crossed, and no amount of pious words could cloak the enormity of David's offence.

Is there a legitimate place for the use of force in modern politics?

1 Kings 2. 13-46

THE REIGN OF SOLOMON (970-930): (1) *Solomon Ascends the Throne*. Solomon ensured his long tenure of the throne (**11**. 42) in true oriental fashion by liquidating or demoting his most probable opponents early in his reign. He began with Adonijah, the person most likely to be the focus of a rebellion. Since a new king inherited his predecessor's harem (2 Sam. **12**. 8), Adonijah's request for Abishag could plausibly be interpreted as a design upon the throne

(**2.** 22; *cf.* 2 Sam. **16.** 21*f.*) whether or not she was technically a concubine of the late king. It may have been that Solomon and his mother took advantage of a thoughtless request to get rid of him.

Next came Adonijah's two principal supporters. Solomon was unwilling to act violently against a priest, though not all kings shared his compunction in this respect, and he exiled Abiathar to Anathoth, a village some three miles N.E. of Jerusalem where priests lived when not on duty in Jerusalem (Jos. **21.** 1-3, 18; Jer. **1.** 1). This act fulfilled the prophecy of 1 Sam. **2.** 27-36.

The news of these events filled Joab, the third member of the rebellious trio, with justifiable alarm, and he followed Adonijah's example in seeking sanctuary at the altar. Benaiah, Solomon's henchman in these matters, was sent to deal with him. He expressed repugnance at killing a man beside the altar, though we need not ascribe his conduct to any higher motive than superstitious fear of a curse upon himself if he shed blood in the shrine; but Solomon showed no such timidity, especially in dealing with a murderer (Exod. **21.** 14), and assured him that in view of Joab's own guilt he could slay him without fear of the consequences. Benaiah then inherited what is described as the army command, but he appears to have behaved more like the unscrupulous chief of an ancient gestapo.

Finally there was Shimei. He was put on parole in Jerusalem, but this prevented him from taking proper care of his property at Bahurim in Benjamin, and (from Solomon's point of view) isolated him from any kinsmen with whom he might have fomented a revolt. When Shimei broke his parole, though not by going north to Benjamin but south to Philistia, Solomon was not slow to take advantage of the opportunity to have him also dispatched.

So the kingdom was established, but it was in danger of becoming a police state, and before long we read of forced labour camps and increasing discontent alongside external splendour. The picture is a harsh one, but Kings does not close its eyes to the realities of human depravity, and continually warns us against that spiritual double-mindedness which forgets to carry over personal religion into the sphere of political and commercial life.

1 Kings 3. 1-28

(2) *The Wisdom of Solomon.* Verses 1-3 make clear three of the essential features of Solomon's reign, all of which led to religious and moral declension in the king's house and ultimately in the whole land. He rested his *political* might on marriage alliances with pagan powers and thus imperilled the purity of the worship of Yahweh

(11. 4); his *economic* policy showed itself in the building of sumptuous prestige buildings, but this was at the cost of temporarily impoverishing the land and requiring high taxes and forced labour from the people; and his *religious* policy was one of syncretism. From the standpoint of the historian this last was an especial fault.

Solomon began his reign with religious ceremonies at the important shrine of Gibeon, six miles N.W. of Jerusalem, where the tabernacle finally came to rest, and in Jerusalem itself. In the former place he had a dream in which God offered him whatever he desired. Solomon asked for wisdom, practical sense in dealing with people, so that he might govern aright. His prayer is worth frequent repetition as we face the continually changing problems of personal relationships in our own lives.

The final part of the chapter gives a practical example of wisdom. It is noteworthy that the king was accessible to ordinary people and that they were not slow to take advantage of their opportunity. Harlots have no great reputation for truthfulness, and it required sagacity on this occasion to effect a decision. Solomon judged rightly that the real mother of the child would be willing for the child's life to be preserved at any cost, even that of losing the right to bring it up herself, and so he gave judgment in favour of the first woman and restored the child to her.

The narrator ascribes such a judgment to the wisdom of God and reminds us that wisdom is His gift, whether it be innate or formed by environment. God can give wisdom in later life to the immature if He so desires. No doubt, as the psychologists teach us, *intelligence* is an innate inherited ability, but the Christian will rightly contend that there is also a *wisdom* not of this world which comes down from above and whose deepest insight is the value of self-giving love—and for this he will pray often with the assurance that his prayer will be answered.

Read James **1.** 5; **3.** 13-18.

1 Kings 4. 1-34

(3) *The Royal Administration.* We now receive an account of the administration and extent of Solomon's empire. First there are listed the leading state officials (**4.** 1-6). These included secretaries of state, the army commander, the priests (Abiathar was on the "retired" list), a chief officer (the inspector of taxes), the king's friend or counsellor, and the forced labour organizer. In a religious state the priests are as important as the secular officials and are named with them; the danger is when the priests become acclimatized to secular ways

and neglect their primary duties—Cardinal Wolsey was not the first to fall into this temptation!

The maintenance of king and government requires a system of taxes, especially if the royal estates (1 Chron. 27. 25-31) are not sufficiently extensive to provide for the needs of the king and court. Solomon provided for his needs by a system of royal imposts and forced labour (4. 7-19, 22f., 26-28). For the purposes of the former the land was divided up into twelve areas, apparently based for the most part on the tribal divisions (see map in *Westminster Historical Maps of Bible Lands*), each under an officer whose duty was to provide the needs of the court for one month in the year. There is some doubt about the precise system used since in fact thirteen areas are enumerated. Either verses 13 and 19 refer to the same area, or Judah was dealt with separately. The amounts of food required for the king and the upkeep of his standing army are listed in verses 22f. and 26-28; it was no small establishment which was maintained (though in verse 26, 4,000 stalls is a more likely figure).

Finally, the extent of the empire is indicated (4. 20f. 24f.).

The evidence suggests that the prosperity was by no means uninterrupted and that it was not shared equally by all the people. The empire enjoyed an enviable reputation in the near east, and Solomon himself had great fame thanks to his reputation for wisdom (4. 29-34). He was considered to be wiser than many other men famous in their own day but now unknown to us, and he expressed his wisdom in proverbs and songs. Some of these were evidently sayings based on the use of Nature to point lessons (for this type of saying, see Prov. 30. 15ff.). The Book of Proverbs represents the accumulated wisdom of Solomon and his successors; Psalms 72 and 127 and Proverbs 10. 1—22. 16; 25. 1—29. 27 are attributed to him.

1 Kings 5. 1—6. 13

(4) *Preparations for Building the Temple.* King Hiram (otherwise Huram or Ahiram) of Tyre maintained with Solomon the friendly relations which had existed between him and David (2 Sam. 5. 11); the two kings entered into a commercial treaty to their mutual profit, Hiram receiving foodstuffs and Solomon building materials for the temple and his other prestige buildings. The story emphasizes the friendliness and helpfulness of Hiram, who was willing to pay lip service to Solomon's God (*cf.* Judg. 11. 24). Would this not also mean, however, that Solomon would have to respond in like manner? And how is a Christian today to pursue a right course in business— *e.g.*, in commercial dealings with countries whose political principles

are contrary to Christian standards, or in transactions with firms whose business (*e.g.*, gambling, armaments) may be questioned, or in making agreements which custom demands shall be sealed with the offer of alcoholic refreshment?

A labour force was required to prepare the materials supplied by Hiram. 30,000 Israelites worked in relays in Lebanon, and a second group of 150,000 Canaanites (*cf.* **9**. 20*f.*), whom it would have been too risky to send abroad, were put on forced labour in Israel itself.

The description of the temple should be read in conjunction with a reconstruction such as that offered in *The New Bible Dictionary*, p. 1244. Unfortunately successive rebuilding on the site has left us with no archaeological remains from Solomon's temple. But the building, which was a novelty in Israel, followed the pattern of similar structures in the Near East. It was a small chapel, 90′ by 30′, divided internally into a nave 60′ long and a chancel 30′ long. At the entrance to the nave was a porch 15′ long, and round the other three sides of the sanctuary ran a series of small rooms in three storeys each $7\frac{1}{2}′$ high; above these were the "clerestory" windows of the main sanctuary. The outside wall of the sanctuary had revetments to support the beams for the small chambers, and so became progressively less thick as it advanced in height. There was a staircase on the south side to provide access to the chambers. The whole structure was supported on a stone platform, and the woodwork for floors and roofing was carried out in cedar.

Ancient temples were not so much places for the worshippers to enter (they were too small for this purpose) as dwelling-places for deities. On what did the presence of God in this temple depend (6. 11-13)?

1 Kings 6. 14—7. 12

(5) *The Construction of the Temple.* The further description of the temple is not easy to follow, and the R.S.V. has often to interpret the obscure Hebrew. (*i*) The inner walls, floor and ceiling were all executed in cedar and cypress wood; the walls were carved decoratively with gourds, flowers, palms and cherubim, and the whole temple was overlaid with gold. (*ii*) A chancel was constructed at the innermost part of the sanctuary, with a lower ceiling than the main sanctuary and no windows (*cf.* **8**. 12); it was shut off from the rest of the sanctuary by two doors which came to an apex at the top, so that the floor, sideposts and the two lintels formed a pentagon. For the main entrance to the sanctuary folding doors were constructed, and there were also chains of gold across the entrance to the inner sanctuary. (*iii*) Within the inner sanctuary was a cedar altar overlaid

with gold, and two large-size cherubim figures with wings out-stretched right across the width of the room. (*iv*) The sanctuary was set in a courtyard built of stone bonded together with cedar. (*v*) The building was commenced in the fourth year of Solomon's reign and took seven years to build (contrast **7.** 1).

The general construction showed a lavish use of good and expensive materials, but the design was reasonably simple. It is probably wrong to look for a detailed typological significance in the description; the writer to the Hebrews, who is our one trustworthy guide in these matters, is remarkably restrained in drawing out the meaning of the various parts even of the tabernacle, and we shall be wise to follow his example.

The new temple was accompanied by a variety of other buildings which gave Jerusalem an appearance worthy of a capital city in a new nation. The House of the Forest of Lebanon was apparently a military storehouse (**10.** 17; Isa. **22.** 8). Next were the Hall of Pillars and a Judgment Hall, and finally Solomon's own palace with a house for Pharaoh's daughter (and possibly also for the rest of the harem). These were all constructed like the temple on a stone platform of massive limestone blocks (which could be trimmed with saws) and woodwork in cedar.

A basic question about the construction of temples was voiced by Solomon himself (**8.** 27) *and echoed by Stephen* (Acts **7.** 47*f.*): *what, then, should be our attitude to the spending of large sums of money to provide lavish places of worship?*

1 Kings 7. 13-51

(6) *The Temple Furniture.* After the digression about Solomon's royal buildings the account now turns to the various furnishings and ornaments of the temple itself. These were constructed under the supervision of a Tyrian craftsman called Hiram; the Israelites lagged behind their neighbours in metal working (1 Sam. **13.** 19*f.*). At the door of the temple were placed two ornamental bronze pillars with capitals decorated with filigree work and rows of pomegranates. It has been suggested that Jachin is the opening word of "He will establish the throne of David and his kingdom for ever", and Boaz is the opening word of "In the strength of the Lord shall the king rejoice". This would indicate the close relationship which was felt to exist between the person of the king and the worship of God.

A second item was a bronze laver standing upon a base of twelve oxen and decorated with gourds. It was of giant size, able to hold some 10,000 gallons of water. Water for ablutions was drawn from it

2 Chron. **4.** 6), but it may also have been symbolic of the sea and the raging waters subdued by God; ancient thought saw in the tremendous power and turbulent might of sea and flood a symbol of the forces of chaos arrayed against God. There were also ten bronze stands on wheels supporting lavers of very ponderous construction (illustration in *The New Bible Dictionary*, p. 1244). These bronze articles were cast in the clay ground of the Jordan valley, a region in which traces of ancient metal-working have been discovered by archaeologists.

How far does this passage support the church's use of aids to worship (buildings, art, music), created by non-believers?

I Kings 8. 1-30

7) *The Dedication of the Temple*. When the temple was completed, it was dedicated to its purpose. The first act was to bring the ark of the covenant containing the two tablets of the law from the tabernacle. A representative gathering of the people was summoned to witness the event in the seventh month at the time of the Feast of Tabernacles. The ark was carried into the inner sanctuary between the cherubim. It was hidden from view, presumably by a curtain (2 Chron. **3.** 14), so that only the ends of the carrying poles which projected at the sides were visible. Then the cloud which symbolized the glory of God filled the building as a sign that God was pleased to dwell there. The words of Solomon in verses 12*f*. are obscure in the Hebrew text, and the R.S.V. offers a reconstruction based on the LXX. The hidden presence of God in the darkness of the sanctuary is contrasted with the splendour of the sun which He created.

Solomon then blessed the people and proceeded to give thanks to God for fulfilling His promises. Although God had refused to choose a city for His dwelling in time past, He had chosen David to be king over His people, and through David's son He had provided both a royal succession on which His favour rested and a house for His name. This thought caused Solomon to break out in further praise of God for the covenant which He made with His people at the Exodus and for His faithfulness in fulfilling His promises to David.

But even heaven cannot suffice as a dwelling for God; how much less can He be confined to a material fixed house! As the New Testament makes clear, a movable tent is a better symbol of His presence among His pilgrim people. Solomon therefore recognizes that it is entirely due to His grace that the God of heaven hears the prayers uttered in His earthly shrine.

For Meditation: 1 Corinthians **3.** 16; **6.** 19.

SOLOMON'S TEMPLE

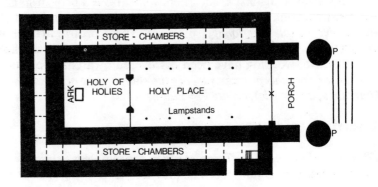

Plan of Solomon's Temple showing the two pillars (P), Jachin and Boaz, and the steps leading up to the Porch.

Orientation was east and west, with the Holy of Holies in the western half.

Dimensions of Porch: 29' x 15'.

Dimensions of Holy Place: 58' x 29'.

Dimensions of Holy of Holies: 29' x 29'.

Height of Main Building: 44'.

Each side wing contained three storeys of auxiliary accommodation, storage rooms, etc.

(All figures are approximate to the nearest foot, allowing for a cubit of 17.49 inches.)

Steven's reconstruction of Solomon's Temple, showing the twin pillars (Jachin and Boaz.), the vestibule porch and side storage chambers.

(8) *Solomon's Prayer in the Temple.* The language of the prayer, as is often the case in Kings, is reminiscent of phrases in the Pentateuch, particularly in Deuteronomy (Lev. 26; Deut. 28). It was once a commonplace of critical scholarship that such "Deuteronomic" passages represent the historian's later writing-up of his story under the influence of the publication of Deuteronomy in the reign of Josiah. But since even critical scholars date Deuteronomy much earlier, and since it is likely that many so-called "Deuteronomic" phrases were stereotyped in prayer, liturgy, and historical writing, this view finds far fewer supporters today. Indeed, there is increasing support for the conservative view of a Mosaic origin for Deuteronomy. But just as we find "*post-Mosaica*" in the Pentateuch, so we must not be surprised to find editorial modifications in other books of the Bible, although the extent of these may well be less than many critics suppose. The spiritual value of the sentiments expressed in this prayer may not be affected should parts of it come from the seventh century rather than the tenth century B.C., but the sense of historical worth would certainly suffer.

In this part of the prayer Solomon appeals to God to hear the prayers of His people in a variety of situations. In legal cases where, in the absence of firm evidence, a man took an oath of innocence, God was called on to vindicate the innocent (31*f*.). Note how the possibility of prayer is not restricted to born Israelites (41-43) or to the temple itself (46-53).

After his prayer Solomon turned to address the people and to bless them; he praised God and prayed that He would keep His people faithful to Himself. Note how this prayer for divine preservation is accompanied by an appeal for human faithfulness – a combination frequent in the New Testament.

The proceedings closed with a feast lasting fourteen days (R.S.V. margin; 2 Chron. 7. 8-10), during which vast sacrifices were offered; the peace offerings were largely consumed by the worshippers. One act is recorded almost in parenthesis—the dedication of the outer court of the temple for the offering of sacrifices. The bronze altar mentioned in 8. 64 is curiously omitted from the earlier lists of temple furniture (but *cf.* 2 Chron. 4. 1).

What conception of God underlies Solomon's prayer?

1 Kings 9. 1—10. 13

(9) *Solomon's Commercial Relationships.* After the completion of the temple there was a further revelation by God to Solomon promising

the eternal welfare of the temple, *provided that* the king kept all God's commandments and ordinances.

Vs. 10-14 indicate that Solomon was in financial difficulties and ceded 20 towns in Galilee to Hiram for 120 talents, but Hiram felt that he had not received value for his money; the etymology of "Cabul" is uncertain. *Cf.* 2 Chron. **8.** 2. A second note tells of Solomon's use of a forced levy of the native population of the land to carry out building operations. Although it is said that the Israelites themselves were not enslaved, we have already seen that they had none the less to do forced labour. With this help Solomon built his new "city centre" and fortifications in Jerusalem; the Millo (**9.** 15, 24; *cf.* 2 Sam. **5.** 9 and 1 Chron. **11.** 8; 2 Kings **12.** 20 and 2 Chron. **32.** 5) was some kind of fortification in the oldest part of the city. He also fortified a number of strategically-placed fortresses, for which consult a map (the sites of Baalath and Tamar are uncertain).

The third note speaks of Solomon's trading operations in company with Hiram. Ezion-geber on the N.E. arm of the Red Sea became an important centre for copper smelting (*i.e.*, a "tarshish"). Ophir is variously identified with S. Arabia, Somaliland, or even India. Hiram provided the fleet, and Solomon brought the goods overland (there being no Suez Canal) to Phoenicia.

The queen of Sheba, the land of the Sabaeans (modern Yemen), was sufficiently impressed by the rumours of the magnificence of Solomon's court and his wisdom to pay a royal visit. The visit was by no means without its more mundane side – dare we call it a trade mission—as there was evidently a considerable exchange of each country's products in connection with the levée. The narrator's emphasis, however, falls upon the testimony of the queen to Solomon's material greatness. If so splendid a person as a queen from the mysterious land of Sheba could bear witness to Solomon's magnificence, then his greatness was amply vindicated. A later Authority saw the significance of the queen in her readiness to come and see for herself concerning what she had heard; she is a standing condemnation of all who fail to inquire further into One greater than Solomon ever was (Matt. **12.** 42).

*1 Kings 10. 14—11. 13

(10) *Solomon's Wealth – and his Folly.* A considerable amount of bullion came in to Solomon annually; the talent weighed about 66 lbs., an amount of gold which would cost about £15,000 ($42,000) today, but this figure does not indicate its actual purchasing power. Although his income was great, it is evident that Solomon's

expenditure was extravagant, and that he was often "in the red". Further wealth came from trade in association with Hiram in "ships of Tarshish"; these were ships capable of going to Tartessus in Spain or of carrying metal ores, but here they were obviously used for eastern trade (*cf.* **9.** 26-28). Another source of wealth was the trade in chariots from Egypt and horses from Kue (Cilicia). Solomon acted as middleman between the suppliers and the Hittites and Syrians around Damascus as well as providing for his own army; stables discovered at Megiddo, once thought to be Solomonic; are now said to date from the time of Ahab. Finally, it would seem that the tourist trade was as profitable then as it is now (**10.** 24*f.*)!

With ch. **11** the picture changes, and attention is directed to a less satisfactory aspect of Solomon's reign. Although it has been suggested that most of the marriages mentioned here were political unions and therefore not simply the result of unchecked lust, it is hard to believe that 700 political unions were either necessary or likely, and though Solomon may have been no worse than his contemporaries he cannot be exculpated even by Old Testament standards. But it is not the size of the harem which arouses the historian's judgment so much as the fact that foreign marriages meant the toleration of foreign religions. At first these would be practised privately, like Mary Queen of Scots's private masses in Holyrood, but, like that unhappy lady's ritual, their influence was felt more widely, and the point was reached where Solomon himself was induced to take part in such worship and to build high places. Thus the fundamental principle of the covenant with Yahweh was broken, and His judgment was threatened; Deut. **17.** 16*f.* could almost have been written with Solomon in mind. What a king tolerates is soon copied by his people, and Solomon's example renewed the popularity of the fertility cults which continued to threaten the worship of Yahweh for the next 350 years.

For meditation: the power of example (1 Cor. **8.** 10*f.*; **11.** 1).

*1 Kings 11. 14-43

(11) *Solomon's Adversaries.* The final part of the story of Solomon tells of the various thorns in his flesh which he experienced. Trouble lasted throughout his reign (**11.** 25) but was intensified in his later years. The first adversary mentioned is Hadad of Edom. After surviving a massacre perpetrated by Joab he had been taken by faithful servants of his father's household southwards *via* Midian and west through Paran in the Sinai peninsula to Egypt where he enjoyed a success story not unlike that of Joseph centuries earlier. When David died and things were safer at home, he returned to

Edom and carried on guerilla warfare against Solomon; this would have the effect of imperilling Solomon's trade connections with Ezion-geber.

A second adversary was Rezon, a vassal of Hadadezer the king of Zobah, an Aramaean kingdom situated north of Israel between Damascus and Hamath. After David's defeat of his master (2 Sam. **8.** 3-12), he put himself at the head of a gang of bandits and succeeded in establishing himself in Damascus, from where he harassed Israel. The ultimate effect would again be to cut trade routes to the north.

The third adversary was nearer home. The split in the kingdom so clearly symbolized was in consequence of Solomon's idolatry, and it was made clear that the prosperity of Jeroboam's line would depend upon a renewed loyalty to Yahweh. Only for David's sake was it promised that the line of Solomon would retain a footing in Jerusalem, like a house with a light in it indicating the presence of living inhabitants. The matter leaked out, and Jeroboam had to flee to Egypt, where opponents of the ruling house in Israel were generally sure of a welcome and support. Here he remained until the time was ripe.

We encounter here a fundamental feature of Old Testament belief in the view that the religious declension of a king or kingdom is judged by God with the rise of enemies, defeat in warfare, and ultimately captivity, and that the future course of history in such circumstances is predetermined by God and made known to prophets.

Do these same principles hold today? For example, is it right for us, in the absence of prophecy, to interpret national disasters as being due to specified acts of national apostasy? Or is there a transfer in God's dealings so that it is now church rather than nation which is the object of His concern?

1 Kings 12. 1-33

THE DIVISION OF THE KINGDOM. More than one interpretation of this incident is possible. It is generally held that, by his reckless folly in following the harsh advice of the younger men instead of the wiser and more moderate counsel of the elder, Rehoboam brought disaster upon himself and lost the greater part of his kingdom to Jeroboam, who appeared at just the right time to win over the alienated people. But H. L. Ellison has suggested that Rehoboam was perhaps not quite such a fool as this view makes him out to be. He was really the victim of a cunning plot by Jeroboam, and he yielded to the suggestion of taking a firm line put forward by advisers who thought that the conspiracy was further advanced than it actually was. A bold line might have won the day. In any case the sending of Adoram, the most hated man in the government, to enforce the king's will was an act of folly. The people promptly lynched him and made what is nowadays known as a Unilateral Declaration of Independence. Only in the case of Judah and Benjamin (the latter possibly under duress from its more powerful neighbour) did the motive of loyalty to the reigning dynasty overcome the appeal to revolt.

Thus the glory of Solomon's kingdom vanished, and his empire disappeared overnight, as neither Israel nor Judah was strong enough to subdue its neighbours.

The narrator now deals first of all with events in the reign of Jeroboam, which was longer than that of Rehoboam, before going back to catch up on the story of Judah. He follows this policy of keeping two narratives in step throughout the record. Shechem was an ancient centre of the Israelite tribal union (Josh. 8. 30ff.; 24. 1; Judg. 9. 6) and the obvious place for a capital. Perhaps because it was not easily defensible Jeroboam later moved to Penuel, due east on the other side of the Jordan, and later still Tirzah became the capital (14. 17). It was essential to provide a religious focus in the kingdom to replace Jerusalem and its fine temple in the affections of the people. The king furnished sanctuaries at Bethel and Dan (the two extremities of the kingdom) each with a golden calf and a priesthood, and he appointed an annual festival, a month later than the corresponding Judaean one (8. 2), at which he himself offered sacrifice. Although W. F. Albright has argued that the calf was a pedestal for the invisible God and not itself an idol to be worshipped, it is unlikely that the people would have risen to such a height of transcendental religion, and indeed the words of the king (12. 28) would encourage idolatry (cf. Exod. 32). In any case the bull was a popular symbol in fertility religions. Thus the way was paved for increasing religious degeneration over the next 200 years.

1 Kings 13. 1-34

PROPHECIES AGAINST JEROBOAM. The story of the prophet from Judah (perhaps the Iddo of 2 Chron. 9. 29) who pronounced judgment upon the worship practised at Bethel is fraught with much difficulty. The point of the main part of the story (13. 1-10, 33f.) is clear enough.

The old prophet at Bethel is one of the most unsavoury characters in the Old Testament; the fact that he lived at Bethel and yet did not speak out against the religious innovations there is tacitly held against him. It is not certain why he was so curious to see the man of God from Judah: was it simply a deliberate attempt to turn the prophet aside from his vow (**13.** 8*f.*) even by means of deceit? In any case the lesson is that the man of God was wrong to accept from somebody else a command purporting to be the word of God when this stood contrary to the word which he himself had received.

It is the tale of the prophet's gory death which causes the most heart-searching. We may be certain that the narrator and original readers of the story would see the main point of the story in the fact that his death was meant to be a sign to the people of Bethel that if God acted so decisively against His own disobedient prophet He would be all the more certain to act in judgment against them.

Nevertheless, the difficulty remains that not only the false prophet from Bethel but also the narrator (*cf.* **20.** 36; 2 Kings **17.** 25) had what appear to us to have been limited views about the nature of God. Evangelical Christians must be prepared to face up to the problems aroused by such a passage as this. We are not meant to find here the full sum of biblical teaching on the nature of God, but must consider this passage in the light of a fuller revelation which knows not only the fact of God's just judgment but also His great mercy and pardon.

On what principles do "the kindness and the severity of God" (Rom. **11.** 22) *operate? How would you deal with the accusation that the Old Testament doctrine cf God is sub-Christian?*

1 Kings 14. 1-31

JEROBOAM I (Israel 930–909). Jeroboam's religious policy had obviously led already to a break with Ahijah, and it was fitting that the prophet who had announced the rise of his house should also pronounce its downfall. We are given an insight into the debased superstition of that day in which people consulted prophets just as they now visit gipsies and fortune-tellers or scan the astrological columns in the press. Jeroboam himself foolishly thought that he could deceive the old, half-blind prophet by the use of disguise, but found he was wrong. Modern critics suggest that the substance of Ahijah's message to the queen is in verses 6 and 12, the rest being an expansion by a pious story-teller, but surely a prophet such as Ahijah would be unable to resist the opportunity, and indeed the divine command, to improve the occasion with a vivid description of the king's evil ways and their inevitable consequences. After this there was nothing more worth recounting about Jeroboam (but see 2 Chron. **13.** 20).

REHOBOAM (Judah 930–913). The narrative now shifts to the southern kingdom and is carried forward to the reign of the first ing to outlive Jeroboam. First, the reign of Rehoboam is brought to a conclusion, two events being recorded which are doubtless to be seen as cause and effect. Idolatry was being practised, very possibly under the influence of the king's foreign mother, and foreign religions were becoming more widespread. The centres of worship were the "high places", local shrines taken over from the Canaanites. The cultic objects were stone pillars and wooden poles ("asherim"), representing the male and female deities respectively, and the shrine personnel included prostitutes. With this apparatus was conducted a cult whose practical purpose was to induce the gods to give fertility to the land and its inhabitants, and whose methods included not only the offering of sacrifices and the celebration of liturgical rituals but also acts of sacred prostitution; these acts were a form of imitative magic to lead the god to grant fertility to the fields and herds. Throughout their history the Israelite people were slow to realize that Yahweh the Creator God was in complete control of natural processes and did not need to be acted on in this way; they tended to identify Yahweh with Baal and to offer Him the type of worship given to Baal.

The invasion of Shishak, *i.e.*, Sheshonq I, ruler of a reinvigorated Egypt, is described in Egyptian sources.

Kings 15. 1-32

ABIJAM (Judah 913–910). Rehoboam's successor in Judah was his son Abijam, whose mother was probably the *grand*daughter of Absalom. His brief reign was not marked by any outstanding event. Indeed it was only due to the memory of David's piety that God allowed the line of Rehoboam to persist in the kingship (*cf.* 11. 36). Verse 6 is an accidental repetition of 14. 30.

ASA (Judah 910–869). By contrast Asa was from the religious point of view one of the best kings of Judah. He carried through a much-needed reformation in doing away with cultic prostitution and removing idolatrous symbols, in particular a pole used in the worship of the goddess Asherah, a Canaanite goddess, which had been erected by his grandmother Maacah (verses 10 and 13 mean this). Maacah had wielded a powerful influence as queen mother, and Asa dealt more firmly with her than his father had done.

Throughout the history of the two kingdoms border warfare and raids were as common as they once were between England and Scotland. The position became serious for Judah when Baasha of Israel built a fortress at Ramah, a mere eight miles north of Jerusalem in Judaean territory. In his fear Asa collected what wealth there was in the temple and royal treasuries and bribed Israel's neighbour Syria to break off alliance with Israel and assist Judah. Syria was not loth to help, profiting both by the bribe and by the excuse thus afforded to capture various northern territories of Israel round Chinneroth (Galilee). Once Baasha's attention was distracted Asa carried out a lightning foray against Ramah and demolished the fortress. He used the materials captured to build two other fortresses at Geba and Mizpah in the same area. But was Asa's action in summoning Syrian help sound policy? See 2 Chron. **16.**

NADAB (Israel 909–908). In the northern kingdom Jeroboam's son carried on his father's policies, but within two years a conspiracy was made against him as he was warring against the Philistine border stronghold of Gibbethon. Baasha, who sounds like a modern dictator raised to power by the army, seized the opportunity to murder him – and the whole royal family – as a precautionary act against reprisals. From now onwards the northern kingdom was subject to dynastic upheavals and never retained the stability of Judah.

Commentary on **15.** 30: *Exodus* **20.** 4*f.*

1 Kings 15. 33—16. 28

BAASHA (Israel 908–885); THE YEAR OF REVOLUTION (885–884). Baasha, the first usurper of the Israelite throne, managed to survive for 24 years, and to die in his bed. But the judgment of God against Baasha and his house had already been spoken by the prophet Jehu (2 Chron. **19.** 2; **20.** 34), who is not to be confused with the "furious rider" who reigned some fifty years later. The prophecy was fulfilled two years later. Baasha's son Elah had succeeded to the throne, but a man of whom the solitary fact worth mentioning was that he was prone to drunkenness was no fit person to rule a turbulent nation. A colonel in the chariot regiment, who was evidently of such low birth that nobody bothered to record his father's name, saw his chance, murdered the drunken monarch and proceeded to liquidate the rest of his family in the typical ancient manner.

His success was short-lived – to be precise, one week. Zimri had omitted to secure the one vital factor, the support of the army. The troops who were still engaged on the protracted siege of Gibbethon – probably a major force was continually posted there for border defence – felt that they had not been consulted, and put up their general, Omri, as king. They marched forty miles to Tirzah and set siege to it. Zimri had the good sense to commit suicide before a worse fate befell him. Even so the dynastic struggle was not over.

OMRI (Israel 884–873). Secular sources indicate that Omri was one of the most powerful of Israelite kings, but the sole event recorded of him here is that he moved the capital from Tirzah to the new site of Samaria, a place of considerable natural strength which Omri and Ahab fortified superbly. His religious policy was sufficient to condemn him in the eyes of the historian, but the world at large remembered him for his conquest of Moab, and for the next 150 years Assyria, which had now begun to menace the west, spoke of Israel as the land of Omri.

The whole story provides an interesting parallel to the dynastic struggles in Rome in A.D.69 (the year of the four emperors). From the religious point of view it illustrates the principle that God may use wicked men as the agents of His judgment, but these same wicked men will not go unpunished if they fall into the sins of the judged (*cf.* Isa. **10.** 5-19). It is sometimes said that the historian glides over the story of Omri because his successful career and peaceful death failed to bear out his thesis that "idolatry doesn't pay", but it should be remembered that for the Israelite what happened to a man's descendants was part of his own fate.

1 Kings 16. 29—17. 24

AHAB (Israel 873–853): (1) *Elijah Prophesies Drought*. With the reign of Ahab, the religious corruption of Israel reached its peak – and its point of no return. Though Ahab was professedly a worshipper of Yahweh, he made a dynastic marriage with the daughter of the king of Tyre and Sidon, and the price of the union was the introduction of the worship of the Phoenician god Melkart, here referred to as Baal. This god was not one of the petty Baalim of the Canaanite shrines whose worship had so often coalesced with that of Yahweh, but the great god himself who typified a way of life in complete contrast to that of Israel.

(As an example of disobedience to Yahweh at this time the historian notes the rebuilding of Jericho (Josh. **6.** 26) at the cost of the life of the builder's two sons.)

The hour of crisis was matched by the appearance of one of the greatest of the prophets who arrived out of the blue on to the stage of history from Tishbe in Gilead, E. of the Jordan, and announced to the king the advent of a drought at the behest of Yahweh, the God of Israel, *and not of Baal*.

The rest of the story is concerned with Elijah's own existence during this perilous period. He was saved from Ahab and from starvation by God's directing him to a perennial stream E. of Jordan, and then, when this dried up, to the house of a widow in Zarephath near Sidon, in Baal's own country! The woman was presumably a pagan, but, like Rahab, she respected the prophet and was ready to trust him even to the extent of preparing a scanty meal for him before she cared for her son and herself. Her faith was amply rewarded. When her son became mortally ill, she thought that God, through the prophet, was visiting her in judgment for her sins. Elijah's act of healing has been interpreted recently as the "kiss of life". Earlier commentators spoke of it as an act of imitative magic or as a transfer of "vital power" from the man of God to the child. But the story ascribes the cure to the prayer of Elijah, whatever other means he may have employed, and emphasizes that Yahweh is Lord of life and death.

For study: *the significance of Elijah in later writings* (Mal. **4.** *5f.*; Luke **1.** 17; Mark **8.** 28; **9.** 1-13; Rev. **11.** 1-13).

1 Kings 18. 1-46

(2) *Conflict on Mount Carmel.* After three years with scarcely any rain Ahab and his chamberlain Obadiah sought out any sources of water which might still remain untapped. In his travels Obadiah met Elijah, for whom the hour of action had come, but feared to tell his master lest, when Ahab came and found that Elijah had melted away into thin air again, he should wreak vengeance on Obadiah for summoning him to a wildgoose chase. But Elijah was now ready to meet Ahab and summoned him to Mount Carmel, a hill sacred to both Phoenicians and Israelites. The conversation with Obadiah indicates the probable reason for the drought; it was because Jezebel was not content to pursue her religion privately, but was prepared to go to any lengths to have it adopted in Israel, that this judgment came upon the land.

The essence of the contest on Mount Carmel was an appeal to the people to give up their religious compromise in favour of Baal or Yahweh; for a primitive people who judged religion by its results such a performance was necessary. Note how Elijah called for a production not of rain but of fire; as a weather-god Baal should have been able to produce both to order. The slaughter of the prophets of Baal may appear to have been a terrible act of persecution, but, as the next chapter shows, the frustrated queen would certainly have had Elijah executed, fire or no fire. It is doubtful whether any other policy would have worked in such a society at such a date.

Elijah's fine satire against the pagan god's failure to respond to his priests, and implicitly also against the process of summoning him, points to a nobler conception of God. But it is by no means obvious that the people "got the message". Certainly the display of fire and the ensuing rainstorm convinced them for the moment of the superiority of Yahweh, but there was no deep-going religious reformation as a result, and Jezebel underwent no change of heart. The corruption of the people had gone too far. While one should not minimise the importance of the incident, one should not exaggerate its effects.

Jesus Himself knew well that people would be saved not by seeing mighty acts of power (Luke **16**. 30*f.*) *but by realizing the spiritual significance of His acts and teaching* (John **2**. 23*f.*; **4**. 46-54).

I Kings 19. 1-21

3) *The Flight of Elijah.* It is psychologically understandable that after the tremendous events on Carmel Elijah should have experienced a sudden change of mood and turned from vigorous confidence to dispirited despair. After the tension had relaxed he was once more an ordinary man feeling exceedingly fearful and longing to flee from the realities of the situation and to indulge in self-pity. Yahweh's word to him can be represented as a rebuke for his weakness and his proud assertion that he alone had remained faithful to Him.

Is this commonly accepted analysis of the situation really correct? The truth is that Jezebel was still very much mistress of the situation; for all their full-throated acclamation of the miraculous power of Yahweh the people were still hobbling between two opinions and were by no means converted in their hearts. Elijah was fully aware of this and knew that there was a price upon his head. Jezebel was not the woman to sit down under the murder of her prophets. It was sound policy for Elijah to make himself scarce, and he departed southwards to Horeb, the place of God's covenant with His people.

A theophany in wind, earthquake, and fire was followed by the faint whisper of God's voice. The intention appears to be to strengthen the conviction that God's voice is ultimately heard, not in the miraculous and tremendous, but in His quiet appeal to the conscience. Then Elijah portrayed the situation as he saw it to Yahweh. He himself was alone left as a representative of true worship; despite Carmel the people had broken the covenant with Yahweh. God replied with a word of judgment upon the royal house and people to be accomplished through Hazael and Jehu and the continuing prophetic witness of Elisha. Yet in the execution of judgment a faithful remnant would be found to remain.

For reasons that are not accessible to us Elijah himself accomplished only one part of this command, the "anointing" of Elisha, upon

317

whom he placed his mantle as a sign of his call to succeed him. The fulfilment of the rest of the prophecy may have been slow, but it was certain.

For study: Elijah as a man of faith (cf. James 5. 17f.)

1 Kings 20. 1-43

(4) *The War with Ben-hadad.* The reign of Ahab saw the expansion of the Assyrian empire westwards, and the smaller states in the Levant found it prudent to ally with each other against their common enemy. Ben-hadad of Syria appears here in command of a coalition of 32 kings, and his purpose in picking a quarrel with Ahab was probably to gain Israel's participation in his alliance. Ahab, however, refused to submit to Syria's overlordship. It is as hard to give a clear interpretation of the diplomatic exchange in verses 2-11 as it is with modern exchanges. Probably verse 4 was spoken sarcastically, or perhaps Ahab, conscious of his inferior strength, was prepared to temporize and grant some part of Ben-hadad's demand in order to save the people from being plundered.

Ben-hadad's proud boast that his forces were so enormous that there would not be enough dust in Samaria for each soldier to have a handful was answered by ignominious defeat. The Syrians ascribed their defeat to the pagan belief that the Israelite gods of the hills had proved superior to their own gods of the plains, and resolved to renew the struggle on terrain where their gods might give better auspices. At the same time they were careful to replace the unreliable foreign kings at the head of the army divisions by their own trained generals. They then marched to Aphek (somewhere in the region of Galilee), where their vast army made the Israelite forces look pitifully small. But Yahweh, the God of plains and hills, demonstrated that He was indeed the Lord, for the Syrians again suffered a crushing defeat. The wall at Aphek was probably undermined by Israelite siege operations. Ben-hadad sued for peace on terms that were very favourable to Ahab.

Although Ahab's policy of leniency may have seemed to be the wisest from a human point of view in that it joined Syria and Israel together against their common foe and forwarded Israel's trade, it was condemned by a prophet who appeared before Ahab and acted a parable against him. From a religious point of view an alliance with Syria could be as harmful as one with Phoenicia, and in the end it was at the hands of the Syrians that Ahab died.

To think over: Do we, as God's people, make the mistake of limiting God's power to protected areas of life from which "the world" is

*excluded? Dare we believe in His sovereignty over the whole of man-
kind?*

1 Kings 21. 1-29

(5) *Naboth's Vineyard.* Naboth was unfortunate enough to possess a
vineyard hard by the king's country residence at Jezreel and bold
enough to hold out for the right to keep his ancestral property against
a compulsory purchase order. Although Ahab behaved like a spoilt
child over his disappointment, he would have acquiesced in the
situation, but Jezebel took action for him. The recipients of the letter
meekly fell in with her royal command (they knew what would
happen to them if they disobeyed), Naboth and his heirs (2 Kings 9.
25, 26) were put to death, and Ahab was able to survey his new estates.

His pride and enjoyment were short-lived. Elijah, the watchdog of
Israelite morality and religion, was fast on the scene and uttered the
condemnation of God upon the evil act. Note that because of Ahab's
repentance, which may have been real enough – he did not necessarily
know or approve of Jezebel's action – the fulfilment of the prophecy
was deferred (2 Kings 9. 25f.).

This is surely one of the most significant stories in 1 and 2 Kings
for the modern church. Jezebel's action was a typical one in a society
in which since Solomon's time the gap between rich and poor had
widened, justice was becoming unknown – except at a price – and
immorality was on the increase. In this situation the prophets of
Yahweh, including many not mentioned in this book, such as Amos,
continually bore a witness to true godliness and the associated way of
life. Christians today have the same inescapable duty to be aware of
what is going on in the political sphere, both domestic and foreign,
so that they may assess the deeds of men from the standpoint of
Christian morality. Commerce and industry are among the areas
where Christian action is demanded. To a genuine insight into the
problems of our day must then be linked the fearlessness of Elijah
in asserting the divine will and pronouncing God's judgment on
infringements of His moral law. We desperately need the "nonconformist conscience" of half a century ago.

*But who is to carry out this task today? The church, or the individual
Christian, or both?*

*1 Kings 22. 1-28

(6) *The Prophecy of Micaiah.* The three years of peace between Syria
and Israel were occupied by their confederacy against Assyria whose

319

king, Shalmaneser III, came west and engaged in battle with them at Qarqar (853 BC). Although he naturally claimed victory in his propaganda documents, the fact that he did not follow up his advance suggests that he exaggerated his success. In the interval of peace that followed the confederates were free to attend to their own interests and Ahab resolved to attack the frontier town of Ramoth-gilead, E. of the Jordan. He enlisted the support of Jehoshaphat of Judah.

Before going to battle it was necessary to consult the prophets to ensure divine approbation of the venture. A vivid picture of ancient superstition and popular prophecy follows. Some 400 prophets proceeded to work themselves up into an ecstatic frenzy, a state in which they were supposed to be susceptible to divine revelation, and announced in chorus the certainty of victory. One man, Zedekiah, went further than his comrades and acted symbolically the victorious advance of Ahab's army; this piece of imitative magic was intended not simply to make clear the prophetic word by action but above all to induce the deity (Yahweh, but it might as well have been Baal, so far as Zedekiah was concerned!) to act in the desired manner.

Jehoshaphat was quite unconvinced by this pantomime and sought independent corroboration. Another prophet, Micaiah, was summoned, and the messenger warned him in advance on which side his bread was buttered. Micaiah entered into the spirit of the occasion and sarcastically confirmed the words of the howling dancers before he uttered a prophecy of impending disaster and stated that the 400 were deceived. Zedekiah was mortally offended by this challenge to his professional reputation and asked how the Spirit had departed from him. The reply was to the effect that if he were to spend some time in quiet and solitude seeking the word of Yahweh instead of capering about in public producing oracles to order he might have some chance of progress in true prophecy. The view of lying spirits from Yahweh expounded by Micaiah is, however, difficult. H. L. Ellison suggests a possible approach when he points out the difficulty of reconciling the sovereignty of God with the acts of evil men, and urges that for men in a primitive society and an undeveloped religion some very elementary form of presentation of this problem and its answer was needed. Biblical doctrine must also take into account James 1. 13f.

*1 Kings 22. 29-50

(7) *The Death of Ahab*. The result of the battle vindicated the prophecy of Micaiah. (We hope he was released from prison.) Ahab's attempt to avoid his prophesied death by disguising himself and

llowing Jehoshaphat to go into battle in his royal robes – surely an
ct of cowardice and treachery (*pace* H. L. Ellison) – came to naught.
A "shot in the air" from a bowman mortally wounded him. In the
our of his death he showed himself a finer man than he had done
arlier. Abandoning his first impulse to flee from the scene of battle,
e remained propped up in his chariot throughout the weary day in
rder to be an inspiration to his men, who would assuredly have
iven up the struggle if they had known that the king was dead or
lying.

EHOSHAPHAT (Judah *872–869*–853). The story now returns
riefly to Judah. Note that the chronology becomes complicated here.
rom now onwards it appears that a system of co-regencies operated,
he king's son being associated with his father during the latter's
ast years on the throne; the lengths given for reigns sometimes
nclude such periods of co-regency. The date of accession as co-
egent is put in italics with each king's years of reign in our section
eadings.

Jehoshaphat was reckoned a good king, since he followed the
olicy of his father, Asa, and did away with the remaining cult
rostitutes. He pursued a policy of peace with Israel (politically
ecessary in view of the Assyrian threat) and retained control of
dom. An attempt at trade with Ophir failed when the fleet was
recked. When Ahaziah of Israel offered to be partner in a fresh
ttempt Jehoshaphat was unwilling to go any further. 2 Chron. **20.**
5ff. describes the first attempt at greater length and shows that
ommercial transactions with the less well-principled king of Israel
ere to be frowned upon.

*For study: What were the causes of Ahab's weakness? Had he any
edeeming features?*

Kings 22. 51-53; 2 Kings 1. 1-18

AHAZIAH (Israel 853–852). Ahaziah had a brief and undistin-
uished reign, during which Moab seized the opportunity to become
ndependent. The king's early death was brought about by an injury
aused by falling from a lattice – *i.e.*, some kind of projecting oriel
indow. In his anxiety about the outcome of the illness he sought a
ivine oracle concerning his prospects of survival and sent messengers
o a shrine at Ekron in Philistine territory. They were to consult a
od here named "Baal-zebub" or "Lord of the flies"; this name
ppears to be a derisive pun on the god's real name "Baal-zebul"
neaning "'Baal the prince". Ahaziah's act was thus one of apostasy

from Yahweh. The messengers were duly intercepted. They were me
by a man who proclaimed in Yahweh's name the doom of the king
and the force of the man's personality was such that they returned t
the king without accomplishing their original mission. Their earl
return surprised Ahaziah, but when he heard their story he had n
doubts as to the prophet's identity and determined to arrest him an
conceivably to put him to death. The first two posses of police ser
to arrest Elijah met with disaster, but the captain of the third profite
by the example of his predecessors and managed to bring Elijah to th
king with a safe conduct. Nothing, however, could alter the sentenc
of doom against the king.

Like not a few other stories in the Old Testament this is a fearsom
tale. Its lesson is that there can be no mercy for apostasy, and thi
lesson still stands in the New Testament; those who confused th
works of the Holy Spirit with the works of Beelzebul were warned o
the danger of committing a sin for which there is no forgivenes
(Mark **3**. 22, 28*f.*). But so far as the story here is concerned it is wort!
remembering the comment of Jesus on it (Luke **9**. 54*f.*).

2 Kings 2. 1-25

STORIES OF ELISHA (1) *The Translation of Elijah*. As the time fo
Elijah's departure from this world drew near he wished to be left alon
to follow the will of God, but his faithful follower Elisha was unwillin
to desert his master. They went from Gilgal (not the Gilgal of Josh. *5*
9 but another place seven miles N. of Bethel) down to Bethel an
thence to Jericho. At each place a company of local "sons of th
prophets" met them and foretold Elijah's departure. These "sons o
the prophets" were groups of men with prophetic gifts; they were o
very varied spiritual quality, some of them little better than th
prophets of Baal, but here men sympathetic to Elijah are meant. The
Elijah crossed the Jordan and made a farewell offer to Elisha, wh
craved a "double portion" of Elijah's spirit – *i.e.*, not a greater powe
than that possessed by Elijah but the portion conferred on the eldes
son who succeeded to his father's position (Deut. **21**. 17). He wa
promised that he would receive this if he saw Elijah being taken from
him. To attempt to reconstruct in detail what happened to Elijal
is futile. The vital point is that the passing of a true man of God mean
far more to the country than the loss of its chariots and horsemen (*c,*
Zech. **4**. 6).

Here is Elisha's initiation to the prophetic task. Two brief storie
indicate something of his work. The former describes the purifying o
the water at a well in Jericho. The latter is frequently attacked for it

322

"crude" morality. But it should be remembered that the small boys were in reality young men (H. L. Ellison), that "baidhead" was a peculiarly insulting phrase, and that the whole act was one of religious apostasy in insulting the prophet: was he being told to "ascend" like Elijah?

Are the stories of the wonderful deeds of Elisha to be regarded as acted parables and is a deeper meaning to be found in them? The first story could be a hint of the way in which Elisha was to purify the corrupt religion of Israel (Matt. **5.** 13), and the second could suggest the consequences of rejection of the prophet's message. Is this a legitimate method of interpretation?

*2 Kings 3. 1-27

(2) *Jehoram, Israel, and the Moabites.* The structure is complicated at this point by the insertion of a series of stories of Elisha which break up the framework (**2**; **4.** 1—**8.** 15) and by withholding the notice of Jehoram's death until Ch. **9.** Jehoram (852–841) carried on the apostate religious policy of his predecessors, although he did remove a certain pillar of Baal and had some support from Elisha.

Moab had been subjected to Omri and Ahab and had to pay a considerable annual tribute in kind. King Mesha seized the opportunity of a change of overlord to revolt; he has left his own account of the matter in the Moabite Stone. Jehoram acted promptly in sending a punitive expedition for which he enlisted the help of Jehoshaphat of Judah. It may seem strange that Jehoshaphat was so ready to repeat his error at Ramoth-gilead (1 Kings **22.**). The army was swelled by the inclusion of the king of Edom who was a tributary of Judah (1 Kings **22.** 47). When the expedition ran into difficulties it was Jehoshaphat who sought divine guidance, and Elisha was willing to give it for his sake rather than for Jehoram's. Following a common prophetic custom Elisha used music to stimulate his faculties and promised both rain to end the drought and victory. The superior force of the Israelites overcame the Moabites and they were "devoted" to destruction, probably because this was how Mesha had treated Israel. Verse 26 suggests that Mesha thought that the section of the Israelite line defended by Edom would be the weakest point; many commentators, however, emend Edom to "Aram" (*i.e.*, Syria), so that Mesha was trying to break through the lines to gain Syrian help. When his strategem failed, he resorted to human sacrifice, and this act so inspired the Moabites and terrified the superstitious Israelites that the latter fled. It is unlikely in the extreme that the historian thought that Chemosh really did respond to the sacrifice, even in his own land, after all, he has shown us more than once that Baal was quite powerless (1 Kings **18**).

*In what ways does divine blessing come upon the ungodly? For the sake of the godly (**3**. 14; cf. Gen. **18**. 23-33)? Are there any limits set to this principle (cf. Ezek. **18**)?*

*2 Kings **4**. 1-44

(3) *The Shunammite Woman.* Four stories of the prophetic power and insight of Elisha are recorded here.

(*i*) A creditor was within his rights in taking the children of a debtor as slaves (*cf.* Lev. **25**. 39; Isa. **50**. 1). The story is one of many which show the relations of Elisha with ordinary people and the pastoral rôle which he played.

(*ii*) At Shunem, some 20 miles from Carmel, there was a wealthy woman who often gave Elisha a meal on his wanderings and later set aside a room for his use. When her boy had a fatal attack of sunstroke the mother went to summon Elisha. Her husband, from whom she hid the tragedy, was surprised to see her in such haste on a day when no religious duties were demanded, but she made off on the ass, with her servant urging it on from behind. She refused to convey her news to any but the prophet himself and upbraided him that the son whom he had promised to her had died. Elisha sent on his servant to lay his staff, the symbol of his authority, on the child, and himself came and prayed to the Lord and sought to revive the child. We should perhaps not dismiss too lightly the belief in the communication of divine power by touch (*cf.* Mark **5**. 28). One minor point that may need emphasis for Christian workers is the duty of gratitude for hospitality received, as here exemplified at length by Elisha.

(*iii*) At a prophetic feast held in conditions of famine any food-stuff available was pressed into service. One man in his simplicity gathered colocynths, a powerful purgative which made the meal taste bitter and could be poisonous. When Elisha had more meal put in the pot the evil effects were counteracted.

(*iv*) Elisha was offered a gift of first-fruits; these were normally given to priests, but at this time the dividing line between prophets and priests was not strictly drawn. He miraculously multiplied it to provide for the prophets with him, thus foreshadowing the later act of Jesus.

Miraculous activities are for the most part confined to certain periods of biblical history: the Exodus, the ministries of Elijah and Elisha, and the ministry of Jesus and the founding of the church. Why were they particularly characteristic of the ministries of Elijah and Elisha?

(4) *Naaman the Leper*. Feuds between Syria and Israel were common (2 Kings **6**—**7**), and on one of these an Israelite girl was captured as a slave for the army commander. When he fell ill with leprosy, she mentioned the name of the prophet who was famed for his wonderful acts in Israel. Diplomatic relations required that the approach for his services by a Syrian general be made through the proper channels. To the evident surprise of Naaman there were no mighty magic acts, only a command to wash which seemed to be too trivial to be worth carrying out. But Naaman's servants persuaded him that if nothing happened it would be the prophet rather than the general who would lose face. Elisha refused to accept payment for his deed, and the whole incident made a tremendous impression on Naaman, who professed himself ready to worship Yahweh, even though his official position required him to do lip-service in the temple of Rimmon. In order that he might worship Yahweh more effectively he asked for some Israelite earth to take home with him – a superstition more understandable in his time than the apparent feeling of some Christians today that God can scarcely be worshipped effectively outside their particular chapel, or His Gospel preached by somebody who is not a member of their own denomination.

But the good impressions which had formed in the mind of Naaman regarding the grace of Yahweh and the magnanimity of the prophet were very nearly ruined by Gehazi's attempt to line his own pockets in going after the visitor and making request in Elisha's name for a present. Naaman, who may have regarded this as the last stage in an especially long exchange of courtesies and reluctance to receive a gift, willingly granted the request, but the deed did not pass unpunished.

Two of the great principles of missionary work are here illustrated long before New Testament times – going to the heathen (Luke **4**. 27), and accepting nothing from them (3 John 7). God's people are to support God's missionaries. The tricky problem is that of the point at which the heathen become God's people and liable to give materially to missionaries (Gal. **6**. 6; Rom. **15**. 27).

*2 Kings 6. 1-23

(5) *The Hosts of Yahweh*. The first of the two stories in this section deals with the building of some kind of community house for the prophets, possibly at Jericho, in view of the proximity to the Jordan. The Jordan valley is densely wooded in places (the "jungle of

325

Jordan", Jer. **12**. 5). During timber operations there a man lost a borrowed axe in the river, and Elisha recovered it for him.

The second story narrates the ability of Elisha to reveal the whereabouts of Israel's enemies to the king (Jehoahaz or Jehoash). The king of Syria sent a force to surround Dothan by night. In the morning Elisha's servant was filled with fear at the sight, but his master prayed that he might see the invisible forces of divine protection which surrounded them, and the young man had a vision of horses and chariots of fire round about them. Modern people may choose to put the matter in more sophisticated terms, but the basic principle remains firm: God is with His servants to protect them from danger, so that nothing can harm them except by His permission, and nothing can separate them from His love.

The story also tells how Elisha gave a double lesson to the men sent to capture him. They were not able to harm them, and he treated them with a mercy which contrasted with the king's readiness to put them to death. Through this example of clemency peace was brought about and the activities of border raiders were stopped for a time.

> *The hosts of God encamp around*
> *The dwellings of the just;*
> *Deliverance He affords to all*
> *Who on His succour trust.*

*2 Kings 6. 24—7. 20

(6) *The Siege of Samaria.* Probably during the reign of Jehoram Israel was subjected to a major attack from Syria. Samaria, which was strongly fortified, was being starved into submission by the Syrians. Conditions became desperate, with food fetching astronomical prices; the ass (**6.** 25) was an unclean animal, and "dove's dung" some kind of vegetable. Although Elisha had promised deliverance (*cf.* **7.**1), there was no prospect of relief. Even cannibalism was practised. The king threatened to kill Elisha, regarding him as responsible for the conditions, but Elisha repeated that deliverance would come, to the utter disbelief of one of the king's principal officers. In fulfilment of his word the Syrians departed overnight, having heard what they took to be the sound of a relief army approaching, probably from *Muzrim* (Cappadocia) rather than from Egypt (Heb. *Mizraim*).

News of the enemy's departure was brought by four lepers who had decided to give themselves up to the enemy: life as slaves would be preferable to death by starvation. When they reached the enemy amp they had found it deserted and had not been slow to amass plunder for themselves. Then they had recollected the dire need of their fellow-countrymen and hastened back to the city to announce the good news. The king feared that this might well be a typical piece of deceit by the Syrians and took the obvious precautions, but he did not show the incredulity of the captain who had distrusted Elisha's word.

The four lepers no doubt acted as normal men would in not keeping the good tidings of the departure of the enemy to themselves; the Christian reading this story should surely ask whether the church and its members come up even to the standard of normal men in announcing the good news of a defeated spiritual enemy.

2 Kings 8. 1-24

7) *The Murder of Hazael.* As with the other stories of Elisha, it is difficult to place this one chronologically. The king was obviously one friendly to Elisha. There had been a famine in the land, and at Elisha's counsel the woman of Shunem had moved temporarily to Philistine territory. During her absence her lands had been appropriated, and she approached the king for redress. The fact that at this precise moment the king was listening to Gehazi recounting the deeds of Elisha meant that the king could do no other than grant her request.

Gazing intently at Hazael, Elisha foresaw him upon the throne of his master and had a glimpse of the suffering that he would bring upon Israel (*cf.* 1 Kings 19. 17). Hazael protested, but feebly. "They still tell at Princeton University of the visit of Sparhawk Jones to their chapel, and his announcement of the text 'Is thy servant a dog, that he should do this thing?' (2 Kings 8. 13). After a moment's pause, he began crisply: 'Dog or no dog, he did it!' " (W. E. Sangster). The following day, Hazael murdered Ben-hadad and ascended his throne. It has sometimes been suggested that Elisha acted dishonourably in hiding the truth from Ben-hadad, or even that he instigated Hazael to murder. It is more likely that Elisha shrank from "anointing" a man like Hazael at the thought of all that lay ahead.

JEHORAM (Judah. *853*–848–841) At last the author returns to his chronological framework and takes us back (for some of the Elisha stories undoubtedly come after this date) to 848 when Jehoshaphat's son succeeded him in Judah. He explains that it was through no virtue of Jehoram's that the kingdom was saved from divine wrath, but only because God remembered the good deeds of his ancestors (cf. 1 Kings **15**. 4). He fell into the errors of Ahab by marrying his daughter Athaliah, a true child of Jezebel, and, with her, idolatry came officially – it had never been absent unofficially – into Judah. During his reign Edom revolted (cf. 1 Kings **22**. 47), and Jehoram's attempt to reduce it to submission was an ignominious failure. Although his chariotry was successful at Zair, S. of the Dead Sea, his infantry were put to flight. Libnah, a town on the Philistine border, chose the same time to revolt. Thus Judah's strength in the south was seriously crippled.

2 Kings 8. 25—9. 29

AHAZIAH (Judah, 841); JEHU'S REVOLT. Jehoram's successor in Judah, Ahaziah, reigned only one year before he was caught up in the revolution in which Jehu overthrew the monarchy in Israel. The Israelite army was once again (cf. 1 Kings **22**) engaged in battle at Ramoth-gilead, this time defending the town against the Syrians, and Jehoram of Israel had retired from the scene of battle to nurse his wounds at Jezreel, some 35 miles distant; here he was visited by Ahaziah. The situation was propitious for action. Elisha sent one of his young men to anoint the army commander Jehu as king and bid him overthrow the reigning monarch. The young man interrupted an army council meeting to give his message privately to Jehu. The officers were interested to know what the message was; since the young man was obviously a prophet in a state of ecstasy, which they equated with madness (11), possibly it concerned the conduct of the campaign. They refused to be put off by Jehu's prevarication, and when they learned the truth they at once showed that they took seriously "the fellow and his talk". A party was swiftly organized to gallop to Jezreel and assassinate the king, and every precaution was taken to avoid the news leaking out; messengers sent by the king to learn the news were detained by the swiftly advancing troop of chariots. The king was speedily disillusioned by the words of Jehu, who shot at him before he had a chance to escape. Ahaziah fled southwards, but he too was shot before he had gone many miles, and died of his wounds at Megiddo, N.W. of Ibleam.

The first steps had been taken in the extermination of the house of Ahab. But, as so often, the instrument of vengeance was little better than his victim, and in due time the judgment of God had to be proclaimed against the iniquities of Jehu (Hosea **1**. 4f.). That power corrupts is a lesson writ large in Israelite history, and we see the justification for the New Testament teaching that vengeance must be left to God (Rom. **12**. 19).

Is the Christian ever entitled to take the law into his own hands? For example, was a Lutheran minister like Dietrich Bonhoeffer right or wrong in supporting the plot against the life of Hitler?

2 Kings 9. 30—10. 36

JEHU (Israel, 841–813). Jezebel, defiant to the last, perished as prophesied (1 Kings **21**. 23). For her allusion to Zimri see 1 Kings **16**. 10 But it was not yet the end of Jehu's bloody pogrom. The royal family, 70 sons of Ahab by his various concubines, were being brought up in Samaria, and a party opposed to Jehu might easily have put forward one of these as a candidate for the throne. So Jehu challenged the leading men of Samaria to declare on which side their allegiance lay. With a nice sense of the realities of the situation they pledged themselves to him and cheerfully carried out his order for the mass murder of the 70 princes. A grisly exhibition was arranged by night at the gate of Jezreel as a warning to all possible opponents, and in the morning Jehu had the blasphemous audacity to suggest that the princes had been struck down by the hand of God (such is the implication of **10**. 9, 10).

Up to this point Jehu's acts could plausibly be defended as due to the practical necessities of politics in a cruel and chancy world. His next two deeds, however, showed plain thirst for murder. Quite apart from the deceit and cruelty this was an unnecessary refinement of religious persecution. We may be sure that many of the worshippers of Baal were no more sincere in their allegiance than many of the fickle worshippers of Yahweh, and that they would willingly have given up their idolatry to save their own skins. This wanton act may well have lost for Jehu some of the more able people in the land. The same is true of the slaughter of Ahab's officials. As a result the country suffered. The most that the historian has to record of a reign of 28 years is the loss of Israel's possessions in Transjordan, though this would be partly due to the inevitable rupture between Israel and her former allies, Phoenicia and Judah, which would give a powerful Syria the upper hand. One incident not reported in 2 Kings is that the Black Obelisk of Shalmaneser III of Assyria shows Jehu paying tribute (*c.* 841 B.C.).

Finally, mention should be made of Jehonadab, the leader of a group of nationalists who followed the ways of wilderness life and eschewed agricultural and commercial· civilization with its gods. (Jer. **35**). He was willing to be the friend and supporter of Jehu, no doubt out of opposition to the luxurious and apostate ways of the court, and Jehu claimed him as a friend. From this unpromising story John Wesley developed his noble sermon on the value of "A Catholic Spirit" which finds agreement on essentials and does not force conformity in matters of indifference.

*2 Kings 11. 1-21

ATHALIAH (Judah, 841–835). Ahaziah's murder by Jehu gave his mother the chance of doing what Jezebel had not been able to d'o. She promptly put to death all her grandsons, and ruled herself for the next six years. But her plan to remove all possible opposition was defeated by Jehosheba, a princess married to the priest Jehoiada, who successfully hid Jehoash (*or* Joash) in the temple. When the time was ripe a revolution was planned and carried through with the utmost smoothness. Jehoiada gained the support of the royal mercenary guards and arranged a time on the Sabbath when the guard was being changed and a double force was available to bring out the lad and crown him as king. The *coup* had the support of the priesthood, and the people raised no opposition. Athaliah, who bravely came out to challenge the revolutionaries, was the only person to suffer the death penalty. The revolt was thus carried out with very little bloodshed, and it would appear that the religious and political policies of the late queen had been far from popular. The destruction of the chapel of Baal and the lynching of the priest were not simply due to the rivalry of the priests of Yahweh but were supported by popular sentiment. The restored constitutional monarchy was to be in accordance with Judah's ancestral religion; the king was given the testimony (*cf.* Deut. **17**. 18-20; 1 Sam. **10**. 25), and both king and people were bound by a covenant to serve Yahweh. The whole event stands in marked contrast to the unholy scenes in the northern kingdom and afforded a much better augury for the future.

*2 Kings 12. 1-21

JEHOASH (Judah, *841*–835–796). Jehoash's long reign was characterized, initially at least (2 Chron. **24**), by royal support of the worship of Yahweh. The principal event described is his care for the upkeep of the temple. Verses 4*f.* describe the original arrangements made by the king to meet the considerable cost of annual maintenance of the fabric. But by the 23rd year of his reign Jehoash found that nothing had been done, for the priests were evidently using the money to supplement their own incomes. The priests were castigated for their inefficiency, and the responsibilities of collecting the money and of doing the repairs were taken from them. All offerings to the

temple were now to be put in a box made for the purpose and prominently displayed at the entrance (2 Chron. **24**. 8; the reference to
the altar in 2 Kings **12**. 9 is generally regarded as corrupt). The money
was removed from time to time by a royal official and paid over to
the workmen engaged on the temple repairs. Their honesty was
such that written accounts were not required! On the other hand, the
priests received money associated with various offerings.

The concluding part of the chapter indicates a serious decline in
Judah's national strength. Hazael of Syria was able to penetrate far
into the south-west. He finally turned his attention to Jerusalem,
and Jehoash had the utmost difficulty in buying him off. It may well
have been because of this low ebb in the country's fortunes that a
revolt was fomented against the king in the palace and he was put to
death (*cf.* also 2 Chron. **24**. 25).

*There are lessons in this chapter for those concerned with church
finances. It should be read in conjunction with* 1 Cor. **16**; 2 Cor. **8—9**.
*The ideal situation is where the people give spontaneously for the work
of God: what factors can prevent the realization of this ideal?*

2 Kings 13. 1—14. 22

JEHOAHAZ (Israel, 813–798). Jehu was succeeded on the throne of
Israel by his son Jehoahaz. Although the worship of Yahweh was
nominally practised, it was weak and syncretistic, and the historian
saw in the frequent defeats suffered by Israel at the hand of Syria an
indication of the divine wrath against the land. Jehoahaz was left
with a pathetically small army: contrast Ahab's 2000 chariots.
Verses 4-6 speak of a saviour being raised up for Israel; Adadnirari
III of Assyria, Jeroboam II, and Elisha are possible candidates for
the rôle.

JEHOASH (Israel, 798–781). Jehoahaz's son Jehoash was a more
powerful monarch, and his reign marked the prelude to the revival of
Israelite power under Jeroboam II. In his reign came the final illness
and death of Elisha who must now have been of a very great age. The
king was unwilling to display the same enthusiasm as the prophet,
and the size of his prophesied victory was limited. When he sought to
retrieve the losses incurred by his father, he smote the Syrians only
three times; that he was able to do even this was due to the weakness
of both Syria and Assyria in his reign.

AMAZIAH (Judah, 796–767). For a brief space of two years kings
of the same name reigned in both Israel and Judah. When Amaziah

Israel and Judah
after the Disruption

succeeded his murdered father in Judah, he continued to maintain the worship of Yahweh and he took steps to avenge his father's death. He was successful in battle against Edom in the Valley of Salt – *i.e.*, the area S. of the Dead Sea. His victory went to his head and he thought the time was ripe to break a lance with Israel, possibly in order to curb the looting being carried on by Israelite mercenaries (2 Chron. **25**. 6-13). He issued a challenge to Jehoash which the latter with a telling parable disdainfully refused to take up. Amaziah, however, was not to be restrained, and pride suffered its proverbial punishment at Beth-shemesh, W. of Jerusalem. Jerusalem was sacked. The people put the blame for their plight upon the king and attempted to curb him by making Azariah co-regent. Later, a further conspiracy was mounted against Amaziah, and although he fled to Lachish he was assassinated by his opponents.

2 Kings 14. 23—15. 31

JEROBOAM (Israel, *792-781-753*). Jehoash was followed on the throne of Israel by his son Jeroboam II whose long reign represents the Indian summer in the fortunes of the northern kingdom. A combination of external political circumstances had led to the weakening of Syria, so that Jeroboam was able to extend his sphere of influence from the "entrance of Hamath" in the north to the Dead Sea and to weaken the power of Damascus. From a human point of view he was thus a strong and effective monarch, but the evidence of the prophets Amos and Hosea shows all too clearly that the splendour of his kingdom was erected on rotten foundations. If the rich were becoming very rich, the poor were also becoming very poor, and the economic prosperity of the big landowners and merchants rested on oppression and double-dealing.

AZARIAH (UZZIAH) (Judah, *790-767-739*). After the death of Jeroboam there was a period of weakness and anarchy in the north. By contrast Judah was able to enjoy a long spell of stable government and prosperity under Azariah, who is treated to a mere half-dozen verses here; perhaps Isa. **6**. 1 may be taken to indicate the sense of loss felt in the nation at his passing. Yet despite his general maintenance of pure religion, he transgressed grievously in the temple (2 Chron. **26**. 16-23) and was struck with an attack of leprosy which put an end to his public life.

RIVAL RULERS IN ISRAEL (Zechariah, Shallum, Menahem; *753-741*). Meanwhile, Jeroboam's son Zechariah, who was evidently not made of the same stuff as his father, found his throne very uncomfortable. A number of factions arose, and the leader of one, Shallum, assassinated the king at Ibleam. This usurper found that he had no real support, and he swiftly fell at the hands of Menahem who had put himself in control of the old capital of Tirzah. There is reason to suspect that Menahem owed his position as a puppet ruler to Pekah, who reckoned his own tenure of the throne from 752.

PEKAHIAH (Israel, 741–739); PEKAH (Israel, 752–739–731). While this petty bickering was in progress, a far greater menace to the security of Israel had arisen. Jeroboam II had been able to widen his influence, thanks to the weakening of Syria by the growing power of Assyria. Now, however, Assyria altered her policy from the mere collection of tribute to empire-building. When vassal states refused to pay tribute, the new king Tiglath-pileser III (*or* Pul) took stern measures. He came westwards (c. 745–738) and exacted a heavy tribute from Menahem for the privilege of continuing to rule in Israel. The writing was on the wall, but the insane squabbling went on. Menahem's son Pekahiah survived only two years before Pekah, the army commander, deposed and murdered him in order that he might reign himself. Pekah adopted an anti-Assyrian policy, and he suffered the reward of his folly. Israel was subjected to what was to become the familiar policy of deportation and loss of territory, and Assyria backed the conspiracy of Hoshea to get rid of Pekah.

What is the real *menace to the church today? What matters of minor importance may prevent us from fully realizing the major challenges which we must face?*

2 Kings 15. 32–16. 20

JOTHAM (Judah, 750–739–731); AHAZ (Judah, 743–731–715). During the tempestuous events in the northern kingdom Jotham continued the general policy of his father Azariah, and Judah enjoyed a period of quiet. Just before his death, however, the first glimmerings of trouble were seen. Rezin of Damascus and Pekah of Israel launched a coalition against Assyria and sought the help of Judah; when persuasion failed, force was used.

The trouble came to a head in the reign of Ahaz. His full name was Jehoahaz, but the historian could not bring himself to use the "Jeho-" (Yahweh) prefix for this apostate king. During his reign the corruption which had ruined the northern kingdom came to a head in the south. The early prophecies of Isaiah date from this time and show both the immorality of the people and the lack of faith of the king.

Ahaz was panic-stricken by the advance of Tiglath-pileser, whom it was plain folly to resist, and he sought to come to terms with him when he visited Damascus. For the privilege of "independence" he had to pay heavily, not only with a suitable present but also by accepting various tokens of Assyrian overlordship including an Assyrian type of altar. Ahaz's other actions in the temple were to secure enough bronze to pay his debts to Assyria, and offer a parallel to the wholesale uprooting of metal garden railings by British householders in the early years of World War II.

It was against this background of insecurity and irreligion that Isaiah was inspired to compose his greatest prophecies.

2 Kings 17. 1-41

HOSHEA (Israel, 731–722): THE FALL OF SAMARIA. Hoshea, as we have seen (15. 30), probably gained his throne with Assyrian backing, but he soon began to listen to the blandishments of Egypt, an ally constantly condemned by the prophets. "So" is not certainly identified, but was scarcely a power to be reckoned with. When Hoshea failed to send in his annual tribute to Assyria, vengeance was swift. He was imprisoned and the land was left on its own to fight for survival. Samaria was besieged by Sargon II and captured by his successor Shalmaneser V.

Verses 7-23 and 34b-40 discuss the underlying reasons for the fall of Samaria. Four reasons are given: the adoption by the Israelites of the customs of other lands, especially the religious practices of the Canaanites; the refusal of the people to heed the prophets and seers whom God repeatedly sent to warn them; the breaking of the covenant with Yahweh by Israel; and the infiltration of idolatry and immorality into the worship of Yahweh. These reasons are all religious; the historian says little about the low moral tone of the land which was scathingly condemned by Amos and Hosea. Is this because he held that spiritual declension is the cause of moral laxity? The whole passage presents most plainly the Old Testament revelation of God's working in human history.

The newcomers to the land were a set of pagans who did not worship Yahweh; when disaster came upon them, they attributed it to their failure to worship the God of the land, and sought an Israelite priest to teach them the worship of Yahweh – an interesting example of missionary work. Although the worship of Yahweh was established, it existed side by side with a plethora of other faiths, some of them not certainly identified, brought by the settlers from their own lands. Even the worship of Yahweh was in the hands of a very motley collection of priests. The whole situation was thoroughly depressing, and yet this company of people were the ancestors of the Samaritans who gradually changed to a purer form of worship; in the fulness of time some of their descendants gave a warm reception to Christianity. Though the original priest who taught them how to fear (*i.e.*, worship) the Lord may have seen little for his labours in a most discouraging situation, yet in the long run something worthwhile can be seen to have been initiated. There is encouragement in this story for those who evangelize today with little visible fruit for their labours.

2 Kings 18. 1-37

HEZEKIAH (Judah, *729–715–686*): (1) *Sennacherib's Invasion.* Hezekiah was a complete contrast to his father Ahaz in his religious policy and instituted a thorough reformation of the worship of the people. For the first time in 1 and 2 Kings we hear of the removal of the high places and their apparatus for pagan worship. The point had been reached when a policy of centralization seemed to afford the only means of gaining religious purity. Even at Jerusalem itself, however, the brazen serpent associated with the time of Moses had become an object of superstition, probably as a fertility symbol, and it had to be destroyed.

This religious policy was at least partly associated with political motives. It represented one aspect of Hezekiah's attempt to gain freedom from Assyrian domination. For a time Judah enjoyed independence and was even able to make inroads into Philistia. (Verses 9-12 refer to events during the co-regency of Hezekiah with his father.)

As soon as Assyria was free of troubles in other parts of her empire, she proceeded to deal with disobedient Judah and attacked the country with considerable success. Hezekiah had to pay a heavy fine as the price of Assyrian withdrawal from the cities of Judah. But Sennacherib decided that action must be taken against Jerusalem itself and sent three of his principal military officers to claim the surrender of the city. These experts at propaganda and psychological warfare harangued the king's officers in the hearing of the people about the folly of resistance.

Although Hezekiah's advisers sought to have a private interview, the Rabshakeh pressed home his advantage by directly addressing the people and representing to them that Assyria would offer them prosperity in place of their present stringent conditions. No other gods could deliver men from her power: how then could Yahweh save Judah?

That last question was enough! Assyria's fate was sealed: consult Ezek. **36.** 20-23 for the reason.

2 Kings 19. 1-37

(2) *Hezekiah and Isaiah.* Hezekiah is conspicuous in this crisis for the way in which despite all his fear he put his trust in Yahweh. He himself went into the temple to pray, and he sought the intercession of Isaiah the prophet, in whose book this whole narrative is repeated (Isa. **36—39**). Such mockery of the living God as the Rabshakeh had uttered could not pass unchallenged, and Isaiah sent a reply to the king promising that the enemy host would withdraw and the emperor would be slain.

The Assyrian plenipotentiaries left Jerusalem and returned to the army at Libnah. A new threat had appeared in the form of an Egyptian army under Tirhakah, and for the moment Sennacherib was content to forget about Jerusalem, merely repeating his earlier threats in a letter. Once again Hezekiah sought the help of God. The divine reply through Isaiah is given in full as a poetic oracle. Jerusalem could afford to despise the Assyrians because of the overweening pride they had shown against Yahweh. They boasted of their achievements from Lebanon to Egypt. But what they had achieved was accomplished only by Yahweh's plan and will, and now for their arrogance they would suffer the sort of treatment they meted out to their captives.

These words were fulfilled in a disaster which came upon the Assyrian camp and caused the forces to retreat homewards. Herodotus, the Greek historian, tells how mice attacked the Assyrians and chewed their bowstrings (**2.** 141), and it has been conjectured that bubonic plague came with them.

(The mention of Tirhakah raises a historical problem. J. Bright holds that he reigned c. 688–670, and therefore distinguishes an earlier invasion in 701 (**18.** 14-16) from a later one (**18.** 17—**19.** 37) with which it has been conflated. K. A. Kitchen disputes the date of Tirhakah's reign and holds that only one campaign by Sennacherib (in 701) is described. The matter is still *sub judice.*)

For study: Hezekiah as a man of faith – his strength and his weaknesses.

2 Kings 20. 1-21. 18

(3) *Hezekiah's Illness.* Death was even less pleasant in Old Testament times than it is today, for hopes of a life after death were vague and

sporadic. Hezekiah wept bitterly at the prospect (*cf.* Isa. **38.** 10-20), but God healed him from his disease and permitted him an extra fifteen years of life in peace and security. On the occasion of his illness Merodach-baladan, ruler of Babylon (at this time a small state E. of Assyria) sent an embassy to visit him. The reason was not simply disinterested concern for the king's health. Babylon was raising opposition to Assyria in both the east and west and sought Hezekiah's help in the west. His action aroused the censure of Isaiah, who had ceaselessly prophesied the folly of worldly alliances and pride in man-made weapons, and he warned the king about the future captivity of the land. Hezekiah's reply (**20.** 19) sounds self-satisfied, but H. L. Ellison points out that Hezekiah will have realized that his successors could avert the disaster by loyalty to Yahweh.

MANASSEH (Judah, *696*–686–641). This, however, was not to be. Manasseh adopted a totally different policy from his father during his long reign. Circumstances no doubt forced his capitulation to Assyria but did not excuse his wholesale surrender to foreign religious practices and the ways of Canaan. False religion was accompanied by immoral practices and cruelty, human sacrifice and the ruthless suppression of opposition. It is no wonder that the prophets proclaimed the judgment of God upon the land.

Not even the great piety of Josiah and his determined efforts at reformation sufficed to turn the tide. Should one therefore conclude that the effects of evil are more swift and potent than those of good? And if not, why not?

2 Kings 21. 19—22. 20

AMON (Judah, 641–639); JOSIAH (Judah, 639–609): (1) *The Book of the Law*. The policy of Manasseh was continued for a couple of years by his son Amon, but was brought to an end by the murder of the latter in a palace conspiracy. The conspirators were brought to justice by "the people of the land" – *i.e.*, the better-class property-owners in Judah, who more than once opposed the ways of the court (*cf.* **11.** 14-20). They put the king's son Josiah on the throne, and during his long minority they were able to reverse the policy of Manasseh and Amon. The change of policy was not purely religious. The external political situation was easing as Assyria became weaker, and in these circumstances it was not impossible to get rid of the signs of Assyrian worship. But the false religious practices, whose removal was the great feature of Josiah's reign, were not by any means entirely due to Assyrian influence; much was native Canaanite, or taken over from Judah's immediate neighbours, and the king made a determined effort to weed out these also.

According to 2 Chron. **34** the reforms commenced earlier than the eighteenth year of Josiah's reign, but in this year a momentous event took place. Arrangements had been put in hand for a thorough renovation of the temple – it was at least fifty years since Hezekiah's work – and in the course of the work the priest "found the book of the law" in the house of the Lord. Seas of learned ink have been spilt over this phrase. For our purpose it is sufficient to note that the generally held modern view is that the book was some part of the Pentateuch, probably Deuteronomy. It would appear that there was only one copy of the book in existence, and it may have been lost to sight in the reign of Manasseh. The effect of the book was to alarm the king exceedingly as he read the laws which had not been obeyed and saw the threats of God's judgment upon the transgressions of the people. It is highly significant that the book of the law was at once accepted as God's word and taken seriously by the king and his court.

For Meditation: Deuteronomy **5—8.**

2 Kings 23. 1-30

(2) *Josiah's Reformation.* The discovery of the book was followed by a great public assembly at which it was solemnly read before the people and the king led them in a re-dedication of themselves to God. The king also held a celebration of the passover. This feast, if it had not actually fallen into disuse (*cf.* 2 Chron. **30**), had certainly been neglected in previous years. It was the feast which especially reminded Judah of God's redemptive act in bringing His people out of Egypt, and it was therefore more characteristic of true worship than the New Year Feast of Tabernacles which had many counterparts in pagan fertility festivals and which had supplanted it in importance.

Between the record of these two ceremonies is a full list of Josiah's purges of false religious shrines and objects of devotion. He first of all cleansed the temple. Then he deposed all the idolatrous priests in and around Jerusalem; priests of Yahweh from the high places were brought to Jerusalem, but were not given a full share in the temple worship. The various places of corrupt worship were defiled so that they could never be used again. Thirdly, Josiah extended his reforming activities to what had been the kingdom of Israel, especially at Bethel, though he was careful to leave undisturbed the tomb of the prophet of 1 Kings **13.** Finally, he dealt with all the more "private" cults in Judah, spiritistic practices, soothsaying and the like.

Despite these thorough-going measures the doom of God upon Judah was not revoked, but only delayed. It is ascribed here to the provocations of Manasseh (23. 26), but since the judgments of God are conditional we may be certain that, despite the king's sincerity and thoroughness, Josiah's reformation was unable to penetrate beneath the surface and do any lasting good. Such is the impression we gain from Jeremiah, who lived during this period and yet never refers to the reformation with any enthusiasm whatever.

Josiah ended his life tragically. Pharaoh Necho was advancing northwards to help Assyria whose capital Nineveh had fallen to Babylon in 612 B.C. Josiah feared that an Egypto-Assyrian alliance might endanger Judah's independence and went out to fight him at Megiddo. Probably if he had done nothing, the Pharaoh would have ignored the tiny state of Judah. The result was a foregone conclusion, and Josiah perished in the battle.

Could Josiah have gone about his reformation in some other way and been more successful?

2 Kings 23. 31—24. 17

JEHOAHAZ (Judah, 609). After the death of Josiah his third son Jehoahaz (*or* Shallum) was made king by the people of the land. He was presumably more popular than his surviving elder brother, but in his short reign he showed no effort to emulate the piety of his father. Pharaoh Necho, now in control of Palestine and Syria, treated the appointment of a king in Judah as being his affair and declared the appointment null and void. He carried Jehoahaz off to Egypt and installed in his place his brother Eliakim, with the throne-name of Jehoiakim ("Yahu will establish"). He required him to pay a heavy tribute to Egypt which sorely burdened the people.

JEHOIAKIM (Judah, 609–597). The new king survived for eleven troubled years. During his reign the external political situation changed considerably. Egypt was thoroughly defeated by Babylon at Carchemish in 605. Assyria had already succumbed to Babylon, and the latter was now the undisputed mistress of the ancient world. Internally Judah lapsed back into conditions reminiscent of the days of Manasseh, as we learn especially from Jeremiah. Jehoiakim had to yield to the suzerainty of Babylon, but after three years (*c.* 601) he tried to assert his independence while Babylon was otherwise occupied. Babylon allowed various marauders to harry the land until she could take action herself. At this juncture Jehoiakim died; possibly he was assassinated (*cf.* Jer. **22**. 18*f.*; **36**. 30).

JEHOIACHIN (Judah, 597). The dead king was succeeded by his son, but he suffered a parallel fate to that of his uncle Jehoahaz in that Nebuchadnezzar removed him from the throne after three months. A punitive campaign had been launched against Jerusalem; the king was forced to surrender and was carried off to Babylon as a prisoner. Many of the leading men were taken into captivity, and the city and temple were plundered.

How would you answer the criticism of somebody who argues that the captivity of the Jews was not an act of God in judgment upon their sin, but simply a product of external political circumstances which would have happened in any case, whether or not the Jews had been faithful to their God?

2 Kings 24. 18—25. 30

ZEDEKIAH (Judah, 597–587): THE FALL OF JERUSALEM. Under Zedekiah Judah had its very last chance of "home rule". But the new puppet king followed the same fickle policies as his predecessors; Jeremiah's picture of him is far from flattering. Depending on Egyptian help he was so foolish as to rebel against Babylon and thus plunged Jerusalem into all the horrors of an ancient siege. When things became hopeless the king and his army attempted to escape, but were captured in the region of Jericho and taken to Riblah. Nebuchadnezzar, whom nobody could accuse of squeamishness in taking revenge on his enemies, behaved according to pattern. Zedekiah was tortured and the leading officials of Jerusalem were put to death. The principal people were deported, and only the poorer classes were left. The city was razed to the ground and sacked.

The people left behind were put under the governorship of Gedaliah. There is every indication that their lot under him would have been perfectly tolerable, but a dissatisfied group of people, mainly army officers under a prince of the Davidic line, plotted against him and killed both the governor and some of the Babylonian garrison. Revenge was inevitable, and among those who fled the country in the nick of time were Gedaliah's friends and their unwilling companion, Jeremiah (Jer. **40—44**).

Thus the sorry drama reached its tragic conclusion. We have come a long way from the glorious days of David and Solomon, and have seen the outworking of divine judgment in history most clearly expressed. At the end, however, there is one small gleam in the darkness. Jehoiachin, who was evidently regarded as the true ruler of Judah by the Babylonians and by many of the Jews, was released from prison by Evil-merodach (562). The grace of God had not deserted the people in exile, and hope was yet to be rekindled. Of that hope Jehoiachin was a symbol (*cf.* Matt. 1. 11-12).

THE BOOKS OF CHRONICLES

Introduction

At first sight the book of Chronicles (Hebrew: "Events of the Days") appears to consist of nothing more than a series of tedious lists of names joined to a historical account largely plagiarized from the books of Samuel and Kings and with little independent value. Even the most loyal defender of the book must confess that it is dull by comparison with the vigorous narratives of its predecessors and more prone to moralizing.

This, however, would be a superficial estimate of Chronicles. It must be remembered that its aim and contents are quite different from those of Kings. Kings gives a composite history of the united kingdom under Solomon and then of the separated kingdoms of Israel and Judah, with much space being allotted to the northern partner. The Chronicler is concerned simply to give a history of the establishment of the divinely-appointed monarchy and the closely associated worship at the temple. This history really began with David, who united the tribes more thoroughly after the unsatisfactory reign of Saul and brought the ark of the covenant to Jerusalem; after Solomon it continued in the southern kingdom of Judah which alone remained faithful to the house of David and the worship at the temple. The Chronicler's history is the story of the *true* Israel, and therefore he omits the northern kingdom from his consideration. To his story he has prefixed a rapid survey of the origins of his nation by means of his genealogies, and the whole leads up to the story of the re-establishment of the post-exilic Jewish community and the restoration of the temple in Ezra and Nehemiah. It was for this group of people that the Chronicler wrote.

Within this framework the writer had a number of aims. (*i*) He draws from the history the lesson already taught by the book of Kings: faithfulness to God, especially to worship at the temple, brings divine blessing seen in material prosperity, military success, and long life; but apostasy brings divine retribution. (*ii*) The author is particularly concerned with the true ordering of worship, and, more especially, with the place of the Levites in it. The Levites are scarcely mentioned in Kings – we should, after all, hardly expect to find detailed lists of all the Canons of Canterbury Cathedral or Westminster Abbey and their functions in a standard History of England – but the Chronicler constantly draws on the ecclesiastical records to show their place in the life of the temple. (*iii*) One aspect of worship which the Chronicler emphasizes is the use of music, for ideally worship is the joyous praise of God. (*iv*) This last point indicates that the Chronicler is not such a sober-sided ritualist as might be thought. He is well aware of the gracious acts of God which make Old Testament religion something different from a purely legal system. (*v*) If the book of Kings singled out the attitude of the kings to the centralization of worship at Jerusalem in the temple and to the removal of the "high places" with all their pagan associations as one of its main criteria of loyalty to God, the Chronicler lays stress on the way in which the kings responded to or disobeyed the message of the various prophets whom God raised up to guide them.

The date and identity of the Chronicler are uncertain. One view which has much to be said for it would date him around 400 B.C., and some scholars have identified him with Ezra. Critical scholars frequently accuse him of falsifying the historical facts in the interest of his dogmas. It is probable that on occasion he describes events in terms that his readers would best understand from the practices of their own day. His statistics of troops and the like constitute an unsolved problem, since his figures are in general high. But, although some scholars still speak of him as a writer of historical fiction, there is an increasing move amongst critics towards a higher estimate of his historical reliability and to a recognition of the conservative view that where he offers facts not already found in the books of Samuel and Kings he often possessed reliable traditions. Indeed, as David F. Payne has pointed out, where we can check up on the Chronicler from other written sources, he appears as a painstaking and accurate historian. Therefore we should allow him the same degree of accuracy in instances where we have no corresponding material. What his exact sources were is not certain, but it is generally recognized that he used the books of Samuel and Kings together with other sources. There are a lot of differences in the spelling of names between Chronicles and the earlier writings; these must be due in part at least to scribal changes.

The book of Chronicles has been grievously neglected in the past; one has only to compare the amount of space given to it in the commentaries with that allotted to Kings. But one reader at least must confess that study of it for the purpose of this volume has given him a new appreciation of it.

1 Chronicles 1. 1-54

THE EARLY GENEALOGIES OF ISRAEL. The first nine chapters of 1 Chronicles contain a set of genealogies and lists of names which seem about as interesting to read as some modern digest of population statistics. In general they are not of obvious spiritual content for modern readers, and they present the scholar with numerous problems which are far too intricate to be discussed here. Have they, then, any value and purpose?

The Chronicler was presenting a religious history of the united kingdom of Israel and then of the southern state of Judah from the time of David onwards, with a special emphasis upon the temple and its ministers. He was writing for a people returned from exile and re-settled in Judah. In this setting the purpose of the genealogies is twofold. First, the writer aimed to put the portion of history which was his immediate concern into a wider setting. He had no new material to offer for the earlier history of Israel, and he therefore contented himself with prefacing his work with a set of genealogies to span the vast period from the beginning of history to the time of David. There is a special interest in Judah and Benjamin (the southern kingdom) and in Levi. This leads us to the writer's second aim, which was to show the continuity between the people of his own day and their ancestors before the exile. The race of Israel and Judah was one race, united by the ties of blood and the experience of God's grace and judgment.

The opening chapter is relatively clear. It starts with Adam and traces the line of Noah (1-4). It then deals with Japheth (5-7), Ham (8-16), and Shem, who was the progenitor of Abraham, the father of the people of God (17-27). After dealing with Abraham's other offspring by Hagar and Keturah (28-33) the writer turns to Isaac; here again he deals with the offspring of Isaac's other son, Esau, the ancestor of Edom (34-54), before coming to Israel (*i.e.*, Jacob). Thus a process of selection takes place as the writer narrows down his attention to the ancestor of his own people.

The information is taken from Genesis (see a reference Bible for details), but the spelling of the names is not always the same; scribal errors could easily arise in copying strange, unfamiliar names. Note that the relationships are not always indicated exactly (*e.g.*, in **1**. 17 the names after Aram are those of his descendants, not of his brothers).

To think over: "*. . . a poor player,*
That struts and frets his hour upon the stage,
And then is heard no more."

Is this a fair comment on these men, mere names, who appear so briefly on the stage of history and then vanish into obscurity? Or have they a greater, more enduring, significance?

1 Chronicles 2. 1-55

THE DESCENDANTS OF JUDAH. The Chronicler's interest now centres on Israel (**2.** 1-2), and in particular on the descendants of Judah (**2.** 3*ff.*). He is concerned first with the line through Perez, Hezron, Ram, Amminadab, Nahshon, Salma, Boaz ... David – *i.e.*, the succession to the throne; but on the way he has to tidy up various side issues; note the mention of Achar, *i.e.*, Achan, in **2.** 7.

There are omissions and gaps (*e.g.*, the relation of Zimri and Carmi in **2.** 6*f.*; *cf.* Josh. **7.** 18). A problem is caused by the appearance of Chelubai, *i.e.*, Caleb, in **2.** 9. He is generally identified with the Caleb, son of Jephunneh, who was Joshua's contemporary, and a member of a non-Israelite race, the Kenites. If this is so, a large part of the genealogy would really refer to non-Israelites and would represent an attempt to give them an honourable pedigree. H. L. Ellison has suggested, however, that the reference here is to a different, earlier Caleb. It is true that both Calebs then had daughters called Achsah (Josh. **15.** 17), but Ellison thinks that this is a possible coincidence.

Many of these names are not known to us from other sources. But others we do know more clearly; there are bad men (Er, Achar) and good (Caleb, Boaz, David) in the lists, and we are reminded that men do not merely live to themselves, but also form part of a community. Though their deeds may not be recorded in the history books, their influence was not confined to their own lives. It is a characteristic emphasis of the Old Testament that men are closely bound to each other through family and community connections. The New Testament also reminds us that "None of us lives to himself" (Rom. **14.** 7), and this is true not only of our relation to God but also of our relation to the rest of mankind.

1 Chronicles 3. 1—4. 43

THE DESCENDANTS OF DAVID. In a sense this chapter forms an "index" to the ensuing narrative; it provides a list of the sons of David and then traces the royal line from Solomon to the last king of Judah. Among the later descendants of the royal line after the exile Zerubbabel, the leader of the Jewish community, finds a place, together with a number of his relatives. This final part of the list was evidently kept "up to date", for we find that it is continued to later generations of descendants in the Greek translation of Chronicles; consequently attempts to date the writing of Chronicles with the aid of the list are liable to some uncertainty.

One or two difficulties may be noted. "Bathshua" in **3. 5** is Bathsheba; for the first "Elishama" in the list of David's sons (**3. 6**) substitute "Elishua". The "Eliada" of **3. 8** occurs as "Beeliada" in **14. 7**, a circumstance which reminds us that the name "Baal" was used in early times in Israel despite its possible pagan associations (it is a perfectly good Hebrew word meaning "master, owner"), but was altered in later times to the more pious-sounding "El" form. In **3. 15** Johanan was not a king of Judah, and in **3. 16** Zedekiah was the uncle of Jeconiah.

THE TRIBES OF JUDAH AND SIMEON. The remainder of the portion gives a fragmentary set of genealogies of the tribe of Judah which cannot easily be fitted into any kind of scheme (**4. 1-23**), and genealogies of the tribe of Simeon (**4. 24-43**). The tedium of the names is relieved by the brief note about Jabez who belied his unfortunate name ("He giveth pain") by his faith in God. We also find comments on the conquests of Simeon near the unidentified "Gedor" and their exploits near Mount Seir in Edom, these events are not mentioned elsewhere. For the "Meunim", see 2 Chron. **20. 1**; **26. 7**; they were an Edomite people.

One reason for the insertion of these genealogies was to enable the Chronicler's contemporaries to establish their lineage and position in Israel; what are the value and the danger of this practice? See Rom. **3. 1f.**; **9. 4f.**; Phil. **3. 4-7**; Matt. **3. 7-10**; Rom. **2. 25-29**. *What are the modern parallels?*

1 Chronicles 5. 1—9. 44

THE OTHER TRIBES OF ISRAEL. In succession the Chronicler takes us through the tribes of Reuben (**5. 1-10**), Gad (**5. 11-17**) and Manasseh (**5. 23-26**). Note the comment on Reuben and Judah in **5. 1f.** There is a reference to the captivity of the trans-Jordanian tribes in **5. 6**; the Chronicler omits mention of this later in his history at the appropriate chronological point, since his interest is then concentrated on Judah. The war with the Hagrites (**5. 10, 18-22**) is not described elsewhere.

The survey of the tribes is interrupted by a lengthy discussion of the priestly tribe of Levi. There is a list of the high-priestly line (**6. 1-15**), from which certain names, both notable and notorious, are missing; then come the genealogies of Gershom, Kohath and Merari (**6.** 16-30), and the genealogies of the singers, Heman, Asaph and Ethan (**6.** 31-48 – note that these are given in reverse order); verses 49-53 repeat the sons of Aaron, and finally there is a list of Levitical cities (**6.** 54-81; *cf.* Josh. **21.** 1-42). A familiar figure in **6.** 28, 33 is Samuel (in **6.** 27 the words "Samuel his son" should be inserted).

After Issachar (**7.** 1-5) we are surprised to find "Benjamin" (**7.** 6-12); that tribe is given a full treatment in **8.** 1-40, since it formed an integral part of the southern kingdom. It has therefore been suggested that originally there was a list of the tribe of Zebulun (otherwise unmentioned) at this point. This same obscurity of the text has left only the last two names in **7.** 12 from a list of the tribes of Dan. Then follow the other tribes, Naphtali (**7.** 13), Manasseh (**7.** 14-19), Ephraim (**7.** 20-29), and Asher (**7.** 30-40).

Such is the general framework of the history of Israel. But before taking up his major theme the author has two more tasks to perform. First, he gives a table of the leaders of Judah (**9.** 1-16; *cf.* Neh. **11.** 3-18) and the temple staff (**9.** 17-34) who formed the nucleus of the people after the exile. (Something has been lost between **9.** 33 and 34). Second, he repeats the line of Saul (**9.** 35-44; *cf.* **8.** 29-38) as an immediate introduction to the story of that king's death with which the narrative proper commences.

1 Chronicles 10. 1—11. 9

THE REIGN OF DAVID: (1) *The Foundation of the Kingdom.* The history of the monarchy in Israel and Judah really begins for the Chronicler with the death of the first king, Saul. From a secular point of view Saul had been a powerful leader under whom the kingdom had achieved a certain measure of unity and strength, but from a religious point of view his career was so unsatisfactory that the Chronicler was prepared to pass over it altogether. One must consult 1 Samuel 9*ff.* for the story of Saul's early promise and his later decline. All that is recorded here, therefore, is the account of Saul's death in battle against the Philistines, the story being repeated from 1 Sam. **31.** 1-13. The Chronicler emphasizes that the battle meant the end of Saul's "house" (**10.** 6), although in fact some of his descendants survived.

The Chronicler now takes up the narrative in 2 Sam. **5.** 1-3, 6-10 of the acclamation of David by all Israel at Hebron. He passes over the struggle for power with the remnant of Saul's followers, and concentrates his attention on the positive side, the ready response of the people to David as they followed up his earlier anointing by Samuel, by entering into a covenant with him.

We see from this passage the typical procedure of the Chronicler. He follows closely the story already known to us from 1 and 2 Samuel, and indeed presupposes that we have already read it for ourselves. At the same time he draws out the meaning of the story in a fresh way, and he is able to add extra information from other sources; for example, he knows how the Philistines treated the head of Saul, and he also tells how Joab became the commander-in-chief of David's forces as a result of his successful attack on Jerusalem and how he repaired the city.

What is the ultimate significance of secular greatness in the sight of God? Is a man's religious attitude the only thing that really matters? How does Rev. 21. 24-26 fit in with the Chronicler's attitude?

1 Chronicles 11. 10—12. 22

(2) *The Mighty Warriors.* The list of David's mighty men in **11.** 11-41a is reproduced from 2 Sam. **23.** 8-39; it is supplemented with a further list (**11.** 41b-47) from another source. The Chronicler's emphasis is on the way in which these men supported David in the establishment of the kingdom, although some of the men may have served him only at a later date. What is particularly brought out, therefore, is not only the fact that these brave men did notable exploits but also that they were motivated by loyalty to their leader.

Some words appear to have dropped out between verses 12 and 13; it was Shammah who acted valiantly in the plot of barley; the plural in verse 14 may show "that this was a joint act of Eleazar and Shammah" (D. J. Wiseman). In verse 22 "ariel" probably means a hero.

Chapter **12.**, which is peculiar to 1 Chron., lists other warriors who threw in their lot with David while he still had to face the opposition of Saul. A group of Benjaminites, from Saul's own tribe, were particularly useful because of their prowess at long-range warfare with arrows and slings. A second group of Gadites were short-range warriors; they left their homes on the far side of Jordan to help David when he was in the stronghold (Adullam), and they showed their resource and determination by crossing the Jordan when it was in spate. A third group of men from Benjamin and Judah were received by David with suspicion, as they could have been spies from Saul (*cf.* 1 Sam. **23** for the atmosphere of this time). He sternly threatened them with divine vengeance if they proved disloyal, but their leader addressed David under the influence of the Spirit and swore loyalty. The final group from Manasseh came to David when he was seeking

349

sanctuary among the Philistines and then when he returned to Ziklag. They were experienced men who could act as officers in the rapidly increasing host that assembled round David as Saul's fate became more and more obvious. An "army of God" means an army of great size.

The imagery of warfare and battle is often used of the Christian life; what qualities can we, as Christian warriors, find to emulate in David's warriors? Consider also the variety of gifts they displayed.

1 Chronicles 12. 23—13. 14

(3) *The Army Groups; The Removal of the Ark.* In **12.** 23-40 we have a list of the numbers of troops who supported David in his assumption of the throne at Hebron. It covers the various tribes of Israel now united as one kingdom. (It should be remembered that in the reign of Saul the kingdom was not fully united, and after the death of Solomon the latent divisions immediately expressed themselves). The list contains various items of information about the different contingents. The men of Issachar "had understanding of the times", practical wisdom in time of battle.

The numbers in the list are strange. The total number of warriors, over 300,000, is very high, and the distribution of men among the individual tribes is also strange; Judah has an extremely low number in comparison with the other tribes; D. J. Wiseman suggests that this means that most of the tribe had long been with David. The numbers may have suffered in transmission, as has happened elsewhere in Chronicles. Nevertheless, they were sufficiently high for the author to think it worthwhile to mention the special arrangements made for their maintenance during their review at Hebron. The omission of horses (40) is significant as they were not yet commonly introduced to Palestine.

The first major item in the newly inaugurated reign was the moving of the ark of God to a place of honour. It had been left at Kiriath-jearim, otherwise Baalah (*cf.* Josh. **15.** 9; the "baal-" name was changed to a less offensive form) after it had been brought back from Philistine territory (1 Sam. **6.** 21—**7.** 2) and had been neglected during the reign of Saul. The event was of such importance to the Chronicler that he relates it out of its true historical order, drawing attention to David's early concern for religious propriety. After consultation with his leaders (*cf.* 2 Sam. **6.** 1) David summoned all Israel – *i.e.*, representatives of all the people – to bring the ark on its journey. The task was interrupted by the untimely death of Uzza, who sought to steady the ark when it was in danger of falling. His death was understood as due to the anger of God, an interpretation rejected by some commentators on the grounds that it implies an unworthy conception of God. However. one must assume some fundamental fault in Uzza's attitude to have merited such a judgment. For a fuller discussion of the matter see A. M. Renwick (*New Bible Commentary*, pp. 283*f.* [first edition]).

1 Chronicles 14. 1-17

(4) *War Against the Philistines.* At this point in the story the Chronicler uses the events recorded in 2 Sam. **5.** 11-25 to fill in the gap before the bringing of the ark to Jerusalem, although in fact these events preceded the removal of the ark to the house of Obed-edom. This demonstrates that the Chronicler was not aiming to produce a chronological account, and his history should therefore not be judged by wrong standards. The narrative recounts the aid sent by Hiram to help David in building a palace in Jerusalem; this fact indicates the spread of David's reputation outside his own country. Second, there is a list of David's sons; it contains a couple of names not found in 2 Sam. **5.** 14-16. (For "Beeliada" see **3.** 8). Third, two victories over the Philistines are noted. The Philistines would have observed with alarm the establishment of a strong monarchy in Israel and sought to weaken it. But with the help of God David was able to overcome their attacks at Baal-perazim and in the valley of Rephaim, not far from Jerusalem.

It is noteworthy how success in battle is attributed to the guidance and help of God. The prosperity and the fame of the kingdom were due to the Lord's bringing the fear of David upon all the nations.

This may be a suitable occasion to ponder what the Bible has to teach about: (i) the origins of material success; and (ii) the Christian attitude to war. Can the biblical teaching be summed up in such simple propositions as, "Godliness leads to prosperity", and "Success in battle is due to the help of God"?

1 Chronicles 15. 1—16. 6

(5) *The Ark Comes to Jerusalem.* After the interval of three months the task of bringing the ark up to Jerusalem was resumed and completed. Since the original tabernacle was to remain at Gibeon (*cf.* **16.** 39), a new tent was provided for the ark in Jerusalem. The distinctive feature of the story as recorded here in comparison with the

351

account in 2 Sam. **6** is the place accorded to the Levites in the ceremony. The calamities which befell the ark earlier were due to failure to let the Levites care for it in the proper manner. On this occasion they had to sanctify themselves (*i.e.*, wash and avoid defilement of any kind, *cf.* Exod. **19.** 10-15) before they carried the ark. One person viewed the proceedings with disdain; Michal perhaps typifies the religious indifference of Saul and his family (note the description: "Saul's daughter").

The detailed descriptions of the various duties of the Levites tend to be regarded by critical scholars as late and even fictional compositions, since the earlier records in Samuel and Kings make so little mention of them. But it must be urged that the Chronicler, writing as he did from the point of view of one deeply interested in the second temple and its worship, would naturally stress ecclesiastical details not found in a history written from a more secular point of view. The vital point for us to observe is that the Chronicler stresses for his readers (and for us) that the worship of God must be conducted in a manner both orderly and joyous, and that the best that music can offer is to be used in divine praise. The common sense of **15.**22 ought not to be overlooked! (In **15.** 20*f* (Alamoth and Sheminith are musical terms of uncertain meaning; thus Sheminith = either an eight-stringed instrument or bass [male] voices, says D. J. Wiseman.)

Is only the best music good enough for divine worship? What are the standards of judgment which we should apply?

1 Chronicles 16. 7-43

(6) *The Praise before the Ark.* Having described the instrumental praise of God, the Chronicler now takes up the mention in verse 4 of verbal praise offered to God, and gives us an example of such praise. The psalm which is quoted at this point is a combination of various passages in Psalms: verses 8-22 are from Psalm **105.** 1-15; 23-33 are from Psalm **96.** 1-13; 34 from Psalm **106.** 1 (*cf.* **107.** 1; **118.** 1; **136.** 1); and 35*f.* from Psalm **106.** 47*f.* It is sometimes held, rather unnecessarily, that this psalm represents the type of praise that would be used rather than the words actually used on the occasion of bringing up the ark. The psalm calls the worshippers to the praise of God Who has done wonderful deeds in the past and in particular has fulfilled His covenant promises by giving His people a secure dwelling in their land. Then the whole earth is summoned to praise a God Who does such wonderful acts in contrast with the powerless idols of pagans. The tone throughout is of praise, thanksgiving, and adoration, and may well

move us to ask whether our prayers are truly vehicles of praise to God.

The final paragraph deals with regulations for the future worship which was to be carried on both in Jerusalem and in Gibeon. (For the problems surrounding the functions of Obed-edom, **16.** 38, see H. L. Ellison in *New Bible Commentary*, p. 348). In verse 41 the words "for His steadfast love endures for ever" give the actual text of the prayer to be used.

Notes: V. 9. "tell"—Heb. "meditate on". V. 29: "the beauty of holiness" is rendered variously by the versions—*e.g.*, "Bow down to the Lord in the majesty of His holiness." The beauty may refer either to the Lord or to the worshipper—imputed, in the latter case.

Chronicles 17. 1-27

7) *David's Request to Build the Temple.* The bringing of the ark to Jerusalem was followed after some time by David's expression of his desire to build a permanent temple which would be a worthy edifice alongside his own palace (contrast the attitude expressed in Haggai **1.** 4!). Nathan's first favourable reaction was followed by a detailed oracle from God in which permission was refused (*cf.* **22.** 8-10). God would in fact give David a settled "house" in a country that enjoyed peace and security, and one of David's own sons would be charged to build a house for Him. The words are undoubtedly prophetic of Solomon, but both Jews and Christians have seen in them an ultimate messianic reference. The prophecy did not reach its final fulfilment in Solomon, but (according to Christians) in Jesus Christ, Who was the Son of God in a different and deeper sense from that in which any merely human king could be so called; His kingdom is truly eternal, and He prophesied that He would build a new house of a spiritual nature (Acts **2.** 30*f.*; Heb. **1.** 5). Note the difference between v. 14 and 2 Sam. **7.** 13; the Chronicler makes clear Who was the real King in Israel.

Many men have wished to perform some task for God but have not been given permission to do so, or the resources to reach a successful conclusion. Not all such have accepted the answer of God to their prayers in the spirit of David. It is therefore worthwhile to study the prayer of David in **17.** 16*ff.* and to note the spirit of thankfulness and praise which animated him.

1 Chronicles 18. 1-17

(8) *David's Military Successes*. According to **22.** 8 the reason why David was prevented from building a temple for God was that he had been a man of war. These wars were fought with the help of God, as is evident from this chapter (**18.** 6, 13), so that we must assume that David had a different rôle in the economy of God from that assigned to Solomon.

In his various wars David systematically overcame his rivals on every side of his kingdom. A further (*cf.* **14.** 8*ff.*) campaign against the Philistines led to accessions of territory around Gath. On the east Moab became subject to Israel. Hadadezer, king of Zobah, (1 Kings **11.** 23; 2 Chron. **8.** 3), was defeated near Hamath on the R. Orontes; his allies the Syrians suffered the same fate, and David gained considerable booty from the campaign which was later used for the temple (the sites in verse 8 are unidentified). The successful outcome of the campaign encouraged Tou, the king of Hamath, to make an alliance with David.

A brief note follows on the administration of David. It lists his army commander, his chamberlain, the chief priests (H. L. Ellison has "Abiathar the son of Ahimelech" here), the secretary, the captain of the foreign mercenaries who served as the royal bodyguard, and the king's sons who acted as "chief officials"; this last expression has been substituted for the word "priests", which is used in 2 Sam. **8.** 18. By this change of word the Chronicler meant to show that they were not the kind of priests known in his own day. He thought that the use of the word "priest" would convey a misleading impression and felt justified in altering it. This may sound to some people today like a wilful alteration of historical facts, but this is to judge the Chronicler by the wrong kind of standard.

Note: V. 4: similar large numbers of combatants and chariots occur in contemporary documents (D. J. Wiseman).

To think over: verse 13 speaks of David's success in battle. It was not matched by his success in domestic life. How is it possible for a man of God to fall into such inconsistency? What is the remedy?

1 Chronicles 19. 1-20. 8

(9) *David's Wars with Ammon and Syria*. The story in ch. **19** is a reproduction of that in 2 Sam. **10**. When David sent an embassy to Ammon to console the son of king Nahash on the death of his father,

and no doubt also to confirm the existing alliance between the two countries, the servants of the new king saw an opportunity to break an alliance which they felt was not to the advantage of their country. David's envoys were dismissed with pointed insults (the beard was a token of manhood and possibly of rank) and preparations were made for the inevitable consequences; it looks very much as though the Ammonites felt sufficiently confident of success to provoke David to war. As a result of the campaign the allies of Ammon were brought into nominal subjection to David. The war with Ammon itself was finished off by Joab who captured the capital city of Rabbah (modern Amman); David appeared on the scene only in time for the victory procession when he wore the defeated king's crown.

Between 20. 1 and 2 the Chronicler passes over in silence the story of David's dealings with Bathsheba and Uriah the Hittite. It may be argued, however, that the story was not germane to his purpose and he could therefore justifiably omit it (2 Sam. 11. 1-12. 25). He does, however, recount the slaying of the Philistine giants in a final note on the wars of David. The story has raised difficulties. Compare 1 Sam. 17 and 2 Sam. 21. 19 (the passage parallel to the present one). Most critics regard the text here as the Chronicler's attempt to gloss over a difficulty, but others (*e.g.*, A. M. Renwick, *op. cit.*, pp. 290*f.*) hold that the text of 2 Sam. 21. 19 should be emended to agree with that of 1 Chron.

How deeply and sincerely the rough and unscrupulous soldier Joab meant his words in 19. 13 is uncertain. But the sentiments which he expressed may surely be taken to heart by all who must fight in the name of the Lord.

Note: V. 18: the number of chariots given in 2 Sam. 10. 18 (700) is more likely. Note that the word used for chariots here can refer to men mounted on any animal or vehicle. The "foot soldiers" are called "horsemen" in 2 Sam. 10. 18 – this is not a contradiction, for in ancient Near Eastern warefare at this time, horsemen dismounted in order to fight (D. J. Wiseman).

1 Chronicles 21. 1—22. 1

(10) *David's Sin and the Choice of the Temple Site.* One of the 'warts' of David which the Chronicler did not omit from his picture was his sin in numbering the people. The story is told in 2 Sam. 24 with the well-known difference that there it is God Who stirred up David to number Israel whereas here it is Satan. The later author of 1 Chronicles

was aware of the activity of Satan in tempting mankind. As von Rad remarks, "This certainly gives us a more exact picture of God, but it does not remove the great paradox inherent in the whole belief in the Devil." In other words, it remains incomprehensible how Satan came into existence in God's Universe or how he can appear (as here) as God's servant. But one day we will understand, and meanwhile we can trust both the righteousness and the power of God's actions.

It is not made clear why the act of numbering the people was sinful, but probably in this case it represented a reckoning up of human resources with the consequent possibility of distrust in God. The numbers in **21**. 5 differ from those in 2 Sam. **24**. 9, and various suggestions have been made to harmonize them. Possibly the Chronicler was taking figures from a different record here. The result of the act was divine punishment carried out by the angel of the Lord. It was to last for three days, but the punishment was mercifully shortened.

The new feature in the story as told here is the way in which the Lord commanded that an altar be built on the threshing-floor of Ornan (or Araunah) and this site was later used for the building of the temple. The price paid by David for the site is higher than in 2 Sam. **24**. 24, but this may be because the Chronicler had in mind the purchase of a larger area. Sacrifices were then offered, and the Lord indicated His favourable reception of them by sending fire from heaven (as on Carmel). Although Gibeon continued to be a centre for worship, David did not on this occasion go there to offer sacrifice, but marked out the new site for the temple that his son was to build.

For Meditation: Verse 24. *And consider the special effects of sin committed by a leader.*

1 Chronicles 22. 2-19

(11) *Preparations for Building the Temple.* During the last years of his life after Solomon had become his designated successor and co-regent (*cf.* **23**. 1, which may well describe an event which took place before those in ch. **22**.), David made various preparations for the future building of the temple. The story of this is not given in our earlier sources, and the lively activities which David initiates in this last section of 1 Chronicles have seemed to be out of keeping with the picture of the senile king found in 1 Kings **1**—**2**. But David may have been in a low state during 1 Kings **1** and then undergone a measure of recovery before 1 Kings **2**. 1.

The account begins with the preparation of building stones by the forced labour of the resident aliens in the country. The charge which David then delivered to Solomon has some contacts with the speech in 1 Kings 2. 1-4. In it David looked back to the way in which he had been disqualified from building the temple because of his warlike activities. (It is true that Solomon also fought his wars, but these were on a much smaller scale.) He reminded Solomon of the divine promises made to him, and impressed upon him the need for his obedience and piety. Now that preparations for the work were well advanced, let Solomon do his share of the work zealously. Finally, the leading men of Israel were commanded to sustain the king in his task; this they would be able to do, freed as they were from the burdens of war.

(Note that the quantities of gold and silver in verse 14 are incredibly large. Various possibilities have been suggested. W. A. L. Elmslie comments, 'Neither the Jewish Chronicler nor his Jewish readers could have imagined that there would ever be anyone so prosaic as to take the golden words literally'.) There is considerable evidence to show that expressions like 'a thousand', or 'a hundred thousand', etc. represent a large number and a very large number respectively.

David not only exhorted Solomon to serve God; he also gave him material help to do so. In what ways should we give help to younger Christians?

To think over: The balance of faith (8-13, 18) and works (16, 19).

1 Chronicles 23. 1-24. 31

(12) *The Levites and their Divisions.* The opening verses of ch. 23 speak of a solemn assembly called together by David before his death. The account of what took place at this meeting is delayed until ch. 28, and the intervening chapters describe in greater detail the companies of secular officials, priests, and Levites who were appointed to various tasks. Just as it may not be very inspiring to us to read through the lists of pre-Reformation clergy of ancient churches, names of men no doubt often godly and pious in their generation, so here the lists of Jewish names are uninspiring to us, and the attempt to get some order out of the complicated lists is not possible or recommended within the scope of these Notes. Taking the lists as a whole, however, we find that they give us a picture of the continuing worship of God by His people over many centuries and remind us that service rendered to Him is not forgotten by Him.

The material contained in the various lists goes back to ancient records; just as the Pentateuch contains material from various periods in order to keep its legislation up to date, so such chapters as these may reflect the growth and development of the temple service over many years.

The present section gives: (*i*) A division of the Levites into a number of divisions by descent from Levi; the precise number of divisions is not certain (**23**. 6-24). (*ii*) The duties of the sons of Levi. Once the ark had reached its final place and the portable tabernacle had been replaced by a permanent temple, the duties of the Levites became those of assisting the priests in worship (**23**. 25-32). (*iii*) The divisions of the priests. First we are told how the recording of the divisions was carried out, with sixteen divisions from the descendants of Eleazar and eight from the sons of Ithamar (**24**. 1-6). Then there comes the list of 24 groups, each of which did a fortnight's duty at the temple annually in an order chosen by lot. This list gives the background to the priestly duties of Zacharias, who belonged to the eighth group of Abijah, in Luke **1**. 5-23 (**24**. 7-19). (*iv*) A further list of Levitical families, similar to that in ch. **23**. (**24**. 20-31).

Note: Ch. **23**. V. 13: to "burn incense" includes the sacrifices of atonement (Exod. **30**. 10). *Note how standard weights and measures were entrusted to the Levites – honesty in business is a spiritual matter* (Prov. **11**. 1).

1 Chronicles 25. 1—26. 32

(13) *The Singers and the Gatekeepers.* Musicians and choirs have a proper place in the worship of God. What is presented as lists of names in **25** comes to life in the poetry of the Psalms. Prominent names known to us from the Psalter are Asaph (Psalms **50, 73—83**), Jeduthun (Psalms **39, 62, 77**) and Heman (Psalm **88**). It is significant that the task of music in worship can be described as "prophecy" (**25**. 1); this surely indicates its high status. Note too that "small and great, teacher and pupil alike" (**25**. 8) were on an equality in the service of God: is there a lesson here for those of us who cling to our "rightful" seat in the choir (leading soprano, and so on) with jealous care?

The names in **25**. 4 from Hananiah onwards can be differently grouped and vocalized in Hebrew to yield the following piece of verse:

> "Be gracious unto me, O Jah, be gracious unto me!
> Thou art my God, Whom I magnify and exalt.
> O my help when in troubles, I say,
> Give an abundance of visions."

Various explanations of this are possible. One is that an early scribe saw the opportunity of writing the names of Heman's sons in such a way that this verse emerged. (The names, as we have them, are very odd, but the original forms cannot be certainly reconstructed.) Or did the sons themselves compose this "signature tune" employing various nicknames for themselves? It would be pleasant to think that somewhere among the singers of Zion there may have been those with a gentle sense of humour!

Ch. 26 contains miscellaneous lists, beginning with the gatekeepers. There were 24 of these, but they were not organized in divisions like the priests. They guarded the four sides of the temple with its store-house and the "parbar" (some kind of open space). The temple treasurers and their duties are listed (**26.** 20-28), and a number of overseers at large who carried out civil duties (perhaps as collectors of taxes) throughout the country (**26.** 29-32).

Not all of us have qualifications for the temple choir, but delight is to be found in serving God in other ways also; see Psalm **84.** 4, 10.

1 Chronicles 27. 1-34

(14) *The Civil Service.* Four concluding lists are given here. In **27.** 1-15 are named the officers in charge of twelve monthly divisions of the people, each of 24,000 men. The impression is given that these men were called to do military service for a month at a time. Most of the names are found in the list of heroes in ch. **11,** but the relation between the precise organization here and the less orderly list there is not easy to define.

Verses 16-24 give a list of twelve tribal leaders, which oddly includes Aaron and omits Gad and Asher. H. L. Ellison suggests that they were appointed at the time of the ill-fated census to which allusion is made in the context.

The third list (**27.** 25-31) gives the officials who looked after the royal estates, both in the region of Jerusalem and also further afield in the low-lying plain of Sharon and the foothills of the Shephelah. The passage gives an interesting summary of Israelite agriculture – ploughing, viticulture, the growing of olives and sycamores, and the keeping of herds.

Finally, there is a list of the king's closest counsellors (*cf.* **18.** 14-17 for the royal officials). Jonathan (otherwise unknown) and Jehiel tutored the king's sons. Ahithophel and Hushai are remembered from 2 Sam. **15.** 31*ff.* for their varying attitudes during Absalom's revolt. The title of "king's friend" (1 Kings **4.** 5) was used in ancient courts for a close associate of the king. For Abiathar see 1 Sam. **22.** 20-23.

To Think Over: Note v. 23; *a sinful act given a pious flavour?* *Compare* 1 Sam. **15.** 22; Jer. **7.** 22-23; Mark **7.** 1-23; Acts **5.** 1-10.

1 Chronicles 28. 1-21

(15) *Plans for the Temple.* After the introductory reference at 23. 1*f.*, the assembly of the leaders of Israel is now described at length. It had the twin purposes of establishing Solomon on the throne as David's successor and of raising popular enthusiasm for the building of the temple. There is nothing about this in 2 Samuel or 1 Kings, but the hasty anointing of Solomon in 1 Kings **1.** 39 could well have been followed by a more solemn and public ceremony.

The first part of David's speech recounts in language already familiar to us how he was prevented from building the temple and how the task had been reserved by God for his successor. It is again emphasized that Solomon's success would depend upon keeping the commandments of God, and therefore the people themselves were called to render obedience to Him. Solomon also received the same command.

At this point David gave Solomon plans for the construction of the temple. Like the tabernacle built by Moses, the temple was to follow a divine pattern; we may also compare the plan given by God to Ezekiel at a later date (Ezek. **40***ff.*). We see how the successful completion of the task depended upon the willing co-operation of king and people. We should remember that the king occupied a far more important place in ancient religion than he does today. In a very real sense he was "Defender of the Faith". But at the same time, as the history of Israel shows again and again, a godly king was heavily dependent upon the support of the people if his lead was to prove effective. The commandment in 1 Timothy **2.** 1 *and* 2 is a very wise one.

Question: Is there any truth about the Christian Church to be learned from this reading? If so, what is it?

1 Chronicles 29. 1-30

(16) *Gifts for the Temple.* Good intentions are useless in God's service apart from the willing provision of the resources with which to carry them out. Much had already been provided from the royal revenues for the building of the temple, but now the king made a further offering from his own private resources. For the sums stated,

360

see comment on **22.** 14; but it is made clear that the honour of God required lavish giving. (The daric (**29.** 7) was a coin in use at a later period, the name being used here to convey a certain value to the Chronicler's readers.)

The effect of giving to God should be rejoicing; note continuous tense (13). This is brought out in David's prayer which stresses that all that we have and possess comes from God. When, therefore, we who are but shadows upon the earth and pilgrims give gifts to God we are simply returning what has already been given to us, and have no cause for boasting about our generosity. Thus David could refer without either pride or false humility to his uprightness and pray that the disposition shown on this occasion might be maintained by the people and by Solomon.

The assembly then moved to its climax as the people blessed God and offered sacrifices. On the second day they anointed Solomon as king (*i.e.*, co-regent) and pledged allegiance to him. Only the death of David remained to be recorded.

For guidance in our prayers: David's prayer (cf. verse 11 with Matt. 6.13b [A. V., K. J. V.] and R. S. V footnote).

2 Chronicles 1. 1—2. 18

THE REIGN OF SOLOMON: (1) *Preparations for the Temple.* Originally 1 and 2 Chronicles formed one book, so that we should pass straight from the story of David to that of Solomon. The story is close to what we have already read in 1 Kings (1 Kings 3. 4-15; **10.** 26-29; **5.** 1-18), but differs considerably in the manner of its telling. Two paragraphs illustrate the theme of the opening verse that God was with Solomon and made him exceedingly great. First, we have the story of how Solomon, accompanied by the representatives of the people, went to the sanctuary at Gibeon which was still the chief place of worship. For the bronze altar, see Exod. **31.** 9: **38.** 1–7; "thousand" = "myriad" – used of any very large number. By night he had a dream in which God invited him to ask for what he wanted. Those who may misconceive the God of the Old Testament as a remote and unfeeling judge should observe that the Old Testament knows well the truth that "He giveth more grace" (Jas. **4.** 6); Soloman received more than he asked for.

Second, we are reminded of the greatness of Solomon's kingdom in terms of the size of his armed forces, the wealth of the country in bullion, and the extent of the trade which Solomon carried on, especially as a middleman in the horse market.

After these preliminaries the theme of the building of the temple is

361

taken up. (**2. 2** seems to be an accidental anticipation of **2. 18**.) Solomon renewed his father's trade alliance with Huram of Tyre, and sought both skilled workers and materials in exchange for natural produce. Huram responded willingly; his praise of Yahweh is not surprising in a diplomatic document in a polytheistic society. The name of the master workman was Huramabi, elsewhere abbreviated to Huram or Hiram.

"Wisdom and knowledge" cover both general religious knowledge (Deut. **4.** 6) and secular cleverness as aids to good government; the more "spiritual" word for insight or discernment is not used.

"Ask what I shall give you": what would you automatically ask for (*cf.* Mark **10.** 51)?

2 Chronicles 3. 1—5. 1

(2) *The Construction of the Temple.* The description of the temple here is much briefer than that in the corresponding section of 1 Kings (1 Kings **6—7**) and should be supplemented from that source. One or two additions are of interest. It is only in **3.** 1 that we find the identification of the temple site with "Mount Moriah"; according to Gen. **22.** 2 Abraham went to one of the mountains in the land of Moriah when he was commanded to sacrifice Isaac. The cubit "of the old standard" (**3.** 3) was about 20·5 inches, equal to a normal cubit (17·7 inches) and a handbreadth in length (Ezek. **40.** 5; **43.** 13); the "common cubit" (Deut. **3.** 11) was a round measure. "Parvaim" (**3.** 6) is unknown; the meaning is no doubt that gold of the finest quality was used. The large amount employed fits in with contemporary practice in Assyria, Babylon, and Egypt. In **3.** 14 there is mention of a veil which is not described in 1 Kings, but on the other hand 2 Chronicles is silent about the doors described in 1 Kings; some scholars think that a reference to the veil has dropped out of the text of 1 Kings. For the description, *cf.* Exod. **26.** 31.

The bronze altar (**4.** 1) is not mentioned in the description in 1 Kings, but see 1 Kings **8.** 64; **9.** 25. For the "3,000" baths of **4.** 5 substitute "2,000" as in 1 Kings. The bath is generally reckoned to have been about 4 gallons, 6¾ pints (22 litres).

The tables in **4.** 8 were probably for the lamps; the suggestion in verse 19 that they were for the bread of the Presence is probably due to a scribal error ("tables" for "table") in that verse.

Meditation: **4.** 21, 22 – *the smallest details must be of the highest quality in God's service.*

(3) *The Dedication of the Temple*. The chief item in the opening ceremony for the new temple (1 Kings **8.** 1-21) was the bringing up of the ark of the covenant from the site it occupied in the older part of the city which lay to the south of the new buildings (*cf. New Bible Dictionary*, p. 616, fig. 119, and Map 11). The Levites carried the ark from one site to the other, but it was the prerogative of the priests to bring it into the sanctuary itself. In **5.** 9 "to this day" shows how a post-exilic writer would follow an earlier manuscript exactly (D. J. Wiseman). The presence of all the priests on this occasion, and not simply one particular division of them, provided a splendid array for the ceremony. The Chronicler also draws attention to the activity of the singers and trumpeters who accompanied the proceedings with stirring praise. In Chronicles praise and thanksgiving are the constant accompaniments of true religion, and it was amid an atmosphere of joyful song that the glory of God was seen to fill the new house of God.

After the ark had arrived Solomon took the lead in the ceremony by blessing the assembly and giving a brief recital of the events which had led up to the present occasion. Thus God now had both a prince over His people and a place of worship in which stood the ark, the symbol of the lasting covenant made with His people at the Exodus.

The Chronicler attached great importance to the ark of the covenant. When the covenant is given its rightful place, the Lord reveals Himself in cloud and glory. How far is this kind of outward and visible continuity important in religion? What happened to the Jewish religion when the ark was lost? Is there anything corresponding to this in Christianity?

2 Chronicles 6. 12-42

(4) *Solomon's Prayer in the Temple*. In v. 13 there is mention of a bronze platform in front of the altar from which Solomon offered his prayer to God; a reference to this may have been lost from the text of 1 Kings **8.** (For Solomon's act of kneeling in prayer see 1 Kings **8.** 54). At the end of the prayer Solomon quotes the words of Psalm **132.** 8-10 (slightly altered), in which the presence of God in His temple is invoked and His blessing and favour sought for the people and the king: note how the national and personal are interwoven.

Since the Chronicler, after considerably abbreviating various parts of the earlier description of the temple, has thought it right to retain this account of the dedication ceremony in detail, this passage deserves our fresh study and meditation. We may note, therefore, that *the whole possibility of prayer is seen to rest upon the faithfulness of God* Who gives evidence of fulfilment of His promises to particular individuals in the present time and Who can therefore be relied upon to fulfil His further promises regarding the future. A second point, which cannot be too heavily underlined, is that *God is concerned about the moral character of His people.* Sin is not simply a failure to worship God correctly but is also the attitude which treats one's fellow-men wrongly, for God's commandments are concerned with the life of the whole community. Thirdly, the prayer shows that *forgiveness is abundantly available to those who are truly penitent.* Even when God has given up His people to the ultimate earthly punishment – *viz.,* captivity – it is still open to them to repent and receive His forgiveness. A fourth point that follows from this is *the necessity of forgiveness.* No man who has sinned can enjoy life and the blessing of God until he has been restored to a right relationship with Him.

Are there any situations in which God is unwilling to hear the prayers of His people? What has the New Testament to add to the concept of prayer which is found in the Old Testament?

2 Chronicles 7. 1-22

(5) *The Dedication Feast.* (*cf.* 1 Kings **8**. 62 – **9**. 9). In response to Solomon's prayer for the presence of God a further visible token was now given in the kindling of the sacrifices upon the altar with heavenly fire (Lev. **9**. 24; 1 Kings **18**. 38; 1 Chron. **21**. 26) – symbol of a holy, cleansing, purifying, judging, energizing Presence. In this way God declared His approval of the new temple and at the same time assured them that as He had been present at their former places of worship so He would now be with them in the temple.

Sacrifices were now offered in great quantities, as befitted this special occasion, and we are again reminded of the music which accompanied them. So great was the amount of the offerings that the middle courts of the temple had to be used in addition to the altar. The feasting lasted seven days (8-14 Tishri); it was followed by the feast of tabernacles (15-21 Tishri) and a solemn closing ceremony (22 Tishri), after which the people returned home. The corresponding verses in 1 Kings are not clear as they stand (1 Kings **8**. 65*f.*; see R.S.V. margin).

The Lord is well aware of the fickleness of men and of the way in which religious enthusiasm can speedily be followed by degeneration.

It is still common to see large crowds present in church on anniversary occasions with meagre attendances on the remaining Sundays of the year. Therefore the consequences of disobedience and idolatry are most clearly set out. If one thing is made abundantly plain in the Old Testament it is surely this: that when Israel did finally incur the wrath of God and go into exile for their sins, nobody could say that they had not been warned time and time again. Well might the Lord say, "I spread out My hands all the day to a rebellious people" (Isa. **65**. 2; Rom. **10**. 21).

Commentary: "Oh, that today you would hearken to His voice! Harden not your hearts" (Psalm **95**. 7*f.*). *It is a lesson for* us also: *read* Hebrews **3**. 7—**4**. 13.

2 Chronicles 8. 1—9. 31

(6) *Solomon's Wealth and Wisdom.* These two chapters contain a miscellaneous collection of information, mostly taken from 1 Kings **9**. 10—**10**. 29; **11**. 41—43, about the remainder of Solomon's reign. We may group the material under various headings as follows:

(*i*) The extent of Solomon's kingdom. **8**. 2 tells how Solomon gained twenty cities in Galilee from Huram and settled them with an Israelite population. These were the cities of 1 Kings **9**. 10-14 which Solomon had given to Huram and which the latter had viewed with scorn; it appears that in due course Solomon was able to redeem them. For Hamath-zobah see 1 Chron. **18**. 9*f.* Tadmor lay NE of Israel; later it was named Palmyra. The mention of these two places well outside the borders of Israel suggests that Solomon maintained far-flung trade connections. Upper and Lower Beth-horon were near Jerusalem; Baalath is unknown. They were all military ports.

(*ii*) The commercial wealth of the kingdom was erected on the foundations of slave labour (**8**. 7-10) and successful trading (**8**. 17*f.*; **9**. 10-28). The 250 chief officers of **8**. 10 with the 3,600 overseers of **2**. 18 are equivalent to the 550 officers of 1 Kings **9**. 23 with the 3,300 overseers of 1 Kings **5**. 16. "Algum" (**9**. 10*f.*) is probably a scribal error for "almug" (1 Kings **10**. 11*f.*), red sandalwood, but "algum" in **2**. 8 is probably a different, coniferous tree.

(*iii*) The fame of Solomon is illustrated by the story of the Queen of Sheba and the congratulations which she showered upon the magnificent monarch.

(*iv*) The religious ordinances of Solomon form the object of especial mention by the Chronicler. The regular festivals laid down in the law were observed by Solomon, and the divisions of priests and Levites carried out the duties for which provision had been made by

David. We are reminded how Solomon kept his wife away from the holy places associated with worship. The objection to her presence apparently lay not only in her nationality but also in her sex; as a woman she was liable to be religiously unclean. Mark **7** reminds us that this aspect of Jewish religion is permanently and fully done away with in Christ.

(*v*) Other interesting material about Solomon has not been included in the account which the Chronicler now closes (**9.** 29-31), but the reader is referred to various sources. These are not now identifiable, but some scholars think that certain of the references may simply be to different parts of the Books of Kings. "Iddo" is identified with the unnamed prophet of 1 Kings **13**. 1. Absence of references to Solomon's great sin suggest that the Chronicler seeks to portray the monarchy as an institutional rather than a personal office.

2 Chronicles 10. 1-11. 12

REHOBOAM (930–913): (1) *The Division of the Kingdom.* We have already seen on numerous occasions how the Chronicler has left out considerable amounts of material found in the Books of Samuel and Kings as being irrelevant for his particular purpose. There is considerable evidence that the Chronicler expected his readers to be familiar with the contents of the earlier histories before they started to read his work. For example, "**10.** 2 presupposes a knowledge of 1 Kings **11**. 26-40, and thus supports the accuracy of this narrative" (D. J. Wiseman).

We now come to his most important omission. In the history of the period after the death of Solomon he ignores almost completely the story of the northern kingdom. For him there is but one kingdom, what the Books of Kings call Judah, the southern part that remained loyal to the Davidic line, that possessed the temple in Jerusalem and that offered a relatively orthodox worship to Yahweh. By its secession the northern kingdom of Israel forfeited the right to be called a kingdom; it is noteworthy how in the present passage, which repeats 1 Kings **12**. 1-24 almost word for word, the verse which tells how Jeroboam became king in the north (1 Kings **12**. 20) is omitted. Moreover, except where the Chronicler takes over the usage of Kings in giving the name of "Israel" to the northern kingdom, he gives that name to the southern kingdom. It is, however, important to observe that it is the northern *kingship* to which he objects; the people of the land were still Israelites and could return to Yahweh if they so desired (*cf.* **11**. 13-17; **15**. 9; **30**. 1-12).

As indicated above, the story of the disruption of the kingdom is virtually identical with that in 1 Kings **12.** One new feature is the description of the building, or, more probably, strengthening of certain military bases in Judah. It was essential to prepare a country diminished in size and resources for possible invasion from Egypt. The measures described may have been taken after the Egyptian invasion described in the next chapter.

2 Chronicles 11. 13-12. 16

(2) *Rehoboam's Religious Decline.* There was not (and in those days could not be) an iron curtain between the northern and southern kingdoms, so that it was easy to pass from the one to the other. Israelites who kept up their loyalty to the worship at Jerusalem could fairly easily go up as pilgrims (*cf.* 1 Kings **12.** 27; Jer. **41.** 5). Priests who refused to serve at the shrines set up by Jeroboam lost no time in finding their way to Judah where they settled permanently. (The "satyrs" in **11.** 15 were demonic objects of worship.) It would appear from **11.** 17a that some of the common people also came up to Judah and settled there on a permanent basis. No doubt, however, some of the priests were content to stay in Jeroboam's service and "put their pocket before their conscience".

The modern reader may perhaps ask whether in such conditions as these it is a Christian duty to stay in an apostate country and exercise a leavening influence or to seek a more godly environment. Equally difficult in these days of lax and even erroneous doctrinal standards in some churches and in proposed schemes of church unity is the problem of whether one stays in or comes out: what does the Bible in general teach about secession?

The mention of Rehoboam's harem in **11.** 18-23 may be meant as an indication of his apostasy from Yahweh, although admittedly the general tone of the paragraph is favourable to him. In any case, however, Rehoboam was not faithful to his God, and the Chronicler saw in the invasion of Shishak of Egypt (recorded in his temple inscriptions at Karnak as taking place in 925 B.C.) a judgment on his apostasy. This was made clear by the intervention of Shemaiah the prophet who pointed out the lesson of the invasion to the king. Since the people responded to the message and repented at the eleventh hour, the invasion was milder in its effects than they might have expected, although Egypt overlordship lasted for some years. **12.** 12b implies that faithful, orthodox worship was fairly well rooted in Judah compared with the rapid apostasy in the north, though in view of 1 Kings **14.** 22-24 we cannot say that the situation was as good as might have been desired. The concluding estimate of Rehoboam is far from good. *What has he taught us about the way we should live?*

2 Chronicles 13. 1-22

ABIJAH (913–910). The short reign of Abijah (or Abijam) is passed over quite briefly in 1 Kings 15. 1-8. It is left to the Chronicler to give a fuller account of the war with the northern kingdom. The size of the forces in 13. 3, which is comparable with the census figures in 2 Sam. 24. 9; 1 Chron. 21. 5, shows that this was a full-scale war between the two countries. Abijah probably relied on support from Damascus to threaten Israel's rear (*cf.* 1 Kings 15. 19). In the speech of Abijah before action commenced the battle is represented as an invasion by Judah to conquer the apostate north. While the covenant made between Yahweh and David's line was to last for ever (a "covenant of salt", an inviolable pact consecrated by sacrifices), Jeroboam and his worthless young men had opposed the king chosen by Yahweh. They now felt confident for battle because they possessed a large army and the idolatrous calves instituted by Jeroboam. But these were paltry bulwarks! Had they not driven out those who wished to serve God aright, and was it not true that Judah continued in the orthodox ways of worship? Surely then God would support Judah in the battle! And so it proved to be. Jeroboam's sound tactics – envelopment of the enemy from two sides – proved futile, for with divine help Abijah won a resounding victory. He slew a considerable number of men ('500,000' probably means a large number) and captured a number of border towns, thus strengthening himself against any further moves from the north.

Speeches before battle and the use of martial music were not uncommon in ancient battles. Abijah's speech was by no means free from that exaggeration and misstatement which is characteristic of propaganda. 1 Kings 15. 3 and 2 Chron. 14. 3-5 demonstrate effectively that the religion of Judah was not as pure and undefiled as the king made it out to be. All we can say is that Israel went down the path of religious decline more quickly than did Judah.

To Think Over: "The first casualty of war is truth"—no sooner do we find ourselves committed to taking sides in controversy than we are liable (a) to justify ourselves hypocritically, (b) to denigrate the other side harshly.

2 Chronicles 14. 1—15. 7

ASA (910–869): (1) *His Prosperity*. The reign of Asa (*cf.* 1 Kings 15. 9-24) began with a period of peace in which two measures were taken by the king for the good of the kingdom. He began with a religious reformation to deal with the various abuses which had never been wholly absent from the country and which had probably become more powerful in the previous reign. Asa's second act was to renew and strengthen the fortifications of the kingdom and to keep his army up to scratch.

The value of these preparations became evident during the invasion of Zerah the Ethiopian or Cushite. The identity of this adventurer is uncertain. The old identification with Pharaoh Osorkon I or II is now generally abandoned, and he is thought to be an Egyptian or Arabian chieftain out for spoil. He may have been the leader of mercenary troops left near Gerar after the withdrawal of Shishak. The number of troops assigned to him should be interpreted to mean simply an enormous army. Battle was waged with him south of Jerusalem near the border with Philistia (for Mareshah *cf.* **11.** 8).

15. 1-7 tells how the prophet Azariah encouraged Asa to further acts of reformation after his successful battle. Evidently the task took some years and at this point Asa needed this admonition to spur him on to complete it. Verses 3-6 draw an example from the time of the Judges and teach the lesson that those who seek after God will know His blessing. What evidence can be adduced to show that verse 2 is only partly true – *i.e.*, that God seeks out His people even before they begin to seek for Him (*e.g.*, Isa. **65.** 1; Rom. **5.** 6, 8)?

For Discussion: Re **14.** *1-5: how far does the Old Testament teach that reformation in the Church should be a continuous process rather than an occasional crisis?*

2 Chronicles 15. 8—16. 14

(2) *Asa's Reforms – and his Weakness.* The prophecy of Azariah achieved its object. The far-reaching nature of the changes was seen above all in the deposal of the queen mother and the destruction of her favourite idol. The high places, however, still remained (**15.** 17; *cf.* 1 Kings **15.** 14). This is an apparent contradiction of **14.** 3, 5; this is usually dealt with by distinguishing between high places which were thoroughly idolatrous and required to be purged and those high places where a comparatively pure worship was carried on and which could be allowed to remain.

In his later years Asa showed a certain declension from his earlier piety. (Note that the date in **15.** 19; **16.** 1 is calculated from the date of the disruption; Baasha died before Asa's 36th year.) He found himself threatened on his north border by Israel, and in his extremity he sought a renewal of an earlier alliance with Damascus. We may compare how in the years before the Reformation the Scots used to ally with the French against England, thus exposing that country to attacks from two sides. So it was that while Damascus made diversionary attacks in the north of Israel, Asa was able to force Baasha to give up his activities in the south and strengthen the frontier on his own side. This reliance on outside help was characterized by the prophet Hanani as lack of fatih in God and he told the king so to his face. This provoked Asa to anger against the prophet and his followers, and he showed a cruelty towards them that was frequently imitated by later kings. The Chronicler does not definitely state that the disease of Asa in his later years was a consequence of his disbelief, but notes how even in his extremity Asa did not return to faith in God. The doctors whom the king consulted no doubt practised magic and even foreign arts of healing, and it would be quite wrong to take from these verses a wholesale condemnation of medical science. Despite his lapse, Asa died in honour, and his funeral was celebrated with a great bonfire (not with cremation).

Question: What distinctive characteristics of the prophet has the Chronicler taught us so far?

2 Chronicles 17. 1-19

JEHOSHAPHAT (*872–869–848*): (1) *The Teaching of the Law.* Jehoshaphat undoubtedly ranks as one of the best kings of Judah in the eye of the Chronicler, and he devotes considerable space to his activities (*cf.* 1 Kings 15. 24; 22. 1–36, 41–50). Three features of his reign are depicted in this chapter.

(*i*) Jehoshaphat continued in the good ways of his father Asa. It is not clear whether verse 1 means that he took defensive measures against Israel (the northern kingdom) or that he established his strength over Israel (the southern kingdom). In any case he kept his military installations up to strength. He also corrected various religious laxities which had survived Asa's reign; such reforming measures were continually necessary. In view of 20. 33, verse 6 is probably to be understood in the same way as 14. 3, 5. Note how his temporal welfare is related to his devotion to God – "because" (3), "therefore" (5).

(*ii*) He organized teaching of the law in the cities of Judah, apparently for the first time. This is a passage of some importance, since it indicates knowledge of the law at a date well before the reign of Josiah which is often thought to be the earliest date for anything of the kind. There would appear to be no good grounds for denying

370

that the Chronicler is here retailing sound history. It is impossible to tell exactly what was comprised in the "book of the law" used on this occasion.

(*iii*) Finally, we observe that the kingdom of Judah enjoyed the respect of her neighbours including the Philistines and the Arabs (who had caused trouble in the previous reign). A problem is raised by the closing verses of the chapter which give Judah an army far larger than she can have possessed at the time; H. L. Ellison reckons that one tenth of the totals given here would be more realistic. D. J. Wiseman comments, "The term 'thousand' may be a group term, and not necessarily a numeral".

The centralization of sacrificial worship at Jerusalem which took place increasingly during the monarchy according to the ideal set out in Deut. 12 no doubt made for increased purity of worship. We may perhaps wonder, however, what its effects would be as regards the level of local religious fervour and devotion. After the exile the development of synagogue worship overcame this lack in the religious life of the people. *Is the teaching of the law instituted by Jehoshaphat to be seen as an earlier attempt to meet this need? Has his action any lessons for contemporary church life and evangelism?*

2 Chronicles 18. 1—19. 3

(2) *Jehoshaphat and Ahab.* The story here is a simple repetition of that in 1 Kings 22. It does not show Jehoshaphat in the best light. He appears in collaboration with the ungodly king of Israel as the result of a marriage alliance and he succumbed to the persuasion of Ahab to join him in an expedition to invest Ramoth-gilead; was he aiming to re-unite the divided monarchy? The venture was far from successful, culminating as it did in the death of Ahab and the indictment of Jehoshaphat by the prophet Jehu.

On the other hand, it may be reckoned to the credit of Jehoshaphat that he had the godly wisdom to seek the guidance of Yahweh before setting out for battle, and that he was not fobbed off by the ravings of the professional prophets as they uttered their superstitious disabling oracles against the enemy but rather pushed the matter until he heard the voice of a more reliable prophet. It is admittedly surprising that in the face of Micaiah's ill-omened message Jehoshaphat still set out for battle, but it is likely that for all we are told about the strength of his kingdom he was to some extent under the influence of Israel and had to accompany his ally.

It is an old question how far one could distinguish between the activities of true and false prophets; does the Old Testament give any criteria? (See Deut. **13**. 1-11; **18**. 15*ff.*; Jer. **23**. 9*ff.*; Ezek. **12**. 21—**14**. 11; also the discussion by J. A. Motyer in *New Bible Dictionary*, pp. 1041*f*.). Compare the New Testament teaching on testing the spirits (1 Cor. **12**. 1-3; 1 John **4**. 1-6). *Is the modern Christian required to distinguish between true and false preachers, and, if so, what are the criteria?*

2 Chronicles 19. 4—20. 37

(3) *The Appointment of Judges.* After his hapless venture at Ramothgilead Jehoshaphat "dwelt at Jerusalem" – *i.e.*, he stayed at home and devoted himself to the affairs of his own land and people. He regularized and renovated the judicial system. The judges were strictly charged to act as the servants of Yahweh and to avoid all partiality and corruption. **19**. 8 distinguishes religious from civil cases, and in **19**. 10 the "statutes" are categorical commands, while the "ordinances" are laws applying to particular situations (for the distinction see, *e.g.*, F. F. Bruce in *New Bible Dictionary*, pp. 268*f*.). The policy followed here is very similar to that enacted in Deut. **16**. 18-20; **17**. 8-13.

Since it is axiomatic for some critics that the Deuteronomic legislation dates from just before or during the reign of Josiah, some 200 years later, it follows for them that this account cannot be historical. Wellhausen suggested that this story was attached to the reign of Jehoshaphat because his name means "Yahweh judges"! W. Rudolph, however, in the latest critical commentary on Chronicles, holds that there is a historical kernel to the story here, although he then goes on to argue that the story has been "touched up" in the light of the Deuteronomic laws. It is surely legitimate to argue that this account demonstrates that the Book of Deuteronomy is by no means a creation of the time of Josiah, although it assumed great importance then, but that it has a much earlier origin.

(4) *The Lord Fights for Judah.* The final episode in the reign of Jehoshaphat to be related at length was an invasion by Judah's eastern neighbours; the Meunites or Meunim (1 Chron. **4**. 41) were a people resident in Edom near Petra (*cf.* **26**. 7). The news of their advance caused the king and his people to seek divine help. In his prayer the king appealed to the sovereignty of God, to His action in giving the land to His people, and to the building of the temple in which God had promised to hear their prayers; on this basis he claimed the help of God to act in judgment. The prayer was answered by the inspired utterance of a prophet who assured the people that the Lord would fight for them. On the next day the invading armies were

strangely thrown into confusion and internecine conflict, so that they destroyed themselves; Judah was left to gather the booty and to give praise to God.

20. 31ff. sum up the reign of Jehoshaphat largely in the words of 1 Kings. The last paragraph warns that even a godly ruler can be led astray by allying with the ungodly; the final event recorded in this reign ended in disaster.

Compare Jehoshaphat's experience with that of Asa, his father.

2 Chronicles 21. 1-20

JEHORAM (*853*–848–841; *cf.* 2 Kings 8. 16-24). As is not infrequently the case, the godliness of the father was not handed down to the son. In this case, however, the father would appear to have been partly to blame for the situation, for Jehoram had been joined in marriage to the house of Ahab by wedding Athaliah, the daughter of Jezebel. He began his reign with an act of fratricide. (The existence of two brothers of the same name, **21.** 2, is unlikely; the second "Azariah" appears as "Azariahu" in Hebrew). The reasons for this violent behaviour are not clear. It may be that Jehoram feared the possible rivalry of young men possessed of fortified cities, or perhaps their religious policy was more orthodox than his own, as the verdict of Elijah (**21.** 13) would suggest. We may wonder whether Athaliah incited the king to the murder. Divine grace tolerated this ungodly monarch, but there came a time when grace found a limit to its patience. The divine disfavour with Jehoram was seen in the diminution of Judah's territory by the revolt of Edom in the south and Libnah on the western border with Philistia, and also in the invasions carried out by the Philistines and Arabs who on this occasion found no strange, supernatural power to repulse them.

The letter from Elijah the prophet has caused some historical difficulty because in the opinion of many scholars he had departed this life some time earlier (2 Kings **2.**11), and also because there is no mention of the letter in 2 Kings. See *Note*. No solution has as yet won wide support. Whatever be the origin of the oracle, it was prophetic of the disasters that befell Jehoram in later life; all his family died except Jehoahaz his youngest son. "Jehoahaz" and "Ahaziah ' (**22.** 1) are alternative ways of writing a name meaning "Yahweh has grasped"; many Israelite names were compounded with the name of "Yahweh", either with the prefixes " Jeho-" and "Jo-" or with the suffixes "-iahu" and "-iah". Jehoram himself perished horribly, and it is an awful epitaph that he departed with no one's regret.

Note: D. J. Wiseman comments: "Elijah was probably still alive. 2 Kings 3. 11 could imply that Elisha, servant of Elijah, may have taken office while Elijah was living. Otherwise we must take the general view that the letters were written by Elijah in anticipation of such a period of failure, and were forwarded by a successor".

2 Chronicles 22. 1—23. 21

AHAZIAH (841). The reign of Ahaziah is recounted with little change from the narrative in 2 Kings 8. 25—9. 29, except that the parts of the story dealing specifically with the northern kingdom are as usual omitted. With his statement that it was the inhabitants of Jerusalem who made Ahaziah king, the Chronicler perhaps implies that the choice was not universally popular in the country at large. In any case the king reigned only a year before he met his death. (He was 22 years old (2 Kings 8. 26), not 42, as in 22. 2.) The account here puts the death of Ahaziah's nephews before his death, and locates the latter at Samaria, whereas in 2 Kings 9-10 Ahaziah died at Megiddo before his nephews. It has been suggested that in this account Samaria may mean the realm rather than the town of that name.

ATHALIAH (841–835). Ahaziah's true successor was Joash, but for the first few years of his reign the throne was usurped by Athaliah. After some six years of rule she was deposed by a rising in favour of the young king led by Jehoiada the priest; it is the Chronicler who tells us that Jehoshabeath, who kept the boy hidden, was the wife of this priest. The story of the installation of the new king and the assassination of Athaliah follows the account in 2 Kings 11, but the narrative has been considerably modified in order to indicate the part played by the priests and the Levites. This has led to an under-emphasis on the rôle of the secular forces. The Chronicler makes clear that no unseemly events took place in the temple precincts. The number of people who took part in the covenant ceremony is also larger than in 2 Kings (23. 2). Since it is unlikely that a movement of revolt on so large a scale could have taken place without the queen hearing of it, we should perhaps suppose that the large assembly of people took place at a later point in the story (23. 16). Thereafter steps were taken to see that the temple services continued undisturbed.

For Meditation: The "Usurper" as a title of Satan. How true is it to experience? What can be done about it? Does this chapter help?

JOASH (*841*–835–796). The reign of Joash falls into two parts. During the first years of his reign he was under the good influence of Jehoiada, who appears to have acted as his guardian. The one matter singled out for mention from this period is the work undertaken to restore the temple and maintain it in good repair. When the priests proved to be dilatory, the king took the matter into his own hands. The Chronicler lays stress on the fact that the money contributed was the tax laid down in the law of Moses (Exod. **30**. 12*ff.*; **38**. 25*f.*; Neh. **10**. 32-38). The money was taken out from time to time and used to pay the workmen. Although the account in 2 Kings **12**. 13*f.* states that the money was used exclusively for temple repairs, the Chronicler states that the excess money collected was used to provide various temple utensils; this may mean that the temple utensils were purchased only after the repairs had been completed.

The second part of Joash's reign after the death of Jehoiada showed a fall from grace. There was evidently a party growing up which followed the ways of Israel, and Joash now fell under its influence and turned to religious syncretism. Various prophets warned the king of the consequences of his act, in particular Zechariah the son of Jehoiada, who suffered martyrdom for his fidelity (*cf.* **16**. 10). The incident was referred to by Jesus as the last of the murders of the prophets perpetrated by the Jews; this was according to the order of the books in the Jewish Bible of His day which placed Chronicles at the end (Matt. **23**.35; Luke **11**. 51). When an enemy invasion took place, the result was inevitable. Unlike Jehoiada, the king received an ignominious burial.

The apostasy of Joash is not recorded in 2 Kings **12**, except if it is to be inferred from the mention of the way in which he bought off the Syrian invaders by means of bribes from the temple treasures. The verdict passed upon him is not unfavourable, though by no means lavish in praise. Some scholars have been tempted to assume that the story of his apostasy is an invention of the Chronicler in order to fit the life of this pious king and his sad end into his philosophy of history. There are, however, indications of the use of another source at this point, and it would be most rash to yield to a sceptical verdict about a story which is perfectly credible in itself.

"May the Lord see and avenge!" (**24**. 22). *Should a Christian ever pray this prayer?* Cf. Luke **23**. 34; Acts **7**. 60; Rom. **12**. 19*f.*; 1 Peter **2**. 19-23; Rev. **6**. 10*f.*

2 Chronicles 25. 1-28

AMAZIAH (796–767). Amaziah (2 Kings **14.** 1-20) is yet another example of a king whose reign began well but nevertheless ended in disaster. He began by executing his father's assassins. He then carried out a military census, the results of which indicated that the kingdom had declined in strength. The king felt compelled to supplement his forces with warriors from Israel. The "100,000" who came to help him were probably a body of mercenaries rather than an official detachment; in view of 2 Kings **13.** 7 the number needs careful interpretation. A prophet forbade the king to make use of these troops, recruited as they were from the apostate northern kingdom, and they were dismissed from service without having to strike a blow. They were now in a position rather like that of many a modern salesman who is expected to supplement his low basic salary by commission on what he sells; they were therefore ill-pleased that they had not been able to supplement their official wages with the spoils of battle, and proceeded to conduct a plundering campaign in the north of Judah as they moved homewards. Even without their help, however, Amaziah was able to wage a successful campaign against Edom. The success was tarnished by three facts: (*i*) the cruel treatment of the Edomites. (*ii*) The capture of the Edomite gods in order to worship them and obtain their blessing; this was a common practice among pagans. But Amaziah "had better have thrown the idols down the cliff of Petra than his unfortunate Edomite captives" (F. F. Bruce). (*iii*) The consequent pride of the king who determined to break a lance with Joash of Israel. He was answered with a fine specimen of an Old Testament parable; this was followed up by a crushing defeat in which the king himself was captured, his capital city was attacked, and his treasures in the temple were plundered.

How is Proverbs **16.** 18, 19 *illustrated here?* Compare 2 Kings **14.** 8-14.

2 Chronicles 26. 1-23

UZZIAH (*790–767–739*). We are not told a very great deal about Uzziah in 2 Kings (2 Kings **14.** 21*f*.; **15.** 1-7), and for many of us the most vivid fact about him is his death by which Isaiah's vision in the temple is dated (Isa. **6.** 1). But archaeological evidence suggests that he was far from being an insignificant monarch during his lengthy reign, and the details of the picture are partly filled in by the Chronicler. He tells us that there was a revival in the military power of Judah during the early part of Uzziah's reign. He attacked the

Philistines and the Arabs who were old thorns in the side of Judah. For Gath see 1 Chron. **18.** 1, 2 Kings **12.** 17; it was now captured again and defortified so effectively that it does not figure again in lists of Philistine strongholds; (*cf.* Amos. **1.** 6-8). "Gurbaal" (**26.** 7) may be a scribal error for "Gerar" (2 Chron. **14.** 9-15 records operations in this area); for the Meunites see **20.** 1*ff.* In this way the power and prestige of Judah were re-established in the south as far as Eloth (Elath) on the Red Sea. At home Uzziah refortified Jerusalem and improved the condition of agriculture. The Shephelah (1 Chron. **27.** 28) is the low hill country W. of Jerusalem, and the "plain" is the tableland E. of Jordan; the *Negeb* or hill country S. of Jerusalem is also known to have been heavily populated at this time. Finally, Uzziah brought the army up to strength and furnished it with the latest "secret weapons" for hurling missiles (similar siege weapons can be seen on contemporary Assyrian reliefs); W. Rudolph notes how the Hebrew language had no word of its own to give to these "engines" and simply called them "inventions". Thus the country recovered from its decline under Amaziah to the prosperity described by Isaiah.

Despite all this, the ultimate verdict on Uzziah was a negative one. Like Amaziah he exemplified the proverb that a haughty spirit goes before destruction. In his earlier years when he had followed the instruction of Zechariah (possibly the man named in Isa. **8.** 2) things went well. Later in life he attempted to fulfil the functions of a "divine king". In the ancient Near East the king was a person of central importance in the religion of the nation and took a leading part in offering sacrifices. We have already seen how the maintenance of religion in Israel and Judah depended very much upon the king, but the law of Moses laid it down that the laity were not to offer sacrifices personally; that was the prerogative of the priests (Num. **16.** 40; **18.** 7). But the temptation to the king to follow the practices of his neighbours proved too strong for many kings, especially in the northern kingdom. In the case of Uzziah, who sought to burn incense in the sanctuary by himself, the effects were disastrous.

The lesson that pride comes before a fall is one that is repeated several times in 2 Chronicles because so many rulers in Judah failed to learn it. No Christian can afford to ignore warnings against what has been called "the Devil's masterpiece". See 1 Corinthians **10.** 11*f.*

2 Chronicles 27. 1—28. 27

JOTHAM (*750*–739–731). The reign of Uzziah, who, despite his lapse in the temple, was certainly one of Judah's better kings, was followed by the briefer but equally good rule of his son Jotham (*cf.* 2 Kings 15. 32-38). He strengthened the wall of the Ophel—*i.e.*, the temple hill in Jerusalem. He is credited with further fortifications in the countryside of Judah, especially the building of forts in wooded regions where it would have been impracticable to build towns of any size. He also subdued the Ammonites and forced them to pay a very considerable tribute. (The cor was roughly equal to six bushels.) These military operations were no doubt connected with the wider political situation. From now onwards Assyria began to threaten the west, and various of the smaller states formed a defensive alliance against her. They tried to force Judah to join them (2 Kings 15. 37).

AHAZ (*743*-731-715). Judah very nearly came to destruction in the ensuing reign. Ahaz is marked out as one of the most godless kings of Judah in the account in 2 Kings 16. 1-20. His failure to depend upon Yahweh bore bitter fruit in the military chaos which he experienced. Rezin, the king of Syria, and Pekah of Israel inflicted heavy losses upon Judah when she refused to join their anti-Assyrian coalition, although they were unable to take Jerusalem itself (2 Kings 16. 5; Isa. 7).

When the Israelite army brought a large number of captives home with them from Judah, a prophet urged the release of the prisoners; analyze the principles on which he based his appeal. Do these apply to any current problems? With a clemency that must have been almost unheard of in those cruel days the army leaders yielded to his command and returned the prisoners to their own land. In this way the action of the good Samaritan was anticipated by several hundred years, and the godlessness of Ahaz and Judah was shown up by contrast with the northern kingdom which they despised. This example incidentally shows that the Chronicler's estimate of the northern kingdom was not a wholly negative one.

Ahaz, however, descended yet further in faithlessness towards Yahweh by appealing for help against his enemies to Tilgath-pilneser (as his name is here spelled) – a case of casting out the Devil by the aid of Beelzebub, as W. Rudolph drily comments. Freedom was purchased for the moment – but at a heavy price. Verse 20 speaks not of an invasion but of crippling impositions which had to be paid to Assyria out of the temple treasures. Assyrian gods had to be acknowledged, and pagan altars were set up. The false worship appears to have been carried on in the temple precincts (2 Kings 16. 12-16).

2 Chronicles 29. 1-36

HEZEKIAH (729–715–686): (1) *The Reformation.* Of all the kings of Judah after David and Solomon it is Hezekiah whose reign receives the most attention from the Chronicler. This was principally because of the very considerable religious reformation which he carried through after the apostasy of Ahaz.

Hezekiah started his reign by undoing the evils of his predecessor. He summoned together the priests and Levites and required them to sanctify both themselves and the temple. In his speech he associated the coming of the Lord's anger upon Judah with the neglect of the temple. The worship which had been offered in the reign of Ahaz had been so corrupt that it could not truly be regarded as worship of Yahweh, the God of Israel (**29. 7**). The priests and Levites then systematically cleared up the rubbish in the temple and prepared everything necessary for orthodox worship. All was now ready for a re-dedication ceremony at which sin offerings and burnt offerings were made as an atonement for the sins of the nation. First a sin offering for the king, the temple, and the country as a whole was offered. The laity participated in the offerings by placing their hands upon them, but it was the priests who carried out the actual sacrifices upon the altar. These and the ensuing burnt offerings were accompanied by music, after which the people bowed themselves in worship.

The official sacrifices were followed by the freewill offerings of the people. The burnt offerings were completely consumed by fire, leaving nothing to be eaten. The peace offerings (otherwise called thank offerings or consecrated offerings) were partly burned, the flesh being left for the worshippers to eat. Libations accompanied the burnt offerings. Usually the preparation of the burnt offerings was the duty of the worshippers (Lev. **1.** 5, 11) or the Levites (Ezek. **44.** 11), but the flaying of them was carried out by the priests or, as on this occasion, by the Levites. The note in verse 34 about the priests may reflect the decadent conditions under Ahaz when Urijah aided the king in his apostate ways.

Have the sacrifices offered by the people any parallels in Christian worship and life (Rom. **15.** 16; Phil. **2.** 17; **4.** 18; Heb. **13.** 15*f.*; 1 Pet. **2.** 5)? *Note* "*suddenly*" (36) – *ought we to be afraid of a sudden revival?*

2 Chronicles 30. 1—31. 1

(2) *The Great Passover.* During the reign of Ahaz there had taken place the fall of Samaria and the carrying away of a large part of the populace of Israel as captives to Assyria. Judah was therefore now

the sole remaining representative of the united kingdom, and so when Hezekiah decided to hold a passover celebration at the restored temple it was eminently fitting to summon to it representatives from the north; we remember how pilgrims had come from the north in earlier days (**11**. 13-17). Many scholars deny the historicity of this appeal to the north, but we may agree with J. Bright that such scepticism is unjustified. Some would even deny the historicity of the passover celebration itself on the grounds that it appears to be a copy of the later celebration under Josiah, and that the Book of Deuteronomy, which alone requires the celebration of the passover in Jerusalem (Deut. **16**. 5*f*.), had not yet been discovered. Neither of these objections is firmly based. (The student interested in these problems may be referred to the discussion in G. T. Manley's, *The Book of the Law*.)

The passover was held in the second month of the year rather than the first (*cf.* Num. **9**. 1-14 for this possibility) because it was too late to hold it at the right time and the king was unwilling to postpone the event for the best part of a year. The people from the north were summoned in a tone both firm and gracious, but few responded to the invitation to share in the feast. It was an encouragement to seek spiritual union, despite divisions. Some people had begun to eat the passover while in a state of uncleanness. This was a severe transgression of the law, but Hezekiah sought forgiveness from God on their behalf, and his prayer was heard. In this way the Chronicler illustrates plainly that the ultimate thing in religion is not the fastidious observance of cultic rules but the devout heart which seeks to worship God. There are occasions when the rules are "over-ruled". (Are there any modern applications of this principle?)

So successful was this feast of passover and unleavened bread that a further week of festivity followed. It could truly be said that there had never been a passover like this one since the time of Solomon (**30**. 26: the verse does not mean that passover had not been celebrated in the interim). Finally, the people completed the task of reformation in the countryside and returned to their homes.

Question: Does Hezekiah's invitation to Israelites from the north have any bearing on contemporary ecumenical situations – e.g., the practice of united Communion services?

2 Chronicles 31. 2-21

(3) *Tithes and Offerings.* The cleansing and re-dedication of the temple were negative acts of reformation. It was still necessary to make

arrangements for the continuing worship of Yahweh which had been so seriously disturbed in the previous reign. Hezekiah therefore restored the divisions of priestly and Levitical service which had been instituted by Solomon. It was also necessary to make provision for the supply of sacrifices and for the maintenance of the priests. The king himself made a substantial contribution from his own resources. The people also were required to bring their gifts, the first-fruits and the tithes which were prescribed in the law. O. Eissfeldt has significantly pointed out that the word for "first-fruits" at the same time means the "best fruits". When the people took this command seriously, the king and his officers were very considerably surprised by the amount of the gifts which were brought in. There can be little doubt that the officers of many a modern church would have an even greater surprise if the congregation began to approach anything like the Old Testament standard of giving. (Have *you* ever worked out what a tithe of your income would be, compared it with what you actually do give – assuming that you do act as a faithful steward and keep an account – and then prayerfully sought the Lord's guidance concerning your gifts? Needless to say, the tithe is not a legalistic prescription for all Christians, but it makes a useful standard of comparison.) So great were the amounts contributed that special arrangements had to be made for the storage of the produce at the temple.

At this time also an enrolment had to be made of those who were qualified to receive the people's gifts in order that there might be no misappropriation of the funds. Special care was taken to see that the country priesthood were not forgotten in the distribution; their modern counterparts are sometimes forgotten, too!

The chapter makes it clear that God's blessing rests upon those who give generously to Him. But let it be far from our minds to give to God in order that we may benefit from it! Would you agree with the paradoxical dictum: "Jesus promises reward to those who are obedient without thought of reward"?

Discuss standards of Christian stewardship – are they anything other than wholly personal and subjective?

2 Chronicles 32. 1-33

(4) *Sennacherib's Invasion.* It is against the background of Hezekiah's religious zeal and his faithfulness to Yahweh that the Chronicler would now have us view the remaining significant events in his reign. The most important of these was the invasion of Judah by Sennacherib. The history is confirmed by discoveries in Assyria which depict Sennacherib (705–681 B.C.) before Lachish (9),

give his account of the siege of Jerusalem, and record his assassination. Hezekiah prepared for the danger by fortifying Jerusalem, including the Millo (1 Kings 9. 15, 24), and by sealing up sources of water outside the city of which a besieger might make use. The "brook that flowed through the land" is the Siloam tunnel which brought water from outside the city to within its walls (*New Bible Dictionary*, Plate XVc and Fig. 193). The people were also trained in warfare and encouraged to rely upon the power of God; is there an allusion in verse 8 to Isa. 7. 14? But did the people take Hezekiah's exhortation to heart? Isa. 22. 1-14 is an interesting commentary on this episode.

The actual invasion was on a greater scale than might be thought on the basis of the account here. Most of Judah was invested and Jerusalem was in the greatest danger. A very considerable tribute had to be paid to the conqueror. Nevertheless, Jerusalem itself, unlike Samaria a few years earlier, was not taken.

The Chronicler briefly passes over the story of Hezekiah's sickness and the visit of the ambassadors of Merodach-baladan, and assumes familiarity with the account in 2 Kings 20. But he makes it plain that Hezekiah's pride in displaying his possessions to the Babylonians displeased the Lord Who had allowed him to undergo this temptation (31). Isaiah prophesied the wrath of God upon the country, but its execution was stayed until after Hezekiah's death. We may presume that, since many of God's prophecies are conditional, a different attitude on the part of Hezekiah's successors and the people of the land would have led to a different result, but the reigns of Manasseh and even of Josiah were to show that the kingdom was corrupt in many ways. The last words spoken of Hezekiah convey a picture of a good king who experienced divine blessing, but the coming of judgment upon the land was by now almost inevitable.

To Consider: Does Hezekiah's folly in showing the treasures to the enemy have any parallel in spiritual experience today?

2 Chronicles 33. 1-25

MANASSEH (696–686–641). In 2 Kings Manasseh ranks among the very worst of Judaean kings; the account of his doings here reproduces a picture of complete apostasy from Yahweh with no essential variations from the earlier narrative (*cf.* 2 Kings 21. 1-18). There is, however, a new element in the story; he is seen as an Old Testament Prodigal Son. According to the Chronicler, after Manasseh had refused to hear the words of the prophets he was carried away captive to Babylon and later allowed to return to his kingdom; this event caused him to repent and to alter his religious policy in the later years of his reign. This story has been subjected to the severest criticism. It is argued that nothing is known of this story of the captivity of Manasseh from other sources; 2 Kings is silent about it, and no historical value is to be attached to the Prayer of Manasseh in the Apocrypha. The story of his repentance is therefore said to be a concoction by the Chronicler to explain why this flagrant sinner was granted such a long reign by God.

Once again we need not capitulate to scepticism. W. Rudolph has argued that there are no convincing grounds against the historicity of the captivity itself. It is possible that Manasseh was thought to be associated with the risings of Pharaoh Psammetichus I or of Shamashshumukin (the brother of Ashurbanipal) against Ashurbanipal, *c.* 655–648, and was summoned to Babylon to answer for his sins. We know that Esarhaddon and Ashurbanipal dwelt for periods in Babylon. His release and return to his own kingdom may be paralleled by the earlier release of Pharaoh Necho I by the same Assyrian monarch. (If this is so, the wall which Manasseh built in Jerusalem would be for defence against Egypt rather than against his own overlord.) Now whether Manasseh interpreted all this as a divine chastisement and repented is a possibility which Rudolph denies, since our other sources imply that the false religion of the earlier part of his reign still needed to be dealt with at the end. However, more weight than Rudolph allows should be given to the suggestion of earlier commentators that Manasseh's repentance left no lasting impression on the land, especially as it took place late in his reign.

AMON (641–639). No comment is needed on this reign in which all the sins of Manasseh were continued. That the king's policy was disliked is evident from his assassination (*cf.* 2 Kings **21.** 18-26).

Why in your opinion did the Chronicler include the story of Manasseh's repentance? What lesson has it to teach us?

2 Chronicles 34. 1-33

JOSIAH (639–609): (1) *The Reformation.* Josiah is ranked with Hezekiah as one of the two great reforming kings of Judah, although his measures came too late to arrest the degeneration of the country. An important difference between the accounts of his work in 2 Kings **22.** 1—**23.** 30 and in 2 Chronicles is that the former places first the temple repairs and the discovery of the book of the law (probably Deuteronomy – compare verse 24 with Deut. **27.** 15*ff.*, **28.** 16*ff.*) in his eighteenth year, and then describes his reforms, whereas the latter has Josiah instigate a number of reforms some six years earlier so that the finding of the book was not the immediate cause of the reformation. The matter is discussed at length by D. W. B. Robinson (*Josiah's Reform and the Book of the Law*), who comes to the conclusion that the Chronicler's representation is to be preferred. It is probable that both accounts are somewhat schematic and that we ought to envisage a programme of reform occupying several years, both before and after the finding of the book, without our being able to specify too closely the precise course of the reforms. A further difference is that since the Chronicler had already told that Manasseh had done away with foreign cults (33. 15), he omits mention of these in his account of Josiah's reforms.

When allowance is made for these differences in order and content, the narrative is seen to be close to that in 2 Kings. It is interesting to note what seems to be the introduction of "Music While You Work" (or Muzak) long before the invention of transistor radios! This practice is also attested for Assyria and Egypt where heavy work was done to the accompaniment of musical signals. Verse 14 does not say whether the book of the law was actually found during or as a result of the repairs, but the narrative gives no reason to suspect that it was "found" for the occasion, like Aaron's calf (Exod. 32. 24).

Verse 33 gives an excellent impression of the king's zeal for reformation, but one is bound to ask whether one can really "make" people to "serve the Lord their God". In fact the outward reformation lasted only as long as Josiah was there to enforce it (see Jer. 11. 13; 13. 10).

How can a Christian placed in a position of leadership or influence best convey his zeal for the Lord to his fellow men and women?

2 Chronicles 35. 1-27

(2) *The Second Great Passover.* As in the reign of Hezekiah the celebration of the passover formed the culmination of the reformation of worship. It took place under the direction of the king who gave instructions to the Levites to carry out the slaughter of the passover lambs for the people since they now no longer needed to carry the ark of the covenant. The sacrificial animals for the occasion were given by the king, the princes, and the chiefs of the Levites. We have previously commented how the passover was especially fitted to be the climax of the reformations undertaken by Hezekiah and Josiah since it commemorated the redemption of Israel from Egypt by the hand of God. The tragedy of Israel's history was that this feast and the events which it celebrated had been thoroughly neglected throughout the monarchy. It took place just before the fall of Jerusalem – as did that more notable passover when Jesus gave His

disciples the sacrament of the Lord's Supper. The command to *repeat* it in memory of Him was made with full wisdom, for He knew how easily we too can forget the significance of the cross; it is at our peril that we come to the Lord's Table irregularly and perfunctorily, or surround the simple rite with such elaborate ritual and formal reverence that it can no longer speak plainly to us of the sacrificial death of the Saviour.

Perhaps if Josiah had lived the history of Judah might have turned out differently, although one fears that the end would simply have been delayed. As it was, he perished as a result of a foolish political move. He went out to oppose Pharaoh Necho II who was on his way to help the tottering Assyrian empire against the growing power of Babylon. He no doubt feared that a strengthened Assyria would have curtailed his own freedom; he had after all done away with the Assyrian gods introduced by Ahaz. Necho warned him against any attempt at resistance, but Josiah refused to listen. The outcome of the unequal struggle was what might have been expected. Josiah perished as a result of his wounds. The laments which were written concerning him have not survived.

Verse 21 implies that Necho would have by-passed Judah – how could a godly king have made Josiah's mistake? How does this square with your doctrine of providence?

2 Chronicles 36. 1-23

THE LAST KINGS OF JUDAH: *Jehoahaz, Jehoiakim, Jehoiachin and Zedekiah* (609–587). The final quarter-century of the kingdom is passed over with great speed; the account in 2 Kings 23. 31—25. 30 is a little more leisurely. Evidently the biblical historians could not bring themselves to tarry over the sorry tale of the last kings of Judah; we must turn to Jeremiah for a fuller account in which the worthlessness of these men is pitilessly exposed. Jehoahaz was replaced by his brother Eliakim, or Jehoiakim, the nominee of Egypt. The new monarch survived for eleven years until the expedition made in 605 by Nebuchadnezzar, who was then still the crown prince. The interpretation of verse 6 is disputed. W. Rudolph holds that the Hebrew text implies only a threat of transportation and that Jehoiakim capitulated under this threat. This interpretation would appear at first sight to be contradicted by Dan. 1. 1*f.*, but that passage may perhaps speak not of the captivity of the king but only of the carrying away of the temple vessels to Babylon.

Jehoiakim's son Jehoiachin (he was eighteen, not eight, years old – 2 Kings 24. 8) had a reign as short as that of Jehoahaz before the

Babylonian government caught up with him and deposed him in favour of his uncle ("brother" in verse 10). The temple treasures were carried off – a sign to the people that their God *could* not (as Nebuchadnezzar would have put it) or rather *would* not (as Jeremiah would have put it) defend them any longer.

The account of Zedekiah's reign is used to underline the lessons of Judah's history. Since the king and people had repeatedly refused to hear the word of God, especially from the mouth of Jeremiah the prophet, the patience of God had at last reached its limit and "there was no remedy". The king of Babylon overran the land and took Jerusalem. He destroyed its fortifications and the temple, and carried many of the people into exile. This exile was to last until the Persians took over the Babylonian empire, a period of some seventy years for the land to enjoy its sabbaths. These events are attested by contemporary secular documents. Nebuchadnezzar's Chronicle claims the capture of Jerusalem in March 597 B.C., and to have carried Jehoiachin to Babylon (2 Kings 25.27). Records from that city show him prisoner also under Nebuchadnezzar's son, Evil-merodach (*cf.* Jer. 52).

But a biblical writer could not end his history on this despondent note. Just as 2 Kings closes with a gleam of hope, so the end of 2 Chronicles looks forward into the future as though the seventy years had already run their course. The decree of Cyrus, which is contained in the opening verses of Ezra (1. 1-4) has been added to the end of the book. Originally this addition was unnecessary because the books of Chronicles, Ezra, and Nehemiah were meant to be read in the order stated. But this order was disturbed by the fact that Ezra and Nehemiah were received into the canon first and Chronicles came last in the series. The Hebrew Bible could not end with tragedy, and so the verses containing the promise of restoration were inserted to give the book a fitting conclusion. "Speak tenderly to Jerusalem, and cry to her that her warfare is ended, that her iniquity is pardoned, that she has received from the Lord's hand double for all her sins." The last event, therefore, is the act of God, Who promises through Cyrus that a house will be built for His worship and on the basis of this Gospel message issues His evangelistic appeal: "Whoever is among you of all His people, may the Lord his God be with him. *Let him go up.*"

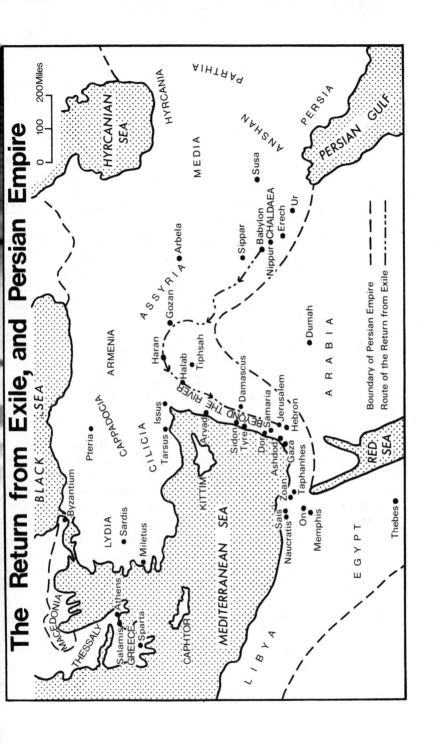

The Return from Exile, and Persian Empire

0 100 200 Miles

HYRCANIAN SEA

HYRCANIA

PARTHIA

MEDIA

ANSHAN

PERSIA

PERSIAN GULF

Susa

Sippar

Babylon

Nippur • CHALDAEA

Erech

Ur

ASSYRIA

Gozan • Arbela

Haran

Halab

Tiphsah

Damascus

Dumah

ARABIA

BEYOND THE RIVER

Samaria

Jerusalem

Hebron

Sidon

Tyre

Dor

Ashdod

Gaza

Arvad

Issus

Tarsus

CILICIA

KITTIM

Pteria

CAPPADOCIA

ARMENIA

BLACK SEA

Byzantium

LYDIA

Sardis

Miletus

MACEDONIA

THESSALY

Athens

Salamis

GREECE

Sparta

CAPHTOR

MEDITERRANEAN SEA

Zoan

Sais

Naucratis

On

Memphis

Taphanhes

EGYPT

Thebes

LIBYA

RED SEA

Boundary of Persian Empire – – –

Route of the Return from Exile –··–··–

EZRA

Ezra 1.1–2.63 Return from Exile

Introduction. Comparison with the closing verses of 2 Chronicles shows that Ezra is a continuation, probably by the same compiler. Originally the Jews counted Ezra and Nehemiah as one Book. The author and compiler could have been Ezra himself.

Jeremiah 25.12 and 29.10 had foretold that release from Babylon would come seventy years after Palestine first came under the Babylonian empire, i.e. 605 B.C. (Jer. 25.1). Ezra 1 records the decree of release in the year when Cyrus conquered Babylon (538 B.C., which is near enough to seventy years). We note the faithfulness of God. The punishment was with a view to restoration.

Contemporary inscriptions show that Cyrus allowed other captive nations to return home with their idols, and he speaks of other gods as he speaks here of Jehovah. Probably this decree for the Jews (2–4) was drawn up by a Jew at Cyrus' request in suitable terms. He was ready to admit that he was the instrument of the one true God (2). Since the Jews had no idols, they were given their captured Temple vessels (7, cf. Dan. 5.2).

Anyone might now leave, but not everyone did. Many had settled and prospered in Babylonia, and vs. 4 and 6 imply that they preferred to pay for others to go rather than go themselves. Life was likely to be hard in Judah. There is an obvious lesson here (cf. Isa. 48.20; 52.11,12; Zech. 2.6,7; Rev. 18.4).

Cyrus appointed a governor for Judah (8). Sheshbazzar is not the same as Zerubbabel, who succeeded him as leader, for 5.14 implies that Sheshbazzar was dead by 520 B.C., whereas Zerubbabel was then a leader. He may be the same as Shenazzar, son of King Jehoiachin, and uncle of Zerubbabel (1 Chron. 3.18,19). The Jews did not creep back, but returned in triumph under a governor appointed by the most powerful monarch of the day. This was God's doing (Psa. 126). It has an application to us (Col. 1. 13).

The list of returning exiles in ch. 2 is repeated in Neh. 7.6–73. They are classified under (*a*) leaders (2), (*b*) families and clans (3–19), (*c*) places of settlement (20–35), (*d*) priests, Levites, Temple servants (36–58), (*e*) alleged priests of uncertain ancestry (59–63).

There is a place for everyone (1 Cor. 12.12).

It was first necessary for the large numbers of returned exiles to settle down (64–70); and Jerusalem itself was in a poor state (Lam. 5.18). They reoccupied the towns and villages round about. God is concerned with material needs. But before they spent all their money on themselves, the wealthy contributed towards the new Temple which Cyrus had authorized them to build (1.3).

The seventh month was an important one for festivals (Lev. 23.24–36; Neh. 8), and the people gathered in the ruined Jerusalem. The priority now was the altar. Note the wording of v.3. They were afraid of the non-Jews who were settled in the surrounding country, and who were naturally jealous of the returned Jews. The answer was to turn to God in sacrifice and prayer (cf. Psa. 56.3,4, 11–13). The initiative was not taken by Sheshbazzar, although as governor he naturally authorized the building of the altar and Temple (5.16). But God had His men whom He used, Joshua the high priest and Zerubbabel of the line of David.

The next priority was the Temple. They used the grant that Cyrus had allowed them to gather material (7). The ruins of the old Temple would supply stone, but all the timber had been burnt (2 Kings 25.9). Then came the great day when the Temple foundation was laid. The Levites were made responsible for the oversight of the work, Once more the trumpets sounded as appropriate psalms of David were sung. Verse 11 shows that the chief psalm was 136, which had been sung at the dedication of Solomon's Temple (2 Chron. 5.13 and 7.3). There is usually a psalm suitable for every occasion in our lives (Eph. 5.19; Jas. 5.13).

We need not be ashamed of emotion. The key emotion here was joy, praise and singing. But the older people, who had waited fifty years for this day, since Solomon's Temple was destroyed in 587 B.C., wept, either for joy at seeing the answer to their prayers, or for sorrow at seeing such narrow foundations in place of the former glorious Temple (Hag. 2.3).

It is good to look back to the past, but not to sigh for the good old days in such a way as to lose the vision of what we must do now (Eccl. 7.10; Phil. 3.13,14).

Ezra 4   Much Opposition

This chapter concerns several occasions of opposition. But opposition does not necessarily mean that we are out of the line of God's will.

Vs. 1–5 continue the story of ch. 3, covering the period 536–520 B.C., and they are picked up again in v. 24. All sorts of people besides Jews and Israelites were in the land. Those mentioned in v. 1 were descendants of peoples who had been settled in the Northern Kingdom by Assyrian kings after many of the Israelites had been deported in 721 B.C. They had adopted a blend of Jehovah worship with worship of their own gods and goddesses (2 Kings 17.24–41). They wanted to help build what to them was just one more shrine in honour of one of their gods. But this sort of mixed worship had done untold damage in Judah before the exile, and Joshua and Zerubbabel would not repeat the mistake. Sometimes the help and affection of the world can be bought at too high a price (Rev. 2.20). Yet refusal may bring strong opposition (4,5).

If we follow the usual Biblical identification of the Persian kings in vs. 6 and 7, Ahasuerus is Xerxes (486–465 B.C.) and Artaxerxes is King Artaxerxes I (464–424 B.C.) who later sent Ezra and Nehemiah to Jerusalem. These verses say nothing about rebuilding the Temple, but only about the city and the walls (12,16). The writer may be collecting together similar cases of opposition as an encyclopedist might. Others identify the kings with Cambyses (529–522 B.C.) and Gaumata (522–521 B.C.).

Consider how helpless the Christian often feels against malicious opposition and such misrepresentation as in v. 13. How important not to give the non-Christian a valid reason for criticism (1 Pet. 3.16,17; 4.15,16). The appeal to the king is on the ground of his own self-interest. This is the sort of thing that Christians meet in some newly independent countries. They are singled out as damaging to the rising state, and persecuted in consequence. These letters and the action of the king must have seemed to the Jews like the end of all their hopes. We now know the end of the story, and remember how the city and the walls were built.

God knows the end of the story also. Our times are in His hand. (Psa. 31.15; Heb. 12.11).

Ezra 5 Revival

Now we return to the story of rebuilding of the Temple. The Jews had lost their enthusiasm for the work under the constant nagging of the enemy. We know from the contemporary Book of Haggai that many of them had begun to build luxury houses for themselves (Hag. 1.4). It is interesting to read Haggai's own words as a supplement to v. 1 here. Suddenly revival came (2). Perhaps Haggai and Zechariah had returned as children in 537 B.C., and now received their call in 520 B.C. They were practical men of action as well. (2) Zerubbabel and Joshua again found willing helpers.

Once more the enemy tried to intervene (3–5) but now the opposition looked different. The people answered the Persian governor boldly, and went on building. About this time the prophet Zechariah was given the great promise from God to pass on to Zerubbabel, probably while the letter was on its way to the king. The great mountain that blocked the way would be levelled to the plain, and the Temple would be finished (Zech. 4.6,7).

Note how the Jews spoke to those who would have stopped them. They interpreted God in language that at least made some sense to those who did not worship Jehovah (11). They freely confessed that they had done wrong in the past through disobeying the God of heaven (12). Compare the argument that the apostles used in Acts 5.29. We must be careful, however, not to make such an argument a pretext for our own self-will.

In this case they had the assurance of God's steady leading in the past (13–15), and they appealed confidently to the document, which must have been preserved, and on which would appear the name of Sheshbazzar and the authorization of Cyrus. There are times when we need not fear to claim our rights in law, without always insisting on every claim that we think is due to us. Paul did not hesitate to claim his rights as a Roman citizen when this was for the glory of the gospel (Acts 16.37–39; 25.11,12.). So we see God reviving His people, giving them wisdom to meet the occasion, and encouraging them through His word by the prophets to look for the perfect fulfilment.

Think of Phil. 1.6.

Ezra 6 Unlikely Support

In the last two chapters we have become so used to persecution by the world that it may surprise us to find the support and sympathy that can come from those who are not true believers. Although King Darius would not want to offend the powerful rulers of the province in the interests of one little city, he was prepared to see justice done. So he instituted an extensive search for the alleged decree (1,2). This decree differs in wording from the published decree of ch. 1. This is the business form in government files. It lists the outside dimensions of the building for which the Persian government would make a grant (3,4). Darius was ready to enforce what his predecessor had sanctioned (6–8). Although the image of God has been marred in man, there is still a feeling for justice (cf. Rom. 13.1–5).

Darius went further. Just as Cyrus had acknowledged the existence of Jehovah (1.3), so now Darius asks the Jews to pray to Jehovah and offer sacrifices on behalf of himself and his sons (9,10). In the New Testament also we are told that prayer for rulers, even non-Christians, must be given a high priority (1 Tim. 2.1-3). Do we not find that apparently unlikely people can be touched by the knowledge that we are praying for them? And such prayer includes other things besides the necessary prayer for their salvation.

So the Jews continued to build, and in 516 B.C., four years from the beginning of the revival (4.24), the Temple was completed (15). What a wonderful experience the dedication must have been! The offerings (17) seem few in comparison with those made by Solomon in 1 Kings 8.5,63, but most of the sacrifices on such an occasion were eaten by the worshippers, and the community now was comparatively small.

Note the new fellowship. Not only did the returned Jews take part, but returned members of the northern kingdom of Israel (16), and members of both kingdoms who had never gone into exile, provided that they made a clean break with paganism (21, cf. 1 Cor. 6.11). The occasion of the dedication was the Passover (22), reminding them of the great occasion of redemption.

Because we have been redeemed through our Lord Jesus Christ, we can build, and be built into, the new Temple (Eph. 2.13, 20-22).

Ezra 7   Man of the Law

There is a gap of nearly sixty years between the end of ch. 6 and the beginning of 7, i.e., from 516 B.C. to 458 B.C. The king is Artaxerxes I (464–424 B.C.) who is probably the same as in 4.7, although at this stage he is friendly towards the Jews. We do not know what has been happening since 516 B.C., although we have some writings from this period, including some of Zechariah, and also probably Malachi, and perhaps Joel. The events of Esther happened in Persia during the reign of Artaxerxes' predecessor.

Ezra was a great student of the Law (6). He was descended from Aaron, and this genealogy picks out some prominent ancestors (1-5). Clearly he held some official position in Persia, perhaps the equivalent of Secretary of State for Jewish Affairs. Note what is said here: he studied the Law thoroughly (6,10,11); he used his knowledge to hold a position in the State, so the king naturally selected him (12); he was prepared to be not merely a student of doctrine but a practical man of action (6,10). It would have been pleasanter to spend his time in Bible study in a remunerative post.

The king sent him to investigate and, if necessary, enforce Jewish observance of the Law (25,26). There is other evidence that Persian kings were concerned with the religious practices of their subjects, as is seen from papyri sent to the Jewish colony at Elephantine in Egypt. Ezra's return encouraged others to accompany him (7, 13). It is surprising what an example will do. Note how Christ is presented as an example (Phil. 2.5–8; 1 Pet. 2.21–23), and, in following Him, we in turn set an example (1 Thess. 1.7; 1 Tim. 4.12). Since he was a trustworthy man, the king was prepared to trust him with large sums of money (15).

From the personal memoirs of Ezra we see something of his inner life, as we do later with Nehemiah. Study his prayer and thankfulness in vs. 27 and 28. He knows that God has inclined the king's heart, and gives glory to Him. Since God has begun this work, he finds assurance and strength, and is able to communicate his confidence to others (Acts 27.22–25; Phil. 1.6).

Why did the others not go before? They were free to do so. Why did they go now?

Ezra 8
A Long Journey

Ezra's journey took him some 900 miles, up the Euphrates and then across to enter Palestine from the north. Although the cavalcade carried treasures that have been estimated at nearly a million pounds (26,27), Ezra refused an escort of troops (22) after committing the whole issue into the hands of God (21). Acts of faith of this kind must not be imposed on every Christian: Nehemiah, who was equally a man of faith and prayer, had no scruples over accepting an escort from the king (Neh. 2.7,9). What to one person is a step of faith may to another be tempting the Lord (Matt. 4.5–7). Ezra did not reach his decision lightly, but knew that it involved fasting and prayer (21,23).

Note again the contrast between those who came and those who were reluctant to come. The list of families in vs. 2–14 is much the same as in chapter 2, and v. 13 suggests, what may be true of the others, that these were going to join members of the family who had already returned.

The most surprising reluctance came from the Levites (15). No reason is given for this, but one might guess that in Babylonia they had considerable position as teachers of the Law. In Judah the most influential Levitical posts would already have been taken.

However, some were willing to come when they were pressed (17–20). We are reminded of the parable of the two sons in Matt.

21.28-31. We may not be too late even though we have held back in the past.

Ezra was a man of great wisdom. He knew how easily people talk scandal, and, if his reforms should prove unpopular, his enemies might whisper that he had diverted some of the silver and gold to his own pockets. So he had the weight of the treasures exactly recorded before and after the journey (24-34). Christians must be careful over such matters, even when they feel that their word should be trusted. Paul did this with the collection money that he handled (2 Cor. **8.**20,21).

The offerings (35) were made on behalf of all the twelve tribes. Many were still scattered, but representatives of both kingdoms were now settled once again in Palestine.

The oneness of Israel is intensified in the oneness of the true Church of Christ. We recognize this oneness in spite of external scattering (Eph. **4.**3,4).

Ezra 9 A Model Prayer

Before the exile there had been too much involvement with Canaanite life, morality, and religion. Some of the trouble had come through mixed marriages, against which special warnings had been given (e.g. Deut. **7.**3,4; Josh. **23.**12,13). In the Books of Ezra and Nehemiah we see the struggle for the restored nation to maintain its separate identity as the people of God. It is vital to watch the first steps of falling in love: there are obviously certain barriers that a Christian should not begin to cross. Experience shows that, almost invariably, the non-Christian drags the Christian down to lower standards. This was the type of situation that distressed Ezra and others (1-6). The longer the marriages went unrebuked, the more families would become involved.

Ezra's physical reactions would be strange to us (3) but would be well understood in his day (cf. Ezek. **7.**18). When the priests and people gathered for the evening sacrifice, they found, not just a formal service, but Ezra pouring out his heart to God.

Ezra's prayer of confession (6-15) ranks with those of Nehemiah (**1.**5-11) and Daniel (**9.**4-19). It is worth analysing to see some of its elements. Thus it contains (*a*) Confession (6,7,10,13). (*b*) Remembrance of God's hand upon the nation in the past (7). This is very evident from our reading of Bible history in our quiet times. (*c*) Grateful remembrance of recent restoration (8,9). Thankfulness has its place in prayer. (*d*) Remembrance of the promises and warnings of God (8,11,12). This involves self-examination. (*e*) The implied desire to put things right, since the prayer would otherwise be empty (14).

Ezra himself was not guilty, but identified himself with the nation, and accepted responsibility as a member of the One people of God.

In v. 9 the margin shows that the Hebrew refers to 'a wall'. This may be interpreted metaphorically, as in RSV, or may refer to the attempt to rebuild the wall in 4.12. (See notes.)

Why should a Christian not contemplate marriage with a non-Christian? (cf. 1 Cor. 7.39; 2 Cor. 6.14). *If both partners are non-Christians, and one is converted, what should be done then?* (see 1 Cor. 7.12–16; 1 Pet. 3.1,2).

Ezra 10   Practical Repentance

Ezra evidently prayed in a voice loud enough to be heard by the people who had gathered for the evening service. Undoubtedly, reports had also been spreading through the city and suburbs all day that the matter of mixed marriages had been reported to Ezra, and that action might be expected. So at the end of the prayer there was a large crowd around Ezra, and, since the problem was one of family life, the record calls attention to the presence of children (1).

The spirit of the crowd was on Ezra's side, and one man acted as spokesman. In spite of their sin, all was not lost. He had faith in the mercy of God (2). But this could only be in response to human action (3,4).

The necessary reforms were done by stages. One cannot always hurry matters that affect people so deeply, even though they are in a minority. First, Ezra retires to the room in the Temple precincts occupied by a son of Eliashib, who may not yet have been high priest (Neh. 3.1). He spent the night fasting (6), and presumably agreed with the leaders in the morning on the terms of the proclamation that should be made, not only in the city, but in all the country round about (7). Actually at this time there were not many houses in the city itself (Neh. 7.4). A date for a national council was fixed for three days later, when all would be involved in the decision (8).

Unfortunately it was a day of heavy rain, and not much could be done, but Ezra again urged the importance of action (10,11). The people saw two things; that the matter was too serious to be settled there and then, and that the local authorities were their proper representatives to deal with individual cases, since they would have personal knowledge of the people involved. The authorities must be responsible for bringing the guilty partners to Jerusalem on some agreed date (12–14). There were four dissentients (15), though they are not listed among the guilty at the end of the chapter.

The guilty were found in a cross-section of the nation, and included priests, Levites, and Temple servants. A call to full-time service of this kind does not render anyone immune to temptation.

We do not know what provision would have been made for the wives and children (44) but presumably the husbands would have been required to make some provision for them. Whether they wished it, or not, they were members of a minority race, and the pagan fathers of the divorced wives would not have allowed their former husbands to escape scot-free.

2 Cor. 7.7–12 *is a general New Testament parallel of a church dealing with some scandal.*

Questions for further study and discussion on Ezra

1. What does this Book indicate about possible working relationships between God's people and secular authorities?
2. What does this Book indicate about problems of relationship between God's people and men of goodwill whose outlook is essentially pagan?
3. What reasons might Jews in Babylon have given for not returning to Judah when they had the opportunity? Consider their relation to Christian service.
4. How far is the average member of the (Christian) community dependent on constant leadership to goad him to action?
5. Was Ezra justified in refusing an escort (8.22)? Why?

NEHEMIAH

Nehemiah 1   Prayer Before Action

Introduction. The Book of Nehemiah is compiled from documents and chronicles, and from personal memoirs of Nehemiah himself in the first person singular. Ezra himself could have been the writer and compiler of the bulk of the Book. Between the end of Ezra and the beginning of Nehemiah we must probably fit the events of Ezra 4.7–23 which ended with the destruction of the rising walls and other buildings.

Ezra was the scholarly man of the Law, but at this moment there was need for a vital man of action. God had prepared Nehemiah for this. He held the important post of cupbearer to Artaxerxes I in 445 B.C., about 13 years after Ezra had gone to Jerusalem. Hanani, his brother (2, cf. **7.**2), brings him news of the fresh disasters at Jerusalem (3). It is less likely that the reference is to the original destruction in 586 B.C.

Nehemiah's immediate response was prayer, and this prayer (4–11) may be compared with that of Ezra in ch. **9.** An analysis of the prayer shows the following: (*a*) Self-reminder of the personal God to whom he is coming (5,6). Prayer is not just talking into the air. (*b*) Confession of sin (6,7). Like Ezra, Nehemiah identifies himself with the nation as a whole. (*c*) Reminder of the warnings and promises of God (8,9). Nehemiah has in mind such passages as Lev. **26.**33–45 and Deut. **30.**1–5. (*d*) Pleading the covenant of God and His redemption of the people (10). (*e*) Specific request for strength and success in the next step to be taken (11).

Nehemiah knew that the answer to his prayer must partly come through him. Oriental kings were particularly fickle, and, although his position as cupbearer meant that he was a favourite of the king, he would have to ask the king to reverse the decision that he had made in Ezra **4.**21. But the end of this verse shows that the king had left the way open if he wished to rescind his decree.

Prayer changes things, and also strengthens us (cf. Acts **4.**31).

Nehemiah 2   A Sacrificial Project

In this Book we shall see several examples of Nehemiah as a man of prayer. The prayer recorded in ch. **1** is only a brief summary of what he was praying continually for a number of days (**1.**4). In fact he received the news in the ninth month (Chislev, **1.**1), and the crisis did not come until the first month (Nisan, **2.**1). We do not know by what method of reckoning this could still be the twentieth year of Artaxerxes (**1.**1), but systems of calendar reckonings were complicated. Some commentators emend **1.**1 to 'nineteenth'.

Now, after days of prayer, Nehemiah sends up what has been called an arrow prayer to God (4; but would the arrow have been effective without the longer period of prayer?). His prayer is answered, but for Nehemiah it involved being uprooted from a pleasant and lucrative post in the centre of civilization and culture at the Persian capital, and undertaking a long journey to be governor (**5.**14) of a depressed group of people struggling to establish themselves in a hostile environment.

Nehemiah was a practical man, and obtained as many concessions from the king as he might reasonably need (7,8). In the hostile situation which then existed—a situation rather different from that which Ezra faced when travelling to Jerusalem—he accepted an escort to prevent his being quietly ambushed on the way (9, cf. Ezra **8.22**).

Sanballat is named as a chief opponent (10). Later documents show that he was governor of Samaria, and no doubt he had hoped to be given Judah as well. Tobiah is thought to have been governor of Ammon. Perhaps 'servant' (10) means he had once been a slave. Geshem was the influential governor of Arabia.

Nehemiah carefully surveyed the extent of the damage before announcing his plan to rebuild (11–16). His route was from the S.W. gate eastwards, following the ruined walls. At the N.E. corner he turned west ('turned back' v. 15) and continued until he once more reached the S.W. gate. At one point he had to dismount and lead his donkey, or mule, over the rubble. His intention to rebuild was met with the insinuation that he wanted to rebel against the king of Persia (17–20, cf. Ezra **4.13,15**).

Diffidence and confidence may both be marks of the man of God (cf. Isa. **40.29–31**).

Nehemiah 3.1–4.23　　　　　　　　Threats to the Work

For devotional reading it is probably sufficient to note that ch. 3 covers the circuit of the walls in order, starting at the N.E., and then moving westward round the city. Each section was allocated to different groups, and some of these were quick enough to do a second stint (e.g. vs. 4,21 and 5,27). There was evidently whole-hearted determination to finish the work, and no suggestion of 'I've done my duty; why should I do any more?' There were, however, a few exceptions (5).

Ezra is not named as an overseer, but possibly worked with Eliashib, the high priest (1). He was a priest himself (**8.2**). Meremoth (4) is also mentioned in Ezra **8.33**. Malchijah (11) is an example of a restored wrongdoer, since he is one of the guilty in Ezra **10.31** (cf. 1 Cor. **6.9–11**). Some of the builders came from outside the official boundaries of Judah (7).

With ch. 4 the opposition begins in earnest with the weapon of mockery and sarcasm. Workers who have refused to join an unofficial strike know the demoralizing effect of this sort of thing. We can be quite sure that the two governors of neighbouring provinces would bring plenty of followers, and v. 2 refers to them as an army. We may not like the tone of Nehemiah's prayer (4,5), but God was being publicly challenged (5), and Nehemiah was calling upon Him to demonstrate who was Lord.

As soon as the wall was up to a respectable height, it was possible to keep the enemies outside. Jeering was insufficient, and more drastic plans were made for attack (6–8). The response was prayer and practical action (9). But the pressure of work was telling on one set of workers (10), and the enemy discouraged others by starting a rumour that at any moment they might launch an attack. It was easy to spread this through the builders who lived near them and came in to work daily (11,12).

Although Nehemiah had authority from the king, an incident could easily be engineered in a remote part of the empire. So he treated the threat seriously by arming all the builders (13), and then keeping half of them permanently on guard (16–20). It was better to deplete the labour force by half than to lose the whole through panic or sudden attack. As many as possible remained all night in the city, householders with their servants (22).

Consider how a sense of inferiority can handicap our Christian activity (cf. 1 Cor. 1.26–29).

Nehemiah 5   Profit and Loss

We should hardly have anticipated the situation of this chapter. Surely all the nation, rich and poor, would have been united to press on with the building of the wall (though cf. 3.5). But human nature is constantly hindering the work of God. The wealthier members of the returned community were not deliberately cheating and oppressing their poorer brethren, as in Isa. 5, but they had not thought out the consequences of standing for what they believed to be their rights. They were loaning money to the poor, and taking interest and security in the form of money, property, and even children (1–5).

The Bible does not regard the taking of interest as wrong in itself (cf. Deut. 23.19,20; Matt. 25.27), but an Israelite was not allowed to take it from a fellow-Israelite (Exod. 22. 25). Whether this rule was ever set aside where money was borrowed for trading at a profit, we do not know: but in the present chapter the money was borrowed because of dire distress in famine conditions (3). So far as slavery was concerned, the release of slaves was ordered every seven years (Exod. 21.2–6).

The plea of the poor was that, as human beings, they and their children were one with the rich (5). Nehemiah supports them (6,7), and reminds the rich that national policy had been to buy back Jewish slaves from the surrounding peoples and set them free (8). It is not certain from v. 10 whether Nehemiah and his servants had or had not asked interest on what they had lent. He does not ask the lenders to remit the capital debt, but to return the mortgaged property from which they would be deriving interest (11). There is a public ceremony with an impressive piece of symbolism (12,13).

Because of the reference to the long period of time in v. 14, it has been supposed that the events of this chapter belong to a later period in the life of Nehemiah. But this comment could have been added by Nehemiah when he put his memoirs together, and v. 16 suggests that the incident came during the building of the wall. The point is that neither then nor subsequently did Nehemiah tax the people to find his legitimate salary. He must have been a wealthy man without greed, and one can appreciate all the more the personal sacrifice involved in leaving his source of income at the Persian court and coming to impoverished Judah.

What relevance has this chapter for interest-free loans for some Christian project?

Nehemiah 6 Stratagems

The opposition faces defeat. Neither sarcasm, show of force, threats, nor internal discontent, has stopped the building. The only hope now is to eliminate Nehemiah himself. Granted that here we have only Nehemiah's own interpretation of the enemy's intention, it is likely that it is correct. If Nehemiah could be enticed out to a conference, it would be easy to arrange an incident in which he could be killed or kidnapped. Nehemiah refuses four times to meet in one of the villages twenty miles north of Jerusalem, on the ground that he cannot interrupt the work he has in hand (1–4). There is a time for work and a time for conferences.

So Sanballat tries to force his hand by sending a note on a slip of papyrus, leather, or potsherd, so that interested bystanders could have a look at it (5). The note stated categorically that Nehemiah wanted to be king and lead a rebellion against Persia (6). The effect of such a letter would be to frighten the cautious and put ideas into the minds of the hotheaded. Moreover, Nehemiah is accused of bribing prophets to speak for him in the name of the Lord (7). He can do no more than flatly deny the charge and again commend the affair to God (8,9).

The next scheme was to make Nehemiah appear a coward. A certain Shemaiah, making a great show of being unable to leave his house in case he was killed for passing on the information, urged Nehemiah to take refuge with him at night in the Temple to escape assassination. Again Nehemiah saw through the trick, and refused to go into the Temple, not being a priest. Tobiah and Sanballat had bribed Shemaiah, and probably also several prophets and prophetesses, to foretell Nehemiah's approaching doom (10–14).

The completion of the wall in the amazing time of 52 days (15,16) was probably possible under God because much of the material was still to hand after the recent destruction. But though the wall could keep the enemy out, they could still infiltrate by way of traitors within. Both through his wife and daughter-in-law Tobiah had links with influential families in Jerusalem (for Meshullam, cf. 3.4,30). Before we sympathize with Tobiah and his friends, we should notice that the more the favour that was shown to him, the greater the neglect of the Temple and the priests (13.7,10).

Consider Nehemiah's wisdom, perseverance, and humility.

Nehemiah 7.1–8.18 Reading the Law

There are three sections in this portion. (*i*) 7.1–4. Although the walls are finished, they must be guarded. Nehemiah is realistic in his assessment of character (2). From v. 1 it seems as though Temple officials were used to guard the gates, since they would not be working in the fields like the rest of the people, and there was no standing army.

(*ii*) 7.5–73a. The genealogy is virtually the same as in Ezra 2. V. 5 explains its insertion here. Nehemiah checks the list of those who returned, so as to be sure that the settled inhabitants are of pure race. The story from v. 5 is taken up again in 11.1.

(*iii*) 7.73b–8.18. A few days after the completion of the walls on the 25th of the sixth month (6.15), the people assemble to dedicate themselves to God. Ezra now appears again as the chief expositor of the Law, although other Levites are linked with him in this (7, cf. Deut. 31.9–13). The seventh month included the Day of Atonement on the 10th, and the Feast of Tabernacles beginning on the 15th. This month had been chosen previously for setting up the altar (Ezra 3.1). Now it is chosen for reading and expounding the Law (1). Probably the only copies were in the hands of the Levites, and the people were instructed orally. Many passages would be repeated so that the hearers might learn them by heart.

Emphasis must have been laid on sections of warning, for the people were sufficiently convicted to weep (9). Nehemiah and Ezra knew that weeping would be appropriate on the Day of Atonement, but the first day of the seventh month was a special day (Lev. 23.23–25), and they wanted rejoicing and thanksgiving for the completion of the wall (10–12).

Next day Ezra announces to the leaders that the Feast of Tabernacles would be in a fortnight's time, and, when the day came the people were ready with their booths of branches in memory of the safe conduct through the wilderness before they had houses in the land (Lev. 23.43).

In v. 17 the word 'so' is significant, and indicates that the feast had not been kept with such enthusiasm since the entry into the land, although it had been kept (cf. Ezra 3.4).

What are the results of hearing the Word of God? Cf. 2 Tim. 3.16,17.)

Nehemiah 9

It was probably fairly common for the people of God to recall their history (e.g. Deut. 26.5–9; Josh. 24.1–13). Sometimes their minds dwelt on God's blessings and promises, as in vs. 6–15 here and in Psa. 105. Sometimes they told the story in sorrow for their rebellion and sin, as in vs. 16 onwards here and in Psa. 106. This remembrance, confession, and rededication followed immediately after the Feast of Tabernacles. The people were concerned that they had been chosen for God's special purposes, and they stood before Him now as a separated people (2). Again they read from the Law (3, cf. 8.3,13,18), since this was the revelation that God had given. They confess their sins, and worship and praise God (3–5).

Ezra leads them in a full prayer. He fixes their minds on God as Creator (6), who made the covenant with Abraham and his descendants (7,8). The Exodus (9–12) was preparatory to the Law on Sinai (13,14). Yet the people had rejected God's orders, even to the extent of trying to return to Egypt (16,17, cf. Num. 14.4). God forgave even rebellion and idolatry (18,19), and continued to teach through His Spirit in Moses and others (20, cf. Num. 11.16,17; Isa. 63.10,11). Finally He brought them into the promised land with all its plenty (21–25).

The prayer now plunges into darkness, but Ezra and his people are determined to face the full facts. The nation had been chosen to be the people of God, and this involved lives that demonstrated the character of God. We note the place that is given to the Law as stating the standards of God (26,29), and also to the prophets, who not only received fresh revelations from God, but who were preachers who tried to recall the people to God's original revelation (26, 30).

The prayer also shows God's forgiveness. This does not come automatically, but is in response to a cry for mercy, which must involve repentance such as Ezra and the people were ready to show now (27,38). One thing that binds the generations together is the covenant (8,32), initiated by God Himself. But once it has been made, it establishes a permanent relationship, which it is wise for man to reassert and reaffirm from time to time, since, while God abides faithful, man is fickle and forgetful. So the nation reaffirms the covenant (38).

The Church also is within the covenant (e.g. Matt. **26.**28; Heb. **12.**24). *What does this involve?*

Nehemiah 10.1–11.36 Pledges

Nehemiah, the governor, takes the lead in setting his seal to the covenant, and various religious and civic leaders follow (1–27). The rest of the people apparently assent verbally, and bind themselves with a solemn oath (28, 29). Several things are mentioned. Mixed marriages had been a problem in the past (e.g. Ezra **9**), and would be again (30, cf. **13.**23–27). The Sabbath must be properly observed (31). Trading on the Sabbath would obviously involve work, and was banned from the beginning (Amos **8.**5). Letting the land lie fallow in the seventh year is the law of Exod. **23.**10,11, and the remission of debts is in Deut. **15.**1,2 (31).

The remainder of ch. **10** makes provision for the worship of God in the Temple, and involves both people and material. Both require money or gifts in kind. The tax for the Tabernacle, which was not an annual one, had been half a shekel per head (Exod. **30.**13), and this amount was the annual tax for the Temple later (Matt. **17.**24). But at this time, perhaps in view of general poverty, a lesser amount was judged to be adequate (32, cf. 2 Cor. **8.**12). The wood offering (34) is not specified in the Law, but was clearly necessary. Financial support is accepted for those who minister in the Temple (35–39).

The lists in **11.**3–19 resemble those in 1 Chron. **9.**2–17. The names seem to be those who were already living in Jerusalem, where not much rebuilding had been done hitherto because of the lack of security while the walls were ruined (cf. **7.**4). The list includes laymen (3–9), priests (10–14), Levites (15–18), and gatekeepers (19). Some general notes follow about the people in general and the priests, Levites, and Temple servants in particular (20–23). The king of Persia had his own representative (24), but we cannot tell how he stood in relation to Nehemiah.

Finally, there is a list of occupied villages in the former tribal

403

territory of Judah and Benjamin (25–36). The area delineated in v. 30 represents the southern point of the original territory up to the northern border of Judah. The word 'encamped' implies that they would be ready to move if the territory were extended. V. 36 perhaps means that some Levite families formerly attached to Judah now lived in Benjamite territory.

What practical work in our church might resemble that of 10.34? When did we last do something towards the wood offering?

Nehemiah 12.1–13.3 Final Ceremony

A fresh list begins in 12.1. This gives the names of priests and Levites who returned with Zerubbabel and Joshua (1–9), and supplements Ezra 2.36–40. V. 9 refers either to antiphonal singing or to alternate spells of service. A second list (10,11) gives the line of high priests from Joshua, and runs down to Jaddua, who, we know from the Jewish historian, Josephus, was high priest when Alexander the Great invaded Persia (333 B.C.). This does not mean that the Book of Nehemiah was written as late as this, for a copyist might add an extra name or two to keep the list up to date. Jonathan (11) and Johanan (22) are equivalent names.

Next comes a list of priests in the time of Joiakim (12–21), and Levites from the time of Eliashib onwards until Darius III (22–26). The chronicles in v. 23 are Temple records. V. 24 refers to 1 Chron. 16.4–6.

After this we take up the narrative again. First the walls had been finished, then the Law had been read and the covenant reaffirmed, and now the walls are dedicated. All the Levites and Temple singers are brought in from the surrounding villages (27–29), and people and walls are purified, perhaps by sprinkling the blood of sacrifice upon them (30).

Then two great processions move off, probably from the same S.W. gate as that by which Nehemiah had gone out not so long before to pick his way over the rubble (2.13–15). Ezra led one procession counter-clockwise (31–37), and Nehemiah accompanied the other clockwise (38,39). For much of the way the processions were on top of the walls, but eventually they came together in the Temple courts (40), where they offered sacrifices and praised God (41–43).

This ceremony was once and for all, but the Temple worship had to continue daily. So the people appointed overseers for the supplies for the ministers in the Temple (44–46). V. 47 means that the people paid tithes and dues to the singers and gatekeepers; after taking their share they passed the balance to the Levites, who did the same for the priests.

Consider the stages of ruin, repair, completion, dedication, joy (cf. 1 Pet. **1.6–9**).

Nehemiah 13 Sad Ending

Vs. 1–3 belong to the time of the previous chapter. The reference is to Deut. **23.3–5**, which barred Ammonites and Moabites from the rights and privileges of Israel.

Note, Tobiah was an Ammonite, which probably accounts for the record immediately continuing with the story of Tobiah's room in the Temple.

'Before this' (4) clearly does not mean before the incident of vs. 1–3, but to something shortly before Nehemiah's return after absence in Persia. We must read it as though it stands for, 'Before this record of my return . . .'

Eliashib the high priest was allied with Tobiah (4), perhaps by marriage as he was with Sanballat (28). The room was no doubt for Tobiah's use when he visited Jerusalem. Nehemiah had evidently been away for some considerable time, and other abuses had crept in. The people had ceased to bring the tithes and offerings (cf. Mal. **3.8–12**, which perhaps belongs to this period). The offerings, though for the support of the ministers, were also offerings to God. What had been pledged in the solemn covenant (**10.35–39**) had been forgotten, and the Levites had dispersed to work on the land (10–13).

Sabbath trading, banned under the covenant (**10.30,31**), was in full swing both with Jews and with pagans (15,16), though some may not actually have sold their goods on the Sabbath, but brought them in to have them ready for sale next day. Nehemiah allowed no evasion (17–22).

Finally, the evil of mixed marriages had broken out again (cf. Mal. **2.11–16**). They had been dealt with by Ezra over twenty-five years before. Children were growing up unable to speak Hebrew and thus to understand the Scriptures (23,24). In his exasperation Nehemiah dealt violently with the offenders, and faced them with the verdict of history. Even the grandson of the high priest was involved (28).

It seems a sad end to Nehemiah's devoted life, but it cannot all have been in vain. A faithful nucleus remained, and, like God, remembered Nehemiah for good (30,31).

Compare Paul's summary at the end of his life (2 Tim. **4.3–18**).

1. What do we know of Nehemiah's prayers?
2. Consider Nehemiah as a man of practical faith.
3. What can we learn from this Book about opposition to God's work from outside?
4. And from within?
5. What place is given here to the written Word of God?

ESTHER

*Esther 1   Fuddled Minds

Introduction. The authorship of this Book is unknown, but it may have formed part of the records of Persia that are referred to in 6.1 and 10.2. This is only a hypothesis, but it would account for the total omission of the name of God. King Ahasuerus is generally identified with Xerxes (486–465 B.C.) whose reign comes immediately before that of Artaxerxes I, of whom we read in Ezra and Nehemiah. There is a possibility that he is Artaxerxes II (404–359 B.C.). Secular records do not throw much light on the domestic life of Xerxes.

In this chapter the king gave a succession of banquets to the dignitaries of his empire (2–4), and then to the people of the capital (5). Drink flowed lavishly, though none was compelled to get drunk (7,8). Men and women were entertained separately (9). On the last day, when even the king was fuddled, he demanded that his chief wife, Vashti (who may be queen Amestris, mentioned by Herodotus), should come and show off her beauty as just one more proud possession of the king (10,11). Vashti reasonably refused (12).

The scene that followed bears all the marks of drunken stupidity, with the childish lower levels of the mind taking over. The king is peevish (12–15), the wise men are touchy at the affront to their dignity (16), and are afraid that their wives will despise them (17, 18), as well they might! They themselves despise a woman who had behaved decently, and propose that she should cease to be queen (19). It is a sad picture of the degradation of man. Yet drink does not create the evils in us; it releases what is there, and we as Christians share in the same selfishness, touchiness, and peevishness, that are in all men, and that may be released by other things besides drink.

There follows the farce of a royal decree to announce solemnly what no oriental ever doubted, that every man should be master in his own house, and should expect foreign wives and servants to understand the master's native tongue, i.e. they could not plead lack of understanding if they failed to obey him.

Since man was made to be a rational being, anything that depresses his reason must be wrong. Compare the extravagance, drink, and suggestiveness here with Phil. 3.17–21 and 4.8.

*Esther 2

Although ch. 2 appears to run on from ch. 1, there is a gap of some three years between them (1.3; 2.16). This period included Xerxes' campaign against Greece, in which he was heavily defeated at Salamis (480 B.C.). Greek records show that Amestris (Vashti?) accompanied him, but on the way home she cruelly mutilated one of the king's mistresses. No doubt this prompted him to look at once for a new queen (1–4).

We now meet Esther and her cousin Mordecai (5–7). The story suggests that Mordecai was not an obscure Jew, and he may be the Marduka who appears on Persian inscriptions as a high official some years before. Obviously he was temporarily out of favour, but he still has influence at court, and Haman hesitates to put him to death on the spot, as he certainly would have done with an ordinary civilian (3.1–6). His great-grandfather, Kish, had gone into exile with king Jehoiachin in 597 B.C. (5,6).

Hadassah (7) is a Jewish name, meaning Myrtle, and Esther is probably from a Persian word for Star. She may have had both names, or her Persian friends may have turned the Jewish name into a name that sounded right to them. Similarly, English children might have turned the name Hadassah into Dusty.

Although the name of God is not found in the Book, the hand of God is certainly seen, and Esther finds herself called to tread the path that, unknown to her, would lead to the salvation of many of her people (8–18).

Why did Mordecai conceal the fact that he and Esther were Jews (10,20)? Possibly as a minority group the Jews were not popular, and he might have endangered such influence as he had as a hanger-on at court (11,19).

In spite of his reticence he becomes the second link in God's purposes, and happens to be on the spot when there is a plot to kill the king; he passes on the information through Esther (19–23).

On what other occasions did God have a man or woman in some position ready to help His people in a crisis? E.g. Gen. 45.7.

Eastern kings were notoriously fickle. They had their favourites in key positions, as Artaxerxes had Nehemiah as cupbearer (Neh. 1 and 2), and Nebuchadnezzar had Daniel (Dan. 2.48). But a favourite could easily be toppled from his position. Now suddenly the king promotes Haman as Grand Vizier, the type of official confidant whom we meet in the Arabian Nights. As an Agagite (1), he was perhaps descended from king Agag, whom Saul spared (1 Sam. 15). His ancestor was one of those who escaped death on that occasion.

At last Mordecai finds the courage to declare himself a Jew (4). We cannot say why he refused to pay Haman the traditional oriental respect (2), but it could be that Haman, with his grandiose ideas, was claiming some sort of divine honours. Or perhaps as a Jew Mordecai would not acknowledge an Amalekite. Haman's reactions suggest the same sort of mental imbalance as affected Hitler. He will not be revenged on Mordecai alone, but on the whole Jewish race (5,6).

He is also profoundly superstitious. If he is to embark on a massacre, he must have a lucky day for it, and he employs experts to cast lots, working through the months and days until the lot came out for the 12th month (7), and presumably the 13th day, though this is only implied (13). Haman would have to curb his impatience for nearly a year (7), but this gave time for his preparations.

These began with the accusation that has often been employed against Jews and Christians; they are different, awkward, and lawbreakers (8). The charge was backed by a substantial bribe (9). Haman does not have to pay this immediately, but presumably he calculates that he will more than cover it by his confiscations of Jewish property. The king's refusal to take the money (11) is merely oriental courtesy (cf. 7.4).

So Haman has a free hand, and the royal office is filled with translators and secretaries writing out enough decrees for the whole empire (12). It was to be total massacre of the Jews, including presumably those in Palestine. The king and Haman had a drink on it (15), but the average man, who often sees the truth, was worried. The Jews this year; who next year?

Do not be too surprised when letters to the press show astounding ignorance of what Christians really stand for (cf. 1 Pet. 3.14–17; 4.14–16).

Esther 4 and 5 Resistance

What a study this Book is in human reactions! We know the end of the story, so it is not easy to get the feel of the situation as it was. Humanly speaking, it was impossible for Mordecai and his people to escape the massacre, unless some miracle happened in the intervening period, for the king's decree could not be changed (**8.8**, cf. Dan. **6.8**). However, Mordecai and the Jews accepted the possibility of a miracle, and their fasting would naturally include prayer (3,16). Groping for some indication of the hand of God, Mordecai remembered Esther and her position with the king (14).

But would Esther realize her responsibility, since the matter could not be left passively to God? She might well have reminded Mordecai that up till now he had insisted on her concealing her Jewish ancestry (**2.20**). Now he blackmails her with the threat that she would die too as a Jew (13). We are not required to condone Mordecai's conduct simply because he is in the Bible and on the side of the Jews.

In the seclusion of the women's quarters Esther is taken by surprise at the news which had shaken the city (8). But she rises to the occasion, and agrees to risk her life in the face of court procedure, which was not so simple as Mordecai imagined (11–16).

With ch. **5** Esther has found the germ of a plan. It must have come to her during the three days of prayer. The account that follows is true to life. Esther is intensely nervous, and in a sense is feeling her way. So, when the king receives her kindly, she cannot say what she wants, but postpones the crisis until the banquet next day (1–5). There again her courage fails, and she invites the king and Haman to yet another banquet (6–8).

The double invitation went to Haman's head. No doubt in view of the strained relations between him and Mordecai, Esther had hitherto treated him coldly. Now he is delighted to find that he has made a conquest (12). One thing came between him and his cup of bliss. Mordecai sat sullenly by the gate and would not salute him. His wife had the solution, and, before he even considered going to bed, he ordered gallows to be erected, so that he could hang Mordecai in the morning (14,15).

Prov. **16.12–20**.

Esther 6 and 7 Divine Coincidence

One of the awe-inspiring experiences of life is to be able to trace the hand of God in seemingly natural events, which become coincidences of God's plan. Certainly ch. 6 is a thrilling account of God's timing of events.

The king on that critical night was suffering from insomnia, and the record suggests that this was unusual (1). For bedtime reading he chose the annals of his reign, which would contain frequent and soothing references to his great deeds. The reader chose the passage containing the abortive plot, and the king was sufficiently awake to enquire about a reward for Mordecai.

The king was not the only one who could not sleep, and by divine coincidence Haman was at the door to ask for Mordecai's execution if the king was still awake. In his exalted state of mind, he naturally took the king's question in the wrong way (6), and was overwhelmed to find himself parading Mordecai in triumph through the streets (10, 11). Presumably this parade did not happen until the morning, and, when Haman returned home, his superstitious wife and friends regarded it as a bad omen that his campaign against the Jews had started so disastrously (13). At this moment of deep depression, the escort arrived to take him to the palace (14).

In ch. 7 Esther speaks at last. She confesses that she is a Jewess, and begs for the life of herself and her people. She knows the terms of the transaction, and the loss in money which the king would sustain if he went back on Haman's plan with its accompanying bribe (4, cf. 3.9); but it is not even a question of slavery; it is life or death (4).

The king at first does not realize what Esther is referring to, but he is wholly on her side when she denounces Haman (5,6). His interpretation of the situation in v. 8 may be due to a look of triumph that he had previously seen on Haman's face.

They covered Haman's face as a condemned criminal (8), and hanged him on the gallows that he had prepared for Mordecai (9,10). Cruelty breeds cruelty, and Haman reaped what he had sown. The king was pacified (10). He had lost one favourite, but could soon find another.

Matt. 7.1,2.

Esther 8 The Way Out

The new favourite was at hand. Mordecai had once saved the king's life, and the king had recently seen fit to reward him. He was Esther's cousin, and she had given the king the pleasant feeling of being a benefactor and saving a large number of his subjects, though it was true that he had first been willing to have them killed. So he handed Mordecai the signet ring that he had once given to Haman, and appointed him vizier in Haman's place. Esther had received Haman's property as a reward (1), and, since she was confined to the palace, she handed it over to Mordecai (2).

Although Mordecai had the signet ring, he could not make a major policy decision without the royal permission. It was felt that Esther again was the most likely person to obtain this (3–6). The problem was how to evade the original decree, since legally it could not be reversed. Mordecai found the solution, and, once the king had given permission in principle, he set the translators to work on a fresh set of decrees. There were still nearly nine months to go before the massacre, but the empire was extensive, and every place that had received the original decree must have the new one (9), so that it could be read aloud to the people (13).

The evasion of the original decree was ingenious. The king gave every encouragement to the Jews to defend themselves on the day of the massacre (11,13). This would naturally deter the local authorities from enforcing the original decree. If the king was on the side of the Jews, he would show small mercy to anyone who was known to have attacked them.

The change of vizier was popular in the capital (15). It remained to be seen whether Mordecai would be a better man for the post. Meanwhile, where a few days earlier it had been dangerous to be recognized as a Jew, it now became attractive (16). Throughout the empire there were a number of converts (17). This need not only have been through fear of possible consequences. The fear (17) includes the sense of awe that recent events had engendered. The God of the Jews was the living God.

1 Pet. 2.12.

Esther 9 and 10   Vengeance

Much of ch. 9 leaves an unpleasant taste behind it, and there is nothing in Scripture which would incline us to support the Jews in the wholesale massacre of their enemies. While they killed some in self-defence (2), other verses suggest the slaughter of any whom they regarded as their enemies (5–10). Certainly the extra massacre in Susa on the following day (13,15) was wholly unwarranted, since Haman's original decree had specified one day only for the massacre of the Jews. Unfortunately mass excitement brings out the worst elements in human nature. Many of the citizens of Susa must have wished that Haman was back in place of Mordecai, who, being the chief man in Susa, must bear considerable responsibility for the extra massacres. He was popular with the Jews (10.3), but it is not said that he was popular with the people in general. A good point is that the Jews did not loot (10,15). The Bible reports the facts, and leaves us to form our own moral judgement in the light of total Scripture, and the judgement of these notes is not infallible!

When the excitement has died down, Mordecai institutes the Feast of Purim (20–28), still observed by the Jews, who then read Esther aloud, and boo every mention of Haman. The feast is named after the word for 'lot' (26, cf. **3**.7). *Pur* (plural *Purim*) probably means a stone, or pebble, specially shaped for casting lots.

Esther and Mordecai now send out a more pleasant communication to all Jews about the proper celebration of the festival (29–31), and presumably the writing (32) included the story of its origin. A version may have gone into the royal records.

Finally Mordecai is seen in a position of great honour. The date is about 473 B.C. (**3**.7). We do not know how long he held office.

Psalm **18**.16–19.

Questions for further study and discussion on Esther

1. 'In this Book we see men and women at their worst and at their best.' Give examples. Are we called upon to make moral judgements on Bible characters?
2. Although the name of God is not mentioned in this Book, what indications are there of the hand of God at work?
3. What place has this Book in the total revelation of the Bible?
4. Is it wise to look for type pictures of Christ or the Church in this Book? If so, is Mordecai in any way a picture of Christ, or Esther of the Church?
5. How would you compare Mordecai's life with the lives of other Hebrews in foreign lands, e.g. Joseph, Moses, Daniel, Nehemiah?

JOB

INTRODUCTION

Apart from being inspired Scripture, this Book is one of the literary masterpieces of the world. It is well worth reading aloud, especially in the RSV. When the AV translation of Job was made, the meaning of certain unusual words and phrases was uncertain, and the RV and RSV have the advantage of further discoveries.

The author is unknown, as is the date when the Book was written. But the Book contains in verse the record of an argument between

Job and his friends in, probably, patriarchal times. Early Egyptian and Babylonian literature show that from at least 2000 B.C., people were concerned with the problem of evil.

The theme of Job is not simply the problem of evil. The key verses are **1**.9–11 and **2.4,5**, where Satan maintains that a man serves God only for His gifts. If these are withdrawn and suffering comes, he will turn from God. Keep this in mind as you read, and notice how Job continually casts himself upon God as his only hope, even though his pain drives him to violent words that he later regrets. It is for this steadfastness that he is commended in Jas. **5.11**.

Job 1 Challenge to God

The scene is Edom, the chief character is one of the notable righteous men of Scripture (Ezek. **14**. 14), who worshipped the true God, and who, like the patriarchs, acted as priest for his household (5). The next scene, in heaven, must have been revealed to the author by God Himself, since we are nowhere told that Job himself ever knew of it. The picture of Satan in the Bible is consistent, and is too strange to have been invented, since, although evil, he has access to God with the angelic sons of God (Rev. **12.10**), obtains permission from God to test God's people (Luke **22.31,32**), and inflicts suffering on them (1 Pet. **5.8**).

In the first test he is allowed to manipulate people and things so that almost simultaneously Job loses his possessions and his children. Most of us have experienced a succession of major or minor disasters. Because he could do nothing to prevent or remedy them, Job commends himself to God in the faith that somewhere there is a hidden blessing that he could not as yet understand.

The one experience may be a permitted temptation from Satan to break us and also a testing from God to make us (e.g. 2 Sam. **24.1**; 1 Chron. **21.1**; Luke **22**. 31,32).

Job 2 and 3 The Outcast

The angelic sons of God are God's messengers on earth, and in Zech. **1.11** they, like Satan here, go through the earth. Notice that Satan is not a neutral being, but is actively against God and righteousness (3). He makes the profound observation that many a person can sacrifice even his nearest and dearest, but his faith will collapse when he has to bear physical suffering himself (4,5). God allows the test, but again sets a limit (6, cf. **1.12**).

Job's affliction may have been elephantiasis. It drove him from the village to the ashpit as a loathsome object. His wife now became Satan's agent, as Peter later was for Jesus Christ (Matt. **16**. 22,23). Beware of this when you give and seek advice. The advice to Job is to renounce his faith and let God kill him, presumably in the hope that the unknown future would be better than the agony of the present. Remember that the nature of the future life had not yet been revealed. Job's answer now is magnificent (10).

His three comforters proved to be an additional trial. Eliphaz came from Teman, in Edom (Amos **1**.12). The name is Edomite (cf. Gen. **36**.4), and Edom was noted for wisdom (Jer. **49**.7). Bildad may be a descendant of Shuah (Gen. **25**.2). Zophar may come from the place of Naamah of Josh. **15**.41; but we cannot be certain of the meaning of Shuhite and Naamathite.

In ch. 3 Job cries in anguish, but he does not curse God. Like Jeremiah (**20**.14–18) he curses the fact of his birth. *Oh that I had never been born!* (3–10). Job calls on those who professed to pronounce effective curses. Leviathan (8) may be a mythical monster, or Satan himself (Isa. **27**.1), or the crocodile, as later in Job **41**. In the last case, the phrase in v. 8 would be comparable to our 'put your head in the lion's mouth', i.e. do something particularly daring.

Oh that I had died at birth! (11–19). Death means release from the physical sufferings of life.

Oh that I might die now, since life is so bitter! (20–26). Yet Job knows that suicide is not the way out. If God means him to die, God must let his illness be fatal.

Where are my breaking points?

Job 4 A Religious Experience

Each of the friends has a real faith in God as One who must be concerned with human righteousness. Each expresses his faith from a different angle, and probably Eliphaz has the deepest experience of all, even though intellectually he is unable to interpret the ways of God's working. We must bear in mind all the time how little had been revealed to mankind as yet. Clearly a real experience of God had been possible ever since the Fall, but men had little knowledge of doctrine, except for the doctrine of the covering of sin through sacrifice (**1.5**).

Note first of all the account of something equivalent to conversion (12–21). Eliphaz became the godly man that he was through a vision and a word. The word was the more important, as it was with Samuel (1 Sam. 3, especially vs. 1,21), and the prophets (e.g. Jer. **1**.9; Ezek. **3**.1–3). God continually uses His written Word today

414

both for conversion and for building up, and we must not normally expect to see visions and hear voices.

The content of the word to Eliphaz is a miniature of the total Word of the Bible—the majesty and holiness of God, and the littleness and failure of man. The Bible is the record of the reconciliation of man with God. Man as he is cannot save himself (17), nor have angels the wisdom and life in themselves to do it. Vivid language expresses their inadequacy (18).

In the light of his experience Eliphaz deals with Job. Job has put others right in the past, but, now that he is suffering himself, he has collapsed (1–6). Now Eliphaz asserts what Job's friends keep asserting. He assumes that reward and punishment are measured out in this life exactly according to what one deserves. Hence Job must be a great sinner (7–11).

Obviously Eliphaz himself is living by theory. He was a good man and he had prospered. Consequently he could give good advice as Job had done (1–6). But evidently he had not suffered personally.

Experience of God must go hand in hand with experience of life.

Job 5 How to be Blessed

In general, God censures the view of the friends that He sends exact retribution for sin and righteousness in this life, and commends Job for asserting the reverse of this (42.7,8). On the other hand, Job is driven to admit that he has spoken foolishly about God, and he repents in dust and ashes (42.1–6). Thus we must distinguish between the general point of view of Job and his friends, and their particular utterances. Many things that the friends say are true, and other things that Job says are false. Thus, if we preach or meditate on an isolated text from this Book, we must test it against the rest of the teaching of the Bible.

Eliphaz now continues his argument based on the purity and holiness of God. The angels will not take your part in defying God's laws (1, cf. 15.15 for 'holy ones'). If you become impatient of God and jealous of those whom He blesses, you declare yourself on the side of the fools who defy God (cf. Psa. 14.1). The fool may seem to prosper for a time, and then suddenly his possessions are destroyed and we recognize that God has cursed them (2,3). His sons are condemned by the court that sits at the gate of the city (4, cf. 29.7) and the needy help themselves to his stores, even though there is a thorn hedge, like barbed wire, to fence them in (5). Suffering does not grow like flowers, but men bring it on themselves through their own innate folly, as inevitably as sparks fly upward (6,7).

If I were in your position, I would turn to God, who crushes the wicked, and blesses the needy and the righteous (8–16). Then He will restore you and give you every material blessing that you can wish for (17–27).

In this final section we have one of the few verses in this Book which are directly quoted in the N.T., i.e. v. 13; quoted in 1 Cor. 3.19.

Consider v. 7 in the light of such passages as Mark 7.20–23; Jas. 1.14; Rom. 8.22,23.

Job 6 Need for Sympathy

We become aware of the pattern of the Book as we read. At first each friend speaks in turn, and in turn Job replies to him. Eliphaz has begun mildly, not accusing Job directly of being a great sinner, but implying that he is on the side of the foolish man who defies God. Job understands the hint, and in this chapter insists on bringing it into the open. But first he justifies himself for his extravagant outcry in ch. 3. Two things drew the cry from him. (*a*) The sheer weight of his suffering, which none of his friends can estimate (2,3). (*b*) The fact that it is God Himself who is inflicting these sufferings upon him (4). We note that, like his friends, Job believes that the sufferings have come from God: the point in dispute is whether they have come as punishment for personal sin.

Job continues: There is always a reason for the cries of animals; when they are satisfied, they are silent. So there is a reason for my cry in my distress (5). The meaning of vs. 6,7 is uncertain. There is a clear reference to insipid food, such as the tasteless purslane, sometimes used in salads, but is Job referring to the platitudinous sentiments of Eliphaz? Or does he mean his sufferings, which he speaks of in general terms as 'them', and which are like a continuous meal of insipid or bad food which he cannot endure?

Next Job desires God to end his life and relieve him of his pain. If he knew that this would be so, he would bear his pain cheerfully, since he does not fear death as a rebel against God (8–10). But he fears what may happen to his inner attitude if his weak body has to go on suffering indefinitely (11–13).

He addresses his friends directly: You disappoint me. In my fever you should have been as cooling ice-water, but I am like a traveller in the desert who counts on finding water in the usual places, and now it has vanished in the sand. (Tema [19] was in north Arabia; cf. Isa. 21.14. Sheba; perhaps the same Arab tribe as the Sabeans in 1.15). I did not ask you for some sacrificial gift, but only for sympathy (14–23). Instead you give forceful and vague rebukes for my words,

416

as wild as the wind, rebukes which show how hard and unsympathetic you are (27). Tell me exactly what I have done wrong (24–30).
Contrast vs. 15–20 with Isa. 32.1,2.

Job 7   Not Worth Punishing

The greater part of this chapter is directed towards God. Pessimistically Job sees all mankind like slaves and servants, longing for knocking-off time in the evening and for their wages at the end (1,2). So, he says, I continue in the toils of my pain, waiting—for what? (3). Night is but a restless longing for daylight, with the pain of my sores (4,5).

It may seem inconsistent that, after complaining of the longdrawn wearisomeness of his life, Job in v. 6 now complains of its brevity. Presumably RSV has made a fresh paragraph before v. 7 because here Job addresses God directly. But, in view of the sequence of theme, it might be best to begin the paragraph before v. 6. Although the hours drag for me because of my suffering, yet in the sight of God my life is so brief that surely He need not spend time afflicting me. Death will take me from my friends and I shall not return again to this earth (6–10). We shall note how Job gradually comes to a hope beyond Sheol, the state of the departed, in chs. 14 and 19.

What are You, God, trying to do with me? Am I like Noah's flood, or some threatening monster, whom You must subdue? (12). Suffering by day and terrifying dreams by night make me wish that I could choke to death instead of continuing life so emaciated that all my bones stand out. Is little man so important to You that You must always keep Your eye on him and seize every opportunity to punish him? (17,18, cf. 14.1–3). If only You would relax for the twinkling of an eye! (19—this is an English equivalent).

If I have sinned, how can my sin affect You, so that You need to shoot me down like someone aiming at a target, and cast me away like a heavy burden? (20). Surely it would be better to take away my sin, but, if You wait much longer to show Your pardon by relieving my sufferings, You will be too late: I shall be dead (21).

Job describes his sufferings as though God cannot feel them. What difference has the Incarnation made? (Heb. 2.9,10,17,18; 4.15).

Questions for further study and discussion on Job, chapters 1–7

1. How does Satan work against God?
2. What other passages in Scripture speak of revelation through a word from God?

3. Are Eliphaz and Job correct in their views of the littleness of man?
4. What does the Bible mean by the fool?
5. If you have to choose between sympathy and advice, which is the more important?
6. Would Job have been justified in committing suicide?

Job 8 Wisdom of the Ancients

Whether we regard the Book of Job from a literary or factual angle —and why not both?—we are bound to notice the consistent presentation of the characters. Eliphaz tries to comfort on the basis of his own experience, which is good as far as it goes, but unfortunately has never been touched by any vestige of personal suffering. He has spoken first, probably as the eldest.

Now Bildad makes his first contribution to the argument—one can hardly call it 'discussion'. He is a traditionalist, who puts great store in the wisdom of the ancients, and has a stock of religious platitudes to direct pointedly at Job. It would not seem that he has suffered personally.

At first he asserts as a strong possibility ('if') that either Job or his children have sinned, and so God has given them into the grip of sin's consequences. If Job is really innocent, he has only to appeal to God to give him back his lost blessings even more abundantly than before (2–7).

He asks: What is the value of your opinion, with your brief experience, compared with the accumulated wisdom of the ancients, which I have at my fingertips? (8–10).

Then come the parables from nature. Take the papyrus and reed. They need plenty of water, and wither without it. The godless man loses the water of God's blessings (11–13). He thinks his home and possessions are secure, but they are brushed aside as easily as a spider's web (14,15). Or compare him to a quick-growing plant that reaches upwards in the sunshine and twines its roots round firm rocks. When he is uprooted, he is quickly forgotten, and is replaced by others (16–19).

The underlying theme is loss of the good things of life, and, after all, Job has lost them. Surely he must draw the proper conclusions! His innocence can be proved by his restoration (20–22).

Bildad's views cannot be totally rejected, but compare them with Luke **13**.4 *and* John **9**.2,3.

The Book is not a string of haphazard arguments. Not only do the friends each have their consistent approach, but Job keeps turning his mind in first one direction and then another in his efforts to find some solution. As we read, we can discover an important line of thought, which begins in this chapter, i.e. the longing for a mediator to represent him before the unseen and inscrutable God.

Job agrees with Bildad in general about God's moral government (2) but how can we meet God face to face when His actions appear to contradict our established beliefs? He could always overwhelm us with His superior wisdom and power (3,4). Suppose I look for Him in nature? If I am honest, I find that nature speaks of apparently irrational violence (5–7), as well as of the creation of the heavens, with their splendid constellations and empty blacknesses, and the sea under God's control (8,9—the meaning of 'chambers of the south' can only be guessed at). God in nature cannot interpret my problem of suffering (10–12).

V. 13 speaks of Rahab, who appears to be some dragon-opponent of God. After the time of Job, it is applied to Egypt as the defier of God (Psa. **87**.4. and Isa. **51**.9). Mesopotamian and Canaanite stories of warfare between the gods and dragon monsters may well be based on the truth of Satan's original rebellion.

So Job says: God overthrew rebellious supernatural powers, and now He has overthrown me as though He is angry with me. My only hope would be to meet Him face to face and force Him to give me justice, but He remains out of reach, and even in court He could treat me as an unjust judge would do (13–20).

Since it is all one to me whether I live or die, I must speak as I see it. Innocent and wicked alike suffer, and God must be held responsible (21–24). I cannot forget my suffering (25–28), and God persists in making me appear filthy and guilty, however much I try to make myself as white as snow or as clean as potash can make me (29–31). If only I had a mediator, or that God would lay aside His rod of authority and be human for once! (32–35).

How far has Job understood God's part in cleansing? (cf. Isa. **1**.16–18,25).

Job 10   **Is Predestination the Answer?**

If we have not suffered like Job, do not let us judge him too harshly. We have a fuller revelation of Satan, sin, and the future life than he had, but again and again we find problems of divine government that we cannot understand.

In this chapter Job probes the idea of an extreme predestination as a possible solution. He addresses God: If You cannot give convincing grounds for Your treatment of an innocent man (2,3), and if You cannot be deceived as human judges can be (4, 5), have You determined from the beginning to treat me as a sinner whether or not I am guilty? Am I, as it were, predestined to (earthly) damnation? (6,7).

Yet how could this be consistent with the miracle of my creation when You transformed the materials of earth into the soft foetus, which eventually became flesh and bones? (8–11). Up till now You have given me life and care (12), but apparently You were all the time secretly predestinating the destruction of all that You had given (13). So it makes no difference whether I am good or bad (14,15), or whether I can lift myself up and prove my innocence; You are determined to hunt me down, and provide torments and afflictions that in the eyes of the world will witness to my guilt (16,17).

Surely it would have been better never to have brought me to birth or to have let me be stillborn (18,19). But once I am alive, my life at the best is so short that You could afford to relax Your tortures in the knowledge that You will soon be rid of me in death, that dark and final state (20–22). Note how Job piles on the words to describe utter darkness.

Note how in both his replies Job begins by speaking about God, and ends by speaking to Him. Which is better? (cf. 2 Cor. 12.8).

Job 11 and 12 Theories and Realities

The man of religious experience and the man with his mind stored with traditional wisdom have both failed to move Job one inch from his position. Can Zophar do better? He is perhaps the most simple-minded of the three. He may or may not have had a real experience of God, but he gives no testimony to having suffered. He is shocked that anyone should maintain his innocence when facts proved that God was punishing him for his sin. He is the practical, devout churchgoer who has not had much cause to think out the relation between God, goodness, and happiness. He is the first to become rude to Job (2,3). He has listened to Job protesting his innocence, but if he stood face to face with God he would find that he was such a great sinner that he would be surprised he had suffered so little (4–6).

In vs. 7–10 Zophar speaks of the omnipotence and unsearchability of God in a way of which we approve, but the lesson he draws is that guilty Job cannot hope to hide his sin from Him (11–14). So he must repent and put away his sin, and pass into the life of prosperity and peace (15–20).

At the end of the first round of arguments, Job speaks at greater length. He accuses Zophar and his friends of refusing to face the realities of life. After the opening sarcasm (2), he declares that he also knows the standard answers (3), but what he needs now is understanding sympathy from those who have themselves known the seamy side of life (4,5). Face the fact that the wicked, whose god is their strong right hand and what it brings them, do prosper (6).

He continues: Nature witnesses to the life-giving God (7–10, cf. 9.5–12). Here Job uses the Name YAHWEH (JEHOVAH) as the capitals in v. 9 show. The only other place in the Book where it is used by one of the speakers, as distinct from the narrator, is 1.21. On both occasions the context shows it has the significance of HE IS (Exod. 3.14,15 with marginal notes) as the Life-giver, and it is not as yet the Covenant Name.

Job also admits the importance of traditional wisdom (11,12), but points out the sudden reversals of status that traditional wisdom may overlook (13–25, cf. Luke 1.51–53).

Consider 11.7–9 *in the light of such verses as* John 1.18 *and* Heb. 1.1,2.

Job 13.1–22 Defendant in Court

Job assures his friends that he and they start with the same set of facts (1,2), and with the belief that God is omnipotent and all-wise (1,2). But, since this has not solved the vital problem, he wishes to speak directly to God about it (3). God is, in fact, more honest than Job's friends. Here again we see Job moving towards God as his only hope and vindicator, and this longing will keep emerging. His rebuke of his friends in vs. 4–12 is one we should take to heart. They have given him the impression that they have not spoken out of sympathy and understanding of the situation, but have spoken the orthodox language so as to keep on good terms with God. Is Job right in holding that God will not be pleased with such an attitude? (10).

So he turns to speak boldly to God, even though he takes his life in his hand and may be killed for his presumption (13–15). Parallelism suggests that the first line of v. 14 must have a similar meaning to the second, though the metaphor is not clear. But perhaps a beast's teeth correspond to a man's hand. Most modern commentators follow RSV and reject the magnificent AV of v. 15., 'though He slay me, yet will I trust Him'. The AV sentiment is true, even though this is probably an incorrect translation here.

Job continues: I should not have a right to defend myself in God's court if I were sinful and godless, but I have a watertight case, and no prosecuting counsel can find a flaw. If he can, I will gladly accept my fate (16–19). But, since I am defending myself before the great God and not before human judges, I must ask Him not to punish me as guilty before the case is heard, and not to reveal His overwhelming majesty in such a way that I dare not speak (20,21). Then I shall be happy to speak in my own defence, or answer any specific charges (22).

In the light of vs. 4–12 consider the sort of situations when we should (i) keep silent; (ii) listen to the problems of others in an unjudging way; (iii) discuss; (iv) give what we believe to be the Biblical answer without further discussion.

Job 13.23–14.22   Speech for the Defence

We must read this as the speech that Job wishes to make in God's court. He begins by demanding to know the precise charge against him. Before the hearing he is already suffering the penalty of the guilty (23–25). The theme is a favourite one with modern existentialist writers. Obviously the charge, which has not been read out in court, is a serious one, and must go right back to long-forgotten misdemeanours of youth (26, cf. 1.5). Meanwhile Job says, I am a condemned prisoner, in the stocks, under police guard, and under house arrest (27). And, after all, I am no more than an ordinary frail man (28).

Job for the time being abandons his plea of innocence, since God is still silent and has not declared what the charge is. Indeed, Job admits that he has sinned in some measure (13.26; 14.17), though certainly not enough to justify such terrible sufferings.

In ch. 14 he paints a picture of the human race, of which he is a member, so as to move the Prosecutor to pity. Man's life is brief, and he is hardly worth God's attention, certainly not His punishment (1–3). No one (not even God?) can make him clean (4), so why not let him live his predestined span of life with such enjoyment as he can get, even though he is no more than a hired servant? (5,6).

Now comes an important advance in Job's thinking. He contrasts the hope of a felled tree with the destiny of a dead man. The tree can return to life on earth, while man cannot (7–12, cf. 10. 21,22).

If only this need not be the end! Suppose Sheol, the state of death, were not the end, but only a hiding place in which my body was not suffering the punishments of God. Suppose that in the end God were to call me out to meet Him face to face. Then I could bear my present sufferings, and would gladly come forth to meet God, for I should know that He had taken away my sins for ever (13-17).

But the light of hope fades as quickly as it has come, though it will appear again in ch. **19.** Man is not like the living tree, but like the crumbling mountain, gradually being worn away by God until he loses all concern even for his own family. He has the self-concern that often characterizes old age, and that is easy to criticize so long as we are not too old ourselves (18-22).

Consider how far one can go with natural arguments and hopes for immortality. What better arguments are found in Christ?

Questions for further study and discussion on Job, chapters 8-14

1. How much weight should be given to Christian tradition, and how should its truth be estimated?
2. How far are the friends making statements about God's moral government that are true in general?
3. How far does nature provide an adequate revelation of God and His working?
4. When Job wants to be justified before God, does he approximate at all to the New Testament presentation of justification?
5. What other passages in the Bible find lessons in the growth of a tree? What pictures are applicable to the Christian?

Job 15 Dangerous Talk

The first group of speeches is ended, and we may summarize them. *Eliphaz:* God is pure. *Job:* Yet He torments me. *Bildad:* God governs rightly. *Job:* Yet He will not let me stand before Him. *Zophar:* God is all-wise. *Job:* Yet I would plead before Him.

Now Eliphaz begins his second argument with a disgruntled attack. You call yourself a wise man, but you do not talk like one. Your line of reasoning would destroy the fear of God altogether. Your irreverence proves your guilt (1-6).

Have you the wisdom of Adam, who, as the direct creation of God might be expected to have the fullest knowledge of His ways; or, like the angels, were you created before the world? (7, cf. 38.4-7). Unless you have had the privilege of access to the council of God, you cannot claim to know more than we do, when we come with the God-given words of comfort that you despise as inadequate (8-11).

You have agreed that man is hopelessly unclean (**14.4**), and yet you think that the holy God, before whom even the angels and heaven itself are inferior, must put Himself in your hands to be criticized, you whose sin is like meat and drink to you (12–16, cf. similar words of Eliphaz in 4.17–19).

Listen again to the opinions of wise men, who have inherited a pure tradition uncontaminated by strangers who have come into the land with newfangled notions (17–19). The wicked man is racked with pain (so is Job). He is cut down in the midst of prosperity (so was Job). He sees no hope (nor does Job). Although Job is not yet reduced to begging, this could well be the next step for the outcast (20–24, cf. Job's state in 30. 27–30).

Why does the wicked (and Job) suffer? He has made a personal attack on God, like a soldier who thinks he can protect himself with a heavy embossed shield (25,26). He has grown fat, flabby, and insensible to the spiritual and moral demands of God (27, cf. Deut. 32.15; Psa. 73.7). He is the sort of man who chooses to rebuild and inhabit wicked cities that God has cursed (28, cf. Josh. 6.26; 1 Kings 16.34. Note also Rev. 18.4,5). The remainder of the speech uses various metaphors of destruction (29–35).

Was Job 'doing away with the fear of God' (4) in what he said?

Job 16 and 17 Hope of a Mediator

Job turns the charge of windy words back on Eliphaz (3, cf. 15.2). The trouble is that, as so often happens in arguments, the speakers are not on the same wave-length. If the positions of the speakers were reversed, Job could just as easily pour out unfeeling consolation (4,5).

But facts are facts, says Job, and there is still no answer to God's apparent attack on my body. He has made me a despised outcast, shrivelled my skin, and emaciated me as a clear proof of my guilt in the eyes of my friends (6–8).

As frequently happens after a sudden reversal of fortune, every Tom, Dick and Harry has turned to insult the once successful man (9–11, cf. 30.1), and Job sees God Himself as a brutal warrior who is shooting him down, cutting him to pieces, and destroying his defences like breaking a city wall (12–14). Meanwhile Job wears the sackcloth of humiliation and mourning, even though he cannot see any sin for which to humble himself (15–17).

Then comes another mediator passage (18–22). Job as it were splits God in two. His friends fail through lack of sympathy, but surely God understands and will mediate for Job with Himself. Thus the Old Testament lays the foundations for the New Testament revelation, though Job's idea of the mediator is still crude. Yet we see how he is defeating Satan, who had declared that Job would renounce God. Instead of that, he has turned to God as his sole confidence.

Ch. **17**.3,4 continues this. No one else will stand up for me, but God will surely guarantee me to Himself as innocent.

The Hebrew of v. 5 is literally 'He telleth friends to a portion, the eyes of his children shall fail'. The RSV interprets it as a proverbial description of a merciless man, such as Job's friends are. The other proverbial interpretation is 'One invites friends to a meal, while his own children are starving', i.e. the friends invite Job to share their wisdom when they have not enough for themselves.

Job continues: I am a cursed monster in the eyes of my fellows, so that they spit to avert the evil contagion (6, cf. **30**.10. Or perhaps they actually spit contemptuously on Job, cf. Isa. **50**.6). A truly righteous man must be amazed at God's strange treatment of me, and angry when he sees the godless prospering, yet he will not be deflected from the way of righteousness in the hope of sharing godless prosperity (8,9).

My friends are wrong in holding out hopes of my sudden restoration when they say it will soon be morning for me (10–12). All I can look for now is death and the extinction of hope (13–16).

Consider **16**.19–21 *in the light of* 2 Cor. **5**.19–21.

Job 18   Pictures of Destruction

Bildad has the hardness and lack of sympathy which can so easily mark the traditionalist who has all the answers. It is irritating to find a man like Job who cries out of his own experience and refuses to hunt up sensible wordy answers to what the friends are saying (2,3). Job is only damaging himself when he demands that God should change His moral government of the earth. One might as well expect Him to move mountains (4).

The remainder of his speech adds nothing to what Bildad has said earlier. He comes up again with his vivid metaphorical illustrations of the fate of the wicked. There is little point in trying to find spiritual lessons in most of these descriptions, though v. 14 supplies one exception. Instead, if we have the opportunity of speaking or teaching, we can learn from the Bible how to communicate by picture.

Note the pictures of the wicked. No money for light or warmth in his home (5,6). Hesitant, shuffling, steps as he loses his way in the dark, misses his path through his own fault, and is caught in an animal trap (7–10). He runs like a hunted animal, but starvation has sapped his strength, and when he falls he knows it will mean the end (11,12). For already disease and the most powerful form of death are devouring him (13, surely a hit at Job). He is dragged from his comfortable home and handed over to grim King Death (14, an amazing title of death, cf. Heb. 2.15). Others take over his home, or it is destroyed like Sodom and Gomotrah (15). He and his family are blotted out root and branch, and pass violently from the light of this world into the darkness of death (16–19). Their fate is a byword of horror in the world.

Consider death as the king of terrors in the light of Heb. 2.14,15 *and* 1 Cor. 15.26,54–57.

Job 19

Job goes too far in v. 4; no man's sin is private to himself (contrast 1 Cor. 4.4). But, he says, if you use my wretched state as an argument, I can only reply that God has chosen to make me falsely appear a sinner in the eyes of the world. Not only my friends, but my wife and close relatives treat me as an outcast (13–19). My body wastes away, and I am practically destroyed (20). Surely, you, my friends, could give me the pity that God denies me! (21,22).

Yet, is God really my enemy? He is my only hope. This is the theme of vs. 23–27, which are notoriously difficult to translate in detail. In vs. 23,24 Job wants his words recorded indelibly to be a witness of his innocence, for one day God will appear as his next of kin (Hebrew: *Goel*) whose duty it was to avenge the blood of a kinsman (e.g. Num. 35.19), and He will stand up as a witness in Job's favour.

Commentators disagree over whether Job visualizes vindication before or after death, and, if the latter, whether he has the concept of the resurrection of his body. Job's death is suggested by his contrasting use of '*my Redeemer lives*', and by the word translated 'earth' which is literally 'dust' (margin, as in Gen. 3.19), and could refer to Job's body turned to dust (25). V. 26 apparently implies the destruction of Job's flesh, yet it could be the wasting away of his skin right to the point of death, but still leaving him in the body to see the vindication of God.

The turning point in favour of interpreting it of Job's death is the sequence of thought from 14.13–17. There he has expressed the longing that, after his time in Sheol, God would call him out and vindicate him. Now he asserts in faith that this must be so.

This does not solve the question of the resurrection of the body. 'From' can be taken in either sense (26, see margin). But since the Hebrew mind has difficulty in thinking of proper human existence apart from the body, and since Job here refers to 'my eyes', the RSV is probably correct in the translation that implies resurrection.

Job's vindication will mean the condemnation of his friends, who hunt him down, determined that the cause of his suffering is to be found in some inwardly-concealed sin (28,29).

What does 'I know that my Redeemer lives' mean to us? (cf. Rev. 1.18).

Job 20 and 21 — Barren Examples

Job might just as well not have spoken. Zophar sees the answer too quickly (2) and confuses the slight to his self-respect with a proper understanding of the situation (3).

Once again he produces a highly-coloured picture of the brief prosperity of the wicked. The metaphors and descriptions are mostly clear.

How far is Zophar speaking the truth? It is possible to be selective over examples of wickedness, and undoubtedly long-term history shows that tyrants, great and small, generally lose all that they have wrongfully accumulated. Zophar's mistake was in applying this to all sinners, and especially to Job.

V. 26—'a fire not blown upon . . .'. His goods are so inflammable that an ordinary fire will destroy them.

If only Job's faith in ch. 19 could have been sustained and discussed sensibly, the conversations might have had a different conclusion. But Job is stung by Zophar's declamation into a correspondingly wordy answer.

He agrees that this is the way we should expect God to govern. Why he is so appalled and dismayed is that His moral government does not work out like this with Job or with the wicked.

Then he quotes examples as Zophar has done, and again the descriptions are mostly clear.

V. 16: They hold their prosperity fast in defiance of God. But immediately Job feels bound to assert his own innocence in case his friends should draw the conclusion that he is being secretly wicked in order to get prosperity.

In vs. 19–21 Job deals with an argument, based on such passages as 18.15–19, that at least the children of the wicked are punished. But how is this just if the criminals themselves are spared?

Vs. 32,33: The wicked man has a spectacular funeral and a pleasant grave, and he has numerous imitators just as he had numerous predecessors.

Is Job as one-sided as his friends in this chapter?

427

Questions for further study and discussion on Job, chapters 15–21

1. Consider the work of Christ in the light of **15.**14–16.
2. Find further references to God as Redeemer (e.g. Psa. **19.**14; **103.**4; Isa. **49.**7,26). How is He Redeemer in the Old Testament?
3. What can one learn from these discussions about not being on the same wave-length in arguing?
4. Films of growing plants can be speeded up to show plan and purpose in apparently meaningless single movements. Can one speed up history to show moral developments including rewards and punishments?

Job 22 Specific Charges

The second round of arguments is over, and it may be summarized as follows: *Eliphaz:* God is pure, and destroys the wicked. *Job:* And me, the innocent. *Bildad:* God governs rightly, and destroys the wicked. *Job:* If God governs rightly, He will vindicate me. *Zophar:* The prosperity of the wicked is short. *Job:* The wicked prosper to the end.

In the third round only Eliphaz, with his deep religious experience, feels able to speak at the same length as before. In his two previous contributions he has been comparatively moderate in his attack, but now he accuses Job of specific sins.

God is complete in Himself without depending on man's righteousness or sin for His satisfaction. He gains nothing by making Job appear a sinner if he is innocent. So the reason for Job's sufferings must lie in himself (2–5).

Eliphaz accuses Job of some of the typical sins of a man in power and favour (6–9. Job answers this in **29.**12–17). He seizes on Job's cries for God to reveal Himself, and twists them to mean that Job supposed that the unseen God could not, or would not, notice his wickedness (12–14). He compares Job to the sinners at the time of the Flood (15,16), and paraphrases Job's own words, even to the repudiation of the counsel of the wicked, although he significantly reverses Job's words about the source of the unacknowledged blessings (17,18, cf. **21.**14–16).

The speech ends by calling Job to deliberate repentance, and includes the much quoted v. 21. In vs. 24–26 Eliphaz is saying what Christ says in the Sermon on the Mount (Matt. **6.**19–21,24) about the proper attitude to money: God, not mammon, is the proper end of our devotion.

428

If the RSV is correct with its suggestion for the difficult Hebrew of v. 29 (see margin), it could be the source of 1 Pet. 5.5. In v. 30 the harder reading *'not innocent'* (margin) could be correct, and is more likely to have been altered by copyists because of its difficulty. In its context it would mean that through Job's intervention God would even pardon the guilty—an unexpected anticipation of 42. 8,10.

Consider v. 21 in the light of the New Testament.

Job 23   The Silence of God

Job at least listens to what his friends say, and now he takes up the point that Eliphaz made about the unseen God (22.12–14). So far from wanting to hide from God in order to enjoy his sins without punishment, as Eliphaz suggested, he longs to meet Him, plead his innocence, and hear what God has against him (3–5). Since God is just, He would be bound to acquit him (6,7, cf. 9.33–35).

But God refuses to reveal Himself to Job (8,9). How shall we interpret the much quoted v. 10? By itself it is a magnificent declaration of faith, and we may well take it as one of the flashes of faith that occasionally shine out in Job (cf. 19.25–27), even though, true to human experience, he fails to maintain such a position under pressure. The alternative interpretation in the context is that God hides Himself because He knows that, if He allowed Job to plead his case, He would be forced to acquit him.

Job is still confronted with the problem of his sufferings, which he and his friends believe to have come from God, and which we know were permitted by God. Job again declares not merely his negative innocence, abstinence from sin, but his positive clinging to what he knew of God's words (11,12). He has done all that Eliphaz suggested in 22.22,24,25, but God's purposes towards Him remain unchanged (13,14, cf. 22.27–30).

Note how Job in v. 15 distinguishes between the general presence of God, which was compatible with his continued suffering, and the face-to-face presence for which he longed.

In v. 17 the RSV has again abandoned the negatives of the Hebrew (cf. 22.30), and this fits the theme of the chapter. If they are kept, Job may mean that he is not so blinded as Eliphaz had suggested in 22.11. In this case one would translate as, 'thick darkness is away from my face.'

Consider v. 3 in the light of Eph. 2.18 and John 14.6.

429

Job continues his theme of the search for God, but with a slight variation. Why does not God at least appoint certain days when He would be in session to hear cases? (1). Others besides Job would be glad to take the opportunity of coming to ask for justice, and he lists some examples. The fatherless and widows were always liable to be victims of human injustice, as also were the poor who could not afford to bribe the judges (2–4, cf. Psa. 94.6 and Amos 5.11,12).

They become outcasts, wandering through the countryside, with no proper homes, glad to get occasional employment from their wealthy oppressors (5–11). V. 9 sounds abrupt, but means that some cannot even keep their children, since their rich creditors seize them as slaves to be pledges for payment of debts (cf. Neh. 5.5).

If they go to the cities, their fate is no better. In the midst of the crowds they are left alone to die, and they cannot get through to God to help them (12).

The people who are responsible may be highly respected members of the State. But what about the obvious criminals, the men who sleep by day and work by night, who say 'It is morning' when others are going to bed? (13–17).

Commentators differ over the translation and application of vs. 18–24. The RSV legitimately inserts 'You say' before v. 18. In speaking these words, the sarcasm in Job's voice would show his meaning. In v. 21 Job jumps back to the thought of the oppressors, since Eliphaz had accused him of oppressing the widow (22.9). God lets them go on living in their brutality, and even heals them when at the point of death (22,23). Their life is extended, but not so long as to be a burden to them, and their dying is not prolonged (24. It is also possible to change the punctuation: 'They are exalted; a little while and then they are gone'). Probably Job is implying that, since God is letting him die in agony, he is not guilty as the friends suppose.

How far can God be blamed for refugees and oppressed persons? If they cry to God, should He answer by intervention from heaven, or by us?

Job 25 and 26   Wonders of Heaven and Earth

These notes assume that the present form of the Book in the Hebrew is correct. Many commentators believe that some rearrangement is needed at this point, so as to tidy up the third round of speeches. Whether we are dealing with fact, or with great literature, we must not let our desire for tidiness run away with what is true to life. Eliphaz, with his religious experience, speaks a third time. Bildad finds his stock of platitudes running out. Zophar, with his even more formal religious views, cannot speak at all, but keeps an injured silence.

In ch. 25 Bildad praises the omnipotence of God, who rules autocratically in heaven, and sends His messengers through the earth which His light illumines (2,3). (Alternatively, we may interpret this as: He stills the storms that sweep across the skies, brings out the countless armies of the stars, and illumines the earth.) Even the bright heavenly bodies are inferior to Him, and more so is man the maggot, with all his sin (4–6, cf. Eliphaz in 4.17–19).

Job sarcastically takes up the argument, such as it is, in ch. 26, and adds to it. Bildad has praised God's omnipotence in heaven and earth, but why stop there? The Bible regards the seas as lower than the land—as obviously they are—and also knows of the subterranean waters from which come the springs and wells. Sheol and Abaddon, names for the place or state of the dead, are metaphorically regarded as 'below', since the dead are buried under the earth, and have not ascended to heaven 'above'. So Job says God rules below, as well as above; in fact, in every part of the universe (5,6).

What follows is poetical truth. The northern stars, so important for the traveller, hang unsupported, as does the earth (7). There is the marvel of the heavy rain suspended in the clouds (8). There seems no reason for the RSV to alter the reading 'His throne' in v. 9 (margin). None can see into heaven through the heavens.

The circle of the horizon marks the spot where the sun rises and sets (10). The mountains tremble (11. In the light of v. 7 Job cannot have believed that the sky was supported by mountains.) For Rahab and the serpent (12,13) see notes on 3.8 and 9.13, though here the serpent may be some constellation such as Draco, the Dragon. Gen. 1.6,9 describes the stilling of the sea and clearing of the heavens.

These chapters may be compared with Isa. 40.21–26.

Job 27   Removing Misunderstanding

We may well consider whether vs. 7–23 can be part of Job's speech, or whether they are from a lost speech by Zophar. Thousands of words have been written on the interpretation of Hamlet's character, with its swings of mood. Few critics feel justified in rejecting or rearranging sections of the play in order to iron out apparent inconsistencies. Our first duty is to see whether a passage has a meaning as it stands. A depiction of character that is true to life is enriched by many elements that superficially appear contradictory.

Job waits for Zophar to answer, but he is silent. So are Eliphaz and Bildad. Job therefore has unexpectedly won. When a good man wins an argument, he can afford to relax and reconsider. Has he perhaps been too extreme? Was there some truth on the other side? Might he perhaps have created a false impression by some of his remarks?

The opening words of v. 1 introduce a fresh phase. Job no longer has to *answer* his friends (cf. **26.1**). He begins by summing up his position: he is innocent and intends to maintain his righteousness in word and deed, even though God appears to treat him as guilty and his friends believe him to be so (2–6).

But have his exaggerated statements suggested that it pays to be wicked? His friends may then have the last word. They will say that Job is hugging his secret sins because of his theory that the sinner really comes off best, and is in fact healed of his diseases (**24.22-24**). Job has already seen this possible interpretation in **21.16** (cf. also **31.3,4**).

Thus v. 7 follows on logically from v. 6, which states that Job intends to be righteous to the end of his days. Moreover, he sees that fellowship with God, which the wicked rejects, is essential, and it would be terrible to die in one's sin without God (8–11). Earlier he has found consolation in vindication by God if he dies innocently under his sufferings (**19.25-27**).

Finally, he is prepared to concede that the wicked do not ultimately prosper (13–23). As we saw in chs. **20** and **21**, much depends on the examples of wickedness that we select.

Note, in support of this being Job's speech and not Zophar's, the plural 'you' and 'yourselves' (not 'thee' and 'thyself') in vs. 11,12.

Let us watch ourselves in argument in case we are goaded into exaggeration.

Job 28 Wisdom

We continue to read responsibly, and see how the theme of this superb chapter fits into Job's pattern of thinking at the moment. The temperature of the discussion has fallen, and Job now is almost talking to himself.

His theme is a quiet approach to what he has vehemently demanded before when his friends had stung him with their accusations. How can one come face to face with God and have the ultimate wisdom which explains everything? The conclusion brings Job back to his old perplexities. God alone has ultimate wisdom, and He will not reveal it. He has shown man that his highest wisdom is to fear God and to depart from evil. This is, of course, what Job has done. And yet he suffers.

The chapter begins with man's search for treasure underground with all the scientific techniques of the day. There were mines in the Sinai Peninsula and in Egypt, among other places. V. 5 probably refers to the farmer at work on the surface, and fires lit below ground to help crack the rocks. Man's search takes him where no bird or beast penetrates (7,8). V. 10 refers to galleries and adits, and v. 11 to the diversion of underground streams which could stop the mining, as indeed they have done in modern mining ventures.

Wisdom cannot be dug out from the earth or from the sea, yet it is more valuable than any gold or jewels (12–19). If we die without it, shall we find it in the state of death? No, for death has heard no more than a rumour of it (20–22 [Why do people who try to consult the spirits of the departed always assume that they are so much wiser than the living?]).

God, the Creator, alone is perfectly wise, and His creation of the universe is the manifestation of supreme wisdom. Man was made to rule the universe as God's vicegerent, God-centred in everything (23–28). Job does not speak of the Fall, but we know how mankind failed to be wise. (For Wisdom in creation, cf. Prov. 8.22–31. For Wisdom in life, cf. Prov. 1.7; 9.10).

Consider the relation between science and wisdom.

Job 29   A Good Man

Job pauses again, but as yet no one attempts to answer him. The excitement of attacking a noisy heretic has died down. So Job carries on from his conclusion in ch. 28, and describes the ways in which he had feared God and departed from evil. At that time all went smoothly, and the blessings of God were showered upon him as tradition expected. This chapter is Job's own detailed description of what was summarized briefly in 1.1–5.

Job does not think only of material happinesses. What he valued was the friendship of God (4,5). Satan had said in his challenge that the two things were inextricably tied together, and that, if the material things were touched, Job would lose all desire for God and would renounce Him utterly (1.9–11; 2.4,5). Job demonstrates that this is not so.

There is no reason to doubt Job's description of himself as probably the chief man in the city. A reading of the prophets (e.g. Isa. 5; Amos 5.10–12) shows how frequently the rulers misused their position, and for personal gain did the opposite of what Job did here.

The gate of the city with its square (7) was the place where the elders gathered for parliament and law court. Here Job's wisdom was paramount (8–10), and it was the type of wisdom that he commended in 28.28, since it was always on the side of the needy who had no advocate when they were wrongly accused, or when they had a case against some person of influence (12–17). Job would certainly not have been popular with some of his fellows, and this could account for the way they turned against him when he was humiliated by his terrible disease.

Meanwhile Job anticipated that God would give him a long and fruitful life, with his honour undimmed, and his powers to contend for righteousness as fresh as ever (18–20).

In addition to his words in court, Job's advice was highly valued at all times. Men drank it in, and Job was able to cheer them with his smile without being sucked under by their depression (21–25).

Compare righteous Job with the perfect Messiah of, e.g. Isa. **11**.1–5.

Job 30 Depth of Suffering

In chs. **29–31** Job takes up three subjects. In ch. **29** we saw the picture of his former prosperity and the respect that deservedly was his. Now he looks by contrast at his present state. We can imagine him turning his exhausted gaze on the riff-raff who came round to make sport of him. Something of snobbish dignity comes out as he describes them (1–8), and the description reveals a darker side of his personality to which he was blind. No doubt many of these were criminals whom Job had condemned, in contrast to the innocent whom he had acquitted in ch. **29**. But he shows a hardness towards them, which, to be fair, must have been intensified by the way in which they were now having their revenge on him (9–15), since God had snapped his bow-string and left him defenceless (11, cf. **29**.20).

Naturally they withdrew at night, but the silence of night made him all the more conscious of the pains that tortured him (17, cf. **7**.4,5). As he writhed in agony his clothes were twisted around him and he had the sensations of choking to death (18). He rolled in pain in the dirt and the ashes (19, cf. **2**.8). Now God's storm winds were whirling him away to the land of destruction (20–23).

There follows one of the most pitiful passages in the Book, raising an argument that Christians must face from time to time. Surely, cries Job, I may be expected to call for help like a man trapped under a heap of rubble. I wept for the sufferer and tried to help him. But no corresponding help has come to me from God when I have called to Him (24–26). I suffer inwardly and outwardly, my body turned black with sores, and no one in the crowd can help me (28,30).

It seems that vs. 29 and 31 balance one another as do 28 and 30. It is unlikely that there were ostriches so close to the city, but both jackal and ostrich have a mournful wail. In 39.13 another Hebrew word for 'ostrich' is used, which means literally 'wailer'. Job howls with pain, and the only fit music for him now is the dirge of mourners.

Contrast this chapter with 1 Pet. **2.**19–23.

Job 31 Self-examination

Job has spoken of the splendours of the past and the horrors of the present. Now he goes back to search his life, to see whether he has been guilty of any of the secret sins that his friends have imputed to him.

He firmly asserts that God is concerned to punish sin (2–4), and, if he had been guilty of any of these things that he now mentions, he would deserve the sentence of the righteous Judge, and in some cases, of human judges also. But, as it is, he confidently lays his life open to God's scrutiny.

Job's self-examination goes almost as deep as does the Sermon on the Mount. Immorality can be immorality of the eyes as well as of act (1, cf. Matt. **5.**28). Vs. 5–8, in the light of the curse in v. 8, probably refer to covetousness which tried to attain its desires through some dishonest practice. In vs. 9–12 Job speaks of adultery with a married woman, which, unlike v. 1, could bring him before the courts if he were discovered. Even if he were not discovered, adultery is deadly and destructive to the personality (12). The reference in v. 10 is to a slave-concubine.

Vs. 13–15 show a truly Christian attitude to servants who are slaves, and remind us of Eph. **6.**9. Do we employ others?

Vs. 16–20 again go beyond what the average person would have expected. Job has gone out of his way to feed and clothe the needy, even to the extent of caring for some of them from childhood. If the literal Hebrew is kept (18, margin), Job says 'I acted as his father from my earliest days, and similarly I looked after the widow.' V. 21 speaks of a secret attack on someone with the knowledge that Job had influence in court.

Trust in money or superstitious worship of the sun and moon both draw devotion away from God, and would have deserved human condemnation also (24–28, cf. Matt. **6.**24).

The attitude to enemies in vs. 29,30 is not unlike Matt. **5**.21,22, 43–45, while Job also goes out in positive kindness to anyone in need (31,32).

Then Job declares that he has not been guilty of hypocrisy (33. Margin shows that the Hebrew has 'like Adam' or 'like man'. The reference to Adam is perfectly possible, cf. Gen. **3**.8). He has not lacked moral courage (34, cf. Matt. **5**.11,12).

Now despairingly he puts his signed plea into court (35). If God would also put in His charge against him, Job would proudly display it, because everyone would know it to be false.

The addition of vs. 38–40 may seem an anticlimax, but it is certainly a human touch. When we are justifying ourselves, we keep wanting to add something else so as to block every possible attack. So Job denies that any of his lands were acquired unjustly.

Consider this chapter in the light of New Testament standards.

Questions for further study and discussion on Job, chapters 22–31

1. What more could Job have done in his search for God?
2. What does the Bible mean by Wisdom?
   (Note Jas. **1**.5; **3**.13–17; 1 Cor. **1**.24, 30.)
3. Is Job in his prosperity (ch. **29**) the sort of man you would turn to in trouble?
4. How far can we argue from our own feelings and actions to those of God (**30**.24–26)?
5. What place is there for self-scrutiny (ch. **31**)?

Job 32   Youth Must Speak

It is a surprise to find a new speaker suddenly introduced, and many commentators regard the Elihu speeches as a later addition by a reader who felt that the friends had overlooked some points. But if the Book already existed, with the speeches by God to round it off, the Elihu speeches seem a strange addition, especially as they do not add anything of significance, apart from laying a stronger emphasis on suffering as a discipline. So these notes will continue to consider the Book as it stands, and look for the life situation, as well as the literary significance, of this section.

Elihu has not been mentioned before, because he is only one out of many in the crowd around Job. Apart from the rabble who made sport of Job whenever the friends withdrew (**30**.9–15), the arrival of three famous wise men to debate with the leading wise man of the city must have drawn a host of seriously-minded listeners. There was little point in singling one of these out for mention at the beginning, and no doubt, as is the way with conferences, others also interjected points from time to time.

It is hardly to be wondered at that an intelligent young man should be bursting to say something, and indeed he tells us that he felt like exploding (19,20). He may have been descended from Buz, a nephew of Abraham (Gen. 22.21), and Ram may be the equivalent of Aramaean, or Syrian.

He has all the marks of sensible godly youth. He is astounded that his seniors, older in the faith, have not been able to silence the unsound utterances of Job, but he has had respect for their seniority. He rightly sees that it is not simply a matter of dry debate, but he is emotionally roused, and angry, at what he has heard (1–5).

What encourages him to speak is that wisdom comes from God, and He gives it to the young as well as to the old (6–10). Elihu has followed every argument keenly (11,12), and in his speeches he is able to take up points that have been made. Do not let the friends excuse themselves by saying that they have found an unexpected wisdom in Job, so that only God can refute him (13). Elihu will make a different approach (14), and when he speaks, it will be with a passionate desire for truth (21,22).

Note: 1 Tim. 4.11–16.

Job 33   God's Interpreter

Elihu has listened to Job's cry for a mediator to come between him and the unseen, terrifying God (e.g. 9.33–35). He offers himself. Job need not be afraid of him, as he would naturally be afraid of God, since Elihu, like Job, is formed of dust and God has breathed the spirit of life into them both (1–7).

Elihu first takes up Job's argument that, although he is innocent, God is treating him as an enemy (8–11, cf. 13.24–27). God is not answerable to man for His doings (12,13). Note that the original Hebrew may be followed in v. 13 (margin), and 'words' can be translated legitimately as 'affairs'.

Elihu, like Eliphaz (4.12–17), may well have had his religious experience supported by a dream or vision. Perhaps he hints that, if only Job would be quiet, he would have a dream that he would recognize as from God (14–16). But Elihu is confident that he already knows the interpretation of such a dream: it would be to force Job from his pride to repentance, so that he would not be cut off in his sin (17,18).

Suppose no vision comes? Then sickness itself is the voice of God —and Elihu evidently describes Job's present state (19–21). What is

needed now is an interpreter, who will make the sick man understand his sin, and mediate his return from it, so that God redeems
him from the grave and restores him (22–25). The Hebrew word for
'angel' and 'messenger' (23) is the same, and it seems likely that
Elihu is offering himself as the messenger of God. Nothing is said
about the nature of the ransom, and, whatever foretaste we may find
of the atonement, the emphasis is here, not on the price or the
recipient of the money, but on the restored state (cf. Psa. **103.4**).

Ultimately Elihu holds the same position as the friends, and
believes that Job can be restored only when he has confessed his
sin (**27,28**). It would seem that Elihu also resembles the friends in
never having suffered acutely. Because he has been a good man and
has enjoyed a good life, he assumes that this is the invariable rule.

*There is no reason why we should not find for ourselves a fresh
meaning in v. 24 in the light of the New Testament (e.g. Tit. **2.14**).*

Job 34 Consider your Verdict

Elihu pauses for Job to reply, as he has done to each of the friends.
But Job unfortunately has a certain contempt for young men (**30.1**)
and he retains some of his pride of being free to speak without
contradiction (**29.8**). Thus Job's silence is not necessarily a mark of
the late insertion of these chapters, but is true to life.

Annoyed by Job's silence, Elihu turns away from him and
addresses the crowd, including the three friends, flattering them as
men of discrimination (2–4, 34–37). He calls on them to find Job
guilty.

Job's blasphemous language ranks him with the wicked. Not only
has he accused God of treating him as guilty when he is innocent
(5–8, cf. **27.2**–6), but he has even said that friendship with God does
not bring rewards (9—Job has not said this in so many words, but
he has virtually maintained it). What a terrible libel on God! Of
course He rewards men according to their works (10–12)! One can
hear the grunts of applause from the more fortunate members of the
audience. God is absolutely Sovereign. He has not been elected to
the throne of creation by someone else to whom He is answerable
(13). He has a perfect right to withdraw anyone's life at any
moment (14,15).

A supreme governor cannot govern by ignoring justice, and we
have no more right to question God than we have a king or others in
authority (16–18. Is Elihu more emotional than logical here?).
Certainly God works fairly without respect of persons, as the universal fact of death shows (19,20).

Job argues absurdly in suggesting that God should fix times for hearing human complaints (24.1), since God knows without legal arguments whether a man is good or bad, and acts accordingly (21–30).

Vs. 31–33 are very difficult to translate from the existing Hebrew text. Certainly Elihu suggests penitence, humility, and repentance (31,32. There is a misprint in some editions of RSV, which fail to close the single inverted comma after v. 32). Perhaps the RSV of v. 33 means, 'Will you then be satisfied with the reward He will give you for your repentance, since you now reject the recompense He has given you for your unrepented sin? It is up to you to decide.'

It is very pleasant to play to the gallery, but it may be at someone else's expense.

Job 35.1–36.23 Unanswered Prayer

The openings of these two chapters show that once again Elihu has waited for Job to speak. In ch. 35 he takes up his paraphrase of Job's argument that he has mentioned in 34.9. Is it true that religion and righteousness are not profitable to men (3)? God is so lofty and transcendent that man's sin cannot injure Him, nor man's righteousness benefit Him, in the way that sin and righteousness affect human beings (5–8). The implicit conclusion is that there is no possible reason why God should treat righteousness as punishable sin.

Elihu then realistically raises the question of unanswered prayer, where innocent sufferers cry for help against oppressors (9). The answer is that the prayer is not genuine prayer to God, in order to enjoy the sense of the enlightening presence of God, but rather the automatic responses to pain that one finds in beasts and birds (10,11). This is a profound diagnosis of some of our prayers. Man, like the rest of the animal world, has reflex responses, but he also has a discrimination denied to the others. Our cries for deliverance from evil men may be empty prayers (12,13). Job's impatient demands are even more reprehensible. He is presuming on what he has seen of God's restraint in the past (14).

Again a pause before Elihu makes his final speech concerning the greatness of God. Unlike Job, he will magnify God's righteousness (2–4). God does not despise anyone who is worthy of regard. He exalts the righteous, and, if they become entangled in troubles, He shows them their sin, restores them if they repent, and slays them if they refuse (5–12).

Only the godless bear a grudge against God for His treatment of them. Therefore implicitly Job is godless; otherwise affliction is the means of recalling the afflicted to sanity (13–16).

God tried to draw Job back to prosperity (16), but Job refused to learn the lessons. He must beware of rejecting the redemptive value of suffering (18), and think that his cries to God are true prayer (19). The darkness of destruction will quickly come (20). Remember that God wishes to teach as only He can teach (22,23).

Consider the quality of some of our prayers for deliverance. Should we conclude that we ought not to pray for deliverance at all?

Job 36.24–37.24 God in the Storm

It is perhaps significant that Elihu's description of the power of God in the storm immediately precedes the coming of the whirlwind out of which God speaks. This is a magnificent description of natural phenomena as testifying to the glory of God (cf. Pss. **19** and **104**).

Evaporation is followed by rain, and the thick thunder clouds are pictured as the pavilion in which the royal majesty dwells (27–30). The final words in v. 30 are difficult to interpret. They could mean that the rains keep the seas full. Some amend slightly to 'the tops of the mountains', which are covered with clouds. Storm and rain are God's agents for judgement and blessing (31), and God hurls the lightning against wicked men (32,33).

In 37.1–5 Elihu calls attention to approaching thunder. Thunder is poetically spoken of as God's voice, though no one would suppose that it was God actually shouting (cf. Psa. **29**): it is a translation of God's majesty into sound.

Next Elihu speaks of frost, ice, and snow (6–10), which seal up men's hands by stopping them from working. Then there are the clouds that move over the heavens to fulfil God's purposes (11–13).

Job understands so little of all these wonders, except that he benefits from them (14–17). The comparison of the sky to a smooth metal mirror is understandable poetry (18). We ourselves on a blazingly hot day sometimes speak of the sky as being like brass, and we use the metaphor of rending the heavens. Note also a different metaphor in **38.37**.

In humility Elihu declares that man's mind is too dark to argue with such a great God, and, if he did, he must expect to be destroyed (19,20). Just as the clouds roll away and leave sunlight too bright for the eyes, so, if God were to reveal Himself, He would be seen in the overwhelming brightness of majesty (21,22). We must be content to know that He acts justly (23,24).

Does this type of argument still have a place in a scientific age? Have you ever heard God in the storm?

Job 38   The Inanimate Creation

As Elihu ends his speech, the storm that he has seen approaching is on top of them, and unexpectedly the voice of God is heard addressing Job (1. The word 'whirlwind' may equally be translated 'storm'). We cannot say whether others heard the voice also, since in John 12.29 and Acts 22.9 individuals heard the words of God from heaven, while others heard the voice only as a noise (cf. Acts 9.7).

It is just possible that v. 2 refers to Elihu, although Job later takes the words to himself (42.3). Certainly, v. 3 refers to Job. Job had stood firm in face of Satan's challenge, but he had made some extreme statements about God's treatment of him.

God in fact speaks in terms that remind us of Elihu's final chapter, though the examples are more detailed. The impression that God leaves is that, if He controls the intricate orders of creation, which Job can only dimly understand, surely Job can trust Him to order his life, even though there too he cannot understand.

God begins with the creation of the world, long before the time of Job, when only the angels were present to rejoice in the wonder of the event (4–7. Parallelism suggests that 'morning stars' and 'sons of God' are the same, cf. Isa. 14.12).

The restraint of the seas while the clouds brooded over them (8–11, cf. Gen. 1.6–10) is followed by a description of the succession of day and night. The dawn makes the night criminals run for home, like pests shaken out of a garment (12,13), while early morning with its low sun makes objects stand out like the imprint on clay, and puts colour into them. The light withheld from the wicked in v. 15 is the normal person's night (cf. 24.16,17).

The rest of the chapter needs few comments, with its vivid description and gentle sarcasm. Apart from vs. 39–41, God is speaking of the wonders of the inanimate creation. With vs. 22,23, cf. Josh. 10.11; Judg. 5.21. Vs. 26,27: God provides for others besides man. The picture of ice-locked seas in v. 30 is remarkable, but ships were sailing from Palestine and Egypt to Scandinavia before 2000 B.C., so Job could have been aware of what God was talking about. In

441

v. 32, the Mazzaroth could be the signs of the Zodiac, or some unidentified constellation.

Angels are concerned to observe other things besides creation, cf. 1 Pet. 1.12.

Job 39 The Animal Creation

We noted the transition from the inanimate to the animal creation in **38.39**. Now God goes beyond anything that Elihu had said. A Christian who tries to understand nature is continually amazed by the intricacies of the life of the animal world, and the way in which an interlocking and balance of nature is preserved, whether it has come through direct creation or planned evolution. If Job had had a microscope, God could have included the wonders of the insect world as well. The savage lion and fierce raven of **38.39**–41 are succeeded by the timid goats, which bring forth their young without any help from man (1–4). The wild ass roams untamed (5–8). The wild ox (probably the now extinct aurochs) does not work for man (9–12). The ostrich, which seems so foolish and cruel in risking survival by laying her eggs in the open, where they can easily be found, has the compensation of enormous speed of foot. Apparent foolishness of instinctive behaviour in any creature is always balanced by some compensating quality (13–18).

These creatures are not tamed, but a horse can be trained for battle. In the days when war was fought on foot, the appearance of war-horses from about 2000 B.C. was a frightening thing. But what a picture we have here! (19–25, cf. Judg. **5.22**.)

Finally, there are the birds of prey, hawks and eagles, with their incredibly keen powers of vision at a distance, and their habits of building in inaccessible sites (26–30). Could the last line of v. 30 have been in Christ's mind in Matt. **24.28**?

An astounding range of knowledge is shown in these chapters, far wider than, for example, in Psalm **104**. This tallies with their claim to be the real words of God and not the work of some literary encyclopaedist steeped in travellers' tales. With one possible exception (to be discussed) there is not a single error of fact, since it is now admitted that the *unicorn* of **39.9** is a fiction of the AV translators.

> *'All things bright and beautiful,*
> *All creatures great and small,*
> *All things wise and wonderful,*
> *The Lord God made them all.'*

The order of nature is complicated and intricate. We may be tempted to find fault with aspects of it, and, for example, treat the ostrich as an example of God's foolishness, or cruelty, but the wisdom of God is at work all the time (**39.16–18**). So let not Job find fault with any of the ways of God (1,2).

Job is virtually speechless and mumbles a brief reply. For the moment he wishes to be silent (3–5), but he has not yet given the answer for which God is looking (7,8). So God continues and asks Job whether he would like to take His power and produce a better form of government in which all evil men were blotted out of the world (9–14). The moment we accept a challenge of this kind, we are faced with an all-or-nothing. There is no point at which we can logically stop, and say that we, as upholders of absolute righteousness, will punish evil up to grade X, but not beyond. Job and we must end by blotting out the whole human race, including ourselves. The alternative would be to make a race of puppets, which would have to obey, but could not have the spontaneous love and friendship which, after all, Job and we long for.

It is not that God is too weak to crush wicked men, and He playfully demonstrates this by the examples of two mighty beasts which He was strong enough, and daring enough, to create.

The first is Behemoth (15–24), which the RSV margin, like most commentaries, interprets as the hippopotamus. If so, there are two errors in the description. The tail of the hippo is insignificant (17) and he does not go up into the mountains (20). The description would just as well fit the elephant (AV margin), provided that the word for tail is applied to the trunk. Neither the hippo nor the elephant ever lived in the Jordan valley, and Jordan in v. 23 must simply be quoted as typical of a great river, just as we might say, 'The building would not be dwarfed by the Eiffel Tower.'

In v. 19 the thought is that he is one of the chief of God's creatures.

The power of God in creation is matched by His power in the Resurrection (Rom. **1**.4; Eph. **1**.19,20; Phil. **3**.10).

Job 41   An Untamed Monster

It may sound ludicrous to think of God dealing with profound problems of faith by talking about the crocodile, but Christ taught by analogies from nature (e.g. Matt. **6**.26–33), and God here is making Job feel the sense of power. He is no longer pressing Job so hard, and in the contemplation of this horrific and beautiful monster, Job's attention is distracted from himself.

There is no doubt that Leviathan is here the crocodile. How would Job care to go crocodile fishing, and bring home a big one to run round the house as a pet, or to sell in the market (1–6)? May we deduce that God has a sense of humour?

Why not go out and fight him? If you catch him once, you won't want to do it again! (7,8). One look at him is enough (9,10). Yet he is only a creature, and Job has suggested challenging his Creator (10). No one has any claim upon God, in the sense that, by giving Him something, he has put God under an obligation, for the whole world is His by right of creation (11—quoted in Rom. 11.35). The argument here is that even if Job dared to face God, he could claim nothing as of right.

A vividly poetical description follows, describing the armour plating of the crocodile (12–17), and then the way in which he sneezes air and water, which sparkle in the sun like fire bright enough to kindle fuel. The eyes of the crocodile appear red under the surface of the water, and in Egyptian hieroglyphics they stood for the dawn (18–21). The Hebrew for 'sneezings' in v. 18 is *atishah*!

His body is invulnerable to the weapons of the day (22–29). His tracks on the mud are as though a threshing-sledge with teeth had been drawn across (30), and he leaves a trail of white foam behind him (31,32).

So God has unfolded the world before Job's eyes, with the initial creation, the heavens and the earth, and typical animals weak and powerful. He made them all, and cares for them all, and He made Job also (40.15).

Read Psalm 104.23–30.

Job 42   The Final Scene

At last Job answers. He has demanded to meet God face to face and argue his case. Now he has met Him, he has nothing of himself to plead. So will it be with each one of us. Job accepts God's supremacy, and, if He does not work as Job would wish, it is not through inability, but for some deeper reason beyond Job's understanding (2,3). In vs. 3 and 4 Job quotes God's question in 38.2 and His invitation to speak in 38.3 and 40.7, but now he has nothing to say. For he sees himself as he is, and he repents humbly before God (5,6). To his dying day Job probably never knew the reason for his sufferings, and the way in which he had demonstrated that Satan was wrong. He became a pioneer of men and women who can dis-

444

entangle the love and service of God from the material blessings of life, though they give thanks for the latter when they come.

Since Job admits that he has no claim upon God, he knows that his restoration, if it comes, will be through the undeserved grace of God. He is in a sense justified by faith, and not, as he previously imagined (e.g. 27.4–6), by his good works.

God's verdict on the debate (7–9) is on the basic positions of Job and his friends as to whether suffering is the result of personal sin. The friends had refused to face life as it is. Job had protested against God's treatment of him, but he had longed to vindicate the goodness and justice of God in the light of facts as they were. Now Job's restoration comes from the moment when he forgot his sufferings and interceded for his friends. It says much for his friends that they accepted the position of sinners in the eyes of the spectators.

God does not include Elihu in the condemnation. He had realized something of the disciplinary nature of suffering, and had in small measure anticipated the answer that God Himself gave.

Once the trial is over, it would have been pointless to leave Job to die in agony. God made man to enjoy the blessings of life, and Job is therefore restored to more than his previous prosperity, while, we imagine, Satan licked his wounds. One day Satan would have permission to try again with the Son of God Himself, and then he would taste final defeat. Job's sufferings are an example, but Christ's greater sufferings are redemptive.

Note the New Testament comment on Job in Jas. **5**.10,11.

Questions for further study and discussion on Job, chapters 32–42

1. How far is Elihu the sort of man to whom you would turn for advice and help in trouble?
2. What is the value of regarding suffering as discipline? Consider this in the light of 2 Cor. **12**.7–9, especially in view of the mention of Satan.
3. If you are keen on some branch of natural history or physical science, or if you watch nature programmes on TV, in what ways do these speak to you of God?
4. How far is ch. **42** a satisfying ending to the Book?
5. How great a handicap is it not to have suffered either emotionally or physically?